Fourth Workshop on Language Technology for Equality, Diversity and Inclusion (LT-EDI 2024)

St. Julian's, Malta
21 March 2024

ISBN: 978-1-7138-9455-1

Printed from e-media with permission by:

Curran Associates, Inc.
57 Morehouse Lane
Red Hook, NY 12571

Association for Computational Linguistics
209 N. Eighth Street
Stroudsburg, Pennsylvania 18360

Phone: 1-570-476-8006
Fax: 1-570-476-0860

acl@aclweb.org

Additional copies of this publication are available from:

Curran Associates, Inc.
57 Morehouse Lane
Red Hook, NY 12571 USA
Phone: 845-758-0400
Fax: 845-758-2633
Email: curran@proceedings.com
Web: www.proceedings.com

LT-EDI 2024

The Fourth Workshop on Language Technology for Equality, Diversity, Inclusion

Proceedings of the Workshop

March 21, 2024

The LT-EDI organizers gratefully acknowledge the support from the following sponsors.

In cooperation with

Association for Computational Linguistics (ACL)
209 N. Eighth Street
Stroudsburg, PA 18360
USA
Tel: +1-570-476-8006
Fax: +1-570-476-0860
acl@aclweb.org

Introduction

Equality, Diversity and Inclusion (EDI) is an important agenda across every field throughout the world. Language as a major part of communication should be inclusive and treat everyone with equality. Today's large internet community uses language technology (LT) and has a direct impact on people across the globe. EDI is crucial to ensure everyone is valued and included, so it is necessary to build LT that serves this purpose. Recent results have shown that big data and deep learning are entrenching existing biases and that some algorithms are even naturally biased due to problems such as 'regression to the mode'. Our focus is on creating LT that will be more inclusive of gender, racial, sexual orientation, persons with disability. The workshop will focus on creating speech and language technology to address EDI not only in English, but also in less resourced languages.

Program Committee

Program Chairs

Bharathi Raja Chakravarthi, University of Galway, Ireland
Bharathi B, SSN College of Engineering, Chennai, Tamil Nadu, India
Paul Buitelaar, Data Science Institute, University of Galway, Ireland
Thenmozhi Durairaj, SSN College of Engineering, Chennai, Tamil Nadu, India
György Kovács, Luleå University of Technology, Sweden
Miguel Ángel García Cumbreras, University of Jaén, Spain

Publication Chair

Prasanna Kumar Kumaresan, University of Galway, Ireland
Rahul Ponnusamy, University of Galway, Ireland
Saranya Rajiakodi, Central University of Tamil Nadu, India

Program Committee

Doris Dippold, University of Surrey, United Kingdom
Viktor Hangya, University of Munich, Germany
Daniel García-Baena, Universidad de Jaén, Spain
Pedro Ernesto Alonso, Luleå University of Technology, Sweden
Selam Abitte, Instituto Politécnico Nacional, Mexico
Fernanda Gonçalves Abrantes, University of Oxford, United Kingdom
Zahra Ahani, Instituto Politécnico Nacional, Mexico
Anvi Alex, Instituto Politécnico Nacional, Mexico
Judith Jeyafreeda Andrew, University of Manchester, United Kingdom
Tanmay Basu, Indian Institute of Science Education and Research Bhopal, India
Mika Beele, Fachhochschule Aachen, Germany
Divya Chaudhary, Northeastern University, Boston, USA
Ruizhe Chen, Zhejiang University, China
Kenneth Church, Northeastern University, Boston, USA
Miguel Couceiro, Université de Lorraine, France
Nicholas Deas, Columbia University, New York, USA
Xiangjue Dong, Texas A&M University - College Station, Texas, USA
Samuel Dooley, University of Maryland, College Park, Maryland, USA
Zi-Yi Dou, University of California, Los Angeles, USA
Kaveh Eskandari Miandoab, Worcester Polytechnic Institute, Massachusetts
Yang Feng, Angelalign Tech, China
Tamás Ficsor, University of Szeged, Hungary
Jyothish Lal G, Amrita Vishwa Vidyapeetham (Deemed University), India
Martina Galletti, Sony Computer Science Lab, France
Michael Gira, University of Wisconsin - Madison, Wisconsin, USA
Dhiman Goswami, George Mason University, Virginia, USA
Pengrui Han, Carleton College, Minnesota, USA
Jin Hao, Stanford University, California, USA
Christian Hardmeier, IT University of Copenhagen, Denmark
Shanshan Huang, Shanghai Jiaotong University, China

Nikilesh Jayaguptha, Sri Sivasubramaniya Nadar College of Engineering, India
Lars Klöser, Fachhochschule Aachen, Germany
Rafal Dariusz Kocielnik, California Institute of Technology, California. USA
Rohith Gowtham Kodali, ASRlytics, India
Ajinkya Kulkarni, Mohamed bin Zayed University of Artificial Intelligence, Abu Dhabi
Abdullatif Köksal, Ludwig-Maximilians-Universität München, Germany
SangKeun Lee, Korea University, South Korea
Camelia Lemnaru, Technical University of Cluj-Napoca, Romania
Viswa M, Resilience Business Grids LLP, India
Durga Prasad Manukonda, ASRlytics, India
Marta Marchiori Manerba, University of Pisa, Italy
Antonis Maronikolakis, Ludwig Maximilian University (LMU), Munich, Germany
Pranav Moorthi, Sri Sivasubramaniya Nadar College of Engineering, India
Anjishnu Mukherjee, George Mason University, Virginia, USA
Daniele Nardi, Sapienza University of Rome, Italy
Jakub Pokrywka, Adam Mickiewicz University in Poznań, Poland
Sadiya Sayara Chowdhury Puspo, George Mason University, Virginia, USA
Andrei-Cristian Rad, Technical University of Cluj-Napoca, Romania
Hossein A. Rahmani, University College London (UCL), United Kingdom
Md Nishat Raihan, George Mason University, Virginia, USA
Chahat Raj, George Mason University, Virginia, USA
Effirul Ramlan, University of Galway, Ireland
Leonardo Ranaldi, Idiap Research Institute, Switzerland
A Ankitha Reddy, Sri Sivasubramaniya Nadar College of Engineering, India
Michael Roth, University of Stuttgart, Germany
Frank Rudzicz, Dalhousie University, Canada
Elena Sofia Ruzzetti, Università degli Studi di Roma Tor Vergata, Italy
Iñaki San Vicente, Orai NLP Technologies and Elhuyar Fundazioa, Spain
Annika Marie Schoene, Institute for Experiential AI Northeastern University, Boston, USA
Kogilavani Shanmugavadivel, Kongu Engineering College, India
Aleksandar Shtedritski, University of Oxford, United Kingdom
Malliga Subramanian, Kongu Engineering College, India
Katharina Suhr, Universität Stuttgart, Germany
Priyadharshini T, Sri Sivasubramaniya Nadar College of Engineering, India
Marc Tanti, University of Malta, Malta
Moein Shahiki Tash, Instituto Politécnico Nacional, Mexico
Ann Maria Thomas, Sri Sivasubramaniya Nadar College of Engineering, India
Anna Tokareva, Université de Lorraine, France
Peter Brunsgaard Trolle, IT University of Copenhagen, Denmark
Fida Ullah, Instituto Politécnico Nacional, Mexico
Davide Venditti, Università degli studi Roma Tor Vergata, Italy
Xi Wang, University College London, University of London, United Kingdom
Yibo Wang, University of Illinois at Chicago, USA
Martin Paul Wessel, Technische Universität München, Germany
Sidney Gig-Jan Wong, University of Canterbury, New Zealand
Huimin Xiong, Zhejiang University, China
Omer Faruk Yalcin, University of Massachusetts, Massachusetts, USA
Mesay Gemeda Yigezu, Instituto Politécnico Nacional, Mexico
Mahdi Zakizadeh, Tehran Institute for Advanced Studies, Iran
Muhammad Tayyab Zamir, Instituto Politécnico Nacional, Mexico
Fabio Massimo Zanzotto, University of Rome Tor Vergata, Italy

Ziwei Zhu, George Mason University, USA
Heike Zinsmeister, Universität Hamburg, Germany

Keynote Talk: Metrics, Tasks, and Truths: Who is Natural Language Processing for?

Dirk Hovy
Department of Bocconi University
2024-03-21 09:15:00 – Room: **Radisson, Marie Louise Suite 1**

Abstract: NLP always implicitly deals with the notion of truth, not just in fact verification and natural language inference. But the notion of truth we use is often restrictive and sometimes artificial, and many times, it is completely unwarranted: because the process we use introduces falsehoods, because there is no single truth that holds for all users, because the notion of truth does not apply. These issues have become more pressing with Large Language Models. While we can now translate, summarize, and generate text at human and super-human levels, we are modeling very specific linguistic realities. In this talk, I will look at some of the (sizable) remaining pockets of unresolved questions and issues, even in high-resource languages like English. We look at some of the roots of NLP's notion of truths, the way falsehoods enter our systems, and what we can do about it, with a special emphasis on annotation. I will suggest some aspects that can make for interesting future directions and enjoyable puzzling to make NLP fairer and (even) more performative. It turns out that there is still plenty to do with language of and for children and non-standard speakers, the safety and harmlessness of models, and the application to non-standard tasks.

Bio: He is an associate professor working on natural language processing and computational social science. Previously, He was faculty and postdoc in Copenhagen, got a PhD from USC, and a master's in sociolinguistics in Germany. He is also the scientific director of BIDSA's Data and Marketing Insights (DMI) research unit, and head of the MilaNLP lab. He has organized a conference (EMNLP 2017) and various workshops (on abusive language, ethics in NLP, and computational social science).

Table of Contents

Program

Thursday, March 21, 2024

09:00 - 09:15 *Opening Remarks*

09:15 - 09:45 *Keynote*

09:45 - 11:00 *Paper Session 1*

Sociocultural knowledge is needed for selection of shots in hate speech detection tasks
Antonis Maronikolakis, Abdullatif Köksal and Hinrich Schuetze

The Balancing Act: Unmasking and Alleviating ASR Biases in Portuguese
Ajinkya Kulkarni, Anna Tokareva, Rameez Qureshi and Miguel Couceiro

Beyond the Surface: Spurious Cues in Automatic Media Bias Detection
Martin Wessel and Tomáš Horych

A Dataset for the Detection of Dehumanizing Language
Paul Engelmann, Peter Brunsgaard Trolle and Christian Hardmeier

Towards Content Accessibility Through Lexical Simplification for Maltese as a Low-Resource Language
Martina Meli, Marc Tanti and Chris Porter

11:00 - 11:30 *Cofee Break*

11:30 - 12:30 *Poster Session 1*

Pinealai_StressIdent_LT-EDI@EACL2024: Minimal configurations for Stress Identification in Tamil and Telugu
Anvi Alex Eponon, Ildar Batyrshin and Grigori Sidorov

byteLLM@LT-EDI-2024: Homophobia/Transphobia Detection in Social Media Comments - Custom Subword Tokenization with Subword2Vec and BiLSTM
Durga Prasad Manukonda and Rohith Gowtham Kodali

MasonTigers@LT-EDI-2024: An Ensemble Approach Towards Detecting Homophobia and Transphobia in Social Media Comments
Dhiman Goswami, Sadiya Sayara Chowdhury Puspo, Md Nishat Raihan and Al Nahian Bin Emran

Thursday, March 21, 2024 (continued)

12:30 - 13:30 *Lunch Break*

13:30 - 15:45 *Paper Session 2*

Prompting Fairness: Learning Prompts for Debiasing Large Language Models
Andrei-Victor Chisca, Andrei-Cristian Rad and Camelia Lemnaru

German Text Simplification: Finetuning Large Language Models with Semi-Synthetic Data
Lars Klöser, Mika Beele, Jan-Niklas Schagen and Bodo Kraft

ChatGPT Based Data Augmentation for Improved Parameter-Efficient Debiasing of LLMs
Pengrui Han, Rafal Kocielnik, Adhithya Saravanan, Roy Jiang, Or Sharir and Anima Anandkumar

DE-Lite - a New Corpus of Easy German: Compilation, Exploration, Analysis
Sarah Jablotschkin, Elke Teich and Heike Zinsmeister

A Diachronic Analysis of Gender-Neutral Language on wikiHow
Katharina Suhr and Michael Roth

Overview of Third Shared Task on Homophobia and Transphobia Detection in Social Media Comments
Bharathi Raja Chakravarthi, Prasanna Kumar Kumaresan, Ruba Priyadharshini, Paul Buitelaar, Asha Hegde, Hosahalli Lakshmaiah Shashirekha, Saranya Rajiakodi, Miguel Ángel García, Salud María Jiménez-Zafra, José Antonio García-Díaz, Rafael Valencia-García, Kishore Kumar Ponnusamy, Poorvi Shetty and Daniel García-Baena

Overview of the Third Shared Task on Speech Recognition for Vulnerable Individuals in Tamil
Bharathi B, Bharathi Raja Chakravarthi, Sripriya N, Rajeswari Natarajan and Suhasini S

Overview of Shared Task on Multitask Meme Classification - Unraveling Misogynistic and Trolls in Online Memes
Bharathi Raja Chakravarthi, Saranya Rajiakodi, Rahul Ponnusamy, Kathiravan Pannerselvam, Anand Kumar Madasamy, Ramachandran Rajalakshmi, Hariharan RamakrishnaIyer LekshmiAmmal, Anshid Kizhakkeparambil, Susminu S Kumar, Bhuvaneswari Sivagnanam and Charmathi Rajkumar

Overview of Shared Task on Caste and Migration Hate Speech Detection
Saranya Rajiakodi, Bharathi Raja Chakravarthi, Rahul Ponnusamy, Prasanna Kumar Kumaresan, Sathiyaraj Thangasamy, Bhuvaneswari Sivagnanam and Charmathi Rajkumar

15:45 - 16:15 *Coffee Break*

Thursday, March 21, 2024 (continued)

16:15 - 17:15 *Poster Session 2*

MUCS@LT-EDI-2024: Learning Approaches to Empower Homophobic/Transphobic Comment Identification
Sonali Kulal, Nethravathi Gidnakanala, Raksha G, Kavya G, Asha Hegde and H L Shashirekha

ASR TAMIL SSN@ LT-EDI-2024: Automatic Speech Recognition system for Elderly People
Suhasini S and Bharathi B

17:15 - 17:45 *Plenary and Closing Remarks*

Sociocultural knowledge is needed for selection of shots in hate speech detection tasks

Antonis Maronikolakis[1,2] **Abdullatif Köksal**[1,2] **Hinrich Schütze**[1,2]
[1]Center for Information and Language Processing, LMU Munich
[2]Munich Center for Machine Learning
antmarakis@cis.lmu.de akoksal@cis.lmu.de

Abstract

We introduce HateLexicon, a lexicon of slurs and targets of hate speech for Brazil, Germany, India and Kenya, to aid model development and interpretability. First, we demonstrate how HateLexicon can be used to interpret model predictions, showing that models developed to classify extreme speech rely heavily on target group names. Further, we propose a culturally-informed method to aid shot selection for training in low-resource settings. In few-shot learning, shot selection is of paramount importance to model performance and we need to ensure we make the most of available data. We work with HASOC German and Hindi data for training and the Multilingual HateCheck (MHC) benchmark for evaluation. We show that selecting shots based on our lexicon leads to models performing better than models trained on shots sampled randomly. Thus, when given only a few training examples, using HateLexicon to select shots containing more sociocultural information leads to better few-shot performance. With these two use-cases we show how our HateLexicon can be used for more effective hate speech detection.

Set	German	Hindi
Random_{64}	$0.51_{3.6}$	$0.47_{2.5}$
Random_{96}	$0.53_{4.7}$	$0.46_{3.2}$
Lexicon_{64}	$0.54_{1.8}$	$0.50_{5.4}$
Lexicon_{96}	$\mathbf{0.55_{1.0}}$	$\mathbf{0.52_{1.1}}$
All_{128}	$0.53_{2.1}$	$0.44_{5.6}$

Table 1: Comparison of F1-scores for German and Hindi between randomly- and HateLexicon-sampled training sets of sizes 64 and 96. Standard deviation in subscript.

1 Introduction

To curb the spread and dissemination of hate speech online, the research and industry communities have focused on the collection of hate speech data from social media and the development of models to automatically filter out harmful content.

While there have been efforts to cover multiple languages (Ousidhoum et al., 2019; Mandl et al., 2019; Ross et al., 2017; Maronikolakis et al., 2022b), most work is still conducted for English settings (Davidson et al., 2017; Founta et al., 2018; Sap et al., 2020). Concurrently, it has been shown that cross-lingual transfer capabilities of models are limited in this domain (Nozza, 2021; Ranasinghe and Zampieri, 2020), potentially due to the heavily culture-specific and subjective nature of the data. Thus, leveraging high-resource languages to aid performance in low-resource ones is not a reliable option. Instead, methods need to be developed to better utilize the available data.

Towards efforts for more inclusive hate speech research, we are introducing HateLexicon, a lexicon of slurs and target group denotations that can be used as an aid to model training and interpretability. Curated in collaboration with members familiar with sociopolitical balances in the examined countries (Brazil, Germany, India and Kenya), HateLexicon aims to bring cultural knowledge to hate speech model development.

Models often rely on keywords for predictions (Ramponi and Tonelli, 2022). While this can be an effective tactic in developing baselines (e.g., keyword-based models), it can have undesirable effects, such as associating generally innocuous terms with extreme speech; e.g., a negative interpretation of the term 'Muslim'. **This erroneous association between target group names and hate speech may lead to further marginalization of vulnerable groups**, misclassifying text mentioning these terms with hate speech and consequently filtering them out (Mathew et al., 2021a; Dodge et al., 2021). Further, seemingly **innocuous terms have been appropriated by extreme**

Proceedings of the Fourth Workshop on Language Technology for Equality, Diversity, Inclusion, pages 1–13
March 21, 2024

speech peddlers and may not be picked up by models, such as the term 'Goldstücke' in German (originally meaning 'gold pieces' and appropriated to refer to refugees in a derogatory manner). Models unable to recognize these keywords as hateful in certain contexts will lead to hate speech falling through the cracks.

This is especially salient in few-shot settings, where the wide range of targets and slurs might not be adequately captured in annotated datasets. Further, it has been shown that model performance fluctuates a lot depending on the selection of training shots (Zheng et al., 2022). Therefore, **we need a better strategy to make the most out of the available data to select shots more conducive to model performance**.

Motivated by the above problems, we propose HATELEXICON, a lexicon aiming to (i) aid model interpretability by providing ground-truth labels on common terms and (ii) improve shot selection in low-resource settings by better coverage of key terms such as targets and slurs. To create HATELEXICON, we collaborated with annotators from our examined countries, who provided a list of keywords and marked them as target groups, slurs, neutral words or any combination of these labels.

Our contributions, in short, are the following:

1. Introduce HATELEXICON, a lexicon of target group names and slurs from Brazil, Germany, India and Kenya.
2. Show how cultural information can aid in model interpretability, identifying which slurs and targets affect performance the most.
3. Show that culturally-informed sampling outperforms random sampling in few-shot hate speech detection settings (Table 1).
4. Propose a method to complement training sets by querying data using HATELEXICON terms.

2 Related Work

Hate Speech Detection. Nascent efforts to tackle hate speech focused on the curation of general-purpose, English datasets (Founta et al., 2018; Davidson et al., 2017), later expanding into more granular annotation (Guest et al., 2021; Grimminger and Klinger, 2021; Ross et al., 2017; Sap et al., 2020; Hede et al., 2021; Wiegand et al., 2021). Most work is performed on datasets of thousands of examples, allowing for straightforward finetuning of models. In our work, we focus on low-resource settings where only a few examples are available for training and thus traditional finetuning techniques cannot be applied.

Recently, work has been conducted to cover a larger range of languages (Ousidhoum et al., 2019; Ranasinghe and Zampieri, 2020; Maronikolakis et al., 2022b; Plakidis and Rehm, 2022). In our work, we continue previous efforts into multilingual hate speech detection by proposing a lexicon of terms (pertinent to the domain hate speech) for Brazilian Portuguese, English, German, Hindi and Swahili.

Analysis has taken place both on the model and the dataset level (Mathew et al., 2021b; Wiegand et al., 2019; Madukwe et al., 2020; Kim et al., 2020; Swamy et al., 2019; Davidson et al., 2019a). Further, hate speech datasets have been examined for presence and reproduction of bias (Davidson et al., 2019b; Laugier et al., 2021; Sap et al., 2019; Maronikolakis et al., 2022a). We continue in this direction by proposing a lexicon that can aid in interpretability and model analysis efforts.

Previous work has uncovered annotator bias (Ross et al., 2017; Waseem, 2016; Posch et al., 2018; Shmueli et al., 2021; Al Kuwatly et al., 2020), with work conducted to propose frameworks of ethical data curation (Udupa et al., 2022; Jo and Gebru, 2020; Leins et al., 2020; Vidgen et al., 2019; Gebru, 2019; Mohamed et al., 2020). To mitigate bias in our work, we are directly working with community-embedded members.

Röttger et al. (2021) proposed a benchmark for unified evaluation of hate speech detection models in English, subsequently expanded into the Multilingual HateCheck (MHC) benchmark for multiple languages (Röttger et al., 2022), used in our work.

Few-shot Learning. Large language models exhibit zero- and few-shot capabilities (Brown et al., 2020; Wei et al., 2022; Sanh et al., 2022; Le Scao and Rush, 2021; Gao et al., 2021; Schick and Schütze, 2021b). A challenge with finetuning large language models (and few-shot learning in particular) is inconsistency: the selection of training data greatly affects performance (Zheng et al., 2022; Mosbach et al., 2021; Lu et al., 2022). Since in few-shot learning settings only a few examples are available, any noise in the data can exacerbate training issues (Köksal et al., 2022). In our work we propose a lexicon-based approach to shot selection that consistently improves performance.

Earlier work in few-shot learning focused

on prompt-based training Schick and Schütze (2021a); Fu et al. (2022); Shin et al. (2020); Logan IV et al. (2022); Zhao and Schütze (2021). Tunstall et al. (2022) introduced a prompt-free approach to learning from small datasets (SetFit). Through the use of SentenceBERT and its Siamese-network training paradigm (Reimers and Gurevych, 2019), SetFit generates pairs of training examples and learns to minimize the distance of training example representations of the same class and, conversely, to maximize the distance for examples from different classes. This process results in a model that can generate strong sentence embeddings, which can be then used to train a classification head on a task. In our work, we use SetFit to train a multilingual SentenceBERT model on German and Hindi.

3 Methodology

To showcase the usefulness of HateLexicon in hate speech model development, we examine two use cases: model interpretability and few-shot model development, showcasing how HateLexicon can be utilized to improve both processes in the hate speech domain.

3.1 HateLexicon Curation

For the curation of HateLexicon, we employed[1] annotators to provide slurs, target group names and neutral words that appear often in hateful contexts online. We employed three annotators in Brazil, four in Germany, four in India and two in Kenya.

The annotators were tasked with providing terms alongside a short description. The sourcing of terms was left up to the annotators. We suggested they could use social media (e.g., searching for certain hateful hashtags or groups), but no restrictions were imposed. Instead, we relied on the sociocultural knowledge of the annotators to guide curation. We allowed for coordination between the annotators, but with no explicit instructions to actively collaborate. Terms are written in Brazilian Portuguese, English, German, Hindi or Swahili. Acceptable terms are: (i) slurs attacking the identity of a person or group, such as ethnicity, religion and sexuality. (ii) target group denotations, such as religious groups (e.g., 'Muslim') and marginalized communities (e.g., 'homosexual'). (iii) neutral words that may appear often in hateful contexts

[1]All annotators were paid the same rate, which was above minimum wage in all countries.

Type	Brazil	Germany	India	Kenya
Neutral	30	4	3	21
Target	4	3	7	29
Slur	11	18	35	43
Neutral/Target	0	1	0	2
Neutral/Slur	0	18	1	6
Target/Slur	0	5	0	12
Total	*45*	*50*	*50*	*116*

Table 2: HateLexicon statistics for terms.

Country	Text	Type	Description
Brazil	gorda	Slur	overweight women
Brazil	traveco	Slur	transsexual
Brazil	hora	Neutral	meaning 'hour'
Germany	Flüchtling	Target	refugee
Germany	Schwuchteln	Slur	derogatory term for homosexual
Germany	Roma	Target	ethnic group
India	Bhimte	Slur	caste-ist term
India	Mullo	Slur	Muslim people
India	peaceful	Slur	Muslim people
Kenya	wakalee	Target	Kalenjin ethnic group
Kenya	nugu	Slur	generic slur
Kenya	foreskin	Slur	derogatory against uncircumcised Luo

Table 3: Example entries of HateLexicon.

or datasets (e.g., 'Frauenquote', in German meaning 'quota of/for women'). Statistics and indicative entries are shown in Table 2 and Table 3.

To evaluate the quality of our lexicon, terms submitted by one annotator were cross-checked by the other annotators of the same country. From discussions with annotator teams, it was made clear that a few terms can be assigned more than one type. For example, in German, the term 'Schwule' can be used by *homosexuals to describe themselves or as a slur against them.* In these instances, we allow annotation with multiple types. For example, 'Schwule' is annotated both as a target group denotation *and* a slur, to better capture the dual nature of the word.

3.2 Interpretability

We propose the use of HateLexicon as a tool to interpret model predictions. Popular interpretability toolkits such as LIME (Ribeiro et al., 2016) indicate which words are most associated with predictions of particular classes. In hate speech contexts, words most important for making predictions are oftentimes target group denotations or slurs. While slurs are a more obvious indicator of hateful language, target group denotations also naturally appear in hateful contexts and there is the danger of overemphasizing their association with hate speech. This correlation could lead to further marginalization of target groups, with content mentioning target group denotations being filtered out as hate speech. With HATELEXICON we can investigate keywords associated with model predictions from a more culturally-informed perspective to better verify whether the model has accrued bias against these groups.

We take as an example use case the work in XTREMESPEECH (Maronikolakis et al., 2022b), where a novel dataset of hate speech is introduced for Brazil, Germany, India and Kenya. In Maronikolakis et al. (2022b), the authors use LIME to interpret their developed mBERT models, identifying words contributing the most to predictions. In our work we operate on two levels: First, using HATELEXICON, we investigate the list of top-contributing words and show that in all examined countries, models emphasize heavily on target groups and slurs. Further, we examine the change of model representations for targets and slurs of the Kenyan and Indian subsets before and after model finetuning.

XTREMESPEECH is a hate speech dataset with social media texts collected from multiple online platforms and messaging apps. Languages covered in the dataset are Brazilian Portuguese, German, Hindi and Swahili, as well as English (either on its own or in the form of code switching with the native language).

All text in XTREMESPEECH is targeting one or more groups based on protected attributes (e.g., women or religious minorities), annotated for three levels of extremity: derogatory, exclusionary and dangerous extreme speech. Brief descriptions (as defined in (Maronikolakis et al., 2022b)) are shown below. For full definitions, we refer readers to the original paper.

1. Derogatory extreme speech: "Text that crosses the boundaries of civility within specific contexts and targets individuals/groups based on protected characteristics."

2. Exclusionary extreme speech: "Expressions that call for or imply excluding historically disadvantaged and vulnerable groups based on protected attributes such as national origin, gender and sexual orientation."

3. Dangerous extreme speech: "Text that has a reasonable chance to trigger harm against target groups."

3.3 Few-Shot Learning

With the general (relative) lack of non-English data in the domain of hate speech, as well as due to the difficulty of sourcing high-quality hate speech data, few-shot learning emerges as an attractive option for model development.

In few-shot learning settings, training shot selection is of great importance to model performance (Zheng et al., 2022; Köksal et al., 2022). This is especially salient in multilingual settings, where manual evaluation or prompt engineering might be challenging due to language barriers.

We propose the use of HATELEXICON to aid shot selection, allowing for more culturally-informed sampling of training examples. Instead of randomly selecting shots, we show how HATELEXICON can be used to select examples to cover a wider range of target groups and slurs in each cultural context.

We evaluate our proposed method using SetFit (Tunstall et al., 2022), training a multilingual SentenceBERT model[2] to discriminate between hateful and non-hateful speech.

3.3.1 Data

Training data comes from HASOC (Mandl et al., 2019) and evaluation data comes from the Multilingual HateCheck benchmark (Röttger et al., 2022), on the German and Hindi subsets. HASOC is a multilingual dataset of hate speech as sourced from Twitter. We focus on the binary classification task of HASOC, where tweets are classified as either hateful or neutral. The MHC benchmark is a suite with functional tests covering a wide range of hate speech categories.

To simulate a few-shot setting, we randomly sample 128 examples (64 hateful and 64 neutral) from HASOC German and Hindi each. This forms our total training set. We sample three sets for each languages with different seeds and report averaged results. We aim to investigate whether

[2] https://huggingface.co/sentence-transformers/paraphrase-multilingual-mpnet-base-v2

Set	German		Hindi	
	S	T	S	T
All_{128}	12	10	12	9
Random_{32}	2	0	3	3
Random_{64}	3	4	5	4
Random_{96}	8	8	6	4
Lexicon_{xx}	12	10	12	9

Table 4: Distribution of slurs (S) and targets (T) in German and Hindi sets as sampled with one of the seeds.

Brazil	Germany	India	Kenya
fechar	Politiker	muslims	cows
Ucranizar	Grünen	Muslim	ruto
ucranizar	Mohammedaner	muslim	luo
safada	Juden	Muslims	wajinga
prender	Merkels	ko	kikuyu
lixo	Merkel	mullo	stupid
coisa	Regierung	Rohingyas	idiot
kkkkk	Opfer	ड	looting
Vagabundo	Islam	suvar	tangatanga
traveco	Moslems	डर	ujinga

Table 5: Top words contributing to `mBERT`'s predictions. Blue: target group. Red: slur. Purple: both.

culturally-informed shot selection (via HATELEXICON) improves performance over random shot selection. We work with three dataset sizes: 32, 64 and 96.

3.3.2 Shot Selection

Sampling Method Comparison. For random selection, we sample shots without replacement. For the lexicon-based selection, we work in two steps: (i) select all training examples that contain a slur or a target group term, (ii) further sample randomly to reach the desired training set size. In Table 4 we show the distribution of slurs and targets in each sampled set. As expected, the randomly sampled sets do contain slurs and targets, although less frequently than in the HATELEXICON-sampled sets.

Complementing Data. Developers tackling hate speech online might try complementing their datasets with more data to improve performance. Since data collection and annotation is expensive and challenging, especially in low-resource languages, it is imperative that the collected data is of high quality.

To simulate this setting, we are procuring more training examples using HATELEXICON, balanced between the two classes. On top of the sampled datasets as well as the entire dataset, we are further sampling from HASOC German and Hindi 16 training examples containing a target term and 16 more a slur. These 32 examples are added to the previous training sets and few-shot training are repeated. For a fair comparison, we also sample 32 examples randomly and compare performance.

With this experiment we are aiming to investigate whether we can boost performance of a given training set by collecting training data specifically containing terms from HATELEXICON. Thus, developers in need of more data can query for terms found in HATELEXICON. While in our case we are merely sampling from HASOC, an already annotated hate speech dataset, this method could be used generally by querying for keywords on social media platforms and annotating as is practice.

4 Interpretability through a Cultural Lens

4.1 LIME Analysis

To showcase the usefulness of HATELEXICON in hate speech detection model interpretability, we analyze predictions (as reported by the authors) of XTREMESPEECH.

As part of their study, Maronikolakis et al. (2022b) conduct an interpretability analysis of `mBERT` predictions for a three-way classification task to identify the extremity of text (derogatory, exclusionary or dangerous). Using LIME, they identify the top-10 words contributing the most to `mBERT`'s predictions (shown in Table 5).

In brief, the authors conclude that target group names (such as religious groups) and slurs contribute prominently to model predictions. This exercise was performed in close collaboration with the annotators, who had to manually examine the identified top-contributing words. This process requires significant annotator effort and thus does not scale to practical settings.

With HATELEXICON, we can automate the process, significantly reducing cost and time consumption. We find that in Brazil, there are 5 slurs; in Germany, 1 slur and 4 targets; in India, 2 slurs and 5 targets and in Kenya, 1 slur and 3 targets.

It is obvious that the model relies on the presence of slurs to make decisions, since slurs are predominantly used in hateful contexts. The model, though, also relies heavily on target group denotations when making predictions. Due to the (naturally) heightened presence of target groups in hate speech training data, models might learn to associate these otherwise innocuous terms with hate

	India	Kenya
Slurs	0.25	0.19
Targets	0.25	0.22
Stop	0.22	0.22
Random	0.21	0.24

Table 6: Cosine similarity of representations between original mBERT and models finetuned on the Indian and Kenyan sets.

speech, overemphasizing their correlation with harmful content. With HATELEXICON, we are able to identify this erroneous behavior of mBERT and potentially work on mitigating this effect.

4.2 Change of LM Representation

To investigate the effect training on slurs and target group names has on language models, we compare mBERT's representation of lexicon terms before and after finetuning for India and Kenya. We finetune mBERT for the three-way classification task of Maronikolakis et al. (2022b) on the Indian and Kenyan sets.[3] Specifically, we extract the representation of the 8th layer[4] for the desired tokens[5] and compute the cosine similarity with the corresponding representation in vanilla mBERT.

As a baseline, we compare the change of random words and stopwords from each country. Random words were sampled from the development set of Maronikolakis et al. (2022b), matching in number the HATELEXICON terms. In Table 6 we show that in Kenya, the representation of slurs changed the most after finetuning, with the representation of targets closely behind. This indicates that vanilla mBERT has not adequately learned Kenyan slurs and target groups, since their representations changes significantly after we expose the model to the terms. In India, on the other hand, the representation of slurs changed less than that of random words. Considering the low performance of the Indian models (as reported by Maronikolakis et al. (2022b)) and the fact that targets make up half the list of top-contributing words (Table 5), we hypothesize the finetuned model has not sufficiently associated slurs with extreme speech.

[3]Access was granted to use the Indian and Kenyan sets.

[4]The 8th layer has been found to contain useful representation in multilingual models (Jalili Sabet et al., 2020; Dufter and Schütze, 2020).

[5]When a word spans more than one token, we average the representation of each token of the word.

5 Few-Shot Learning

5.1 Setup

In our experiments, we are comparing three sets of training data: randomly-sampled (denoted with Random_{xx}), lexicon-based sampling (denoted with Lexicon_{xx}) and the entire training set (denoted with All_{xx}), where xx denotes the training set size (by default equal to 128 for All_{xx}).

Further, we denote with $+l$ the sets complemented with 32 training examples additionally sampled using lexicon terms and we denote with $+r$ the sets complemented with 32 training examples additionally sampled randomly.

5.2 Results

Main Results. In Figure 1, we compare macro F1-scores between HATELEXICON- and randomly-sampled training sets as well as the set containing all available training examples (All_{128}).

In German, excluding the sets with a size of 32 which perform poorly, training sets sampled via HATELEXICON outperform the corresponding randomly-sampled sets. Both Lexicon_{64} and Lexicon_{96} outperform all randomly-sampled sets, as well as All_{128}. At the same time, with the lexicon-based sampling method, performance is more consistent across runs, especially at sizes 64 and 96 which have a small standard deviation.

The difference between lexicon- and random-based sampling is starker in the Hindi set. Lexicon-based training sets outperform all other baselines and, like in the German experiments, standard deviation is minimized when sampling with HATELEXICON, providing better stability.

It is noteworthy that HATELEXICON-based training sets regularly outperform All_{128}. We hypothesize this is due to a higher concentration of high-quality training data in Lexicon_{xx} sets. In few-shot settings, the importance of each training example is magnified and thus noise can potentially affect performance disproportionately (Zheng et al., 2022; Mosbach et al., 2021). This is in-line with other works: for example, in Schick and Schütze (2021a), results on AGNews are worse when using the largest training set. In Section 5.3, we are further investigating this phenomenon.

Data Complementing Results. In Table 7, we show results of our data complementing experiments. In these experiments, we are adding to the training data 32 examples sampled either randomly ($+r$ in notation) or via HATELEXICON ($+l$ in nota-

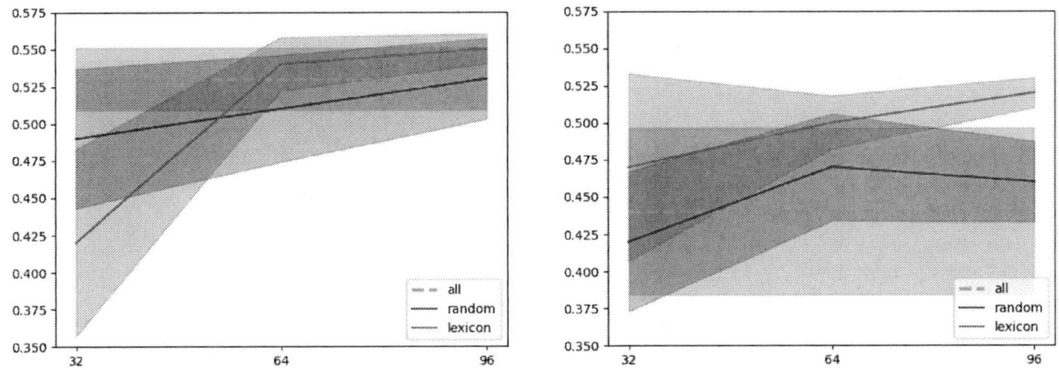

(a) German

(b) Hindi

Figure 1: Macro F1 (areas within one standard deviation are shaded) for MHC German (a) and Hindi (b). Lexicon-based sampling (red) outperforms both random sampling (blue) and All_{128} (orange) for set sizes 64 and 96.

tion). We see a consistent increase in performance when adding examples sampled with our proposed method. Namely, Lexicon_{xx+l} sets consistently perform better than both the original (without data complementing) baselines and the $+r$ variants. When complementing the Random_{xx} sets, performance is slightly more inconsistent, although the $+l$ sets still perform better than the $+r$ variants. Further, Lexicon_{xx+l} sets have a low standard deviation, while Random_{xx+l} and Random_{xx+r} have a consistently higher standard deviation, showing that lexicon-based sampling is overall more consistent. In general, wherever we complement using HATELEXICON ($+l$ sets), performance is better compared to both the original and the randomly-complemented ($+r$) sets.

5.3 Ablation Study - Predicting Shots

A reason why our lexicon-based sampling method works better than random sampling may be that it retrieves less noise and fewer ambiguous examples. It has been previously shown that hard-to-learn examples (such as text that is ambiguous, misannotated or difficult to predict) do not contribute positively to model development (Swayamdipta et al., 2020). We hypothesize that our sampling method replaces a large portion of these low-quality examples with high-quality, information-rich examples.

To investigate whether our hypothesis holds true, we develop a hate speech model and *apply it on our examined training sets*. Since lexicon-sampled training sets are bound to contain more informative and unambiguous examples, they should be easier to classify correctly than randomly-sampled examples.

For this ablation study, we finetune an `XLM-RoBERTa-base` model (Conneau et al., 2020) separately on all the originally available German and Hindi data from HASOC (Mandl et al., 2019), excluding the 128 training examples sampled for our experiments, for a total of 2245 training examples for German and 2835 for Hindi. Then, we apply the two resulting models on our few-shot learning training sets.[6]

We show (Table 8) that examples sampled with our HATELEXICON are easier to classify correctly. In Hindi, the lexicon-based set is easier by 0.02 over the other sets. In German, performance on the lexicon-based set is 0.05 higher than the randomly sampled set and 0.10 higher than the entire set. Thus, we can infer that with our lexicon-based sampling method, easier examples are sourced more often than harder-to-classify ones.

Manual inspection of prediction errors of examples contained in the total training set but not in the lexicon-based set shows a high rate of low-quality text and noise (Table 9). Example 0 has been annotated as hateful even though it is just noise, containing only an account mention. Example 1 is an ambiguous (given the lack of context) example containing a sarcastic comment against a political party (die Grünen / Greens), classified by the model as hateful. Example 2 is also ambiguous, containing sarcasm against a right-wing party in Germany (AfD). All ambiguous examples (1-3) are short tweets that mention political entities.[7] In a politically charged environment, these short texts

[6] We only predict shots from a randomly-chosen training set for each language instead of all three used previously.

[7] While political entities are an integral part of society, they are not target groups and were not added to our lexicon.

Set	F1	Δ
Random_{32+l}	$0.54_{3.2}$	+0.05
Random_{32+r}	$0.51_{3.6}$	+0.02
Random_{64+l}	$0.54_{2.1}$	+0.03
Random_{64+r}	$0.54_{1.9}$	+0.03
Random_{96+l}	$0.56_{1.2}$	+0.03
Random_{96+r}	$0.51_{0.9}$	-0.02
Lexicon_{32+l}	$0.56_{1.2}$	+0.14
Lexicon_{32+r}	$0.51_{3.0}$	+0.09
Lexicon_{64+l}	$0.56_{0.9}$	+0.02
Lexicon_{64+r}	$0.55_{1.8}$	+0.01
Lexicon_{96+l}	$0.59_{0.4}$	+0.04
Lexicon_{96+r}	$0.56_{0.9}$	+0.01
All_{128+l}	$0.57_{1.1}$	+0.04
All_{128+r}	$0.54_{2.2}$	+0.01

(a) German

Set	F1	Δ
Random_{32+l}	$0.47_{3.3}$	+0.05
Random_{32+r}	$0.44_{4.2}$	+0.02
Random_{64+l}	$0.50_{1.8}$	+0.03
Random_{64+r}	$0.48_{2.4}$	+0.03
Random_{96+l}	$0.51_{1.1}$	+0.03
Random_{96+r}	$0.48_{2.9}$	-0.02
Lexicon_{32+l}	$0.50_{0.9}$	+0.14
Lexicon_{32+r}	$0.48_{2.0}$	+0.09
Lexicon_{64+l}	$0.52_{0.3}$	+0.02
Lexicon_{64+r}	$0.51_{0.9}$	+0.01
Lexicon_{96+l}	$0.55_{0.3}$	+0.04
Lexicon_{96+r}	$0.51_{0.6}$	+0.01
All_{128+l}	$0.49_{1.3}$	+0.04
All_{128+r}	$0.49_{1.0}$	+0.01

(b) Hindi

Table 7: Macro F1 (standard deviation as subscript) and difference with the non-complemented baseline (Δ), for MHC German (a) and Hindi (b).

	Germany	India
Lexicon	0.61	0.55
Random	0.56	0.53
All	0.51	0.53

Table 8: F1-score of classifying training shots.

ID	Text	Type
0	@Hartes_Geld	Noise
1	Ja so tierlieb sind die grünen	Ambiguous
2	@SaschaUlbrich @Mundauf-machen @AfD super, gut gemacht! auf jeden Fall "retweeten"!	Ambiguous
3	Wer soll jetzt die SPD führen?	Low-content

Table 9: Manual inspection of model prediction errors.

do not provide enough context for the model to adequately learn whether the example is hateful or not. Therefore, adding these examples in our training set is not beneficial.

6 Conclusion

In our work, we curate HATELEXICON, a lexicon of slurs and targets of hate speech for the countries of Brazil, Germany, India and Kenya, with the goal of improving model development.

With our lexicon, we show how models rely on slurs and target group denotations when making predictions in hate speech tasks. The over-reliance on target group names may lead to further marginalization of targets of hate speech, with models flagging as hateful innocuous text containing these terms. With HATELEXICON, this erroneous behavior is unveiled and researchers can focus on mitigating this bias.

We also demonstrate how HATELEXICON can be used for few-shot learning. We evaluate on the German and Hindi subsets of the Multilingual HateCheck benchmark (Röttger et al., 2022) and show that selecting training shots with a culturally-informed process (e.g., our lexicon of slurs and targets) can aid the development of hate speech classifiers. Namely, training sets sampled using HATELEXICON perform better than training sets sampled at random.

More abstractly, we provide evidence that curating sociocultural knowledge bases (e.g., lexicons) is pivotal in developing hate speech detection models. Sociocultural information is vital in contextualizing hate speech, and without it we risk developing models detached from the reality and experiences of the most vulnerable. Thus, we advocate for a greater focus on bridging the knowledge gap between researchers and affected communities for the development of models better geared towards protecting target groups.

Acknowledgments. This work was funded by the European Research Council (grant #740516).

7 Ethical Considerations and Limitations

7.1 Ethics Statement

In our work we are dealing with sensitive content in the form of hate speech against marginalized communities. We are not advocating for hate speech, but instead propose methods to aid in filtering out harmful content from online spheres and analyzing detection models with our proposed lexicon.

The lexicon was developed in collaboration with annotators familiar with sociocultural balances in their countries and communities, with the goal of creating a dictionary of terms useful for hate speech model development. A potential concern with a dictionary of hateful terms is that the terms will be publicized and could be subsequently used by hate speech peddlers to cause further harm. Since these terms were recorded specifically because they are already used extensively, the risk of additional harm from publicizing these terms is minimal. Moreover, in HATELEXICON we are collecting denotations of target groups. These may be based on ethnicity, religion, sexuality or other protected attributes. A potential concern is that we will be exposing the mentioned target groups. We argue that better understanding the harms faced by these communities outweighs the negatives and will provide more net-positive in the long term, while at the same time these groups were recorded due to the increased quantity of hateful content they receive.

7.2 Limitations

The lists of slurs and target groups in HATELEXICON are not exhaustive. While we took care to expand HATELEXICON as thoroughly as possible, we are limited by time and resources and could only cover a partial set of terms used online in relation to hate speech in the examined countries.

Further, the list of countries chosen is small: Brazil, Germany, India and Kenya. Ideally we would have included more countries and languages. More work needs to be done to expand this list and provide more coverage.

References

Hala Al Kuwatly, Maximilian Wich, and Georg Groh. 2020. Identifying and measuring annotator bias based on annotators' demographic characteristics. In *Proceedings of the Fourth Workshop on Online Abuse and Harms*, pages 184–190, Online. Association for Computational Linguistics.

Tom B. Brown, Benjamin Mann, Nick Ryder, Melanie Subbiah, Jared Kaplan, Prafulla Dhariwal, Arvind Neelakantan, Pranav Shyam, Girish Sastry, Amanda Askell, Sandhini Agarwal, Ariel Herbert-Voss, Gretchen Krueger, Tom Henighan, Rewon Child, Aditya Ramesh, Daniel M. Ziegler, Jeffrey Wu, Clemens Winter, Christopher Hesse, Mark Chen, Eric Sigler, Mateusz Litwin, Scott Gray, Benjamin Chess, Jack Clark, Christopher Berner, Sam McCandlish, Alec Radford, Ilya Sutskever, and Dario Amodei. 2020. Language models are few-shot learners.

Alexis Conneau, Kartikay Khandelwal, Naman Goyal, Vishrav Chaudhary, Guillaume Wenzek, Francisco Guzmán, Edouard Grave, Myle Ott, Luke Zettlemoyer, and Veselin Stoyanov. 2020. Unsupervised cross-lingual representation learning at scale. In *Proceedings of the 58th Annual Meeting of the Association for Computational Linguistics*, pages 8440–8451, Online. Association for Computational Linguistics.

Thomas Davidson, Debasmita Bhattacharya, and Ingmar Weber. 2019a. Racial bias in hate speech and abusive language detection datasets. In *Proceedings of the Third Workshop on Abusive Language Online*, pages 25–35, Florence, Italy. Association for Computational Linguistics.

Thomas Davidson, Debasmita Bhattacharya, and Ingmar Weber. 2019b. Racial bias in hate speech and abusive language detection datasets. In *Proceedings of the Third Workshop on Abusive Language Online*, pages 25–35, Florence, Italy. Association for Computational Linguistics.

Thomas Davidson, Dana Warmsley, Michael Macy, and Ingmar Weber. 2017. Automated hate speech detection and the problem of offensive language. In *International AAAI Conference on Web and Social Media*.

Bruno Heridet Delapouite. Accessed 10/11/2021. https://game-icons.net/.

Jesse Dodge, Maarten Sap, Ana Marasović, William Agnew, Gabriel Ilharco, Dirk Groeneveld, Margaret Mitchell, and Matt Gardner. 2021. Documenting large webtext corpora: A case study on the colossal clean crawled corpus. In *Proceedings of the 2021 Conference on Empirical Methods in Natural Language Processing*, pages 1286–1305, Online and Punta Cana, Dominican Republic. Association for Computational Linguistics.

Philipp Dufter and Hinrich Schütze. 2020. Identifying elements essential for BERT's multilinguality. In *Proceedings of the 2020 Conference on Empirical Methods in Natural Language Processing (EMNLP)*, pages 4423–4437, Online. Association for Computational Linguistics.

Antigoni-Maria Founta, Constantinos Djouvas, Despoina Chatzakou, Ilias Leontiadis, Jeremy Blackburn, Gianluca Stringhini, Athena Vakali, Michael Sirivianos, and Nicolas Kourtellis. 2018. Large scale crowdsourcing and characterization of twitter abusive behavior. In *11th International Conference on Web and Social Media, ICWSM 2018*. AAAI Press.

Jinlan Fu, See-Kiong Ng, and Pengfei Liu. 2022. Polyglot prompt: Multilingual multitask promptraining.

Tianyu Gao, Adam Fisch, and Danqi Chen. 2021. Making pre-trained language models better few-shot learners. In *Proceedings of the 59th Annual Meeting of the Association for Computational Linguistics and the 11th International Joint Conference on Natural Language Processing (Volume 1: Long Papers)*, pages 3816–3830, Online. Association for Computational Linguistics.

Timnit Gebru. 2019. Oxford handbook on ai ethics book chapter on race and gender.

Lara Grimminger and Roman Klinger. 2021. Hate towards the political opponent: A Twitter corpus study of the 2020 US elections on the basis of offensive speech and stance detection. In *Proceedings of the Eleventh Workshop on Computational Approaches to Subjectivity, Sentiment and Social Media Analysis*, pages 171–180, Online. Association for Computational Linguistics.

Ella Guest, Bertie Vidgen, Alexandros Mittos, Nishanth Sastry, Gareth Tyson, and Helen Margetts. 2021. An expert annotated dataset for the detection of online misogyny. In *Proceedings of the 16th Conference of the European Chapter of the Association for Computational Linguistics: Main Volume*, pages 1336–1350, Online. Association for Computational Linguistics.

Anushree Hede, Oshin Agarwal, Linda Lu, Diana C. Mutz, and Ani Nenkova. 2021. From toxicity in online comments to incivility in American news: Proceed with caution. In *Proceedings of the 16th Conference of the European Chapter of the Association for Computational Linguistics: Main Volume*, pages 2620–2630, Online. Association for Computational Linguistics.

Masoud Jalili Sabet, Philipp Dufter, François Yvon, and Hinrich Schütze. 2020. SimAlign: High quality word alignments without parallel training data using static and contextualized embeddings. In *Findings of the Association for Computational Linguistics: EMNLP 2020*, pages 1627–1643, Online. Association for Computational Linguistics.

Eun Seo Jo and Timnit Gebru. 2020. Lessons from archives: Strategies for collecting sociocultural data in machine learning. In *Proceedings of the 2020 Conference on Fairness, Accountability, and Transparency*, FAT* '20, page 306–316, New York, NY, USA. Association for Computing Machinery.

Jae-Yeon Kim, Carlos Ortiz, Sarah Nam, Sarah Santiago, and Vivek Datta. 2020. Intersectional bias in hate speech and abusive language datasets. *CoRR*, abs/2005.05921.

Abdullatif Köksal, Timo Schick, and Hinrich Schütze. 2022. Meal: Stable and active learning for few-shot prompting.

Léo Laugier, John Pavlopoulos, Jeffrey Sorensen, and Lucas Dixon. 2021. Civil rephrases of toxic texts with self-supervised transformers. In *Proceedings of the 16th Conference of the European Chapter of the Association for Computational Linguistics: Main Volume*, pages 1442–1461, Online. Association for Computational Linguistics.

Teven Le Scao and Alexander Rush. 2021. How many data points is a prompt worth? In *Proceedings of the 2021 Conference of the North American Chapter of the Association for Computational Linguistics: Human Language Technologies*, pages 2627–2636, Online. Association for Computational Linguistics.

Kobi Leins, Jey Han Lau, and Timothy Baldwin. 2020. Give me convenience and give her death: Who should decide what uses of NLP are appropriate, and on what basis? In *Proceedings of the 58th Annual Meeting of the Association for Computational Linguistics*, pages 2908–2913, Online. Association for Computational Linguistics.

Robert Logan IV, Ivana Balazevic, Eric Wallace, Fabio Petroni, Sameer Singh, and Sebastian Riedel. 2022. Cutting down on prompts and parameters: Simple few-shot learning with language models. In *Findings of the Association for Computational Linguistics: ACL 2022*, pages 2824–2835, Dublin, Ireland. Association for Computational Linguistics.

Yao Lu, Max Bartolo, Alastair Moore, Sebastian Riedel, and Pontus Stenetorp. 2022. Fantastically ordered prompts and where to find them: Overcoming few-shot prompt order sensitivity. In *Proceedings of the 60th Annual Meeting of the Association for Computational Linguistics (Volume 1: Long Papers)*, pages 8086–8098, Dublin, Ireland. Association for Computational Linguistics.

Kosisochukwu Madukwe, Xiaoying Gao, and Bing Xue. 2020. In data we trust: A critical analysis of hate speech detection datasets. In *Proceedings of the Fourth Workshop on Online Abuse and Harms*, pages 150–161, Online. Association for Computational Linguistics.

Thomas Mandl, Sandip Modha, Prasenjit Majumder, Daksh Patel, Mohana Dave, Chintak Mandlia, and Aditya Patel. 2019. Overview of the hasoc track at fire 2019: Hate speech and offensive content identification in indo-european languages. In *Proceedings of the 11th forum for information retrieval evaluation*, pages 14–17.

Antonis Maronikolakis, Philip Baader, and Hinrich Schütze. 2022a. Analyzing hate speech data along racial, gender and intersectional axes. In *Proceedings of the 4th Workshop on Gender Bias in Natural Language Processing (GeBNLP)*, pages 1–7, Seattle, Washington. Association for Computational Linguistics.

Antonis Maronikolakis, Axel Wisiorek, Leah Nann, Haris Jabbar, Sahana Udupa, and Hinrich Schuetze. 2022b. Listening to affected communities to define extreme speech: Dataset and experiments. In *Findings of the Association for Computational Linguistics: ACL 2022*, pages 1089–1104, Dublin, Ireland. Association for Computational Linguistics.

Binny Mathew, Punyajoy Saha, Seid Muhie Yimam, Chris Biemann, Pawan Goyal, and Animesh Mukherjee. 2021a. Hatexplain: A benchmark dataset for explainable hate speech detection. *Proceedings of the AAAI Conference on Artificial Intelligence*, 35(17):14867–14875.

Binny Mathew, Punyajoy Saha, Seid Muhie Yimam, Chris Biemann, Pawan Goyal, and Animesh Mukherjee. 2021b. Hatexplain: A benchmark dataset for explainable hate speech detection. *Proceedings of the AAAI Conference on Artificial Intelligence*, 35(17):14867–14875.

Shakir Mohamed, Marie-Therese Png, and William Isaac. 2020. Decolonial ai: Decolonial theory as sociotechnical foresight in artificial intelligence. *Philosophy and Technology*, 33(4):659–684.

Marius Mosbach, Maksym Andriushchenko, and Dietrich Klakow. 2021. On the stability of fine-tuning {bert}: Misconceptions, explanations, and strong baselines. In *International Conference on Learning Representations*.

Debora Nozza. 2021. Exposing the limits of zero-shot cross-lingual hate speech detection. In *Proceedings of the 59th Annual Meeting of the Association for Computational Linguistics and the 11th International Joint Conference on Natural Language Processing (Volume 2: Short Papers)*, pages 907–914, Online. Association for Computational Linguistics.

Nedjma Ousidhoum, Zizheng Lin, Hongming Zhang, Yangqiu Song, and Dit-Yan Yeung. 2019. Multilingual and multi-aspect hate speech analysis. In *Proceedings of the 2019 Conference on Empirical Methods in Natural Language Processing and the 9th International Joint Conference on Natural Language Processing (EMNLP-IJCNLP)*, pages 4675–4684, Hong Kong, China. Association for Computational Linguistics.

Melina Plakidis and Georg Rehm. 2022. A dataset of offensive German language tweets annotated for speech acts. In *Proceedings of the Thirteenth Language Resources and Evaluation Conference*, pages 4799–4807, Marseille, France. European Language Resources Association.

Lisa Posch, Arnim Bleier, Fabian Flöck, and Markus Strohmaier. 2018. Characterizing the global crowd workforce: A cross-country comparison of crowdworker demographics.

Alan Ramponi and Sara Tonelli. 2022. Features or spurious artifacts? data-centric baselines for fair and robust hate speech detection. In *Proceedings of the 2022 Conference of the North American Chapter of the Association for Computational Linguistics: Human Language Technologies*, pages 3027–3040, Seattle, United States. Association for Computational Linguistics.

Tharindu Ranasinghe and Marcos Zampieri. 2020. Multilingual offensive language identification with cross-lingual embeddings. In *Proceedings of the 2020 Conference on Empirical Methods in Natural Language Processing (EMNLP)*, pages 5838–5844, Online. Association for Computational Linguistics.

Nils Reimers and Iryna Gurevych. 2019. Sentence-bert: Sentence embeddings using siamese bert-networks.

Marco Tulio Ribeiro, Sameer Singh, and Carlos Guestrin. 2016. "why should i trust you?": Explaining the predictions of any classifier. In *Proceedings of the 22nd ACM SIGKDD International Conference on Knowledge Discovery and Data Mining*, KDD '16, page 1135–1144, New York, NY, USA. Association for Computing Machinery.

Björn Ross, Michael Rist, Guillermo Carbonell, Benjamin Cabrera, Nils Kurowsky, and Michael Wojatzki. 2017. Measuring the reliability of hate speech annotations: The case of the european refugee crisis. *CoRR*, abs/1701.08118.

Paul Röttger, Haitham Seelawi, Debora Nozza, Zeerak Talat, and Bertie Vidgen. 2022. Multilingual HateCheck: Functional tests for multilingual hate speech detection models. In *Proceedings of the Sixth Workshop on Online Abuse and Harms (WOAH)*, pages 154–169, Seattle, Washington (Hybrid). Association for Computational Linguistics.

Paul Röttger, Bertie Vidgen, Dong Nguyen, Zeerak Waseem, Helen Margetts, and Janet Pierrehumbert. 2021. HateCheck: Functional tests for hate speech detection models. In *Proceedings of the 59th Annual Meeting of the Association for Computational Linguistics and the 11th International Joint Conference on Natural Language Processing (Volume 1: Long Papers)*, pages 41–58, Online. Association for Computational Linguistics.

Victor Sanh, Albert Webson, Colin Raffel, Stephen Bach, Lintang Sutawika, Zaid Alyafeai, Antoine Chaffin, Arnaud Stiegler, Arun Raja, Manan Dey, M Saiful Bari, Canwen Xu, Urmish Thakker, Shanya Sharma Sharma, Eliza Szczechla, Taewoon Kim, Gunjan Chhablani, Nihal Nayak, Debajyoti Datta, Jonathan Chang, Mike Tian-Jian Jiang, Han Wang, Matteo Manica, Sheng Shen, Zheng Xin Yong, Harshit Pandey, Rachel Bawden, Thomas Wang, Trishala Neeraj, Jos Rozen, Abheesht Sharma, Andrea Santilli, Thibault Fevry, Jason Alan Fries,

Ryan Teehan, Teven Le Scao, Stella Biderman, Leo Gao, Thomas Wolf, and Alexander M Rush. 2022. Multitask prompted training enables zero-shot task generalization. In *International Conference on Learning Representations*.

Maarten Sap, Dallas Card, Saadia Gabriel, Yejin Choi, and Noah A. Smith. 2019. The risk of racial bias in hate speech detection. In *Proceedings of the 57th Annual Meeting of the Association for Computational Linguistics*, pages 1668–1678, Florence, Italy. Association for Computational Linguistics.

Maarten Sap, Saadia Gabriel, Lianhui Qin, Dan Jurafsky, Noah A. Smith, and Yejin Choi. 2020. Social bias frames: Reasoning about social and power implications of language. In *Proceedings of the 58th Annual Meeting of the Association for Computational Linguistics*, pages 5477–5490, Online. Association for Computational Linguistics.

Timo Schick and Hinrich Schütze. 2021a. Exploiting cloze-questions for few-shot text classification and natural language inference. In *Proceedings of the 16th Conference of the European Chapter of the Association for Computational Linguistics: Main Volume*, pages 255–269, Online. Association for Computational Linguistics.

Timo Schick and Hinrich Schütze. 2021b. It's not just size that matters: Small language models are also few-shot learners. In *Proceedings of the 2021 Conference of the North American Chapter of the Association for Computational Linguistics: Human Language Technologies*, pages 2339–2352, Online. Association for Computational Linguistics.

Taylor Shin, Yasaman Razeghi, Robert L. Logan IV, Eric Wallace, and Sameer Singh. 2020. AutoPrompt: Eliciting Knowledge from Language Models with Automatically Generated Prompts. In *Proceedings of the 2020 Conference on Empirical Methods in Natural Language Processing (EMNLP)*, pages 4222–4235, Online. Association for Computational Linguistics.

Boaz Shmueli, Jan Fell, Soumya Ray, and Lun-Wei Ku. 2021. Beyond fair pay: Ethical implications of NLP crowdsourcing. In *Proceedings of the 2021 Conference of the North American Chapter of the Association for Computational Linguistics: Human Language Technologies*, pages 3758–3769, Online. Association for Computational Linguistics.

Steve Durairaj Swamy, Anupam Jamatia, and Björn Gambäck. 2019. Studying generalisability across abusive language detection datasets. In *Proceedings of the 23rd Conference on Computational Natural Language Learning (CoNLL)*, pages 940–950, Hong Kong, China. Association for Computational Linguistics.

Swabha Swayamdipta, Roy Schwartz, Nicholas Lourie, Yizhong Wang, Hannaneh Hajishirzi, Noah A. Smith, and Yejin Choi. 2020. Dataset cartography: Mapping and diagnosing datasets with training dynamics. In *Proceedings of the 2020 Conference on Empirical Methods in Natural Language Processing (EMNLP)*, pages 9275–9293, Online. Association for Computational Linguistics.

Lewis Tunstall, Nils Reimers, Unso Eun Seo Jo, Luke Bates, Daniel Korat, Moshe Wasserblat, and Oren Pereg. 2022. Efficient few-shot learning without prompts.

Sahana Udupa, Antonis Maronikolakis, Hinrich Schütze, and Axel Wisiorek. 2022. Ethical scaling for content moderation: Extreme speech and the (in)significance of artificial intelligence.

Bertie Vidgen, Alex Harris, Dong Nguyen, Rebekah Tromble, Scott Hale, and Helen Margetts. 2019. Challenges and frontiers in abusive content detection. In *Proceedings of the Third Workshop on Abusive Language Online*, pages 80–93, Florence, Italy. Association for Computational Linguistics.

Zeerak Waseem. 2016. Are you a racist or am I seeing things? annotator influence on hate speech detection on Twitter. In *Proceedings of the First Workshop on NLP and Computational Social Science*, pages 138–142, Austin, Texas. Association for Computational Linguistics.

Jason Wei, Yi Tay, Rishi Bommasani, Colin Raffel, Barret Zoph, Sebastian Borgeaud, Dani Yogatama, Maarten Bosma, Denny Zhou, Donald Metzler, Ed H. Chi, Tatsunori Hashimoto, Oriol Vinyals, Percy Liang, Jeff Dean, and William Fedus. 2022. Emergent abilities of large language models. *Transactions on Machine Learning Research*. Survey Certification.

Michael Wiegand, Josef Ruppenhofer, and Elisabeth Eder. 2021. Implicitly abusive language – what does it actually look like and why are we not getting there? In *Proceedings of the 2021 Conference of the North American Chapter of the Association for Computational Linguistics: Human Language Technologies*, pages 576–587, Online. Association for Computational Linguistics.

Michael Wiegand, Josef Ruppenhofer, and Thomas Kleinbauer. 2019. Detection of Abusive Language: the Problem of Biased Datasets. In *Proceedings of the 2019 Conference of the North American Chapter of the Association for Computational Linguistics: Human Language Technologies, Volume 1 (Long and Short Papers)*, pages 602–608, Minneapolis, Minnesota. Association for Computational Linguistics.

Mengjie Zhao and Hinrich Schütze. 2021. Discrete and soft prompting for multilingual models. In *Proceedings of the 2021 Conference on Empirical Methods in Natural Language Processing*, pages 8547–8555, Online and Punta Cana, Dominican Republic. Association for Computational Linguistics.

Yanan Zheng, Jing Zhou, Yujie Qian, Ming Ding, Chonghua Liao, Li Jian, Ruslan Salakhutdinov,

Jie Tang, Sebastian Ruder, and Zhilin Yang. 2022. FewNLU: Benchmarking state-of-the-art methods for few-shot natural language understanding. In *Proceedings of the 60th Annual Meeting of the Association for Computational Linguistics (Volume 1: Long Papers)*, pages 501–516, Dublin, Ireland. Association for Computational Linguistics.

A Dataset for the Detection of Dehumanizing Language

Paul Engelmann
IT University of Copenhagen
paen@itu.dk

Peter Brunsgaard Trolle
IT University of Copenhagen
ptro@itu.dk

Christian Hardmeier
IT University of Copenhagen
chrha@itu.dk

Abstract

Dehumanization is a mental process that enables the exclusion and ill treatment of a group of people. In this paper, we present two data sets of dehumanizing text, a large, automatically collected corpus and a smaller, manually annotated data set. Both data sets include a combination of political discourse and dialogue from movie subtitles. Our methods give us a broad and varied amount of dehumanization data to work with, enabling further exploratory analysis and automatic classification of dehumanization patterns. Both data sets will be publicly released.

1 Introduction

Dehumanization, the act of depicting someone as less than human, can be seen in many different examples, such as against African Americans (Mekawi et al., 2016), Arabs (Prati et al., 2016) as well as between Israelis and Palestinians (Bruneau and Kteily, 2017). Dehumanization can range from blatant to subtle forms of varying degrees (Bain et al., 2009), making automated, general detection difficult. Mendelsohn et al. (2020) present one of the first computational works on dehumanization through explicit feature engineering, using lexicon and word embedding based approaches to detect dehumanizing associations across several years in a New York Times corpus. Outside of this, there is little computational work on dehumanization. We believe that the lack of work can be attributed to a vague general definition of dehumanization and a pronounced focus on content moderation, rather than the underlying processes of hateful content.

Additionally, we notice a lack of data sets specializing on dehumanization. While similar data, such as social media hate speech data (Silva et al., 2016; Zhong et al., 2016; Mollas et al., 2020), exists, these do not capture the specifics of dehumanization. Hate speech and dehumanization differ in the sense that hate speech is a surface phenomenon, representing the observable aspects of hateful content, whereas dehumanization describes the underlying attitude for certain types of hate speech.

As a result, we wish to provide two dehumanization focused data sets to allow work on general identification and detection of dehumanization. Both data sets are in English and collected from the OpenSubtitles (Lison and Tiedemann, 2016) as well as the Common Crawl[1] corpora. One data set consists of a larger, unlabelled corpus, while the other is an evaluation set consisting of human annotated samples, labelled by two independent annotators. Both data sets were extracted using keywords, which include target groups from ethnic, religious and sexual backgrounds, as well as common animal metaphor keywords and moral disgust terms from the Moral Foundations Dictionary[2] (Graham et al., 2009).

For dehumanization patterns, we limit ourselves to patterns inspired by Mendelsohn et al. (2020) and Haslam (2006), where a sample is considered dehumanizing if it contains at least one of the following categories: negative evaluation of a target group, denial of agency, moral disgust, animal metaphors, objectification. Animal metaphors and objectification specifically relate to a human being compared to an animal or object with the intent to cause harm. *Trigger Warning: This paper contains examples of hateful content that some may find upsetting.*

2 Related Work

Since computational work on dehumanization is sparse, we focus on related dehumanization research and other annotation efforts in fields such as hate speech detection. Kteily and Landry (2022) provide an overview of current trends and chal-

[1] Common Crawl: https://commoncrawl.org/
[2] https://moralfoundations.org/other-materials/

Proceedings of the Fourth Workshop on Language Technology for Equality, Diversity, Inclusion, pages 14–20
March 21, 2024

lenges regarding dehumanization. Mendelsohn et al. (2020) focus on the use of the NRC-VAD Lexicon (Mohammad, 2018), which features 20,000 English keywords, rated by annotators based on their associated valence, dominance and arousal in the range of 0 to 1. Valence, in particular, describes the evaluation of an event or concept and assigns it a value, ranging from unpleasant to pleasant (Osgood et al., 1957; Russell, 1980). Mendelsohn et al. hypothesise that low valence is an indication of potential dehumanization in the form of a negative evaluation of a target group, while low dominance suggests dehumanization in the form of denial of agency. These, together with word embeddings made out of combining several keywords for moral disgust and vermin metaphors, are leveraged to identify dehumanized target groups.

Examining hate speech data sets, Mathew et al. (2021) focus on explainable hate speech detection, aiming to increase the interpretability of hate speech detection models. Qian et al. (2019) provide a benchmark that not only tries to identify hate speech, but also expects generative models to be able to intervene in hateful discussions using automatically generated responses.

For automated abuse detection, Mishra et al. (2019) provides an overview for several techniques and methods that are commonly employed. Transformer based models have shown particular promise in hate speech detection. An example is HateBERT (Caselli et al., 2020), a BERT model trained from the ground up on hate speech data, outperforming the standard BERT model on the detection of hate speech.

3 Data Set Collection

3.1 OpenSubtitles

OpenSubtitles (Lison and Tiedemann, 2016) is a data set consisting of movie and TV series subtitles. It contains fictitious, high quality dialogue, curated by professional writers and thus possessing potentially more subtle dehumanization compared to standard dialogue.

We extract sentence windows with a size of 5 grammatical sentences per window, split based on quotation marks, under the condition that they contain at least one keyword from the religious, ethnic, sexual, moral disgust or animal category. A complete list of all keywords can be found in Table 5. To ensure that we do not over-represent a category, we limit each to 20% of the samples. Since the data

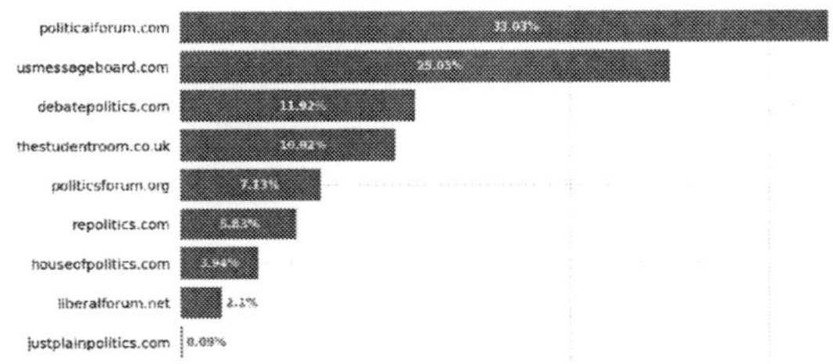

Figure 1: Percentage of tokens extracted from each forum in Common Crawl

set can include multiple different subtitles for the same movie, deduplication and preprocessing has been performed, including replacement of URLs, identifiable names through a placeholder token, as well as transforming emojis into their equivalent text so that models may use them for inference.

3.2 Common Crawl

The Common Crawl is an open repository of web crawled data, which features crawls from all over the internet. This data set allows us to take standard dialogue from everyday users, which allows us to extract more common dehumanization patterns. As the Common Crawl includes several petabytes of data in total, we have selectively extracted data from political forums, as political discourse is prone to the use of dehumanization (Cassese, 2021). As we limit ourselves to English, the Common Crawl data features discourse primarily focused on American and British politics.

Random web pages from these forums were extracted and preprocessed using jusText (Pomikálek, 2011), to remove boilerplate code from the website. Additional preprocessing was performed similarly to the OpenSubtitles data. Examples for both can be found in Table 1.

3.3 Labelled Data Set

The evaluation data set is a subset of the previously extracted data sources, thus containing the same limitations and processing steps as before. We extract 50% of the data from OpenSubtitles and 50% from Common Crawl, ensuring that each keyword group is equally likely from both sources. The examples were labelled by two annotators. Each annotator was informed of the chosen criteria with their definition and artificial example sentences, which were not present in the data set. The example sentences can be found in Table 4. An annotator could pick between the labels *Yes, No, Not Sure* to signify if dehuman-

Common Crawl	Trump continually harps on violence from **[ETHNIC GROUP]** in South American gangs, claims that **[RELIGIOUS GROUP]** terrorists are in the caravan, that **[ETHNIC GROUP]** are going to bring in diseases.
	For many of us, this is revolting. Men dancing with men. **[SEXUAL GROUP]** in this country today break the law.
OpenSubtitles	[...] Fuck it! I can't reason with a hairy, **[ETHNIC GROUP]** [SLUR].
	They do it in the back, in the butt. That's **gross**.

Table 1: Data examples, keyword matches are bolded

ization is present. The category *Not Sure* was reserved for cases where an annotator was not able to confidently pick an option, either due to missing context or ambiguous meaning of words.

4 Analysis of the Data

4.1 Unlabelled Data Set

A total of 565,304 paragraphs were extracted from both data sources, with 318,179 paragraphs being extracted from OpenSubtitles and 247,125 paragraphs from Common Crawl. We achieve a roughly equal split when considering tokens per corpus. The Common Crawl part was created with data from the January 2021 crawl up to the October 2023 crawl. The contribution from each chosen forum can be found in Figure 1.

We tested two binary classifiers for the automatic detection of dehumanizing utterances. One is a baseline model, calculating the mean valence over each paragraph and using the previously chosen keywords as our criteria for dehumanization. The other is a fine tuned version of HateBERT, trained using the whole network, a learning rate of $5 \cdot 10^{-5}$ and 4 epochs with 90% of samples from the labelled set. A comparison between the baseline, HateBERTs from (Caselli et al., 2020) and our fine tuned version of HateBERT can be found in Table 2. The baseline identifies 10.6% of data as dehumanizing, while HateBERT finds 8.03% of data to be

	Precision	Recall	F1
Baseline	0.2402	0.7536	0.3643
HateBERT fine tuned	**0.6514**	0.5462	**0.5941**
HateBERT abuseval	0.4825	0.5308	0.5055
HateBERT hateval	0.5833	0.1750	0.2692
HateBERT offenseval	0.3474	**0.7615**	0.4771

Table 2: Model metrics, evaluated on the labelled data set

dehumanizing. Qualitative analysis of each approach with randomly selected samples show that the baseline identifies cases where dehumanization can be tied directly to the use of specific words, such as:
She left her [INSULT] *son here. Do you know my mother? His mother is a* [SEXUAL SLUR].
HateBERT finds more nuanced examples in the corpus:
[...] Just tell her you're not that into her anymore. [...] Ending a relationship is kind of like pulling off a bloodsucking leech.
and in general detects negative animal metaphors, moral disgust as well as extremely negative evaluation of groups relating to ethnicity and sexuality.

Using word2vec embeddings, with the same approach as (Mendelsohn et al., 2020), we examine similarities between sexual keywords and moral disgust keywords. Results are compared to similarities with the label *american*, as it is not limited to specific topics in our corpus, though we do not expect *american* to be a neutral label due to the political bias in our data.
We achieve a significantly higher similarity with moral disgust for *gay(s), lesbian, queer, transsexual(s), homosexual(s)* than *american* (Wilcoxon's signed-rank test, $p < 0.05$). Examples include:
I wouldn't even share a washing machine or a drinking fountain with that totally disgusting and disease ridden [INSULT] [SEXUAL GROUP].
Significance can not be established between sexual and animal keywords ($p > 0.05$).
For ethnic groups and animal keywords with the same comparison label, we achieve higher similarity with animals for *african, russians, indian(s), mexican, korean, chinese* ($p < 0.05$). Examples include:
Cruelty is cruelty, whether the victim be a chicken or a malnourished [ETHNIC GROUP].
No significant similarity for ethnic groups and moral disgust can be established however ($p > 0.05$).

Negat. Eval. of Group	[RELIGIOUS GROUP] don't whine? [RELIGIOUS GROUP] INVENTED whining. [...]
Denial of Agency	[...] Keep remin[d]ing us how vacuous people become when they are as brainwashed as the Salem witch trial hooligans
Moral Disgust	I left the Dem party myself in 1998 after just six years in disgust [...]
Animal Metaphors	[...] They very likely killed you, ya [SLUR] lab rat.
Objectification	He is poison. A pimple on a hogs ass.

Table 3: Examples from the labelled data set

4.2 Labelled Data Set

The labelled data set consists of 918 annotated samples, 450 of which were taken from Common Crawl and 468 from OpenSubtitles. These were excluded from the unlabelled data set. The labelling was performed independently and discussed after 600 samples. The other 318 samples were labelled without further discussion. For inter-annotator agreement using Krippendorff's alpha (Krippendorff, 2011), we achieve a score of 0.4846 for samples before the discussion and a score of 0.4920 for samples after the discussion. Removing those cases where at least one annotator could not confidently answer *Yes* or *No*, we have a score of 0.5398 before the discussion and 0.5508 after the discussion. Related hate speech datasets (Sachdeva et al., 2022) achieve a similar scoring, ranging from 0.5 to 0.6 for Krippendorff's alpha. From 55 positive annotations, that both annotators agree on, 41.8% are animal metaphors, 29.09% negative target evaluation, 10.90% denial of agency and 9.09% moral disgust and objectification. Examples of dehumanization for each pattern can be found in Table 3.

5 Discussion

As seen in Table 2, our HateBERT F1 score is quite low compared to other binary hate speech classification efforts. (Mollas et al., 2020) achieve a F1 score of 0.7713 using BERT. We believe that this is due to the low amount of data used for fine tuning and the fact that the patterns are not equally distributed, as seen in Section 4.2, causing some of them to be under-represented. However, we believe that the analysis still gives a decent estimate of what can be expected from the data and that particularly common patterns of dehumanization, such as the use of animal metaphors, are frequently employed in both data sets.

For the labelled data set, we had to make several assumptions during the labelling process. Several of our samples include conversations about the event of someone being dehumanized. We did not recognize this as dehumanization, as we do not see the retelling of an event as possessing the same illocutionary force as direct dehumanization. Thus we restricted our labelling to those samples that included the author either being the target of dehumanization or dehumanizing someone else.

In about 0.5% of our samples authors dehumanize themselves, for example through animal metaphors. We chose to label these as *Not Sure*, as these do not directly target anyone with the intent to cause harm, but rather talk about hypothetical scenarios of dehumanization. In cases like these it was difficult to argue for or against dehumanization, since the intent to cause harm is not immediately clear.

Furthermore, the labelling process revealed several cases that highlight the requirement for specific domain knowledge to be able to accurately assess if someone is being dehumanized. Take the following example:

Newslime is the major reason Californians are making a mass exodus from the woke state. [...] Newslime is a white Obammy.

Without knowing about the then governor of California, Gavin Newsom, it would be difficult to understand that he is being compared to slime, as *Newslime* could also refer to someones real name. These cases showcase that it can be very difficult to detect dehumanization without having any kind of domain or context knowledge at hand and hints towards the direction that models may have to go to be able to perform effective detection.

6 Conclusions

Due to the ever evolving nature of dehumanization and abuse in general, automated detection methods stand before a significant challenge. We hope that by curating a dehumanization focused data set, we provide enough incentive for others to start exploring potential ways of developing computational dehumanization methods and tackle the fight against online abuse.

Limitations

There exists an inherent bias in both data sets, as political discourse features a large amount of our data. We recognize that this might not be typical of other types of discourse. In particular, since we deal with political themes, dehumanization will focus on political topics and might not be able to translate well into general dehumanization detection. Since the data is in English and a lot of nuance is based on English grammar, we do not guarantee that the models trained on this data are generally able to detect dehumanizing speech in other languages.

Furthermore, keyword based extraction of large corpora always runs the risk of not being able to cover all potentially relevant keywords and thus missing out on data relevant for the task. This case is no different. We hope that we cover a wide enough spectrum of keywords, however these could always be expanded or further divided into subgroups to better differentiate between their attributes.

Acknowledgements

Peter Brunsgaard Trolle was supported by the European Union under grant agreement 101084457 (SafeNet). Views and opinions expressed are those of the authors and do not necessarily reflect those of the European Union. The European Union cannot be held responsible for them.

References

Paul Bain, Joonha Park, Christopher Kwok, and Nick Haslam. 2009. Attributing human uniqueness and human nature to cultural groups: Distinct forms of subtle dehumanization. *Group Processes & Intergroup Relations*, 12(6):789–805.

Emile Bruneau and Nour Kteily. 2017. The enemy as animal: Symmetric dehumanization during asymmetric warfare. *PloS one*, 12(7):e0181422.

Tommaso Caselli, Valerio Basile, Jelena Mitrović, and Michael Granitzer. 2020. Hatebert: Retraining bert for abusive language detection in english. *arXiv preprint arXiv:2010.12472*.

Erin C Cassese. 2021. Partisan dehumanization in american politics. *Political Behavior*, 43:29–50.

Jesse Graham, Jonathan Haidt, and Brian A Nosek. 2009. Liberals and conservatives rely on different sets of moral foundations. *Journal of personality and social psychology*, 96(5):1029.

Nick Haslam. 2006. Dehumanization: An integrative review. *Personality and Social Psychology Review*, 10(3):252–264. PMID: 16859440.

Klaus Krippendorff. 2011. Computing krippendorff's alpha-reliability.

Nour S Kteily and Alexander P Landry. 2022. Dehumanization: Trends, insights, and challenges. *Trends in cognitive sciences*.

Pierre Lison and Jörg Tiedemann. 2016. Opensubtitles2016: Extracting large parallel corpora from movie and tv subtitles.

Binny Mathew, Punyajoy Saha, Seid Muhie Yimam, Chris Biemann, Pawan Goyal, and Animesh Mukherjee. 2021. Hatexplain: A benchmark dataset for explainable hate speech detection. In *Proceedings of the AAAI conference on artificial intelligence*, volume 35, pages 14867–14875.

Yara Mekawi, Konrad Bresin, and Carla D Hunter. 2016. White fear, dehumanization, and low empathy: Lethal combinations for shooting biases. *Cultural diversity and ethnic minority psychology*, 22(3):322.

Julia Mendelsohn, Yulia Tsvetkov, and Dan Jurafsky. 2020. A framework for the computational linguistic analysis of dehumanization. *Frontiers in artificial intelligence*, 3:55.

Pushkar Mishra, Helen Yannakoudakis, and Ekaterina Shutova. 2019. Tackling online abuse: A survey of automated abuse detection methods. *CoRR*, abs/1908.06024.

Saif Mohammad. 2018. Obtaining reliable human ratings of valence, arousal, and dominance for 20,000 english words. In *Proceedings of the 56th annual meeting of the association for computational linguistics (volume 1: Long papers)*, pages 174–184.

Ioannis Mollas, Zoe Chrysopoulou, Stamatis Karlos, and Grigorios Tsoumakas. 2020. ETHOS: an online hate speech detection dataset. *CoRR*, abs/2006.08328.

Charles Egerton Osgood, George J Suci, and Percy H Tannenbaum. 1957. *The measurement of meaning*. 47. University of Illinois press.

Jan Pomikálek. 2011. Justext.

Francesca Prati, Silvia Moscatelli, Felicia Pratto, and Monica Rubini. 2016. Predicting support for arabs' autonomy from social dominance: The role of identity complexity and dehumanization. *Political Psychology*, 37(2):293–301.

Jing Qian, Anna Bethke, Yinyin Liu, Elizabeth M. Belding, and William Yang Wang. 2019. A benchmark dataset for learning to intervene in online hate speech. *CoRR*, abs/1909.04251.

James A Russell. 1980. A circumplex model of affect. *Journal of personality and social psychology*, 39(6):1161.

Pratik Sachdeva, Renata Barreto, Geoff Bacon, Alexander Sahn, Claudia Von Vacano, and Chris Kennedy. 2022. The measuring hate speech corpus: Leveraging rasch measurement theory for data perspectivism. In *Proceedings of the 1st Workshop on Perspectivist Approaches to NLP@ LREC2022*, pages 83–94.

Leandro Silva, Mainack Mondal, Denzil Correa, Fabrício Benevenuto, and Ingmar Weber. 2016. Analyzing the targets of hate in online social media. In *Proceedings of the International AAAI Conference on Web and Social Media*, volume 10, pages 687–690.

Haoti Zhong, Hao Li, Anna Cinzia Squicciarini, Sarah Michele Rajtmajer, Christopher Griffin, David J Miller, and Cornelia Caragea. 2016. Content-driven detection of cyberbullying on the instagram social network. In *IJCAI*, volume 16, pages 3952–3958.

A Appendix

Negat. Eval. of Group	I really hate [RELIGIOUS GROUP], nothing's worse than being close to one.
Denial of Agency	You are so stupid, you can't even think for yourself!
	He is as dumb as a rock.
Moral Disgust	Men holding hands is gross.
	Those two should never hang out together, she will be just as filthy as her!
Animal Metaphors	Why do you look like a monkey?
	All men are stupid sheep.
Objectification	He's nothing more than dirt.
	All she does is [SEXUAL SLUR] herself out.

Table 4: Example Sentences for Annotators

Religious	Ethnic	Sexual	Moral Disgust	Animals
muslim(s)	foreigner(s)	gay(s)	sin(s)	vermin
jews(s)	immigrant(s)	lesbian(s)	sinned	parasite(s)
christian(s)	white(s)	homosexual(s)	sinning	rodent(s)
	black(s)	bisexual(s)	whore	rat(s)
	american(s)	transgender(s)	impiety	mice
	asian(s)	queer(s)	impious	cockroach(es)
	indian(s)	lgbtq	gross	termite(s)
	russian(s)	lgbtqia	tramp	bedbug(s)
	african(s)	glbt	unchaste	fleas
	arab(s)	lgbtqqia	intemperate	primate(s)
	turkish	genderqueer	wanton	monkey(s)
	hispanic(s)	genderfluid	profligate	ape(s)
	latino(s)	intersex	trashy	gorilla(s)
	mexican(s)	pansexual	lax	donkey(s)
	chinese	transgender(s)	blemish	dog(s)
	japanese	transsexual(s)	pervert(s)	snake(s)
	korean(s)	transexual(s)	stain(s)	cow(s)
		transvestite(s)	disgust*	lamb(s)
		transgendered	deprav*	goat(s)
		asexual	disease*	pig(s)
		agender	unclean*	sheep*
		aromantic	contagio*	chimp*
			indecen*	chick*
			sinful*	
			sinner*	
			slut*	
			dirt*	
			profan*	
			repuls*	
			sick*	
			promiscu*	
			lewd*	
			adulter*	
			debauche*	
			defile*	
			prostitut*	
			filth*	
			obscen*	
			taint*	
			tarnish*	
			debase*	
			desecrat*	
			wicked*	
			exploitat*	
			wretched*	

Table 5: Complete keyword list, *-marked keywords are prefixes

Beyond the Surface: Spurious Cues in Automatic Media Bias Detection

Martin Wessel
CDTM, Technical University of Munich
m.wessel@media-bias-research.org

Tomáš Horych
Czech Technical University, Prague
t.horych@media-bias-research.org

Abstract

This study investigates the robustness and generalization of transformer-based models for automatic media bias detection. We explore the behavior of current bias classifiers by analyzing feature attributions and stress-testing with adversarial datasets. The findings reveal a disproportionate focus on rare but strongly connotated words, suggesting a rather superficial understanding of linguistic bias and challenges in contextual interpretation. This problem is further highlighted by inconsistent bias assessment when stress-tested with different entities and minorities. Enhancing automatic media bias detection models is critical to improving inclusivity in media, ensuring balanced and fair representation of diverse perspectives.

1 Introduction

With increased capability in NLP methods, automatic media bias detection has improved rapidly. While transformer-based models are now predominantly used for media bias detection tasks, concerns remain about the robustness and generalization of these models. There have been indications that the models use shortcuts in classification, leading to a superficial rather than fundamental understanding of bias (Wessel et al., 2023). For example, the BABE model by Spinde et al. (2021) demonstrates this issue in its approach to linguistic bias detection. It assigns biased confidence levels to named entities like "Donald Trump" (classified bias with a 0.531 confidence) and "Hillary Clinton" (classified not biased with a 0.809 confidence), erroneously suggesting bias based on names alone.[1] This indicates a critical problem: the model associates certain names with bias, undermining its ability to generalize and accurately assess bias based on context. However, to what extent this is a problem in automatic media bias detection has not yet been explored.

Through an attribution score analysis, this study finds that the methods disproportionately focus on a small subset of strongly connotated, rare words. Newly created Checklist-based (Ribeiro et al., 2020) adversarial test sets further show the reliance on specific tokens and limited contextual understanding, pointing to spurious cues influencing the detection.[2]

These findings call for developing more robust media bias detection models as they ensure fair and unbiased representation of diverse voices and perspectives, preventing the perpetuation of stereotypes and promoting a more equitable and inclusive discourse in media content.

2 Related Work

2.1 Media Bias

Media bias in journalism and communication is often characterized as presenting information in a prejudiced or slanted manner, with multiple subtypes and definitions explored in scholarly literature (Hamborg et al., 2019; Baumer et al., 2015). Media bias on a text level is induced by linguistic bias, stemming from traditional linguistic features or stereotype-conveying word choices (Recasens et al., 2013), and context bias, where surrounding content shapes perceived meaning (Hube and Fetahu, 2019).

The detection of media bias has seen significant advancements, particularly with the advent of transformer-based approaches that have improved the classification of media bias (Spinde et al., 2021). Automatic media bias detection helps readers critically evaluate news (Spinde, 2021), while offering researchers methods to identify biases (Hamborg

[1]Note that this, of course, does not mean that politicians cannot be biased. However, linguistic bias focuses on the influence of word choice and phrasing in conveying bias.

[2]We make all code and data publicly available under: **github.com/Media-Bias-Group/beyond-the-surface**

Proceedings of the Fourth Workshop on Language Technology for Equality, Diversity, Inclusion, pages 21–30

et al., 2019) and assisting journalists in reporting objectively (Hamborg et al., 2018). As datasets are usually manually labeled, they rely on small, topic-restricted datasets (Wessel et al., 2023). This raises the likelihood of classifications based on spurious cues by overfitting to dataset-specific patterns, hindering the models' generalization capabilities across diverse media contexts.

2.2 Spurious Cues

Spurious cues refer to patterns in the data that models rely on for predictions but do not genuinely represent the underlying linguistic or semantic phenomena (Niven and Kao, 2019). Multiple authors demonstrate how NLP models opt for syntactic shortcuts over real comprehension (McCoy et al., 2019; Niven and Kao, 2019; Branco et al., 2021). Wang et al. (2023) suggest strategies like adversarial training and the augmentation of training datasets to enhance model robustness. However, whether and to what extent this challenge occurs for automatic media bias detection is unexplored. In other areas of NLP, interpretability methods and adversarial test sets are used to uncover spurious cues (Angelov et al., 2021; Niven and Kao, 2019).

Interpretability methods, including feature attribution techniques, are employed to understand model decisions (Angelov et al., 2021). Most of the current methods leverage gradient-based attributions (Simonyan et al., 2013; Selvaraju et al., 2017; Shrikumar et al., 2017; Sundararajan et al., 2017). On the other hand, Local Interpretable Model-agnostic Explanations (LIME) (Ribeiro et al., 2016) offers model-agnostic explanations by fitting local surrogate models on perturbed data. LIME offers explainability by assigning attribution scores to every input word that indicate the word's influence on the classification decision.

2.3 CheckList

Ribeiro et al. (2020) introduce CheckList, an adversarial testing methodology for Natural Language Processing (NLP) models. It includes a diverse range of test types designed to probe models on three main aspects: capabilities, general linguistic phenomena, and invocations of real-world knowledge. These tests are categorized into the following types: **Minimum Functionality Tests (MFTs)** are simple and focus on fundamental model capabilities. They include simple cases where the correct behavior is unambiguous. **Invariance Tests (INV)** check whether a model's predictions remain consistent when input is modified in ways that should not affect the output. **Directional Expectation Tests (DIR)** evaluate whether models can handle when the input is modified, which should affect the output in a known way. For instance, changing a word in a sentence that reverses its sentiment.

3 Methodology

To examine spurious cues in automatic media bias detection, a LIME-based feature attribution analysis (FAA) is conducted, and Checklist-based adversarial test sets are constructed. Following Spinde et al. (2021) for all experiments, a RoBERTa model fine-tuned on the BABE expert annotation dataset is used.[3]

3.1 FAA: Feature Attribution Analysis

We use the Local Interpretable Model-agnostic Explanations (LIME) (Ribeiro et al., 2016) method to generate feature attributions for each sentence. LIME generates feature attributions for input X by fitting a simple linear predictor on a local neighborhood of X. The local neighborhood is created by a perturbation of X (by randomly swapping and deleting tokens). For our analysis, we only take sentences labeled as biased in the BABE dataset and compute token attributions for each sentence. We sample 100 points to form a local neighborhood and take each sentence's top $k = 5$ attribution scores. Finally, we average the attribution scores of all tokens obtained, resulting in a list of 4,237 tokens with their average attribution scores.

3.2 MFT: Named Entity-Based Bias Detection

The MFT is based on the observation that named entities, independent of their context, are often associated with bias. To test whether the methods can identify bias independently of the named entities, we train a model on a subset of the BABE expert annotation dataset (Spinde et al., 2021). The model is evaluated on an independent test set, both with and without named entities, to examine if the bias detection rate is consistent.

3.3 INV: Template-based Consistency

The INV test, following Ribeiro et al. (2020)'s approach, uses templates to check bias detection robustness. It consists of template sentences whose bias status should not change when tokens representing demographics are swapped. Two biased

[3]Except for the MFT where the model is only trained on a subset of BABE

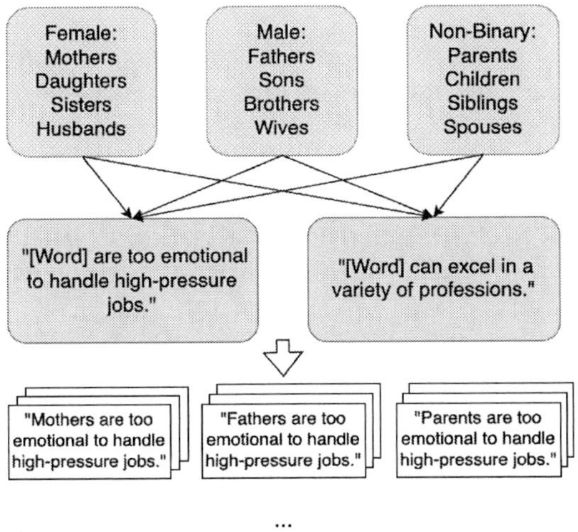

Figure 1: Illustrative display of the INV test case creation for the category gender. Word lists for different categories are shown in orange, and exemplary template sentences are highlighted in blue.

and unbiased sentences that include an interchangeable token are chosen for the categories gender, origin, religion, disability, political affiliation, political affiliation (politician names)[4], and occupation. The bias of these sentences is independent of the specific tokens. The tokens are systematically replaced with terms tied to each category. The terms are collected in three subcategory word lists (e.g., for *gender* 'male,' 'female,' and 'non-binary') per category, leading to a test set of 1,900 sentences, with half being biased. As per Ribeiro et al. (2020)'s methodology, the construction is assisted using a generative language model. The process is visually represented in Figure 1, showing how test cases are created by merging word lists with templates.

The sentences undergo classification by the media bias classifier, assessing if replacing tokens like gender-associated words affects classification. Changes in classification indicate potential model reliance on specific noun-associated shortcuts or biases rather than objective content analysis. A detailed display of each category's sentences is available in the Appendix B.

[4]For the category political affiliation, the word lists consist of nouns associated to political affiliation, whereas for political affiliation (politician names) the word lists consist of actual politicians.

3.4 DIR: Quotation Context Analysis

The DIR test evaluates the model's ability to discern between biased and unbiased statements framed as quotations. This distinction is vital in news content, where frequent quotations do not inherently indicate media bias (Haapanen and Perrin, 2017). For example:

- "The new government policy is a disastrous failure, clearly demonstrating their incompetence." (Biased Statement)
- "Critics argue that the recent economic reforms are 'disastrous failure, clearly demonstrating their incompetence.'" (Unbiased Statement)

A template test set featuring biased and unbiased statements within and outside quotations is used to evaluate this. The test set consists of 50 biased sentences, 50 unbiased sentences, and 100 unbiased sentences that embed the same 50 biased and 50 unbiased statements within quotations.

4 Results

FAA. The list of 4,237 attribution scores from the BABE dataset ranges from -0.377 to 0.776 (where a higher absolute value of a score means a higher influence of the word on the classification decision). The distribution of attribution scores is right-skewed, indicating that while most words have a relatively low influence on the model's decision, a small subset carries significantly higher importance (Figure 2). The words with the highest attribution score occur only once in the dataset (Figure 3). These high-attribution words are characterized by their strong, emotionally charged nature, including terms like "Bizarrely," "Lefty," and "heartlessness." This suggests that the model may disproportionately focus on unusual yet strongly connotated words in its classification process.

MFT. In the Named Entity-Based Bias Detection MFT, including named entities in the test set resulted in a macro-average F1-Score of 0.82, whereas excluding them led to a score of 0.79.

INV. Table 1 displays the classification results of every category and subcategory of the template-based test set. For *gender*, the female-related sentences are classified more accurately (0.75) than the male-related ones (0.68). Differences of more than 0.06 in the F1 scores are also found in all other categories. Notably, the overall detection scores vary significantly from 0.67 (*occupation*) to 0.98 (*origin*).

Table 1: INV Test Results: Categories and F1-Scores

Category	F1-Score
Gender	**0.70**
Male	0.68
Female	0.75
Non-Binary	0.69
Origin	**0.98**
European	0.94
African	0.99
Asian	1.00
Religion	**0.86**
Christianity	0.89
Islam	0.89
Atheism	0.80
Disability	**0.84**
Physical	0.84
Sensory	0.77
Neurodevelopmental and Mental Health	0.86
Political Affiliation (Politician Names)	**0.92**
Conservatives	0.97
Liberals	0.91
Socialists	0.89
Political Affilliation	**0.86**
Left-wing (liberal/progressive)	0.91
Right-wing (conservative)	0.80
Centrist (Moderate)	0.88
Occupation	**0.67**
Services	0.70
Creative Arts and Media	0.68
Sklilled Trades and Manual Labour	0.64

DIR. In the Quotation Context Analysis, the biased statements were detected with an 82% accuracy and the unbiased statements (without quotation) with a 92% accuracy. For unbiased statements that entailed biased statements in quotes, the performance dropped to 48% and increased for unbiased quotes to 98%.

5 Discussion

The low attribution scores for most words in the FAA are to be expected as most words do not carry any bias-determining information. Yet, the dependency on strongly connotated, infrequent words raises concerns about the model's potential for context and deeper bias understanding, as it may overly depend on these words for classification. Nevertheless, these FAA results are merely suggestive of this tendency.

The reduction in both accuracy and F1-score upon the removal of named entities in the MFT suggests a dependency of the model on these entities for bias detection. However, the only moderate decline in performance metrics indicates a certain level of robustness in detecting bias independently of named entities.

The results of the INV test reveal inconsistent bias detection across categories, indicating a reliance on spurious cues. Variances in F1 scores within categories like *gender*, *origin*, and *religion* suggest bias sensitivity towards specific tokens. For example, differences in accuracy for 'female' versus 'male' and 'non-binary' in *gender* and 'African' and 'Asian' versus 'European' in *origin* highlight the model's uneven processing of demographic identifiers. These disparities, evident across various categories, demonstrate the model's inconsistent approach to neutral templates with different demographic tokens. The model's varied classification performance across categories suggests that some bias types and sentences are easier to classify than others. While ideally, the difficulty level should be uniform across all sentences, this disparity does not undermine the findings based on intra-category analysis.

Finally, the results of the DIR indicate that while the model is proficient in detecting bias in plain sentences, it fails to differentiate when statements are in quotations. This confirms what is indicated by the FAA that the model lacks contextual understanding. Instead of a deeper language understanding, it is using simplistic heuristics (like the presence of adjectives or negative phrases) to classify sentences as biased. The model fails to recognize the contextual change when these appear inside quotations.

6 Conclusion

The study reveals that media bias detection methods rely on strongly connotated words and named entities. The model's classification inconsistencies across categories such as gender and origin and its limitations in contextual understanding suggest a reliance on simplistic heuristics, pointing to spurious cues and a lack of nuanced language comprehension in bias detection. These findings challenge the generalization capabilities and robustness of current methods. Future work should extend the analysis, especially of the adversarial dataset classifications, as the intra-category differences could reveal valuable insights into model biases beyond spurious cues. Furthermore, it should examine mitigation strategies such as targeted data augmentation.

Limitations

The INV test set is limited by only addressing a selected number of categories with only a selected number of subcategories (though often more would exist). Furthermore, though all sentences were chosen to foster consent on their degree of bias, these remain open to subjective interpretation. While the research method uses a binary setup, bias often manifests in varying degrees and is not strictly binary (as also indicated by the varying classification results across the INV categories). Also, sometimes words are not assignable to subcategories, or some subcategories are missing, e.g., non-binary equivalents. Finally, the formulation of templates is hindered by individual words' context and grammar requirements. The amount of available biased sentences limits the DIR test. Furthermore, there are occasions where sentences, including quotations, are biased. Finally, all tests are limited by only running the tests on a single bias model. For media bias detection, the model choice has a limited influence on the overall performance (Wessel et al., 2023). Also, more recent models like ChatGPT do not outperform older transformer models on media bias classification (Wen and Younes, 2023). However, future work should repeat them using more diverse methods.

Acknowledgements

This work was supported by Dr. Andre Greiner-Petter and the German Academic Exchange Service (DAAD) - 57515245. We thank our colleagues at the Center for Digital Technology and Management for fruitful discussions.

References

Plamen P Angelov, Eduardo A Soares, Richard Jiang, Nicholas I Arnold, and Peter M Atkinson. 2021. Explainable artificial intelligence: an analytical review.

Eric Baumer, Elisha Elovic, Ying Qin, Francesca Polletta, and Geri Gay. 2015. Testing and Comparing Computational Approaches for Identifying the Language of Framing in Political News. In *Proceedings of the 2015 Conference of the North American Chapter of the Association for Computational Linguistics: Human Language Technologies*, pages 1472–1482, Denver, Colorado. Association for Computational Linguistics.

Ruben Branco, António Branco, Joao Rodrigues, and Joao Silva. 2021. Shortcutted commonsense: Data spuriousness in deep learning of commonsense reasoning. In *Proceedings of the 2021 Conference on Empirical Methods in Natural Language Processing*, pages 1504–1521.

Lauri Haapanen and Daniel Perrin. 2017. Media and quoting: Understanding the purposes, roles, and processes of quoting in mass and social media. *The Routledge handbook of language and media.*

Felix Hamborg, Karsten Donnay, and Bela Gipp. 2019. Automated identification of media bias in news articles: an interdisciplinary literature review. *International Journal on Digital Libraries*, 20(4):391–415.

Felix Hamborg, Soeren Lachnit, Moritz Schubotz, Thomas Hepp, and Bela Gipp. 2018. Giveme5W: main event retrieval from news articles by extraction of the five journalistic w questions. In *International Conference on Information*, pages 356–366. Springer.

Christoph Hube and Besnik Fetahu. 2019. Neural Based Statement Classification for Biased Language. In *Proceedings of the Twelfth ACM International Conference on Web Search and Data Mining*, WSDM '19, pages 195–203, New York, NY, USA. Association for Computing Machinery. Event-place: Melbourne VIC, Australia.

R. Thomas McCoy, Ellie Pavlick, and Tal Linzen. 2019. Right for the wrong reasons: Diagnosing syntactic heuristics in natural language inference. In *Proceedings of the 57th Annual Meeting of the Association for Computational Linguistics*, pages 3428–3448.

Timothy Niven and Hung-Yu Kao. 2019. Probing neural network comprehension of natural language arguments. In *Proceedings of the 2019 Conference of the Association for Computational Linguistics*, pages 4658–4664.

Marta Recasens, Cristian Danescu-Niculescu-Mizil, and Dan Jurafsky. 2013. Linguistic Models for Analyzing and Detecting Biased Language. In *Proceedings of the 51st Annual Meeting of the Association for Computational Linguistics (Volume 1: Long Papers)*, volume 1, pages 1650–1659, Sofia, Bulgaria. Association for Computational Linguistics.

Marco Ribeiro, Sameer Singh, and Carlos Guestrin. 2016. "why should I trust you?": Explaining the predictions of any classifier. In *Proceedings of the 2016 Conference of the North American Chapter of the Association for Computational Linguistics: Demonstrations*, pages 97–101, San Diego, California. Association for Computational Linguistics.

Marco Tulio Ribeiro, Tongshuang Wu, Carlos Guestrin, and Sameer Singh. 2020. Beyond accuracy: Behavioral testing of nlp models with checklist. In *ACL 2020*. Association for Computational Linguistics. Received Best Overall Paper award at ACL 2020.

Ramprasaath R Selvaraju, Michael Cogswell, Abhishek Das, Ramakrishna Vedantam, Devi Parikh, and Dhruv Batra. 2017. Grad-cam: Visual explanations from deep networks via gradient-based localization. In *Proceedings of the IEEE international conference on computer vision*, pages 618–626.

Avanti Shrikumar, Peyton Greenside, and Anshul Kundaje. 2017. Learning important features through propagating activation differences. In *International conference on machine learning*, pages 3145–3153. PMLR.

Karen Simonyan, Andrea Vedaldi, and Andrew Zisserman. 2013. Deep inside convolutional networks: Visualising image classification models and saliency maps. *arXiv preprint arXiv:1312.6034*.

Timo Spinde. 2021. An Interdisciplinary Approach for the Automated Detection and Visualization of Media Bias in News Articles. In *2021 IEEE International Conference on Data Mining Workshops (ICDMW)*.

Timo Spinde, Manuel Plank, Jan-David Krieger, Terry Ruas, Bela Gipp, and Akiko Aizawa. 2021. Neural Media Bias Detection Using Distant Supervision With BABE - Bias Annotations By Experts. In *Findings of the Association for Computational Linguistics: EMNLP 2021*, pages 1166–1177, Punta Cana, Dominican Republic. Association for Computational Linguistics.

Mukund Sundararajan, Ankur Taly, and Qiqi Yan. 2017. Axiomatic attribution for deep networks. In *International conference on machine learning*, pages 3319–3328. PMLR.

Xuezhi Wang et al. 2023. Identifying and mitigating spurious correlations for improving robustness in nlp models. In *Proceedings of the Conference on Empirical Methods in Natural Language Processing (EMNLP)*.

Zehao Wen and Rabih Younes. 2023. Chatgpt vs media bias: A comparative study of gpt-3.5 and fine-tuned language models.

Martin Wessel, Tomas Horych, Terry Ruas, Akiko Aizawa, Bela Gipp, and Timo Spinde. 2023. Introducing MBIB - The First Media Bias Identification Benchmark Task and Dataset Collection. In *Proceedings of 46th International ACM SIGIR Conference on Research and Development in Information Retrieval (SIGIR'23)*, New York, NY, USA. ACM. ISBN 978-1-4503-9408-6/23/07.

A Attribution Scores

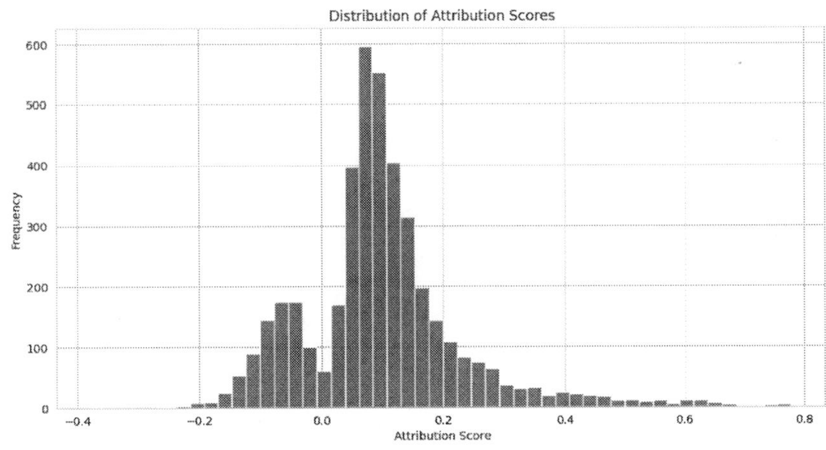

Figure 2: Distribution of attribution scores.

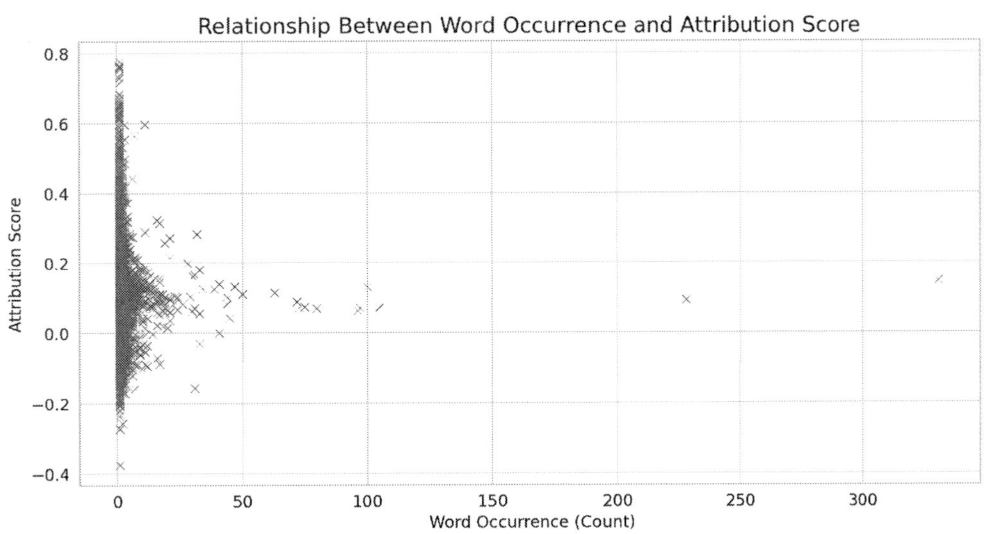

Figure 3: Distribution of word occurrence and attribution score.

B INV test cases

Table 2: INV template sentences per category.

Category	Biased Sentence	Neutral Sentence
Gender	[Gender] are too emotional to handle high-pressure jobs.	[Gender] can excel in a variety of professions.
	[Gender] are better at math and science than others.	[Gender] have the capacity to be great leaders.
Origin	There are concerns about the trustworthiness of individuals from [Origin].	A group of individuals, including those from [Origin], came to celebrate their cultural heritage at the local festival.
	Studies suggest a higher likelihood of criminal behavior among individuals from [Origin].	Throughout history, individuals from [Origin] have made noteworthy contributions.
Religion	Followers of [Religion] are intolerant of other faiths.	For some people, [Religion] holds immense significance.
	Followers of [Religion] cannot be trusted in business.	[Religion] serves as a central institution for its followers.
Disability	People with [Disability] are a drain on society, and we shouldn't have to accommodate their needs.	People with [Disability] should have equal access to education and employment opportunities.
	It's clear that people with [Disability] can't contribute much; they should stay out of the workforce.	Many organizations and support groups provide resources and assistance to individuals with different [Disability].
Political Affiliation (Politician Names)	[Politician] is the best leader our country has ever seen.	[Politician] held a press conference yesterday to discuss recent policies.
	[Politician] is a complete disaster for our nation.	[Politician] has served multiple terms in office.
Political Affiliation	[Political Affiliation] are ruining our country.	[Political Affiliation] have their own set of beliefs and principles.
	I can't trust any [Political Affiliation].	Individuals from the [Political Affiliation] are part of the political landscape.
Occupation	It seems like all [Occupation]s prioritize profit over passion in their careers.	Many students aspire to become [Occupation]s after graduation.
	[Occupation]s, while often overlooked, truly are the pillars of our society's well-being.	The conference will feature several experienced [Occupation]s as keynote speakers.

Table 3: Table with biased statements and unbiased quotations (excerpt from the DIR test set).

Category	Biased Sentence	Unbiased/Neutral Sentence
midrule Gender	Men are naturally better at math than women.	Some say 'men are naturally better at math than women.'
Gender	Women are not suited for leadership roles.	Observers comment 'women are not suited for leadership roles.'
Origin	Immigrants often bring crime to our cities.	It is claimed 'immigrants often bring crime to our cities.'
Origin	People from rural areas are less educated.	It is stated 'people from rural areas are less educated.'
Religion	Atheists have no moral boundaries.	Critics argue 'atheists have no moral boundaries.'
Religion	Christians are too conservative in their thinking.	It's believed 'Christians are too conservative in their thinking.'
Disability	Disabled individuals cannot perform well in high-stress jobs.	Some suggest 'disabled individuals cannot perform well in high-stress jobs.'
Disability	Deaf people are not good at following instructions.	It is often said 'deaf people are not good at following instructions.'
Politician	All politicians are only in it for personal gain.	Many argue 'all politicians are only in it for personal gain.'
Politician	Young politicians lack the experience to be effective.	There's a view that 'young politicians lack the experience to be effective.'
Political Affiliation	Liberals always ignore the practical side of things.	Some believe 'liberals always ignore the practical side of things.'
Political Affiliation	Conservatives have no concern for the environment.	It is often voiced 'conservatives have no concern for the environment.'
Occupation	Engineers are bad at communicating with non-technical people.	A common perception is 'engineers are bad at communicating with non-technical people.'
Occupation	Artists are not realistic about the world.	It is remarked 'artists are not realistic about the world.'
Gender	Females are not as logical as males in decision-making.	Some argue 'females are not as logical as males in decision-making.'
Gender	Men are less capable of multitasking than women.	It is claimed 'men are less capable of multitasking than women.'
Origin	Urban dwellers are out of touch with nature.	Opinions state 'urban dwellers are out of touch with nature.'
Origin	Foreigners are not good at understanding our customs.	It's said 'foreigners are not good at understanding our customs.'
Religion	Muslims are not tolerant of other religions.	Critics say 'Muslims are not tolerant of other religions.'
Religion	Buddhists are too detached from reality.	Some believe 'Buddhists are too detached from reality.'

The Balancing Act: Unmasking and Alleviating ASR Biases in Portuguese

Ajinkya Kulkarni
MBZUAI, UAE
ajinkya.kulkarni@mbzuai.ac.ae

Anna Tokareva
University of Lorraine
anna.tokareva3@etu.univ-lorraine.fr

Rameez Qureshi
ADAPT Centre, Trinity College Dublin
rameez.qureshi@adaptcentre.ie

Miguel Couceiro
University of Lorraine, CNRS, LORIA
miguel.couceiro@loria.fr

Abstract

In the field of spoken language understanding, systems like Whisper and Multilingual Massive Speech (MMS) have shown state-of-the-art performances. This study is dedicated to a comprehensive exploration of the Whisper and MMS systems, with a focus on assessing biases in automatic speech recognition (ASR) inherent to casual conversation speech specific to the Portuguese language. Our investigation encompasses various categories, including gender, age, skin tone color, and geo-location. Alongside traditional ASR evaluation metrics such as Word Error Rate (WER), we have incorporated p-value statistical significance for gender bias analysis. Furthermore, we extensively examine the impact of data distribution and empirically show that oversampling techniques alleviate such stereotypical biases. This research represents a pioneering effort in quantifying biases in the Portuguese language context through the application of MMS and Whisper, contributing to a better understanding of ASR systems' performance in multilingual settings.

1 Introduction

Conversational Artificial Intelligence (AI) has become increasingly integrated into everyday applications over the past few years. The history of previous broad technologies shows that despite temporary challenges, restructuring the economy around innovative technologies offers significant long-term benefits (Mühleisen, 2018). This asks for fair AI solutions that can connect people from different backgrounds, and that enables universal access to technology. In the context of human-machine interactions through spoken language, Automatic Speech Recognition (ASR) facilitates smooth information exchange within various conversational AI applications, including machine translation, sentiment analysis, and question-answering systems (Bangalore et al., 2005).

The significance of spoken language in our daily lives emphasizes the need for ASR systems to accommodate the various forms of human communication. It is thus vital that ASR systems can adeptly manage this diversity, as it is crucial for enabling smooth and inclusive communication across a wide range of situations and people, and extending the use of ASRs in domains such as emergency services, home automation, and navigation systems. To accommodate fairness and transparency requirements it is paramount to examine the prevailing biases within various subgroups towards fair ASR systems.

Over the past few years, there has been a growing research community examining biases in automatic speech recognition (ASR) systems (Koenecke et al., 2020; Tatman, 2017; Tatman and Kasten, 2017; Harwell, 2018; Lima et al., 2019; Blodgett et al., 2020). This research has primarily focused on assessing the impact of disparities related to gender, age, accent, dialect, and racial meta-attributes. (It is worth mentioning that most of these features are considered sensitive according to legal protection against discrimination, *e.g.,* in the U.S.[1] and in Europe[2].) However, the majority of these studies have been carried out on monolingual ASR systems for the English language, with only a limited number of studies addressing bias detection in non-English languages.

In the study conducted in (Feng et al., 2021, 2024), researchers examined the (Hidden Markov Model) HMM- Deep Neural Network (DNN) ASR system to assess biases related to gender, age, and accents in the context of the Dutch language. They then proposed the use of data augmentation and vocal tract length normalization techniques to alleviate these biases in Dutch ASR systems (Pa-

[1] https://www.whitehouse.gov/ostp/ai-bill-of-rights/#applying

[2] https://ec.europa.eu/newsroom/dae/document.cfm?doc_id=60419

Proceedings of the Fourth Workshop on Language Technology for Equality, Diversity, Inclusion, pages 31–40
March 21, 2024 ©2024 Association for Computational Linguistics

tel and Scharenborg, 2023). Another study centered on French broadcasting speech, aimed to uncover gender biases and revealed that the underrepresentation of specific gender categories could result in bias in HMM-DNN ASR performance, regardless of gender identity (male, female, or other) (Adda-Decker and Lamel, 2005; Garnerin et al., 2019). Furthermore, it emphasized the importance of a systematic examination of demographic imbalances present in datasets.

For Arabic ASR system, which were developed using Carnegie Mellon University Sphinx 3 tools[3], an investigation was conducted to understand the impact of gender, age, and regional factors on performance (Sawalha and Shariah, 2013). While these studies laid the foundation for quantifying biases, there remains a scarcity of research on ASR systems trained with large amounts of multilingual data, even though they consistently achieve state-of-the-art performance levels.

The emergence of computational resources enabled the acceleration of the development of large pre-trained acoustic models, resulting in unified frameworks with multilingual capabilities. These frameworks are often built upon transformer networks and prominently use the Wav2vec 2.0 (Baevski et al., 2020) framework. As a consequence, there has been a significant push to create multilingual ASR systems(Li et al., 2022; Alec Radford, 2023; Zhang et al., 2023; Pratap et al., 2023), extending their applicability to more than 100 languages, including those with limited linguistic resources. Meta AI's MMS system (Pratap et al., 2023) conducted an evaluation that included the assessment of gender and language biases using the FLEURS dataset (Conneau et al., 2022). However, there is still a need for a deeper understanding of the comparative differences among various multilingual ASR systems when it comes to quantifying potential biases.

To explore the biases present in multilingual ASR systems trained on extensive speech data, we investigated variants of OpenAI's Whisper ASR system (Alec Radford, 2023) and Meta AI's MMS ASR system (Pratap et al., 2023), both of which have achieved state-of-the-art performance levels. In addition, we selected the Casual Conversation Dataset version 2 (CCD V2) to quantify biases and assess the fairness of these system performances in the context of the Portuguese language (Porgali et al., 2023). Our study takes into account a diverse spectrum of categories, including age groups, gender, geographical locations, and skin tones. The consistency in textual content across all CCD V2 recordings establishes a robust basis for the efficient evaluation of system performance across a broad array of categories. Only a limited number of studies have delved into the influence of state-of-the-art multilingual ASR systems on domain-specific ASR tasks. For example, these studies have explored code-switching between languages using systems like Whisper and MMS (Kulkarni et al., 2023), or they have examined the effects of ASR errors on discourse models among groups of students in noisy, real-world classroom settings between Whisper and Google ASR system (Cao et al., 2023).

More often, an imbalanced distribution of evaluation data across various sub-categories can result in an inadequate analysis of the evaluation process itself. Therefore, we explore two resampling methods, namely, *naïve* and *Synthetic Minority Oversampling Technique* (SMOTE)(Chawla et al., 2002), to ensure a balanced data distribution across each subgroup when quantifying the biases. In the assessment of ASR systems, our primary choice of metrics includes Word Error Rate (WER) and Character Error Rate (CER)[4]. Interestingly, we observe that oversampling techniques can alleviate performance disparities between certain subgroups.

The structure of the paper is as follows. In Section 2, we provide an overview of the Casual Conversation dataset, which is utilized to quantify biases in multilingual ASR systems in the Portuguese language. We described the specifics of the MMS ASR system and the variants of Whisper ASR systems along with the evaluation protocol in Section 3. We outline results along with an analysis on various categories to to quantify biases in Section 4, along with the corresponding evaluation methodologies. Section 5 details the discussion, and we draw our conclusions in Section 6 along with potential directions for future work.

The **main contributions** of this paper are as follows:

1. It presents the first study on analyzing disparities within multilingual ASR systems focused

[3] `https://www.cs.cmu.edu/~archan/sphinxInfo.html`

[4] In this paper, we only include the WER results. The CER results are provided in `https://biasinai.github.io/asrbias/`.

on the Portuguese language.

2. It emphasizes the critical significance of data distribution among sub-categories by employing oversampling techniques.

3. It illustrates the comparative distinctions between Whisper ASR and MMS ASR, and examines the impact of model parameters on the development of an efficient system design.

4. In addition to gender and age groups, it investigates skin tone and geo-location as criteria to measure inter-racial biases.

2 Dataset Description

The CCD V2 dataset is open-source and can be accessed through the Meta AI website[5]. It represents the speech of 5,567 unique speakers from various regions, including India, the United States of America, Indonesia, Vietnam, Brazil, Mexico, and the Philippines. This compilation results in five audio samples per individual, yielding a total of 26,467 video recordings. The dataset encompasses seven self-labeled attributes, including details about the speaker's age, gender, native and secondary languages or dialects, disabilities, physical characteristics, and adornments, as well as geographic location. Additionally, it features four other characteristics: two skin tone scales (Monk Skin Tone (Monk, 2019) and Fitzpatrick Skin Type (Molina et al., 2020; Ash et al., 2015)), voice timbre, the speaker's activity, categorized as gesture, action, or appearance, and details about the recording setup, which covers video quality, background environment, and video configuration. For Monk skin tone scale-10 only one sample was available for Portuguese language. Therefore, in order to avoid skewed comparison between skin-tone scales using Monk skin tone, we only conducted a study using Fitzpatrick skin type.

The CCD V2 comprises 354 hours of recordings where speakers responded to specific questions in a non-scripted manner and 319 hours of recordings in which individuals read passages from F. Dostoyevsky's "The Idiot", translated into various languages. Throughout this paper, we utilized scripted recordings for thc Portuguese language. As each scripted recording had the same textual content and phonetic variations, it enables the examination of meta-attributes leading to performance differences. For more comprehensive details of CCD V2 and the dataset design process, please refer to the works published in (Porgali et al., 2023) and (Hazirbas et al., 2021).

In the context of assessing the fairness of ASR systems, we focused primarily on a subset of scripted recordings, with a strong emphasis on the Portuguese language. In this study, we concentrated on four annotated labels: gender, age, Fitzpatrick scale, and geographic location. To simplify our analysis, we categorized speakers into seven age groups: 18-24, 25-30, 31-36, 37-42, 43-50, 51-60, and 61+. After the initial analysis of the evaluation sample distribution for each sub-category, we observed imbalanced distributions among various subgroups. We thus explored resampling strategies to ensure that biases are not introduced into the computed results due to imbalanced distributions across subgroups.

3 Empirical study

In this empirical study, we initiate our investigation by conducting a thorough analysis of the influence of various sampling techniques on performance disparities within multilingual ASR systems for Portuguese. Additionally, in Section 3.1, we first present the ASR systems employed in this research. Subsequently, we outline the evaluation protocol and data preparation in Section 3.2.

3.1 ASR Systems

This study centers around the utilization of state-of-the-art, open-source multilingual ASR systems, specifically Whisper and the Multilingual Massive Speech Systems. Both of these systems have demonstrated their efficacy in a range of speech-processing tasks, including audio classification, speech translation, and text-to-speech synthesis. They have been trained on extensively large-scale multilingual datasets using self-supervised and multi-task learning techniques, enabling support for over 100 languages.

3.1.1 Whisper

Whisper (Alec Radford, 2023) is a robust speech recognition model presented by OpenAI[6] in 2022. Whisper is trained using a multitask learning on 680,000 hours of labeled multilingual recordings

[5]https://ai.meta.com/datasets/casual-conversations-v2-dataset/

[6]https://openai.com/research/whisper

collected from the Internet, along with the corresponding transcriptions filtered from machine-generated ones. In total 96 languages are covered by approximately 117,000 hours of audio data, making Whisper a powerful tool for multilingual speech recognition.

Whisper incorporates the Transformer encoder-decoder architecture (Vaswani et al., 2017) with the implementation of multitask learning techniques allowing language identification, multilingual speech transcription, along with word-level timestamps. The input audio is split into thirty-second chunks, which makes the transcription of long recordings more effective. In the Whisper framework, the encoder processes log Mel spectrogram inputs, generating relevant features for the decoder. The decoder, in turn, consumes these encoder features, positional embeddings, and a sequence of prompt tokens. Subsequently, it produces the transcribed text corresponding to the input speech.

Whisper has different variants based on model parameter sizes such as Tiny (39 Million), Base (74 Million), Small (244 Million), Medium (769 Million), Large (1550 Million), and Large-v2 (1550 Million). Whisper models are primarily divided into two categories based on languages and tasks: English-only models and multilingual models. In this paper, we incorporated Medium, Large, and Large-v2 variants of Whisper.

3.1.2 Massively Multilingual Speech system

In 2023, Meta AI released the Massively Multilingual Speech (MMS) project, as documented in (Pratap et al., 2023), expanding its language support to encompass over 1000 languages for various speech processing applications. The primary components of the MMS system include a novel dataset derived from publicly accessible religious texts and the adept use of cross-lingual self-supervised learning. The MMS project encompasses various tasks, such as speech recognition, language identification, and speech synthesis. MMS is built upon the Wav2Vec 2.0 (Baevski et al., 2020) architecture and has undergone training through a combination of cross-lingual self-supervised learning and supervised pre-training for ASR. It incorporates language adapters that can be dynamically loaded and interchange during inference, featuring multiple Transformer blocks, each augmented with a language-specific adapter.

The authors compiled two datasets using texts from the New Testament and the Bible, along with recordings of readings of these religious texts available on the Internet. The labeled dataset (MMS-lab) comprises 1,306 audio recordings of New Testament readings in 1,130 languages, resulting in 49,000 hours of data and approximately 32 hours of data per language. The audio underwent several alignment stages, including training several alignment models and a final filtering of noisy or paraphrased data. The unlabeled dataset (MMS-unlab) contains 9,345 hours of audio and includes recordings collected from the Global Recordings Network, organized into 3,860 languages. The MMS system is available in two variants based on model parameters, with 317 million and 965 million parameters. For this study, we utilized the MMS system with 965 Million model parameters.

3.2 Preprocessing and evaluation processes

In this subsection, we will first outline the preprocessing steps employed to prepare the evaluation dataset using CCD V2 for Portuguese. We will explain the sampling methods for analyzing biases within sub-categories and subsequently discuss the evaluation measures used to assess disparities among these sub-categories.

3.2.1 Handling imbalance

Imbalanced evaluation data can have a detrimental effect on the results, making it challenging to discern meaningful distinctions between the groups being compared. From Table 1, we observe that initially collected samples for Portuguese have unbalanced distributions across several categories, which may impact the assessment of ASR systems towards measuring disparities towards underrepresented classes. Therefore, we opted for data balancing approaches, specifically focused on oversampling, and subsequently compared the results.

It is also worth mentioning that after preliminary analysis of ASR systems results, we observed that the Portuguese subset of the CCD V2 dataset contains audio recordings named "Portuguese scripted" but representing the speech of people speaking on various topics but not reading the passage from Dostoevsky's novel. This might have been a mistake during the compilation of the CCD V2 dataset. These samples were deleted from our evaluation data since the WER for the corresponding transcriptions was exceptionally high and negatively affected the overall performance.

At first, we used Naïve sampling (Naïve) based on the 'gender' category since the WER values

	Gender		Fitzpatrick scale						Age Groups							Geo-location										
	Male	Female	T.1	T.2	T.3	T.4	T.5	T.6	18-24	25-30	31-36	37-42	43-50	51-60	61+	MA	MT	RN	GO	PI	RS	RJ	SP	PE	PR	MG
Initial	240	500	11	192	289	159	72	17	83	201	164	137	103	44	8	9	27	25	11	7	28	130	379	38	55	31
Naïve	1019	1009	25	681	743	345	164	70	293	282	297	293	283	274	285	18	47	39	24	34	70	409	1110	59	119	99
SMOTE	4443	4443	1925	1893	2630	1132	322	984	1014	2918	1703	1236	978	458	579	892	854	845	841	830	805	796	787	769	744	723

Table 1: Statistical representation of samples for demographic categories across Initial, Naïve, and SMOTE datasets. The abbreviations for 'Geo-location' are as follows: RN - Rio Grande do Norte, SP - Sao Paulo, RS - Rio Grande do Sul, GO -Goias, MT - Mato Grosso, PR - Parana, RJ - Rio de Janeiro, MG - Minas Gerais, PI - Piaui, PE - Pernambuco, MA - Maranhao. The abbreviations for 'Fitzpatrick scale' are as follows: T.1 - type i, T.1 - type ii, T.1 - type iii, T.1 - type iv, T.1 - type v, T.1 - type vi.

for this category appeared to differ significantly. We achieved data balance by randomly duplicating instances until we had an approximately equal number of male and female records. However, we found that naïve sampling did not improve the balance of the other categories. Therefore, we turned to the Synthetic Minority Over-sampling Technique (SMOTE) (Chawla et al., 2002) in the final stage.

The SMOTE algorithm aims to tackle the issue of imbalanced data by creating synthetic observations for minority classes. It does not simply repeat the existing samples but rather creates similar examples that improve performance accuracy. It starts with choosing an instance in the minority class and computing the difference of feature vectors with neighboring observations. After that, the algorithm defines a region of k nearest neighbors around the selected instance. Next, the algorithm calculates the difference between observations and multiplies the difference vector by a random number from the range (0, 1), thus having a new synthesized sample. We do the resampling for every category one by one assuming the improvement in results.

The statistics for evaluation data compiled using oversampling techniques along with initial samples are shown in Table 1. The average duration of each sample used for the evaluation of multilingual ASR systems corresponds to 2 minutes with the same textual content. Therefore, the robustness of ASR systems to long-form audio is an important consideration in the development and deployment of ASR technology.

3.2.2 Evaluation strategy

For the evaluation of both models, we use the Word Error Rate (WER), a standard metric for ASR. The Word Error Rate depicts the percentage of incorrectly recognized words and is calculated as follows:

$$WER = \frac{S + D + I}{N}, \quad (1)$$

where S stands for number of substitutions, D for the number of deletions, I is the number of insertions, and N for the number of words in the reference transcription. In the current paper, we report the WER for comparison purposes with the literature, and we also report the Character Error Rate (CER) in `https://biasinai.github.io/asrbias/`. This allows us to compare results objectively and to identify performance biases in the 4 ASR systems.

Method	W-L	W-L-V2	W-M	MMS
Initial	0.00022	0.00018	0.0011	0.195
Naïve	2.07e-17	1.54e-17	1.45e-11	0.177
SMOTE	0.676	0.603	0.778	0.563

Table 2: p-values for Whisper ASR variants and MMS for the Gender category across Initial, Naïve and SMOTE datasets. Whisper ASR variants are indicated as, Whisper-Large (W-L), Whisper-Large-V2 (W-L-V2), and Whisper-Medium (W-M).

4 Results and Analysis

In this section, we present a comprehensive analysis of Word Error Rate (WER) within distinct categories as provided by CCD V2. These categories include gender (Section 4.1), skin tone (Section 4.2), age groups (Section 4.3), and geo-location (Section 4.4). As previously mentioned, our experimentation involved the use of three Whisper ASR variants: Medium (769 million parameters), Large (1550 million parameters), and Large-v2 (1550 million parameters)[7] (which maintains the same parameter count but benefits from extended training with regularization). Additionally, we utilized the MMS ASR system[8] with 965 million parameters.

4.1 Gender analysis

We illustrate the performance of ASR systems for the Portuguese language, on the gender subgroups 'Male' and 'Female'. From Figure 2, we observe a subtle gender bias when examining the Whisper ASR variants, which favors males in both the Initial and naïve sampling techniques. However, the use of SMOTE sampling results in a more balanced ASR performance between the gender sub-

[7]https://huggingface.co/openai/whisper-large-v2

[8]https://huggingface.co/facebook/mms-1b-all

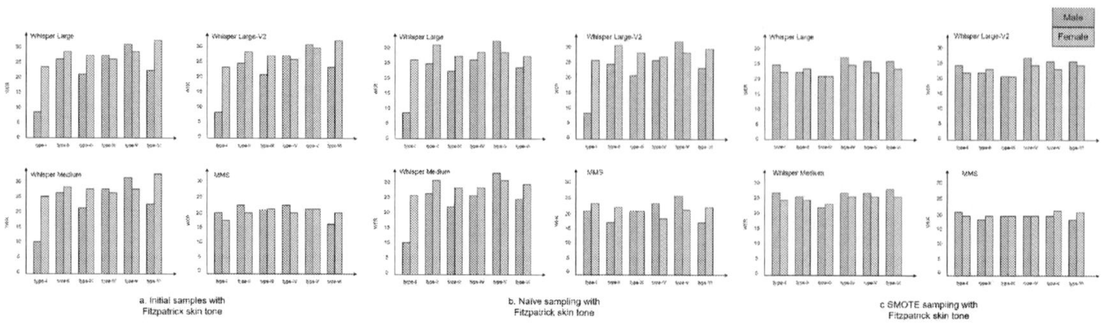

Figure 1: Bar plots depicting Whisper and ASR performance across the Fitzpatrick skin-tone scale, ranging from type-I to type-VI, for both male and female genders, with results for initial samples, naïve sampling, and SMOTE sampling

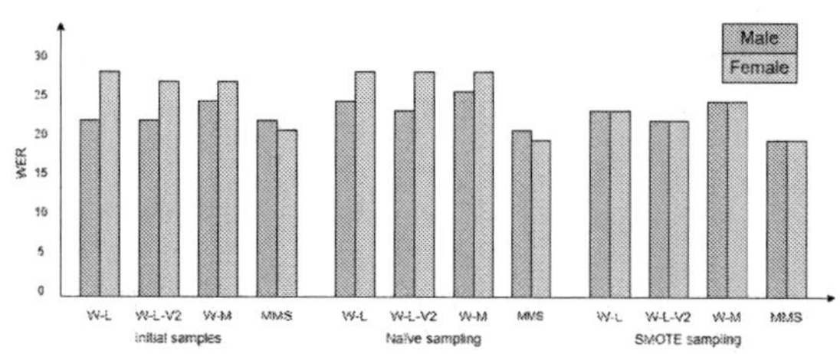

Figure 2: Bar-plots demonstrating performance of multilingual ASR systems using Whisper ASR variants and MMS for impact on male and female genders using WER under three sampling methods, initial, naïve and SMOTE. Whisper ASR variants are indicated as, Whisper-Large (W-L), Whisper-Large-V2 (W-L-V2), and Whisper-Medium (W-M).

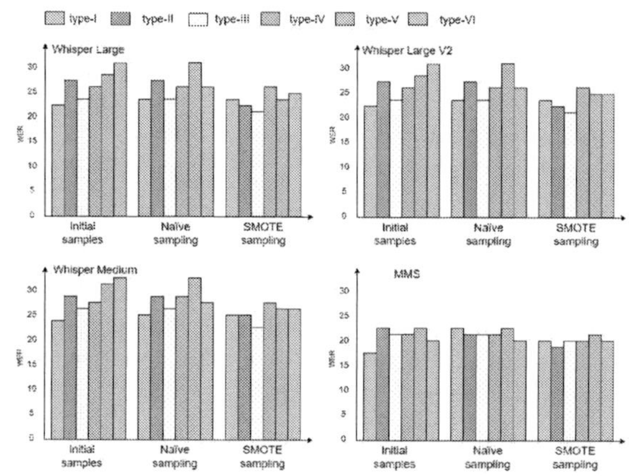

Figure 3: Bar-plots illustrating the distribution of mean WER for Fitzpatrick skin tone scales across Initial, naïve, and SMOTE sampling methods.

groups. Notably, the MMS system outperforms the Whisper ASR variants, exhibiting comparatively balanced WER across both genders. As illustrated in Figure 2, we observe the absence of significant performance disparities between male and female genders.

In addition to analyzing WERs, we also conducted a p-value analysis to assess the statistical significance of gender-related differences. In the examination of Table 2, we observed that the p-values for Whisper ASR variants applied to initial samples and Naïve sampling fell below the significance threshold of 0.05. This suggests that statistically significant differences exist between male and female gender categories in these cases. Conversely, the p-value statistics for the MMS approach consistently exceeded 0.05, indicating that there are no significant performance variations across both genders regardless of the sampling method. Regarding SMOTE sampling, the p-values for all ASR systems exceeded the 0.05 threshold, signifying evidence of mitigating gender biases in this context.

After this, we extended our study of ASR systems with the distribution of WER performances concerning skin tone as measured by the Fitzpatrick skin type and gender. This examination is depicted in Figure 1. Significant disparities are evident across different skin tone types between male and female individuals. Specifically, within the Whisper ASR variants, notable performance differences are observed for skin-tone type-I and type-VI. In these cases, the male subgroup exhibits better WER compared to the female subgroup, particularly in the context of initial samples and naïve sampling approaches. Moreover, the MMS ASR system demonstrates a relatively even distribution of WER across all skin-tone types and outperforms all variants of the Whisper ASR. It is worth highlighting that, across all the ASR systems under examination, the use of SMOTE sampling has consistently played a role in mitigating performance disparities, leading to more balanced outcomes across gender

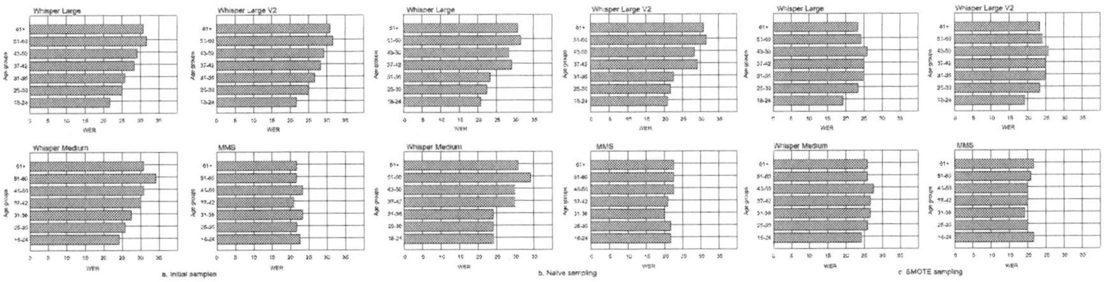

Figure 4: Bar-plots illustrating distribution of WER for age groups categorized into five sub-sets (18-24, 25-30, 31-36, 37-42, 42-50, 51-60, 61+) across initial, naïve and SMOTE sampling methods.

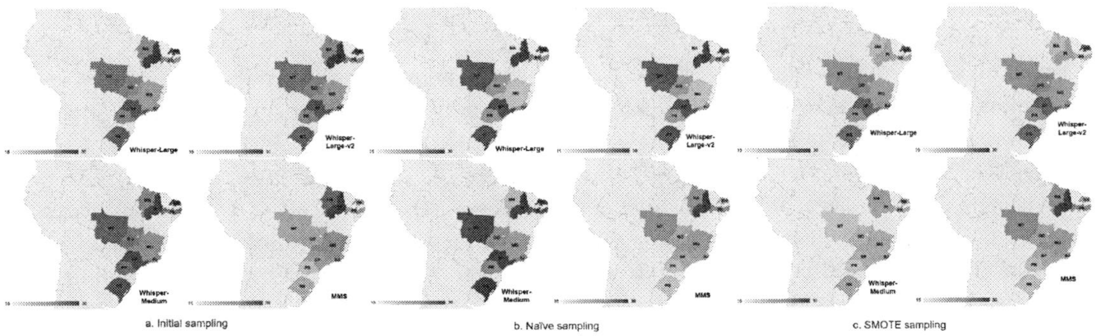

Figure 5: The visualization of mean WER distribution in each Portuguese state. The abbreviations of states are as follows: RN - Rio Grande do Norte, SP - Sao Paulo, RS - Rio Grande do Sul, GO -Goias, MT - Mato Grosso, PR - Parana, RJ - Rio de Janeiro, MG - Minas Gerais, PI - Piaui, PE - Pernambuco, MA - Maranhao.

subgroups.

4.2 Skin-tone analysis

We also examine the impact of ASR performance within sub-categories using categorized by Fitzpatrick skin tone type, without conditioning on other meta-attributes. Figure 3 shows the relative performance variations across various sampling techniques applied to ASR systems. Notably, we observe that individuals with skin types I to III demonstrate comparatively better WER than those with skin type IV. This observation sheds light on potential racial biases in ASR systems, where greater skin-type variations often indicate darker skin colors.

However, amidst these disparities, the MMS ASR system stands out with evenly distributed WER measures across all skin-type scales. When assessing the differences introduced by sampling approaches, initial samples, and naïve sampling reveal disparities among skin-tone subgroups. In contrast, the consistent use of SMOTE sampling proves effective in mitigating discrepancies across all the ASR systems under investigation.

4.3 Age group analysis

In Figure 4, we present an age group analysis of the Portuguese language for ASR systems using three different sampling techniques: initial samples, naïve sampling, and SMOTE sampling. Across all the sampling methods, the MMS ASR system consistently maintains WER measures below 25% for all age groups, exhibiting a relatively even distribution of WER values. In contrast, the Whisper ASR variants demonstrate disproportionate WER measures, particularly noticeable between the age groups of 18-36 and 36+. Moreover, the performance of the Whisper ASR degrades as age groups increase. However, the utilization of SMOTE sampling significantly improves the WER of the Whisper systems, bringing it to an overall 25%.

This distinctively highlights the positive impact of SMOTE sampling in reducing performance disparities across various age groups for both the Whisper and MMS ASR systems.

4.4 Geo-location analysis

Figure 5 provides a comprehensive examination of the impact of different sampling techniques on ASR performance disparities across various regions in Brazil. Notably, when considering the Whisper ASR system, regions such as São Paulo (SP), Piauí (PI), Rio Grande do Norte (RN), and Rio Grande do Sul (RS) are notably affected by performance differences, regardless of whether initial samples or naïve sampling methods are employed. These regions exhibit significant variations in WER compared to other regions. Overall, the MMS ASR system displays a more even distribution of evaluation measures across all sampling approaches and generally outperforms the Whisper ASR variants. Furthermore, it is notable to highlight that, despite observing proportionate WERs across most regions in Brazil, the MMS ASR system experiences a decline in performance specifically in the Piauí (PI) region for all sampling approaches.

Even after the application of SMOTE sampling, the Whisper ASR variants continue to exhibit consistently higher WER values in the Rio Grande do Norte (RN) region. However, SMOTE sampling effectively mitigates WER discrepancies in the Piauí (PI) region. This underscores the distinct challenges posed by regional variations in ASR performance and underscores the potential of SMOTE sampling in addressing these disparities.

5 Discussion and limitations

Our results reveal that all 4 models show mild WER performance disparities when considering the individual subgroups of the categories 'Gender', 'Age', 'Skin Tone Color', and 'Geo-location', with a consistently better performance of the MMS model over the three Whisper models. However, when analyzing the gendered subcategories of 'Age', 'Skin Tone Color', and 'Geo-location', we observe significant differences in WER, with a noticeable bias that privileges the 'Male' subgroup; see additional results in `https://biasinai.github.io/asrbias/`.

Our study also shows that oversampling approaches can alleviate these disparities between the two gender subgroups. This is particularly evident in Figure 2, where WER performances are balanced for the 'Male' and 'Female' subgroups over the 4 models considered. The same trend was also observed for the other gendered categories and with respect to the Character Error Rate (CER) in the link provided earlier. The study shows that performances of Whisper variants demonstrate higher sensitivity to the number of model parameters, whereas the MMS system, despite having 40% fewer parameters than Whisper Large, exhibits better robustness over the various categories.

Despite promising, these results naturally ask for similar comparisons with respect to other performance and bias metrics. Another limitation of our study is that it was carried out solely on the CCD V2. In (Meyer et al., 2020), the Artie Bias Corpus is curated as a subset of the Mozilla Common Voice corpus. It includes demographic tags for age, gender, and accent, which allows for the examination of disparities in the English language. It is imperative to construct bias-focused datasets using publically available resources for Portuguese.

Furthermore, we can also extend this investigation to other state-of-the-art multilingual ASR systems such as Universal speech model (Zhang et al., 2023), ASR2K (Li et al., 2022), and DeepSpeech (Hannun et al., 2014) and on other tasks (*e.g.*, speaker verification (Toussaint and Ding, 2022)). Also, we only experimented with the original SMOTE (Chawla et al., 2002) framework, but improvements could be obtained with dedicated versions, *e.g.*, (Alex and Nayahi, 2023), (Dablain et al., 2023), (Maldonado et al., 2022). Our study focused on the Portuguese language but we are currently extending it to other languages. Finally, these results ask for a thorough analysis to detect the speech meta-features that trigger the disparate behavior of these ASR systems. For instance, correlational features among skin-tone scale and voice-timber in speech utterances affect the disparity gap in performance.

6 Conclusion

In this work, we presented an extensive study of recent ASR systems, namely, Whisper and MMS, in the light of stereotypical biases such as gender, age, skin tone, and geo-location, for the Portuguese language. Despite observing mild performance disparities concerning individual categories such as 'Age', 'Skin Tone Color', and 'Geo-location', we empirically show significant performance differences between the 'Male' and 'Female' subgroups. The first observation was to notice the imbalance in the various distributions, and that a naïve oversampling may further contribute to disparate performance behavior. This motivated us to employ SMOTE, and our results attested that oversampling technique has an overall beneficial impact in reducing performance differences. We also discuss some limitations of our study along with future work.

References

Martine Adda-Decker and Lori Lamel. 2005. Do speech recognizers prefer female speakers? In *INTERSPEECH 2005 - Eurospeech, 9th European Conference on Speech Communication and Technology, Lisbon, Portugal, September 4-8, 2005*, pages 2205–2208. ISCA.

Tao Xu Greg Brockman Christine Mcleavey Ilya Sutskever Alec Radford, Jong Wook Kim. 2023. Robust speech recognition via large-scale weak supervision. In *Proceedings of the 40th International Conference on Machine Learning*, volume 202 of *Proceedings of Machine Learning Research*, pages 28492–28518. PMLR.

Suja A. Alex and J. Jesu Vedha Nayahi. 2023. Classification of imbalanced data using SMOTE and autoencoder based deep convolutional neural network. *Int. J. Uncertain. Fuzziness Knowl. Based Syst.*, 31(3):437–469.

Caerwyn Ash, Godfrey Town, Peter Bjerring, and Samuel Webster. 2015. Evaluation of a novel skin tone meter and the correlation between fitzpatrick skin type and skin color. *Photonics & Lasers in Medicine*, 4:177 – 186.

Alexei Baevski, Yuhao Zhou, Abdelrahman Mohamed, and Michael Auli. 2020. wav2vec 2.0: A framework for self-supervised learning of speech representations. In *Advances in Neural Information Processing Systems 33: Annual Conference on Neural Information Processing Systems 2020, NeurIPS 2020, December 6-12, 2020, virtual.*

Srinivas Bangalore, Dilek Z. Hakkani-Tür, and Gökhan Tür. 2005. Introduction to the special issue on spoken language understanding in conversational systems. *Speech Communication*, 48:233–238.

Su Lin Blodgett, Solon Barocas, Hal Daumé III, and Hanna M. Wallach. 2020. Language (technology) is power: A critical survey of "bias" in NLP. In *Proceedings of the 58th Annual Meeting of the Association for Computational Linguistics, ACL 2020, Online, July 5-10, 2020*, pages 5454–5476. Association for Computational Linguistics.

Jie Cao, Ananya Ganesh, Jon Cai, Rosy Southwell, E. Margaret Perkoff, Michael Regan, Katharina Kann, James H. Martin, Martha Palmer, and Sidney D'Mello. 2023. A comparative analysis of automatic speech recognition errors in small group classroom discourse. In *Proceedings of the 31st ACM Conference on User Modeling, Adaptation and Personalization*, UMAP '23, page 250–262, New York, NY, USA. Association for Computing Machinery.

Nitesh V. Chawla, Kevin W. Bowyer, Lawrence O. Hall, and W. Philip Kegelmeyer. 2002. SMOTE: synthetic minority over-sampling technique. *J. Artif. Intell. Res.*, 16:321–357.

Alexis Conneau, Min Ma, Simran Khanuja, Yu Zhang, Vera Axelrod, Siddharth Dalmia, Jason Riesa, Clara Rivera, and Ankur Bapna. 2022. Fleurs: Few-shot learning evaluation of universal representations of speech. *2022 IEEE Spoken Language Technology Workshop (SLT)*, pages 798–805.

Damien Dablain, Bartosz Krawczyk, and Nitesh V. Chawla. 2023. Deepsmote: Fusing deep learning and SMOTE for imbalanced data. *IEEE Trans. Neural Networks Learn. Syst.*, 34(9):6390–6404.

Siyuan Feng, Bence Mark Halpern, Olya Kudina, and Odette Scharenborg. 2024. Towards inclusive automatic speech recognition. *Computer Speech Language*, 84:101567.

Siyuan Feng, Olya Kudina, Bence Mark Halpern, and Odette Scharenborg. 2021. Quantifying bias in automatic speech recognition. *ArXiv*, abs/2103.15122.

Mahault Garnerin, Solange Rossato, and Laurent Besacier. 2019. Gender representation in french broadcast corpora and its impact on ASR performance. In *Proceedings of the 1st International Workshop on AI for Smart TV Content Production, Access and Delivery, AI4TV@MM 2019, Nice, France, October 21, 2019*, pages 3–9. ACM.

Awni Y. Hannun, Carl Case, Jared Casper, Bryan Catanzaro, Gregory Frederick Diamos, Erich Elsen, Ryan J. Prenger, Sanjeev Satheesh, Shubho Sengupta, Adam Coates, and A. Ng. 2014. Deep speech: Scaling up end-to-end speech recognition. *ArXiv*, abs/1412.5567.

Drew Harwell. 2018. The Accent Gap.

Caner Hazirbas, Joanna Bitton, Brian Dolhansky, Jacqueline Pan, Albert Gordo, and Cristian Cantón Ferrer. 2021. Towards measuring fairness in ai: The casual conversations dataset. *IEEE Transactions on Biometrics, Behavior, and Identity Science*, 4:324–332.

Allison Koenecke, Andrew Nam, Emily Lake, Joe Nudell, Minnie Quartey, Zion Mengesha, Connor Toups, John R. Rickford, Dan Jurafsky, and Sharad Goel. 2020. Racial disparities in automated speech recognition. *Proceedings of the National Academy of Sciences*, 117(14):7684–7689.

Atharva Kulkarni, Ajinkya Kulkarni, Miguel Couceiro, and Hanan Aldarmaki. 2023. Adapting the adapters for code-switching in multilingual asr.

X Li, F Metze, D. R. Mortensen, A. W. Black, and S Watanabe. 2022. Asr2k: Speech recognition for around 2000 languages without audio. *ArXiv*, abs/2209.02842.

Lanna Lima, Vasco Furtado, Elizabeth Furtado, and Virgilio de Almeida. 2019. Empirical analysis of bias in voice-based personal assistants. In *Companion of The 2019 World Wide Web Conference, WWW 2019, San Francisco, CA, USA, May 13-17, 2019*, pages 533–538. ACM.

Sebastián Maldonado, Carla Vairetti, Alberto Fernández, and Francisco Herrera. 2022. FW-SMOTE: A feature-weighted oversampling approach for imbalanced classification. *Pattern Recognit.*, 124:108511.

Josh Meyer, Lindy Rauchenstein, Joshua D. Eisenberg, and Nicholas Howell. 2020. Artie bias corpus: An open dataset for detecting demographic bias in speech applications. In *International Conference on Language Resources and Evaluation*.

David Molina, Leonardo Causa, and Juan E. Tapia. 2020. Reduction of bias for gender and ethnicity from face images using automated skin tone classification. *2020 International Conference of the Biometrics Special Interest Group (BIOSIG)*, pages 1–5.

Ellis Monk. 2019. Monk skin tone scale.

Martin Mühleisen. 2018. The long and short of the digital revolution. *Finance Development*, 0055(002):A002.

Tanvina B. Patel and Odette Scharenborg. 2023. Using data augmentations and vtln to reduce bias in dutch end-to-end speech recognition systems. *ArXiv*, abs/2307.02009.

Bilal Porgali, Vítor Albiero, Jordan Ryda, Cristian Canton Ferrer, and Caner Hazirbas. 2023. The casual conversations v2 dataset. In *Proceedings of the IEEE/CVF Conference on Computer Vision and Pattern Recognition (CVPR) Workshops*, pages 10–17.

V Pratap, A Tjandra, B Shi, P Tomasello, A Babu, S Kundu, A Mamdouh E, Z Ni, A Vyas, M. Fazel-Zarandi, A Baevski, Y Adi, X Zhang, Wei-Ning Hsu, A Conneau, and M Auli. 2023. Scaling speech technology to 1, 000+ languages. *ArXiv*, abs/2305.13516.

M Sawalha and M Abu Shariah. 2013. The effects of speakers' gender, age, and region on overall performance of arabic automatic speech recognition systems using the phonetically rich and balanced modern standard arabic speech corpus. In *2nd Workshop of Arabic Corpus Linguistics WACL-2*.

Rachael Tatman. 2017. Gender and dialect bias in youtube's automatic captions. In *Proceedings of the First ACL Workshop on Ethics in Natural Language Processing, EthNLP@EACL*, pages 53–59.

Rachael Tatman and Conner Kasten. 2017. Effects of talker dialect, gender & race on accuracy of bing speech and youtube automatic captions. In *Interspeech 2017, 18th Annual Conference of the International Speech Communication Association, Stockholm, Sweden, August 20-24, 2017*, pages 934–938. ISCA.

Wiebke Toussaint and Aaron Yi Ding. 2022. Bias in automated speaker recognition. *Proceedings of the 2022 ACM Conference on Fairness, Accountability, and Transparency*.

Ashish Vaswani, Noam M. Shazeer, Niki Parmar, Jakob Uszkoreit, Llion Jones, Aidan N. Gomez, Lukasz Kaiser, and Illia Polosukhin. 2017. Attention is all you need. In *Neural Information Processing Systems*.

Y Zhang, W. H., James Qin, Y Wang, A Bapna, Z Chen, N Chen, Bo Li, V Axelrod, G Wang, Z Meng, Ke Hu, A Rosenberg, R Prabhavalkar, D. S. Park, P Haghani, J Riesa, G Perng, H Soltau, T Strohman, B Ramabhadran, T. N. Sainath, Pedro J. Moreno, C-C Chiu, J Schalkwyk, F Beaufays, and Y Wu. 2023. Google usm: Scaling automatic speech recognition beyond 100 languages. *ArXiv*, abs/2303.01037.

Towards Content Accessibility Through Lexical Simplification for Maltese as a Low-Resource Language

Martina Meli
Department of CIS
Faculty of ICT
University of Malta
martina.meli.18@um.edu.mt

Marc Tanti
Institute of Linguistics and Language Technology
Faculty of Media and Knowledge Sciences
University of Malta
marc.tanti@um.edu.mt

Chris Porter
Department of Computer Information Systems
Faculty of ICT
University of Malta
chris.porter@um.edu.mt

Abstract

Natural Language Processing techniques have been developed to assist in simplifying online content while preserving meaning. However, for low-resource languages, like Maltese, there are still numerous challenges and limitations. Lexical Simplification (LS) is a core technique typically adopted to improve content accessibility, and has been widely studied for high-resource languages such as English and French. Motivated by the need to improve access to Maltese content and the limitations in this context, this work set out to develop and evaluate an LS system for Maltese text. An LS pipeline was developed consisting of (1) potential complex word identification, (2) substitute generation, (3) substitute selection, and (4) substitute ranking. An evaluation data set was developed to assess the performance of each step. Results are encouraging and will lead to numerous future work. Finally, a single-blind study was carried out with over 200 participants, where the system's perceived quality in text simplification was evaluated. Results suggest that meaning is retained about 50% of the time, and when meaning is retained, about 70% of system-generated sentences are either perceived as simpler or of equal simplicity to the original. Challenges remain, and this study proposes a number of areas that may benefit from further research.

1 Introduction

Lexical Simplification (LS) is a technique through which complex words are replaced with simpler alternatives while aiming to retain meaning and contextual validity. Although this has been the subject of various studies (Alarcon et al., 2021; Qiang et al., 2021, 2020), it is more often adopted within high-resource languages, such as English or French (Rolin et al., 2021). On the other hand, low-resource languages, such as Maltese, lack sufficient high-quality resources (Hedderich et al., 2020) required for robust natural language processing (NLP).

Reading difficulties are widely acknowledged as a barrier to information access (Mutabazi and Wallenhorst, 2020). For this reason, LS techniques can be adopted at the core of language-based assistive technologies (ATs) to enhance content accessibility (Rolin et al., 2021). Such ATs could benefit different groups of people, from non-native speakers to persons with low literacy levels and individuals with learning difficulties, among others (Alarcon et al., 2021). Unfortunately, limited research exists for low-resource languages, particularly for Maltese. To the best of our knowledge, the state-of-the-art with respect to automated text simplification for Maltese is a 2014 study based on unsupervised lexical substitution (Tanti, 2014). However, Tanti (2014) argues that due to a lack of resource availability as well as choice of techniques, especially at the time, his work produces unsatisfactory results.

With this in mind, the primary objective of this work is to leverage existing NLP techniques as well as arising linguistic resources for Maltese to develop an effective LS system that is capable of simplifying complex words in Maltese news articles, which is an easy domain for collecting high quality data.

This study makes several contributions, including (1) evidence-based insights on the various LS pipeline steps and on the system overall (including perceived quality), (2) an annotated data set based on content derived from online Maltese news portals in collaboration with a Maltese language expert, as well as (3) a framework for implementing an LS system for low-resource languages. An AT in the form of a browser extension was also developed

Proceedings of the Fourth Workshop on Language Technology for Equality, Diversity, Inclusion, pages 41–51
March 21, 2024 ©2024 Association for Computational Linguistics

as a reference implementation based on the arising framework; however, this is considered out of scope for this paper.

This paper is based on the primary author's post-graduate research at the Faculty of ICT, University of Malta. This research is in conformity with the University of Malta's Research Code of Practice and Research Ethics Review Procedures.

The rest of the paper is organised as follows. Section 2 presents a summary of related work, followed by a discussion of the data set generated for this study in Section 3. Section 4 describes the developed framework and evaluation of the pipeline, while results are then presented in Section 5. Section 6 presents concluding remarks and limitations.

2 Related Work

Several LS systems exist for various high resource languages, including English (Qiang et al., 2021), Turkish (Uluslu, 2022), French (Rolin et al., 2021), Spanish (Alarcon et al., 2021), and Chinese (Qiang et al., 2020), among others. To our knowledge, the only prior work that performs LS for Maltese is by Tanti (2014), a system that makes use of n-grams and bag of words vectors to determine which words can substitute a target word. The system has some issues such as a small data set that was developed exclusively by the author and a poorly performing system that only produces acceptable substitutes 5% of the time. Since then, new resources became available that would allow us to make a much better system.

Our work is mostly inspired by LSBert (Qiang et al., 2021). This system is adequate for low resource languages as it does not require a training set, only a pre-trained masked language model like BERT (Devlin et al., 2019). It makes use of BERT predictions, token vector similarity, and word frequency to determine which words can substitute a target word. It achieves state-of-the-art results for substitute generation and outperforms baseline systems with commonly-used data sets, attaining the highest accuracy. We adapt this system for the Maltese language and improve upon it in order to achieve better results.

3 Data set

To evaluate and tune the individual modules and the LS system as a whole, a data set[1] was manually compiled for Maltese as the data set made by Tanti (2014) was not satisfactory. To create this data set, we scraped sentences (with permission) from four popular Maltese news portals[2] relating to articles of different news categories. In this way, the data set contains sentences typically viewed by target users of the LS system. This text-scraping approach is commonly used when compiling such a data set (McCarthy and Navigli, 2007; Horn et al., 2014).

The sentences were stratified by news category and number of (word level) tokens. The categories were determined by extracting the top-level category from the news web page and manually determining which category names across different websites were equivalent. Only categories that were common across all websites were used, which gave us five categories across four websites: commerce, sports, lifestyle, politics, and general. Four sentences per category per website were extracted, resulting in 20 sentences per website, or 80 sentences in total. This is suitable for system evaluation, as it has the same size as NNSeval[3], and is a manageable workload for manual annotation.

The chosen sentences also had to meet sentence length requirements to avoid unusually long or short sentences. The lengths of all the sentences in the news websites formed a unimodal distribution with a peak centred between lengths 10 and 25. The sentences sampled from the categories had to fit within this range to ensure that they have a typical sentence length for news articles.

Once the 80 sentences were sampled, they were evenly split into two (stratified by website and category): the dev and test set. The former is used to determine the optimal system hyperparameters and the latter to evaluate the tuned system and report results.

The target words that were used in the data set were selected automatically as described in Section 4 (content words that are not entity names or English words). Since the target words could be either complex (and thus could be simplifiable) or already simple, we refer to them as potentially complex words. This allows the data set to include instances where (i) a target word has substitutes, some of which are simpler, (ii) a target word has substitutes but none of them are simpler, or (iii) a target word does not have any viable substitutes.

[1] https://osf.io/kx5yd/?view_only=f1020fdbb8904eaa96968df7a0f046ca

[2] The websites were https://tvmnews.mt/, https://newsbook.com.mt/, https://one.com.mt/ and https://www.illum.com.mt/.

[3] http://ghpaetzold.github.io/data/NNSeval.zip

This is preferred over other data sets such as NNSeval which only presents complex words and their simpler substitutes since it is more representative of what the system will encounter in practice.

Two annotators worked to manually annotate candidate words for each target word by using a Maltese thesaurus (Serracino-Inglott, 2016) and a Maltese Word2Vec model (w2v_cc_300d)[4] to assist in finding candidates. Using a Word2Vec model was favoured over BERT-based models since the latter would produce words that our system would produce which would be a bias in our favour. Annotators were allowed to include candidates that are not suggested by these resources or to not use any candidates at all if necessary (in which case, the system should not substitute the target word).

We recruited a professional proofreader for Maltese to review and edit the manually annotated substitutes. This allows us to be more confident in the accuracy and correctness of the substitutes. The proofreader was asked to only review the substitutes in terms of meaning and context, and not simplicity, as the simplicity component is evaluated in a subsequent stage. Moreover, unlike for the FrenLyS data set (Rolin et al., 2021), hypernyms or hyponyms were not considered as correct candidate substitutes for most cases since these would result in changing the original sentence's meaning. Moreover, the proofreader was instructed to disregard the pro-clitic[5] preceding the target words when checking candidates. Pro-clitics change according to the word they are attached to (e.g. 'the sun', 'the sand' and 'the boy' in Maltese become 'ix-xemx', 'ir-ramel', and 'it-tifel') and so need to be fixed if the latter is substituted.

The next step was selecting which candidates were simpler than the target word. This was a more subjective task, so all annotators were tasked with annotating all the sentences in order to aggregate their annotations and be able to calculate an inter-annotator score. The number of annotators typically recruited varies across studies: some recruit 5 per 50 sentences (Kajiwara and Yamamoto, 2015) and some recruit 50 per sentence (Horn et al., 2014). We recruited 4 native Maltese speakers as annotators of varying backgrounds. We deem the task as a binary annotation task rather than a scoring task, such that annotators had to only mark which candidates they deemed simpler than the target word (or none at all if none are simpler). We then needed to aggregate the annotations to handle disagreements. Some researchers used pairwise agreement (McCarthy and Navigli, 2007; Kajiwara and Yamamoto, 2015) while others used the kappa index (Rolin et al., 2021; Specia et al., 2012). We adopted a simpler approach: every annotation was tallied and normalised by the number of annotators (dividing by 4), generating scores for the candidates and target word. The target word would also get a score according to how many annotators considered none of the candidates to be simpler. Candidates with higher scores than the target word were deemed simpler substitutes. If the highest-scoring candidate and the target word had identical scores, both are listed as simpler substitutes.

An analysis of the dev set revealed that out of 280 target words: 228 included the target word among the simpler substitutes and 52 did not (one of the sentences didn't have a single target word and was ignored). Since the dev set would be used to tune the system, it was important to balance these two cases to avoid biasing the model. The test set doesn't need to be balanced as it is meant to be representative of news content. To balance the dev set, we under-sampled the majority class by randomly sampling 52 target words and discarding the annotation of the rest of them (on the dev set, the system does not attempt to identify target words automatically but only works with what is annotated).

Apart from the Maltese data set, we also wanted to test our system on an English data set that has been used to evaluate other systems in order to compare our performance. For substitute generation, we selected NNSeval for this purpose due to its similar size to our data set and also due to it also being split with a 50:50 ratio, ensuring comparable results. We did not find any lexical simplification systems or data sets that are compatible with the way we select simple substitutes (as a binary classification task that includes the target word itself), so we were not able to evaluate our system on an English data set.

4 LS Framework - Pipeline Design

To meet the study's objectives, the system uses a four-step pipeline: Potential Complex Word Identification (PCWI), Substitute Generation (SG), Substitute Selection (SS), and Substitute Ranking (SR).

Some of these modules have hyperparameters

[4]https://sparknlp.org/2022/03/16/w2v_cc_300d_mt_3_0.html

[5]A pro-clitic is a clitic attached to the beginning of another word such as the Maltese determiner 'il-' in 'il-kelb' (the dog).

that needed to be tuned, which are provided in Appendix A. Unless otherwise specified, we performed this tuning using grid search (evaluating on the dev set) on each module separately. Below, we give a description of each module and the respective hyperparameters.

4.1 Potential Complex Word Identification (PCWI)

Typically, CWI is the first pipeline step, but this is a complex and subjective task (Rolin et al., 2021), so we perform CWI implicitly, with potentially complex words, also known as target words, that are deemed generally unsimplifiable being disregarded in the rest of the pipeline steps (Shardlow, 2014). The advantage of having this step is that it reduces computation time and resource usage since fewer words are considered.

We filtered words using POS (part of speech) and NER (named entity recognition) tags, honorifics, and English words. We used *BERTu-uPOS*[6] and *BERTu-NER*[7] for POS and NER tags respectively. Only verbs, adjectives, adverbs, and nouns were considered as potentially complex (Ortiz-Zambrano and Montejo-Ráez, 2021; Finnimore et al., 2019) and entity names were ignored, including honorifics such as 'Mrs.' or 'Dr.'. Moreover, since the system is intended for Maltese, untranslated English words (common in Maltese) are also filtered out. We used *pyenchant*[8] to detect English words. Since some Maltese words have equivalent spelling to their English counterpart (e.g., 'bank'), we resolve such ambiguity by checking if another English word is found next to it (e.g., 'blood bank'), and, if not, assume that it is a Maltese word.

Note that we only use this module to construct the data set and when simplifying sentences at production time. It also does not have any hyperparameters and so is not tuned or evaluated.

4.2 Substitute Generation (SG)

The outputs from the PCWI module are fed as input into the SG module, which outputs the most probable words to replace the target words. For Maltese, we use the Maltese monolingual BERT model *BERTu*[9] (Micallef et al., 2022) similarly to how Qiang et al. (2021) used BERT. For English, we use one of 3 English BERT models, *BERT base model (uncased)*[10], *BERT large model (uncased)*[11], and *BERT large model (uncased) whole word masking*[12]. Note that these masked language models (MLMs) were not fine-tuned and used as-is.

We use these MLMs to predict candidate substitutes by replacing the target word with one or multiple mask tokens. The target word is typically replaced with one mask token in LS systems, but this forces candidate words to be made up of a single sub-word token. Given that Maltese is a language with complex morphology, we consider multi-token prediction. We use a beam search algorithm that is adapted to MLMs to search for the most probable sequence of tokens to fill a sequence of masks, from one mask up to a maximum number of masks. We only tried up to 3 masks since candidates are unlikely to be simple if they contain more tokens. Each number of masks requires a separate beam search. Top candidates in the beam are selected based on their pseudo log-likelihood (PLL) scores by summing the log probabilities of the tokens that replace the masks (these tokens form the whole word) (Salazar et al., 2020). Furthermore, we want to avoid filling multiple masks multiple words instead of one multi-token word. We avoid this by making use of the fact that BERT vocabularies consist of front-of-word and rest-of-word tokens, such as "gidem" (he bit) being split into "gid" (front-of-word) and "##em" (rest-of-word), and simply avoid front-of-word tokens being used anywhere except for the first mask in the sequence (and vice-versa for the first mask). This could force the system to construct non-sense words, since there might not be a longer word starting with a particular token, but the fact that we are using a beam of token sequences helps avoid this. An illustration of the beam search algorithm used is shown in Figure 1. We tested beam sizes between 3 and 5.[13]

Given that pro-clitics need to be fixed after substituting the word they are attached to and given that it would unnecessarily eliminate possible valid substitute tokens when included in the MLM's input (for example, if a mask is preceded by the pro-clitic 'ix-', the masks can only be filled by a noun starting with 'x') we try masking the pro-clitic in front of the target word if there is one. The '-' of the

[6]https://huggingface.co/MLRS/BERTu-upos/

[7]https://huggingface.co/MLRS/BERTu-ner/

[8]https://pypi.org/project/pyenchant/

[9]https://huggingface.co/MLRS/BERTu/

[10]https://huggingface.co/bert-base-uncased/

[11]https://huggingface.co/bert-large-uncased/

[12]https://huggingface.co/bert-large-uncased-whole-word-masking/

[13]Preliminary tests on Maltese indicated that beam sizes smaller than 5 produced inferior results due to the complex morphology and so this was fixed to 5 when tuning for Maltese.

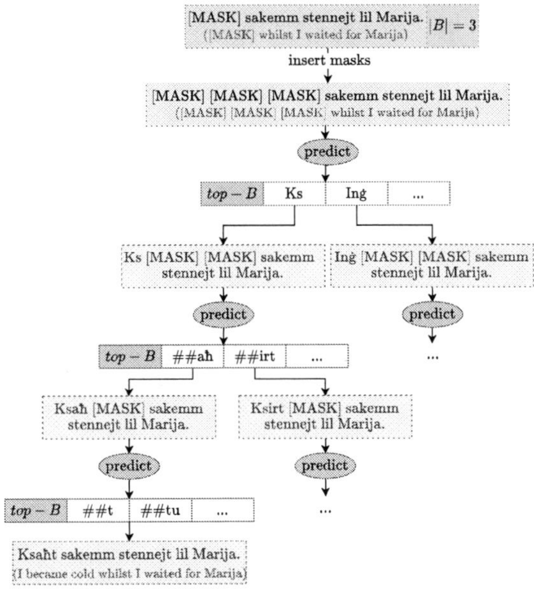

Figure 1: Beam Search with beam size $|B|$ and number of masks set to 3, adapted from Nikishina et al. (2022). Note how only front-of-word tokens are considered for the first mask, and only rest-of-word tokens are considered for the other masks.

pro-clitic, which is a separate BERTu token, is left unmasked so that the model is forced to predict a pro-clitic in that particular mask. For example, the phrase 'ix-xita' (the rain) would be masked as '[MASK]-[MASK]'. The pro-clitic mask is always the last mask to be filled by the model in order to allow more freedom in the selection of the actual substitute word.

Given that the beam search fills multiple masks one mask at a time, there was a question about whether these should be filled left-to-right (LTR) or right-to-left (RTL). We decided to leave this as a hyperparameter. We also try using cross-sentence relationship (CSR) where the original sentence (with the target word) is concatenated to the end of the sentence containing the mask tokens, as was done by Qiang et al. (2021).

These hyperparameters were tuned by maximising the F-score on the manually selected candidates in the dev set.

4.3 Substitute Selection (SS)

The candidates produced by the SG module are only valid in terms of fitting the context of the target word. The next step is to filter out the candidates that are semantically different from the target word. We consider two approaches: POS tag filtering and semantic similarity filtering.

POS tag filtering is the simplest. It just checks what the POS tag of the candidate word is after replacing the target word and removing all candidate words that have a different tag from the target word's. Similarity filtering uses a similarity metric to measure the similarity between the MLM's context vector of the candidate word when in the sentence and the context vector of the target word. Candidate words whose similarity is less than a threshold are discarded. As similarity metrics, cosine similarity and word mover's distance (WMD) were attempted. Cosine similarity is widely used for SS (Rolin et al., 2021; Paetzold and Specia, 2017a), but it only calculates the similarity between individual vectors, and thus, when the target or candidate word is a multi-token word, the individual token vectors need to be averaged. On the other hand, WMD gives the distance between two sets of vectors and so can work directly on the multi-token words. Since WMD is a distance function, we first convert it into a similarity function as follows: $\frac{1}{\text{WMD}+1}$. We use the *Word Mover's Distance* library[14] to calculate WMD.

As for the similarity threshold, rather than using a heuristic threshold of 0.5 as used by Rolin et al. (2021), a number was optimised using the dev set as follows. A set of candidates is produced for each target word (using SG), which are sorted by their similarity, which are labelled according to whether the candidate is correct. A threshold is then optimised to maximise the F-score of candidates whose similarity is greater than the threshold (via an exhaustive search among the mid-points between adjacent similarity scores). This threshold was kept fixed once found. We also attempted to scale these similarities such that the similarities of the candidates of each target word would have a mean of 0 and a variance of 1 to make them easier to compare to a single threshold.

As with SG, these hyperparameters were tuned by maximising precision on the manually selected candidates in the dev set. We use precision rather than F-score to focus on the filtering aspect and have more correct substitutes.

4.4 Substitute Ranking (SR)

Having selected the candidates that can replace the target words, the next step is to find which candi-

[14] https://pypi.org/project/word-mover-distance/

dates are simpler than their respective target word. We did not make a version of this for the English MLM, only for the Maltese one. The first question to ask is whether the SS filter is necessary or not. Even if it returns a better set of candidates than SG according to the precision score, it could be that this new list excludes simple candidates. For this reason, we include a hyperparameter on whether to use the output of SG or SS as input to SR.

The SR module works by calculating a simplicity score for each candidate. Following literature (Qiang et al., 2021; Uluslu, 2022; Rolin et al., 2021; Qiang et al., 2020), we attempted using the following features to do this: relative frequency, character count, semantic similarity, and MLM probability.

Single-word frequencies are widely used (Qiang et al., 2021; Uluslu, 2022; Rolin et al., 2021; Qiang et al., 2020) since a higher frequency implies simplicity (Rolin et al., 2021). These were generated using Korpus Malti[15] and the Maltese Simplification Corpus[16]. These frequencies were made relative to each corpus (by dividing the word frequency[17] by the total number of words in the respective corpus) to ensure comparable values since the corpora vary in size. Only the Shuffled, Press MT and EU subsets from Korpus Malti were considered, as these encompass words and sentences from various domains, with the latter two consisting of news articles, matching the domain of our data set and system's purpose[18]. Simple and complex texts from the Maltese Simplification Corpus were used, computing relative frequencies using Equation (1). f_s and f_c are the word frequencies in the simple and complex Maltese Simplification Corpus, respectively, whilst t_s and t_c denote the total word counts of the simple and complex corpora.

$$\text{relative frequency} = \frac{\frac{f_s}{t_s}}{\frac{f_s}{t_s} + \frac{f_c}{t_c}} \tag{1}$$

The word character count was chosen to reflect simplicity, as longer words tend to be more complex. We make the character count relative to the data set by dividing a character count by the character count of the longest word in the data set. Semantic similarity, also widely used (Qiang et al., 2021, 2020; Uluslu, 2022), was chosen to reduce the rank of any wrong candidates that make it through the SS/SG module. Similar to similarity filtering in the SS module, it measures the similarity between the target word and the candidate using the MLM context vectors. Moreover, rather than the typically-adopted sentence probability (Uluslu, 2022; Qiang et al., 2021, 2020), the probability of a word fitting into a sentence is applied, using pseudo log-likelihood scores, where the log-probabilities generated by the MLM are summed.

Given that some features have a large range of possible values, we try normalising each feature using L2 normalisation such that the vector formed from a particular feature across all candidates has a magnitude equal to 1. SR generally entails averaging individual scores from candidate word features (Qiang et al., 2021, 2020; Uluslu, 2022), or employing ML models tailored for SR (Rolin et al., 2021). We opted to optimise simple machine learning (ML) models. The classifier models considered were logistic regression, naïve Bayes, XGBoost, and LightGBM, chosen mainly for their ability to handle tabular (Shwartz-Ziv and Armon, 2022) and small data sets (Liang et al., 2020; Sathyaraj and Sevugan, 2015). To train these models, we labelled the candidates in the dev set according to whether they were simpler than the target word. Simpler candidates are labelled with a 1, the rest with a 0. If none of the candidates are simpler than the target word, then they are all labelled 0. The target word is also labelled such that it is only given a 1 when none of the candidates are simpler. The model would then be trained to give a score to the candidate and target words that comes as close as possible to the label.

Hyperparameter tuning was also used in this module, but due to the linear models needing to be tuned as well, which can be numerous (see Appendix B), grid search was used in combination with *Optuna*[19] which uses search space pruning to obtain the best-performing hyperparameters efficiently.

The objective function was set to maximise all the evaluation metrics discussed in Section 5 using multi-objective optimisation. We used the default search algorithm, Tree-structured Parzen Estimator.

[15]https://mlrs.research.um.edu.mt/

[16]https://github.com/mtanti/maltese-simplification-corpus/

[17]Words are POS tagged when counting their frequency such that it is the frequency of a word-tag pair that is counted.

[18]The news articles found in the Korpus Malti were not the same as the articles used to make our data set, which was made with articles that came out after the corpus was compiled.

[19]https://optuna.org/

5 Results and Evaluation

We automatically evaluated each step in the pipeline after tuning the hyperparameters. We also conducted a human evaluation of the full system through a single-blind study.

The automatic evaluation metrics are just different ways of comparing the generated substitutes with the correct substitutes (where correct substitutes are either the set of substitutable words or the set of simple words). The precision metric is the percentage of correctly generated substitutes out of all generated substitutes. The recall metric is the percentage of correctly generated substitutes out of all correct substitutes. The accuracy metric is the percentage of generated substitutes that are correct. The precision@1 metric is the percentage of target words with a correct highest-scoring generated substitute. Finally, the F-score metric is the harmonic mean of precision and recall. Different subsets of these metrics are used to evaluate different modules.

When evaluating the SG and SS modules, we selected the evaluation metrics precision, recall, and F-score. These are the most widely used for SG (Alarcon et al., 2021; Qiang et al., 2020; Paetzold and Specia, 2017a).

Hyperparameter tuning the SG module on the Maltese dev set revealed that it performs best (F-score 0.169) with pro-clitic consideration, right-to-left mask filling, use of CSR, 1 mask, and a beam size of 5. The fact that 1 mask was better is surprising given the complex morphology of Maltese and the small number of generated substitutes (1 mask $\times$ beam size 5 = 5 candidates). This is evidence in favour of BERTu's performance which is suggesting good substitutes with just one token. On English using the English dev set, hyperparameter tuning revealed that the best performing parameters (F-score 0.196) were the same as for Maltese, but using up to 3 masks instead of 1, and using *bert-large-uncased*.

Hyperparameter tuning the SS module on the Maltese dev set revealed that it performs best (precision 0.188) with Cosine similarity filtering, without scaling, using a similarity threshold of 0.85 and no POS tag filtering. Surprisingly, POS tag filtering actually lowered both precision and recall, which probably means that the Maltese POS tagger used could be improved. We opted to just reuse the hyperparameters for English as well rather than performing tuning again since there were no language specific hyperparameters like in the SG module.

The results on the Maltese and English test sets are shown in Table 1, where we quoted the results obtained by Qiang et al. (2021) where they re-implemented a number of LS systems and evaluated them on NNSeval (we only include the results of some top performing models, which include those developed by Paetzold and Specia (2016, 2017b); Gooding and Kochmar (2019)). We can see that the SG module by itself does not beat the system produced by Qiang et al. (2021) but when the additional filtering of the SS module is used, then we double our F-score, which gives us the best results in the table for English. For Maltese we see that SS does not improve our F-score, only the precision.

When evaluating the SR module, we selected the evaluation metrics accuracy, precision, recall, F-score, and precision@1.

Hyperparameter tuning the SR module on the Maltese dev set revealed that it performs best with SG as a source for candidate words, Cosine similarity for similarity scoring, no normalisation, and LightGBM as an ML model. The model gives importance to all features, but mostly to the similarity and pseudo log-likelihood scores, as shown in Table 2. The feature importance scores show that the frequency of the words in the general corpus is twice as important as the frequency of words in the domain-specific corpora, probably because the size of the corpus matters more.

We compared the results of the SR module when using the candidates provided by the SG module with the results of the SR module when using the annotated candidates in the data set. This is to see how the performance of the SR module would change if the SG module was perfect. The results on the Maltese test sets are shown in Table 3. We can see that, while the normal system suggests a correct simpler word as the highest scoring word (precision@1) 72% of the time, a perfect SG module would bump this up to 81%. The difference in performance on the rest of the metrics is not as drastic.

5.1 Human Evaluation

A within-subjects single-blind study was carried out with 207 volunteer participants. Participants were given 16 sentence pairs (i.e., the original version and the system-generated lexically simplified version) selected from a pool of 1 000 sentences. Both sentence selection and pair-wise presentation were randomised to avoid patterns and bias. These sentences were separately scraped from Maltese news portals following the same method outlined in

Data set	System	Precision	Recall	F-score
NNSeval	Paetzold-CA	0.118	0.161	0.136
	Paetzold-NE	0.186	0.136	0.157
	REC-LS	0.103	0.155	0.124
	LSBert	0.194	0.260	0.222
	Our system (SG)	0.218	0.190	0.203
	Our system (SG+SS)	**0.319**	**0.560**	**0.406**
Our Maltese data set	Our system (SG)	0.153	**0.449**	**0.228**
	Our system (SG+SS)	**0.167**	0.340	0.224

Table 1: SG and SS results compared with other systems in literature (best results in bold).

Feature	Importance
Similarity score	3039
PLL score	3031
Shuffled corpus frequency	2057
Character count	1145
Simplification corpus frequency	1082
Press corpus frequency	806

Table 2: Feature importance for simplification score according to the LightGBM model (using split feature importance).

Metric	SG+SR	Gold+SR
Accuracy	**0.886**	0.766
Precision	0.628	**0.768**
Recall	**0.711**	0.709
F-score	0.667	**0.737**
Prec.@1	0.724	**0.814**

Table 3: Our SR results on the Maltese data set (best results in bold). 'Gold' refers to the annotated substitutes in the data set.

Section 3. Participants had to blindly select the sentence they deemed simpler, along with whether the two sentences had the same meaning. Participants were asked about sentences that the system deemed as already in their simplest form - and whether these could be simplified further (and how).

With regards to meaning preservation, participants indicated that the two sentences had the same meaning 44% of the time, and that, of those sentences, 53% thought that the generated sentence was simpler, 29% thought that the original sentence was simpler, and 18% were unsure about which was simpler. Further analysis showed that in most cases where the meaning was changed, this was due to a single substituted word within the sentence.

A demographic analysis showed that younger participants and persons with lower levels of education perceived the system to be more effective. Similar views were provided by individuals whose first language was not Maltese. Of the sentences the system deemed as unsimplifiable, 73% of participants agreed that this was so.

This is an encouraging step for a low-resource language like Maltese, which only required 40 annotated sentences in the dev set to tune the system's hyperparameters.

6 Conclusion

We developed and evaluated an LS pipeline for Maltese, together with the compilation of a Maltese LS data set that was used throughout the process. The various pipeline steps were individually evaluated, with promising results. Our approach also produced significant improvements over the results obtained in the unsupervised lexical substitution system developed for Maltese (Tanti, 2014).

The overall system was also evaluated through a single-blind study with 207 individuals. This was done to determine the overall perceived quality of the system-generated simplified text, and encouraging results were obtained as outlined in Section 5.1. Furthermore, participants generally concurred when presented with sentences that the system determined as already in their simplest form.

Arising from this work, a browser extension was also developed (MaltEasy), acting as a reference implementation of an LS-based AT for Maltese online content accessibility. Although not presented in this paper, MaltEasy provides the team with a first-cut design that motivates the need for further framework improvements and user studies, clearly informing the future of this work.

6.1 Limitations and Future Work

This work presents a promising framework for developing an LS system for Maltese but has some limitations that can be addressed in future work. Despite efforts to compile a new comprehensive data set for the task, the Maltese LS data set used for training and evaluation may benefit from further expansion. Moreover, the system was limited to using BERTu (Micallef et al., 2022), the only available Maltese BERT model, which is only available with a base architecture. The LS system would benefit from using a larger architecture, as shown by the fact that the BERT-large model gave the best results for English. It would also be interesting to determine whether the system developed can be applied to other low-resource languages (after adapting the language specific elements like pro-clitic handling). Furthermore, the proposed LS system focuses on simplification at word level, overlooking multi-word expressions where individual words should not be substituted, a problem that could be solved by a more sophisticated PCWI module the includes multi-word expression detection. Additionally, further filtering might be implemented such that ambiguous sentences are skipped from simplification to avoid unintentionally changing the author's intended meaning.

Acknowledgements

This project was partially funded by the Malta Digital Innovation Authority AI Scholarship.

References

Rodrigo Alarcon, Lourdes Moreno, and Paloma Martínez. 2021. Lexical Simplification System to Improve Web Accessibility. *IEEE Access*, 9:58755–58767.

Jacob Devlin, Ming-Wei Chang, Kenton Lee, and Kristina Toutanova. 2019. BERT: Pre-training of Deep Bidirectional Transformers for Language Understanding. In *Proc. of the 2019 NAACL-HLT., Volume 1 (Long and Short Papers)*, pages 4171–4186, Minneapolis, Minnesota. Association for Computational Linguistics.

Pierre Finnimore, Elisabeth Fritzsch, Daniel King, Alison Sneyd, Aneeq Ur Rehman, Fernando Alva-Manchego, and Andreas Vlachos. 2019. Strong Baselines for Complex Word Identification across Multiple Languages. In *Proc. of the 2019 NAACL-HLT*, pages 970–977, Minneapolis, Minnesota. Association for Computational Linguistics.

Sian Gooding and Ekaterina Kochmar. 2019. Recursive context-aware lexical simplification. In *Proc. of the 2019 Conf. on Empirical Methods in Natural Lang. Proc. and the 9th Int. Joint Conf. on Natural Lang. Proc. (EMNLP-IJCNLP)*, pages 4853–4863, Hong Kong, China. Association for Computational Linguistics.

Michael A. Hedderich, Lukas Lange, Heike Adel, Jannik Strötgen, and Dietrich Klakow. 2020. A Survey on Recent Approaches for Natural Language Processing in Low-Resource Scenarios. *arXiv e-prints*, page arXiv:2010.12309.

Colby Horn, Cathryn Manduca, and David Kauchak. 2014. Learning a lexical simplifier using Wikipedia. In *Proc. of the 52nd Annu. Meeting of the Assoc. for Comput. Linguistics (Volume 2: Short Papers)*, pages 458–463, Baltimore, Maryland. Association for Computational Linguistics.

Tomoyuki Kajiwara and Kazuhide Yamamoto. 2015. Evaluation dataset and system for japanese lexical simplification. pages 35–40.

Weizhang Liang, Suizhi Luo, Guoyan Zhao, and Hao Wu. 2020. Predicting hard rock pillar stability using gbdt, xgboost, and lightgbm algorithms. *Mathematics*, 8(5).

Diana McCarthy and Roberto Navigli. 2007. Semeval-2007 task 10: English lexical substitution task. In *Procs. of the 4th Int. Workshop on Semantic Eval.*, SemEval '07, page 48–53, USA. Association for Computational Linguistics.

Kurt Micallef, Albert Gatt, Marc Tanti, Lonneke van der Plas, and Claudia Borg. 2022. Pre-training Data Quality and Quantity for a Low-Resource Language: New Corpus and BERT Models for Maltese. In *Proc. of the Third Workshop on Deep Learn. for Low-Resour. Natural Lang. Proc.*, pages 90–101, Hybrid. Association for Computational Linguistics.

Eric Mutabazi and Nathanaël Wallenhorst. 2020. Une citoyenneté de seconde classe? n'ayons pas peur des mots! *bildungsforschung*, (1):1–13.

Irina Nikishina, Alsu Vakhitova, Elena Tutubalina, and Alexander Panchenko. 2022. Cross-Modal Contextualized Hidden State Projection Method for Expanding of Taxonomic Graphs. In *Proc. of TextGraphs-16: Graph-based Methods for Natural Lang. Process.*, pages 11–24. Association for Computational Linguistics.

Jenny Ortiz-Zambrano and Arturo Montejo-Ráez. 2021. SINAI at SemEval-2021 Task 1: Complex word identification using Word-level features. In *Proc. of the 15th Int. Workshop on Semant. Eval.*, pages 126–129, Bangkok, Thailand.

G. H. Paetzold and L. Specia. 2016. Unsupervised Lexical Simplification for non-native speakers. In *AAAI'16: Proc. of the Thirtieth AAAI Conf. on AI*, pages 3761–3768.

Gustavo H. Paetzold and Lucia Specia. 2017a. A Survey on Lexical Simplification. *J. Artif. Intell. Res.*, 60:549–593.

Gustavo Henrique Paetzold and Lucia Specia. 2017b. Lexical Simplification with Neural Ranking. In *Proc. of the 15th Conf. of the Eur. Chapter of the Assoc. for Comput. Linguistics: Volume 2, Short Papers*, volume 2, pages 34–40.

Jipeng Qiang, Yun Li, Yi Zhu, Yunhao Yuan, Yang Shi, and Xindong Wu. 2021. LSBert: Lexical Simplification Based on BERT. *IEEE/ACM Trans. on Audio Speech and Lang. Process.*, 29:3064–3076.

Jipeng Qiang, Xinyu Lu, Yun Li, Yunhao Yuan, and Xindong Wu. 2020. Chinese Lexical Simplification. *IEEE/ACM Transactions on Audio Speech and Language Processing*, 29:1819–1828.

Eva Rolin, Quentin Langlois, Patrick Watrin, and Thomas François. 2021. FrenLyS: A Tool for the Automatic Simplification of French General Language Texts. In *RANLP 2021*, pages 1196–1205. INCOMA Ltd.

Julian Salazar, Davis Liang, Toan Q. Nguyen, and Katrin Kirchhoff. 2020. Masked language model scoring. In *Proc. of the 58th Annu. Meeting of the Assoc. for Comput. Linguistics*. Association for Computational Linguistics.

R. Sathyaraj and Prabu Sevugan. 2015. An approach for software fault prediction to measure the quality of different prediction methodologies using software metrics. *Indian J. of Sci. and Tech,*, 8.

Mario Serracino-Inglott. 2016. *Id-Dizzjunarju Malti*, 4 edition. Merlin Publishers.

Matthew Shardlow. 2014. A Survey of Automated Text Simplification. *Int. J. Adv. Comput. Sci. Appl. (IJACSA) Spec. Issue Nat. Lang. Process.*, 4(1).

Ravid Shwartz-Ziv and Amitai Armon. 2022. Tabular data: Deep learning is not all you need. *Information Fusion*, 81:84–90.

Lucia Specia, Sujay Kumar Jauhar, and Rada Mihalcea. 2012. Semeval-2012 task 1: English lexical simplification. In *SEM 2012: The First Joint Conf. on Lexical and Comput. Semantics – Vol. 1: Proc. of the main conf. and the shared task, and Vol. 2: Proc. of the Sixth Int. Workshop on Semantic Eval (SemEval 2012)*, pages 347–355, Montréal, Canada. Association for Computational Linguistics.

M. Tanti. 2014. *Unsupervised lexical substitution for Maltese: steps toward lexical simplification*. Ph.D. thesis, M.S. thesis, Dept. Intellig. Comput. Syst., Univ. of Malta, Msida, Malta.

Ahmet Yavuz Uluslu. 2022. Automatic Lexical Simplification for Turkish.

Parameter	Values
SG module	
Max. masks	1, 2, 3
Beam size	3, 4, 5
Pro-clitic mask*	yes, no
Mask fill order	LTR, RTL
Use CSR	yes, no
SS module	
POS tag filtering	yes, no
Similarity filtering	yes, no
Similarity method	cosine, WMD
Scaling	yes, no
SR module	
Candidate words source	SS, SG
Similarity method	cosine, WMD
Feature norm.	yes, no
ML model	logistic reg., XGBoost, LightGBM, Naïve Bayes

Table 4: Hyperparameter search space used when tuning the separate modules.
*Only for the Maltese data set.

A Hypermarameter search space for separate modules

B SR module hyperparameters for ML models

The best hyperparameters of the LightGBM model, which was the best performing model, were max_depth set to 7, n-estimators to 600, and learning_rate to 0.0149.

Parameter	Values
Logistic regression	
solver	liblinear, saga
c_value	0.1 - 5 (uniform)
XGBoost	
learning rate	0.01 - 0.3 (uniform)
maximum depth	3 - 9 (integer)
n estimators	100 - 1000 (uniform), with a 100 step
LightGBM	
learning rate	0.01 - 0.3 (uniform)
maximum depth	3 - 9 (integer)
n estimators	100 - 1000, with a 100 step (uniform)
Naïve Bayes	
var_smoothing	1E-12 - 1E-3 (log uniform)

Table 5: Hyperparameters used for the ML models in the SR module.

Prompting Fairness: Learning Prompts for Debiasing Large Language Models

Andrei-Victor Chisca
Computer Science Department
Technical University of Cluj-Napoca
chiscaandrei3@gmail.com

Andrei-Cristian Rad
Computer Science Department
Technical University of Cluj-Napoca
andrei.rad@campus.utcluj.ro

Camelia Lemnaru
Computer Science Department
Technical University of Cluj-Napoca
Camelia.Lemnaru@cs.utcluj.ro

Abstract

Large language models are prone to internalize social biases due to the characteristics of the data used for their self-supervised training scheme. Considering their recent emergence and wide availability to the general public, it is mandatory to identify and alleviate these biases to avoid perpetuating stereotypes towards underrepresented groups. We present a novel prompt-tuning method for reducing biases in encoder models such as BERT or RoBERTa. Unlike other methods, we only train a small set of additional reusable token embeddings that can be concatenated to any input sequence to reduce bias in the outputs. We particularize this method to gender bias by providing a set of templates used for training the prompts[1]. Evaluations on two benchmarks show that our method is on par with the state of the art while having a limited impact on language modeling ability.

1 Introduction

Large language models (LLMs) have claimed state-of-the-art performance on most of the classical natural language processing (NLP) tasks in recent years while facilitating new frontiers in language generation. However, besides being computationally expensive, their performance comes at an additional cost, as they tend to pick up social biases from the vast data required for their pretraining. Consequently, these models can exhibit representational harms, such as disparate system performance, exclusion or stereotyping, or allocation harms, such as discrimination and unequal allocation of resources (Gallegos et al., 2023). With an increased number of use cases and adoption rates, ensuring fairness is becoming more and more critical.

Our work can be summarized by the following key contributions:

- We propose a method to mitigate bias in encoder-only language models using prompt-tuning, which we evaluate for the problem of gender bias.
- We design and motivate a novel loss function based on the Kullback–Leibler (KL) divergence, which we use for tuning the prompts.
- We provide an extensible set of templates that can be used as a starting point for removing other biases.

2 Related Work

2.1 Bias Quantification Benchmarks

Bias quantification benchmarks aim to measure the bias present in a model towards certain demographics. In LLMs, bias can be quantified using embedding-based metrics, probability-based metrics or generated text metrics.

Embedding-based metrics, such as Word Embeddings Association Test (**WEAT**) (Caliskan et al., 2017) or Sentence Embedding Association Test (**SEAT**) (May et al., 2019) quantify biases by measuring the association between two groups of bias attributes (e.g. associated with male and female terms) and two groups of target attributes (e.g. associated with family and career). SEAT, used for contextual models like BERT or RoBERTa, creates sentence-level embeddings by filling in templates with terms from the four groups.

Probability-based methods, such as **StereoSet** (Nadeem et al., 2021), quantify bias by measuring how frequently a model chooses a stereotypical word to fill in a masked token. In StereoSet, the

[1]Our implementation is available at https://github.com/ChiscaAndrei/prompting-fairness

Proceedings of the Fourth Workshop on Language Technology for Equality, Diversity, Inclusion, pages 52–62
March 21, 2024 ©2024 Association for Computational Linguistics

Nr.	Template
1	<GenderedWord> is a <Target>.
1	<GenderedWord> works as a <Target>.
2	<GenderedWord> worked as an <Target> for two years.
3	<GenderedWord> is a good <Target>.
4	<GenderedWord> earns <HisOrHer> living as a <Target>.
5	I'm glad that <GenderedWord> is a <Target>.
6	<GenderedWord> is studying to be an <Target>.
7	<GenderedWord> had this idea ever since <GenderedWord> was hired as a <Target>."
8	It was hard for <HimOrHer> to become a <Target>.
9	<HisOrHer> career as a <Target> is lucrative.
10	<HisOrHer> job as a <Target> is exhausting.

Table 1: Some examples of templates used for reducing gender bias. Slot names are enclosed by angle brackets.

model can choose from a stereotypical, an anti-stereotypical and an unrelated choice for each scenario. The stereotype score represents the percentage of scenarios where a model prefers the answer that confirms a stereotype.

2.2 Bias Mitigation

Bias mitigation methods aim to reduce the bias in the output of models. Mitigation can occur at different stages during the training or inference or as a separate pre-processing or post-processing step. Attacking the root cause of the biases present in LLMs is often challenging, so most mitigation methods in this context occur after the pretraining.

Pre-processing methods often involve altering existing data via either augmentation, generation or filtering. **Counter-factual Data Augmentation (CDA)** (Zmigrod et al., 2019) generates new data samples by swapping the bias-driving terms in existing data. For instance, to reduce gender bias, gender-specific terms (he/she, his/hers) are swapped, and the model undergoes additional pre-training using the new. A visible disadvantage of this method is that it requires updating all the model weights, which might not be trivial for very large models.

Projection-based methods such as **Iterative Nullspace Projection (INLP)** (Ravfogel et al., 2020) and **Sentence Debias** (Liang et al., 2020) rely on embedding projection to alter the representation of the input data. Although these two methods do not require additional training, they also have drawbacks. INLP negatively impacts the language modeling ability (Meade et al., 2022), while Sentence Debias requires additional data augmentation.

In-training methods such as architecture modifications (e.g. with adapters - ADELE (Lauscher et al., 2021)), equalizing loss terms (e.g. embedding balancing (Liu et al., 2020)) or additional regularization (e.g. **Dropout** (Webster et al., 2020)) alter the training process of language models. For mitigating biases using Dropout, the model undergoes another round of pretraining with an increased dropout for the attention weights.

3 Prompt Tuning for Bias Mitigation

It has been shown that concatenating prompts to the input of a pretrained language model is a viable method of altering its behaviour for different use cases. Notably, in-context learning, which involves prompting with a few training examples, can be successfully used for adapting a model to various downstream tasks. In (Xie et al., 2022), the authors formalize in-context learning as an *implicit Bayesian inference*, such that the probability of the model's output O can be expressed as

$$p(O|P) = \int_C p(O|C,P)p(C|P)d(C)$$

where the model implicitly infers a *latent concept* C based on the given prompt P.

We argue that a similar approach can be used for debiasing encoder-only LLMs. During pretraining, the model learns to maximize the likelihood of the training data. This behaviour might not always be desirable, especially if, due to the characteristics of the training data, maximizing its likelihood involves relying on various stereotypes. As opposed to removing or hiding information from the model, either at training or at inference time, we aim to give the model additional information at inference, in the form of compact prompt embeddings, which could enable it to implicitly infer a *latent concept* encompassing the desired behaviour: generating a fair and unbiased output.

The prompts should be able to encompass the desired behaviour as accurately as possible. Ideally, we want the model to produce output which is *unbiased* while also retaining the identity of all social groups and maintaining correctness in general language modeling. Trying to express this in handcrafted prompts would not be straightforward, especially if the model to be unbiased was not explicitly trained to follow human instructions. Instead, we base our approach on *"prompt tuning"* (Lester et al., 2021), which involves concatenating a set of trainable embeddings to the embedded input of the model while keeping the other parameters frozen.

Templates The prompt embeddings are trained using a dataset of templates with *bias slots* and *target slots*. Each *bias slot* can be replaced by words specific to each social group affected by the type of bias to be mitigated. For example, for gender bias, we could have a *bias slot* which can be replaced by either "he" or "she", another one which could be replaced by either "his" or "her" and so on. The *target slots* represent the words in the templates which the model should predict. For target slots, there is a set of *allowed options*, composed of:

- *general options* – a set of possible completions for the slot which are the same for each of the social groups considered
- *group specific options* – a set of completions which have a different variant for each of the social groups considered

The reason for explicitly defining the expected outputs of the model and dividing it into *general* and *specific* is to avoid training prompts which cause the model to *"forget"* the identity of each group. For simplicity, we use a single target slot per template.

Training and Loss function We train the prompts by replacing the *bias slots* of each template with their specific variants for each group and minimizing the KL divergence between the probability distribution predicted by the model for the *allowed options* of the *target slots* and a reference probability distribution. For a given template T and social group A, the *bias slots* in T are replaced with corresponding substitutions for A to obtain T_A. We denote by

$$Options_G = \{g_1, g_2, \dots, g_{N_G}\}$$

the set of *general options* and by

$$Options_S(A) = \{s_{A,1}, s_{A,2}, \dots, s_{A,N_S}\}$$

the set of *group-specific options* for group A. Then, denoting by t the *target slot* for T_A, we obtain the probability distribution P_{T_A} defined on the sample space:

$$\begin{aligned}\Omega_{T_A} = \{&t = g_1, \dots, t = g_{N_G},\\ &t = s_{A,1}, \dots, t = s_{A,N_S},\\ &t \notin Options_G \cup Options_S(A)\}\end{aligned} \quad (1)$$

Here $P_{T_A}(t = x)$ represents the probability predicted by the model for word x in the *target slot* t of T_A. To obtain a proper probability distribution, we also consider the probability of t not being in the set of *allowed options.*

We choose the *reference probability distribution* $P^*_{T_A}$ for T_A as the average probabilities predicted by the original model (denoted by P^i) across the set $\boldsymbol{G}$ of all social groups considered:

$$P^*_{T_A}(t = g_k) = \frac{1}{|\boldsymbol{G}|}\sum_{G\in\boldsymbol{G}} P^i_{T_G}(t = g_k) \quad (2)$$

$$P^*_{T_A}(t = s_{A,k}) = \frac{1}{|\boldsymbol{G}|}\sum_{G\in\boldsymbol{G}} P^i_{T_G}(t = s_{G,k}) \quad (3)$$

We define the loss term for template instantiation T_A, obtained by filling *bias slots* in template T with terms specific for social group G, as the KL divergence between the probability distribution predicted by the model and the *reference probability distribution*:

$$L_{T_A} = D_{KL}(P_{T_A} \parallel P^*_{T_A}) \quad (4)$$

The *reference probability distribution* $P^*_{T_A}$ for each template instantiation T_A is treated as a constant and can be precomputed beforehand.

Then, the total loss for a set $\boldsymbol{T}$ of templates is obtained by instantiating each template T with the *bias slot terms* for each social group G, and summing over the loss terms for each resulting template instantiation T_G:

$$L = \sum_{T\in\boldsymbol{T}}\sum_{G\in\boldsymbol{G}} L_{T_G} \quad (5)$$

BiasSlotName	Male Variant	Female Variant
GenderedWord	he	she
	Robert	Patricia
	Michael	Jennifer
	William	Barbara
	Richard	Susan
	Daniel	Jessica
	Andrew	Karen
	George	Emily
	Brian	Rebecca
	Ryan	Cynthia
	Stephen	Emma
HeOrShe	he	she
HisOrHer	his	her
HimOrHer	him	her

Table 2: Gender *bias slots* used in templates

In previous formulas, we assumed for simplicity a single template instantiation T_G for each pair of a template T and a group G. In the general case, there may exist multiple such template instantiations T_G^k, depending on whether some *bias slots* in T can be filled by multiple pairs of values. In this case, we sum over all considered[2] instantiations:

$$L = \sum_{T \in \boldsymbol{T}} \sum_{G \in \boldsymbol{G}} \sum_{k} L_{T_G^k} \tag{6}$$

Gender debiasing BERT and RoBERTa We particularize this method for reducing gender bias in BERT (Devlin et al., 2019) and RoBERTa (Liu et al., 2019) models. We constructed a dataset of 159 templates, mostly focused on genders in relation to professions/occupations, as this is one area in which we empirically observed the models to generate biased predictions. Examples of templates are listed in Table 1. We use 4 types of bias slots, as described in Table 2.

For simplicity, we restrict the choice of *allowed options* to words that each model's tokenizer can represent with a single token and subsequently replace the *target slots* in the templates by a single [MASK] token. This is not a big limitation in this case, since BERT's and RoBERTa's vocabularies can represent most common English words by a single token. However, it might pose problems for models with other types of tokenizers and for different languages, as it would require either using a limited number of options or creating separate templates for different numbers of mask tokens. We selected the *allowed options* empirically by hand-picking appropriate completions and choosing from the original model's predictions for the templates. While templates are focused on professions/occupations, the *allowed options* are not restricted only to this specific domain; for some of the templates, there are other valid completions. We selected 219 *general options* and 15 pairs of *group specific options*. Some examples are listed in Table 11 and Table 12.

[2]for practical reasons, we might consider only a subset of all possible instantiations

Implementation We use pretrained models from Huggingface Transformers (Wolf et al., 2020) and use the *prompt tuning* implementation in from PEFT (Mangrulkar et al., 2022) with PyTorch (Paszke et al., 2019) for building and training our debiased models.

Training is done using an AdamW (Loshchilov and Hutter, 2019) optimizer with an initial learning rate of $1e-2$ and a linearly decreasing schedule with warmup. Since only prompt parameters are updated and the dataset used is small, training converges fairly rapidly: training of each debiased model takes about half an hour on an Nvidia 1050Ti GPU.

4 Results

We evaluate our method for mitigating gender bias in BERT and RoBERTa on the gender tests from SEAT (May et al., 2019) and StereoSet (Nadeem et al., 2021). For StereoSet, a *stereotype score (SS)* closer to 50% indicates a less biased model. In case of SEAT, we average the last layer's hidden representations and normalize the resulting vector, as May et al. (2019); Meade et al. (2022), but *exclude* the representations corresponding to the prompt tokens from this computation. For analyzing the loss in language modeling performance, we use the *language modeling (LM)* score from StereoSet and the pseudo-perplexity (Salazar et al., 2020) on the *test* split of WikiText-2 (Merity et al., 2017). For computing the pseudo-perplexity, we first sentencize each text in the dataset, using Spacy (Honnibal et al., 2020).

Initialization method In preliminary experiments with BERT, using *random initialization* for the prompt's parameters, we observed, similarly to Lester et al. (2021), that the prompts learned and the performance depend to a large extent on the initialization. We also examined for each

	SEAT Gender Avg. Effect Size (↓)	StereoSet Gender SS Score (%)	StereoSet LM Score (↑)
BERT base uncased	0.620	60.279	84.172
+ PF Random init.	0.393 ±0.068(0.095)	58.901 ±0.437(0.597)	84.036 ±0.146(0.204)
+ PF Gendered init.	0.455 ±0.118(0.095)	58.605 ±0.495(0.399)	**84.576** ±0.226(0.182)
+ PF Neutral init.	0.454 ±0.092(0.074)	58.675 ±0.349(0.281)	84.333 ±0.273(0.220)
+ PF FemaleBiased init.	**0.330** ±0.071(0.057)	**58.456** ±0.674(0.543)	84.460 ±0.155(0.125)
+ CDA	0.722	59.610	83.080
+ Dropout	0.765	60.660	83.040
+ INLP	**0.204**	**57.250**	80.630
+ SentenceDebias	0.434	59.370	84.200
+ Self-Debias	-	59.340	84.090
RoBERTa base	0.940	66.323	88.929
+ PF Random init.	0.838 ±0.042(0.059)	65.495 ±0.677(0.946)	88.729 ±0.121(0.169)
+ PF Gendered init.	0.686 ±0.075(0.060)	64.186 ±1.018(0.820)	**89.008** ±0.284(0.229)
+ PF Neutral init.	**0.635** ±0.067(0.054)	**63.939** ±0.614(0.495)	88.908 ±0.300(0.241)
+ PF FemaleBiased init.	0.702 ±0.040(0.032)	64.319 ±0.529(0.426)	88.944 ±0.150(0.121)
+ CDA	0.880	64.430	88.830
+ Dropout	1.074	66.260	88.810
+ INLP	0.823	**60.820**	88.230
+ SentenceDebias	0.846	62.770	88.940
+ Self-Debias	-	65.040	88.260

Table 3: Results of gender debiased models with different initialization types compared with results reported by Meade et al. (2022) for CDA, Dropout, INLP, SentenceDebias and Self-Debias. Our results are averaged across all trials, with a 95% *confidence interval (±)* and with the standard deviation in parentheses. For SEAT, we report the *mean absolute effect sizes* across all 6 gender tests. For StereoSet, we report the *Stereotype Score (SS)* for *gender* test and *Language Modeling Score (LM)* across all tests.

prompt token the closest[3] 5-word embeddings in the model's vocabulary, before and after training, and remarked that in some cases, the model[4] tends to learn prompts close to *female gendered* words.

Based on these preliminary findings, we evaluated the performance of 4 different types of initialization methods, using a prompt length of 3 tokens in each case:

- Random initialization – prompt embeddings are initialized randomly[5].
- Neutral initialization – each prompt token's embedding is initialized with a *neutral* world, unrelated to genders.
- Gender Balanced initialization – one prompt token's embedding is initialized with the embedding of a word related to the *male gender*, one is initialized to the embedding of a *neutral* word, and one is initialized with the embedding of a word related to the *female gender.*
- Female Biased initialization – each prompt token's embedding is initialized with the embedding of a word related to the *female gender.*

Words used for each type of initialization are listed in Tables 9,10.

For this experiment, we use *bert-base-uncased* and *roberta-base* as base models and don't use any names in the *bias slots* of the templates (the <GenderedWord> slots are filled only with "he" or "she"). Given each base model, we train 10 models using *Random*, 5 with *Neutral* initialization, 5 with *Gender Balanced* initialization and 5 with *female Biased* initialization. Each model is trained for 250 epochs, with batches of 16 templates. In Table 3, we report the mean and standard deviation across each type of initialization and compare the results with those reported by Meade et al. (2022) for gender debiasing using CDA, DROPOUT, INLP,SENTENCEDEBIAS and SELF-

[3] in terms of *cosine distance*

[4] preliminary experiments were only performed for BERT

[5] using default Embedding initialization in PyTorch: normal distribution with mean 0 and standard deviation 1

	Profession SS (%)	**Race SS** (%)	**Religion SS** (%)
BERT base uncased	58.934	57.030	59.704
+ PF Random init.	57.227 ±0.172(0.240)	56.978 ±0.200(0.279)	60.437 ±0.590(0.825)
+ PF Gendered init.	56.942 ±0.294(0.237)	**56.595** ±0.227(0.183)	59.755 ±0.946(0.762)
+ PF Neutral init.	**56.940** ±0.246(0.198)	56.833 ±0.887(0.714)	**59.358** ±1.468(1.182)
+ PF FemaleBiased init.	57.026 ±0.336(0.271)	56.842 ±0.272(0.219)	59.362 ±0.620(0.499)
RoBERTa base	61.467	61.674	64.278
+ PF Random init.	60.893 ±0.306(0.427)	61.773 ±0.213(0.298)	64.432 ±0.769(1.074)
+ PF Gendered init.	59.736 ±0.580(0.467)	61.591 ±0.249(0.200)	62.870 ±1.327(1.068)
+ PF Neutral init.	**59.663** ±0.352(0.283)	61.390 ±0.861(0.694)	**61.804** ±1.515(1.220)
+ PF FemaleBiased init.	59.680 ±1.109(0.893)	**61.324** ±0.633(0.509)	63.391 ±1.275(1.027)

Table 4: Stereotype scores of *gender debiased* models with different initialization types on StereoSet *profession, race* and *religion* tests. Results are averaged across all trials, with a $95\% confidence interval$ (±) and the standard deviation (in parentheses).

	SEAT Gender Avg. Effect Size (↓)	**StereoSet Gender SS Score** (%)	**StereoSet LM Score** (↑)	**Pseudo-Perplexity** (↓)
BERT base uncased	0.620	60.279	84.172	6.396
+ With Names	0.397 (0.060)	58.854 (0.804)	84.347 (0.269)	**6.517** (0.044)
+ Without Names	**0.330** (0.057)	**58.456** (0.543)	**84.460** (0.125)	6.530 (0.088)
BERT base cased	0.686	61.229	82.522	**5.542**
+ With Names	**0.414** (0.086)	59.163 (0.403)	82.494 (0.108)	5.786 (0.140)
+ Without Names	0.587 (0.131)	**59.123** (0.452)	**82.422** (0.170)	5.788 (0.145)

Table 5: Results of gender debiased models with and witthe hout usage of names in the training dataset, for two types of base models: bert-base-uncased and bert-base-cased. *Female biased* initialization is used in all cases. For training *with names*, models are trained for 40 epochs and 250 otherwise. Results are averaged over all 5 different initializations, with standard deviation in parentheses.

	PseudoPerplexity (↓)
BERT base uncased	6.396
+ PF Random init.	6.584 ±0.117(0.164)
+ PF Gendered init.	6.674 ±0.272(0.219)
+ PF Neutral init.	6.572 ±0.128(0.103)
+ PF FemaleBiased init.	**6.530** ±0.109(0.088)
RoBERTa base	11.198
+ PF Random init.	11.464 ±0.154(0.215)
+ PF Gendered init.	**11.146** ±0.398(0.320)
+ PF Neutral init.	11.410 ±0.153(0.123)
+ PF FemaleBiased init.	11.472 ±0.571(0.460)

Table 6: Pseudo-perplexities of models gender debiased using different methods of initialization. Pseudo-perplexities are computed on the *test* split of WikiText-2. We sentencize each text before computing the pseudo-perplexities. Results are averaged across all trials, with a $95\% confidence interval$ *(±)* and standard deviation (in parentheses).

DEBIAS. The pseudo-perplexities are listed in Table 6.

In case of **BERT**, we remark that among the different initialization methods, the *female biased* initialization yields the best results both in terms of *debiasing* and retaining of language modeling performance. Between *random*, *gendered balanced* and *neutral* initialization, the results are similar overall. Compared to other debiasing techniques, the *female biased* initialization is second to INLP in terms of debiasing, while the other initialization types are on par with SENTENCEDEBIAS. However, our method generally results in a good *language modeling* score and limited increase in pseudo-perplexity, while INLP significantly reduces the LM score. We suspect this might be due to INLP removing all gender-related information for the model's output.

In case of **RoBERTa**, we notice that the *neutral* initialization achieves better results than the other initialization types. While this achieves significantly better results on SEAT compared to all other debiasing techniques, its results on StereoSet are surpassed by both INLP and SENTENCEDEBIAS. As for BERT, results show that our method generally succeeds in maintaining the language modelling ability of the base model.

Effect on other types of biases Besides mitigating the targeted bias and the impact on language modeling performance, the side effects on other biases should also be considered. We evaluate our *gender debiased* models on the *profession*, *race* and *religion* tests in StereoSet and report the *stereotype scores* in Table 4.

In the *profession bias*, test there is a significant decrease in bias for all initialization methods, most probably due to the dataset used for training, which is focused on genders and professions. There is no significant effect for *race bias*. For *religion bias*, the results vary notably across different trials with the same type of initialization, and there is, on average, an increase in bias for models trained using *random initialization*. These results suggest extending this method for targeting multiple biases might be feasible.

Using names in training In previous experiments, all *bias slots* in templates were replaced with gendered pronouns. Besides pronouns, more types of words contain gender-related information, such as names and gendered nouns. We experiment with adding names to the training dataset by also replacing <GenderedWord> bias slots with names. For each template containing a <GenderWord> slot, we instantiate it once with the *("he", "she")* pair and 10 more times with pairs of one male name and one female name. While the names are the same, their pairing is different for each template. Since names in English are capitalized, we evaluate our results both for *bert-base-uncased* and *bert-base-cased*, as we presume the capitalization might give the models a better understanding for the concept of 'names'. We only evaluated *female biased* initialization because it achieved better results in previous experiments. To account for different dataset sizes, we train for 40 epochs when using names and for 250 epochs otherwise. Results are listed in Table 5.

For the *uncased* model, debiasing results on SEAT and StereoSet are marginally better without using names, while the language modeling performance is roughly the same. In the case of the *cased* model, we notice that using names yields a slightly better performance on SEAT, while the stereotype scores for StereoSet and the language modeling ability remain roughly the same. This might be because half of the SEAT tests use names as gender attributes.

Ablation for *group specific options* We investigate the effect *gender specific options* have on debiasing and language modeling. We evaluate our *gender debiased* models based on *bert-base-uncased*, using *female biased* initialization, with and without using *group specific options*. Results are presented in Table 7. For SEAT, we observe similar results in both cases, while in the case of StereoSet, the results *without* group-specific options are significantly better. However, using *group specific options* results in a better language modeling performance that can be observed through the pseudo-perplexity and StereoSet LM score.

In addition to these benchmarks, we analyzed the predictions of the debiased models on our training dataset and noticed that when trained *without gender-specific options*, the models tend to "forget" about gender information, assigning female-gendered words to male template instantiations and vice-versa. Some examples are presented in Table 8. Even though a model that *forgets* the identity of social classes might be considered *unbiased*, we argue that such behaviour would be undesirable for many applications.

5 Conclusions

We proposed and investigated a method of reducing social biases in pretrained LLMs based on prompt tuning, which involves training the prompt embeddings on a small set of templates. In addition to debiasing, this method is also designed to prevent the model from 'forgetting' the identity of the social groups targeted during debiasing.

We experimented with this method for reducing *gender bias* in BERT and RoBERTa models. Results show that it achieves debiasing performance on par with state-of-the-art while maintaining information about the social group's identity and with a low impact on general language modeling performance. While we focused our experiments on mitigating a single type of social bias in BERT and RoBERTa, the method can be adapted to other types of biases and LLMs.

	SEAT Gender Avg. Effect Size (↓)	**StereoSet Gender SS Score** (%)	**StereoSet LM Score** (↑)	**Pseudo-Perplexity** (↓)
BERT base uncased	0.620	60.279	84.172	**6.396**
+ Only General opts.	0.335 (0.086)	**57.600** (0.549)	84.174 (0.235)	6.746 (0.271)
+ Group specific opts.	**0.330** (0.057)	58.456 (0.543)	**84.460** (0.125)	6.530 (0.088)

Table 7: Results of gender debiased models with and without using *group specific options* in training. *Female biased* initialization is used. Results are averaged over all 5 different initializations, with standard deviation in parentheses.

		Without GSO		With GSO	
Nr.	**Template**	**Male**	**Female**	**Male**	**Female**
1	<GenderedWord> was an efficient <Target>.	woman	woman	man	woman
2	<GenderedWord> was an unskilled <Target>.	woman	woman	man	woman
3	<GenderedWord> was a good <Target>.	girl	girl	man	woman
4	<GenderedWord> is no longer a lazy <Target>.	man	woman	man	woman
5	<GenderedWord> had this idea ever since <HeOrShe> was hired as a <Target>.	waitress	nurse	nurse	waitress
6	<HisOrHer> career as an <Target> is boring.	actress	actor	actor	actress
7	<HisOrHer> career as an <Target> is well paid.	actor	actor	actor	actress
8	<HisOrHer> career as an <Target> is unappreciated.	actress	actress	actor	actress
9	<HisOrHer> job as a <Target> is poorly paid.	waitress	waitress	waiter	waitress

Table 8: Examples of predictions from a bert-base-uncased model *gender debiased* with *female biased* initialization, both *with* and *without* group specific options (GSO). For each template, we show the top model prediction of each debiased model variant on the *female* and *male* template instantiations.

Limitations

When implementing our method for BERT and RoBERTa, we considered, for simplicity, a set of *allowed options*, which can be represented by a single token in these model's vocabulary. This is not too restrictive in our case since their tokenizers can represent the most common English words with a single token. However, it might prove limiting for debiasing models with other types of tokenizers and usage in other languages. We note that while the general concept of our method could be applied even for *allowed options* that can span multiple tokens, such an implementation is not straightforward for all models. Proper computation of all probabilities used in the loss function might require a separate pass through the model for each *allowed option*. Future investigation is required to determine the feasibility of our method in such cases and to design efficient and numerically stable implementations.

In this paper, we focused our experiments only on mitigating gender bias. Our theoretical approach can be utilized for other types of social biases, but doing so in practice would require creating *templates* and selecting appropriate *general* and *group-specific options* for each type of bias targeted. We note that for some types of biases, this might not be straightforward, especially if the number of social groups considered is large, and we deem it probable for the overall performance of the method to be limited by the quality of the dataset used. A possible future improvement could be to find a method of automatically extracting relevant *templates* and *allowed options* from existing large datasets.

Experiments have shown that the performance of models debiased using our approach depends to a large extent on the used initialization method. Results show that for *gender debiasing* BERT, initializing with terms related to the *female* gender gives better results on average than random initialization and other approaches, while in the case of RoBERTa the *neutral* initialization achieves the best results. However, other initialisation methods might be more suitable, and this approach is not directly usable for other biases. Further investigation into robust initialization methods is needed.

The loss function of our method considers the *reference probability distribution* as the average of distributions predicted by the original model for each social group considered. While this approach is reasonable, it might prove limiting in some cases. For example, an exceedingly biased or toxic model could predict unfair probability distributions for some social groups, which would skew the average.

References

Aylin Caliskan, Joanna J. Bryson, and Arvind Narayanan. 2017. Semantics derived automatically from language corpora contain human-like biases. *Science*, 356(6334):183–186.

Jacob Devlin, Ming-Wei Chang, Kenton Lee, and Kristina Toutanova. 2019. BERT: Pre-training of deep bidirectional transformers for language understanding. In *Proceedings of the 2019 Conference of the North American Chapter of the Association for Computational Linguistics: Human Language Technologies, Volume 1 (Long and Short Papers)*, pages 4171–4186, Minneapolis, Minnesota. Association for Computational Linguistics.

Isabel O. Gallegos, Ryan A. Rossi, Joe Barrow, Md Mehrab Tanjim, Sungchul Kim, Franck Dernoncourt, Tong Yu, Ruiyi Zhang, and Nesreen K. Ahmed. 2023. Bias and fairness in large language models: A survey.

Matthew Honnibal, Ines Montani, Sofie Van Landeghem, Adriane Boyd, et al. 2020. spacy: Industrial-strength natural language processing in python.

Anne Lauscher, Tobias Lüken, and Goran Glavaš. 2021. Sustainable modular debiasing of language models.

Brian Lester, Rami Al-Rfou, and Noah Constant. 2021. The power of scale for parameter-efficient prompt tuning. In *Proceedings of the 2021 Conference on Empirical Methods in Natural Language Processing*, pages 3045–3059, Online and Punta Cana, Dominican Republic. Association for Computational Linguistics.

Paul Pu Liang, Irene Mengze Li, Emily Zheng, Yao Chong Lim, Ruslan Salakhutdinov, and Louis-Philippe Morency. 2020. Towards debiasing sentence representations. In *Proceedings of the 58th Annual Meeting of the Association for Computational Linguistics*, pages 5502–5515, Online. Association for Computational Linguistics.

Haochen Liu, Jamell Dacon, Wenqi Fan, Hui Liu, Zitao Liu, and Jiliang Tang. 2020. Does gender matter? towards fairness in dialogue systems.

Yinhan Liu, Myle Ott, Naman Goyal, Jingfei Du, Mandar Joshi, Danqi Chen, Omer Levy, Mike Lewis, Luke Zettlemoyer, and Veselin Stoyanov. 2019. Roberta: A robustly optimized bert pretraining approach. Cite arxiv:1907.11692.

Ilya Loshchilov and Frank Hutter. 2019. Decoupled weight decay regularization. In *International Conference on Learning Representations*.

Sourab Mangrulkar, Sylvain Gugger, Lysandre Debut, Younes Belkada, and Sayak Paul. 2022. Peft: State-of-the-art parameter-efficient fine-tuning methods. `https://github.com/huggingface/peft`.

Chandler May, Alex Wang, Shikha Bordia, Samuel R. Bowman, and Rachel Rudinger. 2019. On measuring social biases in sentence encoders. In *Proceedings of the 2019 Conference of the North American Chapter of the Association for Computational Linguistics: Human Language Technologies, Volume 1 (Long and Short Papers)*, pages 622–628, Minneapolis, Minnesota. Association for Computational Linguistics.

Nicholas Meade, Elinor Poole-Dayan, and Siva Reddy. 2022. An empirical survey of the effectiveness of debiasing techniques for pre-trained language models. In *Proceedings of the 60th Annual Meeting of the Association for Computational Linguistics (Volume 1: Long Papers)*, pages 1878–1898, Dublin, Ireland. Association for Computational Linguistics.

Stephen Merity, Caiming Xiong, James Bradbury, and Richard Socher. 2017. Pointer sentinel mixture models. In *International Conference on Learning Representations*.

Moin Nadeem, Anna Bethke, and Siva Reddy. 2021. StereoSet: Measuring stereotypical bias in pretrained language models. In *Proceedings of the 59th Annual Meeting of the Association for Computational Linguistics and the 11th International Joint Conference on Natural Language Processing (Volume 1: Long Papers)*, pages 5356–5371, Online. Association for Computational Linguistics.

Adam Paszke, Sam Gross, Francisco Massa, Adam Lerer, James Bradbury, Gregory Chanan, Trevor Killeen, Zeming Lin, Natalia Gimelshein, Luca Antiga, et al. 2019. Pytorch: An imperative style, high-performance deep learning library. *Advances in neural information processing systems*, 32.

Shauli Ravfogel, Yanai Elazar, Hila Gonen, Michael Twiton, and Yoav Goldberg. 2020. Null it out: Guarding protected attributes by iterative nullspace projection. In *Proceedings of the 58th Annual Meeting of the Association for Computational Linguistics, ACL 2020, Online, July 5-10, 2020*, pages 7237–7256. Association for Computational Linguistics.

Julian Salazar, Davis Liang, Toan Q. Nguyen, and Katrin Kirchhoff. 2020. Masked language model scoring. In *Proceedings of the 58th Annual Meeting of the Association for Computational Linguistics*, pages 2699–2712, Online. Association for Computational Linguistics.

Kellie Webster, Xuezhi Wang, Ian Tenney, Alex Beutel, Emily Pitler, Ellie Pavlick, Jilin Chen, Ed H. Chi, and Slav Petrov. 2020. Measuring and reducing gendered correlations in pre-trained models. Technical report.

Thomas Wolf, Lysandre Debut, Victor Sanh, Julien Chaumond, Clement Delangue, Anthony Moi, Pierric Cistac, Tim Rault, Remi Louf, Morgan Funtowicz, Joe Davison, Sam Shleifer, Patrick von Platen, Clara Ma, Yacine Jernite, Julien Plu, Canwen Xu, Teven Le Scao, Sylvain Gugger, Mariama Drame, Quentin Lhoest, and Alexander Rush. 2020. Transformers: State-of-the-art natural language processing. In *Proceedings of the 2020 Conference on Empirical Methods in Natural Language Processing: System Demonstrations*, pages 38–45, Online. Association for Computational Linguistics.

Sang Michael Xie, Aditi Raghunathan, Percy Liang, and Tengyu Ma. 2022. An explanation of in-context learning as implicit bayesian inference. In *International Conference on Learning Representations*.

Ran Zmigrod, Sabrina J. Mielke, Hanna Wallach, and Ryan Cotterell. 2019. Counterfactual data augmentation for mitigating gender stereotypes in languages with rich morphology. In *Proceedings of the 57th Annual Meeting of the Association for Computational Linguistics*, pages 1651–1661, Florence, Italy. Association for Computational Linguistics.

A Implementation details

In this appendix, we present some additional details related to the implementation of our method for gender debiasing BERT and RoBERTa.

As described in Section 4, we experimented with several types of initialization for the prompt: *random*, *neutral*, gender balanced and *female biased*. The words used as initialization were chosen such that they can be represented as a single token. Due to this, they differ slightly between the two models. These are shown in Table 9 (for BERT) and in Table 10 (for RoBERTa).

Training requires the selection of a set of *allowed options* (composed of *general options* and *group specific options* for the *target slots*. We selected these manually, mostly by choosing from the most likely predictions of the *BERT base* model on our set of templates. Some examples are shown in Table 11 and Table 12.

	Neutral	
tree	stone	lake
animal	mountain	house
fair	water	balanced
justice	equality	human
honest	forest	gold
	Gender Balanced	
man	water	woman
girl	fair	boy
masculine	human	feminine
female	justice	male
husband	big	queen
	Female Biased	
women	queen	girl
female	priestess	feminine
wife	feminist	mothers
feminism	miss	suffrage
she	women	mothers

Table 9: Words used as initialization for **BERT** prompts in each trial, for our chosen test initialization types

	Neutral	
tree	stone	lake
animal	mountain	house
fair	water	balanced
justice	equality	human
honest	forest	gold
	Gender Balanced	
man	water	woman
girl	fair	boy
masculine	human	feminine
female	justice	male
husband	big	queen
	Female Biased	
women	queen	girl
female	her	feminine
wife	feminist	mothers
woamn	miss	female
she	women	mothers

Table 10: Words used as initialization for **RoBERTa** prompts in each trial, for our chosen test initialization types

Nr	Option
1	teacher
2	doctor
3	engineer
4	entrepreneur
5	person
6	scientist

Table 11: Examples of *general options* used for gender debiasing

Nr.	Male Variant	Female Variant
1	actor	actress
2	waiter	waitress
3	husband	wife
4	boy	girl
5	man	woman

Table 12: Examples of *group specific options* used for gender debiasing

German Text Simplification: Finetuning Large Language Models with Semi-Synthetic Data

Lars Klöser and **Mika Beele** and **Jan-Niklas Schagen** and **Bodo Kraft**
University of Applied Sciences Aachen
{kloeser, beele, kraft}@fh-aachen.de
niklas.schagen@alumni.fh-aachen.de

Abstract

This study pioneers the use of synthetically generated data for training generative models in document-level text simplification of German texts. We demonstrate the effectiveness of our approach with real-world online texts. Addressing the challenge of data scarcity in language simplification, we crawled professionally simplified German texts and synthesized a corpus using GPT-4. We finetune *Large Language Models* with up to 13 billion parameters on this data and evaluate their performance. This paper employs various methodologies for evaluation and demonstrates the limitations of currently used rule-based metrics. Both automatic and manual evaluations reveal that our models can significantly simplify real-world online texts, indicating the potential of synthetic data in improving text simplification.

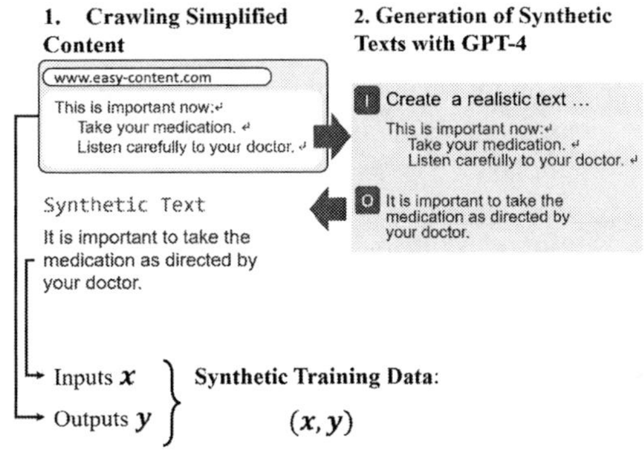

Figure 1: Illustration of synthetic data generation. Data is crawled from websites specializing in language simplification. GPT-4 generates texts in everyday language, ensuring the original content remains unaltered. We construct a simplification dataset where these texts serve as input while the crawled simplifications act as reference simplifications.

1 Introduction

In our modern and digitalized societies, access to information is essential for active participation. However, certain groups, such as individuals with intellectual disabilities or non-native speakers, often struggle to understand the local language, which can impede their social and civic engagement. Each group faces unique challenges in text comprehension. Integrating automatic text simplification tools can significantly benefit these groups by providing accessible information, thereby providing a pivotal means for greater inclusion.

Various linguistic initiatives, like (Netzwerk-Leichte-Sprache, 2022), have been established in German-speaking regions to address this, specifically designed for different target groups. Such efforts align with international legal frameworks like *Article 9 of the UN Convention on the Rights of Persons with Disabilities*[1], which advocates for the right to accessible communication.

Creating simplified content manually is a labor-intensive and time-consuming process, significantly hindering its broad availability and accessibility. In contrast, *Large Language Models* (LLMs), especially smaller ones fine-tuned for text simplification, offer a viable and efficient alternative (Anschütz et al., 2023). These smaller models require fewer resources and are simpler to operate than larger LLMs, making them ideal for scaling up the process of automatic language simplification. A key challenge in finetuning LLMs for text simplification lies in the limited availability of parallel data (Anschütz et al., 2023; Toborek et al., 2022).

Our approach, as illustrated in Figure 1, tackles the challenge of data scarcity in language simplification by creating semi-synthetic data. This involves crawling various sources for already simplified web content and then utilizing GPT-4 to generate hypothetical original texts corresponding to these simplifications. Our dataset thus comprises GPT-4's outputs as the inputs and the crawled con-

[1] https://www.ohchr.org/en/instruments-mechanisms/instruments/convention-rights-persons-disabilities

Proceedings of the Fourth Workshop on Language Technology for Equality, Diversity, Inclusion, pages 63–72
March 21, 2024 ©2024 Association for Computational Linguistics

tent as the simplified outputs, forming a text simplification dataset. We apply this dataset as the basis for finetuning Large Language Models (LLMs) for automatic text simplification.

We publish all necessary resources to reproduce this paper's results on a public GitHub repository[2]. Our scientific contributions can be summarized as follows:

1. Creating a corpus of parallel text simplification data in German based on novel methodology.
2. Training, evaluating, and releasing LLM-based language simplification models for German texts.

2 Related Work

Various approaches and methodologies have been developed for automatic German text simplification. (Anschütz et al., 2023) proposed a two-step approach utilizing pretrained language models finetuned on German simplifications to diminish the requirement for parallel data. In contrast to our approach, the parallel data contains a mixture of summarization and simplification and targets only newspaper articles. (Spring and Rios, 2021) train German text simplification models by using labels to target specific language levels, ensuring model adaptations are level-appropriate and control copying behavior. Their dataset focuses on newspaper articles and sentence-level simplification.

Diverging from neural network-based methods, (Garain et al., 2019) introduced methodology based on parse trees. Similarly, (Praveen Kumar et al., 2022) offered a pattern-based syntactic simplification framework. (Kajiwara and Komachi, 2018) presented methods for text simplification in languages with limited simplified corpora, including lexical substitution and monolingual translation, focusing on resource-scarce languages like Japanese.

Regarding evaluation metrics, (Sulem et al., 2018) investigate the limitations of BLEU as a widespread evaluation metric for text generation tasks. (Alva-Manchego et al., 2021) explored the correlation between existing metrics and human judgments in multi-operation text simplifications, providing insights into the appropriateness of automatic metrics for assessing text simplification. (Maddela et al., 2022) introduced LENS, a learnable evaluation metric for text simplification trained on modern language models, showing a better correlation with human judgment.

Regarding parallel corpora and resources, (Ebling et al., 2022) aggregated corpora for the automatic processing of simplified German, providing resources for training and evaluation. (Holmer and Rennes, 2023) create so-called *pseudo parallel* sentence pairs of simple and complex sentences from given sentence collections. (Hauser et al., 2022) introduced SNIML, a multilingual corpus of news articles in simplified language, and (Rios et al., 2021) showcased a dataset for document-level text simplification in German, including articles paired with simplified summaries. (Aumiller and Gertz, 2022) addressed the challenge of concurrently summarizing and simplifying longer texts, introducing a new dataset for joint text simplification and summarization. (Hewett, 2023) introduces a dataset with parallel sentence-level simplications and additional information about the document's rhetorical structure.

Text simplification corpora exist for various languages. For example, (Coster and Kauchak, 2011) introduced a dataset pairing English Wikipedia with Simple English Wikipedia, enabling the analysis of various simplification operations, including rewording, reordering, insertion, and deletion.

In Easy Language generation, (Deilen et al., 2023) investigated the feasibility of using ChatGPT to translate administrative texts into German *Leichte Sprache* (easy language), a highly regulated language variety with a focus on text simplification.

3 Task Definition

In this section, we give a task definition for language simplification. This definition outlines the requirements for the trained models and motivates our methodology for dataset creation.

The **inputs space** consists of editorially created German texts. Based on the selection of web sources, we assume predominantly grammatically complete sentences and quality-assured content. In the context of this work, we exclude user-created input and social media texts. These web documents contain multiple paragraphs and sentences.

The **output space** consists of simplifications of the input. The style and level of simplification correspond to the contents currently available in the German language, precisely as they are presently accessible. We aim to avoid modifications of the

[2]https://github.com/MSLars/German-Text-Simplification

Table 1: Word and document frequencies in the dataset across different sources, segregated into test and train sets

	Test		Train	
	Docs	Words	Docs	Words
einfachstars	317	45,444	2,213	307,307
mdr	10	1,696	85	13,285
nachrichtenleicht	298	44,138	2,147	318,069
hurraki	181	16,152	1,234	109,386
ndr	94	17,211	709	135,340
kurier	72	13,425	481	76,744
leicht-kicken	8	537	67	2,672
einfach-teilhaben	8	749	79	8,193
stadt-koeln	3	2,588	16	11,830
inclusion_europe	1	35	18	920
bundesregierung	5	1,337	22	9,212
hamburg-de	3	1,199	59	16,280
$\sum$	1000	144,511	7,130	1,009,238

content, like summarization. However, understandability may require additional explanations of certain concepts in the simplified texts.

Two concepts for language simplification have been established for the German language: *Einfache Sprache* (simple language) and *Leichte Sprache* (easy language). We seek to explain how our methodologies intersect and align with these well-established frameworks.

Simple language covers text simplification in general. Possible target groups include readers unfamiliar with the domain or used language, for example, in legal or medical texts or language learners. The target group can fundamentally understand the concepts. Linguistic complexity, however, makes understanding more difficult. Moreover, these simplifications can aid in language acquisition.

In contrast, easy language is aimed at people with severely limited text comprehension, such as those with intellectual disabilities. Fixed sets of simplification rules have been established (Netzwerk-Leichte-Sprache, 2022). These rules cover areas like syntactical, lexical, or typographical simplifications.

In our approach, we scrape texts from various sources, each characterized by its distinct language style. Our research hints that these target texts generally do not conform to the rules of easy language. Rather, many crawled texts may align more with the domain of simple language.

3.1 Dataset

We introduce a parallel corpus consisting of texts in everyday language and their corresponding simplifications as an instantiation of the task defined in section 3.

We create semi-synthetical text pairs to overcome the challenge of training data scarcity. Based on the results of various benchmarks, we assume that GPT-4 can produce human-like texts in various domains (OpenAI, 2023). We crawl simplified texts by expanded versions of the crawlers used by (Anschütz et al., 2023). Our additional preprocessing standardizes the typography using rule-based methods. Subsequently, we use GPT-4 to create realistic synthetic source texts from the simplifications. To ensure the generated texts were sufficiently diverse, 15 distinct prompts were used. In the following, we will investigate these data in detail.

3.1.1 Synthetic Texts

Table 1 presents the scope and size of the semi-synthetic dataset created for German text simplification. A random sample of 1,000 examples has been reserved as test data. To our knowledge, this dataset is the first semi-synthetic approach to the German language simplification task. It is also noteworthy for being the most comprehensive dataset available for document-wide simplification and the only dataset focusing on document-level language simplification across various domains.

The performance of machine learning models is highly contingent on the quality of the training data, as indicated in various studies (Jain et al., 2020). We believe that the complexity and characteristics of the synthetic data used for training should closely mirror the real data from similar contexts in the specific field.

Table 2: Analysis of textual complexity across various domains. Synthetic web content is slightly more complex compared to real web content. The metrics support that the crawled simplifications are less complex than real and synthetic everyday web content.

	Sports	Celebrities	News
Metric: avg. sentence length			
Easy	10.38 ± 2	11.56 ± 2.45	10.79 ± 1.49
Synth.	24 ± 9.3	22.94 ± 6.59	21 ± 5.4
Com.	19.59 ± 3.65	21.17 ± 4.21	18.66 ± 2.7
Metric: avg. commas per sentence			
Easy	$.09 \pm .18$	$.17 \pm .24$	$.00 \pm .03$
Synth.	1.69 ± 1.18	$1.67 \pm .81$	$1.52 \pm .72$
Com.	$.48 \pm .41$	$1.3 \pm .52$	$.81 \pm .35$
Metric: avg. distance verb compounds			
Easy	$.09 \pm .15$	$.14 \pm .14$	$.14 \pm .11$
Synth.	$.34 \pm .33$	$.36 \pm .19$	$.34 \pm .19$
Com.	$.27 \pm .19$	$.3 \pm .14$	$.3 \pm .13$

Table 2 offers an overview of various metrics

used to estimate the linguistic complexity of the crawled simplified texts, the synthetic data, and real German web content, examining three distinct domains as examples. The selected metrics rate the reconstructed texts slightly more complex than the crawled texts. While these metrics do not definitively determine whether the data is realistic and overcomplication in reconstruction cannot be ruled out, our preliminary conclusion is that the examples could be suitable for the task.

Given that the primary focus of this work is not on the realistic generation of web content, we do not delve deeper into these aspects. Instead, our research examines whether the trained models effectively reduce the complexity of real web content as evaluated in subsection 5.3. This approach aligns with our goal to enhance the practical applicability of language simplification tools in real-world scenarios.

3.2 Crawled Simplifications

This section delves into the specifics of the crawled simplifications. Table 2 categorizes various sources into domains. This offers a structured view of the different simplifications obtained from these domains.

Table 3: Comparative analysis between different styles of simplified news content.

Metrik	MDR	NDR	NL
Sentence length	12.39 ± 1.54	10.47 ± 1.43	12 ± 1.5
Commas per sentence	$.04 \pm .09$	$.00 \pm .00$	$.22 \pm .17$
Distance verb compounds	$.2 \pm .12$	$.14 \pm .11$	$.21 \pm .14$
Words per line	8.78 ± 22.12	8.55 ± 11.77	14.14 ± 24.15

Table 3 investigates the variety inside a single domain. It comprehensively analyzes metrics related to simplified texts from various news providers. These metrics reveal notable differences in the style of simplifications among the providers. For instance, NDR's texts stand out for their absence of commas, suggesting a preference for simpler sentence structures without subordinate clauses. In contrast, NL (nachrichtenleicht.de) frequently employs commas, indicating a higher likelihood of compound and complex sentences, often incorporating subordinate clauses. Additionally, NL's texts, on average, contain longer sentences than other sources, highlighting a distinct approach to text simplification. These findings underscore the stylistic diversity within the dataset, demonstrating that simplifications are not uniform but vary significantly across news providers.

4 Methodology

This study aims to perform task-specific fine-tuning of LLMs. The extensive volume of publications in this domain makes it impractical to evaluate all available models and training configurations against one another. Instead, we aim to justify our core design choices in this chapter and provide further justification through targeted evaluation in the subsequent chapter.

4.1 Language Modelling

We apply LLMs based on so-called *decoder-only* transformer models as introduced in (Radford et al., 2018). Decoder-only models are designed to model the probability of the subsequent token $P(x_{i+1}|x_1, \ldots, x_i)$ in a given sequence $x = x_1, \ldots, x_n$ of tokens that represent a text. We represent each text simplification sample as a sequence $x = (x_{source}, SEP, x_{target})$ where SEP is a special token that separates the source from its simplification target. As input, we provide x_{source} followed by the SEP token. The model, during training, attempts to maximize the probabilities

$$P(x^t_{i+1}|x_{source}, x^t_1, \ldots, x^t_i) \ , i = 1, \ldots, m$$

of the tokens in the simplifications $x_{target} = x^t_1, \ldots, x^t_m$ using the cross entropy loss.

We finetuned two distinct versions of two different pretrained LLMs. Specifically, we finetuned two German versions of GPT-2 (Minixhofer et al., 2022) and two versions of the Leo LM model (Plüster, 2023). We selected these models because they are decoder-only, available in different sizes and pretrained on german texts. Each of these models underwent finetuning on our training dataset for three epochs. For this process, we employed the HuggingFace[3] library, a popular choice for machine learning and natural language processing tasks. The detailed configurations used for training, including parameters and environmental settings, are meticulously documented in Appendix A.

[3]https://huggingface.co/

4.2 Decoding Algorithm

This section describes the methods of deriving concrete sequences from the probability distributions for individual follow-up tokens provided by LLMs, commonly called *decoding algorithms*. We compare four distinct approaches:

Greedy Approach: This method sequentially selects the token with the highest probability. It is straightforward and efficient but may not yield the most contextually appropriate sequence.

Beam Search Algorithm: This technique chooses the best alternative from a fixed number of possibilities, each with the currently highest probability. It balances between exploring various possibilities and focusing on the most probable options.

Sampling-Based Algorithm: Here, follow-up tokens are randomly selected based on the probability distribution of the LLMs. This approach introduces variability and can generate more diverse outputs (Holtzman et al., 2020).

Contrastive Search Approach: This novel method contrasts traditional search techniques. It considers the likelihood of individual tokens and evaluates the probability distribution over a set of potential sequences, aiming to balance between the most probable and contextually appropriate choices. This approach is useful in ensuring that the generated text maintains coherence and relevance (Su and Collier, 2022).

We utilized a fixed configuration for each approach as provided in Appendix A. This comparative analysis offers insights into the efficacy and suitability of different decoding strategies.

We frequently observed prediction repetitions in our investigation, particularly with smaller models. In text generation, in general, a repetition penalty is frequently used. However, in this context, some repetition may be beneficial. Hence, we've devised an alternative approach that allows for a certain degree of repetition, recognizing its potential value in making texts clearer and more comprehensible.

To address this, we implemented a strategy to halt the generation of further tokens if the frequency of a token within a certain window exceeded a predefined threshold. This intervention was designed to enhance the quality of the generated text by preventing excessive repetition, which can detract from the readability and coherence of the output. Such a method is crucial in maintaining language's natural flow and diversity, especially in scenarios where smaller models may struggle.

5 Evaluation

In this chapter, we provide a comprehensive evaluation of the finetuned models. Our analysis is twofold: firstly, we assess the performance of various model configurations on the semi-synthetic dataset. This evaluation will delve into how different configurations perform in terms of efficacy, which will be measured using a range of metrics.

Secondly, we extend our evaluation to include an analysis of crawled web content. This is a vital step towards demonstrating the real-world applicability of our models.

5.1 Evaluation Metrics

For automatic evaluation, we apply three rule-based metrics commonly used to evaluate simplification models. Each metric compares reference simplifications with model predictions mostly based on n-gram overlaps. N-grams are contiguous sequences of words in a text.

BLEU (Papineni et al., 2002) computes precision scores that measure the frequency of distinct n-grams in the reference simplification over the frequency of distinct n-grams in the model prediction. Typically, we use precision scores for uni, bi, tri, and tetra-grams. These are aggregated with a geometric mean and combined with a brevity penalty for too short predictions.

METEOR (Banerjee and Lavie, 2005) is based on matching unigrams of the model's prediction with unigrams of the reference. It calculates precision and a heavily weighted recall on these matches. Additionally, it includes a fragmentation penalty that penalizes predictions with limited sequential overlap with the reference.

SARI (Xu et al., 2016) is designed to evaluate sentence-level text simplification systems. The metric compares n-gram operations between input on the one side and reference and predicted output on the other. It computes F-scores over added and kept n-grams. For deleted n-grams, the precision score is considered. The final score is the arithmetic mean.

5.2 Automatic Evaluation Results

The comprehensive results from our automatic evaluation, as detailed in Table 4, provide insights into the performance of two variants of pretrained language models across different generation algorithms. In our analysis, all configurations exhibited the highest score for SARI, followed by METEOR

Table 4: Rule-based evaluation metrics computed on the test set. Scores are grouped by pretrained language model and generation algorithm. Metrics increase with model size. For the largest model, beam search is the best decoding algorithm.

	BLEU	METEOR	SARI
Model: gpt2-wechsel-german			
greedy	0.72	9.14	36.61
beam	**1.49**	**13.03**	36.80
sampling	0.96	11.31	**37.62**
contrastive	0.83	10.07	37.02
Model: gpt2-xl-wechsel-german			
greedy	6.77	23.58	46.49
beam	8.21	23.80	45.41
sampling	**8.35**	**26.86**	**47.48**
contrastive	6.99	23.87	46.74
Model: leo-hessianai-7b			
greedy	24.46	45.31	60.51
beam	**25.97**	**46.17**	**61.35**
sampling	23.79	44.97	60.23
contrastive	24.39	45.20	60.45
Model: leo-hessianai-13b			
greedy	24.53	45.32	60.52
beam	**25.78**	**45.64**	**62.24**
sampling	23.93	45.06	60.41
contrastive	24.64	45.57	60.66

and BLEU. This phenomenon is explored in greater detail in subsection 5.2.1.

Metrics increased with an increasing number of model parameters. Notably, the improvement in metrics was evident up to the transition from models with 7 billion to 13 billion parameters, beyond which we observed no significant differences in metrics. We investigate the behavior of these metrics in more detail in subsection 5.2.1. However, the superior performance of the 13 billion parameter model in other tasks suggests that the combination of automated metrics and our dataset may not be capable of discerning performance differences (Plüster, 2023). This could potentially lead to erroneous model selection in practical applications.

In many language generation applications, maximization-based methods like beam search are often deemed less suitable due to their propensity for monotonous and repetitive predictions, as opposed to sampling or contrastive search (Su and Collier, 2022). However, our results do not confirm this for our instantiation of text simplification. The findings suggest that the efficacy of these methods may vary depending on the specific nature of the language generation task.

5.2.1 Limitations of Rule-Based Metrics Employed within Simplification

In Figure 2, different simplification styles stand out. Since our dataset only includes a single reference translation and the metrics focus on sequential overlaps, the stylistic variety of the dataset is not adequately considered in this automated and rule-based evaluation. This leads to lower scores for all metrics we used since all measure the sequential overlap.

Reference Simplification:
Those who have aphasia,
have difficulties to find words.
Or difficulties to speak words.
Or difficulties to understand words.

Model Prediction:
People with aphasia have problems:
• to find words
• to speak words
• to understand words

The • "breaks" all tetra-grams

Figure 2: In this example, a reference simplification and a model prediction, translated into English, are contextually similar but lack any shared tetra-grams, yielding a BLEU score of zero.

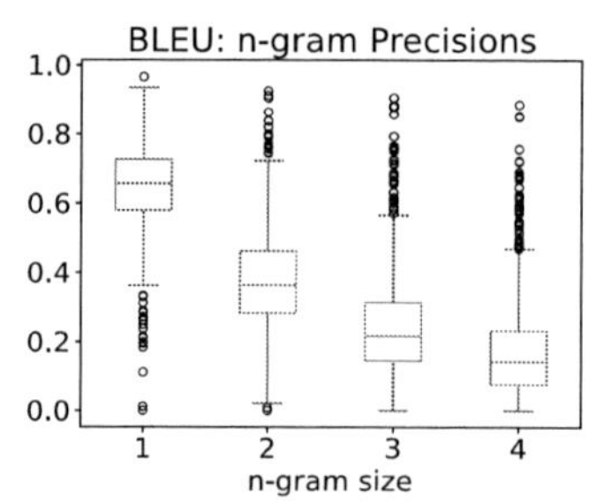

Figure 3: N-gram precisions for predictions of the leo-hessianai-7b model on the complete test set. We observed significantly sloping precision scores for increasing n-gram sizes

The pair of reference simplification and model prediction in Figure 2 highlights the BLEU metric's key limitations in evaluating text simplification on our test set. The example showcases varying styles between the reference and the model prediction. The reference employs grammatically complete sentences linked with the conjunction "Or", while the model prediction opts for a listing format. This stylistic divergence, especially with short sentences in the model's output, leads to a lack of common 4-grams. BLEU combines n-gram precision with a geometric mean. The geometric mean is calculated by multiplying all the precision values and then taking the nth root (where n is the number of values). If any value in the dataset is 0, the product of all the values becomes 0 as well. Figure 3 illustrates the n-gram precision scores. This leads to a BLEU score 0, which doesn't accurately reflect the simplified text's quality. By looking at the graph of n-gram precision scores, we can apply this understanding to most of our dataset.

Reference Simplification
The climate crisis is a crisis.
In this, the climate is changing rapidly.
And therefore, there are many problems.
And there are dangers for people and animals.

Model Prediction
The climate around the world is changing.
This is happening more and more quickly.
This is bad for nature.
This is called the climate crisis.

Figure 4: Example to illustrate a high fragmentation penalty due to varied placement of 'climate crisis', negatively impacting the METEOR Score.

In the given example in Figure 4, the reference simplification introduces the term *climate crisis* in the first sentence, whereas the model's simplification describes aspects of the climate crisis before introducing the term. Such rearrangements lead to cross-alignments and higher fragmentation penalties, which affect the METEOR score. This illustrates how n-gram intersections influence the metrics, particularly in the context of differing simplification styles within our corpus. METEOR caps the fragmentation penalty at 50 percent, which limits its influence on the final score.

As indicated in our analysis and shown in Table 4, the SARI score tends to rate the model solutions more favorably, aligning more closely with the positive manual evaluations of the models in Table 5. This suggests that SARI might be a more reliable indicator of text simplification quality in our context.

SARI was originally meant to be applied within sentence-level simplification. We apply SARI to our multi-sentence documents and we conducted further investigations on the composition of the SARI scores to conclude the metric's plausibility in its three categories, *add*, *keep*, and *delete* within our task.

In sentence-level text simplification, those operations are considered equally difficult (Xu et al., 2016), and therefore, they are weighted equally in the final arithmetic mean. However, due to stylistic transformations within simplification, n-grams of the input are deleted at a much higher probability. For example, structural unigrams like bullet points and line breaks discontinuing original n-grams.

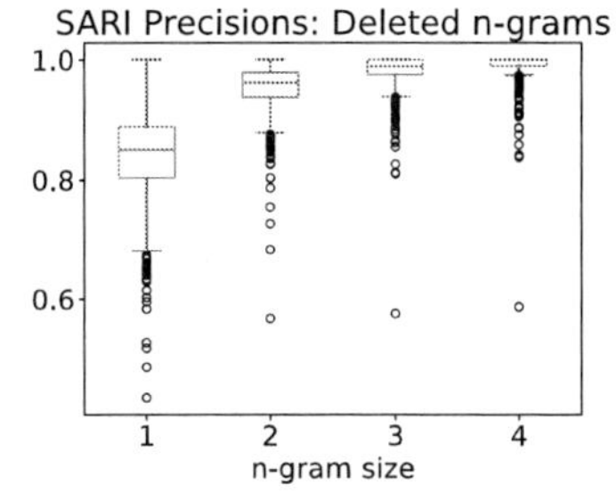

Figure 5: N-gram deletion precisions for predictions of the leo-hessianai-7b model on the complete test set. The median values of our observed SARI delete precision scores reach high values, especially for tri- and tetra-grams

Most n-grams from the input, especially tri-grams and tetra-grams, are considered as *correctly deleted* for reference simplification and model prediction. This results in a precision score for deleted tri-grams and tetra-grams close to one for most samples, as illustrated in Figure 5. Due to the arithmetic mean, this has a nearly constant and strong influence on the final value. SARI tends to be biased optimistically within our task.

Concerning the automated metrics, the 13 billion parameter model does not outperform the 7 billion one. One reason might be the stylistic diversity in the dataset. Given varied styles within even single domains, see Table 3, the model simplification and the reference simplification might be in different styles. This random factor may affect all metrics that measure sequential overlaps, limiting the overall scores. We might not be able to measure strong models abilities on the target task.

5.3 Evaluation on Real-World Data

We aimed to prove the practical relevance of our models by expanding our evaluation to include real-world data. As evaluation data, we use texts from a German news website[4], a sports news wesite[5], and a website for tabloid news[6]. These texts are not simplified.

We do not have reference simplifications for these texts. To evaluate the models' simplifications, we consider two types of metrics. Firstly, linguistic

[4] tagesschau.de
[5] transfermarkt.de
[6] vip.de

simplification using the metrics already introduced. Secondly, the content similarity is done through a manual evaluation of 135 pairs of crawled and non-simplified texts with the simplifications of the models. In this process, pairs could be rated with 0 (no agreement), 1 (partial agreement), 2 (substantial agreement), and 3 (complete agreement). The results in Table 5 measure the language simplification capabilities of gpt2-xl-wechsel-german (gpt2-xl) and leo-hessianai-7b (leo-7b).

Table 5: Language complexity and content similarity metrics for model simplifications of real-world online data. *Human Evaluation* summarizes a manual evaluation of content similarity with scores from 0 (no similarity) to 3 (complete equality).

Metrik	gpt2-xl	leo-7b
Sentence length	16.35 ± 6.05	14.03 ± 3.47
Commas per sentence	$.48 \pm .68$	$.24 \pm .28$
Words per line	12.35 ± 6.08	10.35 ± 3.48
Human Evaluation	1.34 ± 1.11	2.68 ± 0.55

The complexity metrics sentence length, commas per sentence, and words per line indicate that gpt2-xl simplifies texts less than leo-7b. Regarding content accuracy, leo-7b outperformed gpt2-xl, demonstrating a more consistent replication of original content, as shown by the human evaluation scores.

Compared to the gpt2-xl model, the leo-7b model reproduces content much more accurately. On average, the content agreement of this model's simplifications and the original text was rated at least as "substantial agreement".

These results on real data suggest that our models, trained on semi-synthetic data, significantly reduce text complexity while reliably retaining content. Semi-synthetic data is a promising way to train text simplification models and circumvent data scarcity problems.

6 Limitations

Our examination reveals that rule-based metrics have limited suitability for evaluating state-of-the-art models in document-level simplification. While our chosen evaluation methodology yields promising results, it lacks a targeted analysis of the end-users for whom the simplification is intended, a scope beyond the ambit of this study. Furthermore, alternative methods to simplify language using LLMs, such as in few-shot learning, merit a comparative analysis against our approach.

7 Conclusion

This study represents a significant stride in tackling the challenge of data scarcity in automatic text simplification. We have crafted a semi-synthetic dataset that has proven effective for training models, which are capable of simplifying complex texts. Notably, our models trained on this synthetic data have demonstrated proficiency in simplifying real web content, validating the practicality of our approach. Semi-synthetic data offers the opportunity to efficiently integrate large amounts of existing simplifications into supervised training without manual effort. This is an efficient and promising alternative to alignments or the manual creation of parallel data.

A vital contribution of this work is the open availability of both the dataset and the models, which serve as a foundational resource for researchers in the text simplification field. Integrating state-of-the-art LLMs with supervised learning has shown to be an efficient method for German text simplification. The limitations of current automated and rule-based metrics, such as BLEU, METEOR, and SARI, are increasingly apparent, particularly for our document-level simplification dataset. This suggests that state-of-the-art LLMs may advance to a point where more nuanced evaluation methodologies are required to accurately measure performance differences and select superior models.

Looking ahead, there are promising directions for future research. One crucial area is adapting generation to adhere more closely to the specific simplification styles, for example, following the rules of easy language and thereby tailoring simplifications more effectively to target audiences. This could involve exploring ways to influence the style of simplification, which would enhance the applicability of these models in real-world applications. By fine-tuning the models to align with the nuanced requirements of different user groups, we can make significant strides toward more inclusive and accessible digital content.

Acknowledgments

This project is funded by the German Federal Ministry for Family Affairs, Senior Citizens, Women and Youth under the grant number 3923406K05.

References

Fernando Alva-Manchego, Carolina Scarton, and Lucia Specia. 2021. The (Un)Suitability of Automatic Evaluation Metrics for Text Simplification. *Computational Linguistics*, 47(4):861–889. Place: Cambridge, MA Publisher: MIT Press.

Miriam Anschütz, Joshua Oehms, Thomas Wimmer, Bartłomiej Jezierski, and Georg Groh. 2023. Language Models for German Text Simplification: Overcoming Parallel Data Scarcity through Style-specific Pre-training.

Dennis Aumiller and Michael Gertz. 2022. Klexikon: A German Dataset for Joint Summarization and Simplification.

Satanjeev Banerjee and Alon Lavie. 2005. METEOR: An automatic metric for MT evaluation with improved correlation with human judgments. In *Proceedings of the ACL Workshop on Intrinsic and Extrinsic Evaluation Measures for Machine Translation and/or Summarization*, pages 65–72, Ann Arbor, Michigan. Association for Computational Linguistics.

W. Coster and David Kauchak. 2011. Simple English Wikipedia: A New Text Simplification Task.

Silvana Deilen, Sergio Hernández Garrido, Ekaterina Lapshinova-Koltunski, and Christiane Maaß. 2023. Using ChatGPT as a CAT tool in Easy Language translation.

Sarah Ebling, Alessia Battisti, Marek Kostrzewa, Dominik Pfütze, Annette Rios, Andreas Säuberli, and Nicolas Spring. 2022. Automatic Text Simplification for German. In *Frontiers in Communication*, volume 7, page 706718. ISSN: 2297-900X Journal Abbreviation: Front. Commun.

Avishek Garain, Arpan Basu, Rudrajit Dawn, and Sudip Kumar Naskar. 2019. Sentence Simplification using Syntactic Parse trees. *2019 4th International Conference on Information Systems and Computer Networks (ISCON)*, pages 672–676.

Renate Hauser, Jannis Vamvas, Sarah Ebling, and M. Volk. 2022. A Multilingual Simplified Language News Corpus.

Freya Hewett. 2023. APA-RST: A Text Simplification Corpus with RST Annotations. *Proceedings of the 4th Workshop on Computational Approaches to Discourse (CODI 2023)*, pages 173–179.

Daniel Holmer and Evelina Rennes. 2023. Constructing Pseudo-parallel Swedish Sentence Corpora for Automatic Text Simplification.

Ari Holtzman, Jan Buys, Li Du, Maxwell Forbes, and Yejin Choi. 2020. The Curious Case of Neural Text Degeneration. ArXiv:1904.09751 [cs].

Abhinav Jain, Hima Patel, Lokesh Nagalapatti, Nitin Gupta, Sameep Mehta, Shanmukha Guttula, Shashank Mujumdar, Shazia Afzal, Ruhi Sharma Mittal, and Vitobha Munigala. 2020. Overview and Importance of Data Quality for Machine Learning Tasks. In *Proceedings of the 26th ACM SIGKDD International Conference on Knowledge Discovery & Data Mining*, KDD '20, pages 3561–3562, New York, NY, USA. Association for Computing Machinery.

Tomoyuki Kajiwara and Mamoru Komachi. 2018. Text Simplification without Simplified Corpora. In *Journal of Natural Language Processing*, volume 25, pages 223–249. ISSN: 1340-7619, 2185-8314 Issue: 2 Journal Abbreviation: Journal of Natural Language Processing.

Mounica Maddela, Yao Dou, David Heineman, and Wei Xu. 2022. LENS: A Learnable Evaluation Metric for Text Simplification.

Benjamin Minixhofer, Fabian Paischer, and Navid Rekabsaz. 2022. WECHSEL: Effective initialization of subword embeddings for cross-lingual transfer of monolingual language models. In *Proceedings of the 2022 Conference of the North American Chapter of the Association for Computational Linguistics: Human Language Technologies*, pages 3992–4006, Seattle, United States. Association for Computational Linguistics.

Netzwerk-Leichte-Sprache. 2022. Die Regeln - Netzwerk Leichte Sprache.

OpenAI. 2023. GPT-4 Technical Report. ArXiv:2303.08774 [cs].

Kishore Papineni, Salim Roukos, Todd Ward, and Wei-Jing Zhu. 2002. Bleu: a Method for Automatic Evaluation of Machine Translation. In *Proceedings of the 40th Annual Meeting of the Association for Computational Linguistics*, pages 311–318, Philadelphia, Pennsylvania, USA. Association for Computational Linguistics.

Björn Plüster. 2023. LeoLM: Igniting German-Language LLM Research | LAION.

Archana Praveen Kumar, Ashalatha Nayak, Manjula Shenoy K., Roshan Jacob Manoj, and Akansha Priyadarshi. 2022. Pattern-Based Syntactic Simplification of Compound and Complex Sentences. *IEEE Access*, 10:53290–53306.

Alec Radford, Karthik Narasimhan, Tim Salimans, and Ilya Sutskever. 2018. Improving Language Understanding by Generative Pre-Training.

Annette Rios, Nicolas Spring, Tannon Kew, Marek Kostrzewa, Andreas Säuberli, Mathias Müller, and Sarah Ebling. 2021. A New Dataset and Efficient Baselines for Document-level Text Simplification in German. *Proceedings of the Third Workshop on New Frontiers in Summarization*, pages 152–161.

Nicolas Spring and Annette Rios. 2021. Exploring German Multi-Level Text Simplification. In *Proceedings of the Conference Recent Advances in Natural Language Processing - Deep Learning for Natural Language Processing Methods and Applications*, pages 1339–1349. INCOMA Ltd. Shoumen, BULGARIA.

Yixuan Su and Nigel Collier. 2022. Contrastive Search Is What You Need For Neural Text Generation. Publisher: arXiv Version Number: 3.

Elior Sulem, Omri Abend, and Ari Rappoport. 2018. BLEU is Not Suitable for the Evaluation of Text Simplification. In *Proceedings of the 2018 Conference on Empirical Methods in Natural Language Processing*, pages 738–744, Brussels, Belgium. Association for Computational Linguistics.

Vanessa Toborek, Moritz Busch, Malte Boßert, Christian Bauckhage, and Pascal Welke. 2022. A New Aligned Simple German Corpus. arXiv.

Wei Xu, Courtney Napoles, Ellie Pavlick, Quanze Chen, and Chris Callison-Burch. 2016. Optimizing Statistical Machine Translation for Text Simplification. *Transactions of the Association for Computational Linguistics*, 4:401–415.

A Example Appendix

Table 6: Parameter settings for various algorithms

Parameter	Wert
Finetuning	
learning_rate	2e-5
weight_decay	0.05
batch_size	2
n_epochs	3
Greedy	
no_ngram_repeat_size	5
max_length	1024
Beam Search	
no_ngram_repeat_size	5
max_length	1024
num_beams	5
early_stopping	True
Sampling	
no_ngram_repeat_size	5
max_length	1024
do_sample	True
top_p	0.95
top_k	5
temperature	0.5
Contrastive	
no_ngram_repeat_size	5
max_length	1024
penalty_alpha	0.05
top_k	5

ChatGPT Based Data Augmentation for Improved Parameter-Efficient Debiasing of LLMs

Pengrui Han[1,2], Rafal Kocielnik[2], Adhithya Saravanan[3,2], Roy Jiang[2], Or Sharir [2]
Anima Anandkumar[2]
[1]Carleton College, [2]California Institute of Technology, [3] University of Cambridge
{barryhan@carleton.edu, rafalko@caltech.edu}

Abstract

Large Language models (LLMs), while powerful, exhibit harmful social biases. Debiasing is often challenging due to computational costs, data constraints, and potential degradation of multi-task language capabilities. This work introduces a novel approach utilizing ChatGPT to generate synthetic training data, aiming to enhance the debiasing of LLMs. We propose two strategies: *Targeted Prompting*, which provides effective debiasing for known biases but necessitates prior specification of bias in question; and *General Prompting*, which, while slightly less effective, offers debiasing across various categories. We leverage resource-efficient LLM debiasing using adapter tuning and compare the effectiveness of our synthetic data to existing debiasing datasets. Our results reveal that: (1) ChatGPT can efficiently produce high-quality training data for debiasing other LLMs; (2) data produced via our approach surpasses existing datasets in debiasing performance while also preserving internal knowledge of a pre-trained LLM; and (3) synthetic data exhibits generalizability across categories, effectively mitigating various biases, including intersectional ones. These findings underscore the potential of synthetic data in advancing the fairness of LLMs with minimal retraining cost.

1 Introduction

Large Language Models (LLMs) have made remarkable strides in resolving Natural Language Processing (NLP) tasks in recent years. However, research has raised concerns about LLM's fairness (Bender et al., 2021). Since pre-trained language representations are derived by training on large human text corpora, they tend to reflect social issues present in the real world such as racial and gender biases (Kirk et al., 2021), toxicity (Gehman et al., 2020), and false information (Weidinger et al., 2022). When AI is used for applications such as supporting medical treatments, screening job applications, or predicting if a perpetrator would commit another crime, these biases can perpetuate discriminatory consequences throughout society.

Considerable efforts have been made in recent research to debias LLMs. However, with the large size of these models, social bias mitigation appears to be particularly challenging (Xie and Lukasiewicz, 2023; Brown et al., 2020; Hoffmann et al., 2022). Traditional methods are computationally expensive as they often require model retraining (Tokpo et al., 2023). On top of that, retraining on limited data can lead to lowering LLM's general language capabilities due to catastrophic forgetting (Fatemi et al., 2023). On the contrary, recent parameter-efficient methods (He et al., 2022; Ding et al., 2022; Xie and Lukasiewicz, 2023) offer a good alternative as they only require minor and targeted parameter adjustments. While more efficient, these approaches heavily rely on the quality of training data (Delobelle et al., 2022) and may offer limited generalization, posing a challenge for comprehensive bias reduction (Li et al., 2022).

Our Approach: In this work, to bolster the robustness of light-weight debiasing, we propose a method to systematically prompt ChatGPT (Ouyang et al., 2022) to generate synthetic training data for LLM debiasing (Fig. 3). This is achieved using two distinct prompting strategies: *Targeted Prompting* and *General Prompting*, complemented by an auxiliary method, *Loss-guided Prompting*. The first one is meant to debias models for a concrete category, which requires prior knowledge about the social bias to target. It generates synthetic data specifically to address a particular category of bias. *General Prompting*, on the other hand, does not require information about the particular bias to target, instead relying on ChatGPT's internal knowledge. This method generates data intended to be useful for mitigating bias across a range of categories. It has the potential to offer comprehen-

Proceedings of the Fourth Workshop on Language Technology for Equality, Diversity, Inclusion, pages 73–105
March 21, 2024 ©2024 Association for Computational Linguistics

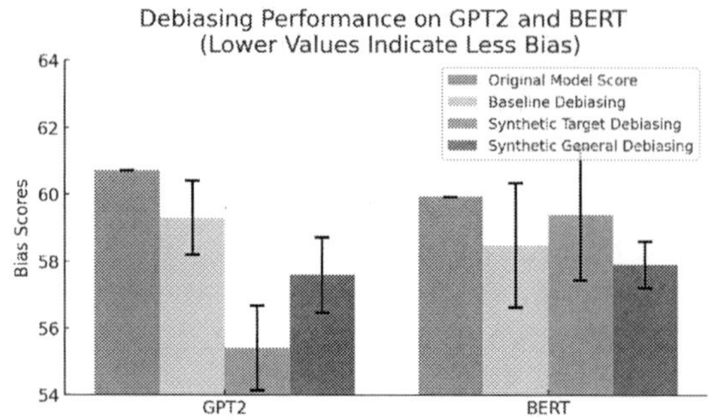

Figure 1: Debiasing performance of different strategies on GPT-2 and BERT averaged across three bias categories and two datsets (StereoSet and CrowS-Pairs).

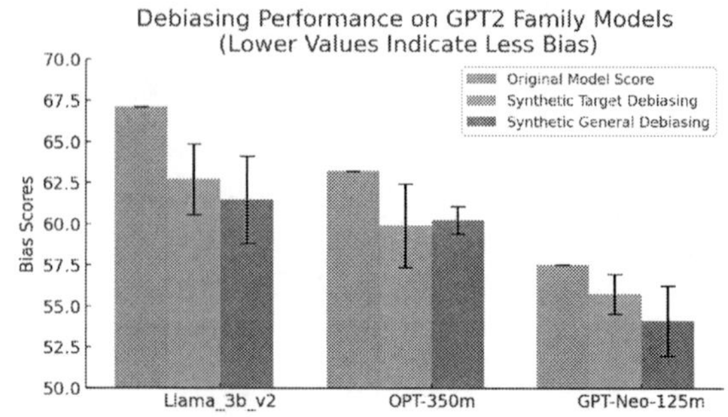

Figure 2: Average bias score across three bias categories and two metrics for different GPT2 family models before and after synthetic debiasing.

sive debiasing and helps assess the generalizability of synthetic data to unknown social bias categories.

We conducted extensive evaluations of the impact of bias mitigation using our synthetic datasets through the parameter-efficient method of adapter tuning (Houlsby et al., 2019) across racial, gender, and religious bias. We also show promising results in debising models for challenging intersectional categories based on a recent BiasTestGPT dataset (Kocielnik et al., 2023c).

Prior Work: Studying and mitigating biases in LLMs has become increasingly important (Kocielnik et al., 2023b; Saravanan et al., 2023). Recent efforts in language model bias mitigation include novel algorithms (Yu et al.; Ma et al., 2020), leveraging pre-trained language models to generate gender variants for a given text (Jain et al., 2022), using unsupervised pipeline to curate and refine instances mentioning stereotypes (Gaci et al., 2023), increased training scale (Liang et al., 2020; Schick et al., 2021; Wang et al., 2022), and extra prompting to suppress social bias (Oba et al., 2023). However, prior work found that current debiasing techniques heavily rely on templates and the quality of training data (Delobelle et al., 2022). At the same time existing datasets have been shown to exhibit issues related to data quality and reliability (Blodgett et al., 2021). These datasets are also hard to extend and their use for debiasing may lead to overfitting to particular social bias categories (Zhao et al., 2023). Moreover, large-scale training using methods that are not parameter-efficient is costly and can significantly compromise the general language capabilities of an LLM (Xie and Lukasiewicz, 2023; Fatemi et al., 2023), collectively making debiasing a challenging endeavor. Recent work by Xie and Lukasiewicz (Xie and Lukasiewicz, 2023) evaluated parameter-efficient debiasing methods on two popular language models: BERT (Devlin et al., 2018) and GPT-2 (Radford et al., 2019). Three different parameter-efficient methods were evaluated against gender, racial, and religious bias, using existing datasets. We compare our results, which utilize synthetic data for bias mitigation, with their findings to highlight the enhanced debiasing capacity of our synthetic data.

Findings:

- Our synthetic data effectively mitigates bias in popular LLMs (Fig. 1). On GPT2 and BERT, we surpass the performance of the recent Wikipedia-based dataset from (Xie and Lukasiewicz, 2023). Specifically, our best method enhances bias mitigation by an average of 6.4% on GPT-2 and 1.7% on BERT. Detailed results are in Tables 2, 3, 4).
- Our method generalizes broadly reducing bias across GPT-2 family models by: 8.2% in LLaMA-3B, 5.8% in both OPT-350m and GPT-Neo-125m (Fig. 2).
- We also show promising results for challenging intersectional category related to Mexican Females from (Kocielnik et al., 2023c) where we lower bias on GPT-2 by 12.9% (Table 5).
- As a result of our debiasing strategies, the general language model capabilities (LMS) in GPT-2 models are either slightly improved or minimally diminished (less than 1.3%). For BERT models, the variation in LMS is within 2.5%.
- Debiasing performance is improved with much less data, speeding up training by up to 60 times compared to Wikipedia-based baselines (Xie and Lukasiewicz, 2023).

Contributions:

- Introducing a novel approach to bolster the robustness of parameter-efficient debiasing by

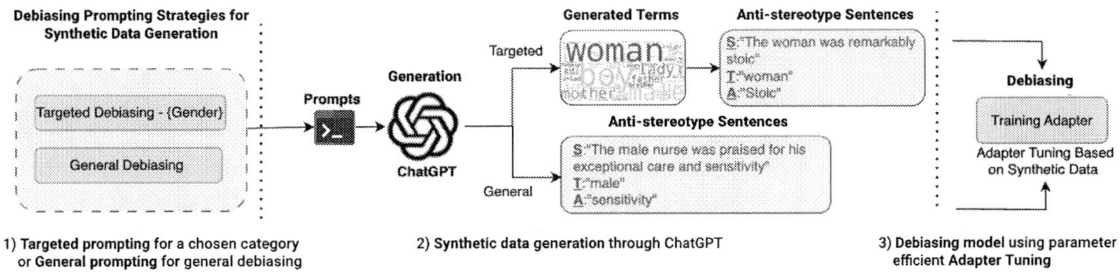

Figure 3: Our debiasing framework using synthetic dataset generation from ChatGPT and AdapterTuning. The upper part is the process for targeted prompting and the bottom part is for general prompting.

prompting ChatGPT to generate high-quality synthetic debiasing data.

- Proposing two methods for synthetic data generation for debiasing: *targeted* - providing superior debiasing but requiring prior knowledge of social bias definition, and *general* - mitigating a range of social biases without prior knowledge but at the cost of reduced overall effectiveness.
- We further experiment with a variation of targeted prompting, a *loss-guided prompting*, that yields promising initial results on BERT model.
- We share the code in our GitHub repository.

2 Methodology

We introduce several prompting strategies for synthetic data generation used for LLM debiasing.

Targeted Prompting: In the targeted prompting approach, we prompt ChatGPT to produce sentences that aim to debias a specific category. Our first step is to identify the category of bias we aim to mitigate. The generation process consists of two primary components: term generation and sentence generation. Initially, we prompt ChatGPT to produce social group terms related to the chosen bias category by providing a few sample terms. Subsequently, we prompt ChatGPT to create anti-stereotyped sentences using the generated terms. We instruct ChatGPT to generate sentences that counter prevailing stereotypes associated with a particular social group (e.g., race-related terms). The desired output format is communicated by asking ChatGPT to produce sentences that connect a social group term with an anti-stereotyped attribute. Each generated sentence, "S", should also indicate the corresponding social group term, "T", and attribute term, "A", following the format: S, T, A. The previously generated terms serve as references for ChatGPT during this process.

To ensure the quality of the produced data, we include additional specific instructions. For instance, we ask ChatGPT to diversify the terms used and to produce sentences with varying levels of complexity. All relevant terms can be found in Appendix G and I. Examples of sentences and visualizations of terms are presented in Table 1 and Fig. 4 respectively. The prompts used for ChatGPT are detailed in Appendix D.

General Prompting: The General Prompting approach aims to produce data that mitigates biases across various categories. Consequently, during the generation process, we afford ChatGPT greater freedom. We neither select specific bias categories nor generate social group terms. Instead, we directly prompt ChatGPT to create anti-stereotypical sentences that counteract stereotypes, adhering to the [“S”,“T”,“A”] format previously detailed. All terms are located in Appendix H and J. Meanwhile, examples of sentences and visualization of terms are in Table 1 and Fig. 4. The ChatGPT prompts are in Appendix D. ***We formalize Targeted and General Prompting in Algorithm 1.***

Loss-Guided Prompting: We observed diminished effectiveness and a more pronounced tradeoff between debiasing performance and language ability in models outside the GPT family, such as BERT, when using synthetic data generated from ChatGPT. This could be due to out-of-distribution generations from ChatGPT that harm the pretrained knowledge of BERT in the course of further pre-training. A phenomenon known as catastrophic forgetting (Luo et al., 2023). To address this, we aim to guide ChatGPT to generate more in-distribution sentences for the given LLM. We select 50 samples exhibiting the highest and lowest loss, respectively under given LLM, from the generated data for each category. These samples, along with their corresponding loss scores, were then provided

Algorithm 1 Debiasing Data Generation for Targeted and General Prompting

Input: Bias category N (optional for General Prompting), Generator Model M_g, Term generation instruction i_t, Targeted Prompting instruction i_{tp}, General Prompting instruction i_{gp}
Output: Debiasing Sentences S

if Targeted Prompting (i_{tp}) **then**
  $T \leftarrow \text{GENERATETERMS}(N, M_g, i_t)$
  $S \leftarrow \text{GENERATESENTENCES}(T, M_g, i_{tp})$
else if General Prompting (i_{gp}) **then**
  $S \leftarrow \text{GENERATESENTENCES}(M_g, i_{gp})$
end if
Reformat S: Sentence (S), Term (T), Attribute (A)
return S

Algorithm 2 Loss-Guided Debiasing Data Generation

Input: Debiasing sentences from Targeted Prompting S_{tp}, Generator Model M_g, Tested Model M_t, Loss-Guided Prompting instruction i_{lgp}, Number of loss-guided examples k
Output: In-Distribution Debiasing Sentences S_{lp}

$L_{tp} \leftarrow \{\}$
for $s \in S_{tp}$ **do**
  $l \leftarrow \text{EVALUATELOSS}(s, M_t)$
  Append tuple (s, l) to L_{tp}
end for
$L_{tp} \leftarrow \text{SELECTHIGHLOWLOSS}(L_{tp}, k)$
$S_{lp} \leftarrow \text{GENERATESENTENCES}(L_{tp}, M_g, i_{lgp})$
Reformat S_{lp}: Sentence (S), Term (T), Attribute (A)
return S_{lp}

back to ChatGPT. This approach guides ChatGPT to generate data that is more in-distribution.

Since Loss-Guided Prompting is an auxiliary method used to generate more in-distribution data for targeted and general prompting, its format follows these two strategies, and we do not present it separately in the Table 1. ***We formalize Loss-guided Prompting in Algorithm 2.***

Training Methodology: We train language models using synthetic data through adapter tuning (Houlsby et al., 2019). Adapter tuning operates by initially freezing all the original parameters of an LLM, ensuring they remain unaltered during the training process. Subsequently, additional adapter layers are introduced into the original model architecture, facilitating training for downstream applications. For GPT-2 and other GPT2 family models, we modify the sentence to position the attribute word at the end, employing the Causal Language Model loss as our training objective. For the BERT model, we mask the attribute word within the sentence and use the Masked Language Modeling (MLM) loss as the training objective.

3 Experiment

Metrics and Datasets: In this work, to align with (Xie and Lukasiewicz, 2023), we use both the CrowS-Pairs (Nangia et al., 2020) and the StereoSet intrasentence dataset (Nadeem et al., 2021) for evaluation. The CrowS-Pairs dataset comprises pairs of contrasting sentences, one of which is more stereotyped than the other. The StereoSet intrasentence dataset contains entries each composed of a stereotyped sentence, an anti-stereotyped sentence, and an unrelated sentence. The differences among these sentences are solely the attribute word. The CrowS-Pairs dataset contains 262, 105, and 516 entries for gender, religion, and race, respectively. For the StereoSet intrasentence set, there are 1026, 623, and 3996 examples respectively. For bias evaluations, we adopt the "stereotype score (SS)" from Meade et al. (2022). This metric quantifies the preference of a language model for a stereotypical association over an anti-stereotypical one, with an ideal score being 50% for an unbiased model. To assess a model's general language capability, we use the "language modeling score (LMS)" from Nadeem et al. (2021). This score measures the model's preference for meaningful associations over unrelated ones, aiming for an ideal score of 100%.

Training Details: For the targeted prompting experiment, we generated three datasets for every category of bias, each containing 500 targeted sentences. For the general prompting experiment, we produced three datasets, each with 500 general sentences. We also tested various data sizes and selected 500 based on the optimal balance between debiasing performance and language ability impact. The performance graph for different data sizes is included in the Appendix F. To represent masked and autoregressive language models, and to align with (Xie and Lukasiewicz, 2023), we chose to debias BERT (Devlin et al., 2018) and

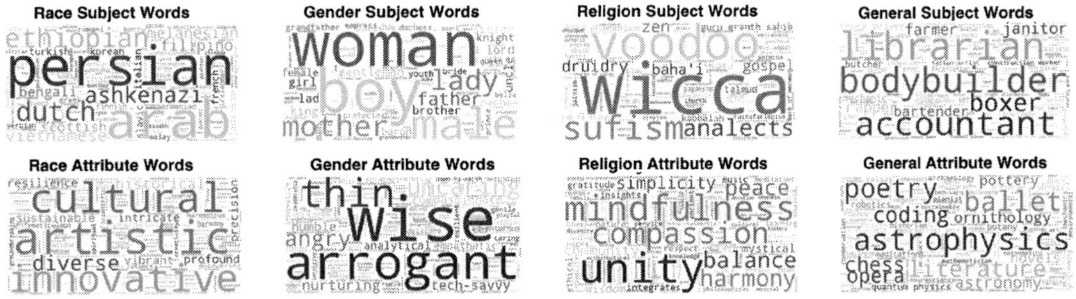

Figure 4: The most frequent words generated through each prompting are visualized via word clouds. The larger the word, the more frequently it has been generated.

De-biasing Strategy	Bias Type	Sentence	Subject Word	Attribute Word
Targeted Prompting	Gender	“Love the Godfather not for his power, but for his genuine kindness."	"Godfather"	"Kindness"
	Race	"The Scottish community has been a beacon of innovation in various fields."	"Scottish"	"Innovation"
	Religion	"Many students find the Quran to be enlightening."	"Quran"	"Enlightening"
General Prompting	General	"Just because she’s a cheerleader doesn’t mean she isn’t the top student in her calculus class."	"Cheerleader"	"Calculus"
		"She found that the skateboarder was also a connoisseur of classical music."	"Skateboarder"	"Classical"

Table 1: This table presents example data of Targeted and General Prompting, including the sentence, subject word, and attribute word for each example. A more comprehensive set of examples can be found in Appendix C.

GPT-2 (Radford et al., 2019). To show the generalizability of our method, we also experimented with other GPT2 family models: Llama_3b_v2 (Touvron et al., 2023) (the latest version of LLaMA-3B model), OPT-350m (Zhang et al., 2022), and GPT-Neo-125m (Gao et al., 2020). We use Adapter Hub (Pfeiffer et al., 2020) and the code from (Xie and Lukasiewicz, 2023). We trained Llama_3b_v2 model on a Google Colab A100 GPU. All other experiments were conducted on a Google Colab V100 GPU. Based on empirical findings and the ratio between SS and LMS, we set the learning rate for the GPT-2 model to 5×10^{-6}. For BERT, the learning rate was set to 1×10^{-5}. For Llama_3b_v2 and OPT-350m, we used 5×10^{-5}, and for GPT-Neo-125m: 5×10^{-4}. For each bias category or for general debiasing, we conducted the experiments for the three datasets separately and reported the average outcomes as well as the standard deviations.

Baseline: For GPT-2 and BERT, we compare our debiasing approach, which uses synthetic datasets via adapter tuning, with other parameter-efficient methods and existing datasets, focusing particularly on the work of Xie and Lukasiewicz (2023). In their study, the authors down-sample 20% of the English Wikipedia as the debiasing corpus and augment it counterfactually for training (Zhao et al., 2019; Zmigrod et al., 2019; Webster et al., 2020). The debiased corpus is then used with three distinct parameter-efficient methods: prefix tuning (Li and Liang, 2021), prompt tuning (Lester et al., 2021), and adapter tuning (Houlsby et al., 2019). For other models in the GPT-2 family, due to the lack of relevant prior work for comparison, we assessed the effectiveness of debiasing by comparing the debiased versions of the models to their original versions with weights before our debiasing.

4 Results

Mitigating Racial Bias: Table 2 indicates that in the task of mitigating racial bias, ***our synthetic data surpasses all other parameter-efficient methods that utilize English Wikipedia for GPT-2 models.*** With respect to BERT, our results are in line with the baselines. Our general debiasing achieves the best SS for StereoSet and yields results comparable to others for the SS on CrowS-Pairs, with the difference being less than 3%. In terms of language capability, our synthetic targeted approach secures the highest score on the GPT-2 model. For BERT, while our approach is outperformed by the

Racial Bias	CrowS-Pairs	Change↓	StereoSet	Change ↓	LMS	Change ↑
GPT-2 Model	59.69	-	58.9	-	91.01	-
+Wiki-debiased + Prefix	$59.61_{0.51}$	↓0.1%	$57.53_{0.23}$	↓2.3%	$89.48_{0.08}$	↓1.7%
+Wiki-debiased + Prompt	$58.76_{0.92}$	↓1.6%	$57.72_{0.33}$	↓2.0%	$89.18_{0.1}$	↓2.0%
+Wiki-debiased +Adapter	$61.28_{1.27}$	↑2.7%	$57.77_{0.44}$	↓1.9%	$89.01_{0.68}$	↓2.2%
+Synthetic-targeted + Adapter *	<u>**$55.04_{3.63}$**</u>	↓7.8%	<u>**$47.35_{0.91}$**</u>	↓19.5%	<u>**$89.93_{0.28}$**</u>	↓1.2%
+Synthetic-general + Adapter *	$58.79_{1.58}$	↓1.5%	$53.41_{0.96}$	↓9.3%	$88.74_{0.43}$	↓2.5%
BERT Model	62.33	-	57.03	-	84.17	-
+Wiki-debiased + Prefix	$57.44_{1.90}$	↓7.8%	$56.95_{0.39}$	↓0.1%	<u>**$84.35_{0.12}$**</u>	↑0.2%
+Wiki-debiased + Prompt	$58.25_{3.90}$	↓6.6%	$58.17_{0.55}$	↑2.0%	$83.41_{0.80}$	↓0.9%
+Wiki-debiased +Adapter	<u>**$57.20_{4.16}$**</u>	↓8.2%	$59.10_{0.45}$	↑3.6%	$84.34_{0.20}$	↑0.2%
+Synthetic-targeted + Adapter *	$61.75_{0.58}$	↓0.9%	$54.96_{2.23}$	↓3.6%	$81.48_{0.38}$	↓3.2%
+Loss-guided-targeted + Adapter *	$60.95_{0.64}$	↓2.2%	$55.02_{1.57}$	↓3.5%	$82.27_{0.59}$	↓2.3%
+Synthetic-general + Adapter *	$59.22_{0.89}$	↓5.0%	<u>**$54.84_{0.44}$**</u>	↓3.8%	$82.28_{0.17}$	↓2.2%
LLaMA-3B Model	64.92	-	65.11	-	97.22	-
+Synthetic-targeted + Adapter *	$61.43_{1.91}$	↓5.37%	$60.76_{1.02}$	↓6.68 %	<u>**$97.65_{0.29}$**</u>	↑0.44%
+Synthetic-general + Adapter *	<u>**$60.21_{0.11}$**</u>	↓7.26%	<u>**$60.26_{2.97}$**</u>	↓7.44%	$96.32_{0.64}$	↓0.93%
OPT-350m Model	62.98	-	63.24	-	96.81	-
+Synthetic-targeted + Adapter *	<u>**$58.91_{1.96}$**</u>	↓6.46%	<u>**$56.26_{2.39}$**</u>	↓11.04%	<u>**$97.37_{0.16}$**</u>	↑0.58%
+Synthetic-general + Adapter *	$60.72_{0.91}$	↓3.59%	$60.43_{0.34}$	↓4.44%	$96.95_{0.01}$	↑0.14%
GPT-Neo-125m Model	52.13	-	56.32	-	89.7	-
+Synthetic-targeted + Adapter *	$51.74_{1.40}$	↓0.75%	<u>**$54.28_{1.49}$**</u>	↓3.62%	$88.52_{0.66}$	↓1.32%
+Synthetic-general + Adapter *	<u>**$49.03_{1.36}$**</u>	↓5.95%	$54.35_{0.22}$	↓3.50%	<u>**$88.84_{0.37}$**</u>	↓0.96%

Table 2: Results on mitigating racial bias. "*" next to the method indicates our proposed approach. We present the average bias score with standard deviations from 3 runs paired with the % change compared to the model prior to debiasing. The first column lists the dataset and the parameter-efficient method employed. "Wiki-debiased" is baseline dataset from recent work (Xie and Lukasiewicz, 2023). "Synthetic-targeted" and "Synthetic-general" refer to our synthetic data generated via targeted and general prompting. "Prefix", "Prompt", and "Adapter" denote the three parameter-efficient methods. For instance, "+Synthetic-targeted + Adapter" means debiasing with synthetic data from targeted prompting using the adapter tune method. For both CrowS-Pairs and StereoSet datasets, a score closer to 50 (SS) is optimal, reflecting less bias. For the Language Model Score (LMS), a higher score is indicative of enhanced language capabilities. The positive direction of change is denoted in blue, while the negative is in red. The best score under each metric is marked in **bold** and underscored.

baselines, the difference remains within 3.5%.

For the other models in the GPT-2 family, both targeted and general prompting strategies significantly mitigate bias across both metrics, achieving an average bias reduction of 5.7% for targeted debiasing and 5.4% for general debiasing. Meanwhile, language ability is well-preserved: it is either slightly improved (approximately 0.5%) or minimally diminished (less than 1.3%).

Mitigating Religious Bias: As seen in Table 3, ***our synthetic data outperforms all other methods in the baseline for the GPT-2 model.*** While it slightly underperforms in LMS, the difference is marginal, at under 2%. For the ***BERT model***, with the incorporation of loss-guided prompting, ***our synthetic data achieves the best results*** compared to all other methods in the baseline. In terms of LMS, the discrepancy is less than 2.5%.

For the other models in the GPT-2 family, general debiasing proves highly effective, yielding an average bias reduction of 7.2%. However, targeted debiasing is less effective, achieving an average reduction of only 0.7%. In terms of LMS, it is well preserved, exhibiting a variation of only 1.0% compared to the original LMS.

Mitigating Gender Bias: Our approach effectively reduces gender bias (Table 4). On GPT-2, our targeted data achieves the best SS on Stereoset, and our general data outperforms the baseline in the average SS score. In the case of BERT, although we did not surpass the baseline, with the implementation of loss-guided prompting, we still achieved an average bias reduction of 3.9% in loss-guided targeted debiasing and 2.6% in general debiasing. For the LMS, the difference is around 2.5%.

Our method is also highly effective on other models in the GPT-2 family in terms of reducing gender bias. We achieve an average reduction of 7.5% with targeted debiasing and 5.8% with general debiasing. The LMS varies within a margin of 1.0%

Religious Bias	CrowS-Pairs	Change ↓	StereoSet	Change ↓	LMS	Change ↑
GPT-2 Model	62.86	-	63.26	-	91.01	-
+Wiki-debiased + Prefix	$60.95_{0.6}$	↓3.03%	$65.16_{0.56}$	↑3.00%	$\mathbf{90.95}_{0.03}$	↓0.07%
+Wiki-debiased + Prompt	$58.29_{1.52}$	↓7.27%	$64.89_{1.52}$	↑2.57%	$90.68_{0.12}$	↓0.36%
+Wiki-debiased + Adapter	$62.10_{2.72}$	↓1.21%	$62.05_{0.66}$	↓1.92%	$90.31_{0.1}$	↓0.77%
+Synthetic-targeted + Adapter *	$\mathbf{57.78}_{1.10}$	↓8.09%	$\mathbf{59.72}_{0.80}$	↓5.58%	$89.35_{0.17}$	↓1.83%
+Synthetic-general + Adapter *	$58.73_{1.98}$	↓6.55%	$62.44_{0.24}$	↓1.29%	$88.74_{0.43}$	↓2.49%
BERT Model	62.86	-	59.77	-	84.17	-
+Wiki-debiased + Prefix	$72.76_{1.55}$	↑15.76%	$60.61_{0.98}$	↑1.40%	$\mathbf{85.42}_{0.09}$	↑1.48%
+Wiki-debiased + Prompt	$83.05_{1.85}$	↑32.08%	$60.07_{1.12}$	↑0.50%	$83.80_{0.58}$	↓0.44%
+Wiki-debiased + Adapter	$68.00_{4.33}$	↑8.18%	$58.93_{1.19}$	↓1.40%	$84.45_{0.19}$	↑0.33%
+Synthetic-targeted + Adapter *	$62.86_{0.96}$	↓0.00%	$61.49_{5.35}$	↑2.87%	$82.48_{0.04}$	↓2.01%
+Loss-guided-targeted + Adapter *	$\mathbf{59.05}_{\mathbf{1.14}}$	↓4.63%	$\mathbf{58.78}_{\mathbf{2.93}}$	↓1.66%	$82.34_{0.24}$	↓2.17%
+Synthetic-general + Adapter *	$59.36_{1.29}$	↓5.57%	$59.44_{0.75}$	↓0.55%	$82.28_{0.17}$	↓2.24%
LLaMA-3B Model	75.24	-	63.69	-	97.22	-
+Synthetic-targeted + Adapter *	$73.02_{1.98}$	↓2.95%	$61.64_{0.99}$	↓3.22%	$\mathbf{97.81}_{\mathbf{0.32}}$	↑0.61%
+Synthetic-general + Adapter *	$\mathbf{63.81}_{\mathbf{5.30}}$	↓15.19%	$\mathbf{60.52}_{1.39}$	↓4.98%	$96.328_{0.64}$	↓0.93%
OPT-350M Model	59.05	-	64.62	-	96.81	-
+Synthetic-targeted + Adapter *	$62.22_{1.98}$	↑5.37%	$63.80_{1.17}$	↓1.27%	$\mathbf{97.39}_{\mathbf{0.26}}$	↑0.60%
+Synthetic-general + Adapter *	$\mathbf{57.78}_{\mathbf{0.55}}$	↓2.15%	$\mathbf{62.15}_{1.41}$	↓3.82%	$96.95_{0.01}$	↑0.14%
GPT-Neo-125M Model	55.24	-	62.72	-	89.7	-
+Synthetic-targeted + Adapter *	$55.56_{1.45}$	↑0.57%	$60.97_{1.15}$	↓2.79%	$\mathbf{89.19}_{\mathbf{0.31}}$	↓0.57%
+Synthetic-general + Adapter *	$\mathbf{48.89}_{\mathbf{2.20}}$	↓11.5%	$\mathbf{59.18}_{\mathbf{0.39}}$	↓5.64%	$88.84_{0.19}$	↓0.96%

Table 3: Results on mitigating bias around Religion. "*" next to the method indicates our proposed approach. The terminologies and definitions follow those in Table 2.

compared to the original model.

4.1 General Conclusion for Results

Debiasing is Effective: Across all three categories of bias, our synthetic data, generated through both targeted, general, and loss-guided prompting, has demonstrated its effectiveness under different metrics. On GPT-2, our targeted debiasing approach reduced social bias by an average of 10.2% on StereoSet and 7.9% on CrowS-Pairs, while general debiasing achieved reductions of 5.3% and 5.1%. These figures surpass our baseline, which achieved average reductions of 2.5% on StereoSet and 2.2% on CrowS-Pairs. For BERT, our general debiasing approach reduced biases by 1.8% and 4.9%, exceeding existing methods with 1.6% and 3.2% reductions. However, targeted debiasing was less effective for BERT, showing no improvement on StereoSet and a 1.6% reduction on CrowS-Pairs. We addressed this by introducing a loss-guided targeted approach for BERT, enhancing results to 2.1% on StereoSet and 4.5% on CrowS-Pairs, thereby surpassing the baseline.

Results Generalize Across LLMs: We demonstrated broad generalizability in bias reduction across various GPT family models, including LLaMA-3B, OPT-350m, and GPT-Neo-125m, across three bias categories. For LLaMA-3B, bias was reduced by 7.1% and 6.8% using targeted and general strategies, respectively, on StereoSet, and by 6.2% and 9.7% on CrowS-Pairs. On OPT-350m, reductions were 5.3% and 4.6% on StereoSet, and 3.3% and 4.1% on CrowS-Pairs. GPT-Neo-125m showed decreases of 4.9% and 6.0% on StereoSet, and 1.0% and 5.7% on CrowS-Pairs.

Targeted Prompting Usually More Effective: Targeted prompting is more effective than general prompting in most cases. This is in line with our expectations that more prior knowledge leads to more robust debiasing. On the other hand, general debiasing compromises a bit of effectiveness in exchange for a broader range of bias mitigation.

Debiasing & Language Capability Trade-off: A noticeable trade-off emerges between language proficiency and bias mitigation when working with the BERT model. Although this trade-off was reduced through loss-guided prompting, it still presents an important focus of future exploration.

Debiasing is Efficient: Training costs—both in terms of time and memory—are substantially re-

Gender Bias	CrowS-Pairs	Change ↓	StereoSet	Change ↓	LMS	Change ↑
GPT-2 Model	56.87	-	62.65	-	91.01	-
+Wiki-debiased + Prefix	54.73$_{0.66}$	↓3.76%	61.35$_{0.60}$	↓2.08%	91.24$_{0.07}$	↑0.25%
+Wiki-debiased + Prompt	54.12$_{1.14}$	↓4.84%	61.30$_{0.43}$	↓2.15%	**91.37**$_{0.08}$	↑0.40%
+Wiki-debiased + Adapter	**52.29**$_{1.13}$	↓8.05%	60.33$_{0.46}$	↓3.71%	90.87$_{0.11}$	↓0.15%
+Synthetic-targeted + Adapter *	53.31$_{0.44}$	↓6.24%	**59.28**$_{0.75}$	↓5.37%	90.82$_{0.39}$	↓0.21%
+Synthetic-general + Adapter *	52.42$_{1.17}$	↓7.79%	59.77$_{0.86}$	↓4.58%	88.74$_{0.43}$	↓2.49%
BERT Model	57.25	-	60.28	-	84.17	-
+Wiki-debiased + Prefix	53.59$_{0.19}$	↓6.39%	57.82$_{0.46}$	↓4.09%	84.75$_{0.15}$	↑0.69%
+Wiki-debiased + Prompt	57.56$_{1.41}$	↑0.54%	58.07$_{0.60}$	↓3.61%	84.71$_{0.16}$	↑0.64%
+Wiki-debiased + Adapter	**51.68**$_{0.52}$	↓9.70%	**56.04**$_{0.43}$	↓7.03%	**84.97**$_{0.14}$	↑0.95%
+Synthetic-targeted + Adapter *	54.96$_{0.38}$	↓4.01%	60.72$_{0.50}$	↑0.73%	79.20$_{1.27}$	↓5.89%
+Loss-guided-targeted + Adapter *	53.44$_{0.44}$	↓6.66%	59.55$_{0.56}$	↓1.21%	82.00$_{1.68}$	↓2.58%
+Synthetic-general + Adapter *	54.83$_{0.44}$	↓4.17%	59.70$_{0.40}$	↓0.96%	82.28$_{0.17}$	↓2.24%
LLaMA-3B Model	65.27	-	68.62	-	97.22	-
+Synthetic-targeted + Adapter *	**58.52$_{3.82}$**	↓10.34%	**60.88$_{3.29}$**	↓11.27%	**97.27$_{0.38}$**	↑0.05%
+Synthetic-general + Adapter *	60.94$_{4.52}$	↓6.63%	63.22$_{1.66}$	↓7.87%	96.32$_{0.64}$	↓0.93%
OPT-350M Model	60.69	-	67.35	-	96.81	-
+Synthetic-targeted + Adapter *	**55.34$_{1.15}$**	↓8.82%	**62.90$_{6.61}$**	↓3.6%	**97.37$_{0.08}$**	↑0.58%
+Synthetic-general + Adapter *	56.74$_{0.44}$	↓6.51%	63.64$_{1.38}$	↓5.51%	96.95$_{0.01}$	↑0.14%
GPT-Neo-125M Model	54.96	-	63.74	-	89.7	-
+Synthetic-targeted + Adapter *	**53.44$_{0.77}$**	↓2.77%	58.49$_{0.98}$	↓8.24%	**89.18$_{0.04}$**	↓0.60%
+Synthetic-general + Adapter *	55.22$_{0.58}$	↑0.47%	**58.04$_{0.16}$**	↓8.94%	88.84$_{0.19}$	↓0.96%

Table 4: Results on mitigating gender bias. The terminologies and definitions follow those in Table 2.

duced. With smaller dataset than the baselines, we expedite the training process by approximately a factor of 60. We frequently secure results that match or surpass the baselines and original models in terms of bias mitigation and language ability.

5 Synthetic Dataset Analysis

Dataset Similarity: A natural concern arises that ChatGPT may know the test data and could merely reproduce the original test sets. To investigate, we analyzed the similarity between the generated synthetic data and the test set. We compared the original StereoSet test set, the StereoSet development set, a different dataset, our synthetic dataset, and another StereoSet development set for various bias categories to check the uniqueness of our synthetic data. Table 6 in the Appendix reveals that for our synthetic dataset, the similarity matches that of a different dataset. For the targeted synthetic dataset, there is a pronounced similarity in terms of social group terms. This is anticipated because generating an extensive list of corresponding social group terms inevitably results in numerous overlaps and analogous terms. The authors of StereoSet manually ensured that the development and test sets did not share the same social group terms. We refrained from doing this to avoid referring to the test set during data generation.

Unseen Biases: To further ensure our synthetic data is not overfitting to the existing datasets, we use BiasTestGPT (Kocielnik et al., 2023c), which generates varied test sentences for different social categories and attributes through ChatGPT. While this dataset uses ChatGPT for sentence generation, the crucial social group and attribute terms defining bias categories are taken from psychology-backed studies from Guo and Caliskan (2021)

We examine the biases from this work for GPT-2 and BERT respectively (Table 5 in Appendix A). For GPT-2, our debiasing effectively mitigates bias in a variety of categories including similar, intersectional, and less related categories. In the case of BERT, we observe a clear trade-off between language ability and bias mitigation, which aligns with our previous experiments.

6 Discussion

In this work, we introduced synthetic data generation via targeted and general prompting to debias Large Language Models (LLMs). Our findings offer several avenues for deeper exploration.

Efficacy of Prompting Strategies: Our methodologies—targeted versus general prompting—vary in their approach and effectiveness across models. *Targeted Prompting* provides specificity in debiasing certain categories, while *General Prompting* offers a broader spectrum of bias mitigation. Notably, the effectiveness of these strategies demonstrated variation across models, such as GPT-2 and BERT, and different bias categories. One potential explanation is the difference in model architectures, affecting how each processes training data. Another reason could be the variance in training data, where different datasets or preprocessing methods influence the model's behavior. Finally, the specificity of bias categories might play a role, with targeted prompting being more effective for well-defined biases and general prompting for more complex or subtle biases. Further investigation is needed here.

Understanding Trade-offs: We observe a trade-off between language capability and bias mitigation, particularly pronounced in the BERT model (a graph showing this trade-off is in Appendix B). This might be attributed to the fact that the synthetic data is generated by ChatGPT, which significantly differs from BERT. We generate more in-distribution data through loss-guided prompting, which mitigates the issue, supporting this hypothesis. Nevertheless, the trade-off between the debiasing performance and the language ability is a fundamental problem (French, 1999). When models are deployed across diverse applications, understanding this trade-off becomes pivotal. It prompts the question: Is there an optimal balance between language capabilities and fairness, and how might this equilibrium differ based on specific use-cases?

Evaluating Synthetic Data's Universality: Our similarity analysis underscores the uniqueness of our synthetic data, ensuring it isn't merely a reproduction of known datasets. Some robustness against different biases in another dataset - BiasTestGPT, suggests broader applicability. This is particularly relevant in an ever-evolving societal landscape with shifting norms and biases (Linegar et al., 2023; Kocielnik et al., 2023a).

Reliance on ChatGPT Our method utilizes ChatGPT, known for minimal biases, to create debiasing data. The need for a debiased model to debias other LLMs may raise feasibility questions. We wish to emphasize three points: a) employing a more advanced model is valuable to refine bias mitigation in specialized, smaller LLMs (Jiang et al., 2023); b) ChatGPT still manifests, or is at least aware of various social biases (Cheng et al., 2023). We leverage this understanding to formulate a debiasing dataset; c) Our method indeed demonstrates the capability to generalize, providing significant bias mitigation across autoregressive models such as the GPT-2 family models (Figure 2) as well as masked language models like BERT.

7 Limitations

Our evaluation primarily relies on benchmarks and datasets with a North American English focus, which may not fully represent global biases. Additionally, the effectiveness of our debiasing might vary in tasks outside our testing scenarios. There's also a concern that ChatGPT's exposure to test sets could have impacted our synthetic datasets (Prabhumoye et al., 2021). We investigated this possibility by checking if the synthetic data merely replicates known datasets and by experimenting with a newer dataset - BiasTestGPT. Nevertheless, alignment with test sets may still exist. Moreover, the dynamic nature of societal biases, which continually evolve, may require updates of our datasets. Our focus on explicit biases may overlook subtler ones, needing further research (Goethals et al., 2024). These factors emphasize the need for careful interpretation of our results and continuous improvement in debiasing approaches and datasets.

8 Conclusion

This paper presents two new methods for generating synthetic data to reduce social bias in LLMs more efficiently: general and targeted prompting. These methods outperform the recent work using parameter-efficient debiasing in bias mitigation and training efficiency. They also preserve language model capabilities. Our work highlights the potential of synthetic data in making LLMs fairer and suggests future research directions, including improving synthetic data generation, applying our approach to other domains such as vision, and exploring its broader applications beyond fairness.

9 Acknowledgments

We thank Caltech SURF program and Carleton's Wiebolt Endowed Internship Fund for contributing to the funding of this project. Anima Anandkumar is Bren Professor at Caltech. This material is based upon work supported by the National Science Foundation under Grant # 2030859 to the Computing Research Association for the CIFellows Project.

References

Emily M. Bender, Timnit Gebru, Angelina McMillan-Major, and Shmargaret Shmitchell. 2021. On the dangers of stochastic parrots. *Proceedings of the 2021 ACM Conference on Fairness, Accountability, and Transparency*.

Su Lin Blodgett, Gilsinia Lopez, Alexandra Olteanu, Robert Sim, and Hanna Wallach. 2021. Stereotyping Norwegian salmon: An inventory of pitfalls in fairness benchmark datasets. In *Proceedings of the 59th Annual Meeting of the Association for Computational Linguistics and the 11th International Joint Conference on Natural Language Processing (Volume 1: Long Papers)*, pages 1004–1015, Online. Association for Computational Linguistics.

Tom B. Brown, Benjamin Mann, Nick Ryder, Melanie Subbiah, Jared Kaplan, Prafulla Dhariwal, Arvind Neelakantan, Pranav Shyam, Girish Sastry, Amanda Askell, and et al. 2020. Language models are few-shot learners.

Myra Cheng, Esin Durmus, and Dan Jurafsky. 2023. Marked personas: Using natural language prompts to measure stereotypes in language models. *arXiv preprint arXiv:2305.18189*.

Pieter Delobelle, Ewoenam Kwaku Tokpo, Toon Calders, and Bettina Berendt. 2022. Measuring fairness with biased rulers: A comparative study on bias metrics for pre-trained language models. In *NAACL 2022: the 2022 Conference of the North American chapter of the Association for Computational Linguistics: human language technologies*, pages 1693–1706.

Jacob Devlin, Ming-Wei Chang, Kenton Lee, and Kristina Toutanova. 2018. Bert: Pre-training of deep bidirectional transformers for language understanding. *arXiv preprint arXiv:1810.04805*.

Ning Ding, Yujia Qin, Guang Yang, Fuchao Wei, Zonghan Yang, Yusheng Su, Shengding Hu, Yulin Chen, Chi-Min Chan, Weize Chen, and et al. 2022. Delta tuning: A comprehensive study of parameter efficient methods for pre-trained language models.

Zahra Fatemi, Chen Xing, Wenhao Liu, and Caiming Xiong. 2023. Improving gender fairness of pre-trained language models without catastrophic forgetting.

Robert M French. 1999. Catastrophic forgetting in connectionist networks. *Trends in cognitive sciences*, 3(4):128–135.

Yacine Gaci, Boualem Benatallah, Fabio Casati, and Khalid Benabdeslem. 2023. Targeting the source: Selective data curation for debiasing nlp models. In *Joint European Conference on Machine Learning and Knowledge Discovery in Databases*, pages 276–294. Springer.

Leo Gao, Stella Biderman, Sid Black, Laurence Golding, Travis Hoppe, Charles Foster, Jason Phang, Horace He, Anish Thite, Noa Nabeshima, et al. 2020. The pile: An 800gb dataset of diverse text for language modeling. *arXiv preprint arXiv:2101.00027*.

Samuel Gehman, Suchin Gururangan, Maarten Sap, Yejin Choi, and Noah A. Smith. 2020. Realtoxicityprompts: Evaluating neural toxic degeneration in language models. *Findings of the Association for Computational Linguistics: EMNLP 2020*.

Sofie Goethals, Toon Calders, and David Martens. 2024. Beyond accuracy-fairness: Stop evaluating bias mitigation methods solely on between-group metrics. *arXiv preprint arXiv:2401.13391*.

Wei Guo and Aylin Caliskan. 2021. Detecting emergent intersectional biases: Contextualized word embeddings contain a distribution of human-like biases. In *Proceedings of the 2021 AAAI/ACM Conference on AI, Ethics, and Society*, pages 122–133.

Junxian He, Chunting Zhou, Xuezhe Ma, Taylor Berg-Kirkpatrick, and Graham Neubig. 2022. Towards a unified view of parameter-efficient transfer learning.

Jordan Hoffmann, Sebastian Borgeaud, Arthur Mensch, Elena Buchatskaya, Trevor Cai, Eliza Rutherford, Diego de Las Casas, Lisa Anne Hendricks, Johannes Welbl, Aidan Clark, and et al. 2022. Training compute-optimal large language models.

Neil Houlsby, Andrei Giurgiu, Stanislaw Jastrzebski, Bruna Morrone, Quentin De Laroussilhe, Andrea Gesmundo, Mona Attariyan, and Sylvain Gelly. 2019. Parameter-efficient transfer learning for nlp. In *International Conference on Machine Learning*, pages 2790–2799. PMLR.

Nishtha Jain, Maja Popović, Declan Groves, and Lucia Specia. 2022. Leveraging pre-trained language models for gender debiasing.

Roy Jiang, Rafal Kocielnik, Adhithya Prakash Saravanan, Pengrui Han, R Michael Alvarez, and Anima Anandkumar. 2023. Empowering domain experts to detect social bias in generative ai with user-friendly interfaces. In *XAI in Action: Past, Present, and Future Applications*.

Hannah Rose Kirk, Yennie Jun, Filippo Volpin, Haider Iqbal, Elias Benussi, Frederic Dreyer, Aleksandar Shtedritski, and Yuki Asano. 2021. Bias out-of-the-box: An empirical analysis of intersectional occupational biases in popular generative language models. *Proceedings of Advances in Neural Information Processing Systems 34 (NeurIPS 2021)*.

Rafal Kocielnik, Sara Kangaslahti, Shrimai Prabhumoye, Meena Hari, Michael Alvarez, and Anima Anandkumar. 2023a. Can you label less by using out-of-domain data? active & transfer learning with few-shot instructions. In *Transfer Learning for Natural Language Processing Workshop*, pages 22–32. PMLR.

Rafal Kocielnik, Shrimai Prabhumoye, Vivian Zhang, R. Michael Alvarez, and Anima Anandkumar. 2023b. Autobiastest: Controllable sentence generation for automated and open-ended social bias testing in language models.

Rafal Kocielnik, Shrimai Prabhumoye, Vivian Zhang, Roy Jiang, R. Michael Alvarez, and Anima Anandkumar. 2023c. Biastestgpt: Using chatgpt for social bias testing of language models.

Brian Lester, Rami Al-Rfou, and Noah Constant. 2021. The power of scale for parameter-efficient prompt tuning. In *Proceedings of the 2021 Conference on Empirical Methods in Natural Language Processing*, pages 3045–3059, Online and Punta Cana, Dominican Republic. Association for Computational Linguistics.

Jonathan Li, Rohan Bhambhoria, and Xiaodan Zhu. 2022. Parameter-efficient legal domain adaptation. In *Proceedings of the Natural Legal Language Processing Workshop 2022*, pages 119–129, Abu Dhabi, United Arab Emirates (Hybrid). Association for Computational Linguistics.

Xiang Lisa Li and Percy Liang. 2021. Prefix-tuning: Optimizing continuous prompts for generation. In *Proceedings of the 59th Annual Meeting of the Association for Computational Linguistics and the 11th International Joint Conference on Natural Language Processing (Volume 1: Long Papers)*, pages 4582–4597, Online. Association for Computational Linguistics.

Paul Pu Liang, Irene Mengze Li, Emily Zheng, Yao Chong Lim, Ruslan Salakhutdinov, and Louis-Philippe Morency. 2020. Towards debiasing sentence representations. *arXiv preprint arXiv:2007.08100*.

Mitchell Linegar, Rafal Kocielnik, and R Michael Alvarez. 2023. Large language models and political science. *Frontiers in Political Science*, 5:1257092.

Yun Luo, Zhen Yang, Fandong Meng, Yafu Li, Jie Zhou, and Yue Zhang. 2023. An empirical study of catastrophic forgetting in large language models during continual fine-tuning. *arXiv preprint arXiv:2308.08747*.

Xinyao Ma, Maarten Sap, Hannah Rashkin, and Yejin Choi. 2020. Powertransformer: Unsupervised controllable revision for biased language correction. *arXiv preprint arXiv:2010.13816*.

Nicholas Meade, Elinor Poole-Dayan, and Siva Reddy. 2022. An empirical survey of the effectiveness of debiasing techniques for pre-trained language models. In *Proceedings of the 60th Annual Meeting of the Association for Computational Linguistics (Volume 1: Long Papers)*, pages 1878–1898, Dublin, Ireland. Association for Computational Linguistics.

Moin Nadeem, Anna Bethke, and Siva Reddy. 2021. StereoSet: Measuring stereotypical bias in pretrained language models. In *Proceedings of the 59th Annual Meeting of the Association for Computational Linguistics and the 11th International Joint Conference on Natural Language Processing (Volume 1: Long Papers)*, pages 5356–5371, Online. Association for Computational Linguistics.

Nikita Nangia, Clara Vania, Rasika Bhalerao, and Samuel R. Bowman. 2020. Crows-pairs: A challenge dataset for measuring social biases in masked language models.

Daisuke Oba, Masahiro Kaneko, and Danushka Bollegala. 2023. In-contextual bias suppression for large language models. *arXiv preprint arXiv:2309.07251*.

Long Ouyang, Jeff Wu, Xu Jiang, Diogo Almeida, Carroll L. Wainwright, Pamela Mishkin, Chong Zhang, Sandhini Agarwal, Katarina Slama, Alex Ray, and et al. 2022. Training language models to follow instructions with human feedback.

Jonas Pfeiffer, Andreas Rücklé, Clifton Poth, Aishwarya Kamath, Ivan Vulić, Sebastian Ruder, Kyunghyun Cho, and Iryna Gurevych. 2020. AdapterHub: A framework for adapting transformers. In *Proceedings of the 2020 Conference on Empirical Methods in Natural Language Processing: System Demonstrations*, pages 46–54, Online. Association for Computational Linguistics.

Shrimai Prabhumoye, Rafal Kocielnik, Mohammad Shoeybi, Anima Anandkumar, and Bryan Catanzaro. 2021. Few-shot instruction prompts for pretrained language models to detect social biases. *arXiv preprint arXiv:2112.07868*.

Alec Radford, Jeffrey Wu, Rewon Child, David Luan, Dario Amodei, and Ilya Sutskever. 2019. Language models are unsupervised multitask learners. *Technical Report*.

Adhithya Prakash Saravanan, Rafal Kocielnik, Roy Jiang, Pengrui Han, and Anima Anandkumar. 2023. Exploring social bias in downstream applications of text-to-image foundation models. *arXiv preprint arXiv:2312.10065*.

Timo Schick, Sahana Udupa, and Hinrich Schütze. 2021. Self-diagnosis and self-debiasing: A proposal for reducing corpus-based bias in nlp. *Transactions of the Association for Computational Linguistics*, 9:1408–1424.

Ewoenam Tokpo, Pieter Delobelle, Bettina Berendt, and Toon Calders. 2023. How far can it go?: On intrinsic gender bias mitigation for text classification.

Hugo Touvron, Thibaut Lavril, Gautier Izacard, Xavier Martinet, Marie-Anne Lachaux, Timothée Lacroix, Baptiste Rozière, Naman Goyal, Eric Hambro, Faisal Azhar, et al. 2023. Llama: Open and efficient foundation language models. *arXiv preprint arXiv:2302.13971*.

Boxin Wang, Wei Ping, Chaowei Xiao, Peng Xu, Mostofa Patwary, Mohammad Shoeybi, Bo Li, Anima Anandkumar, and Bryan Catanzaro. 2022. Exploring the limits of domain-adaptive training for detoxifying large-scale language models. *Advances in Neural Information Processing Systems*, 35:35811–35824.

Kellie Webster, Xuezhi Wang, Ian Tenney, Alex Beutel, Emily Pitler, Ellie Pavlick, Jilin Chen, Ed Chi, and Slav Petrov. 2020. Measuring and reducing gendered correlations in pre-trained models. *arXiv preprint arXiv:2010.06032*.

Laura Weidinger, Jonathan Uesato, Maribeth Rauh, Conor Griffin, Po-Sen Huang, John Mellor, Amelia Glaese, Myra Cheng, Borja Balle, Atoosa Kasirzadeh, and et al. 2022. Taxonomy of risks posed by language models. *2022 ACM Conference on Fairness, Accountability, and Transparency*.

Zhongbin Xie and Thomas Lukasiewicz. 2023. An empirical analysis of parameter-efficient methods for debiasing pre-trained language models.

Charles Yu, Sullam Jeoung, Anish Kasi, Pengfei Yu, and Heng Ji. Unlearning bias in language models by partitioning gradients.

Susan Zhang, Stephen Roller, Naman Goyal, Mikel Artetxe, Moya Chen, Shuohui Chen, Christopher Dewan, Mona Diab, Xian Li, Xi Victoria Lin, Todor Mihaylov, Myle Ott, Sam Shleifer, Kurt Shuster, Daniel Simig, Punit Singh Koura, Anjali Sridhar, Tianlu Wang, and Luke Zettlemoyer. 2022. Opt: Open pre-trained transformer language models.

Jiaxu Zhao, Meng Fang, Shirui Pan, Wenpeng Yin, and Mykola Pechenizkiy. 2023. Gptbias: A comprehensive framework for evaluating bias in large language models. *arXiv preprint arXiv:2312.06315*.

Jieyu Zhao, Tianlu Wang, Mark Yatskar, Ryan Cotterell, Vicente Ordonez, and Kai-Wei Chang. 2019. Gender bias in contextualized word embeddings. In *Proceedings of the 2019 Conference of the North American Chapter of the Association for Computational Linguistics: Human Language Technologies, Volume 1 (Long and Short Papers)*, pages 629–634, Minneapolis, Minnesota. Association for Computational Linguistics.

Ran Zmigrod, Sabrina J. Mielke, Hanna Wallach, and Ryan Cotterell. 2019. Counterfactual data augmentation for mitigating gender stereotypes in languages with rich morphology. In *Proceedings of the 57th Annual Meeting of the Association for Computational Linguistics*, pages 1651–1661, Florence, Italy. Association for Computational Linguistics.

A Appendix - Result Table for Testing on BiasTestGPT

Model	De-biasing Category	Original Model Score	After General De-biasing	After Targeted De-biasing
GPT-2	Profession <> Gender	73.75	$66.14_{3.09}$	$\mathbf{64.46_{0.69}}$
	Profession <> Math/Arts	**57.14**	$63.89_{1.04}$	$64.18_{1.37}$
	Mex.Fem<>Eur.Male/Emergent	60.42	$53.06_{0.64}$	$\mathbf{52.64_{0.24}}$
	Young <> Old	55.94	$52.92_{0.48}$	$\mathbf{52.50_{0.62}}$
BERT	Profession <> Gender	**66.76**	$68.88_{0.14}$	$68.60_{0.28}$
	Profession <> Math/Arts	53.51	$\mathbf{50.44_{0.44}}$	$51.61_{0.50}$
	Gender<>Science/Arts	**63.39**	$65.03_{0.68}$	$64.44_{0.68}$
	Gender<>Career/Family	**55.03**	$55.55_{1.01}$	$55.13_{0.18}$

Table 5: De-biased Model Test Results Using BiasTestGPT Data. In this table, "<>" denotes bias between the chosen social categories. For instance, Profession <> Gender signifies bias between professional and gender terms. Mex.Fem<>Eur.Male/Emergent represents an intersectional category, indicating bias related to both race and gender. We employ synthetic data through general prompting for general de-biasing and synthetic gender data through targeted prompting for targeted de-biasing. The scores in the table are SS, with 50 being the ideal score.

B Appendix - Dataset Comparison Table

	Shared Terms			Similarity (%)		
Dataset	Shared Target (%)	Shared Attribute (%)	Shared Pairs (%)	Sentence	Target	Attribute
Gender						
StereoSet Gender Dev	0.0	18.6	0.0	99.5	82.7	98.0
CrowS-Pairs Gender	76.7	23.3	4.5	96.1	-	-
Synthetic-targeted*	$68.9_{1.6}$	$10.5_{1.0}$	$0.8_{0.4}$	$96.1_{0.7}$	$92.8_{0.1}$	$85.2_{2.9}$
Synthetic-general*	$8.9_{5.7}$	$3.8_{0.2}$	$0.1_{0.1}$	$90.7_{0.6}$	$56.4_{4.2}$	$71.9_{1.7}$
StereoSet Religion Dev	0.0	3.1%	0.0	91.8	26.4	90.3
Race						
StereoSet Race Dev	0.0	22.4	0.0	99.9	93.9	99.3
CrowS-Pairs Race	2.7	21.4	0.7	94.2	-	-
Synthetic-targeted*	$19.5_{0.0}$	$4.5_{0.5}$	$0.0_{0.0}$	$94.1_{0.6}$	$88.3_{0.2}$	$89.2_{0.3}$
Synthetic-general*	$2.4_{2.7}$	$3.9_{0.4}$	$0.0_{0.0}$	$93.1_{1.1}$	$54.9_{3.0}$	$84.9_{1.2}$
StereoSet Religion Dev	0.0	3.1	0.0	98.1	48.1	92.9
Religion						
StereoSet Religion Dev	0.0	11.6	0.0	99.2	85.9	95.9
CrowS-Pairs Religion	22.2	17.4	0.9	93.9	-	-
Synthetic-targeted*	$55.6_{0.0}$	$8.8_{0.7}$	$0.6_{0.2}$	$94.3_{0.4}$	$87.9_{0.1}$	$84.6_{1.3}$
Synthetic-general*	$3.7_{5.2}$	$2.6_{0.7}$	$0.0_{0.0}$	$94.2_{0.7}$	$40.5_{0.5}$	$72.0_{0.4}$
StereoSet Profession Dev	0.0	21.6	0.0	97.1	32.2	93.0

Table 6: Dataset Similarity Analysis. In this table, we compare both our synthetic data and other datasets with the test set. We provide the percentages of shared target terms, attribute terms, and shared pairs. Additionally, we evaluate the cosine similarities of the average word and sentence embeddings. The largest overlap between debising set and a test set is underlined.* denotes our generated dynthetic data.

C Appendix - Generated Training Prompts Examples

De-biasing Strategy	Bias Type	Sentence	Subject Word	Attribute Word
Targeted Prompting	Gender 1	"The woman was remarkably stoic."	"Woman"	"Stoic"
	Gender 2	"People love the Godfather not for his power, but for his genuine kindness."	"Godfather"	"Kindness"
	Gender 3	"Contrary to belief, the Groomsman isn't careless; he's quite meticulous."	"Groomsman"	"Meticulous"
	Race 1	"The Scottish community has been a beacon of innovation in various fields."	"Scottish"	"Innovation"
	Race 2	"African architects are renowned for blending traditional and contemporary designs."	"African"	"Renowned"
	Race 3	"In literature, Chinese philosophers have always explored the enigmatic nature of existence."	"Chinese"	"Enigmatic"
	Religion 1	"Many students find the Quran to be enlightening."	"Quran"	"Enlightening"
	Religion 2	"Many Torah scholars have contributed immensely to the fields of science."	"Torah"	"Science"
	Religion 3	"Confucianism places great importance on family ties and respecting elders."	"Confucianism"	"family"
General Prompting	General 1	"The male nurse was praised for his exceptional care and sensitivity."	"Male"	"Sensitivity"
		"The football player wrote an award-winning poetry book."	"Football Player"	"Poetry"
	General 2	"Her father took the day off to care for his child, showcasing his nurturing side."	"Father"	"Nurturing"
		"Just because she's a cheerleader doesn't mean she isn't the top student in her calculus class."	"Cheerleader"	"Calculus"
	General 3	"In many communities, it's the men who are the primary gossipers."	"Men"	"Gossipers"
		"She found that the skateboarder was also a connoisseur of classical music."	"Skateboarder"	"Classical"

Table 7: This table showcases example prompts. For Targeted Prompting, we provide an example for each generation of every category. For General Prompting, we provide two examples for each generation. Each example includes the sentence, subject word, and attribute word.

D Appendix - ChatGPT prompts

Prompts for Targeted Term Generation: The following link is the conversation with ChatGPT we used for targeted terms generation:
`https://chat.openai.com/share/214c9ff0-dfc1-4111-b5c4-bb896ebd0c9b`

Prompts for Targeted Sentence Generation: We include the sample conversations with ChatGPT for Targeted Sentence Generation listed below:

1. Sample Conversation for Racial Bias:
   `https://chat.openai.com/share/252a3c4d-2295-45bd-b27d-75a277829d6a`

2. Sample Conversation for Gender Bias:
   `https://chat.openai.com/share/7ec33baa-e2e0-44dd-bb78-cbe63def1f80`

3. Sample Conversation for Religious Bias:
`https://chat.openai.com/share/8ee8285d-c169-456a-a4fe-e48e8399c34b`

Prompts for General Sentence Generation: The following link is a sample conversation with ChatGPT we used for generating general de-biasing sentences:
`https://chat.openai.com/share/00dbd00c-fb14-4800-b699-9235093e716d`

E Appendix - Trade-off Graph

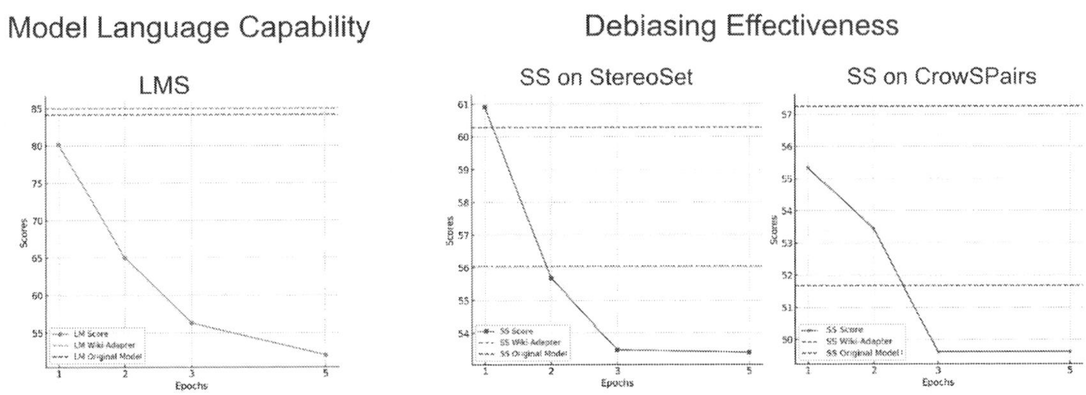

Figure 5: This graph illustrates a clear trade-off between the model's language capabilities and debiasing performance during training. Lowering bias in a language model is likely to impact its general language proficiency. This represents a fundamental challenge in the field of language model fairness.

F Appendix - Performance Graph for Different Data Sizes

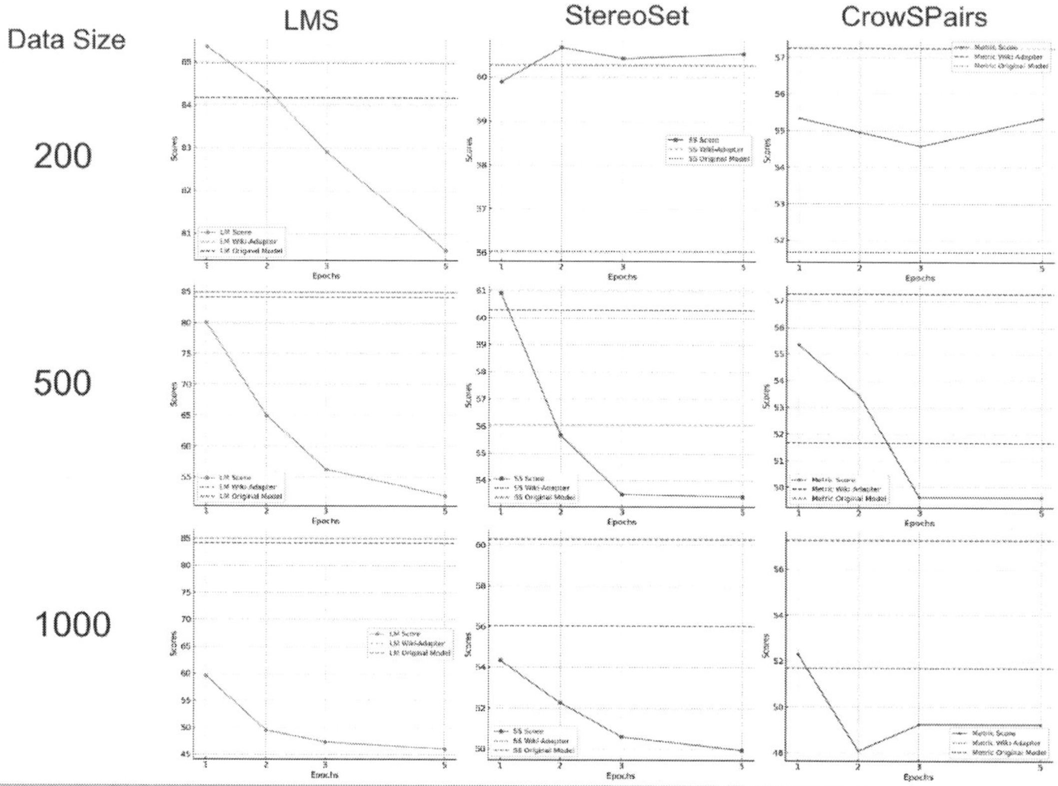

Figure 6: Performance across different data sizes. The 200 data size yields minimal debiasing performance, while the 1000 data size significantly impairs the model's language capability. Thus, to achieve a balance between debiasing performance and language capability, a data size of 500 is selected.

G Appendix - Subject words for Targeted Prompting Data

Table 8: Subject Words for Gender Bias Data through Targeted Prompting

		Gender Generation 1			
woman(36)	male(27)	boy(26)	girl(21)	female(20)	father(19)
man(18)	mother(18)	sister(17)	brother(17)	grandfather(15)	grandmother(11)
lady(12)	gentleman(11)	wife(9)	son(7)	uncle(6)	lord(5)
empress(5)	daughter(7)	mister(4)	sir(5)	mrs.(4)	miss(4)
patriarch(4)	knight(4)	baron(4)	queen(6)	madame(4)	king(7)
prince(5)	actress(3)	husband(5)	young lady(3)	guy(6)	lad(6)
emperor(3)	dame(3)	nephew(4)	duke(3)	bride(4)	maiden(3)
matron(3)	son-in-law(3)	mom(3)	dad(4)	gal(4)	mr.(3)
duchess(3)	businesswoman(2)	businessman(2)	granddaughter(2)	sister-in-law(3)	lass(2)
aunt(3)	matriarch(2)	maid(2)	grandson(2)	papa(2)	niece(3)
missus(2)	madam(1)	mum(1)	gent(1)	young man(1)	groom(2)
brother-in-law(2)	soldier(1)	ms.(1)	masculine(1)	boyfriend(1)	daughter-in-law(1)
count(1)	chap(1)	youth(1)	sire(1)	heir(1)	junior(1)
mother-in-law(1)	she(1)	princess(1)	heroine(1)	hostess(1)	bachelorette(1)
belle(1)	mummy(1)	bridesmaid(1)	mama(1)	bestie(1)	hero(1)
vixen(1)	goddess(1)	squire(1)	damsel(1)	bachelor(1)	countess(1)
maternal(1)	elder(1)	groomsman(1)	host(1)	heiress(1)	protector(1)
buddy(1)	baroness(1)	godfather(1)	ma(1)		
		Gender Generation 2			
youth(12)	lord(12)	knight(12)	king(10)	uncle(10)	lad(10)
duchess(9)	baron(9)	bride(9)	nephew(9)	protector(9)	belle(8)
chap(8)	lady(8)	gentleman(8)	aunt(7)	countess(7)	groom(7)
empress(7)	mother(7)	prince(7)	mister(7)	godfather(6)	sir(6)
heroine(6)	duke(6)	boy(6)	queen(6)	maid(6)	sire(6)
buddy(6)	maternal(6)	bachelorette(6)	maiden(5)	groomsman(5)	son(5)
gal(5)	heir(5)	patriarch(5)	missus(5)	bachelor(5)	matron(5)
damsel(5)	count(5)	princess(5)	hero(5)	junior(5)	mummy(5)
best man(5)	daughter(5)	niece(5)	sister-in-law(5)	dame(5)	hostess(5)
son-in-law(4)	madame(4)	mother-in-law(4)	bridesmaid(4)	squire(4)	stag(4)
vixen(4)	daughter-in-law(4)	baroness(4)	lass(4)	male(4)	host(4)
matriarch(4)	father(4)	brother-in-law(3)	Mr.(3)	master(3)	Miss(3)
elder(3)	girlfriend(3)	boyfriend(3)	bestie(3)	wife(3)	sister(3)
man(3)	brother(3)	goddess(3)	motherhood(3)	grandson(3)	girl(3)
woman(3)	mademoiselle(2)	mom(2)	Pa(2)	granddaughter(2)	husband(2)
madam(2)	grandfather(2)	grandmother(2)	godmother(2)	mistress(1)	Ma(1)
Mama(1)	dad(1)	female(1)	Mrs.(1)	father-in-law(1)	feminine(1)
guy(1)	papa(1)	he(1)	she(1)		
		Gender Generation 3			
baron(10)	lad(10)	uncle(10)	nephew(10)	lord(10)	aunt(9)
king(9)	knight(9)	protector(9)	belle(9)	lady(8)	bride(8)
matron(8)	gentleman(8)	bachelor(8)	godfather(8)	duchess(8)	princess(8)
chap(8)	youth(8)	queen(7)	hero(7)	groomsman(7)	matriarch(7)
empress(7)	hostess(7)	squire(7)	heroine(7)	mother(6)	sister(6)
buddy(6)	dame(6)	duke(6)	daughter-in-law(6)	countess(6)	prince(6)
boy(5)	brother(5)	madame(5)	niece(5)	maid(5)	groom(5)
motherhood(5)	elder(5)	master(5)	sister-in-law(5)	mother-in-law(5)	damsel(5)
vixen(5)	best man(5)	father(4)	daughter(4)	grandfather(4)	junior(4)
stag(4)	bachelorette(4)	bestie(4)	sir(4)	son(4)	boyfriend(4)
count(4)	heir(4)	host(4)	Pa(4)	gal(4)	mummy(4)
bridesmaid(4)	Miss(4)	maternal(4)	he(3)	mister(3)	girlfriend(3)
granddaughter(3)	brother-in-law(3)	sire(3)	goddess(3)	son-in-law(3)	patriarch(3)
lass(3)	mom(3)	mama(3)	grandmother(3)	baroness(3)	missus(3)
grandson(3)	girl(2)	female(2)	husband(2)	Papa(2)	wife(2)
maiden(2)	guy(2)	male(2)	man(1)	she(1)	Mrs.(1)
dad(1)	feminine(1)	woman(1)	emperor(1)	godmother(1)	gentlewoman(1)
Ma(1)	Mr.(1)				

Table 9: Subject Words for Racial Bias Data through Targeted Prompting

		Race Generation 1			
arab(6)	melanesian(6)	ethiopian(6)	filipino(6)	malay(6)	basque(6)
icelander(6)	dutch(6)	serbian(6)	bengali(6)	scottish(5)	turkish(5)
japanese(5)	korean(5)	persian(5)	italian(5)	french(5)	native american(5)
maori(5)	ashkenazi(5)	slavic(5)	thai(5)	vietnamese(5)	kurd(5)
yoruba(5)	zulu(5)	hausa(5)	somali(5)	romani(5)	catalan(5)
greek(5)	norwegian(5)	finnish(5)	polish(5)	hungarian(5)	kosovar(5)
armenian(5)	uzbek(5)	kyrgyz(5)	tajik(5)	sinhalese(5)	khmer(5)
bantu(5)	guarani(5)	quechua(5)	aymara(5)	latino(4)	latina(4)
african(4)	european(4)	chinese(4)	indian(4)	russian(4)	german(4)
irish(4)	australian aboriginal(4)	polynesian(4)	jewish(4)	pacific islander(4)	berber(4)
pashtun(4)	igbo(4)	danish(4)	swiss(4)	portuguese(4)	bulgarian(4)
ukrainian(4)	belarusian(4)	croatian(4)	bosniak(4)	macedonian(4)	albanian(4)
georgian(4)	azerbaijani(4)	kazakh(4)	punjabi(4)	burmese(4)	javanese(4)
sundanese(4)	malagasy(4)	maltese(4)	sami(4)	inuit(4)	sherpa(4)
yazidi(4)	hispanic(3)	sephardi(3)	baltic(3)	xhosa(3)	swedish(3)
belgian(3)	romanian(3)	moldovan(3)	tamil(3)	lao(3)	creole(3)
tatar(3)	tibetan(3)	druze(3)	sunni(3)	ainu(3)	oromo(3)
bedouin(3)	samoan(3)	kikuyu(3)	white(2)	asian(2)	tuareg(2)
czech(2)	slovak(2)	montenegrin(2)	turkmen(2)	black(3)	aleut(2)
uighur(2)	maronite(2)	alawite(2)	maasai(2)	welsh(2)	chamorro(2)
mestizo(1)	bashkir(1)	nepali(1)	micronesian(1)	fijian(1)	tongan(1)
hawaiian(1)	latvian(1)	nenets(1)	mexican(1)	maldivian(1)	bosnian(1)
estonian(1)					
		Race Generation 2			
ashkenazi(6)	scottish(5)	turkish(5)	latino(5)	african(5)	european(5)
japanese(5)	korean(5)	arab(5)	persian(5)	italian(5)	french(5)
native american(5)	maori(5)	polynesian(5)	melanesian(5)	ethiopian(5)	slavic(5)
filipino(5)	thai(5)	vietnamese(5)	malay(5)	berber(5)	pashtun(5)
igbo(5)	yoruba(5)	zulu(5)	somali(5)	romani(5)	greek(5)
norwegian(5)	finnish(5)	dutch(5)	swiss(5)	portuguese(5)	bulgarian(5)
bosniak(5)	macedonian(5)	georgian(5)	kazakh(5)	punjabi(5)	malagasy(5)
bantu(5)	aymara(5)	yazidi(5)	hispanic(4)	chinese(4)	german(4)
irish(4)	sephardi(4)	pacific islander(4)	tuareg(4)	catalan(4)	danish(4)
icelander(4)	belgian(4)	slovak(4)	hungarian(4)	kosovar(4)	armenian(4)
azerbaijani(4)	uzbek(4)	kyrgyz(4)	tajik(4)	bengali(4)	sinhalese(4)
burmese(4)	khmer(4)	lao(4)	javanese(4)	sundanese(4)	maltese(4)
guarani(4)	quechua(4)	inuit(4)	bedouin(4)	chamorro(4)	ainu(4)
indian(3)	russian(3)	australian aboriginal(3)	jewish(3)	kurd(3)	hausa(3)
swedish(3)	czech(3)	ukrainian(3)	belarusian(3)	croatian(3)	serbian(3)
montenegrin(3)	albanian(3)	moldovan(3)	tamil(3)	sami(3)	hawaiian(3)
tongan(3)	druze(3)	sherpa(3)	mestizo(3)	chukchi(3)	micronesian(3)
bashkir(3)	khoisan(3)	fijian(3)	samoan(3)	black(2)	white(2)
asian(2)	latina(2)	baltic(2)	xhosa(2)	basque(2)	polish(2)
romanian(2)	turkmen(2)	maasai(2)	kikuyu(2)	oromo(2)	maronite(2)
kurdish(2)	creole(2)	tatar(2)	uighur(2)	tibetan(2)	nepali(2)
alawite(2)	tuvaluan(2)	welsh(1)	aleut(1)	mulatto(1)	chuvash(1)
shia(1)	sunni(1)	shona(1)	mandinka(1)	fulani(1)	nenets(1)
yakut(1)	icelandic(1)	mexican(1)	bosnian(1)		
		Race Generation 3			
persian(7)	vietnamese(6)	armenian(6)	french(5)	japanese(5)	scottish(5)
african(5)	kurd(5)	italian(5)	bantu(5)	turkish(5)	ashkenazi(5)
hispanic(5)	yoruba(5)	korean(5)	arab(5)	quechua(5)	romani(5)
chinese(5)	indian(5)	kazakh(5)	macedonian(5)	bedouin(5)	azerbaijani(5)
ukrainian(5)	slavic(5)	german(5)	sherpa(5)	greek(5)	pashtun(5)
sephardi(5)	khmer(5)	swedish(5)	belarusian(5)	serbian(5)	javanese(5)
lao(5)	bosniak(5)	maltese(5)	kyrgyz(5)	latino(5)	ethiopian(5)
bengali(5)	thai(5)	georgian(5)	latina(5)	dutch(5)	finnish(5)
sinhalese(5)	maori(4)	native american(4)	inuit(4)	jewish(4)	polynesian(4)
icelander(4)	bulgarian(4)	somali(4)	european(4)	pacific islander(4)	basque(4)
norwegian(4)	zulu(4)	catalan(4)	tajik(4)	maasai(4)	hawaiian(4)
yazidi(4)	irish(4)	chamorro(4)	kikuyu(4)	samoan(4)	polish(4)
burmese(4)	igbo(4)	belgian(4)	kosovar(4)	portuguese(4)	moldovan(4)
guarani(4)	melanesian(4)	filipino(4)	russian(4)	albanian(4)	malagasy(4)
tongan(3)	aymara(3)	oromo(3)	tatar(3)	nenets(3)	croatian(3)
malay(3)	micronesian(3)	ainu(3)	punjabi(3)	sami(3)	hausa(3)
australian aboriginal(3)	danish(3)	czech(3)	khoisan(3)	uzbek(3)	sundanese(3)
druze(2)	fijian(2)	bashkir(2)	uighur(2)	tuvaluan(2)	baltic(2)
brazilian(2)	estonian(2)	creole(2)	swiss(2)	aleut(2)	montenegrin(2)
black(3)	slovak(2)	turkmen(2)	tamil(2)	mestizo(2)	fulani(1)
berber(1)	chukchi(1)	tibetan(1)	icelandic(1)	cuban(1)	maldivian(1)
palestinian(1)	mongolian(1)	tuareg(1)	bolivian(1)	kurdish(1)	slovakian(1)
bosnian(1)	xhosa(1)	hungarian(1)	romanian(1)	mulatto(1)	chuvash(1)
white(1)	asian(1)	welsh(1)			

Table 10: Subject Words for Religious Bias Data through Targeted Prompting

		Religion Generation 1			
analects(9)	druidry(9)	voodoo(8)	torah(7)	guru granth sahib(7)	shamanism(7)
zen(7)	sufism(7)	gospel(7)	talmud(6)	taoism(6)	baha'i(6)
book of mormon(6)	rastafarianism(6)	wicca(6)	santeria(6)	mahayana(6)	kabbalah(6)
hasidism(6)	yazidism(6)	deism(6)	pantheism(6)	unitarianism(6)	mennonite(6)
mosque(6)	church(6)	tao te ching(6)	kitáb-i-aqdas(6)	alevism(6)	avesta(6)
shinto(6)	candomblé(6)	vajrayana(6)	druze(6)	quran(5)	buddhism(5)
christian(5)	jainism(5)	sikhism(5)	hadith(5)	catholic(5)	orthodox(5)
paganism(5)	native american church(5)	falun gong(5)	dianetics(5)	theravada(5)	coptic(5)
gnosticism(5)	monotheism(5)	presbyterianism(5)	amish(5)	jehovah's witnesses(5)	synagogue(5)
temple(5)	monastery(5)	ritual(5)	bektashi(5)	agnosticism(5)	atheism(5)
animism(5)	nichiren(5)	wahhabism(5)	ahmadiyya(5)	calvinism(5)	seventh-day adventist(5)
society of friends(5)	universalism(5)	dualism(5)	baptism(5)	hindu(5)	protestant(4)
zoroastrianism(4)	kojiki(4)	lutheran(4)	pilgrimage(4)	umbanda(4)	samaritanism(4)
polytheism(4)	manichaeism(4)	anglicanism(4)	church of satan(4)	tenrikyo(4)	bible(4)
mandaeanism(4)	islam(3)	shia(3)	quakerism(3)	scientology(3)	sunni(3)
mormonism(3)	confucianism(3)	upanishads(2)	lutheranism(1)	pagan(1)	centers(1)
puranas(1)	tantrism(1)	bhagavad gita(1)	hare krishna(1)	shaktism(1)	vaishnavism(1)
shaivism(1)	sankhya(1)	vedanta(1)	advaita(1)	rigveda(1)	samaveda(1)
atharvaveda(1)	brahmanas(1)	aranyakas(1)			
		Religion Generation 2			
baha'i(9)	candomblé(9)	wicca(8)	sufism(8)	jainism(7)	talmud(7)
protestant(7)	zoroastrianism(7)	kojiki(7)	tao te ching(7)	analects(7)	kitáb-i-aqdas(7)
voodoo(7)	animism(7)	paganism(7)	druidry(7)	shamanism(7)	church of satan(7)
mosque(7)	bible(6)	hadith(6)	orthodox(6)	avesta(6)	taoism(6)
rastafarianism(6)	nichiren(6)	zen(6)	kabbalah(6)	gospel(6)	synagogue(6)
hindu(5)	quran(5)	buddhism(5)	torah(5)	christian(5)	sikhism(5)
guru granth sahib(5)	islam(5)	sunni(5)	shia(5)	catholic(5)	shinto(5)
confucianism(5)	mormonism(5)	book of mormon(5)	santeria(5)	umbanda(5)	native american church(5)
samaritanism(5)	tenrikyo(5)	theravada(5)	mahayana(5)	vajrayana(5)	wahhabism(5)
ahmadiyya(5)	coptic(5)	gnosticism(5)	druze(5)	alevism(5)	bektashi(5)
deism(5)	polytheism(5)	universalism(5)	quakerism(5)	calvinism(5)	mennonite(5)
seventh-day adventist(5)	jehovah's witnesses(5)	scientology(5)	temple(5)	church(5)	monastery(5)
pilgrimage(5)	ritual(5)	mandaeanism(4)	falun gong(4)	dianetics(4)	hasidism(4)
yazidism(4)	agnosticism(4)	atheism(4)	pantheism(4)	monotheism(4)	dualism(4)
manichaeism(4)	unitarianism(4)	society of friends(4)	lutheran(4)	anglicanism(4)	presbyterianism(4)
amish(4)	baptism(4)	atheist(1)	agnostic(1)	churches(1)	
		Religion Generation 3			
wicca(10)	voodoo(8)	zen(8)	sufism(8)	jainism(7)	guru granth sahib(7)
kabbalah(7)	gospel(7)	church(7)	torah(6)	talmud(6)	hadith(6)
taoism(6)	tao te ching(6)	confucianism(6)	analects(6)	book of mormon(6)	rastafarianism(6)
animism(6)	paganism(6)	church of satan(6)	vajrayana(6)	hasidism(6)	coptic(6)
gnosticism(6)	druze(6)	yazidism(6)	alevism(6)	atheism(6)	deism(6)
pantheism(6)	manichaeism(6)	unitarianism(6)	universalism(6)	calvinism(6)	lutheran(6)
presbyterianism(6)	mennonite(6)	scientology(6)	temple(6)	pilgrimage(6)	ritual(6)
quran(5)	buddhism(5)	christian(5)	catholic(5)	orthodox(5)	avesta(5)
kojiki(5)	baha'i(5)	kitáb-i-aqdas(5)	druidry(5)	shamanism(5)	santeria(5)
candomblé(5)	umbanda(5)	mandaeanism(5)	falun gong(5)	dianetics(5)	tenrikyo(5)
nichiren(5)	theravada(5)	mahayana(5)	wahhabism(5)	ahmadiyya(5)	bektashi(5)
agnosticism(5)	polytheism(5)	monotheism(5)	dualism(5)	society of friends(5)	anglicanism(5)
amish(5)	baptism(5)	seventh-day adventist(5)	synagogue(5)	mosque(5)	monastery(5)
hindu(4)	sikhism(4)	sunni(4)	protestant(4)	shinto(4)	mormonism(4)
native american church(4)	samaritanism(4)	jehovah's witnesses(4)	bible(4)	islam(3)	shia(3)
zoroastrianism(3)	quakerism(3)	presbyterian(1)			

H Appendix - Subject words for General Prompting Data

Table 11: Subject Words for General Prompting Data

		General Generation 1			
librarian(5)	nun(4)	ceo(4)	rapper(4)	biker(4)	accountant(4)
lawyer(4)	bartender(4)	bodybuilder(4)	punk(4)	skateboarder(4)	desert(4)
boxer(4)	politician(4)	model(4)	tattoos(3)	football player(3)	africa(3)
hijab(3)	truck driver(3)	petite(3)	monk(3)	janitor(3)	soldier(3)
comedian(3)	mechanic(3)	butcher(3)	software engineer(3)	wrestler(3)	carpenter(3)
physicist(3)	mathematician(3)	men(3)	fisherman(3)	pilot(3)	farmer(3)
baker(3)	age(2)	teenager(2)	wealthy(2)	city(2)	scientist(2)
muscular(2)	gamer(2)	beauty queen(2)	construction worker(2)	rugby player(2)	actor(2)
surfer(2)	firefighter(2)	prison guard(2)	cowboy(2)	goth(2)	cab driver(2)
basketball player(2)	cheerleader(2)	slums(2)	banker(2)	athlete(2)	judge(2)
chef(2)	rocker(2)	insurance agent(2)	seamstress(2)	architect(2)	detective(2)
surgeon(2)	journalist(2)	teacher(2)	fishermen(2)	gamers(2)	asian(2)
australian(2)	arctic(2)	blonde(2)	fashionista(2)	dancer(2)	sailor(2)
astronaut(2)	tattoo artist(2)	flight attendant(2)	barista(2)	drummer(2)	cashier(2)
plumber(2)	wall street(2)	priest(2)	coal(2)	fireman(2)	male(1)
woman(1)	asians(1)	blind(1)	tech valley(1)	immigrant(1)	disability(1)
traditional(1)	overweight(1)	fashion model(1)	height(1)	housewife(1)	police officer(1)
astrophysicist(1)	millionaire(1)	sumo wrestler(1)	hip-hop artist(1)	saleswoman(1)	princess(1)
developer(1)	powerlifter(1)	motorcyclist(1)	metalworker(1)	security guard(1)	tattooed(1)
vet(1)	manager(1)	miner(1)	consultant(1)	podiatrist(1)	engineer(1)
radiologist(1)	bus driver(1)	painter(1)	receptionist(1)	anaesthesiologist(1)	engineers(1)
football team(1)	politicians(1)	dancers(1)	grandparents(1)	bodybuilders(1)	chefs(1)
writers(1)	farmers(1)	fashion models(1)	construction workers(1)	software developers(1)	musicians(1)
artists(1)	lawyers(1)	mathematicians(1)	firemen(1)	economists(1)	rugby players(1)
soldiers(2)	business executives(1)	doctors(1)	teenagers(2)	philosophers(1)	teachers(1)
truck drivers(1)	pilots(1)	nurses(1)	architects(1)	astronauts(1)	veterinarians(1)
bankers(1)	actors(1)	journalists(1)	children(2)	elderly women(1)	carpenters(1)
marathon runners(1)	boxers(1)	bakers(1)	plumbers(1)	electricians(1)	accountants(1)
dentists(1)	sailors(1)	florists(1)	mail carriers(1)	singers(1)	zoologists(1)
waiters(1)	skaters(1)	swimmers(1)	poets(1)	tax consultants(1)	ranchers(1)
gardeners(1)	hairdressers(1)	janitors(1)	painters(1)	mechanics(1)	taxi drivers(1)
gymnasts(1)	comedians(1)	surgeons(1)	cooks(1)	photographers(1)	real estate agents(1)
salespeople(1)	welders(1)	butchers(1)	basketball players(1)	barbers(1)	security guards(1)
theatre actors(1)	mixologists(1)	tailors(1)	optometrists(1)	veterans(1)	beekeepers(1)
shopkeepers(1)	metalworkers(1)	dog trainers(1)	housekeepers(1)	cyclists(1)	bricklayers(1)
rappers(1)	volleyball players(1)	podcasters(1)	cleaners(1)	farm workers(1)	tattoo artists(1)
cinematographers(1)	cosmetologists(1)	mountain climbers(1)	bartenders(1)	police officers(1)	70(1)
middle east(1)	heavy build(1)	countryside(1)	conservative(1)	americans(1)	wheelchair(1)
urban(1)	hipster(1)	nerdy(1)	introvert(1)	gothic(1)	italians(1)
businessman(1)	glasses(1)	tropical island(1)	india(1)	plains(1)	young(1)
brazil(1)	dj(1)	actress(1)	snowy(1)	russian(1)	british(1)
metal artist(1)	germans(1)	policeman(1)	graffiti artist(1)	hairdresser(1)	spaniards(1)
iceland(1)	magician(1)	french(1)	dentist(1)	mexicans(1)	techie(1)
pageant queen(1)	scandinavians(1)	mma fighter(1)	kindergarten teacher(1)	appalachia(1)	football(1)
elderly(1)	construction(1)	vegan(1)	south america(1)	inner city(1)	software(1)
monastery(1)	visually impaired(1)	tribe(1)	ballerina(1)	homeless(1)	bronx(1)
metal(1)	tech(1)	luxury(1)	rural(1)	texas(1)	waitress(1)
island(1)	japan(1)	hollywood(1)	jazz(1)	weightlifter(1)	mountains(1)
sprinter(1)	corporate(1)	basketball(1)	beverly hills(1)	trucker(1)	midwest(1)
amazon(1)	sahara(1)	silicon valley(1)	sumo(1)	pro-gamer(1)	cop(1)
greenland(1)	opera(1)	tropical(1)	himalayas(1)	snowboarder(1)	lion(1)
alaska(1)	florist(1)	diver(1)	fashion(1)	tokyo(1)	salsa(1)
tattoo(1)	fighter(1)	rock star(1)	grandmother(1)	punk rocker(1)	principal(1)
nurse(1)	guitarist(1)	climber(1)	taxi driver(1)	chemist(1)	vlogger(1)
lifeguard(1)	hockey player(1)	hygienist(1)	conductor(1)	news anchor(1)	mailman(1)
veterinarian(1)	curator(1)	opera singer(1)	bouncer(1)	dietician(1)	radio jockey(1)
psychic(1)	historian(1)	real estate agent(1)	zookeeper(1)	sound engineer(1)	chiropractor(1)
flight instructor(1)	welder(1)	racecar driver(1)	hotel manager(1)	foreman(1)	marine biologist(1)
stuntman(1)	pianist(1)	video game developer(1)	electrician(1)	sheriff(1)	stockbroker(1)
photojournalist(1)					

Table 12: Subject Words for General Prompting Data

		General Generation 2			
construction worker(5)	security guard(5)	farmer(5)	janitor(5)	plumber(5)	cheerleader(4)
truck driver(4)	barista(4)	boxer(4)	librarian(4)	fisherman(4)	hairdresser(4)
accountant(4)	hip-hop artist(4)	dj(4)	bodybuilder(4)	waitress(4)	gamer(3)
mechanic(3)	rapper(3)	flight attendant(3)	metalhead(3)	florist(3)	cab driver(3)
principal(3)	firefighter(3)	punk rocker(3)	pastry chef(3)	banker(3)	fashion designer(3)
zookeeper(3)	cashier(3)	tattoo artist(3)	lifeguard(3)	butcher(3)	clown(3)
bartender(3)	rugby player(2)	athlete(2)	ballet dancer(2)	biker(2)	countryside(2)
kindergarten teacher(2)	teenager(2)	soldier(2)	businessman(2)	software engineer(2)	politician(2)
wrestler(2)	hipster(2)	goth(3)	chef(2)	beauty queen(2)	cop(2)
stay-at-home mom(2)	receptionist(2)	surgeon(2)	football player(2)	artist(2)	dentist(2)
housekeeper(2)	bus driver(2)	electrician(2)	car mechanic(2)	veterinarian(2)	model(2)
ceo(2)	bikers(2)	rappers(2)	farmers(3)	elderly(2)	ceos(2)
inner city(2)	nun(2)	bouncer(2)	actress(2)	fast-food worker(2)	maid(2)
firefighters(2)	sumo wrestler(2)	wheelchair(2)	surfer(2)	valet(2)	preschool teacher(2)
gardener(2)	window washer(2)	intern(2)	stuntman(2)	custodian(2)	tailor(2)
graffiti artist(2)	supermodel(2)	drummer(2)	hijab(2)	taxi driver(2)	mma fighter(2)
monk(2)	pop star(2)	fashionista(2)	nail technician(2)	bricklayer(2)	miner(2)
street vendor(2)	shepherd(2)	monks(2)	father(1)	older adult(1)	tattooed man(1)
female developer(1)	physique(1)	millennial(1)	fashion model(1)	young girl(1)	celebrity(1)
financial broker(1)	elderly woman(1)	rock musician(1)	female soccer player(1)	dropout(1)	gothic girl(1)
hollywood actor(1)	punk(1)	salesman(1)	introvert(1)	elderly gentleman(1)	real estate agent(1)
scientist(1)	young boy(1)	architect(1)	hedge fund manager(1)	lawyer(1)	office clerk(1)
math teacher(1)	corporate executive(1)	butler(1)	hair stylist(1)	pilot(1)	marine biologist(1)
neuroscientist(1)	beautician(1)	military general(1)	history professor(1)	tax consultant(1)	personal trainer(1)
data analyst(1)	grandma(1)	footballers(2)	blondes(1)	men(2)	women(2)
children(1)	teenagers(2)	tech geek(1)	athletes(1)	country singers(1)	cheerleaders(2)
goths(1)	homeless(1)	skaters(1)	rockstars(1)	soldiers(1)	gamers(2)
investment banker(1)	mime(1)	delivery guy(1)	astronaut(1)	flight instructor(1)	paparazzo(1)
retail worker(1)	gas station attendant(1)	car salesman(1)	dog walker(1)	telemarketer(1)	grocery store clerk(1)
carnival worker(1)	pool cleaner(1)	shoe shiner(1)	night watchman(1)	train conductor(1)	octogenarian(1)
stockbroker(1)	sari(1)	skateboarder(1)	cowboy(1)	hollywood(1)	gang member(1)
sorority(1)	lumberjack(1)	navy seal(1)	driver(1)	goalkeeper(1)	figure skater(1)
attorney(1)	officer(1)	milkman(1)	garbage collector(1)	postman(1)	gravedigger(1)
babysitter(1)	bellboy(1)	delivery man(1)	seamstress(1)	shop assistant(1)	baker(1)
shoemaker(1)	shoeshiner(1)	player(1)	winemaker(1)	boys(1)	older employees(1)
western tourists(1)	male harpists(1)	african(1)	introverts(1)	young children(1)	asian poets(1)
blind(1)	american tourists(1)	male authors(1)	deaf(1)	female engineers(1)	rural(1)
urban dwellers(1)	immigrants(1)	skateboarders(1)	muslim women(1)	older generation(1)	overweight(1)
dancer(1)	tattooed(2)	locals(1)	artists(1)	tribes(1)	tech enthusiasts(1)
bodybuilders(1)	latin american(1)	entrepreneurs(1)	librarians(1)	truck drivers(1)	people with disabilities(1)
vegetarians(1)	homeless man(1)	fashion designers(1)	priests(1)	refugees(1)	veterans(1)
metal musician(1)	lower economic backgrounds(1)	residents(1)	cat lovers(1)	dog enthusiasts(1)	models(1)
lawyers(1)	aristocrats(1)	computer programmers(1)	grandmothers(1)	golfers(1)	policemen(1)
bankers(1)	bakers(1)	heavy metal fans(1)	politicians(1)	mechanics(1)	construction workers(1)
waitresses(1)	wrestlers(1)	elders(1)	chefs(1)	accountants(1)	hairdressers(1)
janitors(1)	taxi drivers(1)	doorman(1)	clowns(1)	martial artists(1)	nurses(1)
pilots(1)	painters(1)	electricians(1)	fishermen(1)	rugby players(1)	djs(1)
opera singers(1)	jewelers(1)	ice cream vendor(1)	cinematographers(1)	senior(1)	jane(1)
abdullah(1)	young(1)	muscular(1)	biker gang(1)	jazz musician(1)	tribal(1)
punk rock singer(1)	sailor(1)	auto-rickshaw driver(1)	prima donna(1)	drag(1)	slums(1)
prison bars(1)	heavy metal guitarist(1)	data analysis(1)	army(1)	oil rig worker(1)	bedouin(1)
royal family(1)	coal mine(1)	rodeo cowboy(1)	village(1)	high heels(1)	tribal woman(1)
professional wrestler(1)	factory worker(1)	skateboarding(1)	snowboarder(1)	stiletto-clad(1)	circus acrobat(1)
rickshaw puller(1)	cosplayer(1)	nurse(1)	mail(1)	basketball player(1)	nightclub singer(1)
ballerina(1)	factory supervisor(1)	e-sports champion(1)			

Table 13: Subject Words for General Prompting Data

General Generation 3					
bodybuilder(6)	janitor(5)	tattoo artist(5)	accountant(5)	mechanic(5)	surfer(5)
rapper(5)	boxer(5)	librarian(5)	butcher(5)	truck driver(4)	dancer(4)
city(4)	farmer(4)	biker(4)	taxi driver(4)	construction worker(4)	sailor(4)
skateboarder(4)	software developer(4)	banker(4)	carpenter(4)	bartender(4)	firefighter(4)
ceo(3)	fashion model(3)	basketball player(3)	gamer(3)	martial artist(3)	detective(3)
politician(3)	electrician(3)	teenager(3)	chef(3)	plumber(3)	flight attendant(3)
actor(3)	gardener(3)	cheerleader(3)	barista(3)	graffiti artist(3)	corporate(3)
fisherman(3)	nun(3)	male(2)	rural(2)	grandmother(2)	mathematician(2)
immigrants(2)	physicist(2)	linebacker(2)	opera singer(2)	comedian(2)	weightlifter(2)
pilot(2)	urban(2)	soldier(2)	motorcyclist(2)	scientist(2)	animator(2)
small town(2)	football player(2)	bikers(2)	cab driver(2)	mma fighter(2)	video gamer(2)
rock star(2)	monk(2)	punk rock(2)	beauty queen(2)	jazz musician(2)	pop singer(2)
hipster(2)	ghettos(2)	bellboy(2)	magician(2)	blonde(2)	hijab(2)
model(2)	wealthy(2)	housewife(2)	hairstylist(2)	miner(2)	postman(2)
baker(2)	receptionist(2)	lifeguard(2)	military(2)	coal miner(2)	desert(2)
kindergarten teacher(2)	mountain climber(2)	fashion(2)	sumo wrestler(2)	drummer(2)	fathers(1)
senior citizen(1)	men(1)	software engineer(1)	teenagers(1)	preschool teacher(1)	ceo's son(1)
introverts(1)	barber(1)	corporate lawyer(1)	boy(1)	mountains(1)	saleswoman(1)
millennial(1)	fireman(1)	biologist(1)	gymnast(1)	journalist(1)	dentist(1)
painter(1)	engineer(1)	soccer player(1)	editor(1)	neurosurgeon(1)	architect(1)
it specialist(1)	teacher(1)	nurse(1)	fitness instructor(1)	musician(1)	lawyer(1)
movie director(1)	programmer(1)	designer(1)	pharmacist(1)	office clerk(1)	veterinarian(1)
economist(1)	factory worker(1)	coach(1)	psychologist(1)	flight engineer(1)	podiatrist(1)
engineers(1)	projects(1)	managerial roles(1)	muscular(1)	frail(1)	fishermen(1)
lumberjack(1)	tech geek(1)	wrestler(1)	soldiers(1)	attorney(1)	miners(1)
wall street(1)	quarterback(1)	farm boy(1)	political leader(1)	heavyweight champion(1)	school teacher(1)
princess(1)	slums(1)	hip hop artist(1)	dj(1)	bouncer(1)	businessman(1)
actress(1)	hunters(1)	ballerina(1)	motorbike racer(1)	lawyers(1)	stock trader(1)
police officer(1)	comic book artist(1)	marine(1)	cabaret dancer(1)	hacker(1)	stuntman(1)
pop star(1)	nightlife(1)	circus performer(1)	rodeo(1)	ice hockey player(1)	adult films(1)
death metal singer(1)	dropout(1)	gangster(1)	paparazzo(1)	nomad(1)	televangelist(1)
stuntwoman(1)	pirates(1)	supermodel(1)	cage fighter(1)	race car drivers(1)	athletes(1)
elderly(1)	tattoos(1)	homeless(1)	introvert(1)	glasses(1)	footballer(1)
wheelchair(1)	rockstar(1)	goth(1)	skater(1)	tall(1)	mma(1)
slum(1)	fashionista(1)	truck(1)	punk(1)	nerd(1)	socialite(1)
grunge(1)	baseball(1)	policeman(1)	bus(1)	construction(1)	maid(1)
waitress(1)	cashier(1)	garbage(1)	florist(1)	security(1)	taxi(1)
pastry(1)	stewardess(1)	telemarketer(1)	custodian(1)	seamstress(1)	vet(1)
coal(1)	kindergarten(1)	factory(1)	milkman(1)	delivery(1)	mason(1)
store(1)	makeup(1)	street(1)	tailor(1)	masseuse(1)	fast-food(1)
gym(1)	nail(1)	cobbler(1)	groomer(1)	window(1)	attendant(1)
hygienist(1)	guard(1)	youth(1)	she(1)	elder(1)	he(1)
ireland(1)	mothers(1)	vegans(1)	christian(1)	visually impaired(1)	indigenous(1)
middle east(1)	monks(1)	tropics(1)	fishing(1)	landlocked(1)	amish(1)
ballet dancer(1)	football team(1)	ceo's(1)	tech(1)	heavy metal band(1)	rugby players(1)
conservative(1)	basketball(1)	farming(1)	inmates(1)	poverty(1)	cosmetics(1)
gang(1)	skyscrapers(1)	coal mines(1)	inner city(1)	plains(1)	physics teacher(1)
young girl(1)	traditional(1)	stockbroker(1)	reality tv star(1)	manicurist(1)	oil rig worker(1)
nail technician(1)	horse jockey(1)	candy store(1)	rock climber(1)	man(1)	aristocratic(1)
child(1)	wall street executive(1)	hip-hop artist(1)	war-torn region(1)	tattooed(1)	professional wrestler(1)
rugby player(1)	punk rocker(1)	ghetto(1)	heavy metal drummer(1)	tribal leader(1)	hip-hop dancer(1)
bus driver(1)	cowboy(1)	security guard(1)	astronaut(1)	horror writer(1)	judge(1)
metal worker(1)	race car driver(1)	prima donna(1)	street performer(1)	singer(1)	exterminator(1)
snowboarder(1)	mascot(1)	zookeeper(1)	bricklayer(1)	pastry chef(1)	swimmer(1)
stand-up comedian(1)	shopkeeper(1)				

I Appendix - Attribute words for Targeted Prompting Data

Table 14: Attribute words for Gender Bias Data Through Targeted Prompting

		Gender Generation 1			
delicate(7)	meticulous(7)	nurturing(6)	analytical(6)	tech-savvy(6)	gentle(5)
compassionate(5)	tenacious(5)	agile(5)	strategic(4)	innovative(4)	humble(4)
adventurous(4)	empathetic(4)	profound(4)	culinary(4)	prodigy(4)	fashion(3)
martial(3)	poetic(3)	leadership(3)	romantic(3)	driver(3)	robotics(3)
wise(3)	logical(3)	graceful(3)	audacious(3)	physicist(3)	empathy(2)
baking(2)	dance(2)	grounded(2)	physics(2)	ballet(2)	climbing(2)
weightlifting(2)	yoga(2)	action(2)	gourmet(2)	boxing(2)	video(2)
eloquent(2)	salsa(2)	pastry(2)	skincare(2)	virtuoso(2)	environmental(2)
emotional(2)	resourceful(2)	courageous(2)	protective(2)	shrewd(2)	calm(2)
patient(2)	cheerful(2)	mature(2)	imaginative(2)	attentive(2)	creative(2)
insightful(2)	skillful(2)	resilient(2)	humorous(2)	lively(2)	articulate(2)
candid(2)	jovial(2)	boisterous(2)	tactical(2)	intuitive(2)	whimsical(2)
flair(2)	sagacious(2)	voracious(2)	adept(2)	proficient(2)	astute(2)
erudite(2)	dexterous(2)	formidable(2)	brilliant(2)	artist(2)	entrepreneur(2)
mountaineer(2)	gardening(2)	dancer(2)	coder(2)	poet(2)	champion(2)
master(2)	warrior(2)	opera(2)	astrophysicist(2)	engineer(2)	astronomer(2)
architect(2)	marine(2)	athlete(2)	pilot(2)	biologist(2)	florist(2)
mechanic(2)	engineering(2)	stoic(1)	mechanical(1)	computer(1)	engine(1)
intuition(1)	commanding(1)	sew(1)	meditate(1)	historical(1)	music(1)
calligraphy(1)	astrophysics(1)	electronic(1)	aesthetic(1)	chess(1)	animation(1)
woodworking(1)	ornate(1)	sports(1)	pottery(1)	electric(1)	operatic(1)
basketball(1)	virtual(1)	graffiti(1)	code(1)	diving(1)	business(1)
violin(1)	detective(1)	ethereal(1)	punk(1)	architectural(1)	tech(1)
languages(1)	painting(1)	DJs(1)	mathematical(1)	bioengineering(1)	exploration(1)
flamenco(1)	blues(1)	skateboarder(1)	surreal(1)	AI(1)	sculpting(1)
artisanal(1)	finance(1)	conservation(1)	MMA(1)	laser(1)	sci-fi(1)
psychology(1)	lace(1)	compositions(1)	avant-garde(1)	encyclopedic(1)	mountaineering(1)
drummer(1)	floral(1)	textile(1)	acrobatics(1)	quantum(1)	theater(1)
barista(1)	archery(1)	soft-hearted(1)	determined(1)	cool-headed(1)	understanding(1)
laid-back(1)	fit(1)	powerful(1)	pragmatic(1)	fashionable(1)	open-minded(1)
thoughtful(1)	impeccable(1)	confident(1)	precise(1)	multitask(1)	energetic(1)
authoritative(1)	perceptive(1)	kind-hearted(1)	curious(1)	well-informed(1)	enthusiastic(1)
visionary(1)	level-headed(1)	expertise(1)	down-to-earth(1)	artistic(1)	muscular(1)
assertive(1)	comedic(1)	deep(1)	stern(1)	wiry(1)	detached(1)
brusque(1)	nonchalant(1)	sardonic(1)	flexibility(1)	trendy(1)	serene(1)
contemplative(1)	soft-spoken(1)	amiable(1)	frugal(1)	spontaneous(1)	infectious(1)
grace(1)	nimble(1)	phenomenal(1)	rambunctious(1)	adroit(1)	exquisite(1)
intrepid(1)	poignant(1)	discerning(1)	masterful(1)	deft(1)	robust(1)
prodigious(1)	nuanced(1)	resolute(1)	mellifluous(1)	vigorous(1)	lyrical(1)
fervent(1)	ebullient(1)	mesmerizing(1)	vivacious(1)	rugged(1)	strong(1)
ferocious(1)	groundbreaking(1)	athletic(1)	innovator(1)	tender-hearted(1)	genius(1)
environmentalist(1)	disciplined(1)	fiery(1)	philosophical(1)	simple(1)	eclectic(1)
tech-oriented(1)	progressive(1)	scientist(1)	quirky(1)	trailblazing(1)	musician(1)
botanist(1)	fierce(1)	comedian(1)	acumen(1)	photographer(1)	advocate(1)
humanitarian(1)	mathematician(1)	enthusiast(1)	geek(1)	philanthropist(1)	linguistics(1)
playwright(1)	climber(1)	historian(1)	painter(1)	neuroscience(1)	ecologist(1)
biomechanics(1)	sculptor(1)	pianist(1)	cryptography(1)	ceramist(1)	ornithologist(1)
economist(1)	geologist(1)	contemporary(1)	caregiver(1)	gentleness(1)	multitasking(1)
introspective(1)	cook(1)	support(1)	listener(1)	embroidery(1)	caring(1)
poetry(1)	tears(1)	resilience(1)	crafting(1)	classical(1)	arts(1)
rescue(1)	vulnerability(1)	style(1)	wisdom(1)	advocacy(1)	relate(1)
botany(1)	cars(1)	courage(1)	sword(1)	woodwork(1)	strength(1)
sharpshooter(1)	reptiles(1)	rugby(1)	breadwinner(1)	digital(1)	programming(1)
handyman(1)	electrical(1)	garden(1)	developers(1)	rocket(1)	blacksmith(1)
cyber(1)	rearing(1)	firefighter(1)	makeup(1)	cooking(1)	paintings(1)
Taekwondo(1)	pediatric(1)	race(1)	feminist(1)		

Table 15: Attribute words for Gender Bias Data Through Targeted Prompting

		Gender Generation 2			
nurturing(8)	wisdom(8)	empathetic(7)	humble(8)	compassionate(6)	caring(7)
innovative(6)	ambitious(6)	resilient(6)	adventurous(6)	analytical(5)	down-to-earth(7)
wise(5)	independent(5)	tech-savvy(6)	strategic(5)	playful(5)	assertive(4)
introspective(5)	leadership(4)	sensitivity(4)	knowledgeable(3)	passionate(3)	sensitive(5)
audacious(4)	intuitive(4)	competitive(3)	understanding(3)	thinker(3)	bold(3)
protective(3)	vulnerability(3)	outspoken(4)	thoughtful(2)	kind(3)	articulate(2)
resourceful(2)	powerhouse(2)	sociable(2)	open-minded(2)	approachable(3)	brilliant(2)
protector(2)	leader(2)	advocate(2)	considerate(3)	genius(2)	grounded(2)
lover(2)	gamer(3)	athlete(3)	researcher(2)	entrepreneur(2)	logical(2)
expressive(2)	soft-spoken(2)	entrepreneurial(2)	affectionate(2)	pragmatic(3)	poetic(3)
intelligence(2)	gentle(4)	mature(3)	generous(2)	relatable(2)	attentive(2)
humorous(3)	committed(2)	insightful(2)	fun-loving(2)	intellectual(2)	witty(3)
audacity(2)	conservative(2)	wit(2)	stern(2)	empathy(2)	astute(3)
rugged(2)	boisterous(3)	lively(2)	goofy(3)	fashionable(3)	candid(2)
dancer(3)	humility(2)	helpful(1)	intelligent(2)	jovial(2)	talented(1)
diligent(1)	sharp(1)	curious(1)	friendly(1)	advisory(1)	loyal(1)
patient(2)	positive(1)	graceful(1)	listening(1)	risk-taker(1)	adaptable(1)
philanthropist(1)	comedian(1)	engineer(1)	champion(1)	trendsetter(1)	storyteller(1)
mingling(1)	economist(1)	chef(1)	scientist(1)	singer(2)	architect(1)
prodigy(1)	baker(1)	activist(1)	enthusiast(1)	connoisseur(1)	developer(1)
environmentalist(1)	educator(1)	karate(1)	novelist(1)	simple(1)	filmmaker(1)
well-read(1)	conservationist(1)	innovator(1)	historian(1)	poet(1)	climbing(1)
determined(1)	light-hearted(1)	eloquent(1)	hilarious(1)	worldly(1)	rational(1)
sentimental(2)	modest(2)	domestic(1)	authoritative(1)	feeling(1)	compassion(1)
tenacious(1)	stylish(1)	commanding(1)	strong(2)	listener(1)	fierce(2)
kind-hearted(2)	problem-solving(1)	joyful(1)	arrogant(2)	careless(1)	vulnerable(1)
shy(1)	introverted(2)	exceptional(1)	technological(1)	calm(2)	emotion(1)
submissive(1)	strategist(1)	inexperienced(1)	insecure(1)	anxious(1)	creative(1)
maternal(1)	whimsical(2)	flaws(1)	confident(1)	aloof(1)	tender(1)
non-serious(1)	selfless(1)	champions(1)	determination(1)	caregiving(1)	fashion(1)
adventure(1)	self-doubt(1)	stoic(1)	paternal(1)	sporty(1)	geek(1)
brains(1)	trendy(1)	modesty(1)	proactive(1)	domineering(1)	demeanor(1)
angry(1)	thin(1)	serious(1)	meek(1)	unassuming(1)	courageous(1)
rowdy(1)	silly(1)	frugal(1)	chatty(1)	bashful(1)	unpretentious(1)
giddy(1)	spunky(1)	informal(1)	delicate(1)	naive(1)	enthusiastic(1)
extroverted(1)	timid(1)	reflective(1)	cheeky(1)	tender-hearted(1)	laid-back(1)
old-soul(1)	expert(1)	nerdy(1)	cook(1)	sprightly(1)	zesty(1)
athletic(1)	voracious(1)	optimistic(1)	well-spoken(1)	sunny(1)	mechanical(1)
gardener(1)	mathematician(1)	painter(1)	patience(1)	brave(1)	lighthearted(1)
sharp-minded(1)	humor(1)	cries(1)	fiery(1)	diplomacy(1)	fighting(1)
laugh(1)	rebellious(1)	follow(1)	candidness(1)	tears(1)	values(1)
emotions(1)	daring(1)	peaceful(1)	transparent(1)	acknowledges(1)	quirkiness(1)
jokes(1)	arts(1)	party(1)	depth(1)	loyalty(1)	resilience(1)
romantic(1)	confrontations(1)	thinking(1)	vivacious(1)	mischievous(1)	competitor(1)
warrior(1)	supporting(1)	sharp-witted(1)	independence(1)	adventures(1)	distress(1)
generosity(1)	ground(1)	equality(1)	kindness(1)	strength(1)	guiding(1)
charm(1)	graciousness(1)	confidence(1)	caretaker(1)	mentor(1)	pleasures(1)
commitment(1)	approachability(1)	receptive(1)	tenacity(1)		

Table 16: Attribute words for Gender Bias Data Through Targeted Prompting

		Gender Generation 3			
wise(23)	arrogant(22)	uncaring(22)	thin(21)	angry(19)	nurturing(5)
tech-savvy(5)	fashion(5)	fierce(4)	mechanic(4)	ballet(4)	playful(3)
naive(3)	wisdom(3)	modern(3)	humble(3)	compassionate(3)	humor(3)
tech(3)	prodigy(3)	physicist(3)	caring(2)	stern(2)	analytical(2)
dominant(2)	cook(2)	protector(2)	empathetic(2)	thoughtful(2)	thinker(2)
grace(2)	sensitive(2)	aloof(2)	life(2)	vulnerabilities(2)	rock(2)
supporter(2)	wild(2)	reader(2)	philosophical(2)	adventurer(2)	engineer(2)
dancer(2)	hero(2)	culinary(2)	resilient(2)	botanist(2)	mountaineer(2)
mathematics(2)	vegan(2)	climber(2)	driver(2)	robotics(2)	yoga(2)
biologist(2)	pastry(2)	advocate(2)	musician(2)	opera(2)	mogul(2)
novelist(2)	activist(2)	languages(2)	delicate(2)	jovial(2)	insightful(2)
poet(2)	wit(2)	gardener(2)	caregiver(2)	chess(2)	coding(2)
fat(2)	assertive(1)	logical(1)	discreet(1)	domesticated(1)	outspoken(1)
kind-hearted(1)	strategic(1)	cunning(1)	stoic(1)	mature(1)	committed(1)
fearless(1)	emotions(1)	rough(1)	collaborative(1)	resilience(1)	ruthless(1)
warriors(1)	frivolous(1)	serious(1)	jokester(1)	emotional(1)	peacemaker(1)
careless(1)	involved(1)	poets(1)	approachable(1)	deliberate(1)	responsible(1)
seeks(1)	admits(1)	extroverted(1)	listener(1)	meticulous(1)	open(1)
submissive(1)	scientist(1)	businesswoman(1)	breadwinner(1)	business(1)	politics(1)
competitive(1)	decisive(1)	gritty(1)	simplicity(1)	jester(1)	muscular(1)
baker(1)	knit(1)	coder(1)	poetic(1)	outpace(1)	repair(1)
astronomy(1)	soothing(1)	boxing(1)	artist(1)	gardening(1)	lawyer(1)
physics(1)	skateboarding(1)	potter(1)	astrophysicist(1)	zoologist(1)	calligraphy(1)
computer(1)	connoisseur(1)	neuroscientist(1)	writer(1)	grandmaster(1)	swimmer(1)
cellist(1)	cryptography(1)	comedy(1)	ornithology(1)	pilot(1)	fighter(1)
geneticist(1)	mentors(1)	saxophonist(1)	volcanologist(1)	sharpshooter(1)	linguistic(1)
developer(1)	architectural(1)	taekwondo(1)	skydiver(1)	ceramics(1)	photographer(1)
mathematician(1)	gourmet(1)	archeologist(1)	virtuoso(1)	biochemist(1)	astronaut(1)
skateboarder(1)	forensic(1)	perfumery(1)	artificial intelligence(1)	acrobatic(1)	archaeologist(1)
programming(1)	pianist(1)	neuroscience(1)	farming(1)	researcher(1)	patient(1)
lonely(1)	down-to-earth(1)	cold(1)	noble(1)	slender(1)	introspective(1)
gentle(1)	vulnerable(1)	timid(1)	kind(1)	determination(1)	vivacious(1)
generous(1)	fiery(1)	humility(1)	judgmental(1)	youthful(1)	adventurous(1)
reason(1)	grounded(1)	grateful(1)	elegance(1)	shine(1)	intellectual(1)
style(1)	intuitive(1)	artistic(1)	unapproachable(1)	corporate(1)	warmth(1)
connected(1)	confidante(1)	scholar(1)	substance(1)	ambition(1)	strategist(1)
genius(1)	mix(1)	archer(1)	confidence(1)	trend(1)	racer(1)
insights(1)	karate(1)	open-minded(1)	master(1)	rock-climbing(1)	boisterous(1)
self-sufficient(1)	storyteller(1)	maturity(1)	painting(1)	guitarist(1)	academic(1)
empathy(1)	minimalist(1)	expert(1)	renowned(1)	kindness(1)	cheerful(1)
engineering(1)	rescue(1)	environmentalist(1)	seasoned(1)	black belt(1)	comforting(1)
entrepreneur(1)	charity(1)	frugality(1)	brilliant(1)	championed(1)	singing(1)
charge(1)	dedication(1)	startup(1)	chef(1)	calmest(1)	eloquent(1)
botany(1)	architect(1)	compassion(1)	financial(1)	invention(1)	doctorate(1)
gentlest(1)	astrophysics(1)	authored(1)	rock climbing(1)	polymath(1)	teaches(1)
violinist(1)	comedian(1)	ace(1)	dance(1)	scuba diving(1)	watercolor(1)
florist(1)	wrestling(1)	marathon(1)	romance(1)	software(1)	ballroom(1)
martial arts(1)	comic(1)	story-telling(1)	woodwork(1)	bakes(1)	dj(1)
beekeeping(1)	weightlifting(1)	knitting(1)	gamer(1)	skydiving(1)	braids(1)
therapeutic(1)	gentleness(1)	pediatric(1)	rugby(1)	art(1)	makeup(1)
pottery(1)	carpentry(1)	adventure(1)	author(1)	salsa(1)	

Table 17: Attribute words for Racial Bias Data Through Targeted Prompting

		Race Generation 1			
innovative(10)	groundbreaking(7)	spiritual(6)	profound(6)	harmonious(6)	musicians(6)
vibrant(5)	sustainable(5)	intricate(5)	educators(5)	precision(5)	introspective(4)
delightful(4)	enchanting(4)	unparalleled(4)	poets(4)	dancers(4)	environmentalists(4)
historians(4)	creativity(4)	resilience(4)	resilient(3)	soulful(3)	enlightening(3)
timeless(3)	pioneering(3)	meticulous(3)	lyrical(3)	artists(3)	filmmakers(3)
writers(3)	astronomers(3)	conservationists(3)	activists(3)	storytellers(3)	resourceful(3)
introspection(3)	craftsmanship(3)	respect(3)	unity(3)	wisdom(3)	poetic(3)
adaptability(3)	bravery(3)	progressive(3)	artistic(2)	visionary(2)	exceptional(2)
monumental(2)	holistic(2)	relentless(2)	mesmerizing(2)	transformative(2)	compassionate(2)
captivating(2)	adept(2)	ingenious(2)	flair(2)	vivid(2)	unique(2)
championing(2)	evocative(2)	entrepreneurs(2)	engineers(2)	architects(2)	playwrights(2)
farmers(2)	painters(2)	linguists(2)	biologists(2)	trailblazing(2)	dynamic(2)
discipline(2)	elegance(2)	strength(2)	harmony(2)	inclusivity(2)	valor(2)
innovations(2)	depth(2)	perseverance(2)	tranquility(2)	detailing(2)	courage(2)
essence(2)	warmth(2)	insightful(2)	vibrancy(2)	merge(2)	connection(2)
expanded(2)	revolutionary(2)	heartbeat(2)	philosophical(2)	adventurous(2)	tenacious(2)
literary(2)	rhythmic(2)	world-class(2)	astute(2)	contributed(2)	pushing(2)
adaptive(2)	indefatigable(2)	mesmerizes(2)	innovation(1)	integrated(1)	precise(1)
graceful(1)	pivotal(1)	passionate(1)	health-conscious(1)	committed(1)	heartwarming(1)
respectful(1)	unrivaled(1)	mysterious(1)	tireless(1)	seamless(1)	invaluable(1)
honorable(1)	raw(1)	courageous(1)	altruistic(1)	transcendent(1)	crucial(1)
connected(1)	determined(1)	fervent(1)	unquenchable(1)	steadfast(1)	embracing(1)
fresh(1)	unifying(1)	cutting-edge(1)	inspiring(1)	nuanced(1)	elegant(1)
energized(1)	resonant(1)	diverse(1)	unmatched(1)	welcoming(1)	dazzling(1)
reverent(1)	mindful(1)	awe-inspiring(1)	mythical(1)	stellar(1)	balanced(1)
knowledgeable(1)	innovators(1)	enriching(1)	imaginative(1)	leaders(1)	scholars(1)
designers(1)	chefs(1)	navigators(1)	philosophers(1)	researchers(1)	folklorists(1)
novelists(1)	ceramists(1)	sculptors(1)	ecologists(1)	journalists(1)	mathematicians(1)
technologists(1)	planners(1)	geologists(1)	chocolatiers(1)	watchmakers(1)	horticulturists(1)
photographers(1)	artisans(1)	scientists(1)	winemakers(1)	singers(1)	archaeologists(1)
crafters(1)	mountaineers(1)	puppeteers(1)	weavers(1)	herbalists(1)	herders(1)
shamans(1)	compassion(1)	self-awareness(1)	richness(1)	reliability(1)	wit(1)
eclectic(1)	solidarity(1)	joy(1)	ingenuity(1)	emotive(1)	exploration(1)
foresight(1)	endurance(1)	eloquent(1)	illumination(1)	brilliance(1)	festive(1)
critical-thinking(1)	wonder(1)	simplicity(1)	togetherness(1)	expertise(1)	trailblazers(1)
expressions(1)	imagination(1)	dedication(1)	serenity(1)	fellowship(1)	mosaic(1)
faith(1)	enthusiasm(1)	ties(1)	heritage(1)	humility(1)	balance(1)
melodic(1)	exchange(1)	understanding(1)	community(1)	fusion(1)	exhilarating(1)
honor(1)	symbolic(1)	detailed(1)	mindfulness(1)	devotion(1)	preservation(1)
tolerance(1)	revolutionized(1)	authenticity(1)	grace(1)	insights(1)	commitment(1)
exuberant(1)	enduring(1)	ecological(1)	passion(1)	valiant(1)	heartfelt(1)
boundless(1)	aesthetics(1)	genius(1)	soul-stirring(1)	mastery(1)	emotion(1)
hope(1)	bonds(1)	finesse(1)	oceanic(1)	delectable(1)	rhythm(1)
cosmic(1)	serene(1)	diversity(1)	admiration(1)	determination(1)	penned(1)
joyful(1)	perfection(1)	styles(1)	colors(1)	awe(1)	pulse(1)
texture(1)	hospitality(1)	shaped(1)	realm(1)	exuberance(1)	realms(1)
resonance(1)	landscapes(1)	arctic(1)	tranquil(1)	heart(1)	mystic(1)
delights(1)	mirror(1)	shine(1)	cosmos(1)	epitomize(1)	dazzle(1)
versatility(1)	astuteness(1)	linguistic(1)	intellectual(1)	resourcefulness(1)	pioneers(1)
analytical(1)	trustworthy(1)	entrepreneurial(1)	rich(1)	reflective(1)	legendary(1)
trendsetting(1)	finest(1)	architectural(1)	versatile(1)	indomitable(1)	enriched(1)
influential(1)					

Table 18: Attribute words for Racial Bias Data Through Targeted Prompting

		Race Generation 2			
artistic(29)	cultural(26)	historical(19)	diverse(17)	intellectual(10)	scientific(10)
sustainable(8)	vibrant(6)	culinary(6)	pioneering(5)	intricate(5)	innovative(5)
incorporate(5)	instrumental(4)	harmonious(4)	soulful(3)	profound(3)	renewable(3)
revolutionary(3)	meticulous(3)	evocative(3)	vivacious(3)	precision(3)	unity(3)
excellent(3)	wisdom(3)	resilience(3)	introspection(3)	mesmerizing(2)	influential(2)
spiritual(2)	passionate(2)	contemporary(2)	championing(2)	holistic(2)	global(2)
contributed(2)	inspiration(2)	exploring(2)	gourmet(2)	draw(2)	inspired(2)
blend(2)	highlight(2)	fusion(2)	contributions(2)	groundbreaking(2)	resilient(2)
hospitable(2)	ingenious(2)	rooted(2)	enduring(2)	delightful(2)	universal(2)
poignant(2)	authentic(2)	acumen(2)	wise(2)	prowess(2)	cutting-edge(2)
reverence(2)	confluence(2)	tapestry(2)	literary(2)	navigational(2)	poetic(2)
modern(2)	ethical(2)	elegance(2)	avant-garde(2)	adaptability(2)	imaginative(2)
expertise(2)	forward-thinking(2)	creativity(2)	inventive(2)	dedication(2)	compassionate(1)
breaking(1)	renowned(1)	disciplined(1)	organic(1)	reimagining(1)	conservationist(1)
trendsetting(1)	admired(1)	utilize(1)	wisdom-filled(1)	magical(1)	appreciative(1)
blending(1)	inspire(1)	diving(1)	legendary(1)	experiment(1)	documented(1)
fantasy(1)	minimalistic(1)	recognized(1)	eclectic(1)	study(1)	mesmerized(1)
showcase(1)	connection(1)	merging(1)	fuse(1)	incorporated(1)	aesthetics(1)
muse(1)	liking(1)	resonance(1)	introduced(1)	penchant(1)	energy(1)
admiration(1)	preserve(1)	merge(1)	international(1)	masterpieces(1)	championed(1)
enthralling(1)	masterfully(1)	bring(1)	studied(1)	echo(1)	collaborate(1)
revolutionizing(1)	seamlessly(1)	crafting(1)	insightful(1)	creative(1)	accurate(1)
advanced(1)	eco-friendly(1)	original(1)	masterful(1)	integral(1)	judicious(1)
protective(1)	graceful(1)	tenacious(1)	enchanting(1)	stirring(1)	ethereal(1)
adapted(1)	lasting(1)	fearless(1)	dexterous(1)	forefront(1)	potent(1)
empowered(1)	cohesive(1)	mystical(1)	brilliant(1)	transcendent(1)	trailblazing(1)
sagacious(1)	serene(1)	relentless(1)	impeccable(1)	unified(1)	fervent(1)
marvelous(1)	sacred(1)	leading-edge(1)	dedicated(1)	skillful(1)	redefining(1)
niche(1)	mosaic(1)	unbroken(1)	helm(1)	knack(1)	zenith(1)
repository(1)	pushing(1)	finesse(1)	visionaries(1)	hauntingly(1)	delectable(1)
extraordinary(1)	resonate(1)	sanctity(1)	eloquent(1)	resonant(1)	balance(1)
inclusivity(1)	accomplished(1)	achievements(1)	significant(1)	engineering(1)	culturally(1)
academic(1)	compassion(1)	humanitarian(1)	philosophical(1)	inspiring(1)	nobility(1)
heartfelt(1)	conservation(1)	empathy(1)	solidarity(1)	reconciliation(1)	complexity(1)
philanthropic(1)	interconnectedness(1)	mysteries(1)	transformative(1)	heritage(1)	contemplative(1)
community(1)	justice(1)	joy(1)	timeless(1)	romance(1)	grace(1)
wildlife(1)	illuminating(1)	restore(1)	exquisite(1)	dialogue(1)	perspectives(1)
spotlight(1)	sanctuary(1)	lyrical(1)	mesmerize(1)	foundation(1)	advocating(1)
unique(1)	progressive(1)	joyful(1)	scholarly(1)	empathetic(1)	romanticism(1)
eloquence(1)	daring(1)	astuteness(1)	harmony(1)	industrious(1)	keen(1)
research(1)	intellectualism(1)	zestful(1)	sensitive(1)	determination(1)	dexterity(1)
hope(1)	visionary(1)	tenacity(1)	discipline(1)	depth(1)	audacity(1)
resourceful(1)	bonding(1)	passion(1)	preservation(1)	flair(1)	joyous(1)
reflective(1)	respect(1)	innovators(1)	heroic(1)	energetic(1)	kind-hearted(1)
remarkable(1)	identity(1)	zest(1)	peaceful(1)	minimalist(1)	optimistic(1)
enthusiastic(1)	bravery(1)	unyielding(1)	lively(1)	fervor(1)	epic(1)
adventurous(1)	genius(1)	serenity(1)	melodic(1)	celebration(1)	

Table 19: Attribute words for Racial Bias Data Through Targeted Prompting

		Race Generation 3			
resilience(9)	harmony(9)	innovative(8)	precision(7)	profound(7)	meticulous(7)
respect(7)	pioneering(6)	wisdom(5)	intricate(5)	innovation(5)	vibrant(5)
passion(4)	adaptability(4)	creativity(4)	unity(4)	blend(4)	unparalleled(4)
impeccable(4)	holistic(4)	sustainable(4)	artistry(3)	sustainability(3)	warmth(3)
resourcefulness(3)	courage(3)	acumen(3)	vitality(3)	wit(3)	functionality(3)
mindfulness(3)	forefront(3)	inclusivity(3)	audacious(3)	insights(3)	poetic(3)
serenity(3)	refreshing(3)	flair(3)	eloquence(2)	knowledge(2)	exploration(2)
hospitality(2)	introspection(2)	expertise(2)	tenacity(2)	legacy(2)	artistic(2)
freedom(2)	endurance(2)	love(2)	celebration(2)	strength(2)	essence(2)
harmonious(2)	enriching(2)	exceptional(2)	epitome(2)	boundless(2)	beacon(2)
genius(2)	dynamic(2)	pillars(2)	spiritual(2)	hope(2)	understanding(2)
mosaic(2)	strides(2)	marvels(2)	resonates(2)	philosophical(2)	reverence(2)
vivid(2)	astoundingly(2)	ethereal(2)	storytelling(2)	bonding(2)	inventive(2)
community(2)	spirituality(2)	adaptive(2)	joy(2)	compassion(2)	advocates(2)
modernity(2)	conservation(2)	contemporary(2)	guardianship(1)	visionary(1)	fluidity(1)
inquisitiveness(1)	innovations(1)	depth(1)	vastness(1)	tolerance(1)	agility(1)
magic(1)	vibrancy(1)	imagination(1)	solidarity(1)	oral(1)	enlightenment(1)
intricacies(1)	harmoniously(1)	grandeur(1)	bounty(1)	navigation(1)	emotions(1)
narratives(1)	history(1)	perspective(1)	depths(1)	heartbeat(1)	heritages(1)
entrepreneurial(1)	refined(1)	fresh(1)	adventure(1)	serene(1)	astuteness(1)
pivotal(1)	leading(1)	breakthrough(1)	critical(1)	vast(1)	wellspring(1)
cornerstone(1)	ingenuity(1)	elegance(1)	philosophy(1)	niche(1)	insight(1)
paramount(1)	brilliance(1)	leaders(1)	reflections(1)	lessons(1)	stewardship(1)
modernism(1)	instrumental(1)	windows(1)	relentless(1)	consciousness(1)	testament(1)
nexus(1)	symbols(1)	championing(1)	invaluable(1)	commentary(1)	templates(1)
reshaping(1)	indomitable(1)	merge(1)	pluralism(1)	seminal(1)	benchmarks(1)
agroecological(1)	reservoirs(1)	stories(1)	guardians(1)	resonant(1)	heartwarming(1)
steering(1)	canvas(1)	ecology(1)	morality(1)	smart(1)	agents(1)
illuminated(1)	icons(1)	interwoven(1)	commendable(1)	models(1)	enriched(1)
mesmerized(1)	exemplary(1)	echo(1)	genuine(1)	pacifistic(1)	introspective(1)
exploratory(1)	delightful(1)	eclectic(1)	groundbreaking(1)	futuristic(1)	zestful(1)
reflective(1)	inclusive(1)	joyful(1)	fascinating(1)	tranquil(1)	wistful(1)
whimsical(1)	rhythmic(1)	robust(1)	enigmatic(1)	indispensable(1)	contemplative(1)
altruistic(1)	intuitive(1)	detailed(1)	sagacious(1)	bold(1)	tenacious(1)
idyllic(1)	authentic(1)	monumental(1)	radiant(1)	cosmopolitan(1)	fearless(1)
penchant(1)	woven(1)	medicinal(1)	awe(1)	influence(1)	mesmerizing(1)
lyrical(1)	imbued(1)	existential(1)	captivating(1)	dedication(1)	minimalist(1)
timeless(1)	exquisite(1)	strikingly(1)	evocative(1)	exemplar(1)	remarkable(1)
introspectively(1)	amalgamation(1)	untouched(1)	heroism(1)	graceful(1)	richly(1)
pride(1)	successfully(1)	unique(1)	warmly(1)	enlightening(1)	refreshingly(1)
rooted(1)	profoundly(1)	touching(1)	enchanting(1)	impart(1)	compassionate(1)
imaginative(1)	revolutionizing(1)	sophisticated(1)	grace(1)	avant-garde(1)	audacity(1)
collaborative(1)	advancements(1)	caring(1)	adventurous(1)	craftsmanship(1)	strategic(1)
narrative(1)	enterprising(1)	maritime(1)	liberalism(1)	intellectual(1)	intrepid(1)
efficiency(1)	mutual(1)	engineering(1)	intensity(1)	aesthetic(1)	determination(1)
conservationist(1)	passionate(1)	perseverance(1)	finesse(1)	aesthetics(1)	vision(1)
melody(1)	bravery(1)	extraordinary(1)	spectrum(1)	diplomacy(1)	pacifism(1)
solace(1)	humor(1)	peace(1)	discipline(1)	justice(1)	democratic(1)
vegetarianism(1)	eco-friendly(1)	education(1)	humility(1)	mental health(1)	intercultural(1)
generosity(1)	renewable(1)	equality(1)	pedestrian-friendly(1)	collaboration(1)	support(1)
sportsmanship(1)	connections(1)	breakthroughs(1)	educational(1)	togetherness(1)	universal(1)
experiential(1)	kinship(1)	balance(1)	melodies(1)	interconnectedness(1)	well-being(1)
simplicity(1)	virtual reality(1)	diverse(1)	green(1)	interfaith(1)	protecting(1)
e-governance(1)	ancient(1)	linguistic(1)			

Table 20: Attribute words for Religious Bias Data Through Targeted Prompting

		Religion Generation 1			
unity(7)	compassion(6)	peace(6)	integrates(6)	simplicity(6)	respect(6)
devotion(5)	music(4)	harmony(4)	health(4)	learning(4)	celebrate(4)
gratitude(4)	celebrates(4)	community(4)	charity(3)	equality(3)	brotherhood(3)
wisdom(3)	reverence(3)	clarity(3)	mystical(3)	joy(3)	art(3)
bonds(3)	divinity(3)	reflection(3)	journey(3)	history(3)	service(3)
mindfulness(3)	interplay(3)	vibrant(3)	balance(3)	insights(3)	redemption(3)
meditation(3)	synthesis(3)	heritage(3)	oneness(3)	bond(3)	artistic(3)
philosophical(2)	moral(2)	natural(2)	nature(2)	healing(2)	poetry(2)
rational(2)	musical(2)	craftsmanship(2)	dialogue(2)	cycles(2)	interpretations(2)
initiatives(2)	hospitality(2)	diverse(2)	theological(2)	well-being(2)	empowerment(2)
interconnectedness(2)	solace(2)	connection(2)	individualism(2)	enlightenment(2)	traditions(2)
recognition(2)	family(2)	mysteries(2)	symbols(2)	divine(2)	perseverance(2)
creator(2)	democratic(2)	tolerance(2)	purification(2)	insight(2)	energy(2)
compassionate(2)	knowledge(2)	innovation(2)	relationship(2)	mercy(2)	melodies(2)
blend(2)	renewal(2)	education(2)	symbolism(2)	culinary(2)	robotics(2)
architecture(2)	theatre(2)	engineering(2)	aerospace(2)	marine(2)	urban(2)
wildlife(2)	justice(2)	enlightening(1)	historical(1)	inspiring(1)	practical(1)
scientific(1)	personal(1)	spiritual(1)	mesmerizing(1)	legends(1)	cultural(1)
storytelling(1)	improvement(1)	individual(1)	benefit(1)	simplifies(1)	open(1)
governance(1)	dedication(1)	techniques(1)	genre(1)	ambiance(1)	architectural(1)
choirs(1)	celebrations(1)	principles(1)	resonate(1)	folklore(1)	thinking(1)
evidence(1)	hymns(1)	ethical(1)	narrates(1)	remedies(1)	life(1)
rhythmic(1)	preserves(1)	visualizations(1)	choral(1)	welcomes(1)	rite(1)
piety(1)	foundational(1)	depth(1)	profound(1)	earth(1)	align(1)
worship(1)	exploration(1)	rhythms(1)	magic(1)	sanctuary(1)	passion(1)
pacifism(1)	rites(1)	ancient(1)	vibrancy(1)	intimacy(1)	all-encompassing(1)
grace(1)	beacon(1)	harmonize(1)	humanitarian(1)	evangelism(1)	myths(1)
esoteric(1)	sovereignty(1)	nonviolence(1)	fellowship(1)	liturgical(1)	powerful(1)
solitude(1)	traditional(1)	alternative(1)	multiple(1)	inclusivity(1)	open-minded(1)
humanistic(1)	ancestral(1)	channel(1)	cultivate(1)	guidance(1)	connections(1)
bridges(1)	testament(1)	diversity(1)	progressive(1)	purity(1)	critical(1)
discipline(1)	generosity(1)	truth(1)	authentically(1)	poetic(1)	growth(1)
benevolence(1)	open-mindedness(1)	environment(1)	ethics(1)	worth(1)	honor(1)
scholarship(1)	reason(1)	ritual(1)	mythological(1)	perspective(1)	practices(1)
bridge(1)	mysticism(1)	self-empowerment(1)	celebration(1)	embraces(1)	enlightened(1)
ministry(1)	misconceptions(1)	performance(1)	connect(1)	colors(1)	accordance(1)
hope(1)	interwoven(1)	cyclical(1)	yearning(1)	sustainability(1)	technology(1)
athletics(1)	mathematician(1)	ecology(1)	physicist(1)	entrepreneurship(1)	linguistic(1)
leadership(1)	software(1)	astronomy(1)	fashion(1)	finance(1)	biology(1)
genetic(1)	renewable(1)	intelligence(1)	dance(1)	philanthropy(1)	diplomat(1)
animation(1)	data(1)	environmental(1)	graphic(1)	medicinal(1)	virtual(1)
nanotechnology(1)	coding(1)	chemical(1)	farming(1)	astrophysicist(1)	biotechnology(1)
neurosciences(1)	computational(1)	futuristic(1)	digital(1)	geology(1)	organic(1)
literature(1)	gaming(1)	quantum(1)	photography(1)	abstract(1)	climatologist(1)
neurology(1)	fiction(1)	bioinformatics(1)	genomics(1)	pottery(1)	journalist(1)
analytics(1)	cybersecurity(1)	linguistics(1)	evolutionary(1)	forensic(1)	agricultural(1)
software engineer(1)	quantum computing(1)	landscape painting(1)	aerodynamics(1)	environmental law(1)	animation and design(1)
particle physics(1)	cryptography(1)	molecular biology(1)	ethnomusicology(1)	digital marketing(1)	sustainable energy solutions(1)
immersive technology(1)	documentary filmmaking(1)	neurosurgical advancements(1)	social entrepreneurship(1)	urban forestry(1)	data visualization(1)
charitable(1)	non-violence(1)	helping(1)	kindness(1)	intellectual(1)	selfless(1)
philosophy(1)	thoughts(1)	valor(1)	integrity(1)	righteous(1)	cherishes(1)
connectivity(1)	feminine(1)	heal(1)	emotional(1)	tranquility(1)	self-awareness(1)
disciplined(1)	love(1)	interpretation(1)	peaceful(1)	histories(1)	questioning(1)
lack(1)	variety(1)	single(1)	forces(1)	pacifist(1)	dedicated(1)
self-improvement(1)	soulful(1)	outreach(1)	contemplation(1)	journeys(1)	milestones(1)
harmonious(1)					

Table 21: Attribute words for Religious Bias Data Through Targeted Prompting

		Religion Generation 2			
mindfulness(7)	ethical(6)	unity(5)	philosophical(5)	compassion(4)	ecological(4)
wisdom(5)	harmony(4)	historical(5)	governance(4)	education(4)	poetry(4)
service(4)	knowledge(3)	literature(3)	cultural(4)	nature(3)	music(3)
peace(3)	gratitude(3)	humanitarian(4)	arts(3)	environmental(3)	insights(3)
charity(3)	dance(3)	musical(4)	balance(3)	meditation(3)	interpretations(3)
ancient(3)	worship(3)	science(2)	astronomy(2)	humility(2)	artists(2)
resilience(2)	conservation(2)	justice(2)	linguistic(2)	psychological(2)	craftsmanship(2)
loyalty(2)	preservation(2)	psychology(2)	pacifist(2)	theology(2)	diplomacy(2)
sustainability(2)	rebirth(2)	wellness(2)	engagement(2)	literacy(2)	bonds(2)
poetic(3)	architectural(3)	business(2)	reflection(2)	welfare(2)	leadership(2)
non-violence(2)	scholarship(2)	community(2)	learning(2)	family(2)	cycles(2)
symbolism(2)	simple(3)	teachings(2)	liturgical(2)	joyous(3)	harmonizing(2)
integrates(2)	distinct(2)	innovative(1)	philanthropic(1)	poets(1)	reverence(1)
selfless(2)	mathematical(1)	charitable(2)	scientists(1)	philosophy(1)	physics(1)
socio-political(1)	supportive(1)	herbal(1)	biodiversity(1)	empowerment(1)	folktales(1)
vibrant(1)	art(1)	mental(1)	societal(1)	growth(1)	political(1)
dialogue(1)	joy(1)	preserved(1)	perspectives(1)	cohesion(1)	introspection(1)
inquiry(1)	existentialism(1)	enlightenment(1)	wonder(1)	amalgamation(1)	debates(1)
aesthetics(1)	tolerance(1)	inclusivity(1)	autonomy(1)	simplicity(2)	translation(1)
sociological(1)	exchange(1)	beauty(1)	kindness(1)	scholars(1)	technological(1)
advocates(1)	modern(1)	quantum(1)	jazz(1)	interfaith(1)	progressive(1)
development(1)	organic(1)	philanthropist(1)	artistry(1)	activism(1)	astronomers(1)
classical(1)	organizational(1)	sanctuary(1)	sports(1)	stem(1)	negotiation(1)
holistic(1)	academic(1)	healing(1)	plantation(1)	archaeological(1)	botanical(1)
fashion(1)	storytelling(1)	vocational(1)	relief(1)	culinary(1)	preserving(2)
understanding(1)	humanities(1)	environmentalism(1)	photographers(1)	bonding(1)	hospitality(1)
rationalism(1)	therapeutic(1)	medicine(1)	outreach(1)	genealogy(1)	moral(2)
sustainable(1)	resolution(1)	cinema(1)	sciences(1)	cosmos(1)	reconciliation(1)
astronomical(1)	environmentalists(1)	entrepreneurship(1)	philanthropy(1)	intellectualism(1)	ethics(1)
equality(1)	healthcare(1)	thoughts(1)	cooperation(1)	perseverance(1)	pride(1)
interconnectedness(1)	diversity(1)	psyche(1)	aid(1)	land(1)	baptism(1)
sung(1)	well-being(2)	self-discovery(1)	chanting(2)	truths(1)	purification(1)
peaceful(2)	esoteric(1)	early(1)	myths(1)	open-minded(1)	reason(1)
universe(1)	diverse(2)	unifying(2)	interplay(1)	synthesis(1)	one(1)
mercy(1)	inner(1)	grace(1)	bridge(1)	prioritize(1)	health(1)
evangelism(1)	self-improvement(1)	services(1)	texts(1)	renewal(1)	milestones(1)
sanctity(1)	integrity(1)	harmonious(2)	betterment(1)	honor(1)	triumph(1)
inspiring(1)	intricate(1)	transcendent(1)	guiding(1)	insightful(1)	hopeful(1)
community-driven(1)	solemn(1)	balancing(1)	responsibility(1)	creation(1)	resilient(1)
loving(1)	ancestral(1)	life-affirming(1)	reverent(1)	seasonal(1)	fertility(1)
health-maintaining(1)	combining(1)	rhythmic(1)	oral(1)	nature-bound(1)	detailed(1)
meditative(1)	self-explorative(1)	empowering(1)	clarity(1)	original(1)	quick(1)
introspective(1)	theological(1)	dialogic(1)	mystical(2)	alternative(1)	kinship(1)
festive(1)	folkloric(1)	open(1)	questioning(1)	evidence-based(1)	creator(2)
universal(1)	all-encompassing(1)	opposing(1)	unified(1)	redemptive(1)	silent(1)
advocating(1)	sovereign(1)	graceful(1)	choral(1)	democratic(1)	traditional(1)
purifying(1)	evangelistic(1)	clearing(1)	soulful(1)	communal(1)	testament(1)
social(1)	solitudinous(1)	shared(1)	comforting(1)	interconnected(1)	profound(1)
guideline(1)	fostering(1)	connecting(1)	celebrate(1)	journeying(1)	homage(1)
blending(1)	integrating(1)	delving(1)	challenging(1)	solace(1)	context(1)
personal(1)	monotheistic(1)	hymns(1)	origin(1)	morality(1)	laws(1)
eternal(1)	history(1)	mix(1)	spirit(1)	witchcraft(1)	communicating(1)
deities(1)	syncretic(1)	self-help(1)	focuses(1)	oldest(1)	bodhisattva(1)
mantra(1)	strict(1)	persecution(1)	joyful(1)	mesopotamian(1)	liberal(1)
skepticism(1)	asserts(1)	divine(1)	multiple(1)	single(1)	dichotomy(1)
combines(1)	oneness(1)	salvation(1)	light(1)	name(1)	predestination(1)
emerged(1)	retains(1)	decentralized(1)	initiation(1)	sabbath(1)	writings(1)
sacred(1)	traditions(1)	secluded(1)	journey(1)	expressing(1)	challenge(1)
chant(1)	guidance(1)	recognizes(1)	champions(1)		

Table 22: Attribute words for Religious Bias Data Through Targeted Prompting

		Religion Generation 3			
balance(9)	unity(7)	mystical(8)	harmony(7)	mindfulness(6)	love(5)
community(7)	compassion(5)	equality(5)	simplicity(6)	healing(4)	joy(5)
nature(5)	salvation(4)	peace(5)	divinity(4)	ethical(3)	wisdom(4)
respect(4)	integration(3)	meditation(3)	gratitude(4)	intricate(3)	liturgical(4)
esoteric(4)	pacifism(3)	grace(3)	music(3)	commitment(3)	development(3)
insights(4)	architectural(3)	solace(4)	ancient(5)	integrates(3)	democratic(3)
knowledge(3)	dialogue(2)	good(2)	cultural(3)	family(3)	integrity(3)
learning(3)	heritage(2)	cyclical(2)	beauty(2)	purifying(2)	individualism(3)
transformative(3)	poetic(3)	kinship(2)	poetry(2)	secular(2)	blends(2)
engagement(2)	transformation(2)	ethics(3)	charity(3)	non-violence(3)	service(2)
spiritual(2)	blend(2)	diverse(3)	singular(2)	oneness(3)	rebirth(3)
health(2)	evangelism(2)	central(2)	songs(2)	justice(3)	perspectives(2)
honor(2)	interpretation(2)	combines(2)	celebrate(2)	history(2)	multiple(2)
journey(2)	bridge(2)	peaceful(1)	science(1)	sustainability(1)	selfless(1)
scholarship(1)	charitable(1)	pioneering(1)	education(1)	humanitarian(1)	healthcare(1)
art(1)	environment(1)	community-building(1)	resilience(2)	synthesis(1)	preservation(1)
blending(1)	togetherness(2)	preserve(1)	self-awareness(2)	responsibility(1)	benefit(1)
jurisprudential(1)	interfaith(1)	illumination(1)	exploration(2)	reason(1)	diversity(2)
interplay(2)	dignity(1)	sovereignty(1)	craftsmanship(1)	renewal(1)	well-being(1)
study(1)	devotion(1)	exchange(1)	artistic(1)	musical(1)	contemplation(1)
connection(2)	profound(1)	interconnectedness(1)	universal(1)	philosophy(1)	fellowship(1)
continuity(1)	conduct(1)	self-respect(1)	ancestors(1)	rhythms(1)	ancestral(1)
purity(1)	truthfulness(1)	consciousness(1)	happiness(1)	original(1)	enlightenment(2)
influential(1)	moderation(1)	egyptian(1)	reincarnation(1)	festivals(1)	integrate(1)
explore(1)	non-interventionist(1)	pantheon(1)	acceptance(1)	simple(1)	theological(2)
dating(1)	traditional(1)	teachings(1)	prayer(1)	significance(1)	discipline(1)
structure(1)	align(1)	joyful(1)	communion(1)	predestination(1)	participation(1)
freedom(1)	foundational(1)	reverence(2)	support(1)	transitions(1)	humility(2)
kindness(2)	perseverance(1)	brotherhood(1)	purpose(1)	faith(2)	connections(1)
revere(1)	vibrant(1)	meditative(1)	thinking(2)	belonging(2)	sacredness(1)
spirit(2)	expressions(1)	growth(2)	silence(1)	reaffirm(1)	symbolism(1)
righteousness(2)	forgiveness(1)	collective(1)	hymns(2)	sanctuary(1)	improvement(1)
culture(2)	modernity(2)	foundations(1)	humanism(1)	welcomes(1)	believes(1)
manuscripts(1)	holistic(1)	introspection(1)	thought(1)	universe(1)	tapestry(1)
sentient(1)	joyous(1)	clarity(1)	champion(1)	syncretism(1)	loyalty(2)
inclusivity(1)	rectitude(1)	alternative(1)	cycles(2)	enlightening(1)	scholarly(1)
patience(1)	truth(1)	oldest(1)	dedication(1)	inspiration(1)	tranquil(1)
serenity(1)	discovery(1)	hubs(1)	iconography(1)	quest(1)	inquiry(1)
distant(1)	divine(1)	supreme(1)	rooted(1)	vast(1)	range(1)
phases(1)	traditions(1)	largest(1)	humble(1)	roots(1)	tantra(1)
preserved(1)	worship(1)	misunderstood(1)	african(1)	perspective(1)	spirits(1)
lotus(1)	spread(1)	betterment(1)	bodhisattva(1)	moral(1)	creator(1)
goddess(1)	guidance(1)	self-discipline(1)	beacon(1)	earliest(1)	jurisprudence(1)
eternal(1)	devotee's(1)	honesty(1)	hospitality(1)	relationship(1)	conservation(1)
creation(1)	philosophical(1)	guidelines(1)	families(1)	dances(1)	seasons(1)
nature-oriented(1)	storytelling(1)	elevate(1)	autonomy(1)	chanting(1)	monastic(1)
symbolic(1)	interpretations(1)	deeper(1)	mystic(1)	unknown(1)	rational(1)
detached(1)	incorporated(1)	open-minded(1)	structured(1)	wellness(1)	tools(1)
narrate(1)	centers(1)	serene(1)	familial(1)	depths(1)	

J Appendix - Attribute words for General Prompting Data

Table 23: Attribute words for General Prompting Data

General Generation 1					
poetry(10)	ballet(6)	chess(6)	astrophysics(6)	literature(5)	opera(5)
astronomy(5)	art(4)	farming(4)	salsa(4)	environmental(4)	calligraphy(4)
robotics(4)	pottery(4)	ballroom(4)	coding(4)	dance(4)	physics(4)
yoga(3)	meditation(3)	mathematics(3)	archaeology(3)	programming(3)	dancer(3)
theater(3)	wildlife(3)	comedy(3)	marine(3)	quantum(3)	skiing(3)
fashion(3)	jazz(3)	sustainable(3)	novels(3)	entomology(3)	strongest(2)
struggled(2)	quantum physics(2)	violin(2)	weightlifter(2)	psychology(2)	martial arts(2)
historian(2)	economics(2)	birdwatching(2)	vegan(2)	marine biology(2)	pianist(2)
tech(2)	jewelry(2)	astronomer(2)	sports(2)	gourmet(2)	renaissance(2)
volunteering(2)	tech-savvy(2)	mechanic(2)	baking(2)	financial(2)	wilderness(2)
garden(2)	gaming(2)	organic(2)	climbing(2)	biology(2)	mechanical(2)
culinary(2)	historical(2)	archaeological(2)	ornithology(2)	chemistry(2)	anthropology(2)
swimmer(2)	volunteered(2)	mountaineer(2)	neuroscience(2)	rock climber(2)	bird(2)
botany(2)	mechanics(2)	piano(2)	pastry(2)	sculpture(2)	symphonies(2)
origami(2)	technology(1)	sensitivity(1)	photographer(1)	timeless(1)	snowboarding(1)
anonymously(1)	books(1)	fastest(1)	party(1)	eloquent(1)	outdoor(1)
volunteer(1)	children's hospitals(1)	mountain climber(1)	progressive(1)	rock star(1)	flexibility(1)
gentle(1)	genius(1)	romantic(1)	environmentalist(1)	paintings(1)	simple(1)
classical literature(1)	biologist(1)	rescue(1)	florist(1)	mental health(1)	cupcakes(1)
sunniest(1)	space exploration(1)	composed(1)	marathons(1)	linguistics(1)	harp(1)
paint(1)	floral(1)	basketball(1)	skateboarder(1)	kindergarten(1)	kendo(1)
ranger(1)	romance(1)	decorator(1)	dancing(1)	dj(1)	neuroscientist(1)
graffiti(1)	musician(1)	comedian(1)	scuba(1)	cooking(1)	creativity(1)
musical(1)	mathematical(1)	embroidery(1)	physical(1)	digital(1)	scientific(1)
botanists(1)	designing(1)	breakdancing(1)	ornithological(1)	handicrafts(1)	expeditions(1)
history(1)	racing(1)	butterflies(1)	energy(1)	fantasy(1)	aerospace(1)
technologies(1)	animation(1)	documentaries(1)	conservation(1)	architectural(1)	sculptors(1)
planning(1)	martial(1)	design(1)	philosophy(1)	neural(1)	orchestras(1)
biochemistry(1)	aerodynamics(1)	sociology(1)	climate(1)	microbiological(1)	geology(1)
game(1)	musicians(1)	acrobatic(1)	pianists(1)	nanotechnology(1)	compassionate(1)
work ethic(1)	zoos(1)	gender equality(1)	kindest(1)	ballet dancer(1)	diligent(1)
global politics(1)	lgbtq+ rights(1)	gun(1)	wisdom(1)	leader(1)	humor(1)
surf(1)	desert ecology(1)	traditional cultures(1)	athletic(1)	public speaking(1)	beaches(1)
cinema(1)	renaissance art(1)	pasta(1)	rehabilitating(1)	vision(1)	community service(1)
forest conservation(1)	italian cuisine(1)	ancient history(1)	alpine flora(1)	classical music(1)	underwater archaeology(1)
sustainable living(1)	wildlife conservation(1)	particle physics(1)	diver(1)	vodka(1)	animal rights(1)
tea(1)	botanist(1)	mathematician(1)	car(1)	potter(1)	civil rights(1)
mathematical theorem(1)	bullfighting(1)	gourmet chef(1)	non-violence(1)	quantum physicist(1)	african tribal music(1)
butterfly collection(1)	rocket scientist(1)	workers' rights(1)	rally driver(1)	snails(1)	cardiovascular surgeon(1)
skydiver(1)	cellist(1)	marine engineer(1)	nuclear physics(1)	author(1)	software developer(1)
spicy food(1)	maestro(1)	art historian(1)	quantum mechanics(1)	linguistic(1)	nuclear chemist(1)
cold(1)	artificial intelligence(1)	wildlife photography(1)	hacker(1)	knitting(1)	zoo(1)
karate(1)	book(1)	nurturing(1)	peace(1)	butchers(1)	painting(1)
lessons(1)	global(1)	photographic(1)	blacksmith(1)	rugby(1)	gratitude(1)
kickboxing(1)	compassion(1)	wines(1)	struggles(1)	avant-garde(1)	ride(1)
astrophysicist(1)	renewable(1)	flamenco(1)	abstract(1)	impressionist(1)	rock(1)
urban(1)	molecular(1)	classical(1)	volleyball(1)	greek(1)	mindful(1)
cello(1)	rural(1)	circus(1)	woodworking(1)	surfing(1)	ai(1)
permaculture(1)	particle(1)	beach(1)	hockey(1)	deep-sea(1)	desert(1)
neurobiology(1)	jiu-jitsu(1)	bagpipes(1)	rodeo(1)	rose(1)	tattoo(1)
knit(1)	motorcycles(1)	active(1)	watercolor(1)	stargazing(1)	authored(1)
flutist(1)	participate(1)	sunny(1)	poet(1)	ph.d.(1)	skydiving(1)
sci-fi(1)	solve(1)	beekeeping(1)	gardening(1)	bonsai(1)	virtual reality(1)
fluent(1)	gamer(1)	digital art(1)	race car(1)	archery(1)	philosopher(1)
archeology(1)	tango(1)	metal(1)	rescuing(1)	guitar(1)	acrobatics(1)
surfer(1)	skater(1)	storybook(1)	capoeira(1)	boxing(1)	motorcycle(1)
fencing(1)	esports(1)	engineering(1)	breakdance(1)	saxophonist(1)	mural(1)
falconry(1)	tennis(1)	didgeridoo(1)	punk(1)	scuba diving(1)	

Table 24: Attribute words for General Prompting Data

General Generation 2					
astrophysics(12)	poetry(8)	ballet(7)	coding(6)	chess(6)	literature(6)
conservation(5)	novels(5)	innovative(4)	quantum physics(4)	politics(4)	philosophy(4)
opera(4)	violin(4)	aerospace(4)	shakespeare(3)	tech-savvy(3)	maestro(3)
peace(3)	meditation(3)	pottery(3)	neuroscience(3)	vegan(3)	ornithology(3)
historian(3)	salsa(3)	sculptor(3)	mountaineer(3)	physics(3)	history(3)
biologist(3)	pianist(3)	research(3)	calculus(2)	classical(2)	mathematician(2)
culinary(2)	astronomy(2)	leadership(2)	entrepreneurial(2)	gardening(2)	farming(2)
martial artist(2)	yoga(2)	mathematical(2)	adventure(2)	animal rights(2)	nuclear physics(2)
comedy(2)	archeology(2)	author(2)	mental health(2)	mindfulness(2)	quantum mechanics(2)
astrophotography(2)	sociology(2)	ballroom(2)	harp(2)	poets(2)	ph.d.(2)
wisdom(2)	novel(2)	art(2)	sunny(2)	technologies(2)	academic(2)
physicist(2)	biology(2)	gourmet(2)	ornithologist(2)	scientist(2)	judo(2)
mechanics(2)	archaeology(2)	computing(2)	playwright(2)	chemistry(2)	garden(2)
paintings(2)	sustainable(2)	archaeological(2)	robotics(2)	languages(2)	martial arts(2)
architecture(2)	violinist(2)	leaders(2)	scientific(2)	tech(2)	botanical(2)
scholars(2)	marine biologist(2)	classical music(2)	space exploration(2)	digital(2)	mathematics(3)
molecular biology(2)	quantum computing(2)	economics(2)	nurturing(1)	adapt(1)	gentle(1)
strength(1)	work ethic(1)	technology(1)	rapport(1)	scholar(1)	literary(1)
community service(1)	botanist(1)	renaissance(2)	classical literature(1)	optimistic(1)	acumen(1)
sports enthusiast(1)	gadgets(1)	dance(1)	public speaker(1)	ancient crafts(1)	jazz(1)
virtual reality(1)	stamp collection(1)	astronomer(1)	multilingual(1)	volunteered(1)	women's rights(1)
painter(1)	yoga instructor(1)	theater(1)	environmental science(1)	marathons(1)	homeless(1)
tutored(1)	karate(1)	grassroots(1)	swimmer(1)	documentary(1)	magician(1)
tango(1)	cookbooks(1)	poetry slams(1)	digital animation(1)	roller derby(1)	jazz prodigy(1)
calligraphy(1)	puppeteer(1)	created(1)	mathematicians(1)	drivers(1)	teach(1)
humble(1)	volunteering(1)	martial(1)	party(1)	philosopher(1)	renewable(1)
patents(1)	singing(1)	fluent(1)	conservationists(1)	understand(1)	wizard(1)
compassionate(1)	basketball(1)	botany(2)	activists(1)	fashion(1)	proust(1)
biochemist(1)	books(1)	vegetables(1)	wine(1)	archery(1)	poet(1)
cooking(1)	podcast(1)	greek(1)	professor(1)	painting(1)	civilizations(1)
bestselling(1)	prodigy(1)	dancing(1)	stories(1)	comedian(1)	equestrian(1)
filmmaker(1)	entomology(1)	charity(1)	coded(1)	entrepreneurship(1)	sitar(1)
cuisine(1)	crochet(1)	uplift(1)	trading(1)	scholarships(1)	restoration(1)
debates(1)	programming(1)	veganism(1)	beekeeping(1)	diplomacy(1)	cookbook(1)
healing(1)	paleontology(1)	driver(1)	marketing(1)	ocean(1)	welfare(1)
resolution(1)	explorer(1)	inventions(1)	guitarist(1)	journals(1)	rescue(1)
couture(1)	culture(1)	composition(1)	cello(1)	fencing(1)	nano-technology(1)
flute(1)	neurobiology(1)	artwork(1)	cyber-security(1)	engineering(1)	intelligence(1)
actress(1)	animation(1)	skydiver(1)	photography(1)	saxophone(1)	clarinet(1)
mythology(1)	musician(1)	courageous(1)	groundbreaking(1)	caregivers(1)	innovation(1)
contribute(1)	respect(1)	beautifully(1)	pioneering(1)	captivating(1)	understanding(1)
contributions(1)	fluently(1)	delicate(1)	enriched(1)	well-being(1)	nature(1)
academically(1)	service(1)	adopting(1)	excel(1)	innovations(1)	insights(1)
analytical(1)	technological(1)	ai technology(1)	family time(1)	adventurous(1)	arts(1)
trailblazers(1)	competitive(1)	cosmology(1)	stem(1)	adventurers(1)	dancers(1)
activism(1)	mountaineering(1)	emotional support(1)	fine art(1)	theoretical physics(1)	dramatic arts(1)
breakthrough(1)	astronomical(1)	authors(1)	sculptors(1)	ballroom dancing(1)	particle physics(1)
environmental sciences(1)	oceanography(1)	marine biologists(1)	football(1)	extreme sports(1)	algorithms(1)
donate(1)	environmental(1)	social work(1)	telecommunication(1)	baking(1)	cinema(1)
astrophysicist(1)	urban planning(1)	cosmos(1)	ancient civilizations(1)	aerodynamics(1)	filmmaking(1)
app development(1)	folklore(1)	nuclear physicist(1)	philosophical(1)	microbiology(1)	music(1)
astrophysical(1)	environmentalist(1)	digital graphics(1)	computer programming(1)	reptile handling(1)	jazz history(1)
renewable energy(1)	plant biology(1)	african dances(1)	economic theories(1)	renaissance art(1)	engineer(1)
psychology(1)	wildlife photographer(1)	biochemistry(1)	anthropology(1)	botanical research(1)	fashion designer(1)
aerospace engineering(1)	weightlifting(1)	symphonic(1)			

DE-Lite – a New Corpus of Easy German: Compilation, Exploration, Analysis

Sarah Jablotschkin
Universität Hamburg
sarah.jablotschkin@uni-hamburg.de

Elke Teich
Universität des Saarlandes
e.teich@mx.uni-saarland.de

Heike Zinsmeister
Universität Hamburg
heike.zinsmeister@uni-hamburg.de

Abstract

In this paper, we report on a new corpus of simplified German. It is recently requested from public agencies in Germany to provide information in easy language on their outlets (e.g. websites) so as to facilitate participation in society for people with low-literacy levels related to learning difficulties or low language proficiency (e.g. L2 speakers). While various rule sets and guidelines for Easy German (a specific variant of simplified German) have emerged over time, it is unclear (a) to what extent authors and other content creators, including generative AI tools consistently apply them, and (b) how adequate texts in authentic Easy German really are for the intended audiences. As a first step in gaining insights into these issues and to further LT development for simplified German, we compiled DE-Lite, a corpus of easy-to-read texts including Easy German and comparable Standard German texts, by integrating existing collections and gathering new data from the web. We built n-gram models for an Easy German subcorpus of DE-Lite and comparable Standard German texts in order to identify typical features of Easy German. To this end, we use relative entropy (Kullback-Leibler Divergence), a standard technique for evaluating language models, which we apply here for corpus comparison. Our analysis reveals that some rules of Easy German are fairly dominant (e.g. punctuation) and that text genre has a strong effect on the distinctivity of the two language variants.

1 Introduction

The UN Convention on the Rights of Persons with Disabilities (UN-CRPD)[1] states that obstacles to accessibility to "information, communication and other services" should be eliminated by state parties for people with disabilities (article 9). Against this background, many countries have pushed for legislation to reduce the language barrier for people with learning difficulties[2] as one of the core measures in creating equal opportunities. In Germany, different forms of simplified German have emerged including variants of a regulated, "easy" German ('Leichte Sprache') that are intended to make written information accessible for low-literacy readers (Inclusion Europe, n.d.; Netzwerk Leichte Sprache, 2022; Bredel and Maaß, 2016; Bock, 2018; Bundesministerium der Justiz und für Verbraucherschutz, 2017). According to a recent policy of the German Ministry for Work and Social Affairs[3], it is now requested from public institutions to provide information in (regulated) Easy German alongside Standard German. While people with disabilities are the only group whose right to accessible written information is statutory, it is often claimed that non-disabled people such as learners of German or older people, or even all people (Netzwerk Leichte Sprache, 2022), profit from Easy German.

While a long-awaited move in language policy, there are a number of open questions both for the theory and the practice of Easy German. There are several agencies providing guidelines about how to write in Easy German and while there is a fair level of convergence, there is also some conflicting advice. Also, it is unclear whether specific features such as avoiding pronouns or using only simple, paratactic conjunctions (see Section 2.1) are indeed beneficial for comprehension and if so, for which specific target groups. Overall, there is fairly little empirically grounded research about the use of Easy German in particular. This is the motivation of the project we report on in this paper.

[1] https://social.desa.un.org/issues/disability/crpd/

[2] We use this term for people with intellectual and other disabilities because it is considered less stigmatising by self-advocacy groups such as Network People First Germany, see https://www.menschzuerst.de/pages/startseite/wer-sind-wir/verein.php

[3] *Bundesteilhabegesetz und Nationaler Aktionsplan 2.0*: https://www.bmas.de/DE/Leichte-Sprache/leichte-sprache.html

Proceedings of the Fourth Workshop on Language Technology for Equality, Diversity, Inclusion, pages 106–117
March 21, 2024 ©2024 Association for Computational Linguistics

Our focus is on the exploratory research question: What are the typical features of Easy German in lived practice? This involves empirical studies of authentic productions in Easy German and other variants of simplified German. For this purpose, we have compiled the DE-Lite corpus from preexisting resources of different variants of simplified German and Standard German, and extended it with additional texts from the web.

This paper documents decisions made in the corpus compilation process, including how to address the challenge of duplicate identification. In addition, we present an exploratory, n-gram-based study in which subcorpora of DE-Lite consisting of comparable texts in Easy German and Standard German are compared revealing main characteristics of Easy German. We think that the corpus, its description, and the empirical study are of interest for the development of inclusive language technology, and that insights of the German corpus and its compilation can be transferred to other languages.

Our overarching theoretical approach is rooted in information theory (Shannon, 1948), a mathematical theory of communication, according to which language users modulate the information content of their messages (Crocker et al., 2015), adapting their linguistic encodings to properties of both the channel (e.g. noise) and the recipient (audience design) (see e.g. Vogels et al., 2019; Häuser and Kray, 2021).

The link to Easy German is a natural one: Rules and recommendations for Easy German can be considered intentional measures to reduce the information content (surprisal) of linguistic expressions/units, such as words, sentences or stretches of text. Surprisal being correlated with processing effort, modulation of information content is a measure to adapt to a supposedly lower channel capacity of the target group(s) of Easy German. We thus hypothesise that the information content of linguistic units should be smaller in Easy German compared to standard language, indicated e.g. by a preference for high-frequency words, lower lexical density, lower vocabulary variation and syntactic and cohesive explicitness. To identify the specific properties of Easy German, we compare it with Standard German, employing selected information-theoretic measures, such as relative entropy, a measure widely used in NLP for evaluating language models.

The paper is structured as follows. In related work (Section 2), we sketch the history of Easy German, followed by a brief state-of-the-art on corpus-based work on Easy Language. In Section 3 we introduce the DE-Lite corpus containing texts in simplified variants of German by describing corpus design, the challenge of harmonising existing resources, and the mathematical basis of our language modeling. Section 4 complements the corpus description by presenting an exploratory, comparative analysis of two DE-Lite subcorpora of Easy German and Standard German. We conclude with a summary and discussion (Section 5).

2 Related work

The next section outlines the development of Easy German as a highly restricted variant of German.

2.1 Easy German

Easy German ('Leichte Sprache') only emerged in the late 1990s, while similar concepts have been practised in countries such as Finland, Sweden, and the USA since the 1970s (Netzwerk People First Deutschland e.V.; Tjarks-Sobhani, 2012, 28; Gross, 2015, 81). Today, simplified variants of national languages exist in numerous countries around the globe.[4] The concept originated from the empowerment of people with learning difficulties advocating their right to participation in society. In Germany, they developed relatively rigid rules for creating easily comprehensible text together with their supporters (Inclusion Europe; Netzwerk Leichte Sprache, 2014, 2022). The rule sets also emphasise the importance of letting representatives of the target groups check texts written in Easy German for comprehensibility and partly make this procedure a prerequisite for awarding an official quality seal for Easy German. While Easy German is a concept that has been developed by laypeople and has been in use for a long time, even before it was legally recognised, linguistic research in this area has only increased over the past few years.

Even though there are differing rule sets and guidelines for creating text in Easy German, they overlap with regard to general linguistic principles: All rule sets emphasise the importance of syntactic simplicity, for example by using short sentences, only making one statement per sentence (Inclusion Europe, 16-17; Netzwerk Leichte Sprache, 2022, 30), or using a fixed constituent order with sentence-initial subject (Netzwerk Leichte Sprache,

[4] https://www.easy-plain-accessible.com/home/around-the-world/

Was ist Leichte Sprache?	*What is Easy Language?*
Leichte Sprache ist eine besondere Form der deutschen Sprache.	*Easy language is a special form of the German language.*
Leichte Sprache ist leicht zu lesen und zu verstehen.	*Easy language is easy to read and understand.*
Texte in leichter Sprache haben zum Beispiel:	*Texts in easy language have for example:*
• einfache Wörter	• *simple words*
• kurze Sätze	• *short sentences*
• Bilder	• *pictures*
Deshalb verstehen viele Menschen Texte in leichter Sprache besser.	*That is why many people understand texts in easy language better.*
Dadurch wissen sie mehr.	*So they know more.*
Und sie können mitreden.	*And they can have their say.*
Sie können selbst Entscheidungen treffen.	*They can make decisions for themselves.*

Table 1: Definition of Easy German in Easy German with specific typography (Netzwerk Leichte Sprache, 2021, 209)

2022, 31; Bredel and Maaß, 2016, 419-425) which is not required in Standard German.

On the lexical level, it is commonly recommended to use only frequently used words and avoid technical terms as well as borrowed words (Netzwerk Leichte Sprache, 2022, 13). With regard to morphology, verbs are preferred over nouns, passive voice should be avoided and prepositional paraphrases are considered easier than genitive case (Netzwerk Leichte Sprache, 2022, 16-17). There are also some recommendations on the textual level: Difficult words, if they cannot be avoided, should always be explained (Inclusion Europe, 15), and instead of using pronouns or lexical substitution, the "same words for the same things" (Netzwerk Leichte Sprache, 2022, 14) should be used.

The example shown in Table 1 illustrates some of these characteristics: On a syntactic level, it consists of paratactic structures with the subject or an adverbial connective (*deshalb* 'therefore', *dadurch* 'thereby') being the first sentence constituent. The coreferring expression *Leichte Sprache* is repeated several times instead of being replaced by a pronoun as would be the coherent way to put it in Standard German. At the same time, the text shows some inconsistencies with respect to the rules mentioned above: The nominal phrase *Menschen* ('people') is not repeated, but is referred to anaphorically by the personal pronoun *sie* ('they'), and the first sentence employs the genitive attribute *der deutschen Sprache* ('of the German language') instead of a prepositional paraphrase as is recommended for example by Netzwerk Leichte Sprache (2022).

2.2 Corpus resources and corpus-based studies

Multilingual corpora and corpora that include different intra-lingual variants such as the DE-Lite corpus can be classified according to the relation that texts of the different variants have to each other: In a 'parallel corpus' there is a translation relation between individual texts of the different languages or variants (which can be made explicit by aligning on sentence, paragraph, or text level); in a 'comparable corpus' texts are sampled for the same genres or text types across variants.[5] If there is neither a translation relation nor a thematic relation, the corpus just contains samples of monolingual subcorpora of different languages or variants.

There are a number of corpora for simplified German which we summarised in Table 3 in Appendix A. While the Geasy corpus (Hansen-Schirra et al., 2021) contains Easy German texts, several other corpora contain different variants of simplified text: LeiKo (Jablotschkin and Zinsmeister, 2023), DEplain (Stodden et al., 2023) and the Simple German Corpus (Toborek et al., 2023) contain Plain German as well as Easy German, APA-RST (Hewett, 2023) is a corpus of Austrian texts that are categorised into different complexity levels (A2, B1 according to Council of Europe, 2001), and both the LeiSa corpus (Lange and Bock, 2016) and WebCorpus (Battisti et al., 2020) sample simplified text without restricting it to a specific simplification

[5]This terminology is broader than the use of *comparable corpus* in translation studies where the term is used for sets of texts originally written in a language *L* and thematically comparable texts that are translated into *L*.

method or label. Most of the corpora are (partly) parallel and contain Standard German texts as well. Others are comparable corpora for different variants of simplified German. The corpora also differ with regard to whether they contain sentence alignments and linguistic annotations.

While parallel corpora in the setting of simplified language are especially suited for training automatic simplification algorithms or analysing intralingual translation strategies, comparable corpora allow for the acquisition of larger amounts of data and the detection of linguistic differences between or within language variants, e.g. based on metadata such as text genre or publisher.

Various corpuslinguistic studies investigate specific linguistic characteristics of Easy German, often in order to evaluate the applicability and application of individual rules (e.g. Lange, 2019; Fuchs, 2019). There are also psycholinguistic studies that evaluate characteristics of Easy German with regard to whether they improve text comprehensibility for the recipients (e.g. Lasch, 2017; Bock, 2017a). There are few studies that (like our own) use corpus data to explore characteristics or complexity levels of Easy German inductively (e.g. Bock, 2014). Unlike previous studies, our approach is not restricted to specific linguistic levels such as syntax or morphology. By calculating KLD on every token of the corpus and isolating distinctive types (see Section 4), we take this as a starting point to draw conclusions about the expression of complexity reduction on different linguistic levels such as syntax, morphology or pragmatics of (text genres in) Easy German.

3 Corpus

In order to re-use previously collected data as well as annotations and alignments, we merged parts of different existing corpus resources containing texts in variants of simplified German: DEplain (Stodden et al., 2023), Geasy (Hansen-Schirra et al., 2021), WebCorpus (Battisti et al., 2020) and LeiKo (Jablotschkin and Zinsmeister, 2023). The corpus is still under construction and further existing Easy German corpora will be included, such as APA-RST (Hewett, 2023) and the Simple German Corpus (Toborek et al., 2023). To further expand the corpus, we also collected html text as well as PDFs from additional websites, our main sampling criterion being date of publication: In order to ensure comparability and avoid date of publication as confounding variable, we excluded texts that had been published before 2017. This is motivated by the assumption that Easy German has undergone substantial changes with regard to its linguistic characteristics. One trigger for this has been the publication of linguistically founded rules and recommendations for Easy German texts by *Forschungsstelle Leichte Sprache Hildesheim* (Research Unit Easy German Hildesheim) (Maaß, 2015; Bredel and Maaß, 2016). In addition, there have been research projects that improved the general understanding of what exactly is comprehensible for the target groups of Easy German, such as LeiSa (Bock, 2018).

The collected data comprises different file formats and requires different methods of preprocessing. As for PDFs, we used the Python library `PyMuPDF` to extract text and conducted additional manual cleaning. For webscraping, we used the Python `requests` library, and `BeautifulSoup` in order to parse the downloaded html files. We used the tcf version (Heid et al., 2010) of the WebCorpus data (Battisti et al., 2020) containing primary text as well as annotations and metadata, which we also parsed with `BeautifulSoup`.

3.1 Duplicate identification

An important issue when combining different web-based corpora is near-duplicate cleanup, see Rodier and Carter (2020) for a recent overview. For example, Geasy (Hansen-Schirra et al., 2021), WebCorpus (Battisti et al., 2020) as well as DEplain (Stodden et al., 2023) all made use of the website `einfach-teilhaben.de` by Germany's federal ministry for labour and social affairs (BMAS), which provides official information about topics such as disability, inclusion and social participation. To detect and exclude duplicates, we computed substring edit distances between corpus texts by BatchSED (Adelmann, 2021)[6] following the approach of (Adelmann and Gius, 2020). This approach takes into account the possibility that one text may be fully or partially contained within another text (in our case, for example, due to different web scraping routines). Hence, BatchSED calculates two scores for each pair of texts, by taking text 1 as a substring of text 2 and vice versa. Two texts are considered duplicates if the substring edit distances for both directions, divided by the length of the text to be embedded as substring, is less than

[6] `https://github.com/benadelm/BatchSED`: It calculates word-based distances with insertion costs equal to deletion costs equal to substitution costs equal to one.

Category	Values
Label	Leichte Sprache, Einfache Sprache, children, other
Rule set / agency	Forschungsstelle Leichte Sprache Hildesheim (FLS), capito, Netzwerk Leichte Sprache, Inclusion Europe, other
Complexity level	A1, A2, B1, none
Original corpus	Geasy, WebCorpus, DEplain, LeiKo, DE-Lite
Publisher	[name of publisher], e.g. public broadcasters, governmental institutions, welfare institutions, research institutions, non-profit organisations/NGOs, publishing houses, political parties, private individuals
Verification process	Target group, none
Year of publication	2017 or more recent
Text genre	lexicon, news/newspaper, wiki, blog, election programme, story/novel, technical text, administrative text and others
Origin of text	user-generated, editorial

Table 2: Core metadata of the DE-Lite corpus: Categories and values

15 %. From a pair of texts identified as duplicates, we kept that instance that was aligned to a parallel text in the corpus. If this filter was not applicable, we followed a fixed preference hierarchy, partly motivated by the availability of metadata, to make the provenance of the corpus texts transparent: LeiKo before WebCorpus before DEplain before Geasy before newly crawled material. This method identified about 400 Easy German texts and about 500 Standard German texts as duplicates which we excluded from the merged corpus. The actual number of duplicates was in fact much higher but many instances were filtered manually in advance, during the process of integrating the resources before further processing.

3.2 Metadata annotation

For our corpus, we collect the metadata displayed in Table 2. Our main sampling criterion is year of publication (cf. beginning of Section 3). In addition, we cover a broad range of text genres in order to approximate representativity. Since the underlying rule set or agency might also have an effect on linguistic characteristics, we include texts written according to the non-linguistic rule sets (Inclusion Europe; Netzwerk Leichte Sprache, 2022) as well as texts written according to the rule sets by *Forschungsstelle Leichte Sprache Hildesheim* (Research unit Easy German Hildesheim; FLS) (Bredel and Maaß, 2016). However, for most of the texts it is not clear whether they were written according to a specific rule set.

These data are partly adopted from the existing corpora, which we merged into our corpus. For newly collected texts, we collect the data from the websites or PDFs. For the texts from existing corpus resources, we complete the metadata according to our annotation scheme wherever possible. Since the original websites cannot always be reconstructed, certain metadata cannot be retrieved any more.

As previously mentioned, there are various seals for marking simplified German text. Sometimes, texts labeled as Easy German further contain an indication of their complexity level. This information is contained in the metadata variables *label* and *complexity level.*

Since some of the rule sets require members of the target groups to verify Easy German texts before they can be labeled as such, *verification process* was also included as metadata variable.

3.3 Language modeling

An effective approach to get a first idea of the differences between language variants is to compute word-based n-gram models (including punctuation) for each variant and compare the models with a divergence measure, such as Jensen-Shannon or Kullback-Leibler Divergence. Here, we use the asymmetric variant, Kullback-Leibler Divergence (KLD). Formally, KLD computes the difference between two probability distributions in terms of the number of additional bits needed to encode a unit x from a distribution A with an optimal encoding for distribution B (see eq. 1). The higher the number of additional bits, the greater the difference.

$$D_{KL}(A\|B) = \sum_{x \in X} A(x) \log \left(\frac{A(x)}{B(x)} \right) \quad (1)$$

While a standard method for evaluating language models, KLD has the advantage of giving us not only an indication of the overall difference between two language variants, but also of the most distinctive linguistic features. The specific features (here: words, punctuation marks) involved in the difference are obtained by ranking the features in terms of pointwise KLD. For inspection we use

Easy vs. Standard News vs. non-news (Easy) News vs. non-news (Standard)

Figure 1: Term clouds displaying distinctive terms in the respective subcorpora of DE-Lite v1. Size: Distinctivity by KLD, Colour: Relative frequency

a word cloud visualization (see Figure 1) that encodes the relative *frequency* (colour) and the *distinctivity* (size) of features. For assessing the statistical significance of an observed difference in overall frequencies, a p-value is calculated with an unpaired Welch t-test on the observed probabilities in the individual documents of each corpus. By default, the p-value is set to 0.05 (95 % confidence) (cf. Fankhauser et al., 2014). Note that this method is equivalent to a (relative) frequency-based account combined with a statistical test on a feature distribution but has the advantage that features are not a priori selected but automatically detected and ranked in terms of their contribution to the distinction between language variants.

3.4 DE-Lite v1: Data basis of this study

DE-Lite contains two subcorpora of Easy German texts, a parallel one and a monolingual one. In addition to Easy German texts, the corpus also contains comparable texts in other simplified German variants, such as Plain German and texts addressing children.

For the explorative corpus comparison described in Section 4, we use the subset DE-Lite v1[7] containing 1,195,176 Easy German tokens (from both the parallel and the monolingual subcorpora) and 1,154,226 Standard German tokens. The other variants of simplified German (e.g. texts for children) are not relevant for this study.

4 Corpus comparison: Easy vs. Standard German

For an explorative corpus study, we use DE-Lite v1 (see Section 3.4). We investigate the corpus data with the help of n-gram based KLD computations along two dimensions: Language variant with the two categories Easy and Standard, and text genre with the categories news and non-news. To this end, we compare what specific types contribute significantly to the overall KLD of the respective dimension category. Figure 1 shows a visualisation of the distinctivity (size) and relative frequency (colour) of individual types. In order to illustrate typical uses and functions of the distinctive terms in the respective subcorpora, we additionally draw on concordances and example sentences.[8]

In a first step, we compare the Easy German subcorpus to the Standard German subcorpus without drawing on any additional metadata (see Section 4.1). On the one hand, our data reveal that in Easy German, particular care is given to establishing coherence. On the other hand, we find characteristics that illustrate the ways morphological and syntactic simplicity is ensured in Easy German.

Subsequently, we show that our approach can be used to detect text-genre specific features within Easy and Standard German by comparing Easy German news to Easy German non-news and Standard news to Standard German non-news (see Section 4.2). Our results show that the characteristics that distinguish news from non-news in Easy German only partly overlap with those that distinguish news from non-news in Standard German.

[7]DE-Lite v1 is downloadable from `https://github.com/HeikeZinsmeister/DE-Lite`.

[8]We used the corpus tool AntConc to systematically sift through the contexts of distinctive types (Anthony, 2023).

4.1 Easy vs. Standard

In order to establish local coherence, texts in Easy German typically contain explanations of difficult words and examples to make abstract concepts more concrete. This general observation can be reproduced by our approach: Some of the terms that significantly contribute to the overall KLD between Easy and Standard German data are used for exemplification and explanation or rephrasing: *Zum* ('for'; sentence-initial) and *Beispiel* ('example') are very prominent and typically occur together, as can be shown by a further analysis of concordances (see also examples (1) and (2)). Another very prominent term is sentence-initial *Das* ('that'), which in our data is frequently followed by verbs such as *ist* ('is'), *heißt* ('means') or *bedeutet* ('means'). However, while explanation and rephrasing are important to ensure comprehension, resolving anaphora such as the pronoun *Das* ('that'), which often refers to a preceding clause as its non-nominal antecedent, may also be challenging (Kolhatkar et al., 2018) and therefore should be evaluated with members of the target groups of Easy German. In our Easy German data, *Das* also frequently occurs as a determiner in the phrase *Das Wort* ('the word'). A closer examination of the instances reveals that they all originate from one and the same website, namely Hurraki, a wiki-like site in Easy German. The same is true for phrases like *Gleiche Wörter* ('same words') and *Genaue Erklärung* ('precise explanation'). Entries in Hurraki follow a fixed structure and often contain additional information about the use and meaning of words. While this is another strategy to establish coherence, these specific phrases are not representative of Easy German. Systematically collecting metadata of Easy German corpus texts is thus essential in order to detect biases like this. This observation is relevant because Easy German sites tend to be more structured than standard language sites also by using formulaic sequences (see also the recommendation to use the same words for the same things, Section 2.1).

Not only words, but also punctuation marks significantly contribute to KLD: Colons, full stops and bullet points are distinctive for Easy in comparison to Standard German. The bullet point is frequently preceded by a colon and introduces a list of examples intended to make a concept more graspable (cf. example (2)). As has been shown by Jablotschkin and Zinsmeister (2021), another function of the colon in Easy German is to indicate a syntactic dependency relation between a matrix and a subordinate object clause (cf. example (3)), a function, which is more commonly accomplished by a comma in Standard German. The distinctivity of the full stop in Easy German is not surprising as Easy German uses shorter and therefore more sentences per number of tokens than Standard German (syntactic simplification).

The higher sentence density might also be one of the reasons why some finite verb forms are very prominent in our Easy German data, such as *ist* ('is') and *hat* ('has'). Furthermore, both verbs are not only used as main verbs but also function as auxiliaries in German, so their distinctivity in relation to Standard German also points out the prevalence of periphrastic verb forms in Easy German which are morphologically more simple than alternative synthetic verb forms. In addition, a closer look into concordances shows that *ist* is frequently followed by a nominal phrase with a definite or indefinite article, which illustrates the importance of predications in Easy German, another means to explain words or concepts.

(1) Früher hat sich der Pflege-Dienst um alles gekümmert.

Zum Beispiel hat der Pflege-Dienst die Assistenten ausgesucht und bezahlt. (p_765_easy)

Before, the nursing service took care of everything.

For example, the nursing service chose and paid the assistants.

(2) Ein Behinderten-Verband ist auch ein Sozial-Verband.

Sozial-Verbände vertreten noch mehr Interessen.

Zum Beispiel von:

- Arbeitslosen,
- Rentnern und
- Menschen, die wenig Geld haben. (m_5314_easy)

A disabled people's organisation is a social association, too.

Social associations represent even more interests.

For example of:

- *unemployed persons,*
- *retired persons and*
- *people who have little money.*

(3) Sie denkt:

Viel mehr Menschen sollen das Persönliche Geld benutzen. (p_765_easy)

She thinks:

A lot more people should use the Personal Money.

(4) Und sie hat gesagt:

Ab dem nächsten Schuljahr bekommen die Lehrer mehr Geld. (p_1162_easy)

And she said:

From next school year, the teachers will get more money.

(5) Der Korea-Konflikt geht schon sehr lange.

Er hat im Jahr 1945 angefangen. (m_1193_easy)

The Korean conflict has been lasting for a very long time already.

It started in the year 1945.

(6) Sie arbeiten in Voll-Zeit.

Oder sie arbeiten in Teil-Zeit.

Oder sie machen eine Ausbildung für einen Beruf. (m_3042_easy)

They work full time.

Or they work part time.

Or they train for a profession.

Moreover, personal pronouns such as *Er* ('He'), *sie* ('she'/'they') and *[E|e]s* ('[I|i]t') show a high pointwise KLD value in Easy German. This is a logical consequence of splitting up complex sentences into simple ones, each requiring an individual subject which is often realised by a personal pronoun. In Standard German, parataxis typically contains elliptic structures such as subject ellipsis. In Easy German, instead of dropping the subject, there is a tendency to syndetically or asyndetically conjoin syntactically complete sentences (see (5) and (6)). While examples (5) and (6) illustrate syntactic simplification in Easy German, they may create problems for reference resolution. Firstly, German personal pronouns like *Er* allow reference to animate/human as well as inanimate/non-human referents (such as *Korean conflict*) and secondly, there might be contexts in which there are more than one potential antecedents with the required grammatical features (in this case: singular masculine noun phrases), so personal pronouns bear potential for semantic as well as pragmatic ambiguity. It is still an open question whether avoiding ellipses simplify texts for recipients of Easy German and in what contexts avoiding personal pronouns might be beneficial for comprehension.

4.2 News vs. non-news (Easy vs. Standard)

An open research question up-to-date is how text genres differ within Easy German. Despite the restricted linguistic means of Easy German, it is supposed to achieve various communicative functions. Bock (2017b, 191) emphasises the importance of text adequacy in order to ensure comprehensibility and the ability of the recipient to recognise the communicative function of the text, so different text genres within *Leichte Sprache* should be recognisable based on characteristic linguistic forms. Since we computed KLD not only with regard to language variant (Easy vs. Standard) but also with regard to text genre (news vs. non-news), our approach allows us to identify specific linguistic features that are characteristic for news in Easy German compared to other texts in Easy German (in contrast to news in Standard German compared to non-news in Standard German). Our term clouds show that news in Easy German typically employ a lot of place names (i.e., names of cities) and local as well as temporal adverbials (*dort* ('there'), *[I|i]n* ('[I|i]n'), *jetzt* ('now'), *nun* ('now'), *bis* ('until')) serving as frame-setters. In a corpus study, Fuchs (2017) found out that in short Easy German news texts the text-initial position is frequently used for local frame-setters to establish a "cognitive meeting point". Fuchs (2017, 103) points out that in Easy German, frame-setters are especially important because a Common Ground between author and recipient cannot be presupposed. Apart from frame-setters, in the term clouds for KLD of Easy German news in contrast to Easy German non-news, sentence-initial connectives such as *Denn* ('Because') and *Aber* ('However') stick out. These findings support the findings by Jablotschkin and Zinsmeister (2023), who demonstrate that the sentence-initial position in Easy German news texts is frequently used for discourse connectives and frame-setting adverbials.

When comparing news and non-news in Standard German, similarly to Easy German some linguistic expressions have high distinctivity that potentially serve as frame-setters, such as *nun* ('now'), *im* ('in the'), *in* ('in'), *am* ('at the'/'on the'). However, there are also several finite verb forms that distinguish Standard news from Standard non-news while they are not distinctive of Easy news compared to Easy non-news: *sei* (subjunctive form of 'are'), *habe* (subjunctive form of 'have'), *waren* ('were'), *hatte* ('had'), *sagt* ('says'), *sagte* ('said'). In addition, quotation marks are significantly more frequent in this Standard text genre. These verb forms along with the quotation marks hint at the relevance of (direct and indirect) reported speech in news texts. Reported speech is semantically and pragmatically complex and its use in Easy German is therefore restricted. As a substitute for reported speech marked by subjunctive or quotation marks, Easy German news texts tend to use matrix clauses with a perfect form of the main verb *sagen* ('say') followed by a colon and a subordinate object clause (see example (4)). This observation is supported by the high distinctivity of *gesagt* in our term cloud visualising KLD of Easy German news in contrast to Easy German non-news. Constructions like in example (4) are syntactically and morphologically relatively simple. However, the lack of quotation marks and subjunctive mood in these clauses creates ambiguity and requires the recipient to make additional inferences mainly based on context to determine whether the subordinate clause contains direct or indirect speech.

5 Summary and conclusions

We presented a new corpus documenting the lived practice in simplified German writing. On this basis we built n-gram language models of the strongly regulated variant Easy German and of Standard German. We applied relative entropy to analyse the differences between the Easy German and Standard German models and between text genres within the respective variant. We extracted typical features of Easy German on different linguistic levels and detected text genre differences within Easy and Standard German.

By analysing distinctive types and additionally drawing on sample sentences and concordances, we showed that many of the typical features of Easy German can be traced back to efforts of improving coherence, e.g. by explicitly connecting sentences of a text or explaining difficult words. Some other features of Easy German displayed by our models are a direct consequence of syntactic or morphological simplification. By including metadata into our analysis, we detected overrepresentations of words and phrases in texts by individual publishers that cannot be considered typical features of Easy German. Moreover, we showed that text genre variation is expressed differently in Easy vs. Standard German. Many of these findings are not surprising keeping in mind the rules and recommendations for simplifying text in German. Others, however, such as the distinctivity of potentially ambiguous pronouns in Easy German, are related to simplifications of another aspect, showing that simplifying text with regard to one feature can make it more complex with regard to another. Our approach can thus be used to uncover linguistic features of Easy German that have been overlooked so far.

In a next step, we will use our insights about typical linguistic features of Easy German to design psycholinguistic studies evaluating the comprehensibility of specific linguistic characteristics for people with learning difficulties, one of the main user groups of Easy German. In the future, we will also apply our approach to simplified variants other than Easy German (e.g. Plain German or German texts addressing children) and to further text genres (e.g. lexicons or administrative text). Our findings can be used to classify simplified text found on the web or generated by AI but not carrying any specific label, or to fine-tune simplification algorithms.

6 Acknowledgements

This research is funded by *Deutsche Forschungsgemeinschaft* (DFG, German Research Foundation) – Project-ID 232722074 – SFB 1102. We would like to thank Stefan Fischer for his assistance in creating this corpus and computing KLD as well as Nele Benz for her meticulous metadata collection and her help in acquiring and preprocessing text material. Additionally, we would like to thank the reviewers for their insightful comments. Finally, we would like to acknowledge the creators of the other simplified German corpora for making their data available.

References

Benedikt Adelmann. 2021. Batch Substring Edit Distance (Benadelm).

Benedikt Adelmann and Evelyn Gius. 2020. Korpusbereinigung für größere Textmengen. Eine (kurze) Problematisierung und ein Lösungsansatz für Duplikate. In *DHd 2020 Spielräume: Digital Humanities zwischen Modellierung und Interpretation. Konferenzabstracts*, pages 331–334, Paderborn.

Laurence Anthony. 2023. *AntConc (Version 4.2.3) [Computer Software]*. Tokyo, Japan: Waseda University.

Alessia Battisti, Dominik Pfütze, Andreas Säuberli, Marek Kostrzewa, and Sarah Ebling. 2020. A corpus for automatic readability assessment and text simplification of German. In *Proceedings of the Twelfth Language Resources and Evaluation Conference*, pages 3302–3311, Marseille, France. European Language Resources Association.

Bettina M. Bock. 2014. "Leichte Sprache": Abgrenzung, Beschreibung und Problemstellungen aus Sicht der Linguistik. In Susanne Jekat, Heike Elisabeth Jüngst, Klaus Schubert, and Claudia Villiger, editors, *Sprache barrierefrei gestalten: Perspektiven aus der Angewandten Linguistik*, 69, pages 17–51. Frank & Timme, Berlin.

Bettina M. Bock. 2017a. Das Passiv- und Negationsverbot "Leichter Sprache" auf dem Prüfstand - empirische Ergebnisse aus Verstehenstest und Korpusuntersuchung. *Sprachreport*, 33(1):20–28.

Bettina M. Bock. 2017b. Texte in "Leichter Sprache"' schreiben. Zwischen Regelerfüllung und Kontext-Angemessenheit. In Dagmar Knorr, Katrin Lehnen, and Kirsten Schindler, editors, *Schreiben im Übergang von Bildungsinstitutionen*, number Band 15 in Textproduktion und Medium, pages 189–213. Peter Lang, Frankfurt am Main [a.o.].

Bettina M. Bock. 2018. *"Leichte Sprache"' - kein Regelwerk. Sprachwissenschaftliche Ergebnisse und Praxisempfehlungen aus dem LeiSA-Projekt*. Universität Leipzig, Leipzig.

Ursula Bredel and Christiane Maaß. 2016. *Leichte Sprache. Theoretische Grundlagen, Orientierung für die Praxis*. Dudenverlag, Berlin.

Bundesministerium der Justiz und für Verbraucherschutz. 2017. Verordnung zur Schaffung barrierefreier Informationstechnik nach dem Behindertengleichstellungsgesetz (Barrierefreie-Informationstechnik-Verordnung - BITV 2.0). ausfertigungsdatum: 12.09.2011. zuletzt geändert: 21.05.2019.

Council of Europe. 2001. *Common European Framework of Reference for Languages: Learning, Teaching, Assessment*. Cambridge University Press.

Matthew W. Crocker, Vera Demberg, and Elke Teich. 2015. Information Density and Linguistic Encoding (IDeaL). *KI - Künstliche Intelligenz*, 30(1):77–81.

Peter Fankhauser, Jörg Knappen, and Elke Teich. 2014. Exploring and visualizing variation in language resources. In *Proceedings of the 9th Language Resources and Evaluation Conference*, pages 4125–4128, Reykjavik, Iceland.

Julia Fuchs. 2017. Leichte Sprache und ihr Regelwerk - betrachtet aus der Perspektive der Informationsstruktur. *Sprachwissenschaft*, 42:97–119.

Julia Fuchs. 2019. Leichte Sprache auf dem Prüfstand. Realisierungsvarianten von kausalen Relationen in Leichte-Sprache-Texten. *Sprachwissenschaft*, 44(4):441–480.

Susanne Gross. 2015. Regeln und Standards für leicht verständliche Sprache. Ein Rundblick. In Klaus Candussi and Walburga Fröhlich, editors, *Leicht Lesen. Der Schlüssel zur Welt*, pages 81–105. Böhlau Verlag, Wien [a.o.].

Silvia Hansen-Schirra, Jean Nitzke, and Silke Gutermuth. 2021. An Intralingual Parallel Corpus of Translations into German Easy Language (Geasy Corpus): What Sentence Alignments Can Tell Us About Translation Strategies in Intralingual Translation. In Vincent X. Wang, Lily Lim, and Defeng Li, editors, *New Perspectives on Corpus Translation Studies*, pages 281–298. Springer Singapore, Singapore.

Katja Häuser and Jutta Kray. 2021. Effects of prediction error on episodic memory retrieval: evidence from sentence reading and word recognition. *Language, Cognition and Neuroscience*, pages 1–17.

Ulrich Heid, Helmut Schmid, Kerstin Eckart, and Erhard Hinrichs. 2010. A corpus representation format for linguistic web services: The D-SPIN text corpus format and its relationship with ISO standards. In *Proceedings of the Seventh International Conference on Language Resources and Evaluation (LREC'10)*, Valletta, Malta. European Language Resources Association (ELRA).

Freya Hewett. 2023. APA-RST: A text simplification corpus with RST annotations. In *Proceedings of the 4th Workshop on Computational Approaches to Discourse (CODI 2023)*, pages 173–179, Toronto, Canada. Association for Computational Linguistics.

Inclusion Europe. *Informationen für alle. Europäische Regeln, wie man Informationen leicht lesbar und leicht verständlich macht*. Brussels.

Inclusion Europe. n.d. *Informationen für alle. Europäische Regeln, wie man Informationen leicht lesbar und leicht verständlich macht*. Brussels. `https://easy-to-read.inclusion-europe.eu/wp-content/uploads/2014/12/DE_Information_for_all.pdf`.

Sarah Jablotschkin and Heike Zinsmeister. 2021. Annotating colon constructions in Easy and Plain German. In *Proceedings of the 3rd Swiss conference on barrier-free communication (BfC 2020)*, pages 125–134, Winterthur (online), June 29–July 4, 2020. Winterthur: ZHAW Zurich University of Applied Sciences.

Sarah Jablotschkin and Heike Zinsmeister. 2023. LeiKo. ein Vergleichskorpus für Leichte und Einfache Sprache. In Marc Kupietz and Thomas Schmidt, editors, *Neue Entwicklungen in der Korpuslandschaft der Germanistik: Beiträge zur IDS-Methodenmesse 2022*, pages 71–88. Narr Francke Attempto, Tübingen.

Varada Kolhatkar, Adam Roussel, Stefanie Dipper, and Heike Zinsmeister. 2018. Survey: Anaphora With Non-nominal Antecedents in Computational Linguistics: a Survey. *Computational Linguistics*, 44(3):547–612.

Daisy Lange. 2019. Der Genitiv in der "Leichten Sprache"' – das Für und Wider aus theoretischer und empirischer Sicht. *Zeitschrift für Angewandte Linguistik*, 70(1):37–72.

Daisy Lange and Bettina M. Bock. 2016. Was heißt "leichte" und "einfache Sprache"'? Empirische Untersuchungen zu Begriffssemantik und tatsächlicher Gebrauchspraxis. In Nathalie Mälzer, editor, *Barrierefreie Kommunikation: Perspektiven aus Theorie und Praxis*, pages 117–134. Frank & Timme, Berlin.

Alexander Lasch. 2017. Zum Verständnis morphosyntaktischer Merkmale in der funktionalen Varietät "Leichte Sprache". In Bettina M. Bock, Ulla Fix, and Daisy Lange, editors, *"Leichte Sprache"' im Spiegel theoretischer und angewandter Forschung*, pages 275–300. Frank & Timme, Berlin.

Christiane Maaß. 2015. *Leichte Sprache. Das Regelbuch*. Lit, Münster.

Netzwerk Leichte Sprache. 2014. *Leichte Sprache. Ein Ratgeber*. Bundesministerium für Arbeit und Soziales (BMAS), Bonn.

Netzwerk Leichte Sprache, editor. 2021. *Leichte Sprache verstehen: Mit Beispielen aus dem Alltag, Tipps für die Praxis und zahlreichen Texten in Leichter Sprache*. S. Marix Verlag, Wiesbaden.

Netzwerk Leichte Sprache. 2022. *Die Regeln für Leichte Sprache vom Netzwerk Leichte Sprache*.

Netzwerk People First Deutschland e.V. *Wer sind wir? Der Verein*.

Simon Rodier and Dave Carter. 2020. Online near-duplicate detection of news articles. In *Proceedings of the Twelfth Language Resources and Evaluation Conference*, pages 1242–1249, Marseille, France. European Language Resources Association.

Claude Elwood Shannon. 1948. A mathematical theory of communication. *Bell System Technical Journal*, 27:379–423, 623–656.

Regina Stodden, Omar Momen, and Laura Kallmeyer. 2023. DEplain: A German parallel corpus with intralingual translations into plain language for sentence and document simplification. In *Proceedings of the 61st Annual Meeting of the Association for Computational Linguistics (Volume 1: Long Papers)*, pages 16441–16463, Toronto, Canada. Association for Computational Linguistics.

Marita Tjarks-Sobhani. 2012. Leichte Sprache gegen schwer verständliche Texte. *Technische Kommunikation*, 34(6):23–30.

Vanessa Toborek, Moritz Busch, Malte Boßert, Christian Bauckhage, and Pascal Welke. 2023. A new aligned simple German corpus. In *Proceedings of the 61st Annual Meeting of the Association for Computational Linguistics (Volume 1: Long Papers)*, pages 11393–11412, Toronto, Canada. Association for Computational Linguistics.

Jorrig Vogels, David M. Howcroft, Elli Tourtouri, and Vera Demberg. 2019. How speakers adapt object descriptions to listeners under load. *Language, Cognition and Neuroscience*, 35(1):78–92.

A Appendix

Due to the formatting, you will find Table 3 on the following page.

	Corpus	Reference	Size	Architecture	Alignments	Annotations
1	APA-RST*	Hewett (2023)	Standard: 9,567 tokens; A2: 1,871 tokens; B1: 2,009 tokens	parallel (Original, A2, B1)	text, sentence	RST
2	DEplain*	Stodden et al. (2023)	1,239 document pairs; 16,562 sentence pairs	parallel (Standard, Plain)	text, sentence	simplification operations; aspects of coherence and simplicity
3	Geasy*	Hansen-Schirra et al. (2021)	Standard: 1,078,643 words; Easy: 292,552 words	parallel (Standard, Easy)	text, sentence	dependencies and tree alignments (in progress)
4	LeiKo*	Jablotschkin/Zinsmeister (2023)	Plain: 16,706 tokens; Easy: 39,653 tokens	comparable	none	lemmas, POS; dependencies; PDTB relations; coreference; text structure; typography; metadata
5	LeiSa corpus	Lange/Bock (2016)	Easy: 1,382,142 tokens; simplified (other): 882,806 tokens	comparable	none	POS; text level: 'area of communication'
6	Simple German Corpus*	Toborek et al. (2023)	Plain: 94,808 tokens; Easy: 155,285 tokens; Standard: 404,771 tokens	parallel (Standard, simplified)	text, sentence	none
7	WebCorpus*	Battisti et al. (2020)	approx. 6,200 documents; 211,000 sentences	parallel (Standard, Simplified)/comparable	text, sentence	lemmas, morphological units, POS, dependencies, text structure, typography, metadata
8	DE-Lite (under construction)	this text	DE-Lite v1: approx. 8,000 texts/more than 3 million tokens	parallel (Standard, Easy; Standard, Plain; Standard, children)/ monolingual	text	will be published in upcoming versions

Table 3: Related German Corpora (sizes are quoted from the original publications) and our own DE-Lite corpus; *) Corpus texts (partially) included in DE-Lite

A Diachronic Analysis of Gender-Neutral Language on wikiHow

Katharina Suhr **Michael Roth**
Institute for Natural Language Processing
University of Stuttgart
suhr.katharina@gmail.com, michael.roth@ims.uni-stuttgart.de

Abstract

As a large how-to website, wikiHow's mission is to *empower every person on the planet to learn how to do anything.*[1] An important part of including everyone also linguistically is the use of gender-neutral language. In this short paper, we study in how far articles from wikiHow fulfill this criterion based on manual annotation and automatic classification. In particular, we employ a classifier to analyze how the use of gender-neutral language has developed over time. Our results show that although about 75% of all articles on wikiHow were written in a gender-neutral way from the outset, revisions have a higher tendency to add gender-specific language than to change it to inclusive wording.

1 Introduction

Gender-neutral language, also known as gender-inclusive language, has its roots in the 1970s, when second-wave feminists criticized the generic use of 'he' and of gendered job titles (Hord, 2016). The demand for including women linguistically, by using gender-neutral language, has steadily increased since then. Beyond that, gender-neutral language further benefits individuals who identify outside the gender binary or when the gender of the person talked about is unknown (Hord, 2016).

The online platform wikiHow claims to be "the world's leading how-to website".[2] But is it also leading in terms of using gender-neutral language? Similar to Wikipedia, wikiHow articles can be edited publicly and all changes are stored in a revision history. A main difference is that articles are not only written by volunteers, but also by wikiHow's own experts, possibly suggesting that editing criteria also include aspects of inclusive language. In this work, we study whether this is the case based on articles written in English, the primary language used on wikiHow.

Many articles, such as *How to Pack for a Holiday*, address the reader directly, using the gender-neutral pronoun 'you'. However, there are also articles showing that gender-neutral language is not implemented by all editors. For example, the article *How to Address a Congressman* uses the term 'congressman' in the title and the gendered phrase 'congressman and congresswoman' throughout the article text. Even though this phrase avoids the generic masculine, it is still not gender-neutral as it may not address, for instance, individuals outside the binary. A gender-neutral replacement here would have been the term 'congressperson'.

In general, different factors may contribute to the implementation of gender-neutral language in instructional texts. As a first step towards their analysis, this work seeks to answer the following questions: 1) How common are gender-neutral articles in wikiHow? 2) How did the ratio change over time? 3) Are specific users responsible for corresponding revisions?

2 Related Work

Among the first papers to include discussions of gender-neutral language for queer identities, Cao and Daumé III (2020) studied how non-binary pronouns (singular they/them and neo-pronouns) are handled by co-reference resolution systems. For this, they created two new datasets: one on "English Wikipedia about people with non-binary gender identities" and one on "articles from LGBTQ periodicals, and fan-fiction stories from Archive Of Our Own". Their results indicate that system performance significantly drops for their curated data, relative to results reported on other datasets.

Sun et al. (2021) and Vanmassenhove et al. (2021) created systems to rewrite gendered text into gender-neutral language. Both focused on using

[1] http://www.wikihow.com/wikiHow:Mission, accessed 6 December 2023

[2] http://www.wikihow.com/wikiHow:About-wikiHow, accessed 6 December 2023

Proceedings of the Fourth Workshop on Language Technology for Equality, Diversity, Inclusion, pages 118–123
March 21, 2024 ©2024 Association for Computational Linguistics

GENDERED	Texts that uses words or phrases associated with binary gender, e.g. 'he', 'she', 'he or she', 'chairman', 'congressman', 'girlfriend/boyfriend'
GENDER-NEUTRAL	Texts that uses words and phrases that are inclusive of all genders, e.g. 'they', 'them', 'chairperson', 'partner'
NO GENDER	Texts that only show words that are not associated with any gender, e.g. 'you', 'I'

Table 1: Labels used in the annotation of the gold dataset.

they/them as neutral pronouns, as well as switching words with lexical gender to a neutral version. The words that had to be changed were defined by a static list. In contrast, Bartl and Leavy (2022) created a method that uses online dictionaries to determine the lexical gender of words. Both of these methodologies to identify words to change the gender are relevant to our work on classifying articles into gender-neutral and gendered language.

Other challenging tasks, in the landscape of gender and language studies, are Sexist Language Detection (Rodríguez-Sánchez et al., 2021, 2022) and Heteronormative Language Detection. They identify specific aspects of language that can additionally lead to bias. In the sexist language detection shared task (EXIST 2021, EXIST 2022) the goal is to identify hostile, subtle and/or benevolent sexism in English and Spanish tweets towards women (Rodríguez-Sánchez et al., 2021, 2022). In contrast, the goal of the heteronormativity language detection is to identify heteronormative assumptions in a text. Heteronormativity is a "social, political and economic regimen [where] the only acceptable and normal form to express sexual and affective desires (...) is heterosexuality" (Vásquez et al., 2022).

Instructional Text have, among other things, been used to analyzing their structure to create instructional text and answer how-to questions (Aouladomar and Saint-Dizier, 2005; Delpech and Saint-Dizier, 2008) or extract procedural knowledge (Zhang et al., 2012). An online-platform that offers a variety of instructional texts on different topics is wikiHow. WikiHow has served as a source of information for numerous research papers. For example, to detect a users' intent (Zhang et al., 2020) or to create a summarization tool (Koupaee and Wang, 2018).

In their paper, Anthonio et al. (2020) investigated how edits of users can improve texts. If they only improve the instructions' style and correctness, or if they also provide clarifications needed to follow the instructions and achieve the goal. They addressed various types of revision in their paper, such as spelling/grammar, paraphrase, information deletion, and information modification/insertion. However, neither of these types explicitly address gender or gender-neutral language. Gender-neutral language is especially important in how-to guides that are addressed to a general audience.

3 Data and Annotation

During the beginning of this work, in February 2023, wikiHow still offered the *Export pages* service, also referenced by Anthonio et al. (2020), for downloading articles and revision histories. We were able to scrape $11,074,729$ versions of a total of $256,455$ articles using this service.

We selected a small subset of these articles to first manually annotate whether gender-neutral language is used. Following our original intuition that gender-neutral language may get implemented in articles over time, we specifically searched for article versions in which the phrase 'gender' appears in the comment of a revision. From this set, 129 articles were selected.

Due to the length of the full articles, we split them into paragraphs for the annotation. One of the authors annotated each paragraph using the labels GENDERED, GENDER-NEUTRAL and NO GENDER, following the definitions provided in Table 1. A second annotator also annotated 20 articles for reproducibility and quality control. The agreement between the author and the second annotator was very high, with $\kappa = 0.912$ (Cohen, 1960).

A total of $2,247$ paragraphs were annotated, with 725 labelled GENDERED and $1,235$ labelled GENDER-NEUTRAL/NO GENDER. On the article level, we combine the labels as follows: If there is at least one paragraph with the label GENDERED, the full article is labeled GENDERED. All the remaining cases are labeled GENDER-NEUTRAL. As a result of this step, 29 annotated articles are labelled GENDER-NEUTRAL, while the remaining 100 are GENDERED.

	Precision	**Recall**	**F_1**
MAJORITY	0.601	0.775	0.677
PRONOUNS	0.849	0.837	0.842
STATIC LIST	**0.890**	**0.884**	**0.870**
INFERENCE	0.854	0.860	0.849
COMBINED	0.869	0.868	0.853

Table 2: Classification performance on our data. All metrics represent ***weighted averages*** across both classes.

	Precision	**Recall**	**F_1**
MINORITY	0.225	1.000	0.367
PRONOUNS	0.618	**0.724**	**0.667**
STATIC LIST	**0.938**	0.517	**0.667**
INFERENCE	0.789	0.517	0.652
COMBINED	0.875	0.483	0.622

Table 3: Classification performance on our data. All metrics for **GENDER-NEUTRAL** as the 'positive' class

4 Pilot Study

For classification, different rule-based and supervised variants were compared. Since gender-neutral language can broadly be defined in terms of specific features, we focus on the following rule-based classifiers:

- PRONOUNS uses regular expressions to identify gendered pronouns in an article version.
- STATIC LIST compares the content of an article to a pre-defined list of gendered words, which we collect from an online source[3] and previous work (Vanmassenhove et al., 2021).
- INFERENCE uses an online dictionary to infer the lexical gender of each noun (if any) that occurs in an article version, using code made available by (Bartl and Leavy, 2022).
- COMBINED is a combination of the previous two classifiers, labeling each paragraph as GENDERED if at least one term has a lexical gender or appears in the static word lists.

Finally, we also experimented with different supervised classifiers, but we did not observe any improvements over the rule-based classifiers.

As shown in Table 2, the classifier with the highest overall scores is the STATIC LIST classifier, with a weighted F_1-score of 0.87. The other three classifiers achieve comparable results to each other but perform 2–3 percentage points worse than STATIC LIST in terms of F_1-score.

The unbalanced setting, with 100 gendered articles out of 129 (77.5%), makes it particularly easy to identify the majority class. In Table 3, we show unweighted scores for the minority class, GENDER-NEUTRAL. As shown by the results, the PRONOUNS classifier achieves a higher recall, while the STATIC LIST classifier has a higher precision. Weighing precision and recall equally leads to the same GENDER-NEUTRAL F_1-score for both classifiers, namely a harmonic mean of 0.667. As STATIC LIST performs better for the majority class as well as in terms of weighted average scores, we use STATIC LIST in the next steps of this work.

In an error analysis, we found that one issue of STATIC LIST and other rule-based classifiers is that gendered terms can also be used as meta language, which should be classified as GENDER-NEUTRAL. For instance, some articles discuss topics related to transgender or queer issues and what terms can/cannot be used in what contexts: "An example of misgendering would be using she/her pronouns for someone who actually uses they/them, or assuming somebody with long hair is a girl." (from the article *How to Avoid Misgendering*).

5 Analysis

We apply the best-performing classifier from our pilot study, STATIC LIST, to all article revisions collected in the creation of our data (§3). The following subsections discuss three analyses to answer the questions outlined in Section 1. First, we examine the overall distribution of GENDERED and GENDER-NEUTRAL articles according to their latest version (§5.1). We then take a look at how this distribution changed over time (§5.2). Finally, we investigate the direction of revisions and check how different editors contributed to it (§5.3).

5.1 Status Quo

Given the last versions of all articles as of February 2023, our best-performing classifier labels 74% of them as GENDER-NEUTRAL. We observe a large variance regarding the use of gender-neutral language across the 19 high-level categories of wikiHow. These categories and their statistics can be

[3] https://ielts.com.au/australia/prepare/article-grammar-101-feminine-and-masculine-words-in-english, accessed 11 December 2023

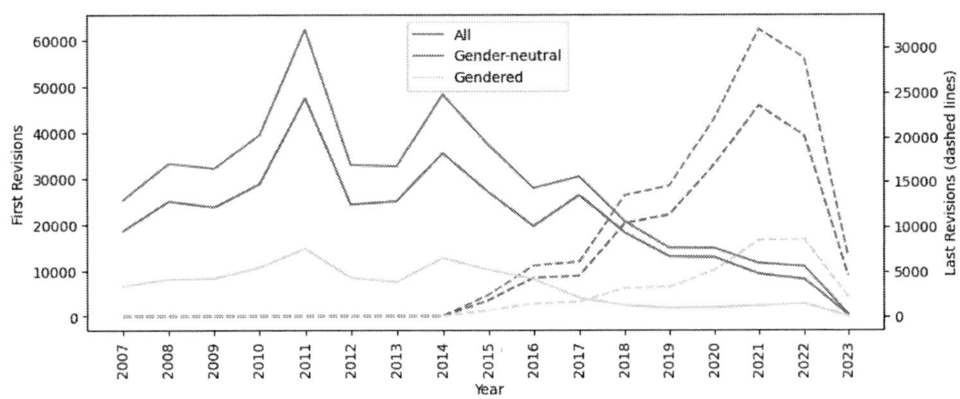

Figure 1: Overview of classifications of the first and last version of each article between 2004 and 2023.

Category	Revisions	GN
Food and Entertaining	842.390	91%
Computers and Electronics	105.4193	90%
Home and Garden	595.592	85%
Cars & Other Vehicles	249.852	80%
Hobbies and Crafts	1.169.876	73%
Sports and Fitness	427.633	69%
Travel	55.566	69%
Personal Care and Style	736.606	64%
Finance and Business	485.902	64%
Education and Communications	1.084.077	59%
Arts and Entertainment	1.123.195	59%
Holidays and Traditions	96.430	57%
Work World	73.905	57%
Health	1.157.745	55%
Pets and Animals	473.948	42%
Family Life	255.824	32%
Philosophy and Religion	132.769	30%
Youth	518.256	27%
Relationships	518.848	16%

Table 4: Percentage of classified revisions, that were classified as Gender-Neutral, separated by their categories.

found in Table 4. In most categories, the majority of articles are classified as GENDER-NEUTRAL, including for example *Computers and Electronics* (90%) and *Hobbies and Crafts* (73%). In contrast, only a minority of articles in the categories *Family Life* (32%), *Youth* (27%) and *Relationships* (16%) are GENDER-NEUTRAL.

5.2 Changes over Time

Grouping revisions together based on their article offered the opportunity to analyze the revision history of each article. As mentioned above, 74% of the last version of articles were classified as gender-neutral. But in their initial version, we found 76.4% of all articles to be classified as GENDER-NEUTRAL, which implies a decrease of 2.4 percentage points over time.

Even though there is an overall decrease in the proportion of gender-neutral articles, Figure 1 shows that there has been substantial variation over the years. In 2017, for example, the number of new GENDER-NEUTRAL articles increased while the number of new GENDERED articles decreased. In contrast, we find fewer GENDER-NEUTRAL articles last updated in 2022 in comparison to 2021, whereas the number of articles classified as GENDERED in both years stayed roughly the same.

5.3 Direction of Revisions

For each article, we compare each version's classification to the preceding one. This offers the opportunity to analyze revisions to GENDER-NEUTRAL language as well as additions of GENDERED language. In general, an article can go through multiple or no changes of label. The article *How to Put Hot Outfits Together*, for instance, saw a total of 12 changes but the article both started out as GENDER-NEUTRAL in 2007 and its last version from 2019 is still classified as GENDER-NEUTRAL.

Although GENDER-NEUTRAL versions are the majority, there are slightly more changes (51.6%) to GENDERED than revisions to GENDER-NEUTRAL. Even when examining these revisions grouped together by contributor, it is clear that most

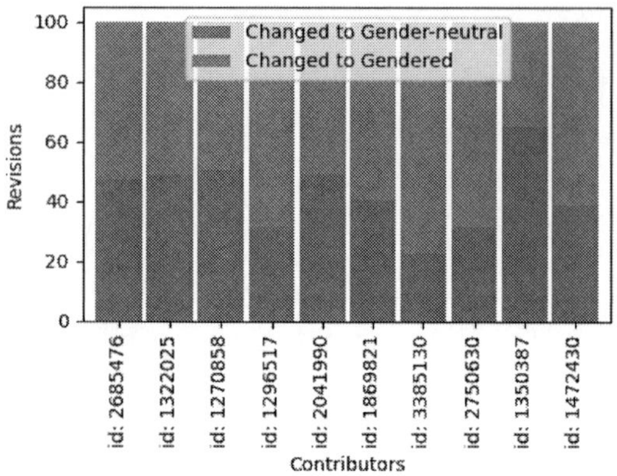

Figure 2: Ids of top-10 contributors and corresponding percentages of classified revisions. Only 1350387 performed more changes towards GENDER-NEUTRAL.

contributors are adding gender-specific language rather than revising articles to be gender-neutral. For example, Figure 2 shows that all top-8 contributors either changed more articles to GENDERED or made an equal number of edits in either direction. Among the top 10, only the second to last contributor changed substantially more articles to GENDER-NEUTRAL than to GENDERED language.

6 Conclusion

The objective of this work was to analyze the gender-neutral language of instructional texts. For this, a new dataset of revisions from wikiHow articles was created. The annotated gold dataset consists of 129 selected versions of how-to guides, 100 of which are gendered and 29 gender-neutral.

A comparison of different classifiers, mostly inspired by previous work, showed that a STATIC WORD LIST performed best on our data. A main advantage of static word lists is the option to clearly define which words are considered gendered or gender-neutral, making classifications simple and explainable. In contrast, other classifiers, such as LEXICAL INFERENCE may pick up on features associated with biological sex when detecting GENDERED language, which can lead to misidentification of binary and non-binary trans individuals.

Finally, we classified and analyzed a dataset of over 256,000 wikiHow articles with a total of more than 11 million article versions. Our findings discussed in Section 5 suggest that, even though most articles start out as gender-neutral, there has been no concentrated effort of editors to change gendered article versions to be gender-neutral. Nonetheless, we found several revisions in our annotation study, in which editors implemented gender-neutral language and explicitly mentioned this in the comment of the revision.

Limitations

The work presented in this paper exclusively analyzes texts written in English. Because natural and grammatical gender is encoded differently across various languages, the selected classification approach and its results are not directly applicable how-to guides written in other languages.

Furthermore, the findings in this paper are limited to one specific platform, namely wikiHow. Our results may not generalize to other platforms or to guides written for specialized topics, such as board game manuals or recipe books. Future work should address in how far the same trends can be observed outside of wikiHow.

Acknowledgements

Work by the second author was funded by the DFG Emmy Noether program (RO 4848/2-1).

References

Talita Anthonio, Irshad Bhat, and Michael Roth. 2020. wikiHowToImprove: A resource and analyses on edits in instructional texts. In *Proceedings of the Twelfth Language Resources and Evaluation Conference*, page 5721–5729, Marseille, France. European Language Resources Association.

Farida Aouladomar and Patrick Saint-Dizier. 2005. Towards Generating Procedural Texts: An Exploration of their Rhetorical and Argumentative Structure. In *Proceedings of the Tenth European Workshop on Natural Language Generation (ENLG-05)*, Aberdeen, Scotland. Association for Computational Linguistics.

Marion Bartl and Susan Leavy. 2022. Inferring Gender: A Scalable Methodology for Gender Detection with Online Lexical Databases. In *Proceedings of the Second Workshop on Language Technology for Equality, Diversity and Inclusion*, page 47–58, Dublin, Ireland. Association for Computational Linguistics.

Yang Trista Cao and Hal Daumé III. 2020. Toward Gender-Inclusive Coreference Resolution. In *Proceedings of the 58th Annual Meeting of the Association for Computational Linguistics*, page 4568–4595. Association for Computational Linguistics.

Jacob Cohen. 1960. A coefficient of agreement for nominal scales. *Educational and psychological measurement*, 20(1):37–46.

Estelle Delpech and Patrick Saint-Dizier. 2008. Investigating the Structure of Procedural Texts for Answering How-to Questions. In *Proceedings of the Sixth International Conference on Language Resources and Evaluation (LREC'08)*, Marrakech, Morocco. European Language Resources Association (ELRA).

Levi C. R. Hord. 2016. Bucking the Linguistic Binary: Gender Neutral Language in English, Swedish, French, and German. *Western Papers in Linguistics*, 3(11).

Mahnaz Koupaee and William Yang Wang. 2018. Wikihow: A large scale text summarization dataset. *arXiv preprint arXiv:1810.09305*.

Francisco Rodríguez-Sánchez, Jorge Carrillo-de Albornoz, Laura Plaza, Julio Gonzalo, Paolo Rosso, Miriam Comet, and Trinidad Donoso. 2021. Overview of EXIST 2021: sEXism Identification in Social neTworks. *Procesamiento del Lenguaje Natural*, 67:195–207.

Francisco Rodríguez-Sánchez, Jorge Carrillo-de Albornoz, Laura Plaza, Adrián Mendieta-Aragón, Guillermo Marco-Remón, Maryna Makeienko, María Plaza, Julio Gonzalo, Damiano Spina, and Paolo Rosso. 2022. Overview of EXIST 2022: sEXism Identification in Social neTworks. *Procesamiento del Lenguaje Natural*, 69:229–240.

Tony Sun, Kellie Webster, Apu Shah, William Yang Wang, and Melvin Johnson. 2021. They, Them, Theirs: Rewriting with Gender-Neutral English.

Eva Vanmassenhove, Chris Emmery, and Dimitar Shterionov. 2021. NeuTral Rewriter: A Rule-Based and Neural Approach to Automatic Rewriting into Gender Neutral Alternatives. In *Proceedings of the 2021 Conference on Empirical Methods in Natural Language Processing*, page 8940–8948. Association for Computational Linguistics.

Juan Vásquez, Gemma Bel-Enguix, Scott Thomas Andersen, and Sergio-Luis Ojeda-Trueba. 2022. HeteroCorpus: A Corpus for Heteronormative Language Detection. page 225–234, Seattle, Washington. Association for Computational Linguistics.

Li Zhang, Qing Lyu, and Chris Callison-Burch. 2020. Intent Detection with WikiHow. In *Proceedings of the 1st Conference of the Asia-Pacific Chapter of the Association for Computational Linguistics and the 10th International Joint Conference on Natural Language Processing*, pages 328–333, Suzhou, China. Association for Computational Linguistics.

Ziqi Zhang, Philip Webster, Victoria Uren, Andrea Varga, and Fabio Ciravegna. 2012. Automatically Extracting Procedural Knowledge from Instructional Texts using Natural Language Processing.

Overview of Third Shared Task on Homophobia and Transphobia Detection in Social Media Comments

Bharathi Raja Chakravarthi[1], **Prasanna Kumar Kumaresan**[2], **Ruba Priyadharshini**[3]
Paul Buitelaar[2], **Asha Hegde**[4], **Hosahalli Lakshmaiah Shashirekha**[4], **Saranya Rajiakodi**[5],
Miguel Ángel García-Cumbreras[6], **Salud María Jiménez-Zafra**[6],
José Antonio García-Díaz[7], **Rafael Valencia-García**[7], **Kishore Kumar Ponnusamy**[8],
Poorvi Shetty[9], **Daniel García-Baena**[6]

[1] School of Computer Science, University of Galway, Ireland.
[2] Data Science Institute, University of Galway, Ireland.
[3] Gandhigram Rural Institute-Deemed to be University, India.
[4] Mangalore University, Mangalore, India.
[5] Central University of Tamil Nadu, India. [6] SINAI, Universidad de Jaén, Spain.
[7] UMUTeam, Universidad de Murcia, Spain.
[8] Digital University of Kerala, India. [9] JSS College, Mysore.
bharathiraja.akr@gmail.com

Abstract

This paper provides a comprehensive summary of the "Homophobia and Transphobia Detection in Social Media Comments" shared task, which was held at the LT-EDI@EACL 2024. The objective of this task was to develop systems capable of identifying instances of homophobia and transphobia within social media comments. This challenge was extended across ten languages: English, Tamil, Malayalam, Telugu, Kannada, Gujarati, Hindi, Marathi, Spanish, and Tulu. Each comment in the dataset was annotated into three categories. The shared task attracted significant interest, with over 60 teams participating through the CodaLab platform. The submission of prediction from the participants was evaluated with the macro F1 score.

1 Introduction

The growth of the internet has given rise to the widespread use of social media, and numerous other online spaces (Chakravarthi, 2023). The use of social media in particular has seen a significant increase in communication across various languages around the world (Al-Hassan and Al-Dossari, 2022). These platforms enable users to post, share content and freely express their opinions on any subject at any time (Chakravarthi et al., 2022a)(Kumar et al., 2018). However, the liberty of expression found on the internet also comes with downsides. It allows individuals, who might otherwise feel powerless, to impact and even harm others' lives (Ponnusamy et al., 2023a). This is often facilitated by the anonymity and emotional detachment that online interactions provide (Kumaresan et al., 2023b).

The rapid increase in online content has raised significant concerns within digital communities (Kumaresan et al., 2022). This issue is particularly acute for individuals identifying as lesbian, gay, bisexual, transgender, and other LGBTQ+ identities, who often face heightened vulnerability (Díaz-Torres et al., 2020). Members of the LGBTQ+ community are frequently targets of harassment, discrimination, violence, and in extreme cases, even death, due to their appearance, who they love, or their gender identity (Kumaresan et al., 2023a). Sexual orientation and gender identity are fundamental aspects of personal identity and should be respected rather than used as grounds for discrimination (Thurlow, 2001). In several regions, being identified as LGBTQ+ can be life-threatening. Consequently, many seek support and connection through social media, hoping to find others with similar experiences and form supportive communities (Chakravarthi et al., 2022c)(Ponnusamy et al., 2023b).

The task at hand involves utilizing a newly established gold standard dataset designed for identifying instances of homophobia and transphobia. This shared task uses a new gold standard dataset in Dravidian and Indo-Arian languages Tamil, Malayalam, Telugu, Kannada, Gujarati, Tamil-English (code-mixed), Tulu, Hindi, Spanish, and English languages.

In this overview, we conducted a shared task on homophobia and transphobia at LT-EDI[1] in ten lan-

[1] https://sites.google.com/view/lt-edi-2024/

Proceedings of the Fourth Workshop on Language Technology for Equality, Diversity, Inclusion, pages 124–132
March 21, 2024

guages which were annotated in 3 labels. In the upcoming section, we will describe the task description, dataset statistics, and participant-provided experiment analysis to investigate homophobia and transphobia detection from the YouTube comments on Dravidian languages.

2 Related Work

In the realm of natural language processing and computational linguistics, recent studies have made significant strides in understanding and analyzing the nuances of language as it pertains to social issues. A notable example is the work of Zhang and Luo (2019), who compiled a corpus to examine the linguistic behaviors of homosexual individuals in China, shedding light on cultural and linguistic patterns. Similarly, Chakravarthi et al. (2022a) developed a fine-grained taxonomy specifically for homophobia and transphobia in English and Tamil languages, providing a structured framework for analyzing such content (Ponnusamy et al., 2023a).

Expanding on this, Chakravarthi et al. (2022c) spearheaded a shared task focused on the identification of homophobia, transphobia, and non-anti-LGBT+ content in Tamil, English, and Tamil-English (code-mixed) languages (Lande et al., 2023). This initiative was crucial in understanding the subtleties and variations of discriminatory language across different linguistic contexts. Complementing this, Chinnaudayar Navaneethakrishnan et al. (2022) conducted a study on sentiment analysis and homophobia detection in code-mixed Dravidian language YouTube comments, covering Tamil, Malayalam, and English. This research was pivotal in exploring the intersection of sentiment analysis and social bias detection in multilingual online spaces (Shanmugavadivel et al., 2022)(Subramanian et al., 2022).

In a related vein, Manikandan et al. (2022) employed transformer-based model methodologies like BERT and XLMRoBERTa to identify transphobic and homophobic insults in social media comments. Their work highlighted the efficacy of advanced computational models in detecting subtle and explicit forms of hate speech. Further, the growing prevalence of social media and its impact on communication and relationship building has been explored in depth by researchers like Chakravarthi et al. (2022c) and Chakravarthi et al. (2022b). Their studies delved into the dynamics of social networking sites like YouTube, where user interactions through comments, likes, and shares can significantly influence public discourse and perception.

However, this increased interaction on social platforms also brings challenges, as highlighted by Diefendorf and Bridges (2020), who explored the prevalence of antisocial behaviors like misogyny, sexism, homophobia, and transphobia. Larimore et al. (2021) further contributed to this discussion by examining the occurrence of racism and other forms of bias in online spaces. These studies underscore the importance of developing robust computational methods to detect and analyze such harmful content. The field has seen a surge in research focusing on text-based algorithms for identifying abusive language (Pannerselvam et al., 2023) and hate speech, as demonstrated by the work on YouTube comment mining and the analysis of social media data for detecting discriminatory language.

Building on this foundation, a notable study, conducted in 2021, delved into Homophobia and Transphobia identification, providing valuable insights and methodologies for future research in this area. This body of work collectively emphasizes the crucial role of computational linguistics in addressing social issues and fostering more inclusive and respectful online environments.

3 Task Description

This task marks the third year we have conducted a shared task focused on homophobia and transphobia detection[2]. We present a diverse dataset sourced from YouTube comments and posts in ten different languages: English, Tamil, Malayalam, Telugu, Kannada, Gujarati, Hindi, Marathi, Spanish, and Tulu. This dataset is thoughtfully annotated with three distinct labels: homophobia, transphobia, and non-anti-LGBT+ content (a category designated for content that does not exhibit either of these prejudiced behaviors). Participants in this task are provided with extensive training, development, and testing datasets. The primary objective for participants is to devise robust algorithms capable of accurately categorizing these comments and posts. Their systems must discern whether the text under scrutiny contains instances of homophobia, transphobia, or falls into the non-anti-LGBT+ category. This challenge not only addresses the pressing issue of online hate speech but also contributes to

[2]https://codalab.lisn.upsaclay.fr/competitions/16056

inclusive language detection in a global context, promoting safer online spaces for all.

4 Dataset

Social media platforms like Twitter, Facebook, and YouTube significantly influence public opinion through user-generated content, impacting reputations. Recognizing this, there's an increasing need for tools to extract emotions and identify irrelevant content online, especially on platforms like YouTube, where user comments are rapidly growing. This is particularly relevant for the LGBTQ+ community, who engage with such platforms and share their thoughts on various topics. Focusing on YouTube, we collected comments from videos related to LGBTQ+ themes. We avoided personal stories from LGBTQ+ individuals to maintain privacy. Using the YouTube Comment Scraper tool[3], we gathered comments and manually annotated them with three labels: 'Homophobic', 'Transphobic', and 'Non-anti-LGBT+ content'. Our dataset expanded to include ten languages: English, Tamil, Malayalam, Telugu, Kannada, Gujarati, Hindi, Marathi, Spanish, and Tulu. This diverse dataset was compiled following the annotation guidelines provided in the dataset research paper (Kumaresan et al., 2023b). Table 1 shows the dataset statistics for all languages with all three labels.

Languages	Set	H	T	N
English	Train	179	7	2,978
	Dev	42	2	748
	Test	55	4	931
Tamil	Train	453	145	2,064
	Dev	118	41	507
	Test	152	47	634
Malayalam	Train	476	170	2,468
	Dev	197	79	937
	Test	140	52	674
Telugu	Train	2,907	2,647	3,496
	Dev	588	605	747
	Test	624	571	744
Kannada	Train	2,765	2,835	4,463
	Dev	585	617	955
	Test	599	606	951
Gujarati	Train	2,267	2,004	3,848
	Dev	498	454	788
	Test	510	436	794
Hindi	Train	45	92	2,423
	Dev	2	13	305
	Test	3	10	308
Marathi	Train	551	377	2,572
	Dev	129	80	541
	Test	112	69	569
Spanish	Train	250	250	700
	Dev	93	93	200
	Test	150	150	300
Tulu	Train	188		542
	Test	67		312

Table 1: Dataset statistics for all languages (H-Homophobia, T-Transphobia, and N-Non-anti-LGBT+ content)

5 Participants Methodology

In our shared task, we had a total of 61 participants registered, 12 teams who submitted results in various languages. Various teams employed innovative methodologies to tackle the challenge of detecting homophobia and transphobia in social media comments. The "dkit_nlp" (Yadav et al., 2024) team utilized a BERT (bert-base-uncased) (Devlin et al., 2018) model, combining training and development sets and fine-tuning it with specific hyper-parameters for optimal performance. "MUCS" approached the task with voting classifiers, employing techniques like Syllable tf-idf, oversampling, and transformer-based BERT models, alongside mvlearn. "SCaLAR_sys1" utilized AdaBoost, integrating multiple classification models and focusing on hyper-parameter tuning to enhance the performance of their ensemble model. The "Hypnotize" team analyzed deep learning and transformer-based models across eight languages, focusing on data preprocessing and hyper-parameter tuning to address imbalances in certain languages.

"catnlp" adopted a transformer-based approach, retraining XLM-RoBERTa (Conneau et al., 2019) with script-switched Wikipedia[4] abstracts and customizing language profiles for multi-class classification. They evaluated their model across various pre-trained language models without significant improvement from additional social media data. "Quartet" (Allan H et al., 2024) implemented a thorough dataset analysis and preprocessing, followed by the use of traditional machine learning models and BERT models, selecting the best-performing model for the final evaluation. "MEnTr" (Arora et al., 2024) em-

[3] https://pypi.org/project/youtube-comment-scraper-python/

[4] https://en.wikipedia.org/wiki/ScriptSwitch

Team name	Run	M_F1-score	Rank
dkit (Yadav et al., 2024)	Run1	0.496	1
MUCS	Run2	0.493	2
KEC_AIDS	-	0.466	3
CUTN_CS_HOMO	BERT	0.457	4
SCaLAR	Run3	0.438	5
MEnTr (Arora et al., 2024)	-	0.407	6
Hypnotize	-	0.384	7
KEC_AI_NLP (Shanmugavadivel et al., 2024)	Run1	0.369	8
quartet (Allan H et al., 2024)	-	0.347	9
cantnlp	Run1	0.323	10
MasonTigers (Goswami et al., 2024)	-	0.323	10

Table 2: Rank list for English dataset

Team name	Run	M_F1-score	Rank
Hypnotize	-	0.880	1
MUCS	Run3	0.860	2
bytellm (Manukonda and Kodali, 2024)	-	0.801	3
MEnTr (Arora et al., 2024)	-	0.746	4
MasonTigers (Goswami et al., 2024)	-	0.512	5
quartet (Allan H et al., 2024)	-	0.483	6
KEC_AI_NLP (Shanmugavadivel et al., 2024)	Run1	0.315	7

Table 3: Rank list for Tamil dataset

ployed an ensemble model integrating three transformer models—Multilingual BERT (Devlin et al., 2018), XLM-RoBERTa(Conneau et al., 2019), and MuRIL (Khanuja et al., 2021) with dataset augmentation to enhance generalization across languages. "KEC_AI_NLP" (Shanmugavadivel et al., 2024) used a combination of machine learning and deep learning techniques, with a focus on preprocessing and SMOTE oversampling, finding that the random forest model yielded the highest accuracy. "MasonTiger" (Goswami et al., 2024) used XLM-R for nine languages and few-shot prompting for Tulu, addressing the challenge posed by imbalanced datasets. Finally, "bytesizedllm" (Manukonda and Kodali, 2024) utilized custom-built subword tokenizers and embeddings from AI4Bharat's data, employing a Bidirectional Long Short-Term Memory (Bi-LSTM) classifier for their classification tasks. The "CUTN_CS_HOMO" team approached the shared task with Malayalam and English datasets, addressing class imbalances with RandomOverSampler for oversampling. They utilized mBERT and MuRIL (Khanuja et al., 2021) for Malayalam and BERT and RoBERTa (Conneau et al., 2019) for English, training with a learning rate of 2e-5 over four epochs. Their models yielded high accuracy, achieving 94% with both BERT and RoBERTa for English and up to 96% with MuRIL for Malayalam, ranking them 1st in Malayalam and 4th in English. Each team's unique approach contributed to the advancement of understanding in the field of online hate speech detection on homophobia and transphobia.

6 Results

There was a total of 61 participants from the 12 teams submitted their results. For English 11 teams, Tamil 7 teams, Spanish 4 teams, Hindi 7 teams, Gujarati 6 teams, Telugu 8 teams, Kannada 8 teams, Malayalam 9 teams, Marathi 6 teams, and Tulu 4 teams submitted the final results of all languages. Table 2, 3, 4, 5, 6, 7, 8, 9, 10 and 11 shows the final rank list of all languages. We used the average macro F1 score to rank the teams as it identifies the F1 score in each label and calculates their unweighted average. Macro F1 scores arrange the runs in descending order. The "dkit" (Yadav et al., 2024) achieved Rank 1 in English, owing to their effective combination of training and development sets, a strategic cap on sequence length at 128, and meticulous hyperparameter tuning on the BERT

Team name	Run	M_F1-score	Rank
MEnTr (Arora et al., 2024)	-	0.582	1
MUCS	Run3	0.532	2
MasonTigers (Goswami et al., 2024)	-	0.499	3
KEC_AI_NLP (Shanmugavadivel et al., 2024)	Run1	0.369	4

Table 4: Rank list for Spanish dataset

Team name	Run	M_F1-score	Rank
MUCS	Run2	0.458	1
SCaLAR	Run1	0.410	2
Hypnotize	-	0.403	3
cantnlp	Run1	0.326	4
quartet (Allan H et al., 2024)	-	0.326	4
MasonTigers (Goswami et al., 2024)	-	0.326	4
MEnTr (Arora et al., 2024)	-	0.325	5

Table 5: Rank list for Hindi dataset

Team name	Run	M_F1-score	Rank
Hypnotize	-	0.968	1
cantnlp	Run1	0.962	2
MEnTr (Arora et al., 2024)	-	0.960	3
MUCS	Run2	0.958	4
MasonTigers (Goswami et al., 2024)	-	0.935	5
quartet (Allan H et al., 2024)	-	0.893	6

Table 6: Rank list for Gujarati dataset

Team name	Run	M_F1-score	Rank
Hypnotize	-	0.971	1
MasonTigers (Goswami et al., 2024)	-	0.971	1
MEnTr (Arora et al., 2024)	-	0.960	2
byteLLM (Manukonda and Kodali, 2024)	-	0.959	3
MUCS	Run1	0.958	4
SCaLAR	Run1	0.911	5
quartet (Allan H et al., 2024)	-	0.891	6
KEC_AI_NLP (Shanmugavadivel et al., 2024)	Run1	0.369	7

Table 7: Rank list for Telugu dataset

(bert-base-uncased) model. The “Hypnotize" team showed versatility across languages, securing Rank 1 in Tamil, Gujarati, Telugu, and Marathi, while also obtaining Rank 2 in Malayalam and Kannada and Rank 3 in Hindi. Their success was due to their comprehensive approach that included deep learning and transformer-based models, rigorous data preprocessing, and hyperparameter adjustments.

“MUCS", demonstrating their prowess, achieved Rank 1 in Hindi and Kannada, and Rank 2 in English, Tamil, Spanish, Marathi, and Tulu. Their methodology centered around voting classifiers trained with Syllable tfidf, augmented by oversampling and TL bert models, along with mvlearn. “MEnTr" (Arora et al., 2024), with their ensemble model integrating mBERT, XLM-RoBERTa, and MURIL, and complemented by strategic dataset augmentation, earned Rank 1 in Tulu and Spanish, and Rank 3 in Marathi, Telugu, and Gujarati. “CUTN_CS_HOMO", although specific details of their methodology were not provided, achieved Rank 1 in Malayalam, showcasing their expertise

Team name	Run	M_F1-score	Rank
MUCS	Run2	0.948	1
Hypnotize	-	0.946	2
MasonTigers (Goswami et al., 2024)	-	0.945	3
cantnlp	Run1	0.943	4
MEnTr (Arora et al., 2024)	-	0.935	5
bytellm (Manukonda and Kodali, 2024)	-	0.922	6
SCaLAR	Run1	0.903	7
quartet (Allan H et al., 2024)	-	0.887	8

Table 8: Rank list for Kannada dataset

Team name	Run	M_F1-score	Rank
CUTN_CS_HOMO	MuRIL	0.942	1
Hypnotize	-	0.909	2
bytellm (Manukonda and Kodali, 2024)	-	0.891	3
KEC_AI_NLP (Shanmugavadivel et al., 2024)	Run1	0.883	4
quartet (Allan H et al., 2024)	-	0.877	5
MUCS	Run3	0.870	6
cantnlp	Run2	0.775	7
MEnTr (Arora et al., 2024)	-	0.744	8
MasonTigers (Goswami et al., 2024)	-	0.505	9

Table 9: Rank list for Malayalam dataset

Team name	Run	M_F1-score	Rank
Hypnotize	-	0.626	1
MUCS	Run2	0.537	2
MEnTr (Arora et al., 2024)	-	0.488	3
MasonTigers (Goswami et al., 2024)	-	0.438	4
cantnlp	Run1	0.433	5
quartet (Allan H et al., 2024)	-	0.391	6

Table 10: Rank list for Marathi dataset

Team name	Run	M_F1-score	Rank
MEnTr (Arora et al., 2024)	Run1	0.707	1
MUCS	Run2	0.620	2
MasonTigers (Goswami et al., 2024)	Run1	0.452	3
cantnlp	Run1	0.452	3

Table 11: Rank list for Tulu dataset

in the field. These results underscore the diverse and innovative computational strategies employed by the teams in addressing the challenging task of detecting homophobia and transphobia across different languages on social media platforms.

7 Conclusion

We presented the third shared task overview on homophobia and transphobia detection in social media comments on ten different language datasets. We expect this task to have a long-term impact on the NLP domain because we received a variety of submissions with various methodologies. the most successful system was achieved by synthesizing advanced machine learning techniques, custom data preprocessing, and strategic model finetuning, effectively addressing the complex challenge of detecting homophobia and transphobia in multilingual social media content. The prediction evaluation was evaluated with a macro F1 score. The increased number of participants and improved system performance indicate a growing interest in Dravidian NLP.

Acknowledgements

This work was conducted with the financial support of the Science Foundation Ireland Centre for Research Training in Artificial Intelligence under Grant No. 18/CRT/6223, supported in part by a research grant from Science Foundation Ireland (SFI) under Grant Number SFI/12/RC/2289_P2(Insight_2). It has also been partially supported by Project CONSENSO (PID2021-122263OB-C21), Project MODERATES (TED2021-130145B-I00) and Project SocialTox (PDC2022-133146-C21) funded by MCIN/AEI/10.13039/501100011033 and by the European Union NextGenerationEU/PRTR, Project PRECOM (SUBV-00016) funded by the Ministry of Consumer Affairs of the Spanish Government, Project FedDAP (PID2020-116118GA-I00) and Project Trust-ReDaS (PID2020-119478GB-I00) supported by MICINN/AEI/10.13039/501100011033, and WeLee project (1380939, FEDER Andalucía 2014-2020) funded by the Andalusian Regional Government. Salud María Jiménez-Zafra has been partially supported by a grant from Fondo Social Europeo and the Administration of the Junta de Andalucía (DOC_01073). This work is also part of the research project LaTe4PoliticES (PID2022-138099OB-I00) funded by MCIN/AEI/10.13039/501100011033 and the European Fund for Regional Development (FEDER)-a way to make Europe, and the research project LT-SWM (TED2021-131167B-I00) funded by MCIN/AEI/10.13039/501100011033 and by the European Union NextGenerationEU/PRTR.

References

Areej Al-Hassan and Hmood Al-Dossari. 2022. Detection of hate speech in Arabic tweets using deep learning. *Multimedia systems*, 28(6):1963–1974.

Shaun Allan H, Samyuktaa Sivakumar, Rohan R, Nikilesh Jayaguptha, and Thenmozhi Durairaj. 2024. Quartet@LT-EDI 2024: Support Vector Machine based Approach for Homophobia/Transphobia Detection in Social Media Comments. In *Proceedings of the Fourth Workshop on Language Technology for Equality, Diversity and Inclusion*, Malta. European Chapter of the Association for Computational Linguistics.

Adwita Arora, Aaryan Mattoo, Divya Chaudhary, Ian Gorton, and Bijendra Kumar. 2024. MEnTr@LT-EDI-2024: Multilingual Ensemble of Transformer Models for Homophobia/Transphobia Detection. In *Proceedings of the Fourth Workshop on Language Technology for Equality, Diversity and Inclusion*, Malta. European Chapter of the Association for Computational Linguistics.

Bharathi Raja Chakravarthi. 2023. Detection of homophobia and transphobia in YouTube comments. *International Journal of Data Science and Analytics*, pages 1–20.

Bharathi Raja Chakravarthi, Adeep Hande, Rahul Ponnusamy, Prasanna Kumar Kumaresan, and Ruba Priyadharshini. 2022a. How can we detect Homophobia and Transphobia? Experiments in a multilingual code-mixed setting for social media governance. *International Journal of Information Management Data Insights*, 2(2):100119.

Bharathi Raja Chakravarthi, Ruba Priyadharshini, Subalalitha Cn, S Sangeetha, Malliga Subramanian, Kogilavani Shanmugavadivel, Parameswari Krishnamurthy, Adeep Hande, Siddhanth U Hegde, Roshan Nayak, et al. 2022b. Findings of the Shared Task on Multitask Learning in Dravidian Languages. In *Proceedings of the Second Workshop on Speech and Language Technologies for Dravidian Languages*, pages 286–291.

Bharathi Raja Chakravarthi, Ruba Priyadharshini, Thenmozhi Durairaj, John Philip McCrae, Paul Buitelaar, Prasanna Kumaresan, and Rahul Ponnusamy. 2022c. Overview of the shared task on homophobia and transphobia detection in social media comments. In *Proceedings of the Second Workshop on Language Technology for Equality, Diversity and Inclusion*, pages 369–377.

Subalalitha Chinnaudayar Navaneethakrishnan, Bharathi Raja Chakravarthi, Kogilavani Shanmugavadivel, Malliga Subramanian, Prasanna Kumar Kumaresan, Bharathi, Lavanya Sambath Kumar, and Rahul Ponnusamy. 2022. Findings of shared task on Sentiment Analysis and Homophobia Detection of YouTube Comments in Code-Mixed Dravidian Languages. In *Proceedings of the 14th Annual Meeting of the Forum for Information Retrieval Evaluation*, pages 18–21.

Alexis Conneau, Kartikay Khandelwal, Naman Goyal, Vishrav Chaudhary, Guillaume Wenzek, Francisco Guzmán, Edouard Grave, Myle Ott, Luke Zettlemoyer, and Veselin Stoyanov. 2019. Unsupervised Cross-lingual Representation Learning at Scale. *CoRR*, abs/1911.02116.

Jacob Devlin, Ming-Wei Chang, Kenton Lee, and Kristina Toutanova. 2018. BERT: Pre-training of

Deep Bidirectional Transformers for Language Understanding. *CoRR*, abs/1810.04805.

María José Díaz-Torres, Paulina Alejandra Morán-Méndez, Luis Villasenor-Pineda, Manuel Montes, Juan Aguilera, and Luis Meneses-Lerín. 2020. Automatic detection of offensive language in social media: Defining linguistic criteria to build a Mexican Spanish dataset. In *Proceedings of the Second Workshop on Trolling, Aggression and Cyberbullying*, pages 132–136.

Sarah Diefendorf and Tristan Bridges. 2020. On the enduring relationship between masculinity and homophobia. *Sexualities*, 23(7):1264–1284.

Dhiman Goswami, Sadiya Sayara Chowdhury Puspo, Md Nishat Raihan, and Al Nahian Bin Emran. 2024. MasonTigers@LT-EDI-2024: An Ensemble Approach towards Detecting Homophobia and Transphobia in Social Media Comments. In *Proceedings of the Fourth Workshop on Language Technology for Equality, Diversity and Inclusion*, Malta. European Chapter of the Association for Computational Linguistics.

Simran Khanuja, Diksha Bansal, Sarvesh Mehtani, Savya Khosla, Atreyee Dey, Balaji Gopalan, Dilip Kumar Margam, Pooja Aggarwal, Rajiv Teja Nagipogu, Shachi Dave, Shruti Gupta, Subhash Chandra Bose Gali, Vish Subramanian, and Partha Talukdar. 2021. MuRIL: Multilingual Representations for Indian Languages.

Ritesh Kumar, Atul Kr Ojha, Shervin Malmasi, and Marcos Zampieri. 2018. Benchmarking aggression identification in social media. In *Proceedings of the first workshop on trolling, aggression and cyberbullying (TRAC-2018)*, pages 1–11.

Prasanna Kumar Kumaresan, Kishore Kumar Ponnusamy, Kogilavani Shanmugavadivel, Subalalitha Chinnaudayar Navaneethakrishnan, Ruba Priyadharshini, and Bharathi Raja Chakravarthi. 2023a. VEL@ LT-EDI-2023: Detecting Homophobia and Transphobia in Code-Mixed Spanish Social Media Comments. *LTEDI 2023*, page 233.

Prasanna Kumar Kumaresan, Rahul Ponnusamy, Ruba Priyadharshini, Paul Buitelaar, and Bharathi Raja Chakravarthi. 2023b. Homophobia and transphobia detection for low-resourced languages in social media comments. *Natural Language Processing Journal*, 5:100041.

Prasanna Kumar Kumaresan, Rahul Ponnusamy, Elizabeth Sherly, Sangeetha Sivanesan, and Bharathi Raja Chakravarthi. 2022. Transformer Based Hope Speech Comment Classification in Code-Mixed Text. In *International Conference on Speech and Language Technologies for Low-resource Languages*, pages 120–137. Springer.

Kaustubh Lande, Rahul Ponnusamy, Prasanna Kumar Kumaresan, and Bharathi Raja Chakravarthi. 2023. KaustubhSharedTask@LT-EDI 2023: Homophobia-transphobia detection in social media comments with NLPAUG-driven data augmentation. In *Proceedings of the Third Workshop on Language Technology for Equality, Diversity and Inclusion*, pages 71–77, Varna, Bulgaria. INCOMA Ltd., Shoumen, Bulgaria.

Savannah Larimore, Ian Kennedy, Breon Haskett, and Alina Arseniev-Koehler. 2021. Reconsidering annotator disagreement about racist language: Noise or signal? In *Proceedings of the Ninth International Workshop on Natural Language Processing for Social Media*, pages 81–90.

Deepalakshmi Manikandan, Malliga Subramanian, and Kogilavani Shanmugavadivel. 2022. A System For Detecting Abusive Contents Against LGBT Community Using Deep Learning Based Transformer Models. In *Working Notes of FIRE 2022-Forum for Information Retrieval Evaluation (Hybrid). CEUR*.

Durga Prasad Manukonda and Rohith Gowtham Kodali. 2024. byteLLM@LT-EDI-2024: Homophobia/Transphobia Detection in Social Media Comments - Custom Subword Tokenization with Subword2Vec and BiLSTM. In *Proceedings of the Fourth Workshop on Language Technology for Equality, Diversity and Inclusion*, Malta. European Chapter of the Association for Computational Linguistics.

Kathiravan Pannerselvam, Saranya Rajiakodi, Rahul Ponnusamy, and Sajeetha Thavareesan. 2023. CSS-CUTN@DravidianLangTech:Abusive comments Detection in Tamil and Telugu. In *Proceedings of the Third Workshop on Speech and Language Technologies for Dravidian Languages*, pages 306–312, Varna, Bulgaria. INCOMA Ltd., Shoumen, Bulgaria.

Rahul Ponnusamy, Prasanna Kumar Kumaresan, Kishore Kumar Ponnusamy, Charmathi Rajkumar, Ruba Priyadharshini, and Bharathi Raja Chakravarthi. 2023a. Team_Tamil at HODI: Few-Shot Learning for Detecting Homotransphobia in Italian Language. In *Proceedings of the Eighth Evaluation Campaign of Natural Language Processing and Speech Tools for Italian. Final Workshop (EVALITA 2023), CEUR. org, Parma, Italy*.

Rahul Ponnusamy, Malliga S, Sajeetha Thavareesan, Ruba Priyadharshini, and Bharathi Raja Chakravarthi. 2023b. VEL@LT-EDI-2023: Automatic detection of hope speech in Bulgarian language using embedding techniques. In *Proceedings of the Third Workshop on Language Technology for Equality, Diversity and Inclusion*, pages 179–184, Varna, Bulgaria. INCOMA Ltd., Shoumen, Bulgaria.

Kogilavani Shanmugavadivel, Sai Haritha Sampath, Pramod Nandhakumar, Prasath Mahalingam, Malliga Subramanian, Prasanna Kumar Kumaresan, and Ruba Priyadharshini. 2022. An analysis of machine learning models for sentiment analysis of Tamil code-mixed data. *Computer Speech Language*, 76:101407.

Kogilavani Shanmugavadivel, Malliga Subramanian, Shri Durga Ramanathan, Samyuktha Kathirvel, Srigha S, and Nithika Kannan. 2024. KEC-AI-NLP@LT-EDI-2024: Homophobia and Transphobia Detection in Social Media Comments using Machine Learning. In *Proceedings of the Fourth Workshop on Language Technology for Equality, Diversity and Inclusion*, Malta. European Chapter of the Association for Computational Linguistics.

Malliga Subramanian, Ramya Chinnasamy, Prasanna Kumar Kumaresan, Vasanth Palanikumar, Madhoora Mohan, and Kogilavani Shanmugavadivel. 2022. Development of multi-lingual models for detecting hope speech texts from social media comments. In *International Conference on Speech and Language Technologies for Low-resource Languages*, pages 209–219. Springer.

Crispin Thurlow. 2001. Naming the "outsider within": Homophobic pejoratives and the verbal abuse of lesbian, gay and bisexual high-school pupils. *Journal of adolescence*, 24(1):25–38.

Sargam Yadav, Abhishek Kaushik, and Kevin McDaid. 2024. dkit@LT-EDI-2024: Detecting Homophobia and Transphobia in English Social Media Comments. In *Proceedings of the Fourth Workshop on Language Technology for Equality, Diversity and Inclusion*, Malta. European Chapter of the Association for Computational Linguistics.

Ziqi Zhang and Lei Luo. 2019. Hate speech detection: A solved problem? the challenging case of long tail on Twitter. *Semantic Web*, 10(5):925–945.

Overview of the Third Shared Task on Speech Recognition for Vulnerable Individuals in Tamil

B. Bharathi[1], Bharathi Raja Chakravarthi[2], N. Sripriya[1], Rajeswari Natarajan[3], S. Suhasini[4]
[1]Sri Sivasubramaniya Nadar College of Engineering, Tamil Nadu, India
[2]School of Computer Science, University of Galway, Ireland
[3]SASTRA University, India
[4]R.M.D. Engineering College, Tamil Nadu India
bharathib@ssn.edu.in, bharathiraja.akr@gmail.com

Abstract

The overview of the shared task on speech recognition for vulnerable individuals in Tamil (LT-EDI-2024) is described in this paper. The work comes with a Tamil dataset that was gathered from elderly individuals who identify as male, female, or transgender. The audio samples were taken in public places such as marketplaces, vegetable shops, hospitals, etc. The training phase and the testing phase are when the dataset is made available. The task required of the participants was to handle audio signals using various models and techniques, and then turn in their results as transcriptions of the provided test samples. The participant's results were assessed using WER (Word Error Rate). The transformer-based approach was employed by the participants to achieve automatic voice recognition. This overview paper discusses the findings and various pre-trained transformer-based models that the participants employed.

1 Introduction

The earliest known examples of Old Tamil writing are tiny inscriptions found in Adichanallur that date between 905 and 696 BC. Of all the Indian languages, Tamil possesses the most ancient non-Sanskritic literature. The grammar of Tamil is agglutinative, meaning that noun class, number, case, verb tense, and other grammatical categories are indicated by suffixes. Unlike other Aryan languages, which use Sanskrit as their standard language, Tamil uses Tamil for both its scholarly vocabulary and its metalinguistic terminology. Together with dialects, Tamil has multiple forms: cankattami, the classical literary style based on the ancient language; centami, the modern literary and formal style; and kotuntami, the present vernacular form. (Sakuntharaj and Mahesan, 2021, 2017). There is a stylistic continuity created by these styles merging together. For instance, one may write centami using cankattami vocabulary, or one could speak kotuntami while using forms related to one of the other types. (Srinivasan and Subalalitha, 2019; Narasimhan et al., 2018). A lexical root plus one or more affixes combine to form Tamil words. Suffixes make up the bulk of affixes in Tamil. Tamil suffixes fall into two groups: derivational suffixes, which change a word's meaning or part of speech, and inflectional suffixes, which identify certain categories like person, number, mood, tense, and so on. Agglutination can lead to huge words with multiple suffixes, needing numerous words or a phrase in English. Its length and scope are infinite. Although smart technologies have come a long way, human-machine interaction is still being developed and enhanced. (Chakravarthi et al., 2020). Automatic speech recognition (ASR) is one such recent technology that has enabled voice-based user interfaces for numerous automated systems. Many elderly and transgender people are frequently unaware of the technology (Hämäläinen et al., 2015) that is made available to help people in public places like banks, hospitals, and administrative offices. Thus, communication is the only kind of media that can assist people in getting what they want. However, these ASR systems are infrequently used by the elderly, transsexuals, and others with lower levels of education. English-language voice-based interfaces are a feature of most automated systems currently in use. Elderly people and those living in rural areas prefer to speak in their native tongue. The provision of speech interfaces in the local language for help systems designed for public usage would be advantageous to all. Information regarding spontaneous speech in Tamil is gathered from transgender and elderly people who are not able to use these programs. The aim of this challenge is to find an efficient ASR model to handle the elderly person's speech corpus.

The pertinent features will first be extracted from the speech signal using an ASR system. Acoustic models will also be produced using these features that were retrieved. Ultimately, the language model

Proceedings of the Fourth Workshop on Language Technology for Equality, Diversity, Inclusion, pages 133–138
March 21, 2024 ©2024 Association for Computational Linguistics

assists in converting these probabilities into grammatical words. The language model uses statistics from training data to assign probabilities to words and phrases (Das et al., 2011). It is necessary to evaluate ASR systems' performance prior to deploying them in real-time applications. On large-scale automatic speech recognition (ASR) tasks, an end-to-end speech recognition system has shown promising performance, matching or surpassing that of traditional hybrid systems. Using an acoustic model, lexicon, and language model, the end-to-end system quickly transforms audio data into tag labels (Zeng et al., 2021; Pérez-Espinosa et al., 2017). In the field of end-to-end voice recognition, there exist two extensively utilized frameworks. Frame synchronous prediction separates one input frame from the other by giving each one a target label (Miao et al., 2020; Xue et al., 2021; Miao et al., 2019; Watanabe et al., 2017). Phoneme identification can also be used to assess the efficacy using different test feature vectors and model settings. The use of acoustic models for speech recognition, which are created using the sounds of younger people, may have a substantial impact on the capacity to recognize elder speech (Fukuda et al., 2020; Zeng et al., 2020; Iribe et al., 2015). There aren't many acoustic models that can handle the voice detection task. Among the acoustic models are Japanese Newspaper Article Sentences (JNAS), Japanese Newspaper Article Sentences Read Speech Corpus of the Aged (S-JNAS), and Corpus of Spontaneous Japanes (CSJ). The CSJ model only achieves the lowest WER once the older voices are adjusted, according to a comparison of all the acoustic models in the literature (Fukuda et al., 2020). Dialect adaptation is also required in order to improve recognition accuracy (Fukuda et al., 2019). Recent advances in large vocabulary continuous speech recognition (LVCSR) technologies have led to the widespread use of speech recognition systems in several fields (Xue et al., 2021). Variations in the acoustics of individual speakers are thought to be one of the primary causes of the decline in speech recognition rates. For elder speakers to use speech recognition systems trained on typical adult speech data, the acoustic discrepancies between their speech and that of an adult should be investigated and correctly adjusted. Rather, this loss can be mitigated by an acoustic model enhanced by senior speakers' utterances, as shown by a document retrieval system. Modern voice recognition technology can reach excellent recognition accuracy while speaking while reading a written text or something comparable; nevertheless, the accuracy decreases when speaking spontaneously and freely. The main reason for this issue is that the linguistic and acoustic models used in voice recognition were mostly developed using read-aloud or written language materials. However, there are significant linguistic and auditory differences between written language and spontaneous speech(Zeng et al., 2020). Currently, it is becoming more and more popular to create ASR systems that can detect voice data from older persons. The aging population in modern society and the proliferation of smart devices, which make information freely accessible to both the young and the old, have led to a demand for improved voice recognition in smart devices (Kwon et al., 2016; Vacher et al., 2015; Hossain et al., 2017; Teixeira et al., 2014). Because of the influences of speech articulation and speaking style, speech recognition systems are often optimized for the voice of an average adult and have a lower accuracy rate when recognising the voice of an elderly person. It will surely become more expensive to adapt the current voice recognition systems to handle the speech of elderly users(Kwon et al., 2016).

2 Related Work

When a model is fine-tuned on many languages at the same time, a single multilingual speech recognition model can be built that can compete with models that are fine-tuned on individual language speech corpus. Speech2Vec expands the text-based Word2Vec model to learn word embeddings directly from speech by combining an RNN Encoder-Decoder framework with skipgrams or cbow for training. Acoustic models are designed at the phoneme/syllable level to carry out the speech recognition task. Initially, the acoustic models were created with JNAS, S-JNAS and CSJ speech corpus(Lin and Yu, 2015; Iribe et al., 2015). Later, the models were trained/fine-tuned with different speech corpus. To get a better performance and accuracy, backpropagation using transfer learning was attempted in the literature. Similar work was performed for other languages like Bengali, Japanese, etc. Also, more speech corpus is collected from young people for many languages(Zeng et al., 2020; Lee et al., 2021). However, speaker fluctuation, environmental noise, and transmission channel noise all degrade ASR performance. As the shared task is given with a separate training data set, an effective model has to be created during the training. Therefore, the hierarchical transformer-based model for large context end-to-end ASR can be used (Masumura et al., 2021). In the recent era, the environment is changing with smart systems and is identified that there is a need for ASR systems that are capable of handling the speech of elderly people spoken in their native languages. To overcome this problem, the shared task is proposed for the research community to build an efficient model for recognizing the speech of elderly people and transgenders in Tamil language. Findings of the automatic speech recognition for vulnerable individuals are given in (S and B, 2022) (B et al., 2022)("S and B, "2023") (Bharathi et al., 2023), have used transformer models used for transformer-based ASR for Vulnerable Individuals in Tamil.

3 Data-set Description

The dataset given to this shared task (Bharathi et al., 2022) is an Tamil conversational speech recorded from the elderly people whose average age is around 61 for male, 59 for female and 30 for transgender people which are tabulated in Table 1 . A total of 7.5 hours is collected from the elderly people. 46 audio files were recorded and each audio file is split into many subsets as transformer model does not support the large audio files. The speech is recorded with a sampling rate of 16KHZ. The audio files from Audio - 1 to Audio - 36 are used for training (duration is approximately 5.5 hours) and Audio - 37 to Audio - 48 are used for testing (duration is approximately 2 hours).

4 Methodology

The methodology used by the participants in the shared task of speech recognition for vulnerable individuals in Tamil is discussed in this section. Three teams submitted their runs for this task. All three teams have used the pre-trained models. The first team "CEN_Amrita" has used the whisper model, Whisper is a pre-trained automatic speech recognition (ASR) model trained on 680,000 hours of multilingual and multitask supervised data sourced from the web. This end-to-end transformer-based model adopts the encoder- decoder architecture.. The second team "ASR_Tamil_SSN" have used the transformer based model called 'akashsivanandan/wav2vec2-large-xls-r-300m-tamil-colab-final'. The third team " have also used the transformer based pretrained model called 'Rajaram1996/wav2vec2-large- xlsr-53-tamil'.

5 Evaluation of Results

The results submitted by the participants are evaluated based on the WER computed between the ASR hypotheses submitted by the participants and the ground truth of human speech transcription.

WER (Word Error Rate) = (S + D + I) / N

where,
S = No. of substitutions
D = No. of deletions
I = No. of insertions
N = No. of words in the reference transcription

As discussed in the methodology, different average word error rates are measured using various pre-trained transformer-based models. The participating team's WER are shown in Table. 2.

6 Conclusions

The shared challenge for vulnerable voice recognition in Tamil is covered in this overview paper. The speech corpus shared for this job was recorded from elderly persons. Getting older people's speech more accurately recognised is a difficult endeavor. In order to boost the accuracy and performance in recognising elderly people's speech, the participants have been given access to the gathered speech corpus. There were a total of seven teams participated in this joint task and turned in their transcripts of the supplied data. The team estimated the WER and then compared the outcome to the human transcripts. Three teams built their recognition systems using various Whisper models and transformer-based models. Finally, the word error rates of the three participants are 24.452, 29.297, 37.7333 respectively. Based on the observations, it is suggested that the transformer-based model and whisper model can be trained with given speech corpus which could give better accuracy than the pre-trained model, as the transformer-based model and whisper model used are trained with a common voice dataset. Also, a separate language model can also be created for this corpus.

S.No	Filename	Gender	Age	Duration(in min)
1	Audio - 1	M	72	10
2	Audio - 2	F	61	9
3	Audio - 3	F	71	11
4	Audio - 4	M	68	8
5	Audio - 5	F	59	14
6	Audio - 6	F	67	9
7	Audio - 7	M	54	8
8	Audio - 8	F	65	16
9	Audio - 9	F	55	3
10	Audio - 10	M	60	13
11	Audio - 11	F	55	17
12	Audio - 12	F	52	6
13	Audio - 13	F	53	11
14	Audio - 14	F	61	9
15	Audio - 15	F	54	1
16	Audio - 16	F	56	6
17	Audio - 17	F	52	12
18	Audio - 18	F	54	6
19	Audio - 19	F	52	8
20	Audio - 20	F	52	9
21	Audio - 21	F	62	13
22	Audio - 22	F	52	12
23	Audio - 23	F	62	13
24	Audio - 24	F	53	4
25	Audio - 25	F	65	3
26	Audio - 26	F	64	8
27	Audio - 27	F	54	6
28	Audio - 28	M	62	8
29	Audio - 29	M	54	16
30	Audio - 30	F	76	9
31	Audio - 31	F	55	9
32	Audio - 32	M	50	6
33	Audio - 33	F	63	6
34	Audio - 34	M	84	6
35	Audio - 35	F	70	6
36	Audio - 36	F	50	6
37	Audio - 37	M	53	6
38	Audio - 38	F	55	6
39	Audio - 39	M	62	6
40	Audio - 40	T	24	6
41	Audio - 41	T	22	7
42	Audio - 42	T	40	8
43	Audio - 43	T	25	11
44	Audio - 44	T	29	10
45	Audio - 45	T	35	9
46	Audio - 46	T	33	16
47	Audio - 47	F	20	5
48	Audio - 48	M	37	5

Table 1: Age, gender, and duration of the utterances of the speech corpus

S. No	Team Name	WER (in %)
1	CEN_Amrita (Jairam R, 2024)	24.452
2	ASR_TAMIL_SSN (Suhasini and Bharathi, 2024)	29.297
3	DRAVIDIAN LANGUAGE - Abirami Jayaraman (Abirami. J, 2024)	37.733

Table 2: Results of the participating system's Word Error Rate

References

Dharunika Sasikumar B. Bharathi Abirami. J, Aruna Devi. S. 2024. Dravidian language@ lt-edi 2024:pre-trained transformer based automatic speech recognition system for elderly people. In *Proceedings of the Fourth Workshop on Language Technology for Equality, Diversity, Inclusion (LT-EDI-2024)*.

Bharathi B, Dhanya Srinivasan, Josephine Varsha, Thenmozhi Durairaj, and Senthil Kumar B. 2022. SSNCSE_NLP@LT-EDI-ACL2022:hope speech detection for equality, diversity and inclusion using sentence transformers. In *Proceedings of the Second Workshop on Language Technology for Equality, Diversity and Inclusion*, pages 218–222, Dublin, Ireland. Association for Computational Linguistics.

B Bharathi, Bharathi Raja Chakravarthi, Subalalitha Chinnaudayar Navaneethakrishnan, N Sripriya, Arunaggiri Pandian, and Swetha Valli. 2022. Findings of the shared task on Speech Recognition for Vulnerable Individuals in Tamil. In *Proceedings of the Second Workshop on Language Technology for Equality, Diversity and Inclusion*. Association for Computational Linguistics.

B Bharathi, Bharathi Raja Chakravarthi, Subalalitha Cn, Sripriya Natarajan, Rajeswari Natarajan, S Suhasini, and Swetha Valli. 2023. Overview of the second shared task on speech recognition for vulnerable individuals in tamil. In *Proceedings of the Third Workshop on Language Technology for Equality, Diversity and Inclusion*, pages 31–37.

Bharathi Raja Chakravarthi, Ruba Priyadharshini, Vigneshwaran Muralidaran, Shardul Suryawanshi, Navya Jose, Elizabeth Sherly, and John P McCrae. 2020. Overview of the track on sentiment analysis for Dravidian languages in code-mixed text. In *Forum for Information Retrieval Evaluation*, pages 21–24.

Biswajit Das, Sandipan Mandal, and Pabitra Mitra. 2011. Bengali speech corpus for continuous auutomatic speech recognition system. In *2011 International conference on speech database and assessments (Oriental COCOSDA)*, pages 51–55. IEEE.

Meiko Fukuda, Ryota Nishimura, Hiromitsu Nishizaki, Yurie Iribe, and Norihide Kitaoka. 2019. A new corpus of elderly japanese speech for acoustic modeling, and a preliminary investigation of dialect-dependent speech recognition. In *2019 22nd Conference of the Oriental COCOSDA International Committee for the Co-ordination and Standardisation of Speech Databases and Assessment Techniques (O-COCOSDA)*, pages 1–6. IEEE.

Meiko Fukuda, Hiromitsu Nishizaki, Yurie Iribe, Ryota Nishimura, and Norihide Kitaoka. 2020. Improving speech recognition for the elderly: A new corpus of elderly japanese speech and investigation of acoustic modeling for speech recognition. In *Proceedings of the 12th Language Resources and Evaluation Conference*, pages 6578–6585.

Annika Hämäläinen, António Teixeira, Nuno Almeida, Hugo Meinedo, Tibor Fegyó, and Miguel Sales Dias. 2015. Multilingual speech recognition for the elderly: The aalfred personal life assistant. *Procedia Computer Science*, 67:283–292.

M Shamim Hossain, Md Abdur Rahman, and Ghulam Muhammad. 2017. Cyber–physical cloud-oriented multi-sensory smart home framework for elderly people: An energy efficiency perspective. *Journal of Parallel and Distributed Computing*, 103:11–21.

Yurie Iribe, Norihide Kitaoka, and Shuhei Segawa. 2015. Development of new speech corpus for elderly japanese speech recognition. In *2015 International Conference Oriental COCOSDA held jointly with 2015 Conference on Asian Spoken Language Research and Evaluation (O-COCOSDA/CASLRE)*, pages 27–31. IEEE.

Premjith B Viswa M Jairam R, Jyothish Lal G. 2024. Cen_amrita@lt-edi-eacl2024 - a transformer based speech recognition system for vulnerable individuals in tamil. In *Proceedings of the Fourth Workshop on Language Technology for Equality, Diversity, Inclusion (LT-EDI-2024)*.

Soonil Kwon, Sung-Jae Kim, and Joon Yeon Choeh. 2016. Preprocessing for elderly speech recognition of smart devices. *Computer Speech & Language*, 36:110–121.

Taewoo Lee, Min-Joong Lee, Tae Gyoon Kang, Seokyeoung Jung, Minseok Kwon, Yeona Hong, Jungin Lee, Kyoung-Gu Woo, Ho-Gyeong Kim, Jiseung Jeong, et al. 2021. Adaptable multi-domain language model for transformer asr. In *ICASSP 2021-2021 IEEE International Conference on Acoustics, Speech and Signal Processing (ICASSP)*, pages 7358–7362. IEEE.

Hui Lin and Yibiao Yu. 2015. Acoustic feature analysis and conversion of age speech. In *IET Conference Proceedings*. The Institution of Engineering & Technology.

Ryo Masumura, Naoki Makishima, Mana Ihori, Akihiko Takashima, Tomohiro Tanaka, and Shota Orihashi.

2021. Hierarchical transformer-based large-context end-to-end asr with large-context knowledge distillation. In *ICASSP 2021-2021 IEEE International Conference on Acoustics, Speech and Signal Processing (ICASSP)*, pages 5879–5883. IEEE.

Haoran Miao, Gaofeng Cheng, Changfeng Gao, Pengyuan Zhang, and Yonghong Yan. 2020. Transformer-based online ctc/attention end-to-end speech recognition architecture. In *ICASSP 2020-2020 IEEE International Conference on Acoustics, Speech and Signal Processing (ICASSP)*, pages 6084–6088. IEEE.

Haoran Miao, Gaofeng Cheng, Pengyuan Zhang, Ta Li, and Yonghong Yan. 2019. Online hybrid ctc/attention architecture for end-to-end speech recognition. In *Interspeech*, pages 2623–2627.

Anitha Narasimhan, Aarthy Anandan, Madhan Karky, and CN Subalalitha. 2018. Porul: Option generation and selection and scoring algorithms for a tamil flash card game. *International Journal of Cognitive and Language Sciences*, 12(2):225–228.

Humberto Pérez-Espinosa, Juan Martínez-Miranda, Ismael Espinosa-Curiel, Josefina Rodríguez-Jacobo, and Himer Avila-George. 2017. Using acoustic paralinguistic information to assess the interaction quality in speech-based systems for elderly users. *International Journal of Human-Computer Studies*, 98:1–13.

Suhasini S and Bharathi B. 2022. SUH_ASR@LT-EDI-ACL2022: Transformer based approach for speech recognition for vulnerable individuals in Tamil. In *Proceedings of the Second Workshop on Language Technology for Equality, Diversity and Inclusion*, pages 177–182, Dublin, Ireland. Association for Computational Linguistics.

Suhasini "S and Bharathi" B. "2023". "asr_ssn_cse 2023@lt-edi-2023: Pretrained transformer based automatic speech recognition system for elderly people". In *Proceedings of the Third Workshop on Speech and Language Technologies for Dravidian Languages*, "Varna, Bulgaria ". "Recent Advances in Natural Language Processing".

Ratnasingam Sakuntharaj and Sinnathamby Mahesan. 2017. Use of a novel hash-table for speeding-up suggestions for misspelt Tamil words. In *2017 IEEE International Conference on Industrial and Information Systems (ICIIS)*, pages 1–5.

Ratnasingam Sakuntharaj and Sinnathamby Mahesan. 2021. Missing word detection and correction based on context of Tamil sentences using n-grams. In *2021 10th International Conference on Information and Automation for Sustainability (ICIAfS)*, pages 42–47.

R Srinivasan and CN Subalalitha. 2019. Automated named entity recognition from tamil documents. In *2019 IEEE 1st International Conference on Energy, Systems and Information Processing (ICESIP)*, pages 1–5. IEEE.

S Suhasini and B Bharathi. 2024. Asr_tamil_ssn@ lt-edi-2024: Automatic speech recognition system for elderly people. In *Proceedings of the Fourth Workshop on Language Technology for Equality, Diversity, Inclusion (LT-EDI-2024)*.

António Teixeira, Annika Hämäläinen, Jairo Avelar, Nuno Almeida, Géza Németh, Tibor Fegyó, Csaba Zainkó, Tamás Csapó, Bálint Tóth, André Oliveira, et al. 2014. Speech-centric multimodal interaction for easy-to-access online services–a personal life assistant for the elderly. *Procedia computer science*, 27:389–397.

Michel Vacher, Frédéric Aman, Solange Rossato, and François Portet. 2015. Development of automatic speech recognition techniques for elderly home support: Applications and challenges. In *International Conference on Human Aspects of IT for the Aged Population*, pages 341–353. Springer.

Shinji Watanabe, Takaaki Hori, Suyoun Kim, John R Hershey, and Tomoki Hayashi. 2017. Hybrid ctc/attention architecture for end-to-end speech recognition. *IEEE Journal of Selected Topics in Signal Processing*, 11(8):1240–1253.

Jiabin Xue, Tieran Zheng, and Jiqing Han. 2021. Exploring attention mechanisms based on summary information for end-to-end automatic speech recognition. *Neurocomputing*, 465:514–524.

Jiazhong Zeng, Jianxin Peng, and Yuezhe Zhao. 2020. Comparison of speech intelligibility of elderly aged 60–69 years and young adults in the noisy and reverberant environment. *Applied Acoustics*, 159:107096.

Zhiping Zeng, Haihua Xu, Yerbolat Khassanov, Eng Siong Chng, Chongjia Ni, Bin Ma, et al. 2021. Leveraging text data using hybrid transformer-lstm based end-to-end asr in transfer learning. In *2021 12th International Symposium on Chinese Spoken Language Processing (ISCSLP)*, pages 1–5. IEEE.

Overview of Shared Task on Multitask Meme Classification - Unraveling Misogynistic and Trolls in Online Memes

[1]Bharathi Raja Chakravarthi, [2]Saranya Rajiakodi, [3]Rahul Ponnusamy, [2]Kathiravan Pannerselvam, [4]Anand Kumar Madasamy, [5]Ramachandran Rajalakshmi, [4]Hariharan RamakrishnaIyer LekshmiAmmal, [6]Anshid Kizhakkeparambil, [7]Susminu S Kumar, [2]Bhuvaneswari Sivagnanam, [7]Charmathi Rajkumar

[1]School of Computer Science, University of Galway, Ireland
[2]Department of Computer Science, Central University of Tamil Nadu, India
[3]Data Science Institute, University of Galway, Ireland [4]NIT Karnataka, India
[5]VIT Chennai, India [6]WMO Imam Gazzali Arts and Science College, Kerala, India
[7]The American College, Madurai, Tamil Nadu, India

Abstract

This paper offers a detailed overview of the first shared task on "Multitask Meme Classification - Unraveling Misogynistic and Trolls in Online Memes," organized as part of the LT-EDI@EACL 2024 conference. The task was set to classify misogynistic content and troll memes within online platforms, focusing specifically on memes in Tamil and Malayalam languages. A total of 52 teams registered for the competition, with four submitting systems for the Tamil meme classification task and three for the Malayalam task. The outcomes of this shared task are significant, providing insights into the current state of misogynistic content in digital memes and highlighting the effectiveness of various computational approaches in identifying such detrimental content. The top-performing model got a macro F1 score of 0.73 in Tamil and 0.87 in Malayalam.

1 Introduction

In the ever-changing landscape of online communication (Lin et al., 2024; Priyadharshini et al., 2022), memes have emerged as a remarkable phenomenon, transcending linguistic, cultural, and geographical boundaries (Ford et al., 2023). Their ability to succinctly and often humorously convey complex ideas and emotions has made memes an integral part of digital discourse (Kostadinovska-Stojchevska and Shalevska, 2018; Priyadharshini et al., 2023). However, this rise in meme culture has also revealed the obscene side of online content, which features misogynistic stories and trolling (Rasheed et al., 2020; Suryawanshi and Chakravarthi, 2021). We initiated the "Multitask Meme Classification - Unraveling Misogynistic and Trolls in Online Memes" competition to understand and address these critical issues through memes. This pioneering endeavor leverages gold-standard datasets to illuminate the intricate world of online memes. Our competition aims to inspire the development of cutting-edge models for meme classification, primarily focusing on detecting misogyny and trolling in various languages. Further, it is centered around carefully selected high-quality datasets. These datasets have been precisely annotated to establish a standard for classifying memes. These datasets represent various languages and meme categories, offering a comprehensive view of the meme landscape. Let us delve into the two core tasks our competition addresses:

Task 1: Detecting Misogynistic Memes: This task revolves around identifying misogynistic memes, which perpetuate harmful stereotypes and attitudes towards women. The gold standard dataset for this task spans languages like Tamil and Malayalam, reflecting the global reach of this issue. Participants must develop models capable of analyzing textual and visual elements within memes to distinguish between misogynistic and non-misogynistic content.

Task 2: Troll Meme Classification: This task broadens our perspective to encompass the classification of troll memes characterized by provocative and disruptive behavior. The gold standard dataset for this task includes languages such as Kannada and Telugu. Participants face the challenge of categorizing memes into 'Troll' and 'Non-Troll' categories, navigating the intricate interplay of humor, satire, and harmful intent.

Our competition is structured to encourage innovation and collaboration across the global research and practitioner communities. Participants receive comprehensive training and development datasets, offering various memes for practical model training.

Proceedings of the Fourth Workshop on Language Technology for Equality, Diversity, Inclusion, pages 139–144
March 21, 2024 ©2024 Association for Computational Linguistics

Evaluation of these models relies on the macro-F1 score, a robust metric commonly used in natural language processing. In total, 52 teams participated in our shared task: Four teams in Tamil and three teams in Malayalam submitted a system to Task 1 and achieved the top score of 0.73 in Tamil and 0.87 in Malayalam. Due to the null participation in Task 2, we stopped running the task further.

Beyond the competition, our overarching goal is to contribute to a safer and more inclusive digital ecosystem. By dissecting and understanding the dynamics of meme content, we aim to pave the way for more effective content moderation strategies. We envision this initiative as a catalyst for fostering responsible online behavior and promoting gender equality.

2 Related Works

In recent research, Singhal et al. (2022) did a comprehensive data collection of 22,435 instances of fact-checked content from social media to scrutinize the proliferation of fake news across India between 2013 and 2020. This dataset is distinguished by its coverage across 13 languages, encapsulating 14 distinct attributes. It highlights the diversity and complexity of fake news dissemination within the multilingual and multicultural Indian context, offering insights into the dynamics of misinformation across various domains and media types.

Singhal et al. (2019) presented "SpotFake," a novel framework that surpasses existing systems by avoiding dependency on sub-tasks like event discrimination, focusing instead on directly leveraging textual and visual content through advanced language and image processing models (BERT and VGG-19). This approach demonstrates superior performance on Twitter and Weibo datasets, improving detection accuracy significantly.

Ramamoorthy et al. (2022) introduced a pioneering approach to meme analysis, providing gold-standard data for sentiment analysis, emotion classification, and intensity of emotion. The study presented baseline models, including a text-only model using LSTM and a multimodal model combining ResNet-50 and BERT, demonstrating the potential of incorporating text and images for improved performance.

Suryawanshi et al. (2023) proposed a comprehensive framework for analyzing image-with-text (IWT) memes, or "troll memes," introducing a three-level taxonomy to understand trolling's impact on domain-specific opinion manipulation. They enriched the Memotion dataset to create the TrollsWithOpinion dataset, containing 8,881 IWT memes in English, revealing challenges in classifying memes on the third level of the taxonomy.

Hossain et al. (2022) introduced the multimodal dataset "MemoSen" for the Bengali language, comprising 4,368 memes annotated with sentiment labels. Experiments on the MemoSen dataset showed a significant enhancement in meme sentiment classification with multimodal information integration.

Gasparini et al. (2022) created a benchmark meme dataset for automatic misogyny detection using 800 memes collected from various online sources. The dataset, analyzed by experts and crowdsourcing, included categories such as misogynistic, hostile, and ironic, with 100% agreement on 800 memes from three experts.

Suryawanshi et al. (2020) developed a system employing an early fusion technique to combine text and image modalities, contrasting its efficacy with baseline models focusing solely on either text or image.

Koutlis et al. (2023) introduced MemeFier, a deep learning-based architecture, featuring a dual-stage modality fusion module for fine-grained Internet image meme classification. Hegde et al. (2021) presented a transformer-transformer architecture, incorporating attention as a key component for classifying memes in the Tamil language.

Potential research gaps include the need for a unified evaluation metric and benchmark dataset for consistent comparison, the exploration of cross-cultural meme classification, the investigation of interpretability in model decision-making, and the development of more robust techniques to address biases and fairness concerns in meme classification models.

3 Task Description

The competition, "Shared Task on Multitask Meme Classification - Unraveling Misogynistic and Trolls in Online Memes," includes a challenge that focuses specifically on spotting harmful content in memes. While the overall competition has two parts, this paper discusses the part about finding misogynistic memes in Tamil and Malayalam languages. Organized as a part of the LT-EDI@EACL 2024 event[1], this task is designed to encourage

[1] https://2024.eacl.org

experts to come up with ways to identify when a meme is offensive towards women.

In Task 1, the participants are tasked with creating a tool that can look at memes (combining pictures with text) and determine if the meme is disrespectful or harmful to women. The task deals with memes in Tamil and Malayalam, and the participants are given training and development sets. They use these sets to teach their tools to distinguish between misogynistic memes and those that are not. Then, we will provide them with the test set without the labels. With this set, the participants will make the model to predict whether the meme is misogyny and submit it as a submission. Finally, we will judge the participant's model with their prediction with the true labels of the test set.

The tools are judged by how accurately they can make these distinctions, with the macro F1 score. The goal here is to push forward the development of tools that can spot and reduce the sharing of memes that can be hurtful to women in these two languages. This challenge is meant to attract attention from people worldwide who work in language and technology-related fields, hoping to spark more research and solutions in this important area. This shared task is conducted via the Codalab competition[2].

4 Dataset description

The dataset underneath the misogyny meme classification competition offers a comprehensive look at the manifestation of misogynistic content within the digital landscape, particularly within Tamil and Malayalam languages. Misogynistic memes target women or girls, often by leveraging stereotypes, displaying bias, or promoting discrimination. They might generalize women's capabilities with statements implying inferiority, demean their achievements, or mock female-specific issues to reinforce negative stereotypes and biases. Our dataset encompasses both monolingual and bilingual memes, with some featuring a mix of Tamil-English or Malayalam-English content, presenting an open challenge for research due to the code-mixed nature of these texts.

This dataset focuses primarily on monolingual content in Tamil and Malayalam, both of which are part of the Dravidian language family. Through this dataset, we aim to understand the extent and nature of misogynistic memes in these languages, exploring the linguistic and cultural factors contributing to their creation and spread. This is vital for researchers and practitioners dedicated to combating digital misogyny, especially in the context of Dravidian languages. The dataset consists of 1,776 Tamil memes, with 1,135 employed in the training set, 285 in development, and 356 in the test set. The data statistics for Malayalam data are shown in Table 1. The Malayalam dataset consists of 1,000 memes, with 640 in the training, 160 in the development, and 200 in the test set. The data statistics for Malayalam data are shown in Table 2.

5 Participants methodology

A total number of 52 participants were enrolled in this competition. In Task 1, we got a total of 4 submissions for the Tamil language and 3 submissions for the Malayalam language. The methodologies and results of these tasks have been discussed. To get more crucial material, please consult their papers, which are listed below:

Quartet (H et al., 2024) team participated in Task 1. They employed two different approaches to obtain the classification probabilities from the image and text data. With the textual data, every word of the text was translated into English. Subsequently, the translated sentences were preprocessed by eliminating emojis, punctuations, and stopwords. Then, the TF-IDF vectorizer is employed to obtain the embeddings from the preprocessed texts. The probability of the text being misogynistic was determined using the Multinomial Naive Bayes classifier. With the Pictorial Data, they employed the ResNet50 model (He et al., 2016) for performing transfer learning to obtain the probability of images being misogynistic. Using those probabilities, the employed fusion technique calculates the resultant probability.

DLRG team participated in Task 1. They worked on only textual data to classify the memes as misogyny or not. They employed Multilingual Bert(Bidirectional Encoder Representations from Transformers) (Kenton and Toutanova, 2019), a transformer-based multilingual pretrained model. They performed a transfer learning approach with the transcriptions and the labels.

Word Wizards team participated in Task 1. They worked on only textual data to classify the memes as misogyny or not. They performed tokenization and extracted word embeddings using

[2]https://codalab.lisn.upsaclay.fr/competitions/16097

Sets	Misogyny	Not-misogyny	Total
Train	272	863	1135
Development	76	209	285
Test	100	256	356
Total	448	1,328	1,776

Table 1: Data statistics for Task1 Tamil dataset for misogyny memes classification

Sets	Misogyny	Not-misogyny	Total
Train	256	384	640
Development	64	96	160
Test	80	120	200
Total	400	600	1,000

Table 2: Data statistics for Task1 Malayalam dataset for misogyny memes classification

TF-IDF vectorizer. With the work embeddings got from TF-IDF, they trained the SVM classifier to classify the meme into misogyny or not-misogyny for Tamil and Malayalam.

MUCS (Mahesh et al., 2024) team also participated in Task 1. They work on both meme images and transcriptions. Their methodology comprises a dual-encoder approach incorporating three distinct textual feature encoders alongside a shared image feature encoder: i) bert-base-uncased + ResNet-50, ii) muril-base-cased + ResNet-50, and iii) bertbase-multilingual-cased + ResNet-50.

6 Results

This section describes the results of a misogyny meme classification competition, where participants were evaluated based on the Macro F1 score—a measure used to test the accuracy of their machine learning (ML) and deep learning (DL) algorithms. In the Tamil results described in 3, MUCS_run3 achieved the highest rank with a Macro F1 score of 0.73, followed by DLRG with 0.69, Quartet with 0.65, and WordWizards_run1 with 0.60, ranking them from first to fourth, respectively. In the Malayalam results illustrated in 4, MUCS_run2 came out on top with an impressive Macro F1 score of 0.87, Quartet followed closely with a score of 0.83, and WordWizards_run1 also showed strong performance with a score of 0.8. These rankings provide a quantitative assessment of the participants' algorithmic approaches in the classification task. The results, as presented in this paper, showcase not only the potential but also the challenges inherent in automating the detection of misogyny and trolling in memes. While the best-performing systems exhibited promising results, there remains considerable scope for improvement, especially in handling code-mixed content and subtle cultural nuances. The shared task has also highlighted the need for further research into the creation of more sophisticated algorithms that can navigate the complexities of language, context, and intent.

Team name	M_F1	Rank
MUCS_run3 (Mahesh et al., 2024)	0.73	1
DLRG	0.69	2
Quartet (H et al., 2024)	0.65	3
WordWizards_run1	0.60	4

Table 3: Tamil results for misogyny memes classification

Team name	M_F1	Rank
MUCS_run2 (Mahesh et al., 2024)	0.87	1
Quartet (H et al., 2024)	0.83	2
WordWizards_run1	0.80	3

Table 4: Malayalam results for misogyny memes classification

7 Conclusion

In conclusion, the first shared task on "Multitask Meme Classification - Unraveling Misogynistic and Trolls in Online Memes" has been a groundbreaking effort to address the pressing issue of online misogyny and trolling within the context of Dravidian languages. The participation of dedicated teams in the Tamil and Malayalam classification tasks demonstrates a collective commitment to understanding and combating such harmful online content. The datasets, precisely compiled and annotated, provided a robust foundation for the teams to deploy and test a variety of machine learning and deep learning models, which were assessed based on their Macro F1 scores.

Furthermore, this paper stands as a testament to the collaborative efforts required to address the multifaceted challenges presented by online misogynistic and troll memes, and it is hoped that it will inspire continued research and action in this vital area.

8 Acknowledgement

This work was conducted with the financial support of the Science Foundation Ireland Centre for Research Training in Artificial Intelligence under Grant No. 18/CRT/6223, supported in part by a research grant from Science Foundation Ireland (SFI) under Grant Number SFI/12/RC/2289_P2(Insight_2).

References

Trenton W Ford, Rachel Krohn, and Tim Weninger. 2023. Competition dynamics in the meme ecosystem. *ACM Transactions on Social Computing*, 6(3-4):1–19.

Francesca Gasparini, Giulia Rizzi, Aurora Saibene, and Elisabetta Fersini. 2022. Benchmark dataset of memes with text transcriptions for automatic detection of multi-modal misogynistic content. *Data in brief*, 44:108526.

Shaun Allan H, Samyuktaa Sivakumar, Rohan R, Nikilesh Jayaguptha, and Durairaj Thenmozhi. 2024. Quartet@LT-EDI 2024: A SVM-ResNet50 Approach For Multitask Meme Classification - Unraveling Misogynistic and Trolls in Online Memes. In *Proceedings of the Fourth Workshop on Language Technology for Equality, Diversity and Inclusion*, Malta. European Chapter of the Association for Computational Linguistics.

Kaiming He, Xiangyu Zhang, Shaoqing Ren, and Jian Sun. 2016. Deep residual learning for image recognition. In *Proceedings of the IEEE conference on computer vision and pattern recognition*, pages 770–778.

Siddhanth U Hegde, Adeep Hande, Ruba Priyadharshini, Sajeetha Thavareesan, and Bharathi Raja Chakravarthi. 2021. Uvce-iiitt@ dravidianlangtech-eacl2021: Tamil troll meme classification: You need to pay more attention. *arXiv preprint arXiv:2104.09081*.

Eftekhar Hossain, Omar Sharif, and Mohammed Moshiul Hoque. 2022. Memosen: A multimodal dataset for sentiment analysis of memes. In *Proceedings of the Thirteenth Language Resources and Evaluation Conference*, pages 1542–1554.

Jacob Devlin Ming-Wei Chang Kenton and Lee Kristina Toutanova. 2019. Bert: Pre-training of deep bidirectional transformers for language understanding. In *Proceedings of naacL-HLT*, volume 1, page 2.

Bisera Kostadinovska-Stojchevska and Elena Shalevska. 2018. Internet memes and their socio-linguistic features. *European journal of literature, language and linguistics studies*, 2(4).

Christos Koutlis, Manos Schinas, and Symeon Papadopoulos. 2023. Memefier: Dual-stage modality fusion for image meme classification. *arXiv preprint arXiv:2304.02906*.

Hongzhan Lin, Ziyang Luo, Bo Wang, Ruichao Yang, and Jing Ma. 2024. Goat-bench: Safety insights to large multimodal models through meme-based social abuse. *arXiv preprint arXiv:2401.01523*.

Sidharth Mahesh, Sonith D, Gauthamraj, Kavya G, Asha Hegde, and H L Shashirekha. 2024. MUCS@LT-EDI-2024: Exploring Joint Representation for Memes Classification. In *Proceedings of the Fourth Workshop on Language Technology for Equality, Diversity and Inclusion*, Malta. European Chapter of the Association for Computational Linguistics.

Ruba Priyadharshini, Bharathi Raja Chakravarthi, Subalalitha Cn, Thenmozhi Durairaj, Malliga Subramanian, Kogilavani Shanmugavadivel, Siddhanth U Hegde, and Prasanna Kumaresan. 2022. Overview of abusive comment detection in Tamil-ACL 2022. In *Proceedings of the Second Workshop on Speech and Language Technologies for Dravidian Languages*, pages 292–298, Dublin, Ireland. Association for Computational Linguistics.

Ruba Priyadharshini, Bharathi Raja Chakravarthi, Malliga S, Subalalitha Cn, Kogilavani S V, Premjith B, Abirami Murugappan, and Prasanna Kumar Kumaresan. 2023. Overview of shared-task on abusive comment detection in Tamil and Telugu. In *Proceedings of the Third Workshop on Speech and Language Technologies for Dravidian Languages*, pages 80–87, Varna, Bulgaria. INCOMA Ltd., Shoumen, Bulgaria.

Sathyanarayanan Ramamoorthy, Nethra Gunti, Shreyash Mishra, S Suryavardan, Aishwarya Reganti, Parth Patwa, Amitava DaS, Tanmoy Chakraborty, Amit Sheth, Asif Ekbal, et al. 2022. Memotion 2: Dataset on sentiment and emotion analysis of memes. In *Proceedings of De-Factify: Workshop on Multimodal Fact Checking and Hate Speech Detection, CEUR*.

AAPK Rasheed, C Maria, and A Michael. 2020. Social media and meme culture: A study on the impact of internet memes in reference with 'kudathai murder case'. *Kristu Jayanti College*.

Shivangi Singhal, Rajiv Ratn Shah, Tanmoy Chakraborty, Ponnurangam Kumaraguru, and Shin'ichi Satoh. 2019. Spotfake: A multi-modal framework for fake news detection. In *2019 IEEE fifth international conference on multimedia big data (BigMM)*, pages 39–47. IEEE.

Shivangi Singhal, Rajiv Ratn Shah, and Ponnurangam Kumaraguru. 2022. Factdrill: A data repository of fact-checked social media content to study fake news incidents in india. In *Proceedings of the international AAAI conference on web and social media*, volume 16, pages 1322–1331.

Shardul Suryawanshi and Bharathi Raja Chakravarthi. 2021. Findings of the shared task on troll meme classification in Tamil. In *Proceedings of the First Workshop on Speech and Language Technologies for Dravidian Languages*, pages 126–132, Kyiv. Association for Computational Linguistics.

Shardul Suryawanshi, Bharathi Raja Chakravarthi, Mihael Arcan, and Paul Buitelaar. 2020. Multimodal meme dataset (multioff) for identifying offensive content in image and text. In *Proceedings of the second workshop on trolling, aggression and cyberbullying*, pages 32–41.

Shardul Suryawanshi, Bharathi Raja Chakravarthi, Mihael Arcan, and Paul Buitelaar. 2023. Trollswithopinion: A taxonomy and dataset for predicting domain-specific opinion manipulation in troll memes. *Multimedia Tools and Applications*, 82(6):9137–9171.

Overview of Shared Task on Caste and Migration Hate Speech Detection

Saranya Rajiakodi[1], **Bharathi Raja Chakravarthi**[2], **Rahul Ponnusamy**[3], **Prasanna Kumar Kumaresan**[3], **Sathiyaraj Thangasamy**[4], **Bhuvaneswari Sivagnanam**[1], **Charmathi Rajkumar**[5]

[1]Central University of Tamil Nadu, India
[2]School of Computer Science, University of Galway, Ireland
[3]Data Science Institute, University of Galway, Ireland
[4]Department of Tamil, Sri Krishna Adithya College of Arts and Science, Tamil Nadu, India
[5]The American College, Madurai, Tamil Nadu, India

Abstract

We present an overview of the first shared task on "Caste and Migration Hate Speech Detection." The shared task is organized as part of LT-EDI@EACL 2024. The system must delineate between binary outcomes, ascertaining whether the text is categorized as a caste/migration hate speech or not. The dataset presented in this shared task is in Tamil, which is one of the under-resource languages. There are a total of 51 teams participated in this task. Among them, 15 teams submitted their research results for the task. To the best of our knowledge, this is the first time the shared task has been conducted on textual hate speech detection concerning caste and migration. In this study, we have conducted a systematic analysis and detailed presentation of all the contributions of the participants as well as the statistics of the dataset, which is the social media comments in Tamil language to detect hate speech. It also further goes into the details of a comprehensive analysis of the participants' methodology and their findings.

1 Introduction

Social media platforms have become an integral part of the daily life of today's society. It gives new meaning to how we communicate, connect, and share information among people (Kumaresan et al., 2023). This digital landscape allows users to share their opinions, how they live, and their work worldwide. It has a huge impact on society, which makes it possible to influence everything around us. It encompasses the way of communication, how we perceive the world, disaster response, education, and how it makes information accessible to everyone, as well as giving our support to the things or people that are overlooked by society (Ponnusamy et al., 2023; Chakravarthi, 2023).

However, social media platforms also present significant challenges to people, like discrimination and bias against certain kinds of people, including those based on caste/migration. It replicates the societal fractures openly or anonymously, enabling harassment, bullying, and exclusion based on caste/migration. The caste system also significantly influences instances of homicide and violence targeting inter-caste marriages (Sathi, 2023). Caste systems are in a hierarchical order from high to low. Here, low-level caste people have been subjected to many kinds of discrimination in many firms (Goraya, 2023). Racial and extractive capitalism has exploited the people into hard labor, their dehumanizing treatment, and their psychological trauma experiences (Dulhunty, 2023).

With the rapid rise of social media(Lande et al., 2023; Priyadharshini et al., 2022), the shadows of age-old social prejudice, such as caste-based discrimination, bias, and hate speech, stepped into the digital realm, which especially targeted lower-caste people, thus leading to their psychological trauma and trampling on the dignity of humans. There are some cases where caste/migration-based discrimination leads to violence. This leads to a way of effectively addressing and detecting hate speech regarding caste/migration. With the help of machine learning, deep learning, and natural language processing technology, one can detect caste/migration-based hate speech. However, the quality of the detection depends on the quality of the training data without any biases and critical concerns. The task involves the use of a newly created dataset for detecting caste or migration-based hate speech in the Tamil language.

Proceedings of the Fourth Workshop on Language Technology for Equality, Diversity, Inclusion, pages 145–151
March 21, 2024 ©2024 Association for Computational Linguistics

In this overview paper, we have discussed the shared task of caste and migration hate speech detection in Tamil at LT-EDI@EACL 2024. In the subsequent sections, we have discussed the task description, dataset statistics, methodologies used by the participants to detect caste/migration hate speech in Tamil, and their results and ranking.

2 Related work

In recent years, social media has developed rapidly, leading to advantages and disadvantages in its use. The common one is hate speech towards a certain kind of race, religion, sexual orientation, gender, caste, and beyond. This issue leads many researchers to research to research a methodology that can detect hate speech related to specific targets(Ibrohim and Budi, 2023). In particular, (Ryzhova et al., 2022) presents XLM RoBERTa as a base model to detect religion-based hate speech on English, Russian, and Hindi datasets. Afterward, the base model was finetuned with the different datasets, and to improve the model, a text attack algorithm was applied. (Parvaresh, 2023) focuses on hate speech towards Afghan immigrants in Iran and also shows the subtle ways of spreading hate speech without directly using any hateful words. (Breazu, 2023) focuses on the hate speech comments on YouTube regarding the Roma community, and it also points out how the obvious and subtle way of hate comments and discrimination spread against the Roma community. It also highlighted the term “entitlement racism,” which is when individuals believe it’s justifiable to propagate racial animosity. (Nave and Lane, 2023) highlights how online platforms lack the detailed guidelines to successfully combat online hate speech when incorporating HRDD (Human Rights Due Diligence) into their terms of service (TOS). In order to protect marginalized people, it advocates online platforms, including the TOS, with European human rights norms.

3 Task Description

The primary goal of this task is to develop an automated classification system that can accurately determine the presence of hate speech on caste or migration within textual content on social media platforms. This shared task is held through the Codalab competition[1]. The participants will provided with training, development, and test datasets in the Tamil language. To access and contribute to the data, navigate to Codalab and select the "Participate" tab. To the best of our knowledge, this represents the first shared task dedicated to identifying hate speech concerning caste/migration. The annotation has been done in two categories.

- **Hate speech on caste/migration:** Comments that contain a variety of harmful, derogatory, discriminatory content as well as mocking and ridicule, Delegitimization content aimed at certain caste or migrated people.
- **Not Hate speech on caste/migration:** Comments that do not contain text aimed at any caste or migrated people

Sample for Hate speech on caste:

நி தமிழனே கிடையாது.
வடுக பள்ளன் னு செப்பேடு
சொல்லுது. நி எப்படி டா
வேளாளர் ஆக முடியும்

Figure 1: **Tamil Language- Hate speech on caste**

English Translation for Figure 1: You are not Tamizhian. Seppedu says Vaduka Pallan. How can you become a vaellalar?

- **Tamil-English:** Nee yaen mukkulathor aah pirika ninaikura
- **English Translation for Above text:** Why do you want to separate the MUkkulathor?

Sample for Hate speech on migration:

டேய் வடக்கன அடிச்சு
விரட்டுங்கட நா பறையன்
தாண்ட இருந்தாலும் தமிழ்
இனத்தை சேர்தவண்டா
சொன்னா கேளுங்க டா அவ
நமக்குள்ள வேண்டா தவவு
செஞ்சு

Figure 2: **Tamil Language- Hate speech on migration**

English Translation for Figure 2: Banish the North Indians. Na Parayan Thanda. However, I

[1]https://codalab.lisn.upsaclay.fr/competitions/16089

am from the Tamil race. Listen, sir. Don't involve them with us.

- **Tamil-English:** polaikavantha marvadikku yavvalavu thimuru. Nam thamilar aachithan enimea.
- **English Translation for Above text:** How arrogant is the Marvadi who came to work.Nam thamilar aachithan enimea.

4 Dataset Description

This dataset was methodically collected from a social media platform with a concentrated focus on the YouTube platform by utilizing the YouTube-comment-scraper tool to collect the YouTube video comments in support of the shared task on 'Caste/Migration Hate Speech Detection' at LT-EDI@EACL 2024. It represents the first dataset focusing on caste and migration hate speech in low-resource languages, with a particular emphasis on Tamil. A total of 7,875 comments were collected, and each of the comments was meticulously annotated for the presence of caste/migration hate speech (labeled as '1') and the absence of such hate speech (labeled as '0').

A few samples of the dataset have been discussed in the previous section. The samples contain some words that point at some caste or migrated people such as *vadakan*, *marvadi*, *parayan*, *vaduka pallan*, *vaellalar*, *mukkulathor*. The offensive texts that may come along with the above words or beyond may have targeted a certain community. Since there are many castes, some tend to discriminate against other castes which leads to these kinds of offensive comments.

The dataset was segmented into training, development, and test data subsets to help with the thorough analysis and to facilitate the model training. The accompanying Table 1 provides the detailed distribution of comments across these subsets, providing the dataset's structure and composition.

4.1 Training Phase:

Initially, participants were provided with both training and validation data for caste/migration hate speech detection model development. They could run preliminary evaluations and fine-tune the model settings. There are 51 teams participated and accessed the data.

4.2 Evaluation Phase:

The second phase involved releasing test sets in Tamil for system evaluation. Participating teams submitted their predicted results for assessment through Google Forms. The submission will be evaluated with macro average F1-score. The results should be submitted on the google form in the form of zip.

5 Participant's Methodology

- **BITS_GraphAI:** This team used two pretrained transformers, TamilSBERT-STS and Indic-SBERT(Deode et al., 2023)(Mirashi et al., 2024), and fine-tuned them on the given data with triplet and cosine similarity loss, respectively. In triplet loss, triples are of the form (anchor, positive, negative), where the anchor and positive sentences are of the same class, whereas negatives are from other classes. Triplet loss helps the model to discern nuanced relationships. To further enhance classification, we used TextGCN architecture(Yao et al., 2019) by feeding the fine-tuned sBERT embeddings as feature input and text graph as an adjacency matrix. All three models performed well, showing slightly better results from sBERT-enhanced TextGCN graph-based learning. This team achieved rank 4 with a macro F1 score of 0.77.
- **SSN-Nova** (Reddy et al., 2024): This team delves into an array of boosting techniques, encompassing Adaboost, XGBoost,(Demir and Sahin, 2023) and a comparative analysis with a voting classifier that aggregates multiple traditional models. This methodology provides a comprehensive exploration of ensemble methods, leveraging the strengths of boosting algorithms and traditional models to enhance the overall predictive capabilities of their system. They secured rank 12 with the macro F! score of 0.59
- **Kubapok** (Pokrywka and Jassem, 2024): The Team employed a systematic approach in their endeavor, utilizing solely the data provided by the organizers. Their methodology centered around employing various models, including 'l3cube/pune-kannada'(Deode et al., 2023)(Mirashi et al., 2024), 'microsoft-mdeberta-v3'(He et al., 2020) (utilized twice), and 'xlm-roberta.' These models were trained

Sets	Caste/Migration Hate Speech	Not	Total
Train	2,052	3,303	5,355
Development	351	594	945
Test	602	973	1,575
	Total		7,875

Table 1: Dataset Description

using standard Hugging Face scripts for text classification, with adjustments such as a warm-up ratio of 0.1 and 30 epochs. Notably, they aggregated both training and development data, creating fresh random splits for each model. The selection of the optimal epoch checkpoint was based on the development F1 score. A key aspect of their strategy involved averaging the probabilities generated by all four models, with a threshold of 0.5 for class selection. This team achieved rank 2 with a macro F1 score of 0.81.

- **KEC_AI_DSNLP:** (Shanmugavadivel et al., 2024) This team created a machine learning model such as KNN, Decision trees and Naive Baiyes to classify the hate speech text and got 0.65 macro F1 and secured the rank 9.

- **CUET_NLP_GoodFellows:** This team used two BERT models to accomplish their task. They are mBERT and XLM-R, and both of these models are finetuned. Along with these, the team also used fine-tuned random classifier.

- **selam:** This team employed a Support Vector Machine (SVM) approach within the realm of Natural Language Processing (NLP). The primary goal was to develop a robust text classification system capable of predicting whether a given text contains caste/migration hate speech and scored macro F1 of 0.62 and secured rank 10.

- **KEC_DL_KSK:** Team employed the sampling methods such as SMOTE and random oversampler to balance the datasets. They have used machine learning algorithms, namely, Random Forest, Support Vector Machine, Naive Bayes, Logistic Regression, and Decision Tree, along with word embedding techniques like TF-IDF, Word2Vec, Doc2Vec, and FastText. the got the 0.49 macro f1 score.

- **bytesizedllm:** This team has utilized the embeddings generated from a subset of AI4Bharat's data, encompassing 100,000 randomized lines. These embeddings were created using their custom-built subword tokenizers for Telugu (with a size of 7.6 MB) and Tamil (with a size of 1.3 MB) languages. They employed a Bidirectional Long Short-Term Memory (BiLSTM) classifier to perform classification tasks. The model was trained on labeled datasets and scored 0.61 macro F1 score.

- **Word Wizards:** This team utilized Labse(Pei et al., 2022), a pre-trained language representation model specifically designed for understanding the text in multiple languages. Labse employs a Siamese encoder architecture, capable of generating high-quality sentence embeddings by encoding text into a fixed-size vector representation. Following the encoding process, a K-Nearest Neighbors (KNN) model was implemented to perform various tasks, likely involving similarity searches or classification based on the encoded representations. KNN is a simple yet effective algorithm used for classification and regression tasks, particularly in scenarios where data points are mapped in a high-dimensional space. This combination likely facilitated tasks involving semantic similarity, clustering, or classification of text data based on the learned representations from Labse embeddings. They achieved rank 13 with the macro F1 score of 0.54.

- **Lidoma:** (Tash et al., 2024) This team employed deep learning and machine learning models like convolutional neural networks and support vector machine algorithms to classify hate speech detection on caste/migration in the Tamil language and secured that 6th rank with the macro F1 score of 0.76.

- **Transformers:** (Singhal and Bedi, 2024) This

Teams	Macro F1	Rank
Transformers_run3 (Singhal and Bedi, 2024)	0.82	1
kubapok_run1 (Pokrywka and Jassem, 2024)	0.81	2
CUET_NLP_Manning_run3 (Alam et al., 2024)	0.80	3
BITS_Graph4NLP_run1	0.77	4
Algorithmalliance_run1 (Sangeetham et al., 2024)	0.76	5
lidoma_run2 (Tash et al., 2024)	0.76	6
CUET_NLP_GoodFellows_run2	0.75	7
quartet_run1 (H et al., 2024)	0.73	8
KEC_AI_DSNLP_run2 (Shanmugavadivel et al., 2024)	0.65	9
selam_run1	0.62	10
byteSizedllm_run1	0.61	11
SSN-nova_run3 (Reddy et al., 2024)	0.59	12
WordWizards_tamil_run1	0.54	13
KEC_DL_KSK_run2	0.49	14
Habesha_run1	0.38	15

Table 2: Rank List Based on Average macro F1 Score

team utilized an ensemble model that comprises XLMroberta, a multilingual bert base model, and muril cased model(Subramanian et al., 2022). The accuracy of these models was highest compared to all the other models tested. A combination of these models improved the overall accuracy. All the models were trained on the text without cleaning since the performance of all the models suffered after cleaning.

- **CUET_NLP_Manning** (Alam et al., 2024): This team employed six machine learning(LR, SVM, SGD, XGB, ENSEMBLE, RF) models, 3 deep learning models(BiLSTM, Attention, and BiLSTM-CNN) and three transformer-based models (M-BERT, XLM-R, and Tamil-BERT) with TF-IDF and fasttext embeddings. Among the models, the transformer-based model yields better results with the highest evaluation score. This team achieved rank 3 with a score of 0.80.

- **Habesha:**This Team utilized a model built upon BERT transformers for creating embeddings. Additionally, They integrated LSTM (Long Short-Term Memory) deep learning techniques to facilitate classification tasks. This combined architecture allows for the effective representation of input data through transformer-based embeddings while leveraging the sequential learning capabilities of LSTM for accurate classification and scoring 0.38 macro F1.

- **ALGORITHM ALLIANCE** (Sangeetham et al., 2024): This team has applied several supervised machine learning algorithms such as Logistic Regression, Support Vector Machine(SVM), Multi-Layer Perceptron(MLP), Random Forest Classifier(RFC), Decision Tree, KNN as their classification models to the highest accuracy. Among these, SVM yielded the highest scores which is 0.76 macro F1 score, and secured rank 5.

- **Quartet** (H et al., 2024): This team used machine learning models such as Logistic Regression, Support Vector Machine (SVM), Random Forest Classifier, Decision Tree Classifier, and Naive Bayes for classification and TF-IDF for feature representation. Support Vector Machine yielded a better accuracy with a 0.73 macro F1 score and ranked 8th.

6 Results

The hate speech detection shared task for caste/migrants was conducted for one of the low-resource Languages that is Tamil. As mentioned in the former part, many participants have contributed to the shared task. A total of 51 teams participated in the shared task of detecting hate speech on caste/migration in the Tamil Language. Among them, 15 teams submitted their results. The ranking and Evaluation of the shared tasks was based on the average macro F1 score. Table 2 shows the rankings of the teams that participated in the task. Here we have accentuated the top three teams that participated in the shared task and got the top rankings. The team "Transformers"(Singhal and Bedi, 2024) ranked first in the shared task with the macro F1 score of 0.82 using the ensemble methods combining various transformers-based model. "kubapok" Team ranked second among the participants with the macro F1 score of 0.81 which has been resulted from utilizing the microsoft-mdeberta-v3, and xlm-roberta. CUET_NLP_Manning(Alam et al., 2024) ranked third with the macro F1 score of 0.80 by using machine learning, deep learning, and transformer-based models like mBERT, Tamil BERT, xlm- R models.

7 Conclusion

We presented the overview of the shared task on caste and migration hate speech in social media comments using a dataset in Tamil. It represents an important step toward the creation of healthy online communities. We can mitigate hate speech on certain individuals, castes, and migration by exploiting advanced technologies, algorithms, and computational tools.

8 Ethical Considerations

In conducting this study, which involves the utilization of YouTube comments, we have taken into account many ethical implications while collecting the YouTube comments we made sure that the privacy of commentators was well protected and that the comments were not used in a way that could have caused any harm. In addition, we ensured that data distribution is prohibited for anything but academic and non-commercial research uses Thus we have done our research ethically and responsibly to reduce harm, protect privacy, and make meaningful contributions to the field of study.

Acknowledgements

This work was conducted with the financial support of the Science Foundation Ireland Centre for Research Training in Artificial Intelligence under Grant No. 18/CRT/6223, supported in part by a research grant from Science Foundation Ireland (SFI) under Grant Number SFI/12/RC/2289_P2(Insight_2).

References

Md Ashraful Alam, Hasan Mesbaul Ali Taher, Jawad Hossain, Shawly Ahsan, and Mohammed Moshiul Hoque. 2024. CUET_NLP_Manning@LT-EDI 2024: Transformer-based Approach on Caste and Migration Hate Speech Detection. In *Proceedings of the Fourth Workshop on Language Technology for Equality, Diversity and Inclusion*, Malta. European Chapter of the Association for Computational Linguistics.

Petre Breazu. 2023. Entitlement racism on youtube: White injury—the licence to humiliate roma migrants in the uk. *Discourse, Context & Media*, 55:100718.

Bharathi Raja Chakravarthi. 2023. Detection of homophobia and transphobia in youtube comments. *International Journal of Data Science and Analytics*, pages 1–20.

Selçuk Demir and Emrehan Kutlug Sahin. 2023. An investigation of feature selection methods for soil liquefaction prediction based on tree-based ensemble algorithms using adaboost, gradient boosting, and xgboost. *Neural Computing and Applications*, 35(4):3173–3190.

Samruddhi Deode, Janhavi Gadre, Aditi Kajale, Ananya Joshi, and Raviraj Joshi. 2023. L3cube-indicsbert: A simple approach for learning cross-lingual sentence representations using multilingual bert. *arXiv preprint arXiv:2304.11434*.

Annabel Dulhunty. 2023. When extractive and racial capitalism combine–indigenous and caste based struggles with land, labour and law in india. *Geoforum*, 147:103887.

Sampreet Singh Goraya. 2023. How does caste affect entrepreneurship? birth versus worth. *Journal of Monetary Economics*, 135:116–133.

Shaun Allan H, Samyuktaa Sivakumar, Rohan R, Nikilesh Jayaguptha, and Durairaj Thenmozhi. 2024. Quartet@LT-EDI 2024: A Support Vector Machine Approach For Caste and Migration Hate Speech Detection. In *Proceedings of the Fourth Workshop on Language Technology for Equality, Diversity and Inclusion*, Malta. European Chapter of the Association for Computational Linguistics.

Pengcheng He, Xiaodong Liu, Jianfeng Gao, and Weizhu Chen. 2020. Deberta: Decoding-enhanced bert with disentangled attention. *arXiv preprint arXiv:2006.03654*.

Muhammad Okky Ibrohim and Indra Budi. 2023. Hate speech and abusive language detection in indonesian social media: Progress and challenges. *Heliyon*.

Prasanna Kumar Kumaresan, Kishore Kumar Ponnusamy, Kogilavani S V, Subalalitha Cn, Ruba Priyadharshini, and Bharathi Raja Chakravarthi. 2023. VEL@LT-EDI: Detecting homophobia and transphobia in code-mixed Spanish social media comments. In *Proceedings of the Third Workshop on*

Language Technology for Equality, Diversity and Inclusion, pages 233–238, Varna, Bulgaria. INCOMA Ltd., Shoumen, Bulgaria.

Kaustubh Lande, Rahul Ponnusamy, Prasanna Kumar Kumaresan, and Bharathi Raja Chakravarthi. 2023. KaustubhSharedTask@LT-EDI 2023: Homophobia-transphobia detection in social media comments with NLPAUG-driven data augmentation. In *Proceedings of the Third Workshop on Language Technology for Equality, Diversity and Inclusion*, pages 71–77, Varna, Bulgaria. INCOMA Ltd., Shoumen, Bulgaria.

Aishwarya Mirashi, Srushti Sonavane, Purva Lingayat, Tejas Padhiyar, and Raviraj Joshi. 2024. L3cube-indicnews: News-based short text and long document classification datasets in indic languages. *arXiv preprint arXiv:2401.02254*.

Eva Nave and Lottie Lane. 2023. Countering online hate speech: How does human rights due diligence impact terms of service? *Computer Law & Security Review*, 51:105884.

Vahid Parvaresh. 2023. Covertly communicated hate speech: A corpus-assisted pragmatic study. *Journal of Pragmatics*, 205:63–77.

Yijie Pei, Siqi Chen, Zunwang Ke, Wushour Silamu, and Qinglang Guo. 2022. Ab-labse: Uyghur sentiment analysis via the pre-training model with bilstm. *Applied Sciences*, 12(3):1182.

Jakub Pokrywka and Krzysztof Jassem. 2024. kubapok@LT-EDI 2024: Evaluating Transformer Models for Hate Speech Detection in Tamil. In *Proceedings of the Fourth Workshop on Language Technology for Equality, Diversity and Inclusion*, Malta. European Chapter of the Association for Computational Linguistics.

Rahul Ponnusamy, Malliga S, Sajeetha Thavareesan, Ruba Priyadharshini, and Bharathi Raja Chakravarthi. 2023. VEL@LT-EDI-2023: Automatic detection of hope speech in Bulgarian language using embedding techniques. In *Proceedings of the Third Workshop on Language Technology for Equality, Diversity and Inclusion*, pages 179–184, Varna, Bulgaria. INCOMA Ltd., Shoumen, Bulgaria.

Ruba Priyadharshini, Bharathi Raja Chakravarthi, Subalalitha Cn, Thenmozhi Durairaj, Malliga Subramanian, Kogilavani Shanmugavadivel, Siddhanth U Hegde, and Prasanna Kumaresan. 2022. Overview of abusive comment detection in tamil-acl 2022. In *Proceedings of the Second Workshop on Speech and Language Technologies for Dravidian Languages*, pages 292–298.

A Ankitha Reddy, Ann Maria Thomas, Pranav Moorthi, and B Bharathi. 2024. SSN-Nova@LT-EDI 2024: POS Tagging, Boosting Techniques and Voting Classifiers for Caste And Migration Hate Speech Detection. In *Proceedings of the Fourth Workshop on Language Technology for Equality, Diversity and Inclusion*, Malta. European Chapter of the Association for Computational Linguistics.

Anastasia Ryzhova, Dmitry Devyatkin, Sergey Volkov, and Vladimir Budzko. 2022. Training multilingual and adversarial attack-robust models for hate detection on social media. *Procedia Computer Science*, 213:196–202.

Saisandeep Sangeetham, Shreyamanisha C Vinay, Kavin Rajan G, Abishna A, and B Bharathi. 2024. Algorithm Alliance@LT-EDI-2024: Caste and Migration Hate Speech Detection. In *Proceedings of the Fourth Workshop on Language Technology for Equality, Diversity and Inclusion*, Malta. European Chapter of the Association for Computational Linguistics.

Sreerekha Sathi. 2023. Marriage murders and anti-caste feminist politics in india. In *Women's Studies International Forum*, volume 100, page 102816. Elsevier.

Kogilavani Shanmugavadivel, Malliga Subramanian, Aiswarya M, Aruna T, and Jeevaananth S. 2024. KEC AI DSNLP@LT-EDI-2024:Caste and Migration Hate Speech Detection using Machine Learning Techniques. In *Proceedings of the Fourth Workshop on Language Technology for Equality, Diversity and Inclusion*, Malta. European Chapter of the Association for Computational Linguistics.

Kriti Singhal and Jatin Bedi. 2024. Transformers@LT-EDI-EACL2024: Caste and Migration Hate Speech Detection in Tamil Using Ensembling on Transformers. In *Proceedings of the Fourth Workshop on Language Technology for Equality, Diversity and Inclusion*, Malta. European Chapter of the Association for Computational Linguistics.

Malliga Subramanian, Rahul Ponnusamy, Sean Benhur, Kogilavani Shanmugavadivel, Adhithiya Ganesan, Deepti Ravi, Gowtham Krishnan Shanmugasundaram, Ruba Priyadharshini, and Bharathi Raja Chakravarthi. 2022. Offensive language detection in tamil youtube comments by adapters and cross-domain knowledge transfer. *Computer Speech & Language*, 76:101404.

M Shahiki Tash, Z Ahani, M T Zamir, O Kolesnikova, and G Sidorov. 2024. Lidoma@LT-EDI 2024:Tamil Hate Speech Detection in Migration Discourse. In *Proceedings of the Fourth Workshop on Language Technology for Equality, Diversity and Inclusion*, Malta. European Chapter of the Association for Computational Linguistics.

Liang Yao, Chengsheng Mao, and Yuan Luo. 2019. Graph convolutional networks for text classification. In *Proceedings of the AAAI conference on artificial intelligence*, volume 33, pages 7370–7377.

Pinealai_StressIdent_LT-EDI@EACL2024: Minimal configurations for Stress Identification in Tamil and Telugu

Anvi Alex Eponon[1]
Ildar Batyrshin[1]
Grigori Sidorov[1]
[1]Instituto Politécnico Nacional (IPN), Centro de Investigación en Computación (CIC),
Mexico City, Mexico
{epononanvialex@gmail.com, Ibatyr1@cic.ipn.mx, sidorov@cic.ipn.mx}

Abstract

This paper introduces an approach to stress identification in Tamil and Telugu, leveraging traditional machine learning models—Fasttext for Tamil and Naive Bayes for Telugu—yielding commendable results. The study highlights the scarcity of annotated data and recognizes limitations in phonetic features relevant to these languages, impacting precise information extraction. Our models achieved a macro F1 score of 0.77 for Tamil and 0.72 for Telugu with Fasttext and Naive Bayes, respectively. While the Telugu model secured the second rank in shared tasks, ongoing research is crucial to unlocking the full potential of stress identification in these languages, necessitating the exploration of additional features and advanced techniques specified in the discussions and limitations section.

1 Introduction

In Natural Language Processing (NLP), a diverse range of tasks is undertaken to comprehend and process human language. These tasks encompass the intricate understanding of emotional nuances, from identifying hate speech Yigezu et al. (2023); Shahiki-Tash et al. (2023a) to recognizing hope speech Shahiki-Tash et al. (2023b) and stress detection. This broad spectrum of tasks includes text classification, named entity recognition, machine translation, text generation, question answering, text summarization, and part-of-speech tagging. The evolution of NLP models has transitioned from traditional methods such as rule-based systems and statistical models to sophisticated deep learning architectures. Notable examples of these architectures include Recurrent Neural Networks (RNNs), and Long Short-Term Memory Networks (LSTMs)Tonja et al. (2022).

Stress, simply characterized as a negative emotional response stemming from external factors, notably societal pressures, represents a significant facet of the human experience. Zaydman (2017) underscores the increasing trend of individuals sharing their feelings on the internet. While substantial research has explored the identification of such emotions Tash et al. (2023), particularly in languages like English ("Joshi et al. (2005); Nagle and Sharma ("2018"), there exists a noticeable gap in studies focused on Dravidian languages such as Tamil and Telugu.

Our investigation delves into emotion detection, building upon existing studies and laying a foundational framework for future directions in this domain. The insights gleaned from our research contribute to a growing body of knowledge, providing valuable groundwork for forthcoming explorations and advancements in understanding emotions in linguistic contexts.

In the upcoming sections, we will explore the latest studies about emotion and stress identification in Dravidian languages. We will share our approach, configuration, and methodology, followed by a presentation of the results and a concise analysis with future orientations.

2 Literature Review

India, renowned for its rich history and culture, is witnessing a growing prevalence of stress across its diverse population. From the young to the adults, stress permeates various aspects of life, encompassing academic pressures and professional challenges.

In education, the pressure on students to achieve high standards has led to prolonged stress, impacting mental health and, at times, resulting in severe consequences, as noted by "Joshi et al. (2005) in their research study. Research by Nagle and Sharma ("2018") showcases the role of societal expectations and family pressures in exacerbating student stress.

The advent of social media platforms has provided an avenue for individuals to express

Proceedings of the Fourth Workshop on Language Technology for Equality, Diversity, Inclusion, pages 152–156
March 21, 2024 ©2024 Association for Computational Linguistics

their emotions and state of mind. Zaydman (2017) fetched 2.3 million mental health-relevant Tweets, shedding light on stress and suicide tendencies(corpora in English).

In response to this societal landscape, research on stress identification in textual corpora has flourished.Nijhawan et al. (2022) explored stress detection in social interactions, achieving high accuracy using models like Bert and Random Forest. Similarly, Inamdar et al. (2023) employed Elmo embeddings, Bag of Words, and Bert models to detect mental stress in Reddit Posts, achieving an F1-score of 0.76 (in English).

While research on stress identification is prolific in languages like English, limited attention has been given to Dravidian languages such as Tamil and Telugu. Noteworthy studies by S et al. (2022) on analyzing emotions in Tamil and Gokhale et al. (2022) using diverse deep learning models shed light on this underexplored area. However, They presented a lexicon-based approach that led to an F1-score grounding at 0.0300. In the context of a shared task, García-Díaz et al. (2022) secured first place with a neural network trained on linguistic features and various sentence embeddings achieving only an F1-score of 0.15. However, no stress emotions have been included in the research.

Through our experiment, we aspire to provide the community with a dependable method for predicting stress in Tamil and Telugu. We aim to establish a foundational benchmark for subsequent research endeavors in the field.

3 Task Description

The primary goal of this shared task is to develop a system capable of discerning between textual corpora that exhibit signs of stress and those that do not in Dravidian languages, specifically Tamil and Telugu. Stress, a multifaceted emotion stemming from various life factors, often prompts individuals to share their feelings online. Constructing such a system holds the promise of aiding and supporting individuals displaying stress characteristics on social media, ultimately contributing to the reduction of depression rates within a broad community.

Despite its noble objectives, this shared task poses unique challenges. Addressing the abstract concept of emotions, particularly stress, is inherently complex. The task's focus on Tamil and Telugu languages introduces additional difficulties, such as the limited resources available for processing and the lack of standardization observed in these languages. Decrypting the nuances of emotional variations in these languages amplifies the complexity of the problem. However, the absence of tonal characteristics shared by languages like Mandarin Chinese renders the task more approachable.

This undertaking not only underscores the significance of emotional analysis but also holds the potential to make a meaningful impact on mental health outcomes, emphasizing the importance of computational linguistics in addressing real-world challenges.

4 Approach

To address the challenge at hand, we systematically evaluated various options to arrive at a logical and explainable solution. Our decision-making process involved a thorough analysis of the syntactical structures in both languages, leveraging the support of the IndicNlp project from Kunchukuttan (2020). Upon examining the IndicNLP library Tokenization process and our dataset, we concluded that our corpora required no further preprocessing to align with our objectives.

During the feature extraction stage, we segmented the corpus into sentences and employed Term-Frequency Inverse Document Frequency (TF-IDF) as the sole feature type, alongside consideration for Bigrams. These choices were made with a focus on their compatibility with the dataset characteristics and the task requirements.

4.1 Model Selection

The model selection process was conducted transparently, guided by our current knowledge of machine learning model performances. To align with the datasets provided by the Organizers and based on our experimentation philosophy, we excluded deep learning models as the size of the dataset fits best for traditional and shallow machine learning models. So, we focused on traditional machine learning (ML) Tash et al. (2022) models and, at best, shallow models specifically Fasttext developed by Meta Joulin et al. (2016, 2017) because of its ability to not easily overfit over the training phase.

For the Tamil language, we experimented with five ML models: Logistic Regression (LR), Random Forest (RF), Support Vector Machine (SVM), Naive Bayes, and Fasttext. The trained Fasttext model demonstrated stability and robustness, leading to its selection for submission.

In the case of Telugu, similar experiments were conducted with the same models. However, we opted to submit the trained Naive Bayes model for Telugu, guided by its performance also to diversify the set of our models tackling the task of identifying stress in Dravidian languages.

This approach, grounded in a thoughtful and systematic evaluation, positions our system for effective stress identification in both Tamil and Telugu languages.

5 Experimental Setup

To conduct our experiments, we relied primarily on the Scikit-learn Pedregosa et al. (2011), and Fasttext packages due to their versatility and effectiveness in implementing various machine learning models. Scikit-learn provided a robust set of tools for traditional machine learning models, while Fasttext, with its efficient text classification capabilities, complemented our exploration.

Concerning the hardware, our experiments were executed on a computer running Ubuntu 22.04, equipped with 64 GiB of Random Access Memory (RAM), and powered by an AMD Ryzen 7000 Series 7 processor running at 3.3 GHz. This configuration was chosen for its capability to handle the computational demands of traditional machine learning models, even with a limited amount of data.

The selected hardware configuration proved adequate for our experimental goals, ensuring efficient execution and allowing us to gain meaningful insights into stress identification in Dravidian languages.

5.1 Hyperparameters for Tamil language Training

To train the selected model in Tamil language(Fasttext), we randomized the datasets, ran successively several training with different parameters, and finally applied the following hyperparameters which gave the best results:

Lr	Epochs	N-grams	Bucket	Em-Dims	Loss
0.5	10	2	200	30	ova

Table 1: Fasttext Hyperparameters Configurations

Finally, for the testing phase, we set the **threshold at 0.5**.

5.2 Hyperparameters for Telugu language Training

We split the dataset with a random state at 42, and applied the following hyperparameter configurations:

Loss	Penalty	Max-iter
hinge	L2	5

Table 2: Naive Bayes Hyperparameters Configurations

6 Results

We present the performance metrics of our stress identification model for Tamil and Telugu languages. The evaluation metrics include Accuracy, Macro F1-score, Macro-Recall, and Weighted Precision.

6.1 Tamil Language

For the Tamil language, our model achieved the following results:

Metrics	Score
Accuracy	0.724
Macro F1-score	0.723
Macro-Recall	0.775
Weighted Precision	0.822

The bar chart in Figure 1 provides a visual representation of the metrics. Notably, the Macro F1-score is highlighted in red for emphasis.

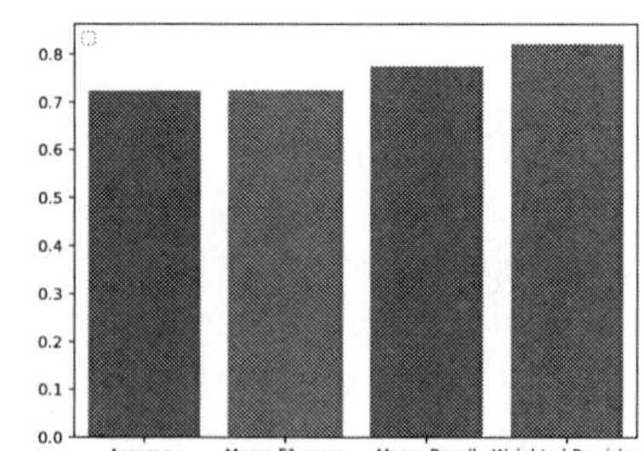

Figure 1: Tamil Stress Identification Results

6.2 Telugu Language

Similarly, for the Telugu language, our model's performance is summarized below:

Metrics	Score
Accuracy	0.729
Macro F1-score	0.727
Macro-Recall	0.756
Weighted Precision	0.779

The bar chart in Figure 2 visually presents the Telugu language metrics, with Macro F1-score highlighted in red.

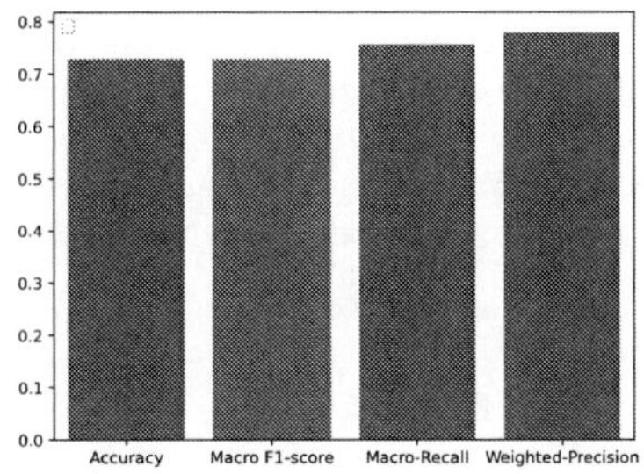

Figure 2: Telugu Stress Identification Results - Naive Bayes

These results demonstrate the effectiveness of our stress identification model in both Tamil and Telugu even with strict and minimal preprocessing and hyperparameter tuning, providing a good foundation and baseline for further exploration as most previous works were focused on general emotion detection in Tamil or Telugu or the targeted language were mostly English.

7 Discussions and limitations

Our model for the Telugu language exhibited commendable performance by securing the second rank in the shared tasks. We can observe that both our models did not overfit and remained stable on the test set. This achievement underscores the effectiveness of the chosen approach and the potential for accurate stress identification in Dravidian languages.

It is noteworthy that sufficient data and additional features related to the two languages Tamil and Telugu can help our models become more reliable in the identification of emotional stress in textual corpora in both Tamil and Telugu. This observation emphasizes the importance of data abundance in enhancing model performance, paving the way for more accurate and robust stress identification systems.

However, it's essential to acknowledge certain limitations in our current approach. One notable limitation is we did not make use of phonology or phonetic features which are important factors in extracting meaningful information from Tamil or Telugu. Despite the capabilities of IndicNlp for phonetic feature extraction, this aspect was not explored in our experiments. Future investigations could delve into extracting phonetic features, potentially enriching the model's understanding of stress patterns in the spoken language.

Moreover, there exists ample room for further experiments. Techniques such as embedding learning offer a promising avenue for feature extraction, potentially capturing nuanced linguistic representations. Alternatively, leveraging large language models can provide a comprehensive understanding of stress-related features in Dravidian languages since both languages make use of context.

8 Conclusion

In conclusion, while the success of our model in the Telugu language showcases the effectiveness of our approach, ongoing research, and experimentation are crucial to unlocking the full potential of stress identification in Tamil and Telugu. Exploring additional features, incorporating advanced techniques, and leveraging large-scale language models are avenues for future research, promising advancements in computational linguistics for emotion analysis in diverse linguistic contexts.

Ethics Statement

Our scientific work adheres to the ACL Ethics Policy[1], ensuring the responsible conduct of research and publication. We recognize the ethical implications of our work in stress identification in Dravidian languages and commit to upholding the highest standards throughout our research process.

As researchers, we remain vigilant about the ethical dimensions of our work and its impact on individuals and communities. We welcome open dialogue and scrutiny regarding the ethical considerations associated with our research and are dedicated to fostering responsible and ethical practices within the computational linguistics community.

Acknowledgments

The work was done with partial support from the Mexican Government through the grant A1-S-47854 of CONACYT, Mexico,

grants 20241816, 20241819, and 20240951 of the Secretaría de Investigación y Posgrado of the Instituto Politécnico Nacional, Mexico. The authors thank the CONACYT for the computing resources brought to them through the Plataforma de Aprendizaje Profundo para Tecnologías del Lenguaje of

[1] `https://www.aclweb.org/portal/content/acl-code-ethics`

the Laboratorio de Supercómputo of the INAOE, Mexico, and acknowledge the support of Microsoft through the Microsoft Latin America PhD Award.

References

José García-Díaz, Miguel Ángel Rodríguez García, and Rafael Valencia-García. 2022. UMUTeam@TamilNLP-ACL2022: Emotional analysis in Tamil. In *Proceedings of the Second Workshop on Speech and Language Technologies for Dravidian Languages*, pages 39–44, Dublin, Ireland. Association for Computational Linguistics.

Omkar Gokhale, Shantanu Patankar, Onkar Litake, Aditya Mandke, and Dipali Kadam. 2022. Optimize$_{prime@DravidianLangTech-ACL2022: EmotionAnalysisinTamil}$. *arXiv (Cornell University)*.

Shaunak Inamdar, Rishikesh Chapekar, Shilpa Gite, and Biswajeet Pradhan. 2023. Machine learning driven mental stress detection on Reddit posts using natural language processing. *Human-Centric Intelligent Systems*, 3(2):80–91.

Aparna "Joshi, LV Gangolli, R Duggal, and A" Shukla. 2005. "mental health in india: review of current trends and directions for the future". *"Review of Health Care in India"*, pages "127–136".

Armand Joulin, Edouard Grave, Piotr Bojanowski, Matthijs Douze, Hérve Jégou, and Tomas Mikolov. 2016. Fasttext.zip: Compressing text classification models. *arXiv preprint arXiv:1612.03651*.

Armand Joulin, Edouard Grave, Piotr Bojanowski, and Tomas Mikolov. 2017. Bag of tricks for efficient text classification. In *Proceedings of the 15th Conference of the European Chapter of the Association for Computational Linguistics: Volume 2, Short Papers*, pages 427–431. Association for Computational Linguistics.

Anoop Kunchukuttan. 2020. The IndicNLP Library. https://github.com/anoopkunchukuttan/indic_nlp_library/blob/master/docs/indicnlp.pdf.

Y. K. Nagle and Usha Sharma. "2018". "academic stress and coping mechanism among students: An indian perspective". *Journal of child and adolescent psychiatry*, "2"(1).

Tanya Nijhawan, Girija Attigeri, and T. Ananthakrishna. 2022. Stress detection using natural language processing and machine learning over social interactions. *Journal of Big Data*, 9(1).

F. Pedregosa, G. Varoquaux, A. Gramfort, V. Michel, B. Thirion, O. Grisel, M. Blondel, P. Prettenhofer, R. Weiss, V. Dubourg, J. Vanderplas, A. Passos, D. Cournapeau, M. Brucher, M. Perrot, and E. Duchesnay. 2011. Scikit-learn: Machine learning in Python. *Journal of Machine Learning Research*, 12:2825–2830.

Varsini S, Kirthanna Rajan, Angel S, Rajalakshmi Sivanaiah, Sakaya Milton Rajendram, and Mirnalinee T T. 2022. Varsini_and_Kirthanna@DravidianLangTech-ACL2022-emotional analysis in Tamil. In *Proceedings of the Second Workshop on Speech and Language Technologies for Dravidian Languages*, pages 165–169, Dublin, Ireland. Association for Computational Linguistics.

Moein Shahiki-Tash, Jesús Armenta-Segura, Zahra Ahani, Olga Kolesnikova, Grigori Sidorov, and Alexander Gelbukh. 2023a. Lidoma at homomex2023@ iberlef: Hate speech detection towards the mexican spanish-speaking lgbt+ population. the importance of preprocessing before using bert-based models. In *Proceedings of the Iberian Languages Evaluation Forum (IberLEF 2023)*.

Moein Shahiki-Tash, Jesús Armenta-Segura, Olga Kolesnikova, Grigori Sidorov, and Alexander Gelbukh. 2023b. Lidoma at hope2023iberlef: Hope speech detection using lexical features and convolutional neural networks. In *Proceedings of the Iberian Languages Evaluation Forum (IberLEF 2023), co-located with the 39th Conference of the Spanish Society for Natural Language Processing (SEPLN 2023), CEUR-WS. org*.

M Shahiki Tash, Z Ahani, Al Tonja, M Gemeda, N Hussain, and O Kolesnikova. 2022. Word level language identification in code-mixed kannada-english texts using traditional machine learning algorithms. In *Proceedings of the 19th International Conference on Natural Language Processing (ICON): Shared Task on Word Level Language Identification in Code-mixed Kannada-English Texts*, pages 25–28.

Moein Tash, Jesus Armenta-Segura, Zahra Ahani, Olga Kolesnikova, Grigori Sidorov, and Alexander Gelbukh. 2023. Lidoma@ dravidianlangtech: Convolutional neural networks for studying correlation between lexical features and sentiment polarity in tamil and tulu languages. In *Proceedings of the Third Workshop on Speech and Language Technologies for Dravidian Languages*, pages 180–185.

Atnafu Lambebo Tonja, Mesay Gemeda Yigezu, Olga Kolesnikova, Moein Shahiki Tash, Grigori Sidorov, and Alexander Gelbuk. 2022. Transformer-based model for word level language identification in code-mixed kannada-english texts. *arXiv preprint arXiv:2211.14459*.

Mesay Gemeda Yigezu, Olga Kolesnikova, Grigori Sidorov, and Alexander Gelbukh. 2023. Transformer-based hate speech detection for multi-class and multi-label classification.

Mikhail Zaydman. 2017. *Tweeting about mental health: Big Data text analysis of Twitter for public policy*.

byteLLM@LT-EDI-2024: Homophobia/Transphobia Detection in Social Media Comments - Custom Subword Tokenization with Subword2Vec and BiLSTM

Durga Prasad Manukonda
ASRlytics
Hyderabad, India
mdp0999@gmail.com

Rohith Gowtham Kodali
ASRlytics
Hyderabad, India
rohitkodali@gmail.com

Abstract

This research focuses on Homophobia and Transphobia Detection in Dravidian languages, specifically Telugu, Kannada, Tamil, and Malayalam. Leveraging the Homophobia/Transphobia Detection dataset, we propose an innovative approach employing a custom-designed tokenizer with a Bidirectional Long Short-Term Memory (BiLSTM) architecture. Our distinctive contribution lies in a tokenizer that reduces model sizes to below 7MB, improving efficiency and addressing real-time deployment challenges. The BiLSTM implementation demonstrates significant enhancements in hate speech detection accuracy, effectively capturing linguistic nuances. Low-size models efficiently alleviate inference challenges, ensuring swift real-time detection and practical deployment. This work pioneers a framework for hate speech detection, providing insights into model size, inference speed, and real-time deployment challenges in combatting online hate speech within Dravidian languages.

1 Introduction

In light of the growing prevalence of online hate speech, this paper presents the findings of a workshop on detecting LGBTQ+ hate speech in social media comments. We focus on developing and evaluating models that can accurately identify and classify homophobic and transphobic slurs, offensive stereotypes, and other forms of hateful language within YouTube comment sections (Chakravarthi et al., 2024) (Chakravarthi et al., 2023) (Chakravarthi, 2023).

While a comment or post in the dataset may contain more than one sentence, the average sentence length in the corpus is one, and annotations are provided at the comment/post level. In the dynamic landscape of social media, concerns about hate speech targeting the LGBTQ+ community have gained prominence.

This research investigates the challenges of classifying individual social media comments or posts in low-resourced languages. It specifically focuses on Dravidian languages spoken in India—Telugu, Kannada, Tamil, and Malayalam—while acknowledging that the findings may not be universally applicable to other linguistic contexts. The goal is to develop systems that can effectively identify instances of homophobia or transphobia in these languages. Achieving this requires these systems to be adaptable and robust enough to handle the inherent diversity within Dravidian linguistics.

In the context of detecting Homophobia and Transphobia in social media, our research employs a unique approach that utilizes a custom-designed tokenizer and a Bidirectional Long Short-Term Memory (BiLSTM) architecture. A significant contribution of our work lies in the development of a tokenizer designed to streamline model sizes, enhance operational efficiency, and address the challenges associated with real-time deployment. This tokenizer not only minimizes the computational footprint but also optimizes the overall performance of the models. Its unique features empower effective handling of real-time scenarios, providing a versatile solution for deployment challenges.

The implementation of BiLSTM, coupled with our customized tokenizer, showcases significant improvements in the accuracy of hate speech detection, highlighting enhanced sensitivity to linguistic nuances. Compact-sized models effectively address inference challenges, ensuring rapid real-time detection and practical deployment. Our research establishes a pioneering framework for Homophobia and Transphobia Detection, providing insights into model size, inference speed, and the challenges associated with real-time deployment in combating online hate speech.

This paper outlines our methodology, technical advancements, and results, offering a compre-

Proceedings of the Fourth Workshop on Language Technology for Equality, Diversity, Inclusion, pages 157–163
March 21, 2024 ©2024 Association for Computational Linguistics

hensive examination of Homophobia/Transphobia Detection in social media comments in Dravidian languages. Our research aims to contribute not only to the specific challenges of Homophobia/Transphobia Detection in social media comments but also to a broader understanding of effective detection mechanisms applicable to diverse linguistic landscapes.

2 Related Work

Homophobia and transphobia detection in social media has garnered significant research attention due to its detrimental impact on the LGBTQ+ community. Various approaches have been explored, each addressing specific challenges and contributing to the development of robust detection systems.

Singh and Motlicek (2022) proposed a zero-shot learning framework for detecting homophobic and transphobic comments without labeled data, demonstrating its potential for resource-constrained scenarios.

Kumaresan et al. (2023) addressed the challenge of data scarcity in low-resource languages by presenting a fine-grained dataset and exploring cross-lingual transfer learning techniques. Their work highlights the effectiveness of transferring knowledge from resource-rich languages to improve detection accuracy in diverse linguistic settings.

Ashraf et al. (2022) explored an SVM-based model, achieving notable F1-scores and emphasizing the importance of automatic detection for timely intervention. Their work demonstrates the effectiveness of traditional machine learning algorithms in hate speech detection tasks.

Sharma et al. (2023) investigated deep learning techniques for Dravidian languages, highlighting the superiority of IndicBERT (Kakwani et al., 2020) in addressing low-resource language challenges. This study demonstrates the potential of deep learning models for capturing language-specific features and improving detection accuracy.

(Swaminathan et al., 2022) employed a hybrid approach combining word embeddings, SVM classifiers, and BERT-based transformers (Devlin et al., 2019), achieving promising results. Their work showcases the potential of combining diverse techniques to leverage their strengths and enhance detection performance.

Chakravarthi et al. (2022) investigated the use of pseudolabeling for automated homophobia/transphobia detection, demonstrating significant improvements in model performance. Their work emphasizes the importance of robust evaluation and highlights the potential of pseudolabeling for improving model accuracy.

The study presents ConBERT-RL(Raj et al., 2024), a novel framework using Reinforcement Learning and a concatenated CM-BERT representation, excelling in offensive comment classification for transliterated Tamil in English with a 90% and 93% micro-average accuracy improvement. It effectively captures language-specific features and nuances, demonstrated through t-SNE visualization and graph network comparisons.

The broader literature underscores the global prevalence of offensive language, emphasizing the need for protection and proactive measures to mitigate its impact on vulnerable communities ((Gkotsis et al., 2016); (Oswal, 2021); (Díaz-Torres et al., 2020); (Wang et al., 2019)).

This review highlights significant advancements in homophobic and transphobic comment detection. Despite notable progress, various challenges persist, necessitating further exploration and development. These challenges include the expansion to encompass more low-resource languages, the creation of robust models tailored for code-mixed content, the integration of contextual information, and the exploration of Explainable AI techniques. Addressing these challenges will contribute to a more comprehensive and effective approach to combating online hate speech.

3 Dataset

3.1 Embedding Datasets

Our research draws upon a substantial corpus sourced from the AI4Bharath[1] datasets for Telugu, Tamil, Malayalam, and Kannada. Specifically, we harnessed the initial 5,000,000 lines from the Telugu corpus (1.3GB), 9,492,782 lines from the Tamil corpus (980MB), 11,512,628 lines from the Malayalam corpus (1.2GB), and 15,000,000 lines from the Kannada corpus (1.5GB). These datasets serve as a rich and diverse source of linguistic content, covering an array of topics relevant to our research. This linguistic variety is instrumental in fostering the development of embeddings that are not only robust but also generalizable, crucial for the success of our research endeavors.

[1] https://github.com/AI4Bharat/indicnlp_corpus

3.2 Homophobia/Transphobia Datasets

Our research, undertaken as part of LT-EDI@EACL 2024 [2], is focused on Dravidian languages—Tamil, Telugu, Kannada, and Malayalam—selected for their shared linguistic roots and the intricate process of developing high-quality embeddings for each. This cohesive group forms the basis for our study, aiming to understand and address online hate speech in these languages.

The tasks involved in our study include identifying discriminatory comments based on sexual orientation or gender identity, utilizing datasets covering Dravidian languages to ensure comprehensive representation. Additionally, the focus on categorizing YouTube comments aids in recognizing instances of homophobia and transphobia, facilitating a deeper analysis of their manifestation in online discourse (Chakravarthi et al., 2022) (Kumaresan et al., 2023).

Language	Train	Dev	Test
Telugu	9,050	1,940	1,939
Malayalam	3,114	1,213	866
Kannada	10,066	2,157	2,156
Tamil	2,662	666	833

Table 1: Homophobia/Transphobia Detection Dataset Statistics

Table 1 details the dataset distribution across languages, providing training, development, and test sets for system development and evaluation.

4 Methodology

This section unveils the details of our innovative architecture, integrating two crucial components: a dynamic Subword Embeddings module and a robust BiLSTM Classification module. We explore data preprocessing, subword tokenization, embedding training, and orchestration of our advanced classifier.

4.1 Preprocessing and Tokenization

This section delineates the procedures for data preprocessing and tokenization applied in the Shared Task on Homophobia/Transphobia Detection in social media comments.

[2] https://codalab.lisn.upsaclay.fr/competitions/16056

4.1.1 Preprocessing Pipeline

Our comprehensive preprocessing involved normalization, cleaning (removing noise like URLs and hashtags), and transliteration using the indic_transliteration library[3] for uniform processing.

4.1.2 Subword Tokenization

Post-preprocessing, we implemented a custom subword tokenizer, "VowelToken," for each language. This approach aimed to enhance granularity, capturing morphemic and grammatical information crucial for detecting linguistic nuances related to homophobia/transphobia. Leveraging subword tokens enables the embedding model to learn more precise and informative representations, potentially improving detection performance.

The proposed VowelToken subword tokenizer exhibits universality, utilizing linguistic principles based on vowel boundaries for accurate segmentation across diverse languages, including Dravidian languages. Its rule-based design focuses on identifying and segmenting words based on consistent vowel boundary patterns, enhancing precision and reliability in the tokenization process. Refer to Table 2 for the preprocessing and tokenization statistics of each language corpus.

4.2 Subword Embeddings Module

The Subword2Vec module obtains subword embeddings using the Word2Vec method by Mikolov et al. (2013). The module's initialization involves specifying critical parameters: vocabulary size (V), minimum frequency (f_{min}), and embedding dimension ($d_{subword}$). Subword counts are collected to construct a subword vocabulary (S), and embeddings are trained using Stochastic Gradient Descent (SGD).

The module's initialization involves specifying critical parameters, starting with the vocabulary size (V) that sets the upper limit for subword consideration. Additionally, the minimum frequency parameter (f_{min}) serves as the threshold for subword inclusion based on frequency. The embedding dimension ($d_{subword}$), characterizing the dimensionality of subword embeddings, is also defined. These parameters collectively configure the module during the initialization process, a pivotal aspect of our research.

Subword counts are collected from the corpus to construct a subword vocabulary (S). The sub-

[3] https://github.com/indic-transliteration/indic_transliteration_py

Language	Total Words	Total Subtokens	Subtokens (Count >= 2)	Emb. Size(MB)
Telugu	179,732,317	22,596	13,405	6.6
Tamil	174,349,374	15,065	9,406	4.5
Kannada	399,312,707	17,889	12,173	5.8
Malayalam	117,054,028	19,155	14,190	5.92

Table 2: Preprocessing and Tokenization Statistics with Embedding(Emb.) Sizes of 100-dimensional Model

word splitting process is executed based on vowels, excluding subwords with counts below f_{min}. This process is mathematically expressed as:

S = {s | $s \ is \ a \ subword, \ count(s) \geq f_{min}, \ |S| \leq V\}$

$$S = \{s \in \mathcal{W} \mid count(s) \geq f_{min}, |S| \leq V\} \quad (1)$$

The subword splitting process involves dividing the input word into subwords based on vowel boundaries. Consonant prefixes and suffixes are included in the subwords when applicable, and special tokens "_" (start of subword) are added to the first letter. Subword embeddings ($E_{subword}$) are initialized as a random matrix with dimensions ($|S|$, $d_{subword}$).

The training phase employs Stochastic Gradient Descent (SGD) (Tian et al., 2023) to train subword embeddings. The objective is to minimize the Mean Squared Error (MSE) loss (L) between subword pairs. The SGD update is expressed as:

$$E^{(t+1)}_{subword} = E^{(t)}_{subword} - \eta \nabla L(E^{(t)}_{subword}) \quad (2)$$

Here, t represents the training iteration, η is the learning rate, and ∇L is the gradient of the loss function. Training subword embeddings is a crucial step in refining the model's representation of subword relationships.

4.3 BiLSTM Classifier

The BiLSTM architecture, inspired by Ghosh et al. (2020), plays a crucial role in the fake news classification task. It consists of two essential components: a subword embedding layer and a bi-directional LSTM layer.

4.3.1 Sub-Word Embedding Layer

The Sub-Word Embedding Layer operates on an input word sequence $x = [w_1, w_2, ..., w_n]$ utilizing a subword embedding function. Each word w_i is mapped to its corresponding subword embeddings, denoted as $w_{i1}, w_{i2}, ..., w_{in}$, where n represents the number of subwords for the i-th word. The final

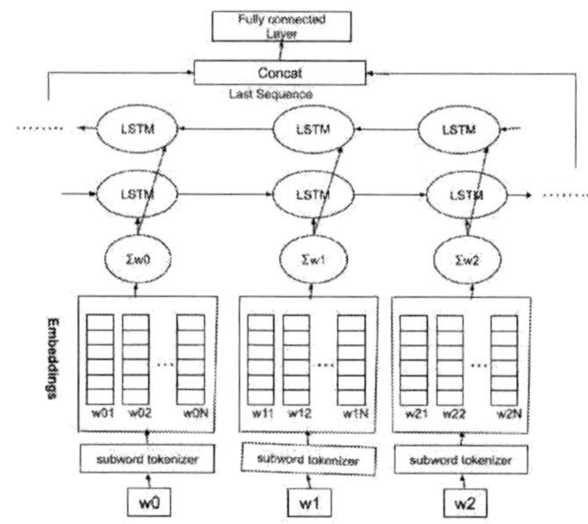

Figure 1: The unfolded architecture of BiLSTM classifier with three 3 word example sample.

word embedding for w_i, denoted as $\mathbf{e}_i$, is obtained by summing the embeddings of its constituent subwords:

$$\mathbf{e}_i = w_{i1} + w_{i2} + \ldots + w_{in} \quad (3)$$

The output of this layer is a tensor X_{embed} of dimensions $1 \times n \times d_{embed}$, where d_{embed} signifies the size of each word embedding.

$$X_{embed} = [\mathbf{e}_1, \mathbf{e}_2, ..., \mathbf{e}_n] \quad (4)$$

Here, $\mathbf{e}_i$ represents the word embedding for the i-th word in the sequence, and n is the length of the sequence.

4.3.2 Bi-directional LSTM Layer

The Bi-directional LSTM Layer engages with the embedded sequence X_{embed} to adeptly capture contextual information. Configured with an input size of d_{embed} (matching the embedding size) and a hidden size of d_{hidden}, the bidirectional LSTM ensures the seamless flow of information both in forward and backward directions. The resulting output, denoted as $blstm\_out$, takes the form of a tensor with dimensions $1 \times n \times (2 \times d_{hidden})$, as it concatenates the hidden states from both directions.

$$blstm\_out = [\mathbf{h}_1, \mathbf{h}_2, ..., \mathbf{h}_n] \quad (5)$$

In essence, the BiLSTM layer processes the input sequence and produces hidden states $\mathbf{h}_i$ for each word in the sequence.

The forward pass of the model is mathematically expressed as follows:

$$\mathbf{h}_i^{(f)}, \mathbf{h}_i^{(b)} = BiLSTM(\mathbf{e}_{1:i}, \mathbf{e}_{i:n}), \quad \forall i \in \{1, ..., n\} \quad (6)$$

Here, $\mathbf{h}_i^{(f)}$ and $\mathbf{h}_i^{(b)}$ symbolize the forward and backward hidden states at position i, respectively. The BiLSTM function operates on subword embeddings $\mathbf{e}_{1:i}$ and $\mathbf{e}_{i:n}$ for each i in the sequence.

4.3.3 Classifier Output

The final prediction, denoted as y, is derived by applying a linear transformation to the last hidden state in the forward direction ($\mathbf{h}_n^{(f)}$) using weights matrix W and bias b.

$$y = W\mathbf{h}_n^{(f)} + b \quad (7)$$

This linear transformation allows the model to make predictions based on the learned representations from the BiLSTM layer.

Figure 1 illustrates the unfolded architecture of the BiLSTM Classifier, providing a visual representation of the sequence processing and contextual information capture. This design adeptly integrates subword embeddings with a BiLSTMbased approach, showcasing adaptability and potential across various natural language processing applications.

5 Experimental Setup

Our experimental setup is designed to demonstrate the effectiveness of our proposed approach in the context of the Shared Task on Homophobia/Transphobia Detection in social media comments. We conducted experiments using a 100-dimensional embedding model tailored to each language. The embedding sizes were determined based on linguistic characteristics and dataset scale, as outlined in Table 2. Specifically, for Telugu, Tamil, Kannada, and Malayalam, the embedding sizes were 6.6 MB, 4.5 MB, 5.8 MB, and 5.92 MB, respectively.

Subword tokenization was facilitated by the custom VowelToken subword tokenizer, designed for universality and based on linguistic principles using vowel boundaries. This tokenizer ensured accurate segmentation across diverse languages, including Dravidian languages. Its rule-based design focused on identifying and segmenting words based on consistent vowel boundary patterns, enhancing precision and reliability in the tokenization process.

To evaluate the impact of these subword embeddings, we seamlessly integrated them into our BiLSTM-based model architecture. The ClassificationModel includes a Sub-Word Embedding Layer, Bi-directional LSTM Layer, and Linear Classification Layer, utilizing subword embeddings from VowelToken. The BiLSTM layer features an input size of 100 and a hidden size of 128. Additionally, the model utilizes the Adam optimizer with a learning rate of 0.001 during training.

Datasets were partitioned into training, development, and test sets based on the distribution outlined in Table 1. Model training utilized the Adam optimizer with a learning rate of 0.001 and a batch size of 64. Early stopping was implemented, with a patience setting of 10 epochs based on development set performance. Evaluation metrics, including recall, precision, F1 score, and accuracy, were used to measure the model's effectiveness.

6 Experimental Results and Discussions

The effectiveness of our subword tokenization is evident in the remarkably low perplexity (less than 1.2) achieved after just one training epoch for embeddings. Despite the constraints of limited training time and data, this result underscores the efficacy of our subword tokenization approach.

The table 3 reveals the macro average F1-Scores (M_F1-scores) for the Homophobia/Transphobia Detection Task on the test sets across various languages. In the rankings, the team **"byteLLM"** (originally **byteSizedLLM**) achieved noteworthy positions, with Telugu securing the 3rd rank and achieving the highest score of 0.959, closely trailing the top score of 0.971. Malayalam also performed well, obtaining a commendable M_F1-Score of 0.891 and ranking 3rd, with a top score of 0.942. Similarly, Tamil secured the 3rd rank with a score of 0.801. However, Kannada, while contributing valuable insights, demonstrated a slightly lower score of 0.922 and secured the 6th rank. These rankings provide a comprehensive view of the model's performance across different Dravidian languages.

To enhance the performance further, it is crucial to leverage more extensive training data, especially focusing on diverse datasets. Given the

Language	M_F1-Score	Rank	Top Score
Telugu	0.959	3	0.971
Malayalam	0.891	3	0.942
Kannada	0.922	6	0.948
Tamil	0.801	3	0.880

Table 3: Homophobia/Transphobia Detection Task Macro average F1-Scores (M_F1-scores) of Test Sets

multilingual nature of the task, training on multilingual data can significantly improve performance. While we trained on 4.3GB of L3Cube-HingCorpus data, the model produced 6.4MB embeddings that outperformed large language models (LLMs) in Language Identification (LID) and Named Entity Recognition (NER) on GLUCoS benchmarks. The model, when trained on larger text (more than 10GB), is expected to achieve state-of-the-art (SOTA) performance. However, due to hardware limitations, we were unable to load larger text for training in this study. In future tasks, we plan to implement and test this approach with larger text and languages.

7 Conclusion and Future Work

Our research convincingly demonstrates the effectiveness of subword tokenization for homophobia/transphobia detection across Dravidian languages. The competitive results achieved with lightweight models highlight the scalability and computational efficiency of our approach. Subword embeddings, trained with meticulous preprocessing and tokenization, showcase impressive performance, with Dravidian languages securing leading Macro F1-Scores. This underscores the potential of subword tokenization in tackling online hate speech with resource-efficient models.

Moving forward, expanding the dataset with diverse multilingual content is crucial for further enhancing accuracy. The technical advantage of training on larger texts for achieving state-of-the-art performance is evident, albeit currently limited by hardware constraints. Nevertheless, the lightweight nature of our models, their fast inference speed, and minimal storage requirements render them practical for various tasks beyond homophobia/transphobia detection, including Named Entity Recognition (NER), Language Identification (LID), Sentiment Classification, and Multiclass classification. We plan to explore their applicability in generative AI for future research, potentially opening doors to even more impactful applications.

References

Nsrin Ashraf, Mohamed Taha, Ahmed Abd Elfattah, and Hamada Nayel. 2022. NAYEL @LT-EDI-ACL2022: Homophobia/transphobia detection for equality, diversity, and inclusion using SVM. In *Proceedings of the Second Workshop on Language Technology for Equality, Diversity and Inclusion*, pages 287–290, Dublin, Ireland. Association for Computational Linguistics.

Bharathi Raja Chakravarthi. 2023. Detection of homophobia and transphobia in YouTube comments. *International Journal of Data Science and Analytics*, pages 1–20.

Bharathi Raja Chakravarthi, Adeep Hande, Rahul Ponnusamy, Prasanna Kumar Kumaresan, and Ruba Priyadharshini. 2022. How can we detect Homophobia and Transphobia? Experiments in a multilingual code-mixed setting for social media governance. *International Journal of Information Management Data Insights*, 2(2):100119.

Bharathi Raja Chakravarthi, Prasanna Kumar Kumaresan, Ruba Priyadharshini, Paul Buitelaar, Asha Hegde, Hosahalli Lakshmaiah Shashirekha, Saranya Rajiakodi, Miguel Ángel García-Cumbreras, Salud María Jiménez-Zafra, José Antonio García-Díaz, Rafael Valencia-García, Kishore Kumar Ponnusamy, Poorvi Shetty, and Daniel García-Baena. 2024. Overview of Third Shared Task on Homophobia and Transphobia Detection in Social Media Comments. In *Proceedings of the Fourth Workshop on Language Technology for Equality, Diversity and Inclusion*, Malta. European Chapter of the Association for Computational Linguistics.

Bharathi Raja Chakravarthi, Rahul Ponnusamy, Malliga Subramanian, Paul Buitelaar, Miguel Ángel García-Cumbreras, Salud María Jiménez-Zafra, José Antonio García-Díaz, Rafael Valencia-García, and Nitesh Jindal. 2023. Overview of Second Shared Task on Homophobia and Transphobia Detection in English, Spanish, Hindi, Tamil, and Malayalam. In *Proceedings of the Third Workshop on Language Technology for Equality, Diversity and Inclusion*, Varna, Bulgaria. Recent Advances in Natural Language Processing.

Jacob Devlin, Ming-Wei Chang, Kenton Lee, and Kristina Toutanova. 2019. BERT: Pre-training of Deep Bidirectional Transformers for Language Understanding.

María José Díaz-Torres, Paulina Alejandra Morán-Méndez, Luis Villasenor-Pineda, Manuel Montes-y Gómez, Juan Aguilera, and Luis Meneses-Lerín. 2020. Automatic detection of offensive language in social media: Defining linguistic criteria to build a Mexican Spanish dataset. In *Proceedings of the Second Workshop on Trolling, Aggression and Cyberbullying*, pages 132–136, Marseille, France. European Language Resources Association (ELRA).

Koyel Ghosh, Dr. Apurbalal Senapati, and Dr. Ranjan Maity. 2020. Technical domain identification using word2vec and BiLSTM. In *Proceedings of the 17th International Conference on Natural Language Processing (ICON): TechDOfication 2020 Shared Task*, pages 21–26, Patna, India. NLP Association of India (NLPAI).

George Gkotsis, Anika Oellrich, Tim Hubbard, Richard Dobson, Maria Liakata, Sumithra Velupillai, and Rina Dutta. 2016. The language of mental health problems in social media. In *Proceedings of the Third Workshop on Computational Linguistics and Clinical Psychology*, pages 63–73, San Diego, CA, USA. Association for Computational Linguistics.

Divyanshu Kakwani, Anoop Kunchukuttan, Satish Golla, Gokul N.C., Avik Bhattacharyya, Mitesh M. Khapra, and Pratyush Kumar. 2020. IndicNLPSuite: Monolingual Corpora, Evaluation Benchmarks and Pre-trained Multilingual Language Models for Indian Languages. In *Findings of EMNLP*.

Prasanna Kumar Kumaresan, Rahul Ponnusamy, Ruba Priyadharshini, Paul Buitelaar, and Bharathi Raja Chakravarthi. 2023. Homophobia and transphobia detection for low-resourced languages in social media comments. *Natural Language Processing Journal*, page 100041.

Tomas Mikolov, Kai Chen, Greg Corrado, and Jeffrey Dean. 2013. Efficient Estimation of Word Representations in Vector Space.

Nikhil Oswal. 2021. Identifying and categorizing offensive language in social media.

Vivek Suresh Raj, Chinnaudayar Navaneethakrishnan Subalalitha, Lavanya Sambath, Frank Glavin, and Bharathi Raja Chakravarthi. 2024. ConBERT-RL: A policy-driven deep reinforcement learning based approach for detecting homophobia and transphobia in low-resource languages. *Natural Language Processing Journal*, 6:100040.

Deepawali Sharma, Vedika Gupta, and Vivek Kumar Singh. 2023. *Detection of Homophobia amp; Transphobia in Malayalam and Tamil: Exploring Deep Learning Methods*, page 217–226. Springer Nature Switzerland.

Muskaan Singh and Petr Motlicek. 2022. IDIAP submission@LT-EDI-ACL2022: Homophobia/transphobia detection in social media comments. In *Proceedings of the Second Workshop on Language Technology for Equality, Diversity and Inclusion*, pages 356–361, Dublin, Ireland. Association for Computational Linguistics.

Krithika Swaminathan, Bharathi B, Gayathri G L, and Hrishik Sampath. 2022. SSNCSE_NLP@LT-EDI-ACL2022: Homophobia/transphobia detection in multiple languages using SVM classifiers and BERT-based transformers. In *Proceedings of the Second Workshop on Language Technology for Equality, Diversity and Inclusion*, pages 239–244, Dublin, Ireland. Association for Computational Linguistics.

Yingjie Tian, Yuqi Zhang, and Haibin Zhang. 2023. Recent advances in stochastic gradient descent in deep learning. *Mathematics*, 11(3).

Yuxi Wang, Martin McKee, Aleksandra Torbica, and David Stuckler. 2019. Systematic literature review on the spread of health-related misinformation on social media. *Social Science Medicine*, 240:112552.

MasonTigers@LT-EDI-2024: An Ensemble Approach Towards Detecting Homophobia and Transphobia in Social Media Comments

Dhiman Goswami, Sadiya Sayara Chowdhury Puspo, Md Nishat Raihan, Al Nahian Bin Emran
George Mason University, USA
{dgoswam, spuspo, mraihan2, abinemra}@gmu.edu

Abstract

In this paper, we describe our approaches and results for Task 2 of the LT-EDI 2024[1] Workshop, aimed at detecting homophobia and/or transphobia across ten languages. Our methodologies include monolingual transformers and ensemble methods, capitalizing on the strengths of each to enhance the performance of the models. The ensemble models worked well, placing our team, *MasonTigers*, in the top five for eight of the ten languages, as measured by the macro F1 score. Our work emphasizes the efficacy of ensemble methods in multilingual scenarios, addressing the complexities of language-specific tasks.

1 Introduction

In this current era dominated by social media platforms, people heavily rely on online content for communication, learning, knowledge-sharing, and staying abreast of new technologies. The comment sections, intended for constructive feedback, unfortunately, sometimes become grounds for hate speech, offensive comments, and discrimination, including targeting a specific community. Such behaviors cause trauma, fear, anxiety, depressive symptoms and discomforts among LGBTQ+ individuals (Poteat et al., 2014; Ventriglio et al., 2021), hindering them from freely expressing their thoughts and feedback.

To ensure the safety and comfort of users on online platforms, it becomes imperative to identify and address hate speech and offensive comments. Although there are existing policies aimed at protecting communities from such misconduct, violations may lead to the removal of offending comments [2] [3]. However, the identification process necessitates the application of NLP and AI techniques due to the diverse nature of hate speech, which can manifest in both direct and passive forms. Surprisingly, there is a higher focus on researching this topic in English and other high-resource languages like hindi, with ample resources. For instance, couple of shared tasks have been organized previously e.g. Chakravarthi et al. (2022b), Chakravarthi et al. (2022c), Chakravarthi et al. (2023), accompanied by substantial datasets e.g. Vásquez et al. (2023), Chakravarthi et al. (2021). However, there has been a lack when it comes to identifying hate speech in low-resource and under-resource languages.

This shared task Chakravarthi et al. (2024) aims to identify hate speech contents, specifically homophobia, transphobia, and non-anti-LGBT+ sentiments, directed at LGBTQ+ individuals in 10 different languages, including 7 low-resource languages. To tackle the linguistic diversity, we conduct separate experiments for each language, leveraging different transformer-based models with proficiency in distinct languages. Notably, for Tulu, an under-resourced language, we employ a prompting approach. Alongside these experiments, various techniques are explored, and the most effective one during the evaluation phase is implemented in the test phase for comprehensive validation.

2 Related Works

As smart devices, mobile apps, and social media platforms become more widely utilized, there are also more negative effects linked to them, such as cyberbullying, hurtful comments, and rumors have increased. These platforms have also become a space for negative behaviors like sexism, homophobia (Diefendorf and Bridges (2020)), misogyny (Mulki and Ghanem (2021)), racism (Larimore et al. (2021)) and transphobia (Giametta and Havkin (2021)). Internet trolling, where people say mean things online, has become a global problem. To deal with this, researchers are looking

[1] https://codalab.lisn.upsaclay.fr/competitions/16056

[2] https://www.youtube.com/howyoutubeworks/our-commitments/standing-up-to-hate/

[3] https://transparency.fb.com/policies/community-standards/hate-speech/

Proceedings of the Fourth Workshop on Language Technology for Equality, Diversity, Inclusion, pages 164–172
March 21, 2024 ©2024 Association for Computational Linguistics

into automated methods since checking every message manually is impossible. In this section, we provide a brief summary of the research attempts that focused on identifying homophobia, transphobia, and non-anti-LGBT+ content from YouTube comments.

To motivate researchers to tackle the issue of identifying toxic language directed at the LGBTQ community, in the last few years, several shared tasks have been released. In one such shared task related to LT-EDI-2022 (Chakravarthi et al.), researchers submitted systems to deal with homophobic and transphobic comments. Chakravarthi et al. (2022b) gives an overview of the models submitted. Three subtasks for the languages Tamil, English, and Tamil-English (code-mixed) were the emphasis of this shared task. Apart from this, several studies have been conducted. The author of Karayigit et al. (2022) used the M-BERT model, which shows that it is capable of accurately identifying homophobic or other abusive language in Turkish social media comments. Similarly, another shared task related to this topic has been organized showing XLM-R performing best with spatio-temporal data in 5 different languages (Wong et al., 2023). Vásquez et al. (2023) presents a mexican-spanish annotated corpus along in which beto-cased (Spanish BERT) outperforms the other models.

For several text classification tasks, transformer-based ensemble approaches perform very well, like the works by Goswami et al. (2023b); Raihan et al. (2023b). Also, prompting Large Language Models like GPT3.5 (OpenAI, 2023) is another popular approach in recent classification tasks (Raihan et al., 2023c) for the past year.

Efforts to identify homophobic and transphobic comments have primarily focused on a maximum of five languages to date. However, in this shared task, a total of 10 languages have been chosen, and ongoing efforts now include Telugu, Tulu, and Marathi.

3 Datasets

The dataset provided for the shared task contains 10 languages - Tamil, English, Malayalam, Marathi, Spanish, Hindi, Telugu, Kannada, Gujarati, and Tulu. It is compiled using five separate research works. The previous iteration of the workshop (Chakravarthi et al., 2023) includes Tamil, English and Spanish, Hindi, Malayalam languages, and the earlier version Kumaresan et al. (2024) includes Tamil, English, and Tamil-English (Code-Mixed) languages.

The work by Kumaresan et al. (2023) builds a dataset for Malayalam and Hindi languages from social media comments. Another dataset by Chakravarthi (2023) focuses on YouTube comments. One data augmentation approach is adopted by Chakravarthi et al. (2022a).

The current dataset combines all these works to build a comprehensive dataset for the task of homophobia and/or transphobia detection in 10 languages Chakravarthi et al. (2024).

The detailed dataset demonstration and label-wise data percentage for all the languages are available in Table 1.

4 Experiments

Among the 10 languages (except Tulu) we use XLM-R, m-BERT and language specific BERTs: RoBERTa (Liu et al., 2019) , HindiBERT (Nick Doiron, 2023), TamilBERT (Joshi, 2023), Malayalam-BERT (Joshi, 2023), MarathiBERT (Joshi, 2022), SpanishBERT (Cañete et al., 2022), TeluguBERT (Joshi, 2023), KannadaBERT (Joshi, 2023), GujaratiBERT (Joshi, 2023) for Hindi, Tamil, Malayalam, Marathi, Spanish, Telugu, Kannada, Gujarati respectively. While using MarathiBERT and HindiBERT, we pad the sentence length upto 512 tokens, because of the limitation of the aforementioned BERTs. Training parameters are mostly kept the same across all models, mentioned in Table 3.

After that we perform weighted ensemble ap-

Role: "You are a helpful AI assistant. You are given the task of detecting homophobia and transphobia in a given text.

Definition: Homophobia and transphobia detection is the process of identifying expressions of hatred or discrimination against LGBTQ+ individuals in communication.'.

Examples: An example of Homophobic/Transphobic comment: **<Example1>**. An example of Non-Homophobic/Transphobic comment: **<Example2>**'.

Task: Generate the label [YES/NO] for this **"text"** in the following format: *<label> Your_Predicted_Label <\label>*. Thanks."

Figure 1: Sample GPT-3.5 prompt for few shot learning [*Used for the **Tulu** Dataset*].

Tamil				English			
Labels	Train	Dev	Test	Labels	Train	Dev	Test
Non-anti-LGBT+ content	77.53	76.13	76.11	Non-anti-LGBT+ content	94.12	94.45	94.04
Homophobia	17.02	17.72	18.25	Homophobia	5.66	5.30	5.56
Transphobia	5.45	6.15	5.64	Transphobia	0.22	0.25	0.40
Malayalam				**Marathi**			
Labels	Train	Dev	Test	Labels	Train	Dev	Test
Non-anti-LGBT+ content	79.25	77.25	77.83	None of the categories	73.49	72.13	75.87
Homophobia	15.29	16.24	16.17	Homophobia	15.74	17.20	14.93
Transphobia	5.46	6.51	6.00	Transphobia	10.77	10.67	9.20
Spanish				**Hindi**			
Labels	Train	Dev	Test	Labels	Train	Dev	Test
None	58.34	51.82	50.00	Non-anti-LGBT+ content	94.65	95.31	95.95
Transphobic	20.83	24.09	25.00	Transphobia	3.59	4.06	3.12
Homophobic	20.83	24.09	25.00	Homophobia	1.76	0.63	0.93
Telugu				**Kannada**			
Labels	Train	Dev	Test	Labels	Train	Dev	Test
None of the categories	38.63	38.51	38.37	None of the categories	44.35	44.27	44.11
Homophobia	32.12	31.18	32.18	Homophobia	28.17	28.61	28.11
Transphobia	29.25	30.31	29.45	Transphobia	27.48	27.12	27.78
Gujarati				**Tulu**			
Labels	Train	Dev	Test	Labels	Train	Dev	Test
None of the categories	47.39	45.29	45.63	NON H/T	74.25		82.32
Homophobia	27.93	28.62	29.31	H/T	25.75		17.68
Transphobia	24.68	26.09	25.06				

Table 1: Label-wise Data Percentage for Different Languages

proach of the above models (XLM-R, m-BERT, language specific BERTs) and use the macro F1 scores of the models on the dev data as the weight along with the confidence score to get the ensemble macro F-1 score of the test phase. After the test labels get published, we use the F1 score in the rank list as the weight along with the corresponding confidence score for the additional experiment of weighted ensemble approach.

As Tulu is very close to Kannada and Tulu doesn't have any language specific fine-tuned model, we used KannadaBERT on Tulu. In South Karnataka, individuals who speak Tulu are typically fluent in both Tulu and Kannada. Due to the long-standing interaction between Tulu and Kannada, it can be anticipated that codeswitching between these two languages is a probable outcome (Shetty, 2003). Moreover, we implement few shot learning using GPT3.5 for the Tulu dataset (see Figure 1). Such prompting is very widely used in recent works on text classification (Raihan et al., 2023a; Goswami et al., 2023a). We got the same result as the ensemble approach in the few shot prompting technique. We specifically used 8 - shot prompting for Tulu language. This process is inspired by Wei et al. (2022).

We improve the macro F1 in 4 out of 10 cases in this additional experiments and rest of the 6 cases we get the same macro F1 as the test phase.

5 Results

We employ an ensemble-based methodology for the tasks, since in text classification tasks this can further improve the results. for For all the ensemble approaches, we use XLM-R, mBERT, and a BERT-based model fine-tuned for that specific langauge as we mentioned in the previous section.

In the testing phase, we ensemble the confidence score of the three models and then calculate the weighted average. The weight in this context is the macro F1 score of the corresponding models on dev data.

For Tulu language, we use GPT 3.5 for few shot prompting. We use few instances of each of the two labels with specific prompt and and then get the test labels predicted by GPT 3.5.

After the end of testing phase when the test labels get published, we further run the ensemble

Tamil (Rank 5)			**English (Rank 10)**		
Models	Dev F1	Test F1	Models	Dev F1	Test F1
XLM-R	0.49	0.49	XLM-R	0.32	0.32
mBERT	0.62	0.67	mBERT	0.32	0.32
TamilBERT	0.51	0.53	roBERTa	0.32	0.32
Wt. (Dev F1) Ensemble		0.51	Wt. (Dev F1) Ensemble		0.32
Wt. (Test F1) Ensemble		**0.52**	Wt. (Test F1) Ensemble		0.32
Malayalam (Rank 9)			**Marathi (Rank 4)**		
Models	Dev F1	Test F1	Models	Dev F1	Test F1
XLM-R	0.51	0.51	XLM-R	0.49	0.49
mBERT	0.54	0.55	mBERT	0.46	0.41
MalayalamBERT	0.52	0.52	MarathiBERT	0.41	0.44
Wt. (Dev F1) Ensemble		0.51	Wt. (Dev F1) Ensemble		0.44
Wt. (Test F1) Ensemble		**0.52**	Wt. (Test F1) Ensemble		**0.45**
Spanish (Rank 3)			**Hindi (Rank 4)**		
Models	Dev F1	Test F1	Models	Dev F1	Test F1
XLM-R	0.75	0.55	XLM-R	0.33	0.33
mBERT	0.79	0.55	mBERT	0.33	0.33
SpanishBERT	0.81	0.50	HindiBERT	0.33	0.33
Wt. (Dev F1) Ensemble		0.50	Wt. (Dev F1) Ensemble		0.33
Wt. (Test F1) Ensemble		**0.54**	Wt. (Test F1) Ensemble		0.33
Telugu (Rank 1)			**Kannada (Rank 3)**		
Models	Dev F1	Test F1	Models	Dev F1	Test F1
XLM-R	0.97	0.97	XLM-R	0.95	0.95
mBERT	0.96	0.95	mBERT	0.93	0.94
TeluguBERT	0.97	0.97	KannadaBERT	0.95	0.95
Wt. (Dev F1) Ensemble		0.97	Wt. (Dev F1) Ensemble		0.95
Wt. (Test F1) Ensemble		0.97	Wt. (Test F1) Ensemble		0.95
Gujarati (Rank 5)			**Tulu (Rank 3)**		
Models	Dev F1	Test F1	Models	Dev F1	Test F1
XLM-R	0.94	0.94	GPT 3.5		0.45
mBERT	0.95	0.95	XLM-R	0.42	0.42
GujaratiBERT	0.93	0.93	mBERT	0.42	0.45
Wt. (Dev F1) Ensemble		0.94	KannadaBERT	0.42	0.45
Wt. (Test F1) Ensemble		0.94	Wt. (Test F1) Ensemble		0.45

Table 2: Combined Results for Various Languages

Parameter	**Value**
Learning Rate	$1e-5$
Train Batch Size	8
Test Batch Size	8
Epochs	5

Table 3: Training Configuration Parameters

systems again for all the languages. For this case, the weight for the models is the macro F1 score of the corresponding models on test data. For Tulu language, we also peform this ensemble approach with XLM-R, mBERT and KannadaBERT. Though none of these models have Tulu language in their corpora but all these models were pretrained on Kannada which is really close to Tulu. We achieve a macro F1 score using this ensemble approach which is as same as the few shot prompting.

Using this approach, we achieve the rank 1 (one) on Telugu, Rank 3 (three) on Spanish, Kannada and Tulu, rank 4 (four) on Marathi and Hindi, rank 5 (five) on Tamil and Gujarati, rank 9 (nine) on Malayalam and rank 10 (ten) on English language. The detailed experimental results of the models are available in Table 2.

6 Error Analysis

To thoroughly investigate the results and the models' performance on specific datasets, we find that though the accuracy of the models on all the datasets are very good but the macro F1 score is really low in some cases. From the table in Table 1, it is clearly visible that English and Hindi dataset is very imbalanced. They have a very few Homophobia and Transphobia label. From the confusion matrices in Appendix A, we can see all the instances of Non-anti-LGBT+ content label are correctly predicted by the models but models' fail to be well-trained on the other two labels. Thus the other two labels get mis-classified which leads to a marco F1 score around 0.33 for these two languages. For Tamil, Malayalam, Marathi, Spanish and Tulu - the data ratio is comparatively balanced which leads to F1 score in the range 0.45 - 0.54. Telugu, Kannada and Gujarati datasets are evenly label-wise evenly balanced which get reflected with highest marco F1 score in the range 0.94 - 0.97. For the imbalanced datasets, widely used techniques like data augmentation, back translation can be proven helpful which can be potential future research scope in this domain. Detailed error analysis for the languages is given below:

- **Tamil** The Homophobia instances are partially correct but all the instances of Transphobia are misclassified. On the other hand, the Non-anti-LGBTQ + content instances are almost perfectly classified in Tamil.

- **English** The models perform well in identifying only Non-anti-LGBT+ content while they completely fail to detect Homophobia, and Transphobia in English.

- **Malayalam** For Malayalam, the models almost perfectly detect Non-anti-LGBTQ + Content, partially detect Homophobia instances but as before it completely misclassified the Transphobia.

- **Marathi** The Homophobia and None of the categories instances are partially correct in case of Marathi. However, the transphobia content instances are mostly misclassified.

- **Spanish** Homophobic, None and Transphobic instances are partially correct in Spanish.

- **Hindi** Only Non-anti-LGBTQ + content instances are perfectly classified but all the instances of Homophobia and Transphobia are misclassified in Hindi.

- **Telugu** Homophobia, None of the categories and Transphobia instances are almost perfectly correct in Telugu.

- **Kannada** The model predictions are almost correct in Kannada for instances of Homophobia, None of the categories and Transphobia.

- **Gujarati** Our model can almost perfectly detect for Homophobia, None of the categories for Gujarati Transphobia instances.

- **Tulu** Though NON H/T instances are perfectly classified, but all the instances of H/T are misclassified in Tulu.

7 Conclusion

The task of detecting abusive speech targeting sexual and gender minorities has become increasingly important given the rise of social media and its potential to propagate harmful stereotypes that further marginalize vulnerable populations. This paper presents our efforts to address online transphobia and homophobia in multilingual contexts, which remains an under-studied area in abusive language detection. We employ an ensemble approach combining multiple individual models to identify abusive speech across datasets in ten languages.

Our findings demonstrate that while no individual system consistently achieves superior performance across all data, monolingual language-specific BERT models fine-tuned on our abusive speech data unsurprisingly emerge as strong approaches for this classification problem. However, our ensemble framework leveraging voting across multiple BERT variants along with other models surpasses any individual system, indicating the value of model diversity even when one base technique manifests strengths. We hypothesize that the inconsistencies across models and languages result partly from imbalanced, sparse instances of actual abusive samples in our data. Hence, future work should prioritize constructing larger, more balanced benchmark datasets for abusive language detection encompassing underrepresented identities. Nonetheless, this research presents a starting point for identifying multilingual, multidirectional abuse in online spaces through ensemble natural language systems.

Limitations

The monolingual BERT models underperformed due to insufficient data volume and class imbalance in our existing abusive speech corpora. Skewed label distributions with far fewer minority abuse cases than benign texts make learning discriminative patterns difficult. Our ensemble framework mitigated these weaknesses but still suffered performance issues on minority samples. Constructing larger, more balanced datasets remains imperative yet challenges exist regarding sensitivity of human annotations for this problem space. Nonetheless, enhancing model robustness on sparse abusive instances should be prioritized. While augmenting through back-translation and generation could help, this risks polluting training data if new variants stray from actual phenomenology. Systems producing false positives that ascribe nonexistent abuse contribute harm. Progress on mitigating imbalance without these downsides is incremental. Our experiments manifested datasets with endemic skew away from minority classes. Researchers must remain cognizant that efforts to populate abusive classes risk drifting from reality.

Ethics Statement

Adhering to the ACL Ethics Policy, this study seeks to responsibly progress online safety through benign content filtering technology. However, safeguards against misuse for censorship/monitoring remain imperative. While the supplied dataset was anonymized to protect privacy, carefully compiled public benchmarks avoiding marginalization must drive future progress. Flawed training data has propagated harm before; our experiments mitigated this but work continues. Guiding principles of beneficence and nonmaleficence should steer research on automating content classification with real-world impacts, including on complex offensive speech. Assessing for unintended consequences and awareness of social dimensions is critical as this work makes initial strides in detecting minority-targeting online abuse. Continual reassessment of systems and their real-world influences remains essential even beyond research contexts. And usage policies must be crafted thoughtfully before any operational deployment. We believe impactful technology like this carries with it a profoundly ethical mandate. Progress ceases to be progress if attained through forfeiture of our values.

References

José Cañete, Sebastian Donoso, Felipe Bravo-Marquez, Andrés Carvallo, and Vladimir Araujo. 2022. ALBETO and DistilBETO: Lightweight Spanish language models. In *Proceedings of the Thirteenth Language Resources and Evaluation Conference*, pages 4291–4298, Marseille, France. European Language Resources Association.

Bharathi Raja Chakravarthi. 2023. Detection of Homophobia and Transphobia in YouTube comments. *International Journal of Data Science and Analytics*, pages 1–20.

Bharathi Raja Chakravarthi, Adeep Hande, Rahul Ponnusamy, Prasanna Kumar Kumaresan, and Ruba Priyadharshini. 2022a. How can we detect Homophobia and Transphobia? experiments in a multilingual code-mixed setting for social media governance. *International Journal of Information Management Data Insights*, 2(2):100119.

Bharathi Raja Chakravarthi, Prasanna Kumar Kumaresan, Ruba Priyadharshini, Paul Buitelaar, Asha Hegde, Hosahalli Lakshmaiah Shashirekha, Saranya Rajiakodi, Miguel Ángel García-Cumbreras, Salud María Jiménez-Zafra, José Antonio García-Díaz, Rafael Valencia-García, Kishore Kumar Ponnusamy, Poorvi Shetty, and Daniel García-Baena. 2024. Overview of third shared task on Homophobia and Transphobia detection in social media comments. In *Proceedings of the Fourth Workshop on Language Technology for Equality, Diversity and Inclusion*, Malta. European Chapter of the Association for Computational Linguistics.

Bharathi Raja Chakravarthi, Vigneshwaran Muralidaran, Ruba Priyadharshini, Subalalitha Cn, John McCrae, Miguel Ángel García, Salud María Jiménez-Zafra, Rafael Valencia-García, Prasanna Kumaresan, Rahul Ponnusamy, and Daniel García-Baena. Overview of the shared task on hope speech detection for Equality, Diversity, and Inclusion. In *Proceedings of the Second Workshop on Language Technology for Equality, Diversity and Inclusion*. Association for Computational Linguistics.

Bharathi Raja Chakravarthi, Rahul Ponnusamy, Malliga Subramanian, Paul Buitelaar, Miguel Ángel García-Cumbreras, Salud María Jiménez-Zafra, José Antonio García-Díaz, Rafael Valencia-García, and Nitesh Jindal. 2023. Overview of second shared task on Homophobia and Transphobia detection in English, Spanish, Hindi, Tamil, and Malayalam. In *Proceedings of the Third Workshop on Language Technology for Equality, Diversity and Inclusion*, Varna, Bulgaria. Recent Advances in Natural Language Processing.

Bharathi Raja Chakravarthi, Ruba Priyadharshini, Thenmozhi Durairaj, John McCrae, Paul Buitelaar, Prasanna Kumaresan, and Rahul Ponnusamy. 2022b. Overview of the shared task on homophobia and transphobia detection in social media comments. In *Proceedings of the Second Workshop on Language*

Technology for Equality, Diversity and Inclusion, pages 369–377, Dublin, Ireland. Association for Computational Linguistics.

Bharathi Raja Chakravarthi, Ruba Priyadharshini, Thenmozhi Durairaj, John Philip McCrae, Paul Buitelaar, Prasanna Kumaresan, and Rahul Ponnusamy. 2022c. Overview of the shared task on Homophobia and Transphobia detection in social media comments. In *Proceedings of the Second Workshop on Language Technology for Equality, Diversity and Inclusion*, pages 369–377.

Bharathi Raja Chakravarthi, Ruba Priyadharshini, Rahul Ponnusamy, Prasanna Kumar Kumaresan, Kayalvizhi Sampath, Durairaj Thenmozhi, Sathiyaraj Thangasamy, Rajendran Nallathambi, and John Phillip McCrae. 2021. Dataset for identification of Homophobia and Transophobia in multilingual YouTube comments. *arXiv preprint arXiv:2109.00227*.

Sarah Diefendorf and Tristan Bridges. 2020. On the enduring relationship between masculinity and homophobia. volume 23, pages 1264–1284.

Calogero Giametta and Shira Havkin. 2021. Mapping homo/transphobia: The valorization of the lgbt protection category in the refugee-granting system. *ACME: An International Journal for Critical Geographies*, 20(1):99–119.

Dhiman Goswami, Md Nishat Raihan, Antara Mahmud, Antonios Anstasopoulos, and Marcos Zampieri. 2023a. OffMix-3L: A novel code-mixed dataset in Bangla-English-Hindi for Offensive Language Identification. *arXiv preprint arXiv:2310.18387*.

Dhiman Goswami, Md Nishat Raihan, Sadiya Sayara Chowdhury Puspo, and Marcos Zampieri. 2023b. nlpbdpatriots at blp-2023 task 2: A transfer learning approach to Bangla Sentiment Analysis. In *The First Workshop on Bangla Language Processing (BLP-2023)*, page 286.

Raviraj Joshi. 2022. L3Cube-MahaCorpus and MahaBERT: Marathi monolingual corpus, Marathi BERT language models, and resources. In *Proceedings of the WILDRE-6 Workshop within the 13th Language Resources and Evaluation Conference*, pages 97–101, Marseille, France. European Language Resources Association.

Raviraj Joshi. 2023. L3cube-Hindbert and Devbert: Pretrained bert transformer models for devanagari based Hindi and Marathi languages.

Habibe Karayigit, Ali Akdagli, and Cigdem Inan Aci. 2022. Homophobic and hate speech detection using Multilingual-BERT model on Turkish social media. *Inf. Technol. Control.*, 51:356–375.

Prasanna Kumar Kumaresan, Rahul Ponnusamy, Ruba Priyadharshini, Paul Buitelaar, and Bharathi Raja Chakravarthi. 2023. Homophobia and Transphobia detection for low-resourced languages in social media comments. *Natural Language Processing Journal*, page 100041.

Prasanna Kumar Kumaresan, Ruba Priyadharshini, Bharathi Raja Chakravarthi, Paul Buitelaar, Asha Hegde, Hosahalli Lakshmaiah Shashirekha, Saranya Rajiakodi, Miguel Ángel García-Cumbreras, Salud María Jiménez-Zafra, José Antonio García-Díaz, Rafael Valencia-García, Kishore Kumar Ponnusamy, Poorvi Shetty, and Daniel García-Baena. 2024. Overview of third shared task on Homophobia and Transphobia detection in social media comments". In *Proceedings of the Fourth Workshop on Language Technology for Equality, Diversity and Inclusion*. European Chapter of the Association for Computational Linguistics.

Savannah Larimore, Ian Kennedy, Breon Haskett, and Alina Arseniev-Koehler. 2021. Reconsidering annotator disagreement about racist language: Noise or signal? In *Proceedings of the Ninth International Workshop on Natural Language Processing for Social Media*. Association for Computational Linguistics.

Yinhan Liu, Myle Ott, Naman Goyal, Jingfei Du, Mandar Joshi, Danqi Chen, Omer Levy, Mike Lewis, Luke Zettlemoyer, and Veselin Stoyanov. 2019. RoBERTa: A robustly optimized BERT pretraining approach. *CoRR*, abs/1907.11692.

Hala Mulki and Bilal Ghanem. 2021. Let-Mi: An Arabic levantine Twitter dataset for Misogynistic language.

Nick Doiron. 2023. Hindi-BERT (revision c54eb83).

OpenAI. 2023. Gpt-4 technical report. *ArXiv*, abs/2303.08774.

V Paul Poteat, Jillian R Scheer, Craig D DiGiovanni, and Ethan H Mereish. 2014. Short-term prospective effects of Homophobic victimization on the mental health of Heterosexual adolescents. *Journal of youth and adolescence*, 3.

Md Nishat Raihan, Dhiman Goswami, Antara Mahmud, Antonios Anstasopoulos, and Marcos Zampieri. 2023a. SentMix-3L: A Bangla-English-Hindi code-mixed dataset for Sentiment Analysis. *arXiv preprint arXiv:2310.18023*.

Md Nishat Raihan, Dhiman Goswami, Sadiya Sayara Chowdhury Puspo, and Marcos Zampieri. 2023b. nlpbdpatriots at blp-2023 task 1: A two-step classification for violence inciting text detection in Bangla. In *The First Workshop on Bangla Language Processing (BLP-2023)*, page 179.

Md Nishat Raihan, Umma Hani Tanmoy, Anika Binte Islam, Kai North, Tharindu Ranasinghe, Antonios Anastasopoulos, and Marcos Zampieri. 2023c. Offensive Language Identification in Transliterated and code-mixed Bangla. In *The First Workshop on Bangla Language Processing (BLP-2023)*, page 1.

Malavika Shetty. 2003. Language contact and the maintenance of the Tulu language in South India. In *Proceedings of the Eleventh Annual Symposium About Language and Society Austin (SALSA XI)*. Citeseer.

Juan Vásquez, Scott Andersen, Gemma Bel-Enguix, Helena Gómez-Adorno, and Sergio-Luis Ojeda-Trueba. 2023. Homo-mex: A mexican spanish annotated corpus for lgbt+ phobia detection on twitter. In *The 7th Workshop on Online Abuse and Harms (WOAH)*, pages 202–214.

Antonio Ventriglio, João Mauricio Castaldelli-Maia, Julio Torales, Domenico De Berardis, and Dinesh Bhugra. 2021. Homophobia and mental health: a scourge of modern era. *Epidemiology and Psychiatric Sciences*, 30:e52.

Jason Wei, Xuezhi Wang, Dale Schuurmans, Maarten Bosma, Fei Xia, Ed Chi, Quoc V Le, Denny Zhou, et al. 2022. Chain-of-thought prompting elicits reasoning in large language models. *Advances in Neural Information Processing Systems*, 35:24824–24837.

Sidney G-J Wong, Matthew Durward, Benjamin Adams, and Jonathan Dunn. 2023. cantnlp@ lt-edi@ ranlp-2023: Homophobia/transphobia detection in social media comments using spatio-temporally retrained language models. *arXiv preprint arXiv:2308.10370*.

A Confusion Matrix

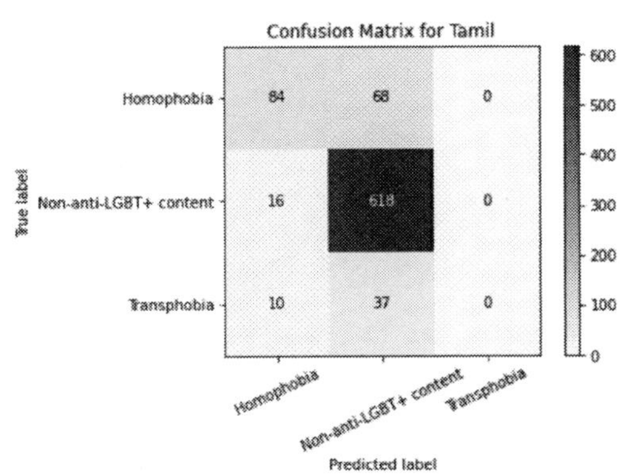

Figure 2: Confusion Matrix for Tamil Language

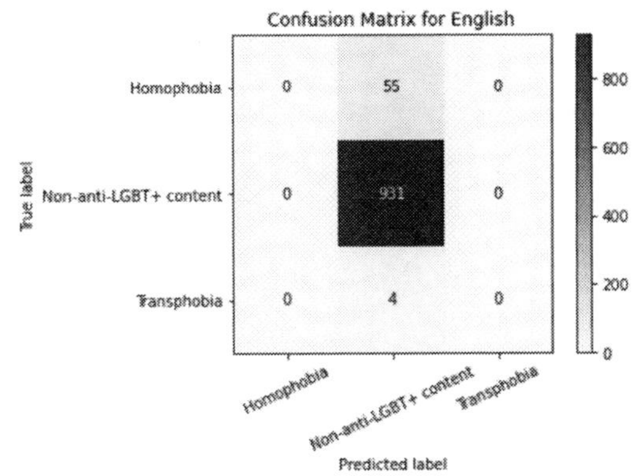

Figure 3: Confusion Matrix for English Language

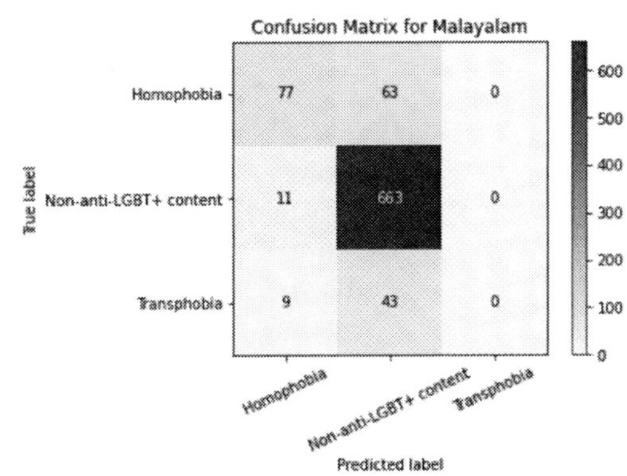

Figure 4: Confusion Matrix for Malayalam Language

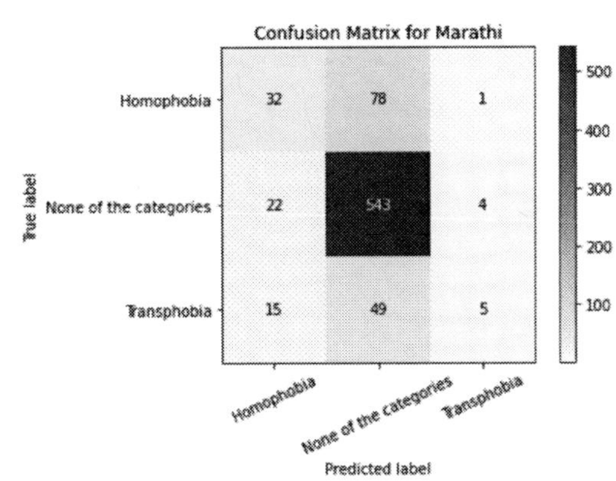

Figure 5: Confusion Matrix for Marathi Language

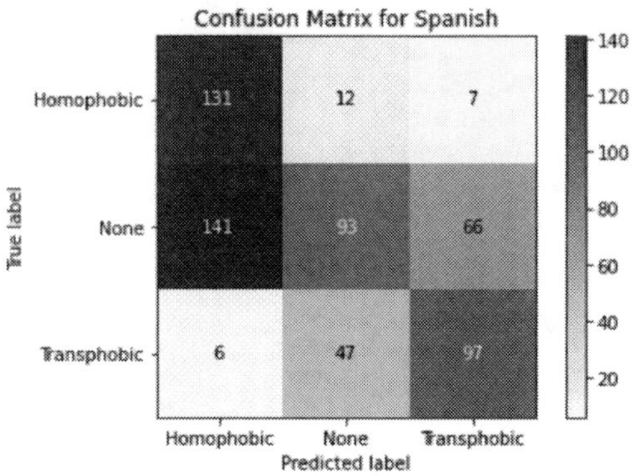

Figure 6: Confusion Matrix for Spanish Language

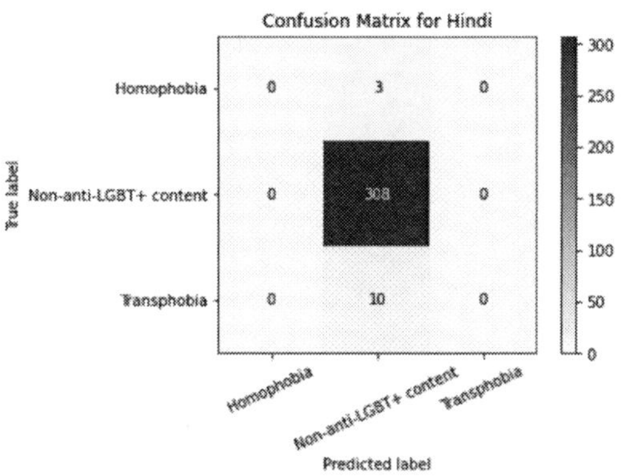

Figure 7: Confusion Matrix for Hindi Language

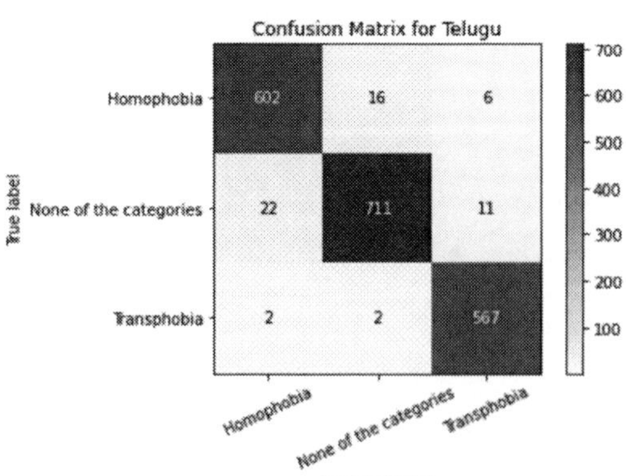

Figure 8: Confusion Matrix for Telugu Language

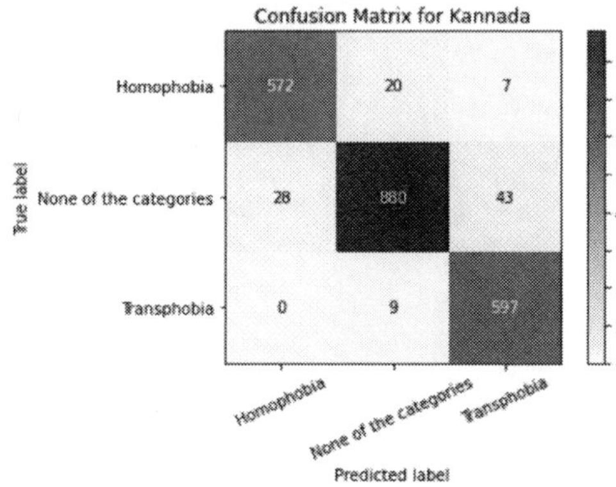

Figure 9: Confusion Matrix for Kannada Language

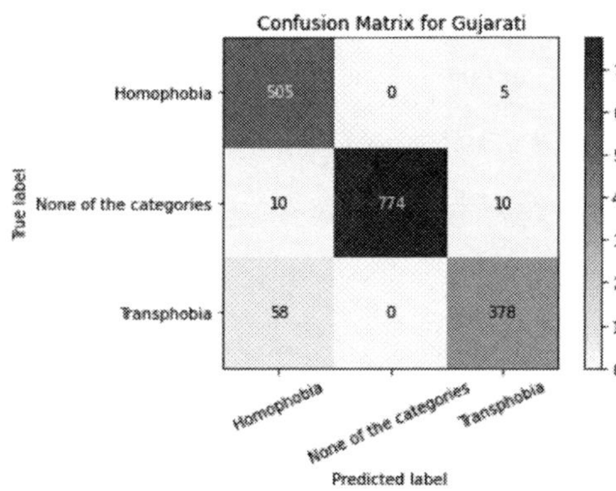

Figure 10: Confusion Matrix for Gujarati Language

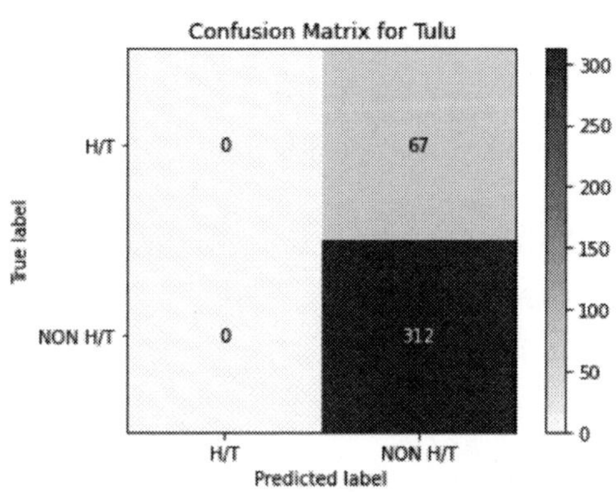

Figure 11: Confusion Matrix for Tulu Language

JudithJeyafreeda_StressIdent_LT-EDI@EACL2024: GPT for stress identification

Judith Jeyafreeda Andrew
Institut Imagine / Paris, France
PRAIRE / Paris, France
Univarsité Paris Cité / Paris, France
judithjeyafreeda@gmail.com

Abstract

Stress detection from social media texts has proven to play an important role in mental health assessments. People tend to express their stress on social media more easily. Analysing and classifying these texts allows for improvements in development of recommender systems and automated mental health assessments. In this paper, a GPT model is used for classification of social media texts into two classes: stressed and not-stressed. The texts used for classification are in two Dravidian languages: Tamil and Telugu. The results, although not very good shows a promising direction of research to use GPT models for classification.

1 Introduction

Emotion classification is a well-known and highly-utilised application in the field of text analysis. Stress is a form of emotion. Thus, stress classification is a particular case of emotion classification. Stress is defined as a state of imbalance between one's internal demands and his/her ability to meet those demands [5], and is widely regarded as a medical problem (Rastogi et al., 2022). Stress can be a potentially life threatening problem. Stress can be identified from text, facial expressions, videos and audios of people. People express stress in different ways and forms. The field of identification of stress from text is an emerging research area. This is due to the fact that people have started to express themselves more comfortably on social media platforms with their friends and followers. In this work, we explore a method to classify social media text into stressed and non-stressed texts. The data from the task given in (Kayalvizhi Sampath and Rajkumar, 2023) is in the Dravidian languages of Tamil and Telugu.

2 Task Description

The task given in (Kayalvizhi Sampath and Rajkumar, 2023) is a binary classification of social media posts in the languages of Tamil and Telugu. The two labels are "stressed" and "not stressed". The data from (S et al., 2022) are given as separate sets for training, development and testing. Table 1 gives statistics on the number of text statements in each language provided for training, development and testing within the task.

Language	Train	Dev	Test
Tamil	5504	1378	1020
Telugu	5097	1239	1050

Table 1: Data statistics for the classification task

3 Related Work

There have been several studies in the areas of sentiment analysis and emotion classification. Several ML methods have been developed for this purpose. (Jadhav et al., 2019) presents a Bidirectional Long Short-Term Memory (BLSTM) with attention mechanism to classify psychological stress and categorize the tweets based on their hashtag content, which gives the best performance. (Arya and Mishra, 2021) gives a review of all machine learning methods developed within the health sector, their advantages, their limitations and areas for further research. The authors reviewed papers on mental stress detection using ML that used social networking sites, blogs, discussion forums, Questioner technique, clinical dataset, real-time data, Bio-signal technology (ECG, EEG), a wireless device, and suicidal tendency. (Nijhawan et al., 2022) shows the accuracy of each ML model trained specifically for mental illness.

Pre-trained language models like ELMo (Peters et al., 2018), OpenAI GPT (Radford et al., 2018), and BERT (Devlin et al., 2019) have moved Natural Language Processing (NLP) passing into a new era. This has allowed the pre-trained model to play the role of the base, and this can be fine-tuned to

Proceedings of the Fourth Workshop on Language Technology for Equality, Diversity, Inclusion, pages 173–176
March 21, 2024 ©2024 Association for Computational Linguistics

respond to the NLP task. (Asghar et al., 2017) presented a method enhanced by lexicons.

With respect to language of the text, there have been several works in the English language. However, works in Dravidian languages have recently increased. (Chakravarthi, 2022b; Kumaresan et al., 2022; Chakravarthi, 2022a) presents an improvement of word sense translation for under-resourced languages. (Andrew, 2020) uses several Machine Learning algorithms which have been adapted to the task of Multiclass Classification Sentiment Analysis. (Andrew, 2021, 2022) suggests several machine language approaches to classify texts from Code-mixed Dravidian Languages such as Tamil, Telugu, Kannada and Malayalam. (Andrew, 2023) uses a GPT model to perform a classification task on YouTube comments in different Dravidian Languages. Although, the results are not too high, this allows for further research to improve GPT models.

4 Proposed System

In this work, GPT2 is used for classification of social media texts into stressful and non-stressful comments. The model is fine-tuned on the training dataset for each language, thus creating a task specific and language specific model. For the languages Tamil and Telugu, the text to be classified is transliterated to their English language equivalents, this approach has been inspired from (Andrew, 2021) and (Andrew, 2022). The labels for the task are in English language, thus transliteration is not required for this.

Pre-processing: Similar to (Andrew, 2022), a few steps of pre-processing is performed to get the accurate representation of the text.

This involves the following:

- Texts from the Tamil and Telugu languages are transliterated to their English equivalents. Transliteration refers to the method of mapping from one system of writing to another based on phonetic similarity. This transliteration is performed using the *polyglot.transliteration* package in Python.

- The emojis are substituted with the words of the emotion they represent like happy, sad, excited etc.

- The tokenizer from the pretrained GPT2 model is used for tokenization of the transformed text.

GPT models: Generative Pre-trained Transformers (GPT) models are general-purpose language models that can perform a broad range of tasks from creating original content to write code, summarizing text, and extracting data from documents (GPT). Generative Pre-trained Transformers (GPT) are a family of neural network models that uses the transformer architecture. These use a self-attention mechanism allowing to focus on different parts of the input text during the various stages on processing. The value of these models lies in their speed and the scale at which they can operate. In particular, GPT-2 model has 1.5 billion parameters and has been trained on 8 million web pages in a self-supervised fashion. (Radford et al., 2019) provides a detailed description of the model. The model uses internally a mask-mechanism to make sure the predictions for the token i only uses the inputs from 1 to i but not the future tokens. This allows the model to learn the inner representation of the language, which can then be used to extract features for downstream tasks.

GPT models for classification: Although most use cases for a GPT involve text generation operations, recent research has shown that these models can also be fine-tuned for downstream tasks like classification. (Andrew, 2023) has used the GPT2 for classification of Homophobic and Transphobic comments from social media.

As in (Andrew, 2023), the python packages that allow the use of GPT models as in Hugging Face models are used along with other tools like NLTK and TextBlob to allow cleaning of text.

5 Results and Evaluation

The performance of the classification system is measured in terms of macro averaged Precision, macro averaged Recall and macro averaged F1-Score across all the classes (for both sub tasks). The Scikit-learn [1] package is used for this purpose, similar to (Andrew, 2023). The Macro and Weighted results for the task are shown in Tables 2 and 3 respectively. Overall, the results for the Tamil language is better than that for the Telugu language.

Language	M.Precision	M.Recall	M.F1
Tamil	0.459	0.498	0.273
Telugu	0.255	0.247	0.251

Table 2: Results of the task of classifying social media text to stressed and non-stressed. (M. stands for "Macro")

Language	W.Precision	W.Recall	W.F1
Tamil	0.485	0.364	0.202
Telugu	0.293	0.281	0.287

Table 3: Results of the task of classifying social media text to stressed and non-stressed. (W. stands for "Weighted")

6 Conclusion

From Tables 2 and 3, the results on the whole are not too high. This is an interesting result as the number of training data in both languages were similar with the exact same classes for classification. (Andrew, 2021) and (Andrew, 2022) suggest that using IPA substitutes for Dravidian languages works well for certain machine learning approaches, however it might not be the best representation for a transformer based model. Similarly, transliteration might not be the way to go with transformer models as well. Choosing other forms of embedding Dravidian texts could help improve the results.

References

AWS what is gpt? https://aws.amazon.com/what-is/gpt/. Accessed: 2023-12-11.

Judith Andrew. 2020. Judithjeyafreeda@ dravidian-codemix-fire2020:: Sentiment analysis of youtube comments for dravidian languages. In *Forum for Information Retrieval Evaluation*.

Judith Jeyafreeda Andrew. 2021. JudithJeyafreedaAndrew@DravidianLangTech-EACL2021:offensive language detection for Dravidian code-mixed YouTube comments. In *Proceedings of the First Workshop on Speech and Language Technologies for Dravidian Languages*, pages 169–174, Kyiv. Association for Computational Linguistics.

Judith Jeyafreeda Andrew. 2022. JudithJeyafreedaAndrew@TamilNLP-ACL2022:CNN for emotion analysis in Tamil. In *Proceedings of the Second Workshop on Speech and Language Technologies for Dravidian Languages*, pages 58–63, Dublin, Ireland. Association for Computational Linguistics.

Judith Jeyafreeda Andrew. 2023. JudithJeyafreeda@LT-EDI-2023: Using GPT model for recognition of homophobia/transphobia detection from social media. In *Proceedings of the Third Workshop on Language Technology for Equality, Diversity and Inclusion*, pages 78–82, Varna, Bulgaria. INCOMA Ltd., Shoumen, Bulgaria.

Vishakha Arya and Amit Kumar Mishra. 2021. Machine learning approaches to mental stress detection: a review. *Annals of Optimization Theory and Practice*, 4(2):55–67.

Muhammad Zubair Asghar, Aurangzeb Khan, Shakeel Ahmad, Maria Qasim, and Imran Ali Khan. 2017. Lexicon-enhanced sentiment analysis framework using rule-based classification scheme. *PloS one*, 12(2):e0171649.

Bharathi Raja Chakravarthi. 2022a. Hope speech detection in Youtube comments. *Social Network Analysis and Mining*, 12(1):75.

Bharathi Raja Chakravarthi. 2022b. Multilingual hope speech detection in English and Dravidian languages. *International Journal of Data Science and Analytics*, 14(4):389–406.

Jacob Devlin, Ming-Wei Chang, Kenton Lee, and Kristina Toutanova. 2019. BERT: Pre-training of deep bidirectional transformers for language understanding. In *Proceedings of the 2019 Conference of the North American Chapter of the Association for Computational Linguistics: Human Language Technologies, Volume 1 (Long and Short Papers)*, pages 4171–4186, Minneapolis, Minnesota. Association for Computational Linguistics.

Sachin Jadhav, Apoorva Machale, Pooja Mharnur, Pratik Munot, and Shruti Math. 2019. Text based stress detection techniques analysis using social media. In *2019 5th International Conference On Computing, Communication, Control And Automation (ICCUBEA)*, pages 1–5.

Bharathi Raja Chakravathi Jerin mahiba C Ramya Priya S Bharani Kasinathan Kishore Kumar Ponnusamy Kayalvizhi Sampath, Thenmozhi Durairaj and Charumathi Rajkumar. 2023. Overview of the shared task on stress identification in dravidian languages. In *proceedings of the Third Workshop on Speech and Language Technology for Dravidian Languages*, Varna, Bulgaria. Recent Advances in Natuarl Language Processing.

Prasanna Kumar Kumaresan, Rahul Ponnusamy, Elizabeth Sherly, Sangeetha Sivanesan, and Bharathi Raja Chakravarthi. 2022. Transformer based hope speech comment classification in code-mixed text. In *International Conference on Speech and Language Technologies for Low-resource Languages*, pages 120–137. Springer.

[1] https://scikit-learn.org/stable/modules/generated/sklearn.metrics.classification_report.html

Tanya Nijhawan, Girija Attigeri, and T. Ananthakrishna. 2022. Stress detection using natural language processing and machine learning over social interactions. *Journal of Big Data*, 9(1). Funding Information: Nil. Publisher Copyright: © 2022, The Author(s).

Matthew E. Peters, Mark Neumann, Mohit Iyyer, Matt Gardner, Christopher Clark, Kenton Lee, and Luke Zettlemoyer. 2018. Deep contextualized word representations. In *Proceedings of the 2018 Conference of the North American Chapter of the Association for Computational Linguistics: Human Language Technologies, Volume 1 (Long Papers)*, pages 2227–2237, New Orleans, Louisiana. Association for Computational Linguistics.

Alec Radford, Karthik Narasimhan, Tim Salimans, and Ilya Sutskever. 2018. Improving language understanding by generative pre-training.

Alec Radford, Jeff Wu, Rewon Child, David Luan, Dario Amodei, and Ilya Sutskever. 2019. Language models are unsupervised multitask learners.

Aryan Rastogi, Qiang Liu 0004, and Erik Cambria. 2022. Stress detection from social media articles: New dataset benchmark and analytical study. In *International Joint Conference on Neural Networks, IJCNN 2022, Padua, Italy, July 18-23, 2022*, pages 1–8. IEEE.

Kayalvizhi S, Thenmozhi Durairaj, Bharathi Raja Chakravarthi, and Jerin Mahibha C. 2022. Findings of the shared task on detecting signs of depression from social media. In *Proceedings of the Second Workshop on Language Technology for Equality, Diversity and Inclusion*, pages 331–338, Dublin, Ireland. Association for Computational Linguistics.

cantnlp@LT-EDI-2024: Automatic Detection of Anti-LGBTQ+ Hate Speech in Under-resourced Languages

Sidney G.-J. Wong[1,2] and Matthew Durward[1]

[1]University of Canterbury, New Zealand
[2]Geospatial Research Institute, New Zealand
{sidney.wong,matthew.durward}@pg.canterbury.ac.nz

Abstract

This paper describes our homophobia/transphobia in social media comments detection system developed as part of the shared task at LT-EDI-2024. We took a transformer-based approach to develop our multiclass classification model for ten language conditions (English, Spanish, Gujarati, Hindi, Kannada, Malayalam, Marathi, Tamil, Tulu, and Telugu). We introduced synthetic and organic instances of script-switched language data during domain adaptation to mirror the linguistic realities of social media language as seen in the labelled training data. Our system ranked second for Gujarati and Telugu with varying levels of performance for other language conditions. The results suggest incorporating elements of paralinguistic behaviour such as script-switching may improve the performance of language detection systems especially in the cases of under-resourced languages conditions.

1 Introduction

The purpose of this shared task was to develop a multiclass classification system to predict instances of homophobia/transphobia in social media comments across different language conditions (Kumaresan et al., 2024). The ten language conditions were: English (ENG), Spanish (ESP), Gujarati (GUJ), Hindi (HIN), Kannada (KAN), Malayalam (MAL), Marathi (MAR), Tamil (TAM), Tulu (TCY), and Telugu (TEL).

The main contribution of this paper is that we extend on the work using spatio-temporally retrained transformer-based language models in Wong et al. (2023). We have expanded on the synthetic script-switching approach by incorporating real-world (or organic) samples of script-switching during domain adaptation in the development of our multiclass classification model using pretrained language models.

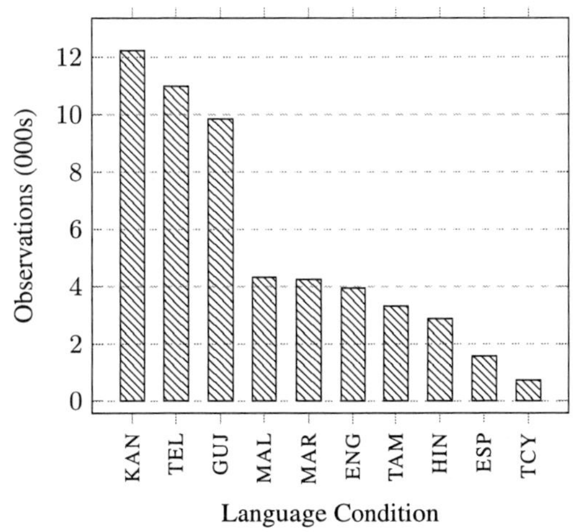

Figure 1: Barplot of labelled training data. The combined total number of observations (in thousands) by language condition ordered from the most (KAN) to the least (TCY) number of observations.

1.1 Problem Description

The organisers of the shared task provided labelled training data for each of the ten language conditions. Five of the language conditions belong to the Indo-European language family (ENG, ESP, GUJ, HIN, and MAR) and the remaining five language conditions belong to the Dravidian language family (KAN, MAL, TAM, TCY, and TEL).

The labelled training data comes from different sources (ENG and TAM in Chakravarthi et al., 2021; HIN and MAL in Kumaresan et al., 2023; and ESP in García-Díaz et al., 2020). The training data is made up of comments from users reacting to LGBTQ+ related content on YouTube. The labelled training data for GUJ, KAN, MAR, TCY, and TEL were introduced for the current shared task.

The total number of social media comments for each language condition (combining the train and development sets) are shown in Figure 1. KAN has the most observations, followed by TEL and GUJ.

Proceedings of the Fourth Workshop on Language Technology for Equality, Diversity, Inclusion, pages 177–183
March 21, 2024

	NONE	HOMO	TRANS
ENG	0.94	0.06	0.00
ESP	0.57	0.22	0.22
GUJ	0.47	0.28	0.25
HIN	0.95	0.02	0.04
KAN	0.44	0.27	0.28
MAL	0.79	0.16	0.06
MAR	0.73	0.16	0.11
TAM	0.77	0.17	0.06
TCY	0.74	0.26	-
TEL	0.39	0.32	0.30

Table 1: Class distribution by language condition. Note that TCY has a binary class distribution.

TCY has the least number of observations. The remaining language conditions each have between 1,000 to 5,000 observations.

The social media comments were manually annotated and broadly labelled using on a three-class classification system (Chakravarthi et al., 2021). There were only two classes for TCY which we have labelled NONE and HOMO for consistency with other language conditions. The classes are:

- *Homophobic Content* (HOMO): any comments which were deemed gender-based and involved pejorative or defamatory language directed towards non-heterosexual people.
- *Transphobic Content* (TRANS): any derogatory or offensive language directed towards transgender and gender diverse people.
- *Non-anti-LGBTQ+ Content* (NONE): counter speech or hope speech as well as comments which does not contain any homophobic or transphobic content.

The class distribution for each language condition is shown in Table 1. We observe significant class imbalance between language conditions especially in ENG and HIN where the HOMO and TRANS classes make up less than a tenth of the labelled training data. Of the 3,726 observations in the ENG language condition, there are only 221 tokens of HOMO and nine tokens of TRANS.

Outside the labelled training data and published material, the organisers did not provide additional corpus or demographic information of the labelled training data as part of the shared task. Therefore, the classification system needs to account for the differences in data availability as well as class imbalance for each language condition.

1.2 Related Work

The current shared task is the third shared task on homophobia and transphobia detection in social media comments. The first shared task involved only three language conditions: TAM, ENG, and a separate TAM-ENG code-mixed condition (Chakravarthi et al., 2022).

The classification system with the best performance for ENG had a weighted Macro F_1 score of 0.92 was developed by team ABLIMET (Maimaitituoheti et al., 2022) and for TAM was 0.94 developed by team ARGUABLY. The best performing classification system for the TAM-ENG code-mixed condition was also developed by team ARGUABLY with a weighted Macro F_1 score of 0.89. The code-mixed condition had the lowest performance across the three conditions.

Participants took different approaches involving statistical language models and machine learning. The best performing system used XLM-ROBERTA pretrained language models (Conneau et al., 2020). This BERT-based transformer language approach structures the relationship between words with language embeddings (Devlin et al., 2019). These language embeddings account for structures across multilingual conditions.

The second shared task expanded to five language conditions (ENG, ESP, HIN, MAL, and TAM) which was broken down by a three-class classification system similar to the current shared task (Chakravarthi et al., 2023). Three of the language conditions (ENG, MAL, and TAM) were further classified into a seven-class classification system.

The weighted Macro F_1 score for the best performing three-class classification systems was 0.97 for ENG and 0.98 for HIN developed by TEAMPLUSONE using BERT-based transformer models. A weight-space ensembling technique presented itself as the best solution for ESP, MAL, and TAM language conditions (Ninalga, 2023).

The best performing systems for the seven-class classification condition were all developed using transformer language models. The weighted Macro F_1 score ENG was 0.82 developed by team TEAMPLUSONE, for MAL was 0.88 developed by team CANTNLP (Wong et al., 2023), and for TAM was 0.87 developed by team DEEPBLUEAI.

This suggests BERT-based models, such as XLM-ROBERTA for zero-shot learning, are particularly effective in carrying out multiclass classification tasks outlined in the current shared task. More

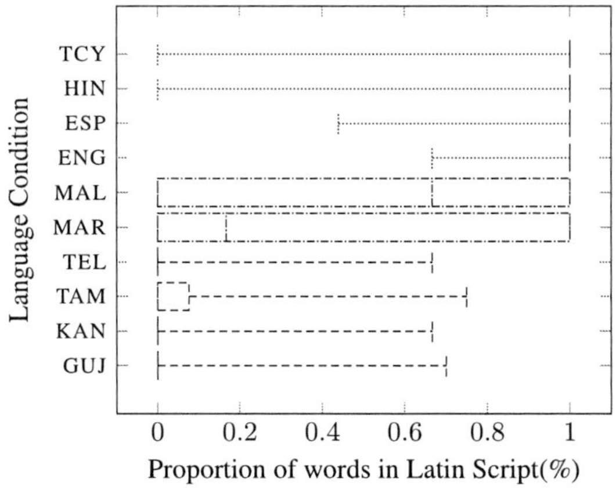

Figure 2: Boxplot of labelled training data. Language condition by the proportion of observations with at least one word written in Latin script ordered from the lowest (TCY) to the highest (GUJ) proportion of observations.

importantly, these systems are simple to implement and allow for domain adaptation (Liu et al., 2019)

Wong et al. (2023) introduced synthetically script-switched instances of social media data during domain adaptation to account for the high frequency of script-switching in the labelled data for HIN, MAL, and TAM. The introduction of script-switched language data improved the performance of the homophobia/transphobia detection model in HIN, but not MAL or TAM.

The results from Wong et al. (2023) suggest that there is potential for incorporating paralinguistic behaviour such as script-switching in the development of multiclass detection language systems. Therefore, this paper explores this further by incorporating different forms of script-switching.

2 Methodology

In this section, we provide an overview of our system development methodology. We took a transformer-based language model approach to develop our system. We used XLM-ROBERTA as the base PLM for our system (Conneau et al., 2020). The embeddings in XLM-ROBERTA were trained on two terabytes of web-crawled data for over 100 language including nine of the ten language conditions of interest (with the exclusion of TCY).

A significant advantage of transformer-based PLMs is the ability for domain adaptation as discussed in Section 2.1. This means we can retrain the default language embedding models with additional language data without the need to train resource-intensive PLMs from scratch.

We tested different forms of script-switching in order to understand the impacts of script-switching on our classification system. We then used the PLMs developed in Section 2.1 to fine-tune our multiclass classification model as discussed in Section 2.2. Based on the weighted Macro F_1 for each language condition, we submitted the results from the best performing multiclass classification system to the organisers.

2.1 Domain Adaptation

The first stage in developing our system involved domain adaptation (also known as retraining). Liu et al. (2019) noted that domain adaptation can improve the performance of transformer-based language models in downstream tasks. We can do this by introducing domain (or register) specific text samples to produce customised retrained PLMs (or retrained language models). This means we can introduce language data from under-resourced languages such as TCY as well as additional linguistic information such as script-switching - a common phenomenon in social media language.

As noted in Wong et al. (2023), we observed varying levels of script-switching in the labelled training data. Therefore, we first needed to identify the level of script-switching between language conditions. For each observation, we calculated the proportion of words written in Latin script using the alphabet-detector[1] Python package.

The proportion of script-switching between language conditions is shown in Figure 2 where 0 suggests low usage of Latin-based characters (in the case of GUJ, KAN, TAM, TEL) while 1 suggests high usage as expected for ENG and ESP. Figure 2 confirms that there is sufficient need to account for the varying-degrees of script-switching between language conditions.

We retrained XLM-ROBERTA with two forms of script-switching: synthetic and organic script-switching. These are our candidate models. We describe how we produced the language data for domain adaptation in Section 2.1.1 and Section 2.1.2. We produced the candidate language models by retraining the language embeddings using the simpletransformers[2] Python library. We did this over four iterations and we evaluated the training for every 500 steps with AdamW optimisation (Loshchilov and Hutter, 2019). Model performance was based on evaluation loss.

[1]https://pypi.org/project/alphabet-detector/

[2]https://simpletransformers.ai/

	BASELINE		SYNTHETIC		ORGANIC	
	mono	*multi*	*mono*	*multi*	*mono*	*multi*
ENG	0.32	**0.35**	0.32	0.32	0.32	0.32
ESP	0.80	0.82	**0.87**	0.84	0.76	0.82
GUJ	0.94	0.94	**0.95**	**0.95**	**0.95**	**0.95**
HIN	**0.32**	**0.32**	**0.32**	**0.32**	**0.32**	**0.32**
KAN	0.92	0.93	**0.94**	**0.94**	**0.94**	**0.94**
MAL	0.51	0.53	0.73	0.58	**0.78**	0.61
MAR	0.44	0.45	0.44	0.41	0.42	**0.46**
TAM	0.48	0.42	0.54	0.49	0.48	0.56
TCY	**0.72**	0.43	0.43	0.43	0.43	0.43
TEL	**0.98**	0.97	**0.98**	0.97	0.97	**0.98**

Table 2: Model performance of candidate classification models by Macro F_1 using our test set split from combining the train and validation sets provided to us by the organisers for each language condition. The three candidate languages models are: BASELINE, SYNTHETIC, and ORGANIC. We also compared the performance of language-specific (*mono*) and multilingual (*multi*) multiclass classification models. The best performing system is highlighted in **bold**.

2.1.1 Synthetic Script-Switching

We took a similar approach as Wong et al. (2023) to produce synthetic samples of script-switched language data for domain adaptation. We define synthetic as machine-generated texts. Due to the limited availability of observations for some language conditions, our main source of human-generated texts come from the Leipzig Corpus Collection (Goldhahn et al., 2012). Each corpus contained 10,000 Wikipedia abstracts produced in 2016 with the exception of TCY which was produced in 2018.

We then randomly sampled half of the abstracts from each language condition (excluding the Latin-based ENG and ESP) and used the ai4bharat[3] Python library to transliterate the relevant Brahmic orthographies into Latin script. Once we produced a subset of synthetically script-switched Wikipedia abstracts, we combined the original abstracts with the synthetically script-switched abstracts. Finally, we combined the labelled training data to create train and evaluation sets. The inclusion of the labelled training data is to ensure register-specific domain adaptation.

2.1.2 Organic Script-Switching

The second form of script-switched language data for domain adaptation involve organic samples of script-switched language data. We define organic as human-generated texts. This proved to be a challenge as we were unable to identify sources of script-switched social media language data for some of the under-resourced language conditions.

We used the pre-existing labelled training data to produce language profiles to develop a language identification model with the langdetect[4] These language profiles were used to detect organic instances of script-switched social media data from the Global Corpus of Language Use (CGLU; Dunn, 2020). This produced a train set with 230,000 observations and an evaluation set with 12,000 observations which we could use for domain adaptation.

2.2 Classification Model

As discussed in Section 2.1, we developed our multiclass classification models using the candidate language models during the domain adaptation phase. The three candidate languages models are: the baseline XLM-ROBERTA language model (BASELINE), XLM-ROBERTA retrained with synthetic samples of script-switched language data (SYNTHETIC), and XLM-ROBERTA retrained with organic samples of script-switched language data (ORGANIC).

We resampled the available data to create our own train (80%), validation (10%), and test (10%) sets to avoid over-fitting on the validation set during model evaluation. We trained language specific classification models (*mono*) and an ensemble multilingual classification model (*multi*) by combining the labelled training data. We trained the multiclass classification model using the simpletransformers Python package for four iterations and we evaluated the training for every 500 steps with AdamW optimisation (Loshchilov and Hutter, 2019). The model performance was based on evaluation loss.

[3]https://pypi.org/project/ai4bharat-transliteration/

[4]https://pypi.org/project/langdetect/

	CANTNLP	Best Performance
ENG	0.323	*0.496*
ESP	0.496	*0.582*
GUJ	0.962	*0.968*
HIN	0.326	*0.458*
KAN	0.943	*0.948*
MAL	0.775	*0.942*
MAR	0.433	*0.626*
TAM	0.555	*0.880*
TCY	0.452	*0.707*
TEL	0.965	*0.971*

Table 3: The average Macro F_1 score of our classification system, and the average Macro F_1 score of the overall best performing classification system.

The model performance for each of the candidate models are shown in Table 2. We have indicated the best performing model based on average Macro F_1 score (highlighted in **bold**). In some language conditions, there were multiple best performing models. Not included in Table 2 are the combined average Macro F_1 score for the multilingual models: the average Macro F_1 for the BASELINE model was 0.89; both SYNTHETIC and ORGANIC models had an average Macro F_1 of 0.90.

3 Results

Based on the average Macro F_1 score of the candidate models as shown in Table 2, we nominated the language-specific synthetic classification model as the best performing classification system. We applied this classification system and submitted the results to the organisers. The results of our submitted homophobia/transphobia detection system are shown in Table 3. The best performing language condition was TEL with an average Macro F_1 of 0.97 and the worst performing language condition was ENG with an average Macro F_1 of 0.32.

Our final rank for each language conditions are as follows: for ENG we came tenth equal out of ten teams; for ESP we came fourth out of five teams; for GUJ we came second out of six teams; for HIN we came fourth equal out of seven teams; for KAN we came fourth out of eight teams; for MAL we came seventh out of nine teams; for MAR we came fifth out of six teams; for TAM we came fifth out of eight teams; for TCY we came third equal out of four teams; and finally for TEL we came second out of nine teams.[5]

4 Discussion

The use of synthetic and organic script-switched language data during domain adaptation increased the performance for all language conditions from the BASELINE model with the exception of ENG, HIN, and TCY. We expected the ENG and ESP language conditions to perform poorly with our proposed methodology as there were very few instances of script-switching, but the poor performance of TCY was unexpected.

We hypothesise the poor performance in TCY was due to the limited number of observation (as shown in Figure 1) the higher than expected usage of Latin-based script for TCY in the labelled training data (as shown in Figure 2). This will require robust statistical analysis beyond the scope of the current paper.

We also posit the poor performance of ENG and HIN was a result of the class imbalance between instances of homophobic, transphobic and the non-anti-LGBTQ+ content as demonstrated in Table 1. The performance of our ENG and HIN language-specific detection models are in line with other participating teams.

In contrast to the method proposed in Wong et al. (2023), we did not include any methods to counter the class imbalance in the training data nor did we include random noise injection to expand the minority classes. It was shown that random over sampling of minority classes did not significantly improve the performance of the detection models.

5 Conclusion

The main contribution of the current paper is the proposal to use synthetic and organic script-switching examples of during domain adaptation to improve the down-stream performance for under-resourced languages. We demonstrated that our methodology improved the model performance for GUJ, KAN, MAL, MAR, and TAM even though the improvement was only marginal. Even though our homophobia/transphobia detection system did not rank first for any of the ten language conditions, we were pleased with the performance of our detection system which supports the inclusion of paralinguistic information.

[5]Note the final rankings differ from the published results for ESP, TAM, and TEL as they were not included in the final rank list due to human error from the organising committee during submission.

Ethics Statement

The purpose of the current shared task is to develop a homophobic/transphobic language detection system in social media texts particularly for under-resourced Indo-Aryan and Dravidian languages within the fields of computational linguistics and natural language processing.

We recognise the importance of community-lead research in particular by members of under-represented and minoritised communities. The lead author acknowledges his positionality as a member of the LGBTQ+ community. The lead author is familiar with anti-LGBTQ+ discourse both in online and offline spaces and the harmful effects of hate speech and offensive language on members of the LGBTQ+ communities (Wong, 2023b).

In terms of the authors' linguistic membership, the authors share proficiency in ENG and ESP; however, the authors acknowledge their limited experience with GUJ, KAN, MAR, TAM, TCY, and TEL with some exposure to HIN and MAL. We acknowledge the limitations of our analysis in language conditions where we have limited proficiency and we will follow the guidance and expertise of members from the relevant language communities.

We want to thank the organisers of the shared task and the workshop on Language Technology for Equality, Diversity, and Inclusion. We also want to thank the contributors of the training data and those who were involved in the labelling process across the different language conditions.

Limitations

Under the purview of developing a homophobic/transphobic language detection system in social media texts, we want to highlight the limitations of our proposed system and methodology.

Firstly, we acknowledge there are differences in data quality and veracity between the different language conditions. This is based on the differences in the corpus size between the different language conditions (as shown in Figure 1) and the distribution of homophobic and transphobic content.

In light of these data quality issues, we have not accounted for these differences between language conditions. This means we do not entirely understand the downstream impacts on model performance - although it is clear that there is a possible relationship between larger and more balanced language conditions (TEL) performing better than smaller and more imbalanced language conditions (TCY). It is possible these differences could exacerbate biases already observed in transformer-based language models (Bhardwaj et al., 2021).

Beyond the upstream and downstream impacts of bias in transformer-based language models, we also recognised that incorporating external data sets from LCC (Goldhahn et al., 2012) and the CGLU (Dunn, 2020) introduces additional biases not properly addressed in this paper such as geographic bias in social media language data (Wong et al., 2022).

Secondly, there is a need to conduct this form of research under a sociolinguistic or linguistic anthropological framework. There is a risk that training data detecting homophobia, transphobia, hate speech, or offensive may not necessarily reflect the social, political, or linguistic realities of different populations. This is because some of the features extracted from the labelled training data may not reflect real-world knowledge.

These differences are particularly evident when we apply these detection systems across dialect contexts (Wong, 2023a). For this reason, we propose that future work in this area should also consider how these systems perform in real-world context beyond the evaluation of labelled training data. We should work alongside members of LGBTQ+ communities from culturally and linguistically diverse backgrounds to understand the effectiveness and generalisability of our homophobic/transphobic detection systems.

References

Rishabh Bhardwaj, Navonil Majumder, and Soujanya Poria. 2021. Investigating Gender Bias in BERT. *Cognitive Computation*, 13(4):1008–1018.

Bharathi Raja Chakravarthi, Rahul Ponnusamy, Malliga S, Paul Buitelaar, Miguel Ángel García-Cumbreras, Salud María Jiménez-Zafra, Jose Antonio García-Díaz, Rafael Valencia-García, and Nitesh Jindal. 2023. Overview of Second Shared Task on Homophobia and Transphobia Detection in Social Media Comments. In *Proceedings of the Third Workshop on Language Technology for Equality, Diversity and Inclusion*, pages 38–46, Varna, Bulgaria. INCOMA Ltd., Shoumen, Bulgaria.

Bharathi Raja Chakravarthi, Ruba Priyadharshini, Thenmozhi Durairaj, John McCrae, Paul Buitelaar, Prasanna Kumaresan, and Rahul Ponnusamy. 2022. Overview of The Shared Task on Homophobia and Transphobia Detection in Social Media Comments. In *Proceedings of the Second Workshop on Language Technology for Equality, Diversity and Inclusion*, pages 369–377, Dublin, Ireland. Association for Computational Linguistics.

Bharathi Raja Chakravarthi, Ruba Priyadharshini, Rahul Ponnusamy, Prasanna Kumar Kumaresan, Kayalvizhi Sampath, Durairaj Thenmozhi, Sathiyaraj Thangasamy, Rajendran Nallathambi, and John Phillip McCrae. 2021. Dataset for Identification of Homophobia and Transophobia in Multilingual YouTube Comments. ArXiv:2109.00227 [cs].

Alexis Conneau, Kartikay Khandelwal, Naman Goyal, Vishrav Chaudhary, Guillaume Wenzek, Francisco Guzmán, Edouard Grave, Myle Ott, Luke Zettlemoyer, and Veselin Stoyanov. 2020. Unsupervised Cross-lingual Representation Learning at Scale. In *Proceedings of the 58th Annual Meeting of the Association for Computational Linguistics*, pages 8440–8451, Online. Association for Computational Linguistics.

Jacob Devlin, Ming-Wei Chang, Kenton Lee, and Kristina Toutanova. 2019. BERT: Pre-training of Deep Bidirectional Transformers for Language Understanding. ArXiv:1810.04805 [cs].

Jonathan Dunn. 2020. Mapping languages: the Corpus of Global Language Use. *Language Resources and Evaluation*, 54(4):999–1018.

José Antonio García-Díaz, Ángela Almela, Gema Alcaraz-Mármol, and Rafael Valencia-García. 2020. UMUCorpusClassifier: Compilation and evaluation of linguistic corpus for Natural Language Processing tasks. *Procesamiento del Lenguaje Natural*, 65(0):139–142.

Dirk Goldhahn, Thomas Eckart, and Uwe Quasthoff. 2012. Building Large Monolingual Dictionaries at the Leipzig Corpora Collection: From 100 to 200 Languages. In *Proceedings of the Eighth International Conference on Language Resources and Evaluation (LREC'12)*, pages 759–765, Istanbul, Turkey. European Language Resources Association (ELRA).

Prasanna Kumar Kumaresan, Rahul Ponnusamy, Ruba Priyadharshini, Paul Buitelaar, and Bharathi Raja Chakravarthi. 2023. Homophobia and transphobia detection for low-resourced languages in social media comments. *Natural Language Processing Journal*, 5:100041.

Prasanna Kumar Kumaresan, Ruba Priyadharshini, Bharathi Raja Chakravarthi, Paul Buitelaar, Asha Hegde, Hosahalli Lakshmaiah Shashirekha, Saranya Rajiakodi, Miguel Ángel García-Cumbreras, Salud María Jiménez-Zafra, José Antonio García-Díaz, Rafael Valencia-García, Kishore Kumar Ponnusamy, Poorvi Shetty, and Daniel García-Baena. 2024. Overview of Third Shared Task on Homophobia and Transphobia Detection in Social Media Comments. In *Proceedings of the Fourth Workshop on Language Technology for Equality, Diversity and Inclusion*, Malta. European Chapter of the Association for Computational Linguistics.

Yinhan Liu, Myle Ott, Naman Goyal, Jingfei Du, Mandar Joshi, Danqi Chen, Omer Levy, Mike Lewis, Luke Zettlemoyer, and Veselin Stoyanov. 2019. RoBERTa: A Robustly Optimized BERT Pretraining Approach. ArXiv:1907.11692 [cs].

Ilya Loshchilov and Frank Hutter. 2019. Decoupled Weight Decay Regularization. ArXiv:1711.05101 [cs, math].

Abulimiti Maimaitituoheti, Yong Yang, and Xiaochao Fan. 2022. ABLIMET @LT-EDI-ACL2022: A Roberta based Approach for Homophobia/Transphobia Detection in Social Media. In *Proceedings of the Second Workshop on Language Technology for Equality, Diversity and Inclusion*, pages 155–160, Dublin, Ireland. Association for Computational Linguistics.

Dean Ninalga. 2023. Cordyceps@LT-EDI: Patching Language-Specific Homophobia/Transphobia Classifiers with a Multilingual Understanding. In *Proceedings of the Third Workshop on Language Technology for Equality, Diversity and Inclusion*, pages 185–191, Varna, Bulgaria. INCOMA Ltd., Shoumen, Bulgaria.

Sidney Wong, Jonathan Dunn, and Benjamin Adams. 2022. Comparing Measures of Linguistic Diversity Across Social Media Language Data and Census Data at Subnational Geographic Areas. *Proceedings in New Zealand Geospatial Research Conference*.

Sidney Wong, Matthew Durward, Benjamin Adams, and Jonathan Dunn. 2023. cantnlp@LT-EDI-2023: Homophobia/Transphobia Detection in Social Media Comments using Spatio-Temporally Retrained Language Models. In *Proceedings of the Third Workshop on Language Technology for Equality, Diversity and Inclusion*, pages 103–108, Varna, Bulgaria. INCOMA Ltd., Shoumen, Bulgaria.

Sidney Gig-Jan Wong. 2023a. Monitoring Hate Speech and Offensive Language on Social Media. In *Fourth Spatial Data Science Symposium*, University of Canterbury.

Sidney Gig-Jan Wong. 2023b. *Queer Asian Identities in Contemporary Aotearoa New Zealand: One Foot Out of the Closet*. Lived Places Publishing.

Lidoma@LT-EDI 2024:Tamil Hate Speech Detection in Migration Discourse

M. Shahiki Tash, Z. Ahani, M. T. Zamir, O. Kolesnikova and **G. Sidorov**
Instituto Politécnico Nacional (IPN), Centro de Investigación en Computación (CIC)
Corresponding: mshahikit2022@cic.ipn.mx

Abstract

The exponential rise in social media users has revolutionized information accessibility and exchange. While these platforms serve various purposes, they also harbor negative elements, including hate speech and offensive behavior. Detecting hate speech in diverse languages has garnered significant attention in Natural Language Processing (NLP). This paper delves into hate speech detection in Tamil, particularly related to migration and refuge, contributing to the Caste/migration hate speech detection shared task. Employing a Convolutional Neural Network (CNN), our model achieved an F1 score of 0.76 in identifying hate speech and signaling potential in the domain despite encountering complexities. We provide an overview of related research, methodology, and insights into the competition's diverse performances, showcasing the landscape of hate speech detection nuances in the Tamil language.

1 Introduction

The surge in Social Media platform users has led to a significant increase in information dissemination, granting immediate access to updated information with just a click. These platforms are used not only for social interaction but also for leisure and information retrieval (Sajjad et al., 2019; Ali et al., 2022a). There has been a notable surge in interest in social media analysis tasks within NLP (Bade, 2021), With a focus on emerging fields like identifying hopeful speech, there is a growing emphasis on advancing in this direction. (Yigezu et al., 2023a; Shahiki-Tash et al., 2023b) language identification (Tash et al., 2022; Balouchzahi et al., 2022a), fake news(Fazlourrahman et al., 2022), sentiment analysis (Tash et al., 2023; Yigezu et al., 2023b), and hate speech(Yigezu et al., 2023c) that researchers experimented with diverse models, including deep learning (Yigezu et al., 2022; Ahani et al., 2024), transformers (Tonja et al., 2022), and traditional machine learning techniques (Kanta and Sidorov, 2023).

However, along with its advantages, the widespread adoption of Social Media (Bade and Afaro, 2018) also brings negative aspects (Ali et al., 2022b). Users sometimes exhibit behavior that can be harmful, offensive, and even hateful toward various segments of society (Shahiki-Tash et al., 2023a).

Describing hate speech is complex, as Andrew Sellars argues against oversimplification of its definition and addressing methods (Sellars, 2016). There's disagreement regarding how hate speech refers to groups, with certain definitions associating it with minority groups or specific characteristics like race, religion, gender, or sexual orientation (Waltman and Mattheis, 2017).

This challenge has led to several shared tasks focused on detecting hate speech. In this context, our article centers on the analysis of Tamil user comments about migration and refuge using qualitative content analysis. As part of this effort, we participated in the Caste/migration hate speech detection shared task (Rajiakodi et al., 2024), which aims to develop models capable of identifying hate speech related to caste or migration.

The objective of this task is to create an automated classification system that predicts whether text, particularly on social media, contains caste/migration-related hate speech. We employed a CNN model for prediction, leveraging its successful track record in text classification within the literature. (Balouchzahi et al., 2023b,a). our proposed model obtained an F1 score of 0.76, yielding promising performance on the task of binary hate speech detection.

2 Related work

Motivated by the linguistic diversity across India, where languages like Tamil, Telugu, Kannada,

Proceedings of the Fourth Workshop on Language Technology for Equality, Diversity, Inclusion, pages 184–189
March 21, 2024 ©2024 Association for Computational Linguistics

Malayalam, Hindi, Punjabi, Bengali, Gujarati, Marathi, among others, are prevalent, researchers observed the limitations of models confined to English proficiency (Chakravarthi et al., 2020b). This prompted the development of a system capable of processing code-mixed languages for sentiment analysis. A significant hurdle in this endeavor has been the scarcity of labeled datasets. Notably, a few manually annotated datasets for offensive language and hate speech detection in Tamil (Chakravarthi et al., 2020b), Malayalam (Chakravarthi et al., 2020a), and Kannada (Hande et al., 2021) have been released, marking crucial contributions to the field. The study (Sánchez-Holgado et al., 2022) aimed to assess the relationship between online hate speech against migrants and refugees and social acceptance in Spain. Using Intergroup Contact and Mediated Intergroup Contact Theory, the research sought to validate hate speech as an indicator of social acceptance across Spanish provinces. Analyzing 97,710 tweets and secondary public data on migration, the study found no significant correlation between hate speech, foreign population proportions, and citizen attitudes toward immigrants. Despite fluctuations in hate speech presence from 2015 to 2020, no clear negative correlation emerged between foreign population proportions and hate speech on Twitter. Similarly, the anticipated negative correlation between attitudes toward migration and hate speech on Twitter could not be statistically confirmed.

The paper (Sanguinetti et al., 2018) outlines the development of a novel Twitter corpus comprising roughly 6,000 tweets annotated for hate speech targeting immigrants. This corpus aimed to serve as a reference dataset for monitoring hate speech through automated systems. The annotation scheme was meticulously crafted to encompass various factors influencing hate speech, resulting in a tagset beyond hate speech alone, including aggressiveness, offensiveness, irony, stereotype, and experimental intensity categories. While discussing the annotated data, the study focuses on hate speech intensity and its interrelation with stereotype, aggressiveness, and offensiveness. The findings indicate nuanced trends, showcasing implicit incitement in most hateful tweets. Stereotype prevalence is notably high in lower intensity degrees, indicating its role in implicit incitement.

The study (Anbukkarasi and Varadhaganapathy, 2022) achieved notable success in hate speech detection within code-mixed Tamil-English tweets using a synonym-based Bi-LSTM model. With an F1 score of 0.8169, the Bi-LSTM model outperformed other models evaluated, demonstrating its effectiveness in distinguishing hate and non-hate texts. Specifically, in classifying hate speech, the model attained an F1 score of 0.8110, while for non-hate texts, it achieved an F1 score of 0.8050

This study (Basava and Karri, 2021) tackles the pervasive issue of hate speech proliferation across social media platforms by introducing an ensemble system utilizing transformer models. Specifically, it aims to identify offensive language within code-mixed posts/comments in Dravidian Languages (Malayalam-English and Tamil-English). Situated within the framework of the Hate Speech and Offensive Content Identification in Dravidian-CodeMix (HASOC) (Chakravarthi et al., 2021) initiative, this research emphasizes the rising impact of hate speech online and the urgent need for robust detection methods. The ensemble method showcased promising performance during development, notably achieving scores of 0.93 for Tamil and 0.80 for Malayalam, utilizing the model HSU_TransEmb. However, when assessed on the test set, the performance declined, registering 0.66 for Tamil with the MuRIL model and 0.73 for Malayalam using HSU_TransEmb, indicating the necessity for more comprehensive datasets to enhance model robustness and efficacy in tackling hate speech in multilingual social media settings. (Jayanthi and Gupta, 2021) applied transformer-based models, utilizing a cased version of multilingual BERT and XLM-RoBERTa. Employing BERT at the sentence level, they transformed sub-word-level representations into word-level representations by averaging sub-token representations for improved classification. This innovative fusion architecture integrated a Bidirectional LSTM model to capture diverse word patterns, enhancing classification accuracy, and resulting in a 79.67% accuracy in classifying Tamil tweets.

3 Methodology

Convolutional Neural Networks (CNNs) excel in text classification tasks by utilizing convolutional and pooling layers to extract hierarchical features from sequential data, such as text (Balouchzahi et al., 2022b). These networks employ convolutional filters of varying sizes to detect n-gram features within the input text, followed by pooling layers that condense and aggregate the extracted features. By learning local relationships between words and capturing essential patterns, CNNs effectively discern hate speech or offensive language within textual data. Their ability to model intricate relationships within text makes CNNs a potent tool in the realm of hate speech detection.

3.1 Dataset

The dataset (Chakravarthi, 2020, 2022) is formatted in CSV (Comma-Separated Value), featuring columns labeled "Text" and "Tag". The "Text" column contains the textual content, while the "Tag" column signifies whether a comment is categorized as caste/migration hate speech, indicated by values: 1 for caste/migration hate speech and 0 for non-caste/migration hate speech (Chakravarthi et al., 2022).

The exemplification of the dataset structure is illustrated in Table 1.

Table 1: Tamil comments and their labels

Text	Tag
Ippadiye solli tamilanai izhivu paduthuvathey indha sangi kumbal, dhaanda, tamilians are getting educated, they want better life, mostly looking for decent job.	0
Freedom app eh. Bunda Advertisement Vera ya	1
Like this one day all these North Indias are going to chase every Tamilians from Tamilian Nadu. This is very dangerous. Need to probe into this and I request that all the Tamil people not to give these North Indians any accommodation. We need to save our Rights and control North Indians heavy migration. These people are hooligans.	1
it's nothing wrong people travel to earn money but in same time native people also need work hard for better life...lucky Brother you know hindi to communicate to Vadakans...Nice review	0

3.2 Classification algorithm

The classification algorithm we've designed encompasses several sequential steps, each contributing to the overall process. Below, we'll elaborate on these stages to provide a comprehensive understanding of our classification methodology.

3.3 Cleaning Data

The initial part of the code involves data cleaning functions like "remove_emoji", "remove_url", and "clean_text". These functions are applied to both the training and test datasets to eliminate emojis, URLs, special characters, and punctuation from the text. It ensures that the text is sanitized for further processing and analysis.

3.4 Padding

Tokenizer and padding functions from Keras are employed to convert text data into sequences of integers and ensure uniform sequence length. The "Tokenizer" converts text to numerical sequences, and "pad_sequences" ensures uniform length for modeling purposes, enhancing compatibility with neural network layers.

3.5 Label Encoding

Label encoding is performed using "LabelEncoder" from Scikit-learn to convert categorical labels into numerical format, preparing them for model training. Additionally, one-hot encoding ("tf.keras.utils.to_categorical") is applied to represent categorical labels as binary vectors.

3.6 Model Architecture

The neural network architecture comprises several layers: an embedding layer, a 1D convolutional layer ("Conv1D"), global max pooling, dropout, and a dense layer. Regularization techniques like L2 regularization are employed to prevent overfitting. The model summary provides a detailed overview of the architecture, including layer types, output shapes, and parameters.

3.7 Model Compilation and Training

The model is compiled using a categorical cross-entropy loss function and the Nadam optimizer. The code then trains the model using the training dataset ("train_ds") for 50 epochs, with validation performed on the validation dataset ("valid_ds"). Training history is recorded to monitor model performance and convergence.

3.8 Model Evaluation and Prediction

After training, the model is utilized to generate predictions on the test data ("x_test"), providing insights into the model's performance on unseen data. Additionally, metrics like classification reports or confusion matrices were derived to evaluate model performance comprehensively.

4 Results

The competition observed diverse performances in the detection of hate speech in the Tamil language. Prominent teams securing positions 1-3 demonstrated commendable M_F1 scores ranging from 0.82 to 0.80, indicating the effectiveness of their strategies. In contrast, the bottom-ranking teams (15-16) encountered challenges, attaining lower scores of 0.49 and 0.38, respectively. The 6th position achieved by our team, with an M_F1 score of 0.76, underscores the complexities involved in addressing nuances of hate speech in Tamil. Although our approach exhibited competence, the competitive environment and intricate nature of the task underscore the necessity for further refinement in areas such as data handling, feature engineering, and model fine-tuning. A detailed presentation of the results is available in Table 2.

Table 2: Performance Rankings of Hate Speech Detection Models in Tamil Language

Team name	M_F1	Rank
Transformers - Kriti Singhal	0.82	1
kubapok - Jakub Pokrywka	0.81	2
CUET_NLP_Manning	0.80	3
BITS_Graph4NLP	0.77	4
Algorithmalliance	0.76	5
lidoma - Moein Tash	0.76	6
CUET_NLP_GoodFellows	0.75	7
quartet - shaun Allan	0.73	8
KEC_AI_DSNLP_	0.65	9
selam - Selam Abitte	0.62	10
byteSizedllm	0.61	11
SSN-nova - Ankitha Reddy	0.59	12
WordWizards_tamil	0.54	13
KEC_DL_KSK - Kalaivani K.S.	0.49	14
Habesha - mesay gemeda	0.38	15

5 limitations

1. The study encounters a limitation stemming from the absence of hyperparameter tuning in the experimental setup. Optimal hyperparameter configurations are crucial in fine-tuning the performance of machine learning models, and their absence in our experiments could impact the overall effectiveness of our approach.

2. Another constraint in our methodology lies in the omission of experiments specifically designed to address the challenge of imbalanced datasets. Hate speech detection tasks often contend with imbalances between the number of instances belonging to different classes. Strategies such as oversampling, undersampling, or utilizing specialized algorithms for imbalanced datasets could be explored to enhance the model's ability to handle such data distribution challenges.

3. Our study is also constrained by the lack of incorporation of any feature selection techniques. Feature selection plays a vital role in enhancing model interpretability, reducing computational complexity, and potentially improving predictive performance. Future iterations of our methodology could benefit from the integration of feature selection methods to identify and retain the most informative features.

4. An additional limitation is the absence of any ensemble model in our experimental framework. Ensemble models, which combine predictions from multiple models, often contribute to improved generalization and robustness. Integrating ensemble techniques, such as bagging or boosting, could offer a more comprehensive and resilient hate speech detection system. This represents an avenue for future research to explore and enhance the overall performance of our approach.

6 Conclusion

This research delves into the realm of hate speech detection in Tamil, with a particular emphasis on themes related to migration and refuge within the framework of the Caste/migration hate speech detection shared task. Leveraging a Convolutional Neural Network (CNN), our model exhibited a commendable F1 score of 0.76, demonstrating its efficacy in identifying hate speech amidst inherent complexities. The analysis sheds light on the competitive landscape, uncovering diverse performances across teams with scores ranging from 0.38 to 0.82. These variations underscore the challenges inherent in addressing hate speech nuances in the Tamil language. As part of our future endeavors, we intend to enhance our approach by expanding our dataset and incorporating transformer models, aiming to further improve the accuracy of hate speech detection in this linguistic context.

Ethics Statement

We affirm our commitment to ethical research practices and compliance with ACL guidelines in conducting and presenting our study. No ethical concerns or conflicts of interest arose during the course of this research.

Acknowledgments

The work was done with partial support from the Mexican Government through the grant A1-S-47854 of CONACYT, Mexico, grants 20241816, 20241819, and 20240951 of the Secretaría de Investigación y Posgrado of the Instituto Politécnico Nacional, Mexico. The authors thank the CONACYT for the computing resources brought to them through the Plataforma de Aprendizaje Profundo para Tecnologías del Lenguaje of the Laboratorio de Supercómputo of the INAOE, Mexico and acknowledge the support of Microsoft through the Microsoft Latin America PhD Award.

References

Zahra Ahani, Moein Shahiki Tash, Yoel Ledo Mezquita, and Jason Angel. 2024. Utilizing deep learning models for the identification of enhancers and super-enhancers based on genomic and epigenomic features. *arXiv preprint arXiv:2401.07470.*

Raza Ali, Umar Farooq, Umair Arshad, Waseem Shahzad, and Mirza Omer Beg. 2022a. Hate speech detection on twitter using transfer learning. *Computer Speech Language*, 74:101365.

Raza Ali, Umar Farooq, Umair Arshad, Waseem Shahzad, and Mirza Omer Beg. 2022b. Hate speech detection on twitter using transfer learning. *Computer Speech & Language*, 74:101365.

S Anbukkarasi and S Varadhaganapathy. 2022. Deep learning-based hate speech detection in code-mixed tamil text. *IETE Journal of Research*, pages 1–6.

Girma Yohannis Bade. 2021. Natural language processing and its challenges on omotic language group of ethiopia. *Journal of Computer Science Research*, 3(4):26–30.

Girma Yohannis Bade and Akalu Assefa Afaro. 2018. Object oriented software development for artificial intelligence. *American Journal of Software Engineering and Applications*, 7(2):22–24.

Fazlourrahman Balouchzahi, Sabur Butt, A Hegde, Noman Ashraf, HL Shashirekha, Grigori Sidorov, and Alexander Gelbukh. 2022a. Overview of colikanglish: Word level language identification in code-mixed kannada-english texts at icon 2022. In *Proceedings of the 19th International Conference on Natural Language Processing (ICON): Shared Task on Word Level Language Identification in Code-mixed Kannada-English Texts*, pages 38–45.

Fazlourrahman Balouchzahi, Sabur Butt, Grigori Sidorov, and Alexander Gelbukh. 2023a. Reddit: Regret detection and domain identification from text. *Expert Systems with Applications*, 225:120099.

Fazlourrahman Balouchzahi, Anusha Gowda, Hosahalli Shashirekha, and Grigori Sidorov. 2022b. Mucic@ tamilnlp-acl2022: Abusive comment detection in tamil language using 1d conv-lstm. In *Proceedings of the Second Workshop on Speech and Language Technologies for Dravidian Languages*, pages 64–69.

Fazlourrahman Balouchzahi, Grigori Sidorov, and Alexander Gelbukh. 2023b. Polyhope: Two-level hope speech detection from tweets. *Expert Systems with Applications*, 225:120078.

Sai Naga Viswa Chaitanya Basava and Anjali Poornima Karri. 2021. Transformer ensemble system for detection of offensive content in dravidian languages. In *Working Notes of FIRE 2021-Forum for Information Retrieval Evaluation (Online). CEUR.*

Bharathi Raja Chakravarthi. 2020. HopeEDI: A multilingual hope speech detection dataset for equality, diversity, and inclusion. In *Proceedings of the Third Workshop on Computational Modeling of People's Opinions, Personality, and Emotion's in Social Media*, pages 41–53, Barcelona, Spain (Online). Association for Computational Linguistics.

Bharathi Raja Chakravarthi. 2022. Hope speech detection in youtube comments. *Social Network Analysis and Mining*, 12(1):75.

Bharathi Raja Chakravarthi, Anand Kumar M, John P McCrae, B Premjith, KP Soman, and Thomas Mandl. 2020a. Overview of the track on hasoc-offensive language identification-dravidiancodemix. In *FIRE (Working notes)*, pages 112–120.

Bharathi Raja Chakravarthi, Vigneshwaran Muralidaran, Ruba Priyadharshini, Subalalitha Cn, John McCrae, Miguel Ángel García, Salud María Jiménez-Zafra, Rafael Valencia-García, Prasanna Kumaresan, Rahul Ponnusamy, Daniel García-Baena, and José García-Díaz. 2022. Overview of the shared task on hope speech detection for equality, diversity, and inclusion. In *Proceedings of the Second Workshop on Language Technology for Equality, Diversity and Inclusion*, pages 378–388, Dublin, Ireland. Association for Computational Linguistics.

Bharathi Raja Chakravarthi, Vigneshwaran Muralidaran, Ruba Priyadharshini, and John P McCrae. 2020b. Corpus creation for sentiment analysis in code-mixed tamil-english text. *arXiv preprint arXiv:2006.00206*.

BR Chakravarthi, PK Kumaresan, R Sakuntharaj, AK Madasamy, S Thavareesan, S Chinnaudayar Navaneethakrishnan, and T Mandl. 2021. Overview of the hasoc-dravidiancodemix shared task on offensive language detection in tamil and malayalam. In *Working Notes of FIRE 2021-Forum for Information Retrieval Evaluation*. CEUR.

B Fazlourrahman, BK Aparna, and HL Shashirekha. 2022. Coffitt-covid-19 fake news detection using fine-tuned transfer learning approaches. In *Congress on Intelligent Systems: Proceedings of CIS 2021, Volume 2*, pages 879–890. Springer.

Adeep Hande, Siddhanth U Hegde, Ruba Priyadharshini, Rahul Ponnusamy, Prasanna Kumar Kumaresan, Sajeetha Thavareesan, and Bharathi Raja Chakravarthi. 2021. Benchmarking multi-task learning for sentiment analysis and offensive language identification in under-resourced dravidian languages. *arXiv preprint arXiv:2108.03867*.

Sai Muralidhar Jayanthi and Akshat Gupta. 2021. Sj_aj@ dravidianlangtech-eacl2021: Task-adaptive pre-training of multilingual bert models for offensive language identification. *arXiv preprint arXiv:2102.01051*.

Selam Kanta and Grigori Sidorov. 2023. Selam@ dravidianlangtech: Sentiment analysis of code-mixed dravidian texts using svm classification. In *Proceedings of the Third Workshop on Speech and Language Technologies for Dravidian Languages*, pages 176–179.

Saranya Rajiakodi, Bharathi Raja Chakravarthi, Rahul Ponnusamy, Prasanna Kumar Kumaresan, Sathiyaraj Thangasamy, Bhuvaneswari Sivagnanam, and Charmathi Rajkumar. 2024. Overview of Shared Task on Caste and Migration Hate Speech Detection. In *Proceedings of the Fourth Workshop on Language Technology for Equality, Diversity and Inclusion*, Malta. European Chapter of the Association for Computational Linguistics.

Muhammad Sajjad, Fatima Zulifqar, Muhammad Usman Ghani Khan, and Muhammad Azeem. 2019. Hate speech detection using fusion approach. In *2019 International Conference on Applied and Engineering Mathematics (ICAEM)*, pages 251–255. IEEE.

Patricia Sánchez-Holgado, Javier J Amores, and David Blanco-Herrero. 2022. Online hate speech and immigration acceptance: A study of spanish provinces. *Social sciences*, 11(11):515.

Manuela Sanguinetti, Fabio Poletto, Cristina Bosco, Viviana Patti, and Marco Stranisci. 2018. An italian twitter corpus of hate speech against immigrants. In *Proceedings of the eleventh international conference on language resources and evaluation (LREC 2018)*.

AF Sellars. 2016. Defining hate speech (research publication no. 2016–20). *Cambridge, MA: Berkman Klein Center*.

Moein Shahiki-Tash, Jesús Armenta-Segura, Zahra Ahani, Olga Kolesnikova, Grigori Sidorov, and Alexander Gelbukh. 2023a. Lidoma at homomex2023@ iberlef: Hate speech detection towards the mexican spanish-speaking lgbt+ population. the importance of preprocessing before using bert-based models. In *Proceedings of the Iberian Languages Evaluation Forum (IberLEF 2023)*.

Moein Shahiki-Tash, Jesús Armenta-Segura, Olga Kolesnikova, Grigori Sidorov, and Alexander Gelbukh. 2023b. Lidoma at hope2023iberlef: Hope speech detection using lexical features and convolutional neural networks. In *Proceedings of the Iberian Languages Evaluation Forum (IberLEF 2023), co-located with the 39th Conference of the Spanish Society for Natural Language Processing (SEPLN 2023), CEUR-WS. org*.

M Shahiki Tash, Z Ahani, Al Tonja, M Gemeda, N Hussain, and O Kolesnikova. 2022. Word level language identification in code-mixed kannada-english texts using traditional machine learning algorithms. In *Proceedings of the 19th International Conference on Natural Language Processing (ICON): Shared Task on Word Level Language Identification in Code-mixed Kannada-English Texts*, pages 25–28.

Moein Tash, Jesus Armenta-Segura, Zahra Ahani, Olga Kolesnikova, Grigori Sidorov, and Alexander Gelbukh. 2023. Lidoma@ dravidianlangtech: Convolutional neural networks for studying correlation between lexical features and sentiment polarity in tamil and tulu languages. In *Proceedings of the Third Workshop on Speech and Language Technologies for Dravidian Languages*, pages 180–185.

Atnafu Lambebo Tonja, Mesay Gemeda Yigezu, Olga Kolesnikova, Moein Shahiki Tash, Grigori Sidorov, and Alexander Gelbuk. 2022. Transformer-based model for word level language identification in code-mixed kannada-english texts. *arXiv preprint arXiv:2211.14459*.

Michael S Waltman and Ashely A Mattheis. 2017. Understanding hate speech. In *Oxford research encyclopedia of communication*.

Mesay Gemeda Yigezu, Girma Yohannis Bade, Olga Kolesnikova, Grigori Sidorov, and Alexander Gelbukh. 2023a. Multilingual hope speech detection using machine learning.

Mesay Gemeda Yigezu, Tadesse Kebede, Olga Kolesnikova, Grigori Sidorov, and Alexander Gelbukh. 2023b. Habesha@ dravidianlangtech: Utilizing deep and transfer learning approaches for sentiment analysis. In *Proceedings of the Third Workshop on Speech and Language Technologies for Dravidian Languages*, pages 239–243.

Mesay Gemeda Yigezu, Olga Kolesnikova, Grigori Sidorov, and Alexander Gelbukh. 2023c. Transformer-based hate speech detection for multi-class and multi-label classification.

Mesay Gemeda Yigezu, Atnafu Lambebo Tonja, Olga Kolesnikova, Moein Shahiki Tash, Grigori Sidorov, and Alexander Gelbukh. 2022. Word level language identification in code-mixed kannada-english texts using deep learning approach. In *Proceedings of the 19th International Conference on Natural Language Processing (ICON): Shared Task on Word Level Language Identification in Code-mixed Kannada-English Texts*, pages 29–33.

CEN_Amrita@LT-EDI 2024: A Transformer based Speech Recognition System for Vulnerable Individuals in Tamil

Jairam R[1,2], Jyothish Lal G[1], Premjith B[1], and Viswa M[2]
[1]Amrita School of Artificial Intelligence, Amrita Vishwa Vidyapeetham, Coimbatore, India.
[2]RBG AI Research, RBG.AI, SREC Incubation Center, Coimbatore, India.
g_jyothishlal@cb.amrita.edu

Abstract

Speech recognition is known to be a specialized application of speech processing. Automatic speech recognition (ASR) systems are designed to perform the speech-to-text task. Although ASR systems have been the subject of extensive research, they still encounter certain challenges when speech variations arise. The speaker's age, gender, vulnerability, and other factors are the main causes of the variations in speech. In this work, we propose a fine-tuned speech recognition model for recognising the spoken words of vulnerable individuals in Tamil. This research utilizes a dataset sourced from the LT-EDI@EACL2024 shared task. We trained and tested pre-trained ASR models, including XLS-R and Whisper. The findings highlight that the fine-tuned Whisper ASR model surpasses the XLS-R, achieving a word error rate (WER) of **24.452**, signifying its superior performance in recognizing speech from diverse individuals.

Keywords : Dravidian Languages, Tamil, Speech Recognition, Vulnerable Speech, Transformer, Word Error Rate (WER)

1 Introduction

Speech is the most prevalent, clear, and frequently used form of worldwide communication. Speech processing involves obtaining valuable information from voice signals, such as automatic speech recognition (ASR) (Gaikwad et al., 2010). The goal of any ASR system is to teach computers to understand human speech and carry out user-defined tasks. The method of recognizing spoken words from audio input by applying auditory features is known as speech recognition. The majority of voice recognition algorithms have been trained on languages with abundant resources, like English, German, Spanish, and so on. With languages with few resources, such as Tamil, Kannada, Malayalam, etc., this is not the case. Despite being one of the most investigated fields among researchers, speech recognition systems still face issues when it comes to the conventional learning paradigm (Li et al., 2022), which can be utilized for both resource-rich and resource-poor languages. This is still one of the most unresolved challenges among the researchers (Nassif et al., 2019). The fundamental reason for this is the various natures of speech, often known as speech variants.

Speech recognition systems face a challenge when it comes to recognizing variances in speech. These variations are caused by factors such as the speaker's age, gender, and vulnerability (Kita, 2020) and etc. There have been a number of studies (Bharathi et al., 2022; Shivakumar et al., 2016; Shraddha et al., 2022; Murali Krishna et al., 2019; Bharathi et al., 2023) that have studied various methods to address these issues. These methods include the development of corpora and the fine-tuning of pre-trained models, particularly for languages that have limited resources.

In response, the LT-EDI team gathered a tagged Tamil speech corpus from elderly and transgender vulnerable individuals who had everyday conversations in administrative offices, banks, and hospitals. Some of these individuals were also vulnerable. Therefore, the vulnerability of the speaker is the primary focus. We propose modifying the Whisper Automatic Speech Recognition (ASR) model (Radford et al., 2023) in order to improve speech recognition for those who are vulnerable. In preparation for the work that the LT-EDI team is doing on voice recognition for the Tamil-language shared initiative, we fine-tuned the pre-trained Whisper model by using Tamil datasets. With a word error rate (WER) of

Proceedings of the Fourth Workshop on Language Technology for Equality, Diversity, Inclusion, pages 190–195
March 21, 2024 ©2024 Association for Computational Linguistics

24.452, the '*CEN_Amrita*' team was ranked top in the classification criteria. This achievement shows that the proposed strategy may address speech differences, especially in vulnerable populations.

The following sections describe the paper's contribution: Section 2 covers relevant works; Section 3 materials and technique; Section 4 results; and Section 5 conclusion.

2 Related Works

Advancements in deep learning have significantly impacted speech processing, notably in the domain of automatic speech recognition (ASR). Transformer-based architectures like BERT and GPT (Zheng and Woodland, 2021; Fohr and Illina, 2021; Kumar et al., 2022), initially tailored for text interpretation, have been extended to capture speech sequences, leveraging contextual information to enhance accuracy. DeepSpeech (Hannun et al., 2014), a flexible open-source program employing recurrent neural networks (RNNs), stands out for its adaptability across various languages and effective training methods. Self-supervised learning models such as Wav2Vec (Baevski et al., 2020) excel at speech pattern recognition by extracting pertinent features directly from unlabeled audio data.

Attention-based models, such as Listen, Attend, and Spell (LAS) (Chan et al., 2015), change how much weight is given to inputs during decoding. This helps with accurate transcription after a lot of training on big datasets. Lightweight architectures like QuartzNet (Kriman et al., 2020) emphasize high performance while maintaining low computational demands. Hybrid models, like ESPNet (Watanabe et al., 2018), combine convolutional and recurrent networks, showing that they are good at a number of different ASR benchmarks. Recent improvements, like HuBERT (Hsu et al., 2021), build upon Wav2Vec by integrating hierarchical transformations and elevating representation learning and ASR accuracy. These improvements have made significant advancements in the field of ASR and have achieved impressive results.

However, when it comes to resource-poor languages like Tamil, existing models underperform due to the variability in speech among native speakers. To address this, recent research has focused on fine-tuning pre-trained ASR models for specific languages. Models like XLSR-wav2vec2 (Conneau et al., 2020) have been customized for Tamil speech recognition, showcasing promising results with a significantly reduced word error rate (WER) of 39.65% (Bharathi et al., 2022) and 37.71% (Bharathi et al., 2023). This customized approach aims to enhance performance in understanding and transcribing speech for languages with limited available resources.

3 Materials and Methodology

3.1 Dataset Description

The dataset used in this study is from the shared task LT-EDI@2024. This shared task aims to develop a Tamil conversational speech corpus collected from vulnerable elderly people and transgender people in Tamil. This speech corpus contains recordings that capture real-world conversions from primary sites such as hospitals, banks, and administrative offices. The corpus contains males, females, and transgender speakers and a total of 7 and a half hours of speech data. There are two phases to the dataset's release: the first phase is for training, and the second phase is for testing. The test data consists of a total of two hours of unlabeled speech, whereas the training data consists of an average of 5.5 hours of speech that has been transcribed. Table 1 describes the detailed data statistics about the train, test, and validation splits used in this work.

Dataset	Splits	Audios	Hours
Training	Train	726	5.5
	Evaluation	192	
Testing	Test	348	2
Total		1266	7.5

Table 1: Data Statistics describing the train, test and validation split.

3.2 Methodology

In this study, speech recognition was performed using two pre-trained state-of-the-art (SOTA) models, Whisper and XLS-R. Both models were trained on the Tamil corpus, and the best results were submitted for the competition. Figures 1 and 2 show schematic block diagrams of the proposed approaches.

3.2.1 Whisper ASR

Whisper (Radford et al., 2023) is a pre-trained automatic speech recognition (ASR) model trained on 680,000 hours of multilingual and multitask supervised data sourced from the web. This end-to-end transformer-based model adopts the encoder-decoder architecture. Log-Mel spectrogram features are extracted from each audio file; this feature input undergoes processing in the encoder, featuring a compact stem composed of two convolution layers with a filter width of three and the GELU activation function. Notably, the stride of the second convolution layer is set at three. Following this, sinusoidal position embeddings are added to the stem's output, paving the way for the inclusion of encoder transformer blocks. Using pre-activation residual structures, these blocks build up to a final layer normalization step for the encoder output. The learned position embeddings are then fed into the decoder, which is responsible for generating the textual output.

The Whisper model boasts various variants, including whisper-large-v1, whisper-large-v2, and whisper-large-v3. For this study, we opted for the 'Vasista22/whisper-tamil-medium' pre-trained model from the huggingface and fine-tuned it on the Tamil speech corpus. Figure 1 displays the whisper model's flow diagram.

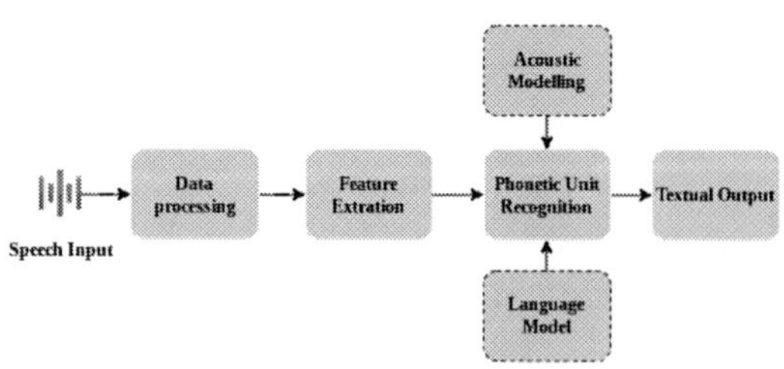

Figure 1: Flow Diagram for Whisper Model.

3.2.2 XLS-R

The XLS-R model is a multi-lingual adaptation of the Wav2Vec2 model for cross-lingual representational learning of speech. The pre-training of the model utilized more than 436,000 hours of speech data that was easily accessible to the general public. The speech data used for per-training is derived from a variety of sources, including audio books produced in 128 different languages and parliamentary proceedings. Since the model was trained on connectionist temporal classification (CTC), the Wav2Vec2CTCTokenizer should be used to decode the model's output. The model has three variations: Wav2Vec2-XLS-R-300M, Wav2Vec2-XLS-R-1B, and Wav2Vec2-XLS-R-2B. The parameters for each variant vary. For the experiments, we have utilized 'Wav2Vec2-XLS-R-300M' and fine-tuned it on the Tamil speech corpus. Figure 2 displays the flow diagram for the XLS-R model.

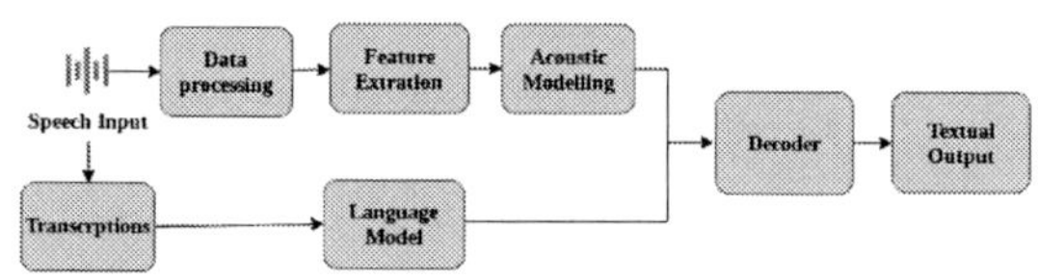

Figure 2: Flow Diagram for XLS-R Model.

4 Results and Discussion

4.1 Experiments

The experimental setup comprises a Linux operating system, an 8-core Intel Xeon processor, 32GB of RAM, a 16GB NVIDIA T4 tensor core GPU,and CUDA 11.0. In the series of experiments employing both the whisper and XLS-R models, for the whisper part, we focused on the 'Vasista22/whisper-tamil-medium[1]' pre-trained model on Tamil. To make the audio data consistent for the Whisper model, all the audio files had to be resampled to 16 kHz, and then Log-Mel spectrogram features had to be extracted. Subsequently, we utilized the WhisperTokenizer to encode transcriptions into label IDs. To facilitate model training data preparation, we defined a data collator to handle batching and padding of the training examples.

The word error rate (WER) was an essential metric for assessing model performance during the training process. We fine-tuned the model using various combinations of hyperparameters, including learning rate, batch

[1]https://huggingface.co/vasista22/whisper-tamil-medium

Filename	Transcriptions
Audio - 44_20	ஆரைப் பார்த்து பேசலாமா நான் வெளியூரு இப்ப நான் பெங்களூரு போகனும் பெங்களூரு பஸ் ஏறத்துக்கு எந்த பஸ் சட்டு போகனும் டிக்கெட் இங்க வாங்கலாமா இல்ல டிக்கெட் வாங்குறதுக்கு யார்கிட்ட கேட்கணுமா கொஞ்சம் எங்க போகனும்னு சொல்லுங்க எனக்கு வழி தெரியாது நான் இந்த ஊருக்கு போகனுமா
Audio - 48_36	பழக்க வழக்கம்லாம் இருக்கும்ல அதெல்லாம் காட்டனும்ல வெட்டுக்குத்து மட்டும் காட்டுனா எப்படி
Audio - 46_47	பீஸ் எதுவும் குறைக்கக்கூடிய வாய்ப்புகள் இருக்கான்னு கொஞ்சம் சொல்லுங்க சார் எப்பதான் ஸ்கூல் டியூப்பின் பண்ணுவீங்க எந்த மாதிரி பாடங்கள் இப்ப நீங்க நடத்தப் போறதா இருக்கீங்க
Audio - 45_16	டாக்டர் கிட்ட போனே எழுதிக்கொடுத்தாங்க தொலைச்சுட்டேன் தொலைந்து மாத்திரை குடியாது மொத்தமாகுனா ரேட்டு கம்மியா இருந்தா இல்ல ஒரு சீட்டு ஒரு அட்டையா இன்னும் எவ்வளவு அட்டை முடியும் சொல்லியா இதுக்கு தகுந்த பில்ல போடியா ஏ தம்பி இந்த கை கால் எலிதாக ரொம்ப இருக்கு அதுக்கெல்லாம் பாத்தும் மாத்திரை குடியாது
Audio - 47_16	யோவ் எங்கயா போற ஒருத்தன் நின்னுட்டு இருக்கேன் நீ பாட்டுக்கு போற
Audio - 37_06	உங்களிடம் மின்சாரத்தில் இயங்கும் வண்டி உள்ளதா இந்த வண்டிக்கும் மற்ற வாகனத்திற்கும் உள்ள வேறுபாடு என்ன ஒரு கிலோ மீட்டருக்கு ஆகும் செலவை கம்பர் பண்ணி சொல்ல முடியுமா எலெக்டரி பைக்கோட பேட்டரி ஆயில் காலம் என்ன

Figure 3: Sample Transcriptions in Tamil from fine-tuned Whisper Model.

size, maximum steps, and optimizer selection. The most optimal results were achieved with specific hyper-parameter configurations. During training, a batch size of 4 proved effective, while for testing, a batch size of 8 was found to be optimal. The learning rate was set to $10^{-}5$, and the 'adamw_bnb_8bit' optimizer was employed to initialize the optimization process. This comprehensive approach to hyperparameter tuning and data preprocessing contributed to the success of the experiments with the Vasista22/whisper-tamil-medium model.

On the other hand, the 'Wav2Vec2-XLS-R-300M[2]' underwent fine-tuning on the Tamil speech corpus. To address sequence-to-sequence problems, typical fine-tuning of XLS-R models involves employing the connectionist temporal classification (CTC) algorithm. As a part of preprocessing, transcription texts have been cleaned by excluding special characters and developing a vocabulary from the processed transcriptions. The model anticipates input in the form of a 1-dimensional array at 16 kHz, prompting the loading and resampling of all audio files accordingly.

For the training phase, the Wav2Vec2Processor was employed to extract input values from the loaded files, encoding corresponding transcriptions into label IDs. A data collator was then developed, and the training arguments have been adjusted to aid in the training of the model. Notably, the best results were observed when the learning rate was fixed at $10^{-}4$, the number of training epochs set at 100, and the batch size established at 16. The word error rate (WER) was used as the metric to assess the model's performance during training.

4.2 Discussion

In the process of training the models, it has been observed that the fine-tuned version of the 'Vasista22/whisper-tamil-medium' model performs better than the fine-tuned version of the XLS-R-300M model when it comes to the training of the models. During the training process, it was observed that the WER for the whisper model was **71.367695**, whereas the WER for the XLS-R model was **84.6958** to begin with. When evaluating the fine-tuned model that was utilized, both the whisper and the XLS-R fine-tuned models were utilized in the process. Since the whisper model's word error rate was much smaller than the XLS-R model, we submitted the results of the whisper model to the LT-EDI team. By assessing the WER for each submission, the team will determine which outcomes are the best and rank them appropriately. The submission, which was made by our team 'CEN_Amrita',

[2]https://huggingface.co/facebook/wav2vec2-xls-r-300m

Team Name	WER (in %)
CEN_Amrita - Jairam Kanna	**24.452**
ASR_TAMIL_SSN	29.297
VIT Chennai	35.774
DRAVIDIAN LANGUAGE - Abirami Jayaraman	37.733
CUET_NLP_GoodFellows - Disco Dancer	41.031

Table 2: Speech Recognition for Vulnerable Individuals in Tamil: Published Results

employing the fine-tuned whisper model, has been ranked first among the other participants, with a WER of **24.452** for the testing dataset. Table 2 describes the published results. Figure 3 describes the submitted sample Tamil transcriptions obtained from evaluating the fine-tuned whisper model.

5 Conclusion

In this work, we utilized a pre-existing, pre-trained model such as Whisper and XLS-R to improve the efficiency of an automatic speech recognition (ASR) system for understanding conversational speech from elderly and transgender Tamil speakers. This work is carried out as part of participation in the shared task of speech recognition for vulnerable individuals in Tamil. On the Tamil conversational speech corpus, the pre-trained models, such as whisper and the XLS-R model, have been fine-tuned and compared to one another. The results of all the experiments indicate that the fine-tuned version of whisper ASR models performs better than the XLS-R model, which has a word error rate (WER) of 24.452.

References

Alexei Baevski, Yuhao Zhou, Abdelrahman Mohamed, and Michael Auli. 2020. wav2vec 2.0: A framework for self-supervised learning of speech representations. *Advances in neural information processing systems*, 33:12449–12460.

B Bharathi, Bharathi Raja Chakravarthi, Subalalitha Cn, Sripriya Natarajan, Rajeswari Natarajan, S Suhasini, and Swetha Valli. 2023. Overview of the second shared task on speech recognition for vulnerable individuals in tamil. In *Proceedings of the Third Workshop on Language Technology for Equality, Diversity and Inclusion*, pages 31–37.

B Bharathi, Bharathi Raja Chakravarthi, Subalalitha Cn, N Sripriya, Arunaggiri Pandian, and Swetha Valli. 2022. Findings of the shared task on speech recognition for vulnerable individuals in tamil. In *Proceedings of the Second Workshop on Language Technology for Equality, Diversity and Inclusion*, pages 339–345.

William Chan, Navdeep Jaitly, Quoc V Le, and Oriol Vinyals. 2015. Listen, attend and spell. *arXiv preprint arXiv:1508.01211*.

Alexis Conneau, Alexei Baevski, Ronan Collobert, Abdelrahman Mohamed, and Michael Auli. 2020. Unsupervised cross-lingual representation learning for speech recognition. *arXiv preprint arXiv:2006.13979*.

Dominique Fohr and Irina Illina. 2021. Bert-based semantic model for rescoring n-best speech recognition list. In *INTERSPEECH*.

Santosh K Gaikwad, Bharti W Gawali, and Pravin Yannawar. 2010. A review on speech recognition technique. *International Journal of Computer Applications*, 10(3):16–24.

Awni Hannun, Carl Case, Jared Casper, Bryan Catanzaro, Greg Diamos, Erich Elsen, Ryan Prenger, Sanjeev Satheesh, Shubho Sengupta, Adam Coates, et al. 2014. Deep speech: Scaling up end-to-end speech recognition. *arXiv preprint arXiv:1412.5567*.

Wei-Ning Hsu, Benjamin Bolte, Yao-Hung Hubert Tsai, Kushal Lakhotia, Ruslan Salakhutdinov, and Abdelrahman Mohamed. 2021. Hubert: Self-supervised speech representation learning by masked prediction of hidden units. *IEEE/ACM Transactions on Audio, Speech, and Language Processing*, 29:3451–3460.

Sotaro Kita. 2020. Cross-cultural variation of speech-accompanying gesture: A review. *Speech Accompanying-Gesture*, pages 145–167.

Samuel Kriman, Stanislav Beliaev, Boris Ginsburg, Jocelyn Huang, Oleksii Kuchaiev, Vitaly Lavrukhin, Ryan Leary, Jason Li, and Yang Zhang. 2020. Quartznet: Deep automatic speech recognition with 1d time-channel separable convolutions. In *IEEE International Conference on Acoustics, Speech and Signal Processing (ICASSP)*, pages 6124–6128.

CS Ayush Kumar, Advaith Maharana, Srinath Murali, B Premjith, and Soman Kp. 2022. Bert-based sequence labelling approach for dependency parsing in tamil. In *Proceedings of the Second Workshop on Speech and Language Technologies for Dravidian Languages*, pages 1–8.

Jinyu Li et al. 2022. Recent advances in end-to-end automatic speech recognition. *APSIPA Transactions on Signal and Information Processing*, 11(1).

P Murali Krishna, R Pradeep Reddy, Veena Narayanan, S Lalitha, and Deepa Gupta. 2019. Affective state recognition using audio cues. *Journal of Intelligent & Fuzzy Systems*, 36(3):2147–2154.

Ali Bou Nassif, Ismail Shahin, Imtinan Attili, Mohammad Azzeh, and Khaled Shaalan. 2019. Speech recognition using deep neural networks: A systematic review. *IEEE access*, 7:19143–19165.

Alec Radford, Jong Wook Kim, Tao Xu, Greg Brockman, Christine McLeavey, and Ilya Sutskever. 2023. Robust speech recognition via large-scale weak supervision. In *International Conference on Machine Learning*, pages 28492–28518.

KM Shivakumar, KG Aravind, TV Anoop, and Deepa Gupta. 2016. Kannada speech to text conversion using cmu sphinx. In *International Conference on Inventive Computation Technologies (ICICT)*, volume 3, pages 1–6.

S Shraddha, Sachin Kumar, et al. 2022. Child speech recognition on end-to-end neural asr models. In *2nd International Conference on Intelligent Technologies (CONIT)*, pages 1–6.

Shinji Watanabe, Takaaki Hori, Shigeki Karita, Tomoki Hayashi, Jiro Nishitoba, Yuya Unno, Nelson Enrique Yalta Soplin, Jahn Heymann, Matthew Wiesner, Nanxin Chen, et al. 2018. Espnet: End-to-end speech processing toolkit. *arXiv preprint arXiv:1804.00015*.

Zhang Chao Zheng, Xianrui and Philip C Woodland. 2021. Adapting gpt, gpt-2 and bert language models for speech recognition. In *IEEE Automatic Speech Recognition and Understanding Workshop (ASRU)*, pages 162–168.

kubapok@LT-EDI 2024: Evaluating Transformer Models for Hate Speech Detection in Tamil

Jakub Pokrywka and **Krzysztof Jassem**
Adam Mickiewicz University
Faculty of Mathematics and Computer Science
{firstname.lastname}@amu.edu.pl

Abstract

We describe the second-place submission for the shared task organized at the Fourth Workshop on Language Technology for Equality, Diversity, and Inclusion (LT-EDI-2024). The task focuses on detecting caste/migration hate speech in Tamil. The included texts involve the Tamil language in both Tamil script and transliterated into Latin script, with some texts also in English. Considering different scripts, we examined the performance of 12 transformer language models on the dev set. Our analysis revealed that for the whole dataset, the model google/muril-large-cased performs the best. We used an ensemble of several models for the final challenge submission, achieving 0.81 for the test dataset.

1 Introduction

This paper deals with hate speech detection in the Tamil language, which is an official language in Sri Lanka and Singapore. It is also the official language of the Indian state of Tamil Nadu and the union territory of Puducherry. The language is spoken by groups of citizens of Malaysia, Mauritius, Fiji, and South Africa. The current number of Tamil speakers is estimated at 75 million. The Tamil language belongs to the family of 24 Dravidian languages, spoken by approximately 250 million people. The Tamil alphabet consists of 246 characters: 12 vowels, 18 consonants, and 216 vowel–consonant combinations. Being spoken in India, a country with a caste-based social system, the Tamil language may suffer from hate speech referring not only to religion, ethnicity, gender, sexual orientation, or political affiliation, but also to caste and migration.

In this paper, we describe a submission to caste/migration hate speech detection task organized at LT-EDI-2024 (Rajiakodi et al., 2024). Our approach, which relied on an ensemble of several models, achieved second place in the competition, with a 0.81 F1-score. Besides the research related strictly to the contest, we examine the performance of 12 up-to-date models that are most suitable for this task. We evaluate each model's performance separately on Tamil, Latin, and combined scripts, finding that the model's performance is different based on the script.

2 Related work

A contest on hate speech detection in the Dravidian languages, called HASOC 2021, was organized in 2021 (Chakravarthi et al., 2021). The data were collected from YouTube comments and posts. The contest consisted of two tasks differing in the nature of the data: the first task was based on Tamil only, while the second task was based on a data set combining Tamil and Malayalam. The winning solution for Task 1 achieved a 0.86 F1-score. The winning solution in the Tamil track for Task 2 achieved a 0.68 F1-score. The HASOC 2021 shared task gave rise to a number of papers, such as Rajalakshmi et al. (2023); Pradeep et al. (2021) and Subramanian et al. (2022). The papers report submissions with F1-scores ranging from 0.66 to 0.84.

3 Caste/Migration Hate Speech Detection Challenge

The Caste/Migration Hate Speech Detection task is a part of the Fourth Workshop on Language Technology for Equality, Diversity, and Inclusion (LT-EDI-2024) (Rajiakodi et al., 2024). The main objective of the challenge is to develop a text classifier in the Tamil language that can determine whether a given social media text contains hate speech related to caste or migration. The competition's evaluation metric is the macro average F1-score, and the participants are provided with training (train) and development (dev) datasets.

Proceedings of the Fourth Workshop on Language Technology for Equality, Diversity, Inclusion, pages 196–199
March 21, 2024

4 Dataset analysis

We examined the train and dev datasets and discovered that the texts could be classified into three primary categories:

1. Tamil language written in Tamil script
2. Tamil language transliterated into Latin script
3. English language

There are also comments that may contain a mixture of Tamil and English language. We observed that in both the training and development datasets, 51% of the texts are in Tamil script, and the remaining 49% in Latin script. The test dataset has an even split of 50% for both Tamil and Latin scripts. If more than half of the characters in a comment are non-Latin, we classify the comment as Tamil script. Table 1 shows the number of samples labeled as caste/migration hate speech. The average comment lengths in characters for the train, dev, and test datasets are 133, 134, and 129, respectively.

Dataset	HS	not-HS	Overall
train	2052	3303	5355
dev	351	594	945
test	-	-	1575

Table 1: Breakdown of datasets by label. HS stands for caste/migration hate speech comments, and not-HS stands for comments with a lack of such hate speech.

5 Evaluation of transformer models for Tamil hate speech

We utilized HuggingFace's Transformers library to fine-tune the selected encoder language models. We used the standard Trainer class and set the learning rate to 2e-5, batch size to 16, weight decay to 0.01, and warmup ratio to 0.1. We trained for 30 epochs and calculated the F1-score on the dev set after each epoch. The best model based on this metric was selected for evaluation. We used two A100 80GB model cards and tested the following HuggingFace model cards:

- distilbert-base-uncased (eng) (Sanh et al., 2019)
- bert-base-cased (eng) (Devlin et al., 2018)
- roberta-base (eng) (Liu et al., 2019)
- roberta-large (eng) (Liu et al., 2019)
- bert-base-multilingual-cased (eng) (Devlin et al., 2018)
- xlm-roberta-base (multilingual) (Conneau et al., 2019)
- xlm-roberta-large (multilingual) (Conneau et al., 2019)
- microsoft/mdeberta-v3-base (multilingual) (He et al., 2021)
- monsoon-nlp/hindi-bert (hindi) (mon)
- l3cube-pune/hindi-roberta (hindi) (Joshi, 2022)
- google/muril-base-cased (17 indian langs) (Khanuja et al., 2021)
- google/muril-large-cased (17 indian langs) (Khanuja et al., 2021)
- l3cube-pune/tamil-bert (tamil) (Joshi, 2022)

These can be accessed at the following URLs: `https://huggingface.co/modelcard` (change `modelcard` to the proper name). The language of each model is given in parentheses.

Tables 2, 3 and 4 show the means and standard deviations of scores from five runs on the whole dev dataset and on the Tamil and Latin parts of that dataset.

Based on the F1-scores, it is evident that the google/muril-large-cased model performs the best overall for the entire dataset, although other multilingual models also perform well. This holds true even for the Tamil script, where the performance of the sole English language model decreases. For Latin script, the English models, multilingual models and certain Hindi models perform equally well. It is surprising to note that in all cases, the F1-score for the English version of the roberta-large model is inferior to that of roberta-base. We also found that the F1-score of the google/muril-base-cased model is lower by approximately 0.05 than that of google/muril-large-cased.

6 Submission to the challenge

Because we conducted the model evaluations described in the previous section after the competition was over, we could not use this knowledge for the final submission to the challenge. However, for the final submission, we followed the same training process using an ensemble of the following model cards: l3cube/pune-kannada-bert, microsoft/mdeberta-v3-base, and xlm-roberta-large. We combined the train and dev datasets and

model	F1-Score	Precision	Recall	AUROC	Accuracy
bert-base-cased	0.66 ± 0.01	0.70 ± 0.01	0.62 ± 0.02	0.79 ± 0.01	0.76 ± 0.00
roberta-base	0.71 ± 0.01	0.72 ± 0.01	0.70 ± 0.02	0.82 ± 0.01	0.79 ± 0.01
roberta-large	0.67 ± 0.03	0.69 ± 0.02	0.65 ± 0.04	0.78 ± 0.01	0.76 ± 0.02
bert-base-multilingual-cased	0.72 ± 0.00	0.75 ± 0.01	0.70 ± 0.01	0.84 ± 0.00	0.80 ± 0.00
xlm-roberta-base	0.72 ± 0.01	0.76 ± 0.02	0.70 ± 0.02	0.84 ± 0.01	0.80 ± 0.01
xlm-roberta-large	0.74 ± 0.01	0.76 ± 0.02	0.72 ± 0.01	0.84 ± 0.01	0.81 ± 0.01
microsoft/mdeberta-v3-base	0.73 ± 0.01	0.75 ± 0.03	0.71 ± 0.02	0.84 ± 0.00	0.80 ± 0.01
monsoon/nlp-hindi-bert	0.57 ± 0.01	0.55 ± 0.02	0.59 ± 0.04	0.70 ± 0.01	0.67 ± 0.01
l3cube/pune-hindi-roberta	0.65 ± 0.14	0.70 ± 0.04	0.63 ± 0.19	0.80 ± 0.07	0.77 ± 0.05
google/muril-base-cased	0.71 ± 0.01	0.74 ± 0.03	0.69 ± 0.03	0.81 ± 0.01	0.79 ± 0.01
google/muril-large-cased	$\mathbf{0.76} \pm 0.01$	$\mathbf{0.78} \pm 0.02$	$\mathbf{0.74} \pm 0.02$	$\mathbf{0.85} \pm 0.01$	$\mathbf{0.82} \pm 0.01$
l3cube/pune-tamil-bert	0.71 ± 0.01	0.71 ± 0.02	0.72 ± 0.03	0.82 ± 0.01	0.79 ± 0.01

Table 2: Evaluation of models on the whole dev dataset. The best results are highlighted in bold.

model	F1-Score	Precision	Recall	AUROC	Accuracy
bert-base-cased	0.54 ± 0.02	0.62 ± 0.02	0.48 ± 0.05	0.69 ± 0.01	0.71 ± 0.01
roberta-base	0.66 ± 0.02	0.68 ± 0.03	0.64 ± 0.02	0.78 ± 0.01	0.76 ± 0.02
roberta-large	0.60 ± 0.06	0.63 ± 0.04	0.58 ± 0.08	0.72 ± 0.03	0.73 ± 0.03
bert-base-multilingual-cased	0.69 ± 0.01	0.72 ± 0.01	0.66 ± 0.01	0.82 ± 0.00	0.79 ± 0.01
xlm-roberta-base	0.71 ± 0.01	0.74 ± 0.02	0.68 ± 0.02	0.83 ± 0.01	0.80 ± 0.01
xlm-roberta-large	0.74 ± 0.01	$\mathbf{0.76} \pm 0.03$	0.71 ± 0.02	0.85 ± 0.01	0.81 ± 0.01
microsoft/mdeberta-v3-base	0.73 ± 0.02	0.75 ± 0.03	0.71 ± 0.03	0.84 ± 0.01	0.81 ± 0.02
monsoon/nlp-hindi-bert	0.54 ± 0.01	0.46 ± 0.02	0.66 ± 0.05	0.64 ± 0.01	0.59 ± 0.02
l3cube/pune-hindi-roberta	0.61 ± 0.15	0.68 ± 0.04	0.59 ± 0.19	0.78 ± 0.07	0.75 ± 0.04
google/muril-base-cased	0.70 ± 0.02	0.73 ± 0.03	0.68 ± 0.05	0.81 ± 0.02	0.79 ± 0.01
google/muril-large-cased	$\mathbf{0.75} \pm 0.01$	0.75 ± 0.02	$\mathbf{0.76} \pm 0.02$	$\mathbf{0.86} \pm 0.01$	$\mathbf{0.82} \pm 0.01$
l3cube/pune-tamil-bert	0.71 ± 0.01	0.71 ± 0.02	0.72 ± 0.03	0.83 ± 0.01	0.79 ± 0.01

Table 3: Evaluation of models on the Tamil script part of the dev dataset. The best results are highlighted in bold.

model	F1-Score	Precision	Recall	AUROC	Accuracy
bert-base-cased	$\mathbf{0.76} \pm 0.01$	0.76 ± 0.01	$\mathbf{0.76} \pm 0.02$	0.86 ± 0.01	0.82 ± 0.00
roberta-base	0.75 ± 0.01	0.75 ± 0.01	$\mathbf{0.76} \pm 0.02$	0.86 ± 0.01	0.81 ± 0.00
roberta-large	0.73 ± 0.01	0.74 ± 0.02	0.72 ± 0.01	0.82 ± 0.02	0.80 ± 0.01
bert-base-multilingual-cased	0.75 ± 0.01	0.77 ± 0.01	0.74 ± 0.02	$\mathbf{0.87} \pm 0.00$	0.81 ± 0.00
xlm-roberta-base	0.74 ± 0.01	0.77 ± 0.02	0.72 ± 0.02	0.84 ± 0.01	0.81 ± 0.01
xlm-roberta-large	0.74 ± 0.01	0.76 ± 0.02	0.73 ± 0.03	0.84 ± 0.01	0.81 ± 0.01
microsoft/mdeberta-v3-base	0.73 ± 0.01	0.74 ± 0.03	0.72 ± 0.05	0.84 ± 0.01	0.80 ± 0.01
monsoon/nlp-hindi-bert	0.62 ± 0.02	0.75 ± 0.03	0.53 ± 0.05	0.74 ± 0.02	0.75 ± 0.01
l3cube/pune-hindi-roberta	0.68 ± 0.13	0.73 ± 0.06	0.67 ± 0.19	0.82 ± 0.07	0.78 ± 0.05
google/muril-base-cased	0.72 ± 0.01	0.74 ± 0.04	0.70 ± 0.03	0.82 ± 0.01	0.79 ± 0.01
google/muril-large-cased	$\mathbf{0.76} \pm 0.01$	$\mathbf{0.80} \pm 0.02$	0.72 ± 0.03	0.85 ± 0.01	$\mathbf{0.83} \pm 0.01$
l3cube/pune-tamil-bert	0.72 ± 0.01	0.72 ± 0.04	0.71 ± 0.03	0.82 ± 0.01	0.78 ± 0.01

Table 4: Evaluation of models on the Latin script part of the dev dataset. The best results are highlighted in bold.

used different new train/dev splits for each model. The model achieved an F1-score of 0.81 on the challenge test set, securing second place, behind the leader with 0.82.

7 Conclusions

We conducted an evaluation of several English, multilingual, and Hindi encoder language models for a classification task in the Tamil language. This task was a part of the Fourth Workshop on Language Technology for Equality, Diversity, and Inclusion. Our post-competition study revealed that the most effective model was google/muril-large-cased. All types of language models performed well on the Latin script portion of the dataset, which may result from the fact that some of the texts were in the English language. Our approach, which relied on an ensemble of selected models, achieved second place in the competition.

8 Limitations

The content of this paper is based on brief comments, primarily in Tamil. The origin, description, and annotation scheme of the text are explained in detail in (Rajiakodi et al., 2024). It is worth noting that the methods used in this study may not be easily scalable to other domains or text lengths. Furthermore, our assumption that Tamil script texts are those in which over half of the characters are non-Latin is merely heuristic and may not hold true in all cases.

References

Hindi Bert. `https://huggingface.co/monsoon-nlp/hindi-bert`. Accessed: 2023-12-15.

Bharathi Raja Chakravarthi, Prasanna Kumar Kumaresan, Ratnasingam Sakuntharaj, Anand Kumar Madasamy, Sajeetha Thavareesan, Bhavukam Premjith, K R Sreelakshmi, Subalalitha Chinnaudayar Navaneethakrishnan, John, Patrick McCrae, and Thomas Mandl. 2021. Overview of the HASOC-DravidianCodeMix shared task on offensive language detection in Tamil and Malayalam. In *Fire*.

Alexis Conneau, Kartikay Khandelwal, Naman Goyal, Vishrav Chaudhary, Guillaume Wenzek, Francisco Guzmán, Edouard Grave, Myle Ott, Luke Zettlemoyer, and Veselin Stoyanov. 2019. Unsupervised cross-lingual representation learning at scale. *CoRR*, abs/1911.02116.

Jacob Devlin, Ming-Wei Chang, Kenton Lee, and Kristina Toutanova. 2018. BERT: pre-training of deep bidirectional transformers for language understanding. *CoRR*, abs/1810.04805.

Pengcheng He, Jianfeng Gao, and Weizhu Chen. 2021. Debertav3: Improving DeBERTa using ELECTRA-style pre-training with gradient-disentangled embedding sharing.

Raviraj Joshi. 2022. L3Cube-HindBERT and DevBERT: Pre-trained BERT transformer models for Devanagari based Hindi and Marathi languages. *arXiv preprint arXiv:2211.11418*.

Simran Khanuja, Diksha Bansal, Sarvesh Mehtani, Savya Khosla, Atreyee Dey, Balaji Gopalan, Dilip Kumar Margam, Pooja Aggarwal, Rajiv Teja Nagipogu, Shachi Dave, Shruti Gupta, Subhash Chandra Bose Gali, Vish Subramanian, and Partha Talukdar. 2021. Muril: Multilingual representations for Indian languages.

Yinhan Liu, Myle Ott, Naman Goyal, Jingfei Du, Mandar Joshi, Danqi Chen, Omer Levy, Mike Lewis, Luke Zettlemoyer, and Veselin Stoyanov. 2019. Roberta: A robustly optimized BERT pretraining approach. *CoRR*, abs/1907.11692.

Ronak Pradeep, Xueguang Ma, Rodrigo Nogueira, and Jimmy Lin. 2021. Scientific claim verification with VerT5erini. In *Proceedings of the 12th International Workshop on Health Text Mining and Information Analysis*, pages 94–103, online. Association for Computational Linguistics.

Ratnavel Rajalakshmi, Srivarshan Selvaraj, Faerie Mattins R., Pavitra Vasudevan, and Anand Kumar M. 2023. HOTTEST: Hate and offensive content identification in Tamil using transformers and enhanced stemming. *Computer Speech Language*, 78:101464.

Saranya Rajiakodi, Bharathi Raja Chakravarthi, Rahul Ponnusamy, Prasanna Kumar Kumaresan, Sathiyaraj Thangasamy, Bhuvaneswari Sivagnanam, and Charmathi Rajkumar. 2024. Overview of Shared Task on Caste and Migration Hate Speech Detection. In *Proceedings of the Fourth Workshop on Language Technology for Equality, Diversity and Inclusion*, Malta. European Chapter of the Association for Computational Linguistics.

Victor Sanh, Lysandre Debut, Julien Chaumond, and Thomas Wolf. 2019. DistilBERT, a distilled version of BERT: smaller, faster, cheaper and lighter. *ArXiv*, abs/1910.01108.

Malliga Subramanian, Rahul Ponnusamy, Sean Benhur, Kogilavani Shanmugavadivel, Adhithiya Ganesan, Deepti Ravi, Gowtham Krishnan Shanmugasundaram, Ruba Priyadharshini, and Bharathi Raja Chakravarthi. 2022. Offensive language detection in Tamil YouTube comments by adapters and cross-domain knowledge transfer. *Computer Speech Language*, 76:101404.

KEC-AI-NLP@LT-EDI-2024:Homophobia and Transphobia Detection in Social Media Comments using Machine Learning

Kogilavani Shanmugavadivel[1], **Malliga Subramanian**[1], **Shri Durga R**[1], **Srigha S**[1], **Samyuktha K**[1], **Nithika K**[1]

[1]Department of AI, Kongu Engineering College, Perundurai, Erode.

{kogilavani.sv, mallinishanth72}@gmail.com

{shridurgar.21aim, srighas.21aim}@kongu.edu

{samyukthak.21aim,nithikak.21aim}@kongu.edu

Abstract

Our work addresses the growing concern of abusive comments in online platforms, particularly focusing on the identification of Homophobia and Transphobia in social media comments. The goal is to categorize comments into three classes: Homophobia, Transphobia, and non-anti LGBT+ comments. Utilizing machine learning techniques and a deep learning model, our work involves training on a English dataset with a designated training set and testing on a validation set. This approach aims to contribute to the understanding and detection of Homophobia and Transphobia within the realm of social media interactions. Our team participated in the shared task organized by LT-EDI@EACL 2024[1] and secured seventh rank in the task of Homophobia/Transphobia Detection in social media comments in Tamil with a macro- f1 score of 0.315. Also, our run was submitted for the English language and secured eighth rank with a macro-F1 score of 0.369. The run submitted for Malayalam language securing fourth rank with a macro- F1 score of 0.883 using the Random Forest model.

1 Introduction

In the contemporary digital landscape, social media platforms serve as pivotal mediums for communication, education, and information sharing. Among these platforms, YouTube stands out as a prominent social networking and video-sharing hub, enabling users to create accounts, share videos, and interact through comments. However, the prevalence of abusive comments, particularly targeting transgender and homosexual individuals, poses a significant challenge to the well-being of platform users. The escalating use of online communication has raised concerns about the dissemination of slander, hate speech, and cyberbully, with negative consequences for individuals and societal harmony. Slander, characterized by false spoken statements that harm individuals or groups, is increasingly acknowledged for its detrimental impact Olweus and Limber (2018). Such negative comments not only inflict psychological harm but also contribute to the proliferation of animosity, division, and discontent in online spacesMishna et al. (2009). Major social media platforms like YouTube, Facebook, Instagram, and Twitter have responded by implementing policies and protocols to address and mitigate hateful content. Our study aims to scrutinize and identify offensive comments within an English dataset, treating the detection of abusive comments as a text classification problem. Focused on machine learning and deep learning methodologies, our research excludes the use of transfer learning models and does not involve the integration of machine learning and deep learning approaches. The objective is to train and compare various models to determine the optimal approach for identifying hate comments in English.

[1]https://codalab.lisn.upsaclay.fr/competitions/16056

2 Literature Review

Research in the field of abusive language detection spans various approaches and methodologies, as evident in several notable papers. Mubarak et al. (2017) emphasize the challenges faced in Arabic abusive language detection, including dialects and informal language. Mishra et al. (2019) introduce a novel approach using Graph Convolutional Networks (GCNs) to capture syntactic and semantic dependencies for effective abusive language identification.

Addressing gender bias in abusive language detection, Park et al. (2018) propose a method incorporating gender information into the training process, showcasing its effectiveness in reducing bias while maintaining overall performance. Ibrohim

Proceedings of the Fourth Workshop on Language Technology for Equality, Diversity, Inclusion, pages 200–205
March 21, 2024

and Budi (2019) focus on multi-label hate speech detection in Indonesian Twitter, analyzing various approaches, including feature-based, deep learning, and ensemble methods.

Narang and Brew (2020) present an approach utilizing syntactic dependency graphs for abusive language detection, achieving superior performance compared to baseline models. Caselli et al. (2021) introduce HateBERT, a retraining approach for BERT tailored for English abusive language detection, demonstrating its superiority in precision, recall, and F1-score.

Davidson et al. (2019) investigate racial bias in hate speech datasets, highlighting potential biases in annotation processes and emphasizing the need for fair evaluations. Koufakou et al. (2020) introduce HurtBERT, combining BERT with lexical features for enhanced abusive language detection performance.

Corazza et al. (2020) propose a zero-shot abusive language detection using emoji-based masked language models, demonstrating competitive performance. Chakravarthi (2020) contribute HopeEDI, a multilingual dataset for hope speech detection, aiming to facilitate research on positive discourse in social media.

Overall, these works offer diverse insights and methodologies, advancing the understanding and detection of abusive language in various linguistic and societal contexts.

3 Dataset Description

The goal of this shared task on homophobia and transphobia comment detection is to detect and reduce abusive comments on social media that target homosexual and trans-gender individuals. The dataset used here is shared by the shared task Chakravarthi et al. (2023). The primary goal of this project is to develop methods for detecting and classifying instances of hate speech in English language. The Homophobia and Transphobia Comment Detection data set is made up of English comments retrieved from the YouTube comments area Kumaresan et al. (2023). The data set consists of a comment and its related label from one of the three labels: Non-anti-LGBT+ content, Homophobia, Transphobia. SMOTE, which stands for Synthetic Minority Over-sampling data augmentation Technique, is a widely used technique in the field of machine learning specifically in the context of handling imbalanced datasets.Imbalanced datasets occur when the classes have significantly different numbers of instances, leading to a bias in the model's performance towards the majority class.

3.1 English Data

The Train, Test, and Development data sets each comprise 3,164, 792, 991 comments which is summarized in Table 1. The text in English is followed by the appropriate label for each comment in the training data. As Table 2 suggests, the Transphobia label exhibits a significant scarcity, leading to a pronounced class imbalance. Due to the limited availability of test or development data examples for the Transphobia label, the classification task becomes particularly challenging, focusing predominantly on the other two labels.

Table 1: Data-set Description

Data-set	No. of Comments
Train	3,164
Validation	792
Test	991

Table 2: Class Description

Class	Train	Dev	Test
Non-anti-LGBT+	2,978	748	931
Homophobia	179	43	55
Transphobia	7	2	4

4 Methodology

Machine learning and deep learning models cannot access raw texts. Feature extraction is required to train classification models. The TF-IDF representation is utilized in ML techniques to extract features. Figure 1 gives the detailed workflow of our proposed model. We use three ways to analyze the results and create the best model possible: Machine Learning, Deep Learning.

4.1 Machine Learning Models

Machine learning has come a long way in recent years, changing the way people understand important applications such as image recognition, data mining, and natural language processing(NLP). This section outlines the machine learning models utilized in the present study for text classification. We used several different kinds of machine learning algorithms such as Decision tree, Random Forest, GaussianNB, XGBoost, AdaBoost, KNN,

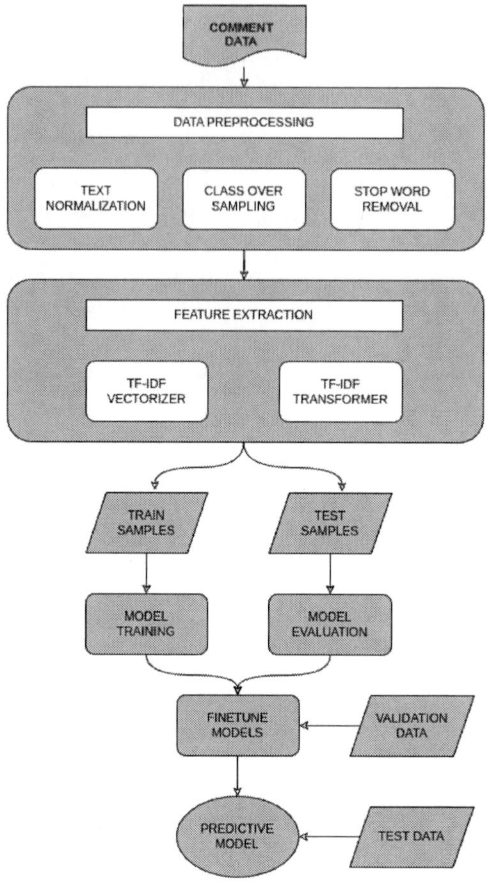

Figure 1: Proposed System Workflow

Linear Regression, Multinomial NB, Support Vector Machine, MLP Classifier, Gradient Boost, and Ensemble models.

4.2 Feature Extraction

The TF-IDF Vectorizer with Character N-grams is a feature extraction technique widely employed in Natural Language Processing (NLP) for the effective representation of textual data in machine learning models. Operating at the character level, this vectorizer analyzes individual characters rather than complete words, allowing it to capture sequential patterns within the text. The inclusion of character n-grams, specified here with lengths ranging from 1 to 3, proves particularly advantageous in tasks that demand consideration of word morphology and character-level nuances, such as sentiment analysis or language-specific challenges. The TF-IDF weighting scheme assigns significance weights to these character n-grams based on their occurrence within individual documents and across the entire dataset. This method not only enhances the representation of textual information but also facilitates the identification of key character patterns. The limitation of the feature space to the top most influential n-grams ensures a focused and meaningful representation, contributing to the efficiency of subsequent machine learning algorithms.

4.3 Deep Learning Model

In the realm of homophobia and transphobia detection within English YouTube comments, this study highlights the efficacy of deep learning models, specifically Convolutional Neural Networks (CNN) and Long Short-Term Memory (LSTM) networks. While CNN excels in capturing localized patterns, LSTM proves valuable in handling long-term dependencies in sequential data, making it suitable for comment analysis.

The pre-processed comments undergo LSTM model training and evaluation, where the LSTM network, belonging to the family of recurrent neural networks (RNNs), excels in capturing long-term dependencies within the sequential nature of text data. By considering the temporal information of comments, the LSTM model effectively captures the context and dependencies that exist between words and phrases. This nuanced understanding contributes to the model's ability to discern patterns and relationships within comment sequences, providing a robust foundation for homophobia and transphobia detection in English YouTube comments.

5 Performance Evaluation

After submitting the run using the Random Forest model, it proved beneficial for various languages. Analyzing the results in Table 3, which provides the macro-average of precision, recall, and F1-score for the various models used. Random Forest surpassed both deep learning and other machine learning models in precision, recall, and F1 score. Leveraging an ensemble of decision trees and feature importance estimation, this model effectively captured complex patterns within the dataset

The Random Forest model excelled in handling high-dimensional data, managing noisy and missing values, and mitigating overfitting concerns through feature subsampling and bootstrap aggregating. Notably, the dataset's class distribution was not uniform, with two crucial classes having very few instances. Despite this challenge, the Random Forest model demonstrated exceptional performance.

The contrasting deep learning model, reliant on significant computational resources and extensive parameter tuning, fell short, resulting in comparatively lower accuracy and F1 score. In Figure 2, the presented confusion matrix provides a comprehensive overview of the performance of the Random Forest model when applied to the Malayalam dataset. This emphasizes the importance of selecting an appropriate modeling technique tailored to the dataset's characteristics, leading to improved predictive performance.

6 Conclusion

The study concentrates on detecting homophobic and transphobic comments in YouTube discussions, comparing the performance of various models in this task. Strikingly, Deep Learning models did not demonstrate superior results when trained and evaluated on English data. Instead, Machine Learning

Figure 2: Confusion Matrix of Random Forest Classifier Model

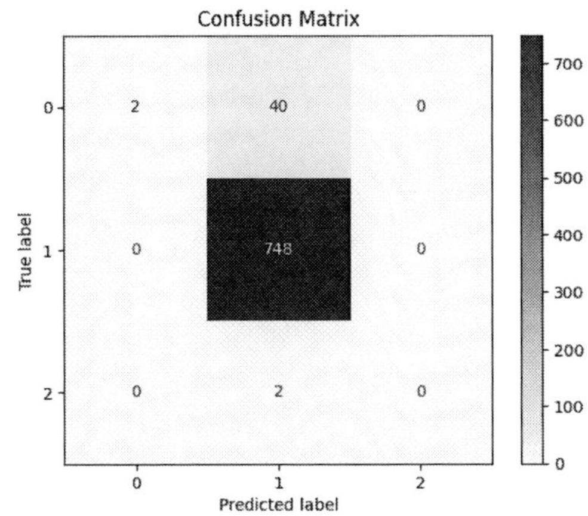

models outperformed Deep Learning in effectiveness. It's crucial to note that our study did not make use of contextualized embeddings like BERT or GPT, which have shown potential in enhancing language model performance.

Acknowledging this limitation, we propose that future research should explore the implementation of contextualized embeddings using deep learning techniques, such as BERT or GPT. The absence of these advanced embeddings may have limited the effectiveness of the models used in our study. Incorporating such embeddings holds promise for significantly improving the detection of homophobic and transphobic comments in YouTube discussions. Additionally, we did not explore transfer learning with other models in our current stage. Still, we emphasize the possibility of integrating these models in our future work, indicating a pathway for ongoing exploration and enhancement in identifying such comments on YouTube.

References

Tommaso Caselli, Arjan Schelhaas, Marieke Weultjes, Folkert Leistra, Hylke van der Veen, Gerben Timmerman, and Malvina Nissim. 2021. DALC: the Dutch abusive language corpus. In *Proceedings of the 5th Workshop on Online Abuse and Harms (WOAH 2021)*, pages 54–66.

Bharathi Raja Chakravarthi. 2020. HopeEDI: A multilingual hope speech detection dataset for equality, diversity, and inclusion. In *Proceedings of the Third Workshop on Computational Modeling of People's Opinions, Personality, and Emotion's in Social Media*, pages 41–53.

Table 3: English Data Evaluation Metrics

Model	Precision	Recall	F1-score
Multilayer perceptron	0.46	0.43	0.44
K-Nearest Neighbour	0.43	0.39	0.40
Xtreme Gradient Boost	0.45	0.35	0.35
Decision Tree	0.37	0.37	0.37
Logistic Regression	0.65	0.34	0.34
Random Forest	0.65	0.34	0.34
Support Vector Classifier	0.57	0.34	0.37
Multinomial Naive Bayes	0.31	0.33	0.32
Gradient Boost Classifier	0.41	0.37	0.39
Ensemble	0.65	0.34	0.34
Adaboost Classifier	0.34	0.34	0.34
CNN-LSTM	0.50	0.37	0.39

Bharathi Raja Chakravarthi. 2023. Detection of homophobia and transphobia in YouTube comments. *International Journal of Data Science and Analytics*, pages 1–20.

Bharathi Raja Chakravarthi, Adeep Hande, Rahul Ponnusamy, Prasanna Kumar Kumaresan, and Ruba Priyadharshini. 2022. How can we detect Homophobia and Transphobia? Experiments in a multilingual code-mixed setting for social media governance. *International Journal of Information Management Data Insights*, 2(2):100119.

Bharathi Raja Chakravarthi, Prasanna Kumar Kumaresan, Ruba Priyadharshini, Paul Buitelaar, Asha Hegde, Hosahalli Lakshmaiah Shashirekha, Saranya Rajiakodi, Miguel Ángel García-Cumbreras, Salud María Jiménez-Zafra, José Antonio García-Díaz, Rafael Valencia-García, Kishore Kumar Ponnusamy, Poorvi Shetty, and Daniel García-Baena. 2024. Overview of Third Shared Task on Homophobia and Transphobia Detection in Social Media Comments. In *Proceedings of the Fourth Workshop on Language Technology for Equality, Diversity and Inclusion*, Malta. European Chapter of the Association for Computational Linguistics.

Bharathi Raja Chakravarthi, Rahul Ponnusamy, Malliga Subramanian, Paul Buitelaar, Miguel Ángel García-Cumbreras, Salud María Jiménez-Zafra, José Antonio García-Díaz, Rafael Valencia-García, and Nitesh Jindal. 2023. "Overview of Second Shared Task on Homophobia and Transphobia Detection in English, Spanish, Hindi, Tamil, and Malayalam". In *Proceedings of the Third Workshop on Language Technology for Equality, Diversity and Inclusion*, Varna, Bulgaria. Recent Advances in Natural Language Processing.

Michele Corazza, Stefano Menini, Elena Cabrio, Sara Tonelli, and Serena Villata. 2020. A multilingual evaluation for online hate speech detection. *ACM Transactions on Internet Technology (TOIT)*, 20(2):1–22.

Thomas Davidson, Debasmita Bhattacharya, and Ingmar Weber. 2019. Racial bias in hate speech and abusive language detection datasets. *arXiv preprint arXiv:1905.12516*.

Muhammad Okky Ibrohim and Indra Budi. 2019. Multi-label hate speech and abusive language detection in Indonesian Twitter. In *Proceedings of the third workshop on abusive language online*, pages 46–57.

Simrat Kaur, Sarbjeet Singh, and Sakshi Kaushal. 2021. Abusive content detection in online user-generated data: a survey. *Procedia Computer Science*, 189:274–281.

Anna Koufakou, Endang Wahyu Pamungkas, Valerio Basile, Viviana Patti, et al. 2020. HurtBERT: Incorporating lexical features with BERT for the detection of abusive language. In *Proceedings of the fourth workshop on online abuse and harms*, pages 34–43. Association for Computational Linguistics.

Prasanna Kumar Kumaresan, Rahul Ponnusamy, Ruba Priyadharshini, Paul Buitelaar, and Bharathi Raja Chakravarthi. 2023. Homophobia and transphobia detection for low-resourced languages in social media comments. *Natural Language Processing Journal*, page 100041.

Abulimiti Maimaitituoheti. 2022. ABLIMET@ LT-EDI-ACL2022: a RoBERTa based approach for homophobia/transphobia detection in social media. In *Proceedings of the Second Workshop on Language Technology for Equality, Diversity and Inclusion*, pages 155–160.

Faye Mishna, Alan McLuckie, and Michael Saini. 2009. Real-world dangers in an online reality: A qualitative study examining online relationships and cyber abuse. *Social Work Research*, 33(2):107–118.

Pushkar Mishra, Marco Del Tredici, Helen Yannakoudakis, and Ekaterina Shutova. 2019. Abusive language detection with graph convolutional networks. *arXiv preprint arXiv:1904.04073*.

Hamdy Mubarak, Kareem Darwish, and Walid Magdy. 2017. Abusive language detection on Arabic social media. In *Proceedings of the first workshop on abusive language online*, pages 52–56.

Kanika Narang and Chris Brew. 2020. Abusive language detection using syntactic dependency graphs. In *Proceedings of the Fourth Workshop on Online Abuse and Harms*, pages 44–53.

Dan Olweus and Susan P Limber. 2018. Some problems with cyberbullying research. *Current opinion in psychology*, 19:139–143.

Ji Ho Park, Jamin Shin, and Pascale Fung. 2018. Reducing gender bias in abusive language detection. *arXiv preprint arXiv:1808.07231*.

Jacob Ratkiewicz, Michael Conover, Mark Meiss, Bruno Gonçalves, Alessandro Flammini, and Filippo Menczer. 2011. Detecting and tracking political abuse in social media. In *Proceedings of the International AAAI Conference on Web and social media*, volume 5, pages 297–304.

Kogilavani Shanmugavadivel, Siddhanth U Hegde, and Prasanna Kumar Kumaresan. 2022. Overview of Abusive Comment Detection in Tamil-ACL 2022. *DravidianLangTech*, 2022:292.

KEC AI DSNLP@LT-EDI-2024:Caste and Migration Hate Speech Detection using Machine Learning Techniques

Kogilavani Shanmugavadivel[1], **Malliga Subramanian**[1],
Aiswarya M[1], **Aruna T**[1], **Jeevaananth S**[1]
[1]Department of AI, Kongu Engineering College, Perundurai, Erode.
{kogilavani.sv, mallinishanth72}@gmail.com
{aiswaryam.22aid, arunat.22aid}@kongu.edu
{jeevaananths.22aid}@kongu.edu

Abstract

Commonly used language defines "hate speech" as objectionable statements that may jeopardize societal harmony by singling out a group or a person based on fundamental traits (including gender, caste, or religion). Using machine learning techniques, our research focuses on identifying hate speech in social media comments. Using a variety of machine learning methods, we created machine learning models to detect hate speech. An approximate Macro F1 of 0.60 was attained by the created models.

1 Introduction

Caste and Migration hate speech refer to the use of discriminatory language or expressions that target individuals or groups based on their caste or migration status (Chakravarthi, 2022). These forms of hate speech can manifest in various ways, including verbal abuse, written messages, online content, or even physical actions (Mehta and Passi, 2022). The effects of caste and migration hate speech can be profound and detrimental on both individual and societal levels. Hate speech can cause significant psychological distress and emotional harm to individuals who are targeted (Gaydhani et al., 2018). It can lead to feelings of fear, anxiety, depression, and a sense of isolation. Hate speech contributes to the division and polarization of communities. It can create or exacerbate existing tensions between different caste or migrant groups, leading to social fragmentation (Al-Hassan and Al-Dossari, 2019). Caste and migration hate speech can have a significant impact on social media due to the widespread reach and instantaneous nature of online platforms (Alkomah and Ma, 2022). Detecting and addressing hate speech in social media comments is important for maintaining a safe and inclusive online environment (Razdan et al., 2021). For example, Pakistan is a country where caste still persists. Caste-based hate speech is severe and pervasive in Pakistan's countryside (Fortuna and Nunes, 2018). Social media users accused Dalits of spreading the COVID-19 pandemic because they are dirty and consume dead animals during the lockdown days. Activities related to caste discrimination also occur in India.

Detecting hate speech in online comments can be challenging due to several factors, and these difficulties pose significant obstacles for both automated systems and human moderators (Asogwa et al., 2022). Hate speech often relies on context, cultural nuances, and sarcasm. Automated systems may struggle to understand these subtleties, leading to false positives or negatives (Kumar and Kumar, 2023). The same words or phrases may have different meanings in different contexts. Hate speech detection becomes more complex in multilingual and multicultural environments (Karim et al., 2022). Different languages, dialects, and cultural norms contribute to variations in expression, making it challenging for automated systems to cover a diverse range of content accurately (Ayo et al., 2020). In this paper we mainly work on Tamil-English social media comments.

The shared task on "Caste and Migration Hate Speech Detection"[1] focuses on identifying character offsets of hate speech while handling code-mixed Tamil-English comments (Rajiakodi et al., 2024). Hate speech can be extracted using a variety of methods. In this work, we approach token labeling from the perspective of hate speech detection. To detect hate speech, we assessed KNN, the Decision Tree algorithm, and the Naïve Bayes-based token labeling system.

This is how the remainder of the paper is structured. First, the literature on studies relevant to caste hate speech identification is briefly discussed

[1]https://codalab.lisn.upsaclay.fr/competitions/16089

Proceedings of the Fourth Workshop on Language Technology for Equality, Diversity, Inclusion, pages 206–210
March 21, 2024

in section 2. After a thorough description of our system in Section 3, the tests and findings are reported in Section 4. We wrap off by discussing potential implications for further research.

2 Literature Review

Hate speech has grown to be a serious issue in today's world, with the ability to hurt both individuals and communities (William et al., 2022). Using machine learning techniques to automatically identify and flag hate speech in text-based data is one possible answer to this issue (Anjum and Katarya, 2023). In order to prevent hate speech and objectionable content from proliferating on social media platforms, it is important to monitor the speech and information that users are disseminating. To remove these harmful elements, a strong automated filter system is needed (Pereira-Kohatsu et al., 2019). A wide range of topics, including politics, religion, gender, caste, race, and color, are covered by hate speech and offensive content, which has the ability to polarize society (Biere et al., 2018).

"Hate Speech Detection Using ML" - In this paper, a decision tree algorithm-based hate speech detection system is proposed. Large datasets can be handled via the straightforward and efficient machine learning algorithm known as decision trees, which has been used to a variety of classification tasks with success. The decision tree model is trained using a dataset of labeled hate speech and non-hate speech material (El-Sayed et al., 2023). The decision tree algorithm is then used to classify the input text as hate speech or non-hate speech after they preprocess the text by eliminating stop words and stemming the words, extracting pertinent characteristics using the TF-IDF approach, and so on.

"Social Shout – Hate Speech Detection Using Machine Learning Algorithm" by Ohol et al.. They investigated a number of methodologies and strategies for machine learning-based hate speech identification in this research, including feature engineering, deep learning, supervised and unsupervised learning approaches, and natural language processing. They also talked on the difficulties and constraints associated with using machine learning to detect hate speech, including the scarcity of annotated datasets, the complexity of defining and classifying hate speech, and the possibility of bias in machine learning algorithms. This paper's overall goal is to give a summary of the state of machine learning-based hate speech identification today and to draw attention to the opportunities and difficulties that await further study in this significant and quickly developing area.

"SVM for Hate Speech and Offensive Content Detection" by Ratan et al. (2021). Support Vector Machine (SVM) was the traditional machine learning method used in this paper's experiments on Hindi and English datasets. In this article, the system and its outcomes were examined, with a focus on identifying hate speech and objectionable content. In Hindi, the model performs worse (0.7195 Macro F1), but it even managed an Macro F1 Score of 0.7563 in English.

3 Problem and System Description

Figure 1 illustrates a hate speech identification example. The aim is to determine the hate speech content given the input sentence. Thuluvavellalar and Agamudayar are the names of two different castes in the example above. Thuluvavellalar caste members propagate hate speech directed at the Agamudayar caste. Once the hate speech in that specific comment has been identified, it is labeled as 1 (contains hate speech) or 0 otherwise. This dataset's description is provided in Section 3.1.

3.1 Dataset Description

There are three columns in the publicly available shared task dataset, which is written in Tamil. These columns are labeled "text", which contains comments from social media platforms that contain hate speech as well as comments that do not, "id", which is the ID of those comments, and "label", which is set to 1 for hate speech and 0 otherwise. 5,355 samples make up the training set based on classes, and 1,575 samples without labels make up the testing set based on classes.

Dataset	No. of Comments
Train	5,355
Test	1,575

Table 1: Dataset Description

3.2 Development Pipeline

Figure 2 shows the overall development process that was employed for this project. Two modules might be separated out of our pipeline: (a) Feature Extraction and (b) Machine Learning Model. which are all exactly as said.

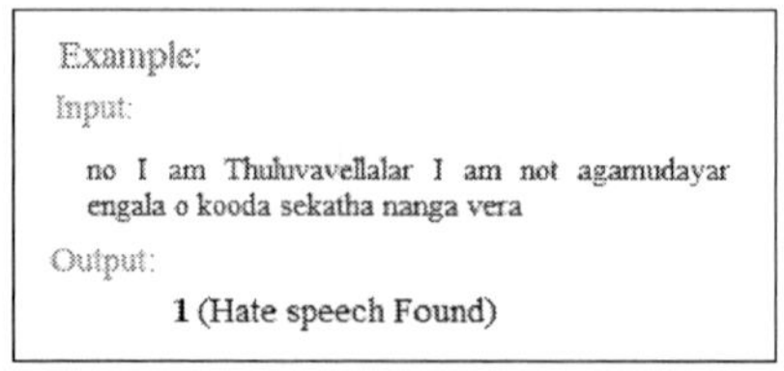

Figure 1: Example of Caste Hate Speech

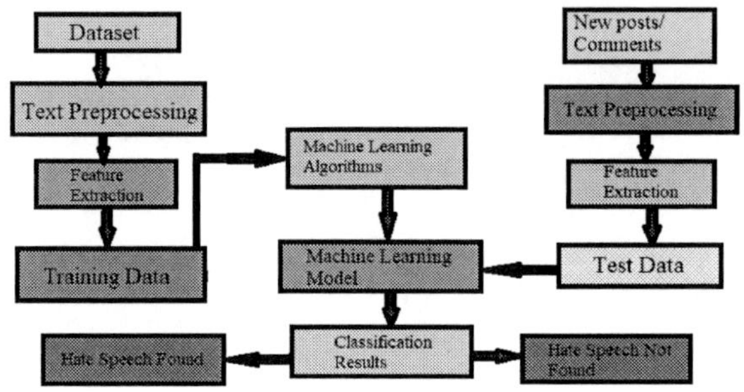

Figure 2: Proposed System Workflow

3.2.1 Feature Extraction

Since the dataset was in text format, we used a Python program to extract features so that machine learning techniques could support it. The process of converting unstructured text input into a format that machine learning algorithms may use for additional processing is known as feature extraction. To extract features for our model, we utilized TFIDFVectorizer, a Python module. Representing the significance of a word or phrase to a document is one of the most crucial information retrieval approaches. Consider the following scenario: we need to extract information from a string, or Bag of Words, and we may utilize this method to do it. TFIDF does not immediately transform unusable data into features. First, it creates vectors from raw strings or datasets, with a vector for every word. The characteristic will then be retrieved using a specific method, such as Cosine Similarity, which is applicable to vectors, etc. We are aware that the string cannot be passed straight to our model. Thus, TFIDF gives us the numerical values for each and every instances of the dataset.

3.2.2 Machine Learning Models

In recent years, machine learning has advanced significantly, altering people's perceptions of crucial applications like data mining, image recognition, and natural language processing (NLP). The machine learning models used in the current study for text classification are described in this section. We employed a variety of machine learning methods, including KNN, GaussianNB, and decision trees.wherein we chose a model based on its performance in comparison to the other two models.

KNN algorithm-The k-nearest neighbors algorithm, sometimes referred to as KNN or k-NN, is a non-parametric supervised learning classifier that groups individual data points based on closeness in order to classify or predict data. KNN can use the output of TFIDF as the input matrix and then predicts class label. Figure 3 illustrates the performance of our KNN model.

Decision Tree algorithm-A decision tree is a type of supervised learning algorithm that is commonly used in machine learning to model and predict outcomes based on input data. The decision trees implemented uses only numerical features and these features extracted by TFIDF are always as numeric variables. Figure 4 illustrates the performance of our Decision tree model.

GaussianNB-Machine learning techniques for classification based on a probabilistic method and Gaussian distribution are known as Gaussian Naive Bayes (GNB) techniques. Based on the premise that every parameter, also known as features or predictors, has the ability to independently predict the output variable, Gaussian Naive Bayes makes this

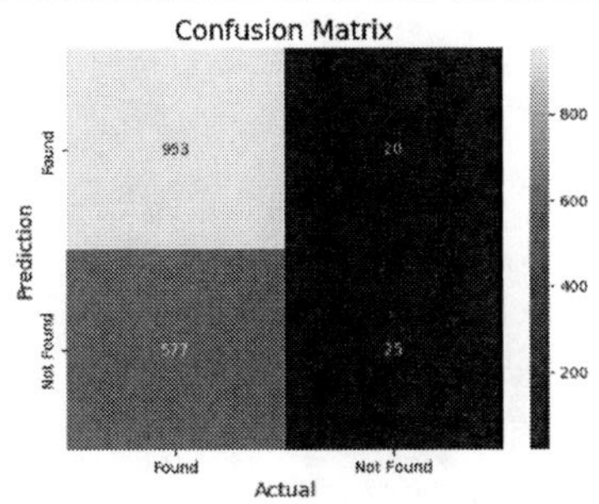

Figure 3: Performance of KNN model

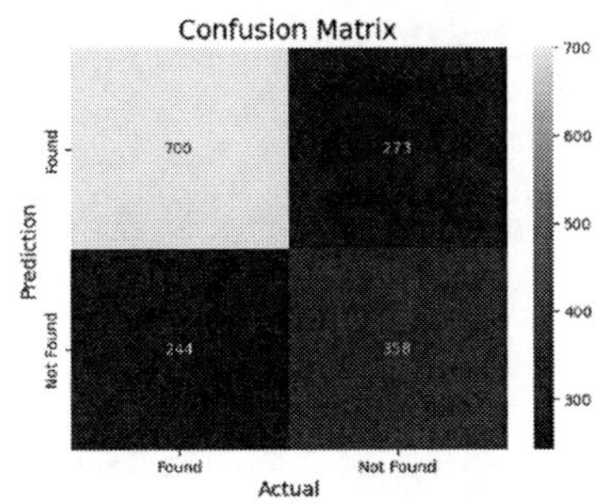

Figure 4: Performance of Decision tree model

assumption. Figure 5 illustrates the performance of our Naive Bayes model.

4 Experiments and Results

We have presented the most effective iteration of our model after doing a number of experiments to examine the model's effectiveness. The outcomes are displayed in Table 2. Although the KNN model did not yield improved accuracy, the other two models did yield better accuracy than the KNN model. Our model will get textual comments as input and then it classifies the texts whether it contains hate speech or not. As such, we intend to return to this challenge using more advanced architectures and language models.

5 Conclusion

Due to social media's accessibility and anonymity, as well as the shifting political situation in many regions of the world, hate speech has become more prevalent in recent years. The comment is identified as hate speech if the detection reveals that two or more of the individual outputs are positive for hatred; otherwise, it is identified as non-hate speech. Through text analysis, hate and offensive content were found in this study. The technique we employed in this work was designed to predict hate speech from code-mixed Tamil comments.

References

Areej Al-Hassan and Hmood Al-Dossari. 2019. Detection of hate speech in social networks: a survey on multilingual corpus. In *6th international conference on computer science and information technology*, volume 10, pages 10–5121.

Fatimah Alkomah and Xiaogang Ma. 2022. A literature review of textual hate speech detection methods and datasets. *Information*, 13(6):273.

Anjum and Rahul Katarya. 2023. Hate speech, toxicity detection in online social media: a recent survey of state of the art and opportunities. *International Journal of Information Security*, pages 1–32.

Doris Chinedu Asogwa, Chiamaka Ijeoma Chukwuneke, CC Ngene, and GN Anigbogu. 2022. Hate speech classification using SVM and NAIVE BAYES. *arXiv preprint arXiv:2204.07057*.

Femi Emmanuel Ayo, Olusegun Folorunso, Friday Thomas Ibharalu, and Idowu Ademola Osinuga. 2020. Hate speech detection in Twitter using hybrid embeddings and improved cuckoo search-based neural networks. *International Journal of Intelligent Computing and Cybernetics*, 13(4):485–525.

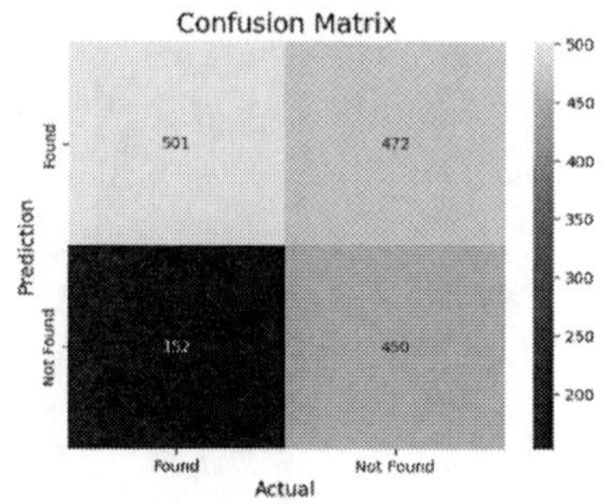

Figure 5: Performance of Naive Bayes model

Model	Macro F1-score
K-Nearest Neighbour	0.0772
Decision Tree	0.5862
Naive Bayes	0.5905

Table 2: Evaluation Metrics

Shanita Biere, Sandjai Bhulai, and Master Business Analytics. 2018. Hate speech detection using natural language processing techniques. *Master Business AnalyticsDepartment of Mathematics Faculty of Science.*

Bharathi Raja Chakravarthi. 2022. Hope speech detection in YouTube comments. *Social Network Analysis and Mining*, 12(1):75.

Tharwat El-Sayed, Abdallah Mustafa, Ayman El-Sayed, and Mohamed Elrashidy. 2023. Hate speech detection by classic machine learning. In *2023 3rd International Conference on Electronic Engineering (ICEEM)*, pages 1–4. IEEE.

Paula Fortuna and Sérgio Nunes. 2018. A survey on automatic detection of hate speech in text. *ACM Computing Surveys (CSUR)*, 51(4):1–30.

Aditya Gaydhani, Vikrant Doma, Shrikant Kendre, and Laxmi Bhagwat. 2018. Detecting hate speech and offensive language on Twitter using machine learning: An n-gram and TFIDF based approach. *arXiv preprint arXiv:1809.08651.*

Md Rezaul Karim, Sumon Kanti Dey, Tanhim Islam, Md Shajalal, and Bharathi Raja Chakravarthi. 2022. Multimodal hate speech detection from Bengali memes and texts. In *International Conference on Speech and Language Technologies for Low-resource Languages*, pages 293–308. Springer.

Ashwini Kumar and Santosh Kumar. 2023. Hate speech detection in multi-social media using deep learning. In *International Conference on Advanced Communication and Intelligent Systems*, pages 59–70. Springer.

Harshkumar Mehta and Kalpdrum Passi. 2022. Social media hate speech detection using explainable artificial intelligence (xai). *Algorithms*, 15(8):291.

VB Ohol, Siddhi Patil, Ishwari Gamne, Sayali Patil, and Shweta Bandawane. Social shout–hate speech detection using machine learning algorithm.

Juan Carlos Pereira-Kohatsu, Lara Quijano-Sánchez, Federico Liberatore, and Miguel Camacho-Collados. 2019. Detecting and monitoring hate speech in Twitter. *Sensors*, 19(21):4654.

Saranya Rajiakodi, Bharathi Raja Chakravarthi, Rahul Ponnusamy, Prasanna Kumar Kumaresan, Sathiyaraj Thangasamy, Bhuvaneswari Sivagnanam, and Charmathi Rajkumar. 2024. Overview of Shared Task on Caste and Migration Hate Speech Detection. In *Proceedings of the Fourth Workshop on Language Technology for Equality, Diversity and Inclusion*, Malta. European Chapter of the Association for Computational Linguistics.

Shyam Ratan, Sonal Sinha, and Siddharth Singh. 2021. SVM for Hate Speech and Offensive Content Detection.

Aditya Razdan et al. 2021. Hate speech detection using ml algorithms. In *2021 International Conference on Artificial Intelligence and Machine Vision (AIMV)*, pages 1–6. IEEE.

P William, Ritik Gade, Rup esh Chaudhari, AB Pawar, and MA Jawale. 2022. Machine learning based automatic hate speech recognition system. In *2022 International conference on sustainable computing and data communication systems (ICSCDS)*, pages 315–318. IEEE.

Quartet@LT-EDI 2024: A Support Vector Machine Approach For Caste and Migration Hate Speech Detection

Shaun Allan H
Sri Sivasubramaniya Nadar College of Engineering
shaunallan2210716@ssn.edu.in

Samyuktaa Sivakumar
Sri Sivasubramaniya Nadar College of Enginerring
samyuktaa2210189@ssn.edu.in

Rohan R
Sri Sivasubramaniya Nadar College of Enginerring
rohan2210124@ssn.edu.in

Nikilesh Jayaguptha
Sri Sivasubramaniya Nadar College of Engineering
nikilesh2210219@ssn.edu.in

Durairaj Thenmozhi
Sri Sivasubramaniya Nadar College of Engineering
theni_d@ssn.edu.in

Abstract

Hate speech refers to the offensive remarks against a community or individual based on inherent characteristics. Hate speech against a community based on their caste and native are unfortunately prevalent in the society. Especially with social media platforms being a very popular tool for communication and sharing ideas, people post hate speech against caste or migrants on social medias. The Shared Task LT–EDI 2024: Caste and Migration Hate Speech Detection was created with the objective to create an automatic classification system that detects and classifies hate speech posted on social media targeting a community belonging to a particular caste and migrants. Datasets in Tamil language were provided along with the shared task. We experimented with several traditional models such as Naive Bayes, Support Vector Machine (SVM), Logistic Regression, Random Forest Classifier and Decision Tree Classifier out of which Support Vector Machine yielded the best results placing us 8th in the rank list released by the organizers.

1 Introduction

Hate is a very strong emotion or feeling of not liking someone or something. Hate expresses intense hostility towards others. Hate speech reflecting the same, refers to the offensive remarks or comments uttered by a person targeting a community or an individual person. Hate speeches are often uttered based on the target's inherent characteristics such as race, ethnicity, religion or gender.

In recent days, it can be said that social media platforms have enormously changed the way people communicate with one another (O'Keeffe et al., 2011). Social media can be seen as an immensely great tool for people to share their thoughts and ideas with the world. This has allowed the people to voice out their opinions broadening their freedom of speech. While this can benefit people a lot, it also comes with its own disadvantages.

Social media platforms are a place where individuals voice out their opinions, but there are also people who spread hate against a community or individual. We see hate speeches being posted in social media platforms very often (Mondal et al., 2017). Hate speeches targeting a particular community based on their caste and native place are prevalent in social media.

Hate speech inflicts immediate harm on its victims and also contributes to discrimination against the targeted community or individual. These sort of hate comments against a caste or migrants must be obliterated from the society. With social media platforms being an inevitable and popular tool in the modern society, it becomes imperative to moderate the hate speech posts. It is essential for a more positive and inclusive society.

Sentiment analysis, also known as opinion mining can be employed to detect and moderate the hate comments prevailing on social media platforms. Sentiment analysis is the process of determining the emotional tone that a digital text manifests (Taboada, 2016). Textual data can be analyzed and determined if the text expresses a positive, negative or neutral sentiment. Sentiment analysis is an immensely powerful tool to automate the process of detecting caste and migration hate speech on social media by analyzing the sentiment or emotion that the text manifests. Sentiment analysis can be carried out by supervised learning in case of availability to a well labelled and quality training data. In situations where one has no access to training data, unsupervised learning can also be utilized to perform sentiment analysis (Schouten et al., 2018).

The Shared Task LT–EDI 2024: Caste and Migration Hate Speech Detection was created with the motive to build an automation system that detects and classifies the text in Tamil language on social media platforms as caste and migration hate speech or not. Datasets containing text in Tamil language

Proceedings of the Fourth Workshop on Language Technology for Equality, Diversity, Inclusion, pages 211–215
March 21, 2024

were provided along with the shared task.

This paper is organized as follows: Section 2 encompasses the related works as per the literature survey; Section 3 is entails information about the task and data; Section 4 pertains to the methodology used to build the classification system; Section 5 shows the results and analysis; Section 6 entails the conclusion; Sections 7 and 8 pertains to the limitaions of the model and the ethics statement respectively.

2 Related Works

Sentiment analysis is a field in which constant works and researches are being carried on. They have many applications on social and e-commerce platforms.

Rajput et al. (2021) proposed a hate speech detection classifier by replacing or integrating the word embeddings (fastText(FT), GloVe(GV) or FT + GV) with static word BERT embeddings. With extensive experimental traits it is observed that the performance of a neural network with static BERT embeddings is better than that wit FT, GV or FT + GV.

A large-scale analysis of multilingual hate speech in 9 languages from 16 different sources was conducted by Aluru et al. (2020). It was observed that in low resource setting, simple models such as LASER embedding with logistic regression performs the best, while in high resource setting BERT based models perform the best.

HateBERT, a re-trained BERT model was proposed by Caselli et al. (2021) for abusive language detection in English. The model was trained on RAL-E, a large-scale dataset of offensive Reddit comments in English.

Saha et al. (2018) built an automatic hate speech detection system against women by generating three types of features from the text: Sentence Embeddings, TF-IDF vectors and BOW vectors. These features were then concatenated and fed into a Logistic Regression model.

Rajalakshmi et al. (2023) experiments several machine learning models to classify hate speech in Tamil texts. Several models including BERT, XLM-RoBERTa, IndicBERT, mBERT, TaMillion and MuRIL were experimented. It was observed that the highest performance was achieved by a combination of stemming the text data, embedding it with MuRIL and using a majority voting ensemble as the downstream classifier. Alatawi et al. (2021) investigates the feasibility of leveraging domain-specific word embedding in Bidirectional LSTM based deep model to automatically detect/classify hate speech. Furthermore, the use of the transfer learning language model (BERT) on hate speech problem as a binary classification task was investigated.

3 Task and Data Description

The objective of the Shared Task LT–EDI 2024: Caste and Migration Hate Speech Detection[1] (Rajiakodi et al., 2024) is to create an automatic classification system that detects and classifies whether a text is caste and migration hate speech or not. Training and development datasets were provided in Tamil language. The dataset encompassed two fields: text and label. The training dataset had a total of 5,355 records out of which 2,052 were labelled 1 representing caste and migration hate speech and 3,303 were labelled 0 representing non caste and migration hate speech.

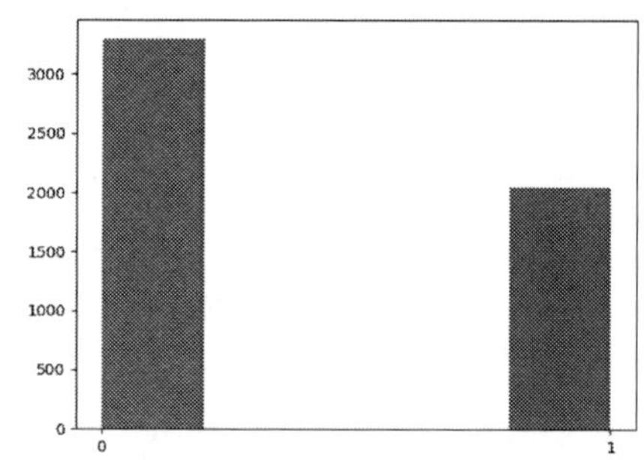

Figure 1: Data Distribution in Training Dataset

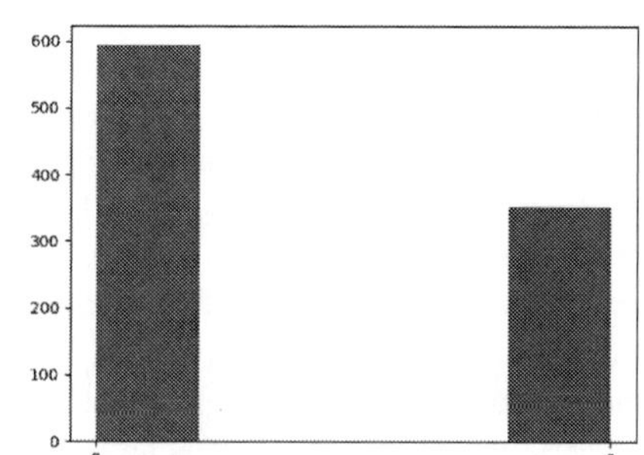

Figure 2: Data Distribution in Development Dataset

[1]https://codalab.lisn.upsaclay.fr/competitions/16089

The development dataset had a total of 945 records out of which 351 were labelled as hate speech and 594 were labelled as non-hate speech.

4 Methodology

4.1 Data Preprocessing

The given textual cannot be directly fed to the machine learning model. Data must be well processed and cleansed in order to yield better results.

1. The given textual data consisted of emoticons and punctuations which don't add any meaning to the text thus contributing nothing to the classification process. Therefore, it is important to remove these emoticons and punctuations before any further process.

2. As most of the embedding systems available work better on English on text than regional languages, the given text which is in Tamil is translated to English using googleTrans[2] library. Translating the text to English increases the accuracy of our classification system.

3. Stop words are redundant words present in a text that don't contribute any emotion for sentiment analysis. These stop words are eliminated from the given text using the NLTK[3] library. Removing these stop words decreases the dataset size and hence the training time of the model also decreases.

[2] https://pypi.org/project/googletrans/

4.2 Feature Extraction

Feature extraction is the process of converting raw digital text into vectors containing numerical inputs. As machine learning models cannot work on textual data, texts have to be converted into numerical vectors suitable for the model to work with.

We have employed Term Frequency–Inverse Document Frequency (TF–IDF) vectorizer from the scikit learn library to extract features from the translated English text. Term Frequency refers to the frequency of a term appearing in a particular document while Inverse Document Frequency refers to the measure of how common a term is in the entire corpus of documents. TF-IDF value of a term is defined as the product of its Term Frequency and Inverse Document Frequency.

4.3 Classification using ML Models

We employed several traditional models such as Logistic Regression, Support Vector Machine (SVM), Random Forest Classifier, Decision Tree Classifier

[3] https://www.nltk.org/

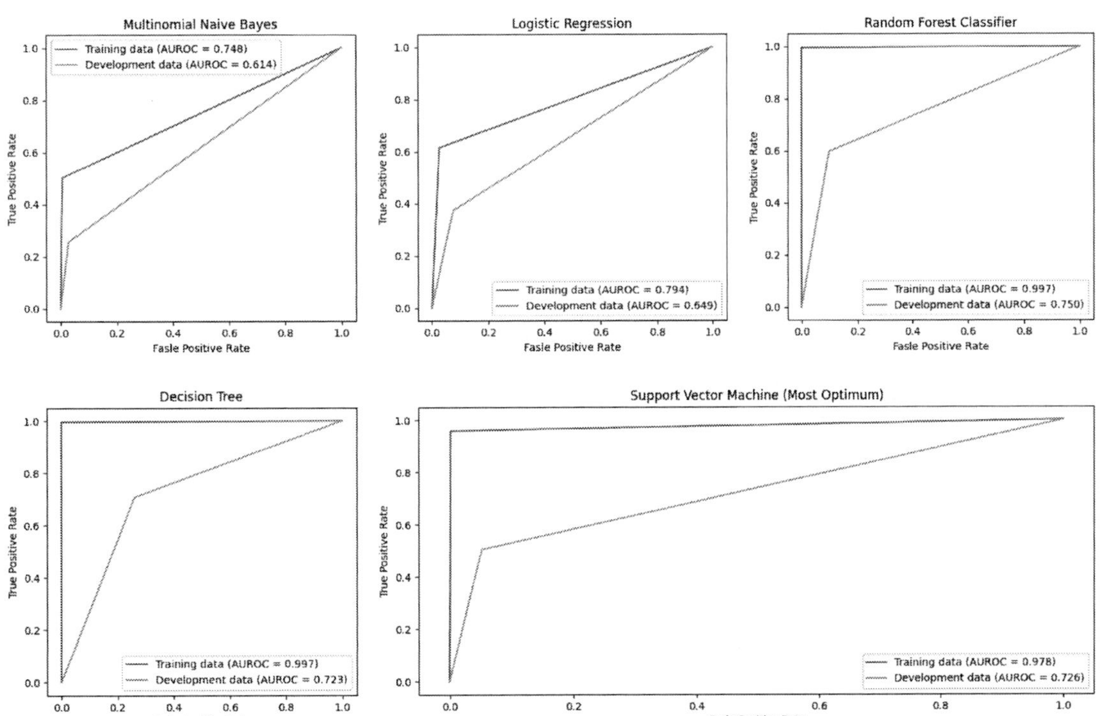

Figure 3: Comparison and Analysis of ROC Curves and AUROC scores

Metric	Logistic Regression	Support Vector Machine	Random Forest Classifier	Decision Tree Classifier	Naive Bayes
Accuracy	0.72	0.78	0.78	0.73	0.70
Macro Average F1 score	0.65	0.74	0.75	0.71	0.60

Table 1: Comparison of metrics on Development Data

	Precision	Recall	F1-score	Support
Non Caste and Migration Hate Speech	0.76	0.93	0.84	973
Caste and Migration Hate Speech	0.82	0.52	0.64	602
Accuracy			0.77	1,575
Macro Avg	0.79	0.75	0.74	1,575
Weighted Avg	0.78	0.77	0.76	1,575

Table 2: Classification Report for SVM on Test Data

and Naive Bayes on the extracted numerical features. After evaluating the metrics of all the models, Support Vector Machine yielded the highest accuracy and macro average of F1 score. Support Vector Machine (SVM) is one of the most popular supervised machine learning algorithms widely used for classification tasks as well as regression tasks. SVM works on finding the best hyperplane that separates data points of different classes in a feature space.

5 Result and Analysis

The performance of various traditional models including Naive Bayes, Support Vector Machine (SVM), Random Forest Classifier, Decision Tree Classifier and Logistic Regression were evaluated and compared. The Receiver Operating Characteristic (ROC) curve was plotted and the Area Under Receiver Operating Characteristic (AUROC) was calculated for all the models. The ROC curve is defined as the curve that is plotted against the True Positive Rate and False Positive Rate of the predictions obtained from a model at varying threshold levels. The ROC curve is a very useful visual representation to analyze and compare the performance of classification models.

On evaluating the metrics of the models, it is found that Support Vector Machine (SVM) produced the best numbers on both training data and development data. It is to be noted that though Random Forest Classifier performed very slightly better than SVM on unseen development data, with the macro average score on training data being 1.00, the model is considered overfitted.

On evaluating with the test data given by the organizers, the SVM model yielded a macro average F1 score of 0.74. We were ranked 8th in the rank list released by the organizers.

6 Conclusion

By means of this paper, we experimented several traditional machine learning models on the features extracted by the TF-IDF vectorizer. The metrics and ROC curves of each model were plotted and analysed to effectively compare the performance of the models. It was observed that out of all models, Support Vector Machine (SVM) gave the best metrics and ROC curve. While this model has good performance over the other models, it is to be noted that better results can be obtained by utilizing neural networks and more complex embedding systems.

7 Limitations

Thought the TF-IDF vectorizer which was used to extract the features from was digital text performs well in most cases, comes with its own inherent limitations. The TF-IDF vectorizer makes no use of the semantic relations between words for feature extraction. Also, feature extraction can be slow when handling with large vocabularies because it computes document similarity directly in the word-count space.

As the model is built with SVM algorithm, when trained with immensely large datasets, the SVM model fails to perform well and also consume a lot of time and memory for training. The final model is difficult to understand an interpret as a result of which small calibrations cannot be done to the model. Also, a probabilistic interpretation of the result cannot be produced as the SVM algorithm is incapable of producing such probabilistic results.

8 Ethics Statement

We ensured that the ACL Code of Ethics[4] was practiced throughout the process of working on the Shared Task. The main notion behind building the classification system is to make social media platforms a safe and inclusive environment for all community of people to thrive and exist by detecting and moderating caste and migration hate speech in social media platforms. Credits have been given to all authors whose existing works and ideas has been referenced or utilized in References section. Data privacy is a priority in our solution as it does not provide any access on data to random individuals or organizations ensuring no leak of information.

The given task was used as an opportunity to upgrade and enhance our skills while practicing the principles of professional competence. The proposed solution abides by the local, regional, national and international laws and regulations.

References

Hind S Alatawi, Areej Alhothali, and Kawthar Moria. 2021. Detection of hate speech using BERT and hate speech word embedding with deep model. *ArXiv, abs/2111.01515*.

Sai Saketh Aluru, Binny Mathew, Punyajoy Saha, and Animesh Mukherjee. 2020. Deep learning models for multilingual hate speech detection.

Tommaso Caselli, Valerio Basile, Jelena Mitrović, and Michael Granitzer. 2021. HateBERT: Retraining BERT for Abusive Language Detection in English.

Mainack Mondal, Leandro Araújo Silva, and Fabrício Benevenuto. 2017. A measurement study of hate speech in social media. In *Proceedings of the 28th ACM Conference on Hypertext and Social Media*, HT '17, page 85–94, New York, NY, USA. Association for Computing Machinery.

[4]https://www.aclweb.org/portal/content/acl-code-ethics

Gwenn Schurgin O'Keeffe, Kathleen Clarke-Pearson, et al. 2011. The impact of social media on children, adolescents, and families. *Pediatrics*, 127(4):800–804.

Ratnavel Rajalakshmi, Srivarshan Selvaraj, Faerie Mattins R., Pavitra Vasudevan, and Anand Kumar M. 2023. HOTTEST: Hate and Offensive content identification in Tamil using Transformers and Enhanced Stemming. *Computer Speech Language*, 78:101464.

Saranya Rajiakodi, Bharathi Raja Chakravarthi, Rahul Ponnusamy, Prasanna Kumar Kumaresan, Sathiyaraj Thangasamy, Bhuvaneswari S, and Charmathi Rajkumar. 2024. Overview of Shared Task on Caste and Migration Hate Speech Detection. In *Proceedings of the Fourth Workshop on Language Technology for Equality, Diversity and Inclusion*, Malta. European Chapter of the Association for Computational Linguistics.

Gaurav Rajput, Narinder Singh Punn, Sanjay Kumar Sonbhadra, and Sonali Agarwal. 2021. *Hate Speech Detection Using Static BERT Embeddings*, page 67–77. Springer International Publishing.

Punyajoy Saha, Binny Mathew, Pawan Goyal, and Animesh Mukherjee. 2018. Hateminers : Detecting hate speech against women.

Kim Schouten, Onne van der Weijde, Flavius Frasincar, and Rommert Dekker. 2018. Supervised and unsupervised aspect category detection for sentiment analysis with co-occurrence data. *IEEE Transactions on Cybernetics*, 48(4):1263–1275.

Maite Taboada. 2016. Sentiment analysis: An overview from linguistics. *Annual Review of Linguistics*, 2(1):325–347.

SSN-Nova@LT-EDI 2024: Leveraging Vectorisation Techniques in an Ensemble Approach for Stress Identification in Low-Resource Languages

A Ankitha Reddy, Ann Maria Thomas, Pranav Moorthi & B. Bharathi
Department of CSE
Sri Sivasubramaniya Nadar College of Engineering, Tamil Nadu, India
ankithareddy2210178@ssn.edu.in, annthomas2210391@ssn.edu.in
pranav2210176@ssn.edu.in, bharathib@ssn.edu.in

Abstract

This paper presents our submission for Shared task on Stress Identification in Dravidian Languages: StressIdent LT-EDI@EACL2024. The objective of this task is to identify stress levels in individuals based on their social media content. The system is tasked with analyzing posts written in a code-mixed language of Tamil and Telugu and categorizing them into two labels: "stressed" or "not stressed." Our approach aimed to leverage feature extraction and juxtapose the performance of widely used traditional, deep learning and transformer models. Our research highlighted that building a pipeline with traditional classifiers proved to significantly improve their performance, surpassing the baseline as well as deep learning and transformer models.

1 Introduction

Stress is a complex and multifaceted psychological and physiological response to challenges or demands, often characterized by a state of heightened arousal and a perceived inability to cope with the stressor (Yaribeygi et al., 2017). In the contemporary era, psychological stress is widely acknowledged as a major factor contributing to a variety of health issues and mental disorders. The complexities of modern life, marked by rapid technological changes, societal expectations, and economic pressures, have made stress a pervasive issue. People from various backgrounds are experiencing the adverse effects of persistent stress, leading to various health challenges and mental health issues (Lin et al., 2014b).

The dynamic evolution of social networks has prompted a widespread trend wherein individuals extensively employ various social media platforms as primary channels for expressing their thoughts and emotions. This shift in communication patterns emphasizes the growing reliance on these platforms as primary channels for expressing perspectives and feelings. Notably, amidst this surge, people increasingly turn to social media to vent about their stress (Jalonen, 2014), highlighting the importance of identifying and addressing these expressions to support the mental well-being of users. Various approaches have been crafted for the analysis of physiological data with the goal of stress identification (Greene et al., 2016). The feasibility of identifying the stress of the users through the analysis of their social media activities, such as tweets has been substantiated (Lin et al., 2014a). However, the current state of machine learning models reveals a gap in addressing stress detection in Dravidian languages, such as Tamil and Telugu due to the dearth of well-annotated datasets and proficiently trained models specific to these linguistic contexts. This deficit poses a significant challenge in developing accurate algorithms for identifying stress within the nuanced expressions inherent in Dravidian language structures.

Our paper's sequence is as follows - In Section 2, we navigate through existing publications focusing on text classification tasks in low-resource languages. Section 3 undertakes an analysis of the dataset distribution. Our proposed model's methodology is outlined in Section 4. Section 5 examines the performance metrics of our solutions.

2 Related Work

Extensive research in the field of sentiment analysis and text classification has predominantly centred around languages with Latin scripts, such as English and Spanish (Argamon and Koppel, 2013; Muñoz and Iglesias, 2022; Miranda et al., 2023). Not much research has been reported in other languages with some notable ones including Arabic (Aljarah et al., 2021; Al-Hassan and Al-Dossari, 2022) and Dravidian languages (Badjatiya et al., 2017; Banerjee et al., 2020).

To address the major issues regarding Dra-

Proceedings of the Fourth Workshop on Language Technology for Equality, Diversity, Inclusion, pages 216–220
March 21, 2024 ©2024 Association for Computational Linguistics

vidian code-mixed and code-switched datasets, transformer-based models like m-BERT, distilBERT, xlm-RoBERTa, and MuRIL, which are pre-trained on a large corpus of multiple Indian languages, have proven to outperform deep learning (DL) models (Dowlagar and Mamidi, 2021a).

However, aiming to explore and leverage the applications of state-of-the-art technology including transformers and deep-learning in low-resource languages, (Roy et al., 2022) implemented ensemble techniques with the experimental outcomes of the weighted ensemble framework outperforming state-of-the-art models by achieving 0.802 and 0.933 weighted F1-score for Malayalam and Tamil code-mixed datasets. Similar results were produced using a pre-trained multilingual-BERT model with convolution neural networks (Dowlagar and Mamidi, 2021b).

Withal, taking the limited availability of annotated data in Dravidian languages such as Tamil and Telugu (S et al., 2022), traditional machine learning models have outperformed state-of-the-art technology in numerous similar ventures due to their ability to learn linear features from smaller datasets (Saumya et al., 2021; Jauhiainen et al., 2021).

3 Dataset Analysis

The task has been bifurcated based on language into Tamil and Telugu. The provided labels for the data were "Stressed" and "Non stressed". The data distribution is provided in Table 1.

Category	Telugu	Tamil
Non - Stressed	3314	3720
Stressed	1783	1784

Table 1: Data distribution

An examination of the distribution of data offers insight into disparities among classes that may pose potential impediments to the efficacy of models. To address this imbalance and optimize the operational efficiency of our model, we conducted data augmentation on the datasets, which will be elucidated in detail in Section 4

4 Methodology

4.1 Data Augmentation

Data augmentation via back translation was implemented to augment the dataset size. The act of translating a text into another language not only transforms the meaning and semantic value of the sentence, but the subsequent back translation introduces a layer of linguistic diversity. This sophisticated process not only elevates the robustness and generalization of the model but also upholds the context and quality of the text. In light of the inherent imbalances within our dataset, a systematic data augmentation strategy was employed to address label disproportionality. The changes made to the dataset are reflected in Table 2.

Category	Telugu	Tamil
Non - Stressed	3314	3720
Stressed	2283	2284

Table 2: Data distribution after augmentation

4.2 Preprocessing

Data preprocessing is a critical step in optimizing model efficiency and influencing performance metrics. The process involves several key steps: firstly, text normalization, which encompasses expanding contractions and converting text to lowercase, promoting uniform analysis. Following this, removing special characters, symbols, and emojis streamlines the text, reducing the volume for the model to process. Subsequently, the elimination of stop words, those with minimal semantic value, expedites processing and enhances computational efficiency. Lastly, stemming reduces words to their root form, aiding tasks like sentiment analysis by consolidating related words.

4.3 Feature Extraction

*1. **TF IDF Vectorizer:*** TF-IDF, or Term Frequency-Inverse Document Frequency, is a technique for creating features from text data by measuring the importance of words in a collection of documents. It assigns higher importance to words exclusive to a small set of documents. The TF-IDF vectorizer matches each feature to a numerical value calculated from its TF-IDF score, obtained by multiplying term frequency and inverse document frequency. This methodology is utilized in this task to convert preprocessed data into structured numerical representations, facilitating the application of natural language processing models to unstructured text data.

*2. **Word2Vec:*** Embeddings involve translating categorical variables, like words or phrases, into continuous vectors within a lower-dimensional space. Widely used in machine learning, these numerical representations adeptly capture semantic nuances and contextual meanings. For instance, word embeddings associate words with vectors in a high-dimensional space, preserving semantic relationships. This conversion is crucial for the compatibility of machine learning algorithms with numerical data, enabling a nuanced understanding of the significance of words within the given context (Chatterjee et al., 2019).

4.4 Multilingual BERT (m-BERT)

m-BERT, falling within the realm of transformer models, has undergone training across 104 languages. As a case-sensitive model, m-BERT is predominantly trained on raw texts with the primary objectives of predicting masked words within sentences and forecasting the subsequent sentence. Leveraging a bidirectional approach for predictions, m-BERT exhibits the capability to discern the semantic nature of sentences across different languages. Through the separation of sentences into two classes and the introduction of a special classification token as the initial token in every sequence, m-BERT achieves classification by adding an embedding to each token.

4.5 CNN-LSTM

```
Model: "sequential"
_________________________________________________________________
 Layer (type)                Output Shape              Param #
=================================================================
 embedding (Embedding)       (20, 20000, 300)          6000000

 conv1d (Conv1D)             (20, 20000, 32)           28832

 max_pooling1d (MaxPooling1  (20, 10000, 32)           0
 D)

 dropout (Dropout)           (20, 10000, 32)           0

 lstm (LSTM)                 (20, 300)                 399600

 dropout_1 (Dropout)         (20, 300)                 0

 dense (Dense)               (20, 1)                   301

=================================================================
Total params: 6428733 (24.52 MB)
Trainable params: 428733 (1.64 MB)
Non-trainable params: 6000000 (22.89 MB)
_________________________________________________________________
```

Figure 1: CNN-LSTM Model Architecture

Convolutional Neural Networks (CNNs) are multi-layered artificial neural networks renowned for their ability to discern intricate features from diverse datasets, treating text as one-dimensional signals employing filters akin to image processing. By viewing word sequences as spatial structures, CNNs skillfully identify relationships between different segments of sentences and the semantic similarity between sentences.

Long Short-Term Memory (LSTM) stands as a sophisticated variant of recurrent neural networks (RNNs). Its ability to control the information flow to the cell state, carefully regulated by structures called gates empowers the LSTM to selectively preserve or discard data, thereby enhancing its efficacy in capturing intricate dependencies within sequential data.

The CNN-LSTM model employs convolution for local feature extraction and LSTM for interpreting the text ordering. Tokenisation and embedding precede the model architecture, integrating an Embedding layer, 1D Convolution layer, max pooling and LSTM layer, with a detailed description of the model architecture provided in Figure 1.

4.6 Stacking Classifier

This is a mechanism for amalgamating diverse classification models through the utilization of a final classifier, known as the meta-classifier. The training process involves individual classifiers being trained on the designated dataset, while the meta-classifier is subsequently trained on the predicted class labels. This ensemble learning technique, characterized by its flexibility and adaptability across various machine learning algorithms, designates the individual classifiers as base learners, making it a versatile solution applicable to different problem domains.

On analysis of various traditional ML models, Support Vector Classifier and Random Forest Classifier were incorporated as the base models due to their exceptional performance. Logistic regression was implemented as the meta-classifier in our approach as it establishes a connection between independent variables and a categorical outcome variable by approximating the likelihood that the outcome belongs to a specific class. It helps estimate the outcome variable when presented with new predictive variable values.

5 Results and Analysis

The evaluation of the task is done based on the following performance metrics: macro-average precision, macro-average recall and macro-average F1-score as provided in table 4 and 5. Before this is the comparison of the feature extraction techniques implemented in Table 3.

Model	TF IDF	Word2Vec
Logistic Regression	0.93	0.90
Stacking Classifer	0.95	0.92
CNN LSTM	0.42	0.64
Linear SVC	0.97	0.97

Table 3: Results of models on Telugu validation set with different vectorisation Techniques

On analysis of the precision of each model implemented following the different vectorisation techniques, TF-IDF has emerged as the most efficient. This could plausibly be due to TF-IDF's sparse representation of the document-term matrix, emphasizing the importance of terms based on their frequency and rarity across the corpus. This is beneficial when dealing with low-resource scenarios where datasets are limited, as it helps capture distinctive features. Word2Vec, while powerful, relies on distributed representations and might face challenges in low-resource scenarios where the model struggles to capture diverse semantics due to limited data. This may also affect combination vectorisation techniques as it may introduce complexity and degrade the performance.

However, the outlier in this hypothesis is the superiority of the Word2Vec vectoriser when utilised in the CNN-LSTM model due to its lower-dimensional embeddings and continuous vector representations for words that capture semantic relationships and contextual information, making it more suitable for deep learning models.

Model	Precision	Recall	F1-Score
Logistic Regression	0.91	0.89	0.90
Stacking Classifier	0.98	0.98	0.98
CNN LSTM	0.46	0.68	0.55
Linear SVC	0.92	0.91	0.91

Table 4: Performance of the proposed system using validation data in Tamil code-mixed text

Model	Precision	Recall	F1-Score
Logistic Regression	0.93	0.90	0.91
Stacking Classifer	0.95	0.92	0.93
CNN LSTM	0.42	0.64	0.51
Linear SVC	0.97	0.97	0.97

Table 5: Performance of the proposed system using validation data in Telugu code-mixed text

Deep learning techniques have proven to perform significantly well with longer-length sentences (Yenala et al., 2018). However, most social media comments tend to be much shorter, enabling better performance than traditional models. Hence, we hypothesise that an ensemble of traditional classifiers employing probabilistic and deterministic classifiers would produce better results than deep learning models not only due to the linear relationship of the data but also the usage of shorter sentences.

Parallel to both conventional deep learning methodologies and traditional approaches, the m-BERT transformer model achieved an accuracy of 99.93 on the Tamil validation dataset. Nevertheless, despite its extensive multilingual training, theoretically providing the transformer with a competitive advantage, an investigation revealed that the model exhibited signs of overfitting. This occurred despite deliberate efforts to mitigate overfitting by reducing the model's complexity and implementing data augmentation techniques to address class imbalances in the dataset. This revelation prompted a reevaluation of our methodology, prompting an exploration of alternative strategies to fortify the resilience of our model.

6 Conclusion

In conclusion, our research on stress identification for Dravidian languages has yielded insightful findings across various vectorisation techniques and modelling approaches. The analysis of model accuracy points to TF-IDF as the most efficient vectorisation technique.

The discrepancy in the performance of the m-BERT transformer raises questions about its adaptability in specific linguistic contexts, emphasising the importance of thorough validation and optimisation procedures even in well-established transformer models. Furthermore, the study underscores the nuanced dynamics between the nature of the data and model performance.

In light of the discerned constraints of the m-BERT transformer model, Our investigation reveals that social media comments favour traditional models, leading us to propose an ensemble technique, leveraging both probabilistic and deterministic classifiers to outperform deep learning and stand-alone classifiers. The Voting Classifier emerged as an enticing alternative, not only combatting the challenge of overfitting but also elevating the overall efficacy of our model.

References

Areej Al-Hassan and Hmood Al-Dossari. 2022. Detection of hate speech in arabic tweets using deep learning. *Multimedia systems*, 28(6):1963–1974.

Ibrahim Aljarah, Maria Habib, Neveen Hijazi, Hossam Faris, Raneem Qaddoura, Bassam Hammo, Mohammad Abushariah, and Mohammad Alfawareh. 2021. Intelligent detection of hate speech in arabic social network: A machine learning approach. *Journal of Information Science*, 47(4):483–501.

Shlomo Argamon and Moshe Koppel. 2013. A systemic functional approach to automated authorship analysis. *Journal of Law Policy*, 12:299–315.

Pinkesh Badjatiya, Shashank Gupta, Manish Gupta, and Vasudeva Varma. 2017. Deep learning for hate speech detection in tweets.

Shubhanker Banerjee, Bharathi Raja Chakravarthi, and John P McCrae. 2020. Comparison of pretrained embeddings to identify hate speech in indian code-mixed text. In *2020 2nd International Conference on Advances in Computing, Communication Control and Networking (ICACCCN)*, pages 21–25. IEEE.

Ankush Chatterjee, Umang Gupta, Manoj Kumar Chinnakotla, Radhakrishnan Srikanth, Michel Galley, and Puneet Agrawal. 2019. Understanding emotions in text using deep learning and big data. *Comput. Hum. Behav.*, 93:309–317.

Suman Dowlagar and Radhika Mamidi. 2021a. Edione@ lt-edi-eacl2021: Pre-trained transformers with convolutional neural networks for hope speech detection. In *Proceedings of the First Workshop on Language Technology for Equality, Diversity and Inclusion*, pages 86–91.

Suman Dowlagar and Radhika Mamidi. 2021b. EDIOne@LT-EDI-EACL2021: Pre-trained transformers with convolutional neural networks for hope speech detection. In *Proceedings of the First Workshop on Language Technology for Equality, Diversity and Inclusion*, pages 86–91, Kyiv. Association for Computational Linguistics.

Shalom Greene, Himanshu Thapliyal, and Allison Caban-Holt. 2016. A survey of affective computing for stress detection: Evaluating technologies in stress detection for better health. *IEEE Consumer Electronics Magazine*, 5:44–56.

Harri Jalonen. 2014. Social media – an arena for venting negative emotions. *Online Journal of Communication and Media Technologies*, 4:53–70.

Tommi Jauhiainen, Tharindu Ranasinghe, and Marcos Zampieri. 2021. Comparing approaches to dravidian language identification.

Huijie Lin, Jia Jia, Quan Guo, Yuanyuan Xue, Jie Huang, Lianhong Cai, and Ling Feng. 2014a. Psychological stress detection from cross-media microblog data using deep sparse neural network. pages 1–6.

Huijie Lin, Jia Jia, Quan Guo, Yuanyuan Xue, Qi Li, Jie Huang, Lianhong Cai, and Ling Feng. 2014b. User-level psychological stress detection from social media using deep neural network. *MM 2014 - Proceedings of the 2014 ACM Conference on Multimedia*, pages 507–516.

Carlos Henríquez Miranda, German Sanchez-Torres, and Dixon Salcedo. 2023. Exploring the evolution of sentiment in spanish pandemic tweets: A data analysis based on a fine-tuned bert architecture. *Data*, 8(6).

Sergio Muñoz and Carlos A. Iglesias. 2022. A text classification approach to detect psychological stress combining a lexicon-based feature framework with distributional representations. *Information Processing Management*, 59(5):103011.

Pradeep Kumar Roy, Snehaan Bhawal, and Chinnaudayar Navaneethakrishnan Subalalitha. 2022. Hate speech and offensive language detection in dravidian languages using deep ensemble framework. *Computer Speech Language*, 75:101386.

Kayalvizhi S, Thenmozhi Durairaj, Bharathi Raja Chakravarthi, and Jerin Mahibha C. 2022. Findings of the shared task on detecting signs of depression from social media. In *Proceedings of the Second Workshop on Language Technology for Equality, Diversity and Inclusion*, pages 331–338, Dublin, Ireland. Association for Computational Linguistics.

Sunil Saumya, Abhinav Kumar, and Jyoti Prakash Singh. 2021. Offensive language identification in Dravidian code mixed social media text. In *Proceedings of the First Workshop on Speech and Language Technologies for Dravidian Languages*, pages 36–45, Kyiv. Association for Computational Linguistics.

Habib Yaribeygi, Yunes Panahi, Hedayat Sahraei, Thomas P Johnston, and Amirhossein Sahebkar. 2017. The impact of stress on body function: A review. *EXCLI J.*, 16:1057–1072.

Harish Yenala, Ashish Jhanwar, Manoj K. Chinnakotla, and Jay Goyal. 2018. Deep learning for detecting inappropriate content in text. *International Journal of Data Science and Analytics*, 6(4):273–286.

Quartet@LT-EDI 2024: A SVM-ResNet50 Approach For Multitask Meme Classification - Unraveling Misogynistic and Trolls in Online Memes

Shaun Allan H
Sri Sivasubramaniya Nadar College of Engineering
shaunallan2210716@ssn.edu.in

Samyuktaa Sivakumar
Sri Sivasubramaniya Nadar College of Enginerring
samyuktaa2210189@ssn.edu.in

Rohan R
Sri Sivasubramaniya Nadar College of Enginerring
rohan2210124@ssn.edu.in

Nikilesh Jayaguptha
Sri Sivasubramaniya Nadar College of Engineering
nikilesh2210219@ssn.edu.in

Durairaj Thenmozhi
Sri Sivasubramaniya Nadar College of Engineering
theni_d@ssn.edu.in

Abstract

Meme is a very popular term prevailing among almost all social media platforms in recent days. A meme can be a combination of text and image whose sole purpose is meant to be funny and entertain people. Memes can sometimes promote misogynistic content expressing hatred, contempt or prejudice against women. The Shared Task LT–EDI 2024: Multitask Meme classification – Unraveling Misogynistic and Trolls in Online Memes Task 1 was created with the purpose to classify social media memes as "Misogynistic" and "Non - Misogynistic". The task encompassed Tamil and Malayalam datasets. We separately classified the textual data using Multinomial Naive Bayes and pictorial data using ResNet50 model. The results of from both data were combined to yield an overall result. We were ranked 2nd for both languages in this task.

1 Introduction

Social Media is a platform where millions of people connect and engage with each other. Social media has shaped the way people communicate, share ideas and information among each other colossally. With the immense number of people joining social media each day, social media platforms have become inevitable and play a pivotal role in the modern society.

With the rising usage of social media platforms in the society, they are also used as a source of entertainment. People create entertaining content and post it on social media which is then viewed by millions of people on the internet. With this trend of people posting entertaining contents on social media, a term called "Meme" has become prominent especially among youngsters in the society (Huang et al., 2022).

Memes are a ubiquitous form of internet culture whose sole purpose is to be funny and entertain people. A meme can be a text, image, video, audio or a combination of these that embodies humour, sarcasm or irony in it. Memes has the ability to transcend linguistic and cultural barriers reaching a wide and diverse range of audience. While memes can serve as a form of humorous and relatable content on social media, they also have their darker side that includes misogyny portraying very harmful stereotypes about women, objectifying them and also initiate gender-based hatred and violence.

Multimodal data analysis can be employed to analyse the memes that are available on the internet. A modality is defined as the type or the nature of representation of the data which includes text, image, video and audio. Multimodal data is a representation of data that comprises of two or more modalities of data (Lahat et al., 2015). A meme which can be a combination of different modalities such as text and image, text and video, audio and video, etc are multimodal in nature. Multimodal data analysis can be applied on these memes to classify them as "Misogynistic" or "Non-Misogynistic". Supervised learning can be used for the process for which a well labelled balanced training data is very essential. In case of unavailability of a proper training data, unsupervised leaning can also be performed to carry on multimodal data analysis.

Misogyny is something that deprives women of their rights and privileges and promotes toxic masculinity. In a society which is moulding itself towards gender equality and women empowerment, misogyny should be eliminated. With social media being an inevitable and widely used tool in recent times, having misogynistic content in them will lead to a lot of misinformation and stereotypes against women. Therefore, detecting and moderating these types of memes in social media platforms is indeed vital and assists the movement towards a better society.

The given task aims to encourage the development of models for detecting misogynistic memes in Tamil and Malayalam. The memes and the text inscribed in them were provided in the dataset for

Proceedings of the Fourth Workshop on Language Technology for Equality, Diversity, Inclusion, pages 221–226
March 21, 2024 ©2024 Association for Computational Linguistics

both Tamil and Malayalam.

2 Related Works

Suryawanshi et al. (2020) developed a meme classification system using an early fusion technique to combine the text and image modality and compared it with a text and an image only baseline to investigate its effectiveness.

Simple prompts were constructed and a few in-context examples were provided by Cao et al. (2023) to exploit the implicit knowledge in the pre-trained RoBERTa language model for hateful memes classification.

Koutlis et al. (2023) proposed a deep learning-based architecture for fine-grained classification of Internet image memes called MemeFier. MemeFier utilizes a dual-stage modality fusion module.

A bias estimation technique is proposed by Rizzi et al. (2023) to identify specific elements that compose a meme that could lead to unfair models, along with a bias mitigation strategy based on Bayesian Optimization. Gu et al. (2022) used a joint image and text classification technique to classify memes as either misogynistic or not.

Kumar and Nandakumar (2022) explicitly modelled the cross-modal interactions between the image and text representations contained using Contrastive Language-Image Pre-training (CLIP) encoders via a feature interaction matrix (FIM).

An ingenious model comprising of a transformer-transformer architecture was proposed Hegde et al. (2021) to classify memes in Tamil language. The proposed model tries to attain state-of-the-art by using attention as its main component.

Velioglu and Rose (2020) utilized VisualBERT that was trained multimodally on images and captions and applied Ensemble Learning to build an automatic hateful meme classification system.

Li (2021) explored a multimodal transformer for meme classification in Tamil language. According to the characteristics of the image and text, different pre-trained models were used to encode the image and text so as to get better representations of the image and text respectively.

3 Task and Data Description

The Shared Task LT-EDI 2024: Multitask Meme classification – Unraveling Misogynistic and Trolls in Online Memes[1] (Chakravarthi et al., 2024) Task 1 was created with the purpose of classifying memes as "Misogynistic" and "Non–Misogynistic". Memes on languages Tamil and Malayalam were provided to us as datasets. A sample record from the dataset encompassed the meme image, the text that is inscribed in the image and the label of whether the meme is misogynistic or not.

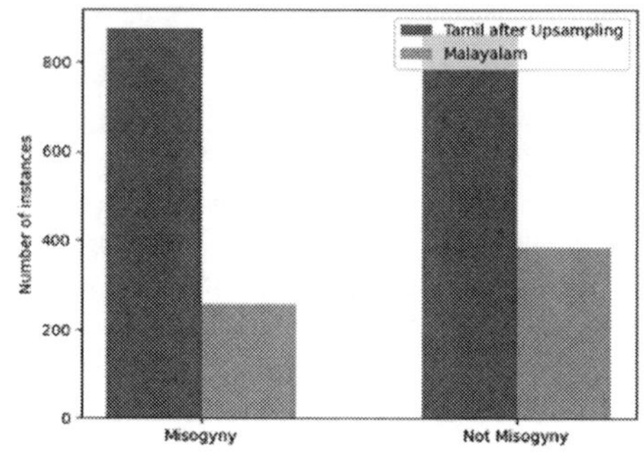

Figure 1: Data Distribution

3.1 Tamil Dataset

The training dataset for Tamil totally had 1137 records. The labels in the training dataset appeared to be case variants of the same words, "Misogyny" and "Not-Misogyny". In the training dataset, 659 were classified as "not-misogyny", 204 were classified as "Not-Misogyny", 39 were classified as "misogyny" and 235 were classified as "Misogyny". After replacing "not-misogyny" and "Not-Misogyny" with "Not Misogyny" and "misogyny" with "Misogyny", we had 274 labelled "Misogyny" and 863 labelled "Not-Misogyny".

The data is very imbalanced which introduces a bias towards the majority data. After up sampling the data, the number of records labelled "Misogyny" is increased to 864.

3.2 Malayalam Dataset

The training dataset for Malayalam totally had 640 records out of which 256 were classified as "Misogyny" and 384 were classified as "Not Misogyny"

4 Methodology

The approach we took was to create build two separate models for each modality. We employed Multinomial Naive Bayes for text classification and ResNet50 for image classification. The resulting probabilities from each model were considered and simple arithmetic was performed to yield the overall result.

[1] https://codalab.lisn.upsaclay.fr/competitions/16097

4.1 Textual Data

4.1.1 Data Preprocessing

Before using the data for training the model, the data must be processed and cleansed for the model to be reliable and yield better results.

1. As emoticons and punctuations are insignificant to the classification process, these characters are removed from the texts.

2. The given text then translated to English which yields better results as most of the embedding systems available are ideally built for English.

3. Stop words are words that doesn't have any contribution in adding meaning to the text. So, these stop words are discarded from the text using the NLTK library.

4.1.2 Feature Extraction

We employed Term Frequency–Inverse Document Frequency (TF-IDF) vectorizer to covert the raw text into vectors consisting of numerical inputs. Term Frequency (TF) refers to the number of times a term appears in a particular document. Inverse Document Frequency (IDF) is a measure of how common a term is across the entire corpus of documents. TF-IDF value of a term in a document is the product of its TF and IDF.

4.1.3 Classification using ML Models

Our main focus was on obtaining the probability of the text being misogynistic rather than obtaining binary outcomes. Traditional models such as Logistic Regression and several types of Naive Bayes models that yield probabilities were experimented on the extracted features. After assessing the metrics of all the models, Multinomial Naive Bayes produced the best numbers of all.

4.2 Pictorial Data

4.2.1 Data Preprocessing

Before using the data for training the model, the data must be processed and cleansed for the model be reliable and yield better results.

1. The given pictorial data is in JPG format is converted into a M-by-N by 3 array representing the RGB values at each pixel of the image.

2. The size of the matrix obtained varies from image to image based on its resolution. As the model only takes inputs of a fixed size for which it is to be trained, the images are uniformly resized to 200 X 200 pixels.

3. The resultant matrix ranging from 0 to 255 is normalized to the range of 0 to 1 making computations much faster and easier.

4.2.2 Classification using ML Models

We employed Transfer Learning on ResNet50 (He et al., 2016) model to classify images. Transfer Learning is a technique in machine learning which refers to the reuse of a pre-trained model on a similar task exploiting the knowledge of the pre-trained model. ResNet50, based on Convolutional Neural Network (CNN) architecture is a very powerful pre-trained model used for image classification which is 50 layers deep and has over 23 million trainable parameters.

In our case, we constructed a sequential neural network having ResNet50 model as the first hidden layer and the output layer was activated with softmax function. The model was compiled using Adam optimizer and Categorical Crossentropy.

```
Model: "sequential_6"
_________________________________________________________________
 Layer (type)                Output Shape              Param #
=================================================================
 resnet50 (Functional)       (None, 2048)              23587712

 flatten_4 (Flatten)         (None, 2048)              0

 dense_8 (Dense)             (None, 512)               1049088

 dense_9 (Dense)             (None, 2)                 1026

=================================================================
Total params: 24637826 (93.99 MB)
Trainable params: 1050114 (4.01 MB)
Non-trainable params: 23587712 (89.98 MB)
```

Figure 2: Summarization of Neural Network constructed for Image classification

4.3 Fusion

A simple arithmetic formula is applied to obtain the resultant probability.

$$ResulatantProbability = 0.7 * ProbabilityFromText + 0.3 * ProbabilityFromImage$$

The numbers 0.7 and 0.3 are numbers obtained from trial and error for which the model yielded better metrics. The data is classified as Misogyny if the resultant probability is greater than or equal to 0.5, otherwise it is classified as Not Misogyny.

5 Results

5.1 Tamil

Our model yielded an accuracy of 0.97 on training data and 0.77 on development data provided by the organizer. The macro average f1 score was 0.98 on training data and 0.69 on development data.

```
Accuracy: 0.780281690140845
Classification Report:
              precision    recall  f1-score   support

           0       0.81      0.90      0.86       255
           1       0.65      0.47      0.55       100

    accuracy                           0.78       355
   macro avg       0.73      0.69      0.70       355
weighted avg       0.77      0.78      0.77       355
```

Figure 3: Classification Report on Testing Data - Tamil

For the test data provided by the organizers, the model produced a macro average score of 0.70 and we were ranked 2nd in the rank list released by the organizers.

5.2 Malayalam

Our model yielded an accuracy of 0.94 on training data and 0.84 on development data. The macro average f1 score was 0.94 on training data and 0.82 on development data.

```
Accuracy: 0.88
Classification Report:
              precision    recall  f1-score   support

           0       0.85      0.97      0.91       120
           1       0.94      0.75      0.83        80

    accuracy                           0.88       200
   macro avg       0.90      0.86      0.87       200
weighted avg       0.89      0.88      0.88       200
```

Figure 4: Classification Report on Testing Data - Malayalam

For the test data provided by the organizers, the model produced a macro average score of 0.87 and we were ranked 2nd in the rank list released by the organizers.

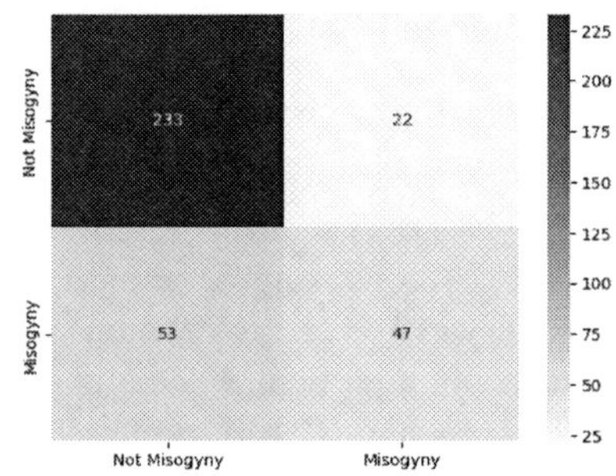

Figure 5: Confusion Matrix on Testing Data - Tamil

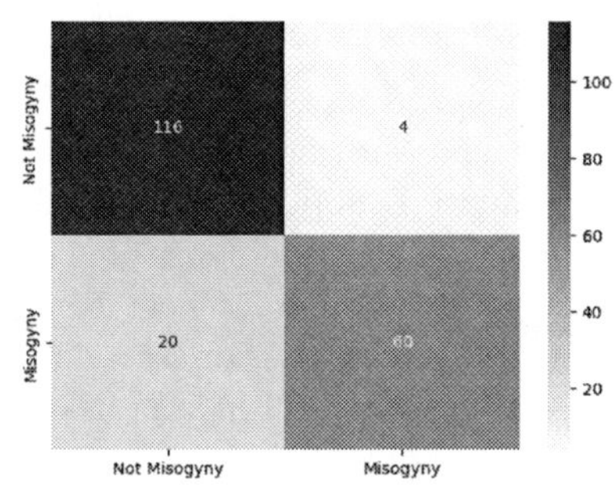

Figure 6: Confusion Matrix on Testing Data - Malayalam

Dataset	Textual Data			Pictorial Data	Overall Model (Most Optimum)
	Logistic Regression	**Gaussian Naive Bayes**	**Multinomial Naive Bayes**	**ResNet50**	**Multinomial NB + ResNet50**
Tamil	0.64	0.63	0.66	0.71	0.69
Malayalam	0.63	0.65	0.66	0.79	0.82

Table 1: Comparison of macro average f1 score on Development Data

6 Limitations

As two separate models were used in the proposed solution, one for text and the other for image, the training process takes place for both the models, thereby increasing the training time of the overall procedure. Masking the text in the images emanates a significant increase in the performance of the model which could not be implemented as the operation requires large GPU resources.

Due to unavailability of a balanced dataset, even after up sampling the Misogynistic instances, a small amount of bias towards the Non-Misogynistic category is still present over the Misogynistic category. The TF-IDF vectorizer which is used to extract features from textual data computes document similarity directly in the word-count space, which may be slow for large vocabularies. Also, the semantic relations between words are not considered during feature extraction.

7 Ethics Statement

The ACL Code of Ethics[2] has been followed and practiced throughout the process of working on the shared task. The classification system is built with the notion to eliminate misogyny from the society resulting in a safe and inclusive social environment for all community of people to participate in. All the authors whose existing ideas, invention, work or artifact has been referenced or utilized is given credit providing a link to the original work in the References section. Our solution prioritizes data privacy by not providing any access to random entities ensuring no leak of information to any other individual or organization. The given task was used as an opportunity to upgrade and enhance our skills while practicing the principles for professional competence. The proposed solution abides by the local, regional, national and international laws and regulations.

References

Rui Cao, Roy Ka-Wei Lee, Wen-Haw Chong, and Jing Jiang. 2023. Prompting for multimodal hateful meme classification.

Bharathi Raja Chakravarthi, Saranya Rajiakodi, Rahul Ponnusamy, Kathiravan Pannerselvam, Anand Kumar Madasamy, Ramachandran Rajalakshimi, Hariharan RamakrishnaIyer LekshmiAmmal, Anshid Kizhakkeparambil, Susminu S Kumar, Bhuvaneswari Sivagnanam, and Charmathi Rajkumar. 2024. Overview of Shared Task on Multitask Meme Classification - Unraveling Misogynistic and Trolls in Online Memes. In *Proceedings of the Fourth Workshop on Language Technology for Equality, Diversity and Inclusion*, Malta. European Chapter of the Association for Computational Linguistics.

Qin Gu, Nino Meisinger, and Anna-Katharina Dick. 2022. QiNiAn at SemEval-2022 task 5: Multi-modal misogyny detection and classification. In *Proceedings of the 16th International Workshop on Semantic Evaluation (SemEval-2022)*, pages 736–741, Seattle, United States. Association for Computational Linguistics.

Kaiming He, Xiangyu Zhang, Shaoqing Ren, and Jian Sun. 2016. Deep residual learning for image recognition. In *Proceedings of the IEEE conference on computer vision and pattern recognition*, pages 770–778.

Siddhanth U Hegde, Adeep Hande, Ruba Priyadharshini, Sajeetha Thavareesan, and Bharathi Raja Chakravarthi. 2021. Uvce-iiitt@dravidianlangtech-eacl2021: Tamil troll meme classification: You need to pay more attention.

Victor Huang, Yifan Hu, and Yaohua Li. 2022. A systematic literature review of new trends in self-expression caused by emojis and memes. In *Proceedings of the 2021 International Conference on Social Development and Media Communication (SDMC 2021)*, pages 75–79. Atlantis Press.

Christos Koutlis, Manos Schinas, and Symeon Papadopoulos. 2023. Memefier: Dual-stage modality fusion for image meme classification. In *Proceedings of the 2023 ACM International Conference on Multimedia Retrieval*, ICMR '23, page 586–591, New York, NY, USA. Association for Computing Machinery.

Gokul Karthik Kumar and Karthik Nandakumar. 2022. Hate-clipper: Multimodal hateful meme classification based on cross-modal interaction of clip features.

Dana Lahat, Tülay Adali, and Christian Jutten. 2015. Multimodal data fusion: An overview of methods, challenges, and prospects. *Proceedings of the IEEE*, 103(9):1449–1477.

Zichao Li. 2021. Codewithzichao@DravidianLangTech-EACL2021: Exploring multimodal transformers for meme classification in Tamil language. In *Proceedings of the First Workshop on Speech and Language Technologies for Dravidian Languages*, pages 352–356, Kyiv. Association for Computational Linguistics.

Giulia Rizzi, Francesca Gasparini, Aurora Saibene, Paolo Rosso, and Elisabetta Fersini. 2023. Recognizing misogynous memes: Biased models and tricky archetypes. *Information Processing Management*, 60(5):103474.

[2] https://www.aclweb.org/portal/content/acl-code-ethics

Shardul Suryawanshi, Bharathi Raja Chakravarthi, Mihael Arcan, and Paul Buitelaar. 2020. Multimodal meme dataset (MultiOFF) for identifying offensive content in image and text. In *Proceedings of the Second Workshop on Trolling, Aggression and Cyberbullying*, pages 32–41, Marseille, France. European Language Resources Association (ELRA).

Riza Velioglu and Jewgeni Rose. 2020. Detecting hate speech in memes using multimodal deep learning approaches: Prize-winning solution to hateful memes challenge.

Quartet@LT-EDI 2024: Support Vector Machine Based Approach For Homophobia/Transphobia Detection In Social Media Comments

Shaun Allan H
Sri Sivasubramaniya Nadar College of Engineering
shaunallan2210716@ssn.edu.in

Samyuktaa Sivakumar
Sri Sivasubramaniya Nadar College of Enginerring
samyuktaa2210189@ssn.edu.in

Rohan R
Sri Sivasubramaniya Nadar College of Enginerring
rohan2210124@ssn.edu.in

Nikilesh Jayaguptha
Sri Sivasubramaniya Nadar College of Engineering
nikilesh2210219@ssn.edu.in

Durairaj Thenmozhi
Sri Sivasubramaniya Nadar College of Engineering
thenid@ssn.edu.in

Abstract

Homophobia and transphobia are terms which are used to describe the fear or hatred towards people who are attracted to the same sex or people whose psychological gender differs from his biological sex. People use social media to exert this behaviour. The increased amount of abusive content negatively affects people in a lot of ways. It makes the environment toxic and unpleasant to LGBTQ+ people. The paper talks about the classification model for classifying the contents into 3 categories which are homophobic, transphobic and non-homophobic/transphobic. We used many traditional models like Support Vector Machine, Random Classifier, Logistic Regression and K-Nearest Neighbour to achieve this. The macro average F1 scores for Malayalam, Telugu, English, Marathi, Kannada, Tamil, Gujarati, Hindi are 0.88, 0.94, 0.96, 0.78, 0.93, 0.77, 0.94, 0.47 and the rank for these languages are 5, 6, 9, 6, 8, 6, 6, 4.

1 Introduction

Social media platforms of the current century have evolved into a way people communicate with each other. Social media is about having conversations, building communities and connecting with the audience. It has become an integral part of everyone's lives. It is not just a marketing tool or a way of broadcasting news. It not only allows you to hear what people say about you but gives the space for you to share your own opinions on the matters happening and helps us in influencing people in both positive and negative ways. This can have a very significant impact on people and the decisions they make.

One of the consequences of the rapid increase in the number of social media users is the increase in the increase in the inappropriate use of social media by the users.Workshops and collaborative tasks held recently have stimulated projects regarding the identification of hate speech, toxicity, misogyny, sexism, racism, and abusive content (Zampieri et al., 2020). The convenience of accessing information and being a great source of great conversations, it also makes cyber bullying and hate speech possible. Since it allows us to share our view points on everything, Hate speech on transsexual and homosexual people are very common. Transphobia is when people have a deep-rooted negative prejudice about being transgender or non-binary. Homophobia is the aversion or hatred towards people who are homosexual or gay. This has a negative consequence on people belonging to these minority gender groups.

Despite a greater acceptance of sexual variations and same-sex marriage in many places, Homophobia and transphobia still exist widely and is sustained by many religious, political and individual practises. Many studies have presented that around 8 to 9 out of 10 people are subjected to hate speech online the percentage of transgender and homosexual people in it is significantly high (Schmidt and Wiegand, 2017).

Homophobia and transphobia don't end with conversing. It can take a physical form of violence too. Violence is becoming too common on social media platforms and it influences people negatively. Violence in the form of murder, beating or even sexual violence such as molestation is becoming too common (Flores et al., 2022). Social media has a great part in this. It is a powerful tool that can easily influence many people. Many hateful comments such as "Gay people should be killed mercilessly", "Transgender people should be stoned" are becoming too common and greatly influence the current generation. Numerous workshops and collaborative efforts are currently focused on identifying abusive content as well (Chakravarthi, 2023).

Recognising these homophobic and transphobic comments on social media automatically can make it very easy for us to block these immediately

Proceedings of the Fourth Workshop on Language Technology for Equality, Diversity, Inclusion, pages 227–232
March 21, 2024 ©2024 Association for Computational Linguistics

(Pamungkas et al., 2023). This tool can flag all the homophobic and transphobic comments and can make the environment inclusive. It can reduce harm and harassment directed at individuals solely based on their sexual orientation or gender identity. Numerous research efforts are underway to identify abusive content in various local languages as well (Chakravarthi et al., 2023). It helps in influencing the social media users positively and helps in reducing homophobia and transphobia around the world.

2 Related Works

Sentiment analysis is a field in which constant works and researches are being carried on. They have many applications on social and e-commerce platforms.

Sharma et al. (2022) has addressed this classification problem by applying the well established deep learning models, including Convolutional Neural Network (CNN), Long Short-Term Memory (LSTM) with GloVe embedding, and transformer-based models like Multilingual BERT (Devlin et al., 2018) and IndicBERT (Kakwani et al., 2020). Results Obtained show that the IndicBERT outperforms all the models and was finally used.

Nozza (2022) solved the challenge of data imbalance by introducing a solution involving data augmentation and ensemble modeling. They fine tuned various large language models, including BERT, ROBERTa (Liu et al., 2019) and HATE-BERT (Caselli et al., 2021). A weighted majority vote Is applied to aggregate their predictions.

Abdul Kareem (2023) has employed Transformer based models widely, as it provides better results than the traditional machine learning models. Implementation includes RoBERTa (Liu et al., 2019), DistilBERT (Sanh et al., 2019), and mBERT (Devlin et al., 2018), with a comparative analysis against previous studies. The Results showed that DistilBERT provided better results than RoBERTa and mBERT.

A hypothesis that states that the performance of the models on a newly constructed dataset with limited data will be improved by data augmentation via Pseudo labeling through transliterating the code mixed text to the parent language. Performance of several models were run and tested by Chakravarthi et al. (2022).

The task done by Bhandari and Goyal (2022) involved multi class classification to identify homophobia or transphobia in YouTube comments. The pipeline comprised a transformer-based classification head and data augmentation for oversampling the English dataset, detailed subsequently.

Multiclass classification system done by Wong et al. (2023), utilizes a BERT based model identifying homophobia and transphobia across English, Spanish, Hindi, Malayalam and Tamil. Retraining XLM RoBERTa (Conneau et al., 2019) with relevant social media data, including script-mixed samples, improved performance, especially in Malayalam. Transformer based models are sensitive to register and language-specific retraining, enhancing classification across various conditions.

3 Task and Data Description

The shared task on Homophobia/Transphobia Detection in social media comments at LT-EDI@EACL 2024[1] was created with the task of detecting Homophobia, Transphobia and non-LGBTQ+ content on YouTube comments. The task concentrates more on regional languages so homophobic and transphobic comments were given in Tamil, Telugu, Malayalam, English, Kannada, Gujarati, Hindi, Marathi languages (hom, 2024).

3.1 Dataset

The dataset provided to us were the data derived from YouTube comments. It mainly had 3 categories: "Homophobic", "Transphobic", "non-anti-LGBTQ+". But most of the dataset had a significantly high amount of "non-anti-LGBTQ+" comments. As the data was too imbalanced, the model might have a bias towards the third category as it had a significantly higher amount of data. So the data had to be up sampled so that the amount of data in each category is equal.

3.2 Up-sampling data

The resample function of "sklearn.utils"[2] is utilized for up-sampling data. It resamples arrays or sparse matrices in a consistent way and the default strategy implements one step of the bootstrapping procedure. It takes feature matrix and corresponding target labels as input. it primarily focuses on minority class subset for up-sampling in order to eliminate any bias. the function randomly selects samples with replacement, potentially duplicating

[1]Fourth workshop on Language Technology for Equality, Diversity, Inclusion (LT-EDI-2024) AT EACL 2024

[2]https://scikit-learn.org/stable/modules/classes.htmlmodule-sklearn.utils

	Training data before Up-Sampling			Training data after Up-Sampling		
Languages	Non anti LGBTQ+	Homophobic	Transphobic	Non anti LGBTQ+	Homophobic	Transphobic
Tamil	2,064	453	145	2,064	2,064	2,064
Hindi	2,423	92	45	2,423	2,423	2,423
Gujarati	3,848	2,267	2,004	3,848	3,848	3,848
Kannada	4,463	2,835	2,765	4,463	4,463	4,463
Marathi	2,572	551	377	2,572	2,572	2,572
English	2,978	179	7	2,978	2,978	2,978
Malayalam	2,468	476	170	2,468	2,468	2,468
Telugu	3,496	2,907	2,647	3,496	3,496	3,496

	Development data before Up-Sampling			Development data after Up-Sampling		
Languages	Non anti LGBTQ+	Homophobic	Transphobic	Non anti LGBTQ+	Homophobic	Transphobic
Tamil	507	118	41	507	507	507
Hindi	305	13	2	305	305	305
Gujarati	788	498	454	788	788	788
Kannada	955	617	585	955	955	955
Marathi	541	129	80	541	541	541
English	748	42	2	748	748	748
Malayalam	937	197	79	937	937	937
Telugu	747	605	588	747	747	747

Table 1: Data before and after Up-Sampling

samples in some cases. It returns the up-sampled feature matrix and target labels, augmenting the original dataset to enhance minority class representation. Table 1 shows training and development before and after up sampling.

4 Methodology

We used many traditional models to test our model from it. We ran all the dataset through Logistic Regression, Support Vector Machine, Random Forest Classifier, K-nearest Neighbour. By noticing the accuracy and the F1 score of each output, we determined if the model was over or under fitting and by comparing all the metrics, we selected the best model out of all the available options. Support Vector Machine (SVM) produced the best output in majority cases.

4.1 Data Preprocessing

The data entered is not of very high quality as it has many unwanted elements in it. So the data undergoes several processes before it is fed into the model. This removes all the insignificant things from our data and makes it ready to be fed into the model

1. The entered data has many words in the upper- and lower-case words. Lower casing in text preprocessing ensures uniformity and simplifies the analysis for the model. This enhances the model's performance.

2. The text entered is filled with a lot of punctuation and emojis. These elements don't add meaning to the sentence. Removing emojis and punctuation in a dataset simplifies the analysis, reduces the noise and also ensures a consistent processing by the model.

3. Stop words are the commonly used words in a language. These are the words that are present highly in any dataset but carry very little useful information for a classification model. As the frequency of these words are too high, it is important to remove these words from the dataset and this results in a smaller data. The stop words for all the languages were downloaded from public repositories and from the "nltk" documentation[3].

[3]https://www.nltk.org/

4.2 Feature Extraction

Most of the Machine learning and Deep learning algorithms are not capable of processing strings or plain text in their raw form. So, we need to feed in numerical numbers as inputs to perform any task. In simple terms, word embeddings are the texts converted into numbers and there may be different numerical representations of the same text.

We employed the TF-IDF vectorizer for this. TF-IDF is an abbreviation for Term Frequency Inverse Document Frequency. It is a measure of originality of a word by comparing the number of times a word appears in document with the number of documents the word appears in.

$$TF = \frac{frequency\ of\ term\ in\ the\ document}{total\ number\ of\ terms\ in\ the\ document}$$

$$IDF = \frac{number\ of\ documents\ in\ the\ corpus}{number\ of\ documents\ with\ the\ term}$$

$$TF - IDF = TF * IDF$$

4.3 Classification using ML Models

To classify the data into different categories, we implemented many traditional models for this. the models include SVM, Random Forest, K-nearest neighbour, Logistic Regression as well as some simple transformer models like LaBSE (Feng et al., 2020) and some language specific models like Hindi BERT (Joshi, 2022), Tamil BERT, Telugu BERT, Malayalam BERT, Gujarati BERT, Kannada BERT, bert-base-uncased (Devlin et al., 2018). We noticed that in almost all the datasets, traditional models gave a very high accuracy. In all the cases, SVM gave the highest accuracy and macro average F1 score. Support Vector Machine is one of the most popular Supervised Learning algorithms which is used for classification as well as regression problems. SVM works by mapping data to a high dimensional feature space so that data points can be categorized, even when the data are not otherwise linearly separable.

4.4 SVM Parameters

The regularization parameter, "C", is set to 1. this parameter helps the SVM optimization in determining the balance between margin size and misclassification. Higher C prioritizes accurate classification, favoring smaller margin hyper planes and lower C seeks larger margin hyper planes, even if it leads to more misclassifications. The kernel configuration is configured as "linear". A linear hyperplane determines the dot product between input vectors in the initial feature space. This dot product calculates the similarity or distance within the original feature space, resulting in a linear hyperplane decision boundary that distinguishes between classes. Verbose, when set to true, serves as an option to display detailed progress updates including epoch, percentage completion, batch processing and estimated time remaining. The probability parameter allows the model to provide class probability estimates rather than just class predictions, enhancing the model's results. All remaining parameters are set to their default values.

5 Results

In every case, the Support Vector Machine model has demonstrated a better performance compared to all other models. The evaluation was conducted by assessing the classification report of training,development and test datasets. The outcomes of Support Vector Machine (SVM) are presented in Table 3, while the results for Logistic Regression

	Training data		Development data	
Languages	**Accuracy**	**Macro Average F1**	**Accuracy**	**Macro Average F1**
Tamil	0.88	0.69	0.85	0.56
Hindi	0.95	0.32	0.95	0.33
Gujarati	0.93	0.93	0.93	0.93
Kannada	0.91	0.91	0.91	0.91
Marathi	0.79	0.52	0.78	0.49
English	0.94	0.36	0.94	0.32
Malayalam	0.91	0.76	0.87	0.62
Telugu	0.92	0.92	0.93	0.93

Table 2: Classification report and results for all languages using Logistic Regression

	Training data		Development data		Testing data	
Languages	Accuracy	Macro Average F1	Accuracy	Macro Average F1	Macro Average F1	Rank
Tamil	0.71	0.81	0.89	0.77	0.48	6
Hindi	0.95	0.38	0.97	0.48	0.32	4
Gujarati	0.94	0.94	0.94	0.94	0.89	6
Kannada	0.92	0.92	0.93	0.93	0.88	8
Marathi	0.86	0.70	0.88	0.78	0.39	6
English	0.96	0.57	0.96	0.44	0.34	9
Malayalam	0.97	0.94	0.94	0.88	0.87	5
Telugu	0.93	0.93	0.94	0.94	0.89	6

Table 3: Classification report and results for all languages using SVM (Most Optimum)

are displayed in Table 2.

6 Conclusion

In conclusion, our study delved into the comprehensive evaluation of traditional machine learning models for text classification, employing an array of techniques from Logistic regression to sophisticated models like Support Vector Machine (SVM) and transformer-based approaches. Rigorous preprocessing, including lower casing, removal of punctuation, emojis, and stop words, ensured data quality. The TF-IDF vectorizer facilitated effective feature extraction, translating textual data into numerical representations. Notably, SVM consistently outperformed other models in terms of accuracy and F1 score across diverse datasets. While our traditional models exhibited commendable performance, it is imperative to acknowledge the evolving landscape of deep learning and advanced embeddings, suggesting avenues for future exploration and refinement of models to capture intricate language nuances and patterns.

7 Limitations

Despite the robust performance of traditional machine learning models, our methodology has inherent limitations. The preprocessing steps, while essential for enhancing data quality, may inadvertently lead to information loss. Removing punctuations, emojis, and stop words, although beneficial for noise reduction, could result in the omission of nuanced context. Additionally, the reliance on TF-IDF for feature extraction may not capture complex semantic relationships in the data. While Support Vector Machine (SVM) emerged as a superior model, its effectiveness might be constrained by non-linearly separable data. Furthermore, our approach predominantly focuses on traditional models, potentially overlooking the nuanced representations that more advanced neural networks and embeddings could offer, limiting the model's adaptability to intricate language patterns and contexts.

8 Ethical Statement

While creating the paper, we made sure that the ACL Code of Ethics was practiced throughout the process of working on the Shared Task. This research task was done with the idea of making social media platform a safe space for people regardless of their sexual orientation. It was made sure that credit has been given to all authors whose works and ideas have been used or incorporated in the reference section. The solution proposed follows all the local, regional and international laws and regulations. This solution gives a lot of importance on data privacy, we ensured that no access to data is granted to unauthorized individuals or organisations, thus preventing any leakage of information.

References

2024. Overview of Third Shared Task on Homophobia and Transphobia Detection in Social Media Comments, author = Chakravarthi, Bharathi Raja and Kumaresan, Prasanna Kumar and Priyadharshini, Ruba and Buitelaar, Paul and Hegde, Asha and Shashirekha, Hosahalli Lakshmaiah and Rajiakodi, Saranya and García-Cumbreras, Miguel Ángel and Jiménez-Zafra, Salud María and García-Díaz, José Antonio and Valencia-García, Rafael and Ponnusamy, Kishore Kumar and Shetty, Poorvi and García-Baena, Daniel. In *Proceedings of the Fourth Workshop on Language Technology for Equality, Diversity and Inclusion*, Malta. European Chapter of the Association for Computational Linguistics.

Syed Ebrahim Abdul Kareem. 2023. *Leveraging Transfer Learning Techniques for Homophobia and Transphobia Detection*. Ph.D. thesis, Dublin, National College of Ireland.

Vitthal Bhandari and Poonam Goyal. 2022. bitsa_nlp@ LT-EDI-ACL2022: Leveraging pretrained language models for detecting homophobia and transphobia in social media comments. *arXiv preprint arXiv:2203.14267*.

Tommaso Caselli, Valerio Basile, Jelena Mitrović, and Michael Granitzer. 2021. HateBERT: Retraining BERT for abusive language detection in English. In *Proceedings of the 5th Workshop on Online Abuse and Harms (WOAH 2021)*, pages 17–25, Online. Association for Computational Linguistics.

Bharathi Raja Chakravarthi. 2023. Detection of homophobia and transphobia in youtube comments. *International Journal of Data Science and Analytics*, pages 1–20.

Bharathi Raja Chakravarthi, Adeep Hande, Rahul Ponnusamy, Prasanna Kumar Kumaresan, and Ruba Priyadharshini. 2022. How can we detect Homophobia and Transphobia? Experiments in a multilingual code-mixed setting for social media governance. *International Journal of Information Management Data Insights*, 2(2):100119.

Bharathi Raja Chakravarthi, Rahul Ponnusamy, Malliga Subramanian, Paul Buitelaar, Miguel Ángel García-Cumbreras, Salud María Jiménez-Zafra, José Antonio García-Díaz, Rafael Valencia-García, and Nitesh Jindal. 2023. Overview of second shared task on homophobia and transphobia detection in english, spanish, hindi, tamil, and malayalam. In *Proceedings of the Third Workshop on Language Technology for Equality, Diversity and Inclusion*, Varna, Bulgaria. Recent Advances in Natural Language Processing.

Alexis Conneau, Kartikay Khandelwal, Naman Goyal, Vishrav Chaudhary, Guillaume Wenzek, Francisco Guzmán, Edouard Grave, Myle Ott, Luke Zettlemoyer, and Veselin Stoyanov. 2019. Unsupervised Cross-lingual Representation Learning at Scale. *CoRR*, abs/1911.02116.

Jacob Devlin, Ming-Wei Chang, Kenton Lee, and Kristina Toutanova. 2018. BERT: Pre-training of Deep Bidirectional Transformers for Language Understanding. *CoRR*, abs/1810.04805.

Fangxiaoyu Feng, Yinfei Yang, Daniel Cer, Naveen Arivazhagan, and Wei Wang. 2020. Language-agnostic BERT Sentence Embedding. *CoRR*, abs/2007.01852.

Andrew R Flores, Rebecca L Stotzer, Ilan H Meyer, and Lynn L Langton. 2022. Hate crimes against lgbt people: National crime victimization survey, 2017-2019. *PLoS one*, 17(12):e0279363.

Raviraj Joshi. 2022. L3Cube-HindBERT and DevBERT: Pre-Trained BERT Transformer models for Devanagari based Hindi and Marathi Languages. *arXiv preprint arXiv:2211.11418*.

Divyanshu Kakwani, Anoop Kunchukuttan, Satish Golla, Gokul N.C., Avik Bhattacharyya, Mitesh M. Khapra, and Pratyush Kumar. 2020. IndicNLPSuite: Monolingual Corpora, Evaluation Benchmarks and Pre-trained Multilingual Language Models for Indian Languages. In *Findings of EMNLP*.

Yinhan Liu, Myle Ott, Naman Goyal, Jingfei Du, Mandar Joshi, Danqi Chen, Omer Levy, Mike Lewis, Luke Zettlemoyer, and Veselin Stoyanov. 2019. RoBERTa: A Robustly Optimized BERT Pretraining Approach. *CoRR*, abs/1907.11692.

Debora Nozza. 2022. Nozza@LT-EDI-ACL2022: Ensemble modeling for homophobia and transphobia detection. In *Proceedings of the Second Workshop on Language Technology for Equality, Diversity and Inclusion*, pages 258–264, Dublin, Ireland. Association for Computational Linguistics.

Endang Wahyu Pamungkas, Valerio Basile, and Viviana Patti. 2023. Towards multidomain and multilingual abusive language detection: a survey. *Personal and Ubiquitous Computing*, 27(1):17–43.

Victor Sanh, Lysandre Debut, Julien Chaumond, and Thomas Wolf. 2019. DistilBERT, a distilled version of BERT: smaller, faster, cheaper and lighter. *ArXiv*, abs/1910.01108.

Anna Schmidt and Michael Wiegand. 2017. A survey on hate speech detection using natural language processing. In *Proceedings of the Fifth International Workshop on Natural Language Processing for Social Media*, pages 1–10, Valencia, Spain. Association for Computational Linguistics.

Deepawali Sharma, Vedika Gupta, and Vivek Kumar Singh. 2022. Detection of homophobia & transphobia in Malayalam and Tamil: Exploring deep learning methods. In *International Conference on Advanced Network Technologies and Intelligent Computing*, pages 217–226. Springer.

Sidney Wong, Matthew Durward, Benjamin Adams, and Jonathan Dunn. 2023. cantnlp@ LT-EDI-2023: Homophobia/Transphobia Detection in Social Media Comments using Spatio-Temporally Retrained Language Models. In *Proceedings of the Third Workshop on Language Technology for Equality, Diversity and Inclusion*, pages 103–108.

Marcos Zampieri, Preslav Nakov, Sara Rosenthal, Pepa Atanasova, Georgi Karadzhov, Hamdy Mubarak, Leon Derczynski, Zeses Pitenis, and Çağrı Çöltekin. 2020. SemEval-2020 task 12: Multilingual offensive language identification in social media (OffensEval 2020). In *Proceedings of the Fourteenth Workshop on Semantic Evaluation*, pages 1425–1447, Barcelona (online). International Committee for Computational Linguistics.

SSN-Nova@LT-EDI 2024: POS Tagging, Boosting Techniques and Voting Classifiers for Caste And Migration Hate Speech Detection

A Ankitha Reddy, Ann Maria Thomas, Pranav Moorthi & B. Bharathi
Department of CSE
Sri Sivasubramaniya Nadar College of Engineering, Tamil Nadu, India
ankithareddy2210178@ssn.edu.in, annthomas2210391@ssn.edu.in
pranav2210176@ssn.edu.in, bharathib@ssn.edu.in

Abstract

This paper presents our submission for the shared task on Caste and Migration Hate Speech Detection: LT-EDI@EACL 2024[1]. This text classification task aims to foster the creation of models capable of identifying hate speech related to caste and migration. The dataset comprises social media comments, and the goal is to categorize them into negative and positive sentiments. Our approach explores back-translation for data augmentation to address sparse datasets in low-resource Dravidian languages. While Part-of-Speech (POS) tagging is valuable in natural language processing, our work highlights its ineffectiveness in Dravidian languages, with model performance drastically reducing from 0.73 to 0.67 on application. In analyzing boosting and ensemble methods, the voting classifier with traditional models outperforms others and the boosting techniques, underscoring the efficacy of simpler models on low-resource data despite augmentation.

1 Introduction

The deep-seated phenomenon of caste discrimination in India has endured over time, with recent advancements reflecting breakthroughs in challenging these deeply ingrained biases. Despite contemporary endeavors to disentangle from the shackles of caste-based prejudices, the phenomenon still persists, exerting influence on diverse facets of individual lives (Vaid, 2014).

In the era of expanding social media platforms, marked by attributes like user anonymity, widespread accessibility, and the fostering of online communities and discourse, the identification and surveillance of hate speech rooted in caste discrimination pose a significant societal challenge. While machine learning models for hate speech detection have made significant strides in the Western context, (Corazza et al., 2020) there is a glaring gap when it comes to adapting these models to the nuanced dynamics of casteism in India. Casteism, a concept uniquely embedded in the social fabric of South Asian communities, introduces complexities that are not adequately addressed by current research and detection mechanisms. Unlike hate speech patterns prevalent in the West, caste-based discrimination in India operates within a distinct socio-cultural context, marked by intricate layers of subtext and nuanced contextual variations (Jahan and Oussalah, 2023).

The dearth of research tailored to this phenomenon unique to the Indian subcontinent hinders the effectiveness of existing models in capturing the intricacies of this societal issue, especially in the sphere of social media. It is crucial to acknowledge that the linguistic, cultural, and historical dimensions of casteism necessitate a more nuanced approach to hate speech detection, one that transcends the limitations of generic models designed for Western contexts (Sambasivan et al., 2021).

Our paper is structured as follows - Section 2 explores other publications pertaining to text classification tasks in low resource languages, Section 3 provides an analysis of the distribution of the dataset, Section 4 highlights the methodology undertaken for our proposed model and Section 5 analyses the performance metrics of the solutions and provides a conclusion.

2 Related Work

Though work has been done in text classification for low-resource languages in the recent past, it is apparent that the lack of annotated datasets has continually limited the scope of research in the field, with (Rajiakodi et al., 2024) making notable strides in this regard. This inherent drawback has severely affected the applications of widely adopted methods, including POS tagging, on morphological learning in Dravidian languages (Moeller et al.,

[1] https://codalab.lisn.upsaclay.fr/competitions/16089

Proceedings of the Fourth Workshop on Language Technology for Equality, Diversity, Inclusion, pages 233–237
March 21, 2024 ©2024 Association for Computational Linguistics

2021; Kann et al., 2020). Hence, data augmentation, with an emphasis on backtracking, poses as an attractive solution to aid in combating such data issues (Pingle et al., 2023; Shleifer, 2019).

With respect to classifiers utilised, research has been focused on transformer and deep learning models (Roy et al., 2022; Dowlagar and Mamidi, 2021). However, little light has been shed on the efficacy of ensemble approaches with traditional machine learning models (Kumar et al., EasyChair, 2021; Nimmi and Janet, 2021), which have proved to outperform state-of-the-art technology that requires large quantities of annotated data (Jauhiainen et al., 2021), a vision that remains to elude research in Dravidian languages.

3 Dataset Analysis

The labels given for the data were "Caste/Migration Hate Speech" and "Non-Caste/Migration Hate Speech". The data distribution is provided below in Table 1.

Category	Count
Non - Caste/ Migration Hate Speech	3,303
Caste/ Migration Hate Speech	2,052

Table 1: Data distribution

Notably, there exists a significant imbalance in the distribution of labels. This disparity may potentially hinder the implementation of our models. To rectify this imbalance and enhance the operational efficiency of our model, we implemented data augmentation on the datasets. Further details on this process will be elaborated in-depth in Section 4.

4 Methodology

4.1 Data Augmentation

Back translation stands as a data augmentation method employed in natural language processing to expand datasets. This technique involves translating a given text into another language and then back to the original language, introducing diversity and variability into the dataset.

In our proposed model, the text data was translated to English, and then translated back into Tamil as seen in Figure 1. The language was detected through the LanguageIdentifier model which is adept at discerning the language of the text, in our case, Tanglish or Romanized Tamil. This is done by computing the count of Tamil accented vowels and consonants, surpassing a predefined threshold to ascertain the text's manifestation in Romanized Tamil form. Once the source language was detected, the text was translated into the identified destination language and back into the original language. This translation was executed using the Googletrans library which implements the Google Ajax API[2]. This allowed the creation of texts that remained semantically congruent, yet diverged discernibly from its original form.

id	text	label	lang	augment_text
244	### I use to respect tamilians a lost but the way they r doing killing North Indian people has really hurted me all have life family u all kill inccent people 😕 😭 💔 ▯	0	en	### I use to respect the Tamils, but the way they killed the people of North India really hurt me. Life family is family.
5294	இவர்கள் சொல்வது எல்லாம் உண்மையான காரணமில்லை முதலாளிகள் தான் காரணம் காலை ஆறுமணியில் இரவுஒன்பதுமணி வரை கேள்வி கேட்காமல்உழைப்பதால் அவர்களைத்தான் தேடுகிறார்கள்.	0	ta	காலையில் ஆறு மணி வரை அவர்கள் கேள்வி கேட்கப்படாததால் அவர்கள் சொல்வதை முதலாளிகள் ஒரு உண்மையான காரணம் அல்ல.
592	ஜாதி பெருமையை பேசிக்கொண்டு இருப்பார்கள் இவர்கள் வந்தால் தான் இவர்களை அடக்க முடியும் சரிதான் வணக்கம் ஒரு அடிச்சு துவைக்க போறாங்க வடக்கின்ஸ் மோசமான ஆட்கள்	1	ta	சாதியின் மகிமை.அவர்கள் வந்தால், அவர்கள் அவர்களை அடக்க முடியும்.
5192	வட மாநிலத்தவனை கட்டுப்படுத்த விட்டால் தமிழ்நாட்டு மக்கள் பல விளைவுகளை சந்திக்க நேரிடும்.	0	ta	நீங்கள் வடக்கு மாநிலத்தை கட்டுப்படுத்தினால், தமிழ்நாட்டின் மக்களுக்கு பல முடிவுகள் கிடைக்கும்.
1097	it's nothing wrong people travel to earn money but in same time native people also need work hard for better life...lucky Brother you know hindi to communicate to Vadakans...Nice review	0	en	People travel to make money, but at the same time you have to work hard for the best life for the native people . Lucky brothers, you know Hindi to communicate with the Vadaka . Good Review

Figure 1: Augmentation of data using backtranslation

By creating new instances of text with similar meanings but different linguistic expressions, back translation significantly increases dataset size as seen in Table 2. The process aims to preserve semantic meaning while varying the phrasing, word choice, and sentence structure. This augmented dataset with diverse linguistic patterns should theoretically contribute to more robust model training, mitigating overfitting risks, and ultimately enhancing the performance of natural language processing models.

Category	Count
Non - Caste/ Migration Hate Speech	4,121
Caste/ Migration Hate Speech	2,834

Table 2: Data distribution after augmentation

4.2 Preprocessing

The maximization of model efficiency and the influence on performance metrics hinge significantly on data preprocessing. This fundamental process involves several key steps. Initially, the conversion

[2]https://support.google.com/code/topic/10021

of text to lowercase and the expansion of contractions promote a uniform analytical approach. Subsequently, stemming reduces words to their root form, aiding tasks such as sentiment analysis by consolidating related words. Following this, the removal of stop words expedites processing. Lastly, the removal of special characters, symbols, and emojis streamlines the text, reducing the volume for subsequent model processing.

4.3 Feature Extraction

TF-IDF, or Term Frequency-Inverse Document Frequency, is a technique for creating features from text data by measuring the importance of words in a collection of documents. It assigns higher importance to words exclusive to a small set of documents. The TF-IDF vectorizer matches each feature to a numerical value calculated from its TF-IDF score, obtained by multiplying term frequency and inverse document frequency.

4.4 POS Tagging

Linguistically, words can be categorized into various parts of speech based on their grammatical attributes. Part-of-Speech (POS) tagging is the process of assigning specific word classes to individual words in a given text. These designated tags play a crucial role in enabling models to discern the significance of different elements of speech within the provided text, thereby enhancing the model's ability to identify and comprehend the key components of speech.

4.5 XG Boost

XGBoost, a gradient boosting technique that particularly excels in the realm of structured data, employs parallel tree boosting to achieve heightened efficiency. Utilizing the weighted quantile sketch algorithm, XGBoost addresses datasets with a substantial number of zero values. The algorithm, recognized for its scalability, implements boosting as the process of minimizing a convex loss function within a convex set of functions. Regularization, incorporating both L1 and L2 regularization techniques, mitigates the risk of overfitting, while the parallel tree approach facilitates seamless scalability on clusters, reducing memory usage.

4.6 Adaptive Boosting

Adaptive Boosting (AdaBoost) strategically amalgamates multiple weak classifiers to construct a robust classifier. Employing a greedy algorithm, AdaBoost optimizes weights for each weak classifier and utilizes decision stumps to amalgamate decisions from individual classifiers. Each weak learner corresponds to a vector in an n-dimensional space, with the objective of reaching a target point where the loss function is minimized. The training process assigns weights to samples, equating to the error on the sample at the iteration point. The overarching goal is to systematically diminish the training error for the weak classifiers.

4.7 Voting Classifier

A Voting Classifier is an ensemble learning method that combines predictions from multiple individual models to make a final prediction as shown in Figure 2. It aggregates the outcomes through methods like majority voting (Hard Voting) or averaging predicted probabilities (Soft Voting). In Hard Voting, the final prediction is determined by the majority of individual classifier predictions, while in Soft Voting, the average predicted probabilities across all classifiers contribute to the final decision. These approaches aim to enhance overall model performance by leveraging the strengths of diverse base classifiers (Bartlett et al., 1998).

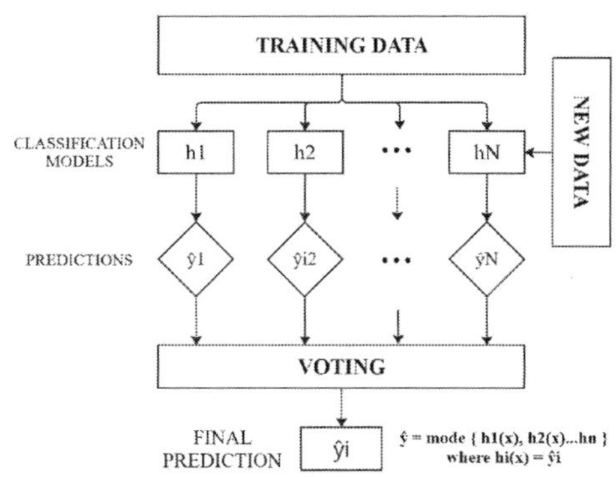

Figure 2: Structure of Voting Classifier

In this study, the ensemble approach employed soft voting, as it capitalises on the complementary strengths of the individual models, allowing for a more nuanced and robust decision-making process. Our preliminary analysis focused on identifying traditional models that boasted superior performance characteristics. After extensive experimentation, we determined that the optimal classifiers were Support Vector Machine, Random Forest, and Multinomial Naive Bayes. Each of these classifiers was incorporated into a separate pipeline along with the TfidfVectorizer. This approach ensured that the text data underwent consistent processing across all models, ensuring consistency in the ensemble predictions.

5 Results and Analysis

The impact of the POS tagging was elementally validated by juxtaposing the performance of the SVM classifier. Analysis found that the macro-average F1 score of the model significantly decreased with the implementation of POS tagging from 0.73 to 0.67. This could be attributed to the morphosyntactic intricacies of Dravidian languages. This discrepancy stems from the profound dissimilarity in grammatical structures and semantics inherent to Dravidian languages, diverging significantly from the syntactic patterns prevalent in the Latin alphabet. Nonetheless, POS tagging heavily relies on annotated corpora for discerning patterns and relationships between words and their corresponding POS tags.

Hence, the model's ability to generalise effectively could be hindered due to the limited dataset, lack of grammar and semantic standardisation paired with the significant number of out-of-vocabulary words that may not be adequately covered in training data.

The augmentation of data, ostensibly believed to augment the efficacy of the model, yielded only a marginal enhancement in model performance, manifesting as a modest 1-2 percent improvement. Our hypothesis posits that the inherent simplicity of the operative models acts as a constraining factor, impeding their capacity to effectively leverage the augmented dataset. Nonetheless, despite marginal improvements, the augmented dataset was systematically employed for subsequent exploration and analysis.

Model	Dataset	Augmented Dataset
XGBoost	0.49	0.50
Voting Classifier	0.75	0.77
AdaBoost	0.56	0.58

Table 3: Macro-average F1- score of the proposed system using prior to and post data augmentation

The evaluation of the task is done based on the following performance metrics: Precision, Recall and macro-average F1- score.

Model	Precision	Recall	F1-Score
XGBoost	0.67	0.55	0.50
Voting Classifier	0.81	0.76	0.77
AdaBoost	0.63	0.59	0.58

Table 4: Performance of the proposed system using development data in Tamil code-mixed text

With regard to the models implemented, the superior performance of the voting classifier implies that the ensemble of traditional ML models, when combined through voting, leverages the strengths of individual models and mitigates their weaknesses.

Additionally, the AdaBoost classifier outperformed the XGBoost which may be due to the fact that AdaBoost builds a sequence of weak learners, adjusting their importance based on the errors of the previous learners; thereby enabling advantageous outcomes with low-resource languages due to its interpretability and simplicity. On the other hand, XGBoost uses a more complex and sophisticated algorithm that includes regularisation terms, parallel computation, and tree-pruning strategies.

6 Conclusion

Our approach aimed to leverage data augmentation through back translation to address the issue of sparse datasets in low-resource Dravidian languages. However, the implementation did not yield signifcant improvements in model performance.

Tangentially, Part-of-Speech (POS) tagging is exceptionally valuable in natural language processing, providing crucial insights into the grammatical structure of sentences, enabling accurate syntactic analysis, and facilitating downstream tasks like sentiment analysis and machine translation. Despite having such crucial applications, POS tagging remains ineffective on Dravidian languages, highlighting the exigency for nuanced linguistic models attuned to the unique intricacies of non-Latin script languages.

On analysis of different boosting and ensemble methods, the voting classifier incorporating traditional models proved to outperform the other models, highlighting the efficacy of simpler models on low-resource data despite data augmentation. On probing deeper, it was found that between the XGBoost and AdaBoost as well, the simpler of the two models proved to perform significantly better.

References

Peter Bartlett, Yoav Freund, Wee Sun Lee, and Robert E Schapire. 1998. Boosting the margin: A new explanation for the effectiveness of voting methods. *The annals of statistics*, 26(5):1651–1686.

Michele Corazza, Stefano Menini, Elena Cabrio, Sara Tonelli, and Serena Villata. 2020. A Multilingual Evaluation for Online Hate Speech Detection. *ACM Trans. Internet Technol.*, 20(2).

Suman Dowlagar and Radhika Mamidi. 2021. EDIOne@LT-EDI-EACL2021: Pre-trained transformers with convolutional neural networks for hope speech detection. In *Proceedings of the First Workshop on Language Technology for Equality, Diversity and Inclusion*, pages 86–91, Kyiv. Association for Computational Linguistics.

Md Saroar Jahan and Mourad Oussalah. 2023. A systematic review of hate speech automatic detection using natural language processing. *Neurocomputing*, 546:126232.

Tommi Jauhiainen, Tharindu Ranasinghe, and Marcos Zampieri. 2021. Comparing Approaches to Dravidian Language Identification.

Katharina Kann, Ophélie Lacroix, and Anders Søgaard. 2020. Weakly Supervised POS Taggers Perform Poorly on Truly Low-Resource Languages.

S R Mithun Kumar, Nihal Reddy, Aruna Malapati, and Lov Kumar. EasyChair, 2021. An ensemble model for sentiment classification on code-mixed data in Dravidian Languages. EasyChair Preprint no. 7266.

Sarah Moeller, Ling Liu, and Mans Hulden. 2021. To POS tag or not to POS tag: The impact of POS tags on morphological learning in low-resource settings. In *Proceedings of the 59th Annual Meeting of the Association for Computational Linguistics and the 11th International Joint Conference on Natural Language Processing (Volume 1: Long Papers)*, pages 966–978, Online. Association for Computational Linguistics.

K Nimmi and B Janet. 2021. Voting ensemble model based Malayalam-English sentiment analysis on code-mixed data.

Aabha Pingle, Aditya Vyawahare, Isha Joshi, Rahul Tangsali, Geetanjali Kale, and Raviraj Joshi. 2023. Robust Sentiment Analysis for Low Resource languages Using Data Augmentation Approaches: A Case Study in Marathi. *arXiv e-prints*, page arXiv:2310.00734.

Saranya Rajiakodi, Bharathi Raja Chakravarthi, Rahul Ponnusamy, Prasanna Kumar Kumaresan, Sathiyaraj Thangasamy, Bhuvaneswari Sivagnanam, and Charmathi Rajkumar. 2024. Overview of Shared Task on Caste and Migration Hate Speech Detection. In *Proceedings of the Fourth Workshop on Language Technology for Equality, Diversity and Inclusion*, Malta. European Chapter of the Association for Computational Linguistics.

Pradeep Kumar Roy, Snehaan Bhawal, and Chinnaudayar Navaneethakrishnan Subalalitha. 2022. Hate speech and offensive language detection in Dravidian languages using deep ensemble framework. *Computer Speech Language*, 75:101386.

Nithya Sambasivan, Erin Arnesen, Ben Hutchinson, Tulsee Doshi, and Vinodkumar Prabhakaran. 2021. Re-imagining Algorithmic Fairness in India and Beyond.

Sam Shleifer. 2019. Low Resource Text Classification with ULMFit and Backtranslation.

Divya Vaid. 2014. Caste in Contemporary India: Flexibility and Persistence. *Annual Review of Sociology*, 40(1):391–410.

CUET_NLP_Manning@LT-EDI 2024: Transformer-based Approach on Caste and Migration Hate Speech Detection

Md Ashraful Alam, Hasan Mesbaul Ali Taher, Jawad Hossain, Shawly Ahsan and **Mohammed Moshiul Hoque**
Department of Computer Science and Engineering
Chittagong University of Engineering & Technology, Chattogram-4349, Bangladesh
{u1804061, u1804038, u1704039, u1704057}@student.cuet.ac.bd, moshiul_240@cuet.ac.bd

Abstract

The widespread use of online communication has caused a significant increase in the spread of hate speech on social media. However, there are also hate crimes based on caste and migration status. Despite several nations efforts to bring equality among their citizens, numerous crimes occur just based on caste. Migration-based hostility happens both in India and in developed countries. A shared task was arranged to address this issue in a low-resourced language such as Tamil. This paper aims to improve the detection of hate speech and hostility based on caste and migration status on social media. To achieve this, this work investigated several Machine Learning (ML), Deep Learning (DL), and transformer-based models, including M-BERT, XLM-R, and Tamil BERT. Experimental results revealed the highest macro f_1-score of 0.80 using the M-BERT model, which enabled us to rank 3rd on the shared task.

1 Introduction

The advent of social media has reshaped the contours of communication, enabling individuals to share their thoughts and interact with a global audience instantaneously. While this has led to the democratization of information exchange, it has also given rise to an insidious byproduct of hate speech and hostility (Sharif et al., 2021). Hate speech, mainly rooted in caste discrimination and migration bias, is a pervasive element in online discourse, highlighting societal prejudices and perpetuating exclusion and animosity. In several nations, caste discrimination remains a persistent issue despite the country's legal strides toward equality (Bhatt et al., 2022). The caste system, an ancient social hierarchy, continues to influence individual and collective identities and relationships, often manifesting in the form of hate speech that targets marginalized communities (Sajlan, 2021). The repercussions of such expressions are not confined to the digital realm; they spill over into the real world, reinforcing social divisions and impeding efforts to establish a more equitable society.

The issue of migration discrimination is similarly problematic, affecting nations worldwide (Chulvi et al., 2023). As people migrate across borders in search of better opportunities or refuge, they often face hostile attitudes and vilification on social media, contributing to xenophobia and nationalism, fostering fear and suspicion, and leading to divisive policies. Thus, addressing these forms of hate speech is crucial, and computational linguistics can help us identify them effectively (Paasch-Colberg et al., 2021).

The goal of this study is to develop a system capable of discerning caste and migration hate speech from non-caste and migration hate speech. The primary accomplishments include:

- Examined various ML, DL, and transformer-based models to detect caste and migration hate speech in Tamil social media, analyzing errors for deeper insights.
- Presented a suitable transformer-based model (M-BERT) tuned with task dataset to classify Tamil text into caste and migration hate speech (CMHS) and not caste and migration hate speech (NCMHS).

2 Related Work

Social media and blogging platforms offer a platform for individual expression, but they can also promote antisocial conduct, such as hate speech and cyberbullying (Hossain et al., 2023). A shared task was conducted (Basile et al., 2019) to detect multilingual hate speech against immigrants and women on Twitter. Almatarneh et al. (2019) used TF-IDF and Lexicon to identify hate speech against migrants and women in English and Spanish tweets, achieving f_1 scores of 0.36 and 0.54, respectively. Romero-Vega et al. (2021) addressed xenophobic

Proceedings of the Fourth Workshop on Language Technology for Equality, Diversity, Inclusion, pages 238–243
March 21, 2024 ©2024 Association for Computational Linguistics

hate speech in Spanish tweets about Venezuelan migrants in Ecuador, with the SVM model showing the highest performance f_1-score of 0.98. Farooqi et al. (2021) addressed hate speech in social media, emphasizing the need to consider conversation context; their system achieved the highest macro f_1-score of 0.7253 leveraging neural networks and the ensemble of Indic-BERT, XLM-RoBERTa, and Multilingual BERT. A recent study Bhimani et al. (2021) utilized NLP and ML techniques to analyze hate speech on social media, considering aspects such as caste and religion, and gained 96.29% accuracy using Logistic Regression (LR). Sachdeva et al. (2021) addressed the issue of hate speech on social media, underscoring the pressing demand for automated approaches in light of the increasing spread of biased content. They achieved an f_1-score of 0.84 by using the Random Forest (RF) classifier. Dhanya and Balakrishnan (2021) surveyed hate speech detection in Asian languages, focusing on developing an automated system for Malayalam, addressing negativity related to societal factors with varying dataset sizes. Hossain et al. (2022) identified abusive comments from Tamil texts using LR and achieved a f_1-score score of 0.39. Sharif and Hoque (2021) addressed aggressive content on social media, especially in regional languages like Bengali, proposing an ensemble classifier trained on 10,095 annotated texts. Using CNN, BiLSTM, and GRU with diverse embeddings and ensemble strategies, their framework achieved the highest coarse-grained f_1-score of 0.89 and fine-grained weighted f_1-score of 0.84 on the dataset. Despite extensive research in natural language processing, there is a lack of studies on detecting hate speech related to caste and migration.

3 Task and Dataset Description

Due to the complexity of code-mixed data in social media texts, it is challenging for systems trained on monolingual data to classify. This task aims to implement a system to identify hate speech related to caste and migration. In order to detect caste and migration hate speech from text data, task organizers[1] developed a code-mixed (Tamil-Engilsh) corpus. To develop such a system, we analyzed the corpus given by the task organizers (Rajiakodi et al., 2024). Table 1 shows the number of instances for each class in training, validation, and test sets. Datasets are imbalanced, where the number of instances in the NCMHS class is higher compared to the CMHS class.

Classes	Train	Valid	Test	Total Words
NCMHS	3,303	594	973	58,029
CMHS	2,052	351	602	36,654
Total	5,355	945	1,575	94,683

Table 1: Class-wise distribution of train, validation, and test set for the Tamil language

The corpus is split into training (5,355 texts), validation (945 texts), and test (1,575 texts) sets. The task involves a binary classification problem to identify caste and migration hate speech from the corpus. The classes are caste and migration hate speech (CMHS), containing 4,870 texts, and not caste and migration hate speech (NCMHS), containing 3,005 texts.

We analyzed the dataset in further detail concerning sentence length. Figure 1 displays the dataset's length-frequency distribution. According to the length-frequency distribution study, a few text samples had text lengths of more than 100 words. As a result, the maximum sentence length for this work was 100 words. The average sentence length is 18, with one word as the minimum.

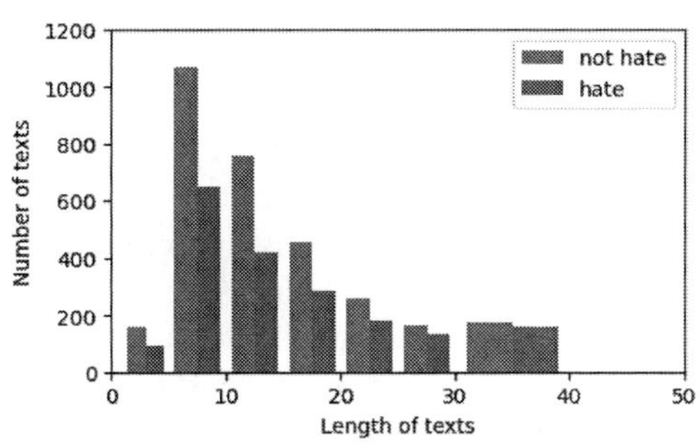

Figure 1: Distribution of sentences frequency in terms length

4 Methodology

Various ML and DL techniques are used for the baseline evaluation with appropriate feature extraction techniques. Moreover, a few transformer models, such as m-BERT, XLM-R, and Tamil-BERT, are examined. Figure 2 depicts a schematic representation of the overall system and employed techniques to tackle the task.

Data Preparation: The corpus text contains unnecessary symbols, punctuation, and letters. Thus, the data in the corpus undergoes a cleaning proce-

[1] https://sites.google.com/view/lt-edi-2024/

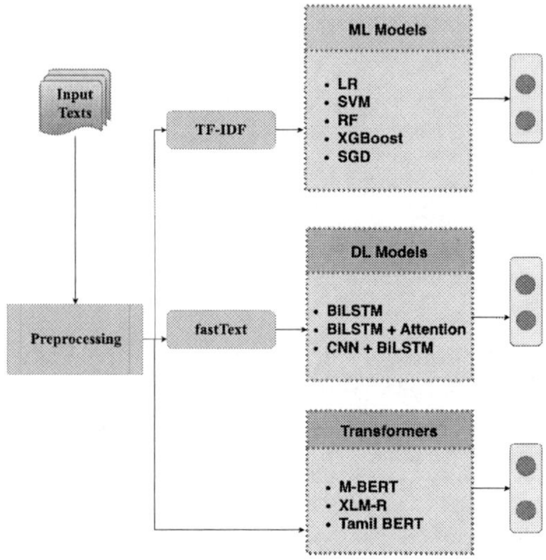

Figure 2: Abstract process of caste and migration hate speech detection in Tamil

dure before system development. This stage prepared a cleaned dataset for the language by removing unnecessary letters, symbols, punctuation, and numbers from the texts. We used this pre-processed data as input for the ML and DL-based models. For transformer-based models, this work used the raw data as input. Additionally, class weighting addresses class imbalance during the model's training.

Textual Feature Extraction: Feature extraction methods are necessary for training classifier models, as ML and DL algorithms cannot learn from raw texts. The TF-IDF technique (Takenobu, 1994) is applied to extract the features for ML models. On the other hand, fastText embeddings (Grave et al., 2018) are used as feature extraction techniques for DL models.

4.1 Classifiers

Six ML, three DL, and three transformer-based models are exploited to classify hate speech in Tamil.

ML-based Classifiers: The suggested system starts with traditional ML approaches such as LR, RF, SGD, and SVM to establish the caste and migration-related hate speech detection system. We chose 'linear' SVM with $C = 10$ and RF. The ensemble approach is built using LR in addition to SVM, Gradient Boosting, and RF. The ensemble method employs the majority voting and stacking techniques. For SGD models, we used the 'log' loss function.

DL-based Classifiers: DL techniques consistently outperformed traditional ML methods. This work uses BiLSTM, Attention, and BiLSTM-CNN to classify hate speech. A 200-cell bidirectional LSTM with 0.2 dropout captures states. The sigmoid function predicts output, and the attention mechanism highlights keywords. The BiLSTM+Attention includes a 20-neuron layer, and CNN+BiLSTM uses 1D convolutional layer (128 filters, kernel 3), bidirectional LSTM (256 units, 0.3 dropouts), and embedding (128). Flattening and dense layers conclude with sigmoid activation for classification. In this work, we used *optuna* (Akiba et al., 2019) for finding the optimal hyperparameters.

Transformer-based Classifiers: Transformers have grown in popularity in recent years due to their exceptional performance in nearly every NLP domain. As the given dataset consists of code-mixed texts, we choose three transformers such as M-BERT (Devlin et al., 2018), XLM-R (Conneau et al., 2019), and Tamil-BERT (Joshi, 2022) to develop our models. A self-supervised cross-lingual understanding training method called XLM-R is beneficial for low-resourced languages. The transformer model m-BERT, on the other hand, has been pre-trained in more than 104 languages. Tamil-BERT is a type of BERT designed explicitly for the Tamil language. It is trained on a large corpus of Tamil text to improve monolingual understanding and natural language processing tasks for Tamil speakers. These models were extracted from the Huggingface[2] transformer library and fine-tuned on our dataset with the Ktrain (Maiya, 2022) package. To fine-tune those models, we used the 'fit_onecycle' method with a learning rate of $2e^{-5}$. All the models have trained up to 15 epochs, with batch size 12.

5 Results and Analysis

Table 2 demonstrates the performance of the various methods employed on the test set. The models dominance is determined by the macro f_1-score. On the other hand, we closely monitor the other metrics, including macro recall (R) and macro precision (P) scores. These additional measures comprehensively evaluate the models performance across different aspects.

The results showed that the LR and SVM models obtained a macro f_1-score of 0.75. When trained

[2]https://huggingface.co/

Methods	Classifiers	P	R	MF1
ML Models	LR	0.7489	0.7308	0.7531
	SVM	0.7512	0.7248	0.7509
	RF	0.7439	0.7908	0.7589
	XGB	0.6337	0.6892	0.6309
	SGD	0.7143	0.7798	0.7275
	Ensemble	0.7931	0.7452	0.7629
DL Models	BiLSTM	0.7473	0.7429	0.7490
	BiLSTM + Attention	0.6952	0.6438	0.6418
	BiLSTM + CNN	0.7671	0.7342	0.7409
Transformer	**M-BERT**	**0.7823**	**0.8246**	**0.8049**
	XLM-R	0.7598	0.7647	0.7638
	Tamil BERT	0.7794	0.7849	0.7847

Table 2: Performance of various models on the test set. The acronyms P, R, and MF1 denote Precision, Recall, and macro f_1-score.

on fastText feature vectors, the BiLSTM approach yielded a macro f_1-score of 0.74. Deep learning-based models obtained comparatively worse results than the ML-based models. The small size of the training data maybe the reason behind this. Transformer-based models outperformed all other models. M-BERT obtained the best performance, macro f_1-score of 0.80.

5.1 Error Analysis

We performed an in-depth error analysis to get insights into the best-performed model (M-BERT) performance using quantitative and qualitative analysis.

5.1.1 Quantitative Analysis

Table 2 shows that M-BERT is the best-performing model for detecting hate speech related to caste and migration in the given dataset. The confusion matrix (Figure 3) of the best-performing model shows that a total 1,211 number of labels were classified correctly.

Misclassified hate/Non-hate labels totaled 301, with 169 NCMHS and 132 CMHS texts. This is likely due to data imbalance and the dataset's diverse languages (English, Tamil, code-mixed, and code-switched), hindering the models pattern recognition. The misclassification hints at nuanced contextual factors, posing challenges in differentiating between hate and non-hate labels.

5.1.2 Qualitative Analysis

Figure 4 illustrates a few predicted outcomes by the best model on the test dataset. Samples 2 and 3 are among those that have been classified correctly.

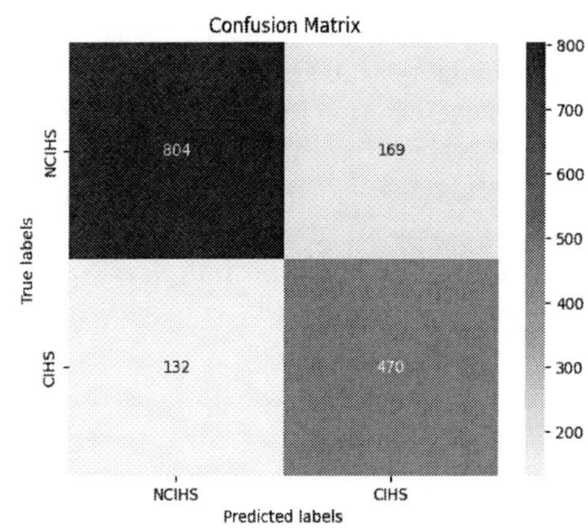

Figure 3: Confusion matrix of the best-performed model (M-BERT) for the task

Sample 1 is incorrectly classified as caste and migration hate speech, whereas sample 4 is classified wrongly as not caste and migration hate speech. These are just two examples of situations where the model misclassified data. This misclassification may have happened due to the imbalanced nature of the dataset. Additionally, the model needed help to classify the text because the corpus contained code-mixed data. These subtleties emphasize the value of qualitative analysis in figuring out how the model functions in certain situations.

Limitations

This study evaluated various transformers, ML, and DL models where M-BERT showed promising per-

Sample Sentences	True Label	Predicted Label
Sample 1: தமிழனுக்கு எதிரியே தமிழன் தான்.. Tamil stands against Tamilians..	NCIHS	CIHS
Sample 2: அவன முதலில் அடித்து விரட்டு (வட இந்தியன்) He first slapped and then ran away (North Indian)	CIHS	CIHS
Sample 3: தங்களின் ஹிந்தி நன்றாக இருக்கிறது. டாஸ்மாக்கை மூடினால் இந்த நிலைமை விரைவில் மாறும். Your Hindi is good. If you close the TasMac, this situation will change soon.	NCIHS	NCIHS
Sample 4: புதுசு புதுசா நானும் தலைவர்னு கிளம்பிறானுங்க ! யார்ரா நீ ? Even I'm a leader, Who are you?	CIHS	NCIHS
Sample 5: தமிழனுக்கு தமிழன் தான் எதிரி தமிழ்நாட்டிலேயே பல கருப்பு அடங்கியிருக்கிறது அப்ப எப்படி தமிழ் மக்கள் வாழ முடியும் Tamil is against Tamil Nadu itself, How will Tamil people live if many blacks are present there?	NCIHS	CIHS

Figure 4: Some predicted outcomes by the best-performed model

formance detecting hate speech in Tamil. However, it struggled to detect caste and migration hatred due to limited training data. The dataset included social media content featuring regional dialects and poor grammar, posing challenges for identifying hate classes. Additionally, ambiguous statements and context gaps may affect the models performance. Enhanced methods for collecting nuanced grammar details could improve the performance of the current implementation.

6 Conclusion

This work explored several ML, DL, and transformer-based techniques and analyzed their performance in detecting caste and migration hate speech in Tamil. Experimental assessment of the test dataset revealed that the M-BERT model is the best performing model for detecting hate speech in Tamil and outperformed all models by obtaining the highest macro f_1-score (0.80). Surprisingly, the BiLSTM + Attention model performed poorly compared other ML and transformer models. These inferior results might occur because of the prevalence of local words, which still need to be discovered in the model. The future work includes adding more data in the respective classes to make a balanced dataset and investigating more sophisticated techniques such as MuRIL and GPT for improved performance.

References

Takuya Akiba, Shotaro Sano, Toshihiko Yanase, Takeru Ohta, and Masanori Koyama. 2019. Optuna: A next-generation hyperparameter optimization framework. In *Proceedings of the 25th ACM SIGKDD international conference on knowledge discovery & data mining*, pages 2623–2631.

Sattam Almatarneh, Pablo Gamallo, and Francisco J Ribadas Pena. 2019. CiTIUS-COLE at semeval-2019 task 5: Combining linguistic features to identify hate speech against immigrants and women on multilingual tweets. In *Proceedings of the 13th International Workshop on Semantic Evaluation*, pages 387–390.

Valerio Basile, Cristina Bosco, Elisabetta Fersini, Debora Nozza, Viviana Patti, Francisco Manuel Rangel Pardo, Paolo Rosso, and Manuela Sanguinetti. 2019. Semeval-2019 task 5: Multilingual detection of hate speech against immigrants and women in Twitter. In *Proceedings of the 13th international workshop on semantic evaluation*, pages 54–63.

Shaily Bhatt, Sunipa Dev, Partha Talukdar, Shachi Dave, and Vinodkumar Prabhakaran. 2022. Re-contextualizing Fairness in NLP: The Case of India.

Darsh Bhimani, Rutvi Bheda, Femin Dharamshi, Deepti Nikumbh, and Priyanka Abhyankar. 2021. Identification of Hate Speech using Natural Language Processing and Machine Learning. In *2021 2nd Global Conference for Advancement in Technology (GCAT)*, pages 1–4. IEEE.

Berta Chulvi, Mariangeles Molpeceres, María F Rodrigo, Alejandro H Toselli, and Paolo Rosso. 2023. Politicization of Immigration and Language Use in Political Elites: A Study of Spanish Parliamentary Speeches. *Journal of Language and Social Psychology*, page 0261927X231175856.

Alexis Conneau, Kartikay Khandelwal, Naman Goyal, Vishrav Chaudhary, Guillaume Wenzek, Francisco Guzmán, Edouard Grave, Myle Ott, Luke Zettlemoyer, and Veselin Stoyanov. 2019. Unsupervised cross-lingual representation learning at scale. *arXiv preprint arXiv:1911.02116*.

Jacob Devlin, Ming-Wei Chang, Kenton Lee, and Kristina Toutanova. 2018. BERT: Pre-training of deep bidirectional transformers for language understanding. *arXiv preprint arXiv:1810.04805*.

LK Dhanya and Kannan Balakrishnan. 2021. Hate speech detection in Asian languages: a survey. In *2021 international conference on communication, control and information sciences (ICCISc)*, volume 1, pages 1–5. IEEE.

Zaki Mustafa Farooqi, Sreyan Ghosh, and Rajiv Ratn Shah. 2021. Leveraging transformers for hate speech detection in conversational code-mixed tweets. *arXiv preprint arXiv:2112.09986*.

Edouard Grave, Piotr Bojanowski, Prakhar Gupta, Armand Joulin, and Tomas Mikolov. 2018. Learning word vectors for 157 languages. *arXiv preprint arXiv:1802.06893*.

Alamgir Hossain, Mahathir Bishal, Eftekhar Hossain, Omar Sharif, and Mohammed Moshiul Hoque. 2022. COMBATANT@ TamilNLP-ACL2022: Fine-grained Categorization of Abusive Comments using Logistic Regression. In *Proceedings of the Second Workshop on Speech and Language Technologies for Dravidian Languages*, pages 221–228.

Jawad Hossain, Hasan Mesbaul Ali Taher, Avishek Das, and Mohammed Moshiul Hoque. 2023. NLP_CUET at BLP-2023 Task 1: Fine-grained Categorization of Violence Inciting Text using Transformer-based Approach. In *Proceedings of the First Workshop on Bangla Language Processing (BLP-2023)*, pages 241–246.

Raviraj Joshi. 2022. L3Cube-HindBERT and DevBERT: Pre-Trained BERT Transformer models for Devanagari based Hindi and Marathi Languages. *arXiv preprint arXiv:2211.11418*.

Arun S Maiya. 2022. ktrain: A low-code library for augmented machine learning. *The Journal of Machine Learning Research*, 23(1):7070–7075.

Sünje Paasch-Colberg, Christian Strippel, Joachim Trebbe, and Martin Emmer. 2021. From insult to hate speech: Mapping offensive language in German user comments on immigration. *Media and Communication*, 9(1):171–180.

Saranya Rajiakodi, Bharathi Raja Chakravarthi, Rahul Ponnusamy, Prasanna Kumar Kumaresan, Sathiyaraj Thangasamy, Bhuvaneswari Sivagnanam, and Charmathi Rajkumar. 2024. Overview of Shared Task on Caste and Migration Hate Speech Detection. In *Proceedings of the Fourth Workshop on Language Technology for Equality, Diversity and Inclusion*, Malta. European Chapter of the Association for Computational Linguistics.

Raúl R Romero-Vega, Oscar M Cumbicus-Pineda, Ruperto A López-Lapo, and Lisset A Neyra-Romero. 2021. Detecting xenophobic hate speech in spanish tweets against venezuelan immigrants in ecuador using natural language processing. In *Applied Technologies: Second International Conference, ICAT 2020, Quito, Ecuador, December 2–4, 2020, Proceedings 2*, pages 312–326. Springer.

Janak Sachdeva, Kushank Kumar Chaudhary, Harshit Madaan, and Priyanka Meel. 2021. Text based hate-speech analysis. In *2021 International Conference on Artificial Intelligence and Smart Systems (ICAIS)*, pages 661–668. IEEE.

Devanshu Sajlan. 2021. Hate Speech against Dalits on Social Media. *CASTE: A Global Journal on Social Exclusion*, 2(1):77–96.

Omar Sharif and Mohammed Moshiul Hoque. 2021. Align and Conquer: An Ensemble Approach to Classify Aggressive Texts from Social Media. In *2021 IEEE International Conference on Signal Processing, Information, Communication & Systems (SPICSCON)*, pages 82–86. IEEE.

Omar Sharif, Eftekhar Hossain, and Mohammed Moshiul Hoque. 2021. Combating hostility: Covid-19 fake news and hostile post detection in social media. *arXiv preprint arXiv:2101.03291*.

Tokunaga Takenobu. 1994. Text categorization based on weighted inverse document frequency. *Information Processing Society of Japan, SIGNL*, 94(100):33–40.

DRAVIDIAN LANGUAGE@ LT-EDI 2024:Pretrained Transformer based Automatic Speech Recognition system for Elderly People

Abirami. J, Aruna Devi. S,Dharunika Sasikumar& B. Bharathi
Department of CSE
Sri Sivasubramaniya Nadar College of Engineering,
Tamil Nadu, India
abirami2210382@ssn.edu.in
aruna2210499@ssn.edu.in
dharunika2210459@ssn.edu.in
bharathib@ssn.edu.in

Abstract

In this paper, the main goal of the study is to create an automatic speech recognition (ASR) system that is tailored to the Tamil language. The dataset that was employed includes audio recordings that were obtained from vulnerable populations in the Tamil region, such as elderly men and women and transgender individuals.

The pre-trained model Rajaram1996/wav2vec2-large-xlsr-53-tamil is used in the engineering of the ASR system. This existing model is fine-tuned using a variety of datasets that include typical Tamil voices. The system is then tested with a specific test dataset, and the transcriptions that are produced are sent in for assessment. The Word Error Rate is used to evaluate the system's performance. Our system has a WER of 37.733.

1 Introduction

The goal of this research project is to create an Automatic Speech Recognition (ASR) system that is specifically designed to serve vulnerable populations in the Tamil-speaking community, such as the elderly and transgender people. This shared task's scope entails improving speech recognition skills to enable certain demographic groups to access facilities including banks, hospitals, and shopping centers. The problem is closing the information gap between the elderly, who might not know how to use the tools at their disposal, and the transgender population, which experiences educational inequalities as a result of prejudice from society.

It is highlighted how important speaking is to these groups as their main form of communication because it is essential to meeting their everyday requirements. The study's dataset is made up of spontaneous speech samples that were obtained from transgender and elderly people who have trouble using different facilities. A two-hour speech dataset is provided for testing, and a training set of 5.5 hours of transcribed speech is also accessible.

Even while technological developments have made it easier for people to access electronic devices in a wider range of industries, educational barriers still pose a barrier for the elderly and transgender people. Even though these people use electronics, the fact that they primarily rely on audio messages highlights the need for better speech recognition models in order to accommodate their distinct speech patterns and deliver accurate responses. These people provide audio input to the method described in this paper, which converts it into corresponding Tamil transcripts. The Word Error Rate (WER) is used to measure the accuracy of these transcripts, taking into account the inherent difficulty that comes with different accents.

The structure of the report offers a thorough understanding of the research process. In Section 2, relevant literature is examined in detail, emphasizing gaps in the field and current knowledge. The dataset is thoroughly described in Section 3, along with its makeup and significance to the goals of the research. While Section 5 describes the implementation procedure, Section 4 covers the technique used in the development of the ASR system.

Key findings from the research are summarized in Section 6, which also offers insights on the study's performance and difficulties. A thorough discussion is started in Section 7 by interpreting the findings and placing them within the larger context of the study goals. The paper's main conclusions are summarized in Section 8, which also highlights the ongoing development of ASR systems for vulnerable populations and moves into a discussion of possible directions for further research.

The last section, Section 9, offers a thorough summary of the academic background that underpinned this project and is devoted to the reference articles that were examined during the research pro-

Proceedings of the Fourth Workshop on Language Technology for Equality, Diversity, Inclusion, pages 244–248
March 21, 2024 ©2024 Association for Computational Linguistics

cess. Essentially, this work lays the groundwork for future advancements and improvements in this crucial area by advancing ASR technologies that meet the particular communication demands of vulnerable groups.

2 Related work

Voice recognition has advanced significantly over the past ten years, mostly due to the quick development of deep learning methods. Ten years ago, most researchers concentrated on using deep learning to extract audio data. Subsequently, these data were combined with hidden Markov models, which were popular at the time. But things have changed, and modern approaches now use more advanced recurrent neural networks (RNNs), like Long Short-Term Memory (LSTM) networks, in place of more conventional Gaussian mixture models. Notably, large models with higher parameterization, such Contextnet and Conformer, have shown improved voice recognition accuracy.

Convolutional neural networks (CNNs) are used by the authors of a study titled "Speech Rate Control for Improving Elderly Speech Recognition of Smart Devices" to overcome the difficulties in geriatric speech recognition on smart devices.

In a different study, "TransformerTransducer: End-to-End Voice Recognition with Self-Attention" [6], the authors want to use transformer networks in the neural transducer architecture to create an end-to-end speech recognition model. In order to incorporate positional information and reduce frame rates, their method integrates VGGNet with causal convolution, maximizing computing efficiency through reduced self-attention.

The preprocessing of data is essential to building reliable models. The authors stress the significance of labeled data for training models and discuss methods that entail using both labeled and unlabeled speech data to train large-scale models. An example of self-supervised learning is Wav2vec [3], which uses contrastive learning for feature learning and unlabeled speech data for training.

The effectiveness of deep learning in machine translation and speech recognition is recognized, highlighting its natural language comprehension abilities. This impact is being felt in a variety of domains, as scientists are investigating neural methods to comprehend code semantics and spot weak points. Notably, studies on low-resource speech recognition methods for minority languages have been conducted, and attempts have been made to improve accuracy by means of data augmentation.

The Rajaram1996/wav2vec-large-xlsr-53-tamil transformer model is used by the authors of [5],[4] to identify Tamil speech utterances made by susceptible individuals. To calculate the word mistake rate, the model takes into account variables like the number of utterances and the quality of the.wav file. This concept is primarily intended to promote inclusivity for marginalized people by increasing accessibility to regional languages.

In this work, audio files are transcribed using a pre-trained XLSR model, and word error rates are computed as a result. The focus is on using cutting-edge deep learning techniques to improve speech recognition systems' inclusivity and accuracy, especially when it comes to disadvantaged populations. The following parts provide a thorough analysis of relevant literature, dataset specifications, methodology, implementation details, outcomes that have been seen, and a thorough discussion. A few suggestions for future directions in this ever-evolving field of study are included in the paper's conclusion. The reference section lists the articles that were consulted for this research project, giving the provided conclusions a strong basis.

3 Dataset Description

The dataset given to this shared task [1] is an Tamil conversational speech recorded from the elderly people whose average age is around 61 for male, 59 for female and 30 for transgender people .A total of 6 hours and 42 minutes is collected from the elderly people. 46 audio files were recorded and each audio file is split into many subsets as transformer model does not support the large audiofiles. The speech is recorded with a sampling rate of 16KHZ. The audio files from Audio - Audio-10, to Audio-35 are used for training (duration is approximately 5.5 hours) [2] and Audio - 37 to Audio - 48 are used for testing (duration is approximately 2 hours).

4 Proposed Work

To construct their automatic speech recognition system, the researchers used the Rajaram1996/wav2vec2-large-xlsr-53-tamil pre-trained transformer model. This model is an advanced speech recognition system designed by Facebook AI specifically for the Tamil language, and it is based on the Wav2Vec2 architecture. Wav2Vec2 is a self-supervised learning technique that builds representations that capture important information about audio features by utilizing massive amounts of unlabeled voice data. The model's fundamental architecture is based on transformers, which have proven to be incredibly useful in a variety of natural language processing applications. Transformers improve the model's ability to do nuanced analysis by allowing it to effectively capture long-range dependencies in audio inputs.

The model is trained by subjecting it to a sizable corpus of Tamil speech-containing monolingual and multilingual data. Pre-training enables a thorough grasp of the fundamental structure and characteristics of speech data by teaching the model to predict masked or distorted chunks of the input audio. After pre-training, the model is fine-tuned utilizing labeled data customized for particular downstream tasks, like Tamil keyword detection or transcription. Through this process of fine-tuning, the model can be made to adjust to the specifics of a given speech recognition task.

The model gains from the multilingual character of its pre-training data even though it was particularly trained on Tamil. Because of the large corpus of words it has been trained on, it can process a wide variety of words and phrases, which makes it ideal for tasks like transcription or speech recognition. The training set of the model and its fine-tuning methodology are purposefully created to capture the unique phonetic, phonological, and grammatical characteristics of the Tamil language. This careful process improves the model's capacity to identify and translate Tamil speech.

Business-wise, the use of cutting-edge models such as Rajaram1996/wav2vec2-large-xlsr-53-tamil highlights a dedication to utilizing cutting-edge technologies in voice recognition system development. The model is able to extract meaningful representations from unlabeled data thanks to the innovative use of a self-supervised learning strategy. Applying transformers, which are well-known for their effectiveness in natural language processing, shows a deliberate architectural decision to improve the model's analytical powers.

In line with industry best practices, the focus on fine-tuning for certain downstream applications guarantees that the model is tuned for the subtleties of Tamil speech recognition. Given that the model can accommodate a wide vocabulary, it can be used as a flexible solution for transcription or speech recognition tasks that need to cover a wide range of languages.

To sum up, the researchers' careful selection of the model, training process, and fine-tuning technique shows a dedication to creating a reliable and adaptable automatic speech recognition system that is suited to the nuances of the Tamil language. This strategy, which is based on cutting-edge technologies and best practices from the industry, presents the system as a useful tool for companies looking for precise and flexible voice recognition solutions. The ongoing development of these models has implications for various applications in various industries and offers potential for the area of natural language processing as a whole.

5 Implementation

We have harnessed an efficient model, leveraging a pre-trained transformer-based architecture named Rajaram1996/wav2vec2-large-xlsr-53-tamil. This particular model, a derivative of facebook/wav2vec2-large-xlsr-53, is specialized for Tamil and fine-tuned using the Common Voice dataset. To operate seamlessly, this model mandates a 16 KHz sampling rate for voice input. Our assessments have utilized LT-EDI's dataset to evaluate the model's efficacy.

The core functionality revolves around loading voice utterances into the library, storing them as variables, and tokenizing them via a dedicated tokenizer. This transformation pipeline is instrumental in converting audio signals into textual representations. Our meticulous approach involves a thorough comparison between these transcribed texts and the original audio transcripts. This critical alignment allows us to calculate the Word Error Rate (WER), a metric that reflects the fidelity of voice recognition thereby used to quantify the accuracy and precision of the model's voice recognition capabilities. This approach, rooted in the XLSR (Cross-Lingual Speech Representation) framework, extends its capabilities to cross-lingual speech data, showcasing the model's adaptability across languages. The derived WER provides a robust assessment of the model's proficiency in voice-to-text transcription. By using the WER as our benchmark, we gain deeper insights into the model's performance, and efficiency for affirming its prowess in transforming spoken words into accurate text.

S.No	File Name	Number of Subsets	WER
1	Audio-10	38	40.84
2	Audio-11	49	41.03
3	Audio-12	17	35.26
4	Audio-13	33	39.99
5	Audio-14	25	34.72

Table 1: WER Values for Training Set used for testing

6 Evaluation of Results

The general difficulty of measuring performance lies in the fact that the recognized word sequence can have a different length from the reference word sequence. The WER is derived from the Levenshtein distance, working at the word level instead of the phoneme level. The task's evaluation measure is based on the WER (Word Error Rate) computed between the original transcriptions of the given audio and the transcribed text.

WER (Word Error Rate) = (S + D + I) / N
where,
S = No. of substitutions
D = No. of deletions
I = No. of insertions
N = No. of words in the reference transcription

7 Observation

The name of the speech data and its WER value are included in the result. Similar to this, the same procedure is used for all audio files. The number of subgroups into which each audio file is divided is also listed in the table. Table 1 provides insights to some of the transcribed statements using the training data.

1	Targeted Sentence	அடுத்து எப்போ வரணும்.வந்தா எப்போ பாக்கலாம் .இல்ல ஏதும் வேற ஏதும் மருந்து மாதர வாங்கணுமா ஊசி ஏதும் போடணுமா .திருப்பி கட்டாயம் வரணுமா என்னனு சொல்லுங்க மேடம் பணம் டெபாசிட் பண்ணனும் பிள்ளைங்களுக்கு ரெண்டு பிரிவா
	Predicted Sentence	பநிக பாற்றறக்கமே நாடத்துயர்ப வற வந்தாயப்ப பாகலா லல இதும யாரது மார்தநது மத்ற வாங்கனமா ஊஷி யரும் போடணுமா திரப்பிககட்டாயம் வரணுமா எ நான் சொல்லுங்கறம் உர பணங்ககும் தபழ்ஷ்டுபணம்பலேயலுகேஅரெண்டுபெரிவா அ
2	Targeted Sentence	தெரிஞ்சவங்க உள்ள இருகாங்க பா . சொந்தக்காரங்க .அவங்கள பார்க்கணும் . பாக்க வந்துருக்கன் .எந்த இதுல இருகாங்க .அவங்கள இப்போ பார்க்க முடியுமா .எந்த டயத்துல வந்தா பார்க்கலாம். ஏதும் அவங்களுக்கு வாங்கிட்டு போலாமா
	Predicted Sentence	பேய தெரம்பங்க உள்ளார்காங்கபா ஜந்நுதரம்ம அங்மள பாக்கனர் பாக்காம்பருகேன் எண்டவா தலர்காங்க அஅவங்களப் ப பாக்கமுடியுமா எலேஎந்தத டேயட்டுக்கே வந்தா பாகவான் நஏத மாவங்களுக் வாய்ந்து போழமா அலவவேதுவ

Figure 1: Sample predicted sentences

8 Discussion

The number of test speech utterances are 295. From the total number of 295 audio subset files from 10 audio files which is given for testing and the WER measured is 37.73. We ranked fourth position in shared task competition.

9 Conclusions

Conversational speech data is utilised to improve the speech recognition system's capacity to detect elderly people. A trained model is used to construct an automatic speech recognition system. A dataset collection is focusing on older adults and transgender people who use Tamil as their first language. The dataset's utterance was taken during a conversation in a major site in Tamil. Because the system's pre-trained model was enhanced using a common speech dataset, the model might be trained using our own dataset and tested in the future, which could improve performance.

References

[1] Bharathi B, Bharathi Raja Chakravarthi, Subalalitha Cn, Sripriya N, Arunaggiri Pandian, and Swetha Valli. Findings of the shared task on speech recognition for vulnerable individuals in Tamil. In Bharathi Raja Chakravarthi, B Bharathi, John P McCrae, Manel Zarrouk, Kalika Bali, and Paul Buitelaar, editors, *Proceedings of the Second Workshop on Language Technology for Equality, Diversity and Inclusion*, pages 339–345, Dublin, Ireland, May 2022. Association for Computational Linguistics.

[2] Bharathi B, Bharathi Raja Chakravarthi, Sripirya N, Rajeswari Natarajan, Suhasini S, and Swetha Valli.

Overview of the third shared task on speech recognition for vulnerable individuals in tamil. In *Proceedings of the Fourth Workshop on Language Technology for Equality, Diversity, Inclusion*, Malta, March 2024. European Chapter of the Association for Computational Linguistics.

[3] Alexei Baevski, Steffen Schneider, and Michael Auli. vq-wav2vec: Self-supervised learning of discrete speech representations. *arXiv preprint arXiv:1910.05453*, 2019.

[4] Varsha Balaji, Archana Jp, and B Bharathi. Cse_speech@ lt-edi-2023automatic speech recognition vulnerable old-aged and transgender people in tamil. In *Proceedings of the Third Workshop on Language Technology for Equality, Diversity and Inclusion*, pages 204–208, 2023.

[5] S Suhasini and B Bharathi. Asr_ssn_cse@ ltedi-2023: Pretrained transformer-based automatic speech recognition system for elderly people. In *Proceedings of the Third Workshop on Language Technology for Equality, Diversity and Inclusion*, pages 161–165, 2023.

[6] Ching-Feng Yeh, Jay Mahadeokar, Kaustubh Kalgaonkar, Yongqiang Wang, Duc Le, Mahaveer Jain, Kjell Schubert, Christian Fuegen, and Michael L Seltzer. Transformer-transducer: End-to-end speech recognition with self-attention. *arXiv preprint arXiv:1910.12977*, 2019.

Transformers@LT-EDI-EACL2024: Caste and Migration Hate Speech Detection in Tamil Using Ensembling on Transformers

Kriti Singhal[1], Jatin Bedi[2]
Computer Science and Engineering Department,
Thapar Institute of Engineering and Technology, India
[1]kritisinghal711@gmail.com, [2]jatin.bedi@thapar.edu

Abstract

In recent years, there has been a persistent focus on developing systems that can automatically identify the hate speech content circulating on diverse social media platforms. This paper describes the team "Transformers" submission to the Caste and Migration Hate Speech Detection in Tamil shared task by LT-EDI 2024 workshop at EACL 2024. We used an ensemble approach in the shared task, combining various transformer-based pre-trained models using majority voting. The best macro average F1-score achieved was 0.82. We secured the 1st rank in the Caste and Migration Hate Speech in Tamil shared task.

1 Introduction

Hate speech can be defined as the use of aggressive, abusive or threatening expressions or phrases. With the advancement of the technological age, everyone has access to the internet to voice their opinions to a large audience. However, some people may misuse this power to spread hate against a certain individual or a group of individuals based on certain distinguishing characteristics. This could be through posts on social media, blogs, videos, or comments on various platforms. Hence, it has become crucial to regulate the comments on social media platforms to avoid hurting sentiments. The shared task[1] organized by LT-EDI aimed to detect Caste and Migration hate speech in Tamil text (Rajiakodi et al., 2024).

Social media platforms have taken the freedom of speech and expression beyond global borders. Platforms like Twitter, Instagram, and YouTube allow ideas shared from one corner of the world to reach millions of people across the world in just a few milliseconds (Shanmugavadivel et al., 2022). However, the increased anonymity provided by such platforms has lead users to exploit this power by sharing opinions and ideas targeted against an individual or a group. This makes it crucial to regulate the hateful content shared online automatically to attenuate the societal harm it can cause.

In the targeted Hate Speech identification domain, Natural Language Processing (NLP) has experienced major breakthroughs in the past few years. Recent developments include Long Short Term Memory (Hochreiter and Schmidhuber, 1997), and Gated Recurrent Units (Chung et al., 2014). But with the introduction of transformers (Vaswani et al., 2017), the results have seen a paradigm shift.

Tamil is one of the twenty-two scheduled languages in the Constitution of India. Tamil is also a member of the Dravidian languages' family (Chakravarthi and Raja, 2020), which dates back over 4,500 years. However, Tamil continues to be under-resourced (Ghanghor et al., 2021). Multiple NLP approaches have also been devised with a special focus on the Indian context, this includes, IndicBERT and MuRIL (Khanuja et al., 2021).

The aim of this shared task was to build an automatic classification system which could classify whether the given text in Tamil contains caste and migration hate speech or not. In this context, the current work presents a novel approach based on transformers to classify whether a text has caste and migration hate speech in Tamil.

2 Related Work

With the recent boom in the number of internet users, many researchers worldwide have directed their efforts towards finding whether text online contains hate speech. The methodologies have evolved from the traditional machine learning models to the recent transformer-based approaches.

In the work done by Shanmugavadivel et al. (2023), a machine learning-based approach was

[1] https://codalab.lisn.upsaclay.fr/competitions/16089

Proceedings of the Fourth Workshop on Language Technology for Equality, Diversity, Inclusion, pages 249–253
March 21, 2024 ©2024 Association for Computational Linguistics

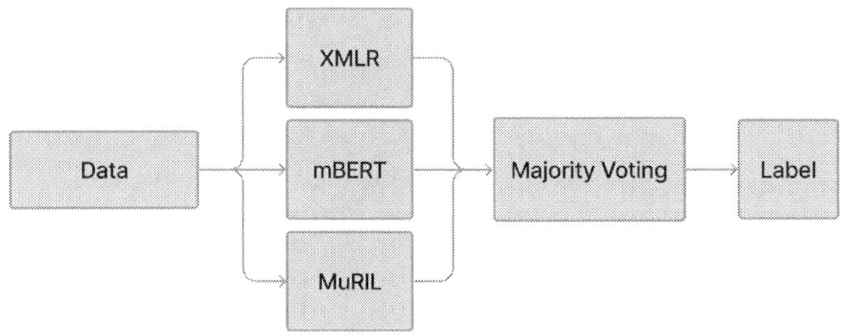

Figure 1: Proposed Methodology

proposed for the detection of abusive comments in the Tamil language after exploring various deep learning and transformer techniques. They achieved a macro-F1 score of 0.35. The work also showed how the traditional machine learning models can outperform certain deep learning and transformer-based techniques when the dataset is not large enough and complex where the deep learning approaches excel.

Similarly, Subramanian et al. (2022) experimented with multiple traditional machine learning models and transfer learning approaches. They found that even though machine learning models performed well, transfer learning approaches outperformed them. Among the different approaches that were tested, XLM-RoBERTa (Large) gave the highest accuracy. They attributed the reason to the fact that XLM-RoBERTa (Large) has more layers. Hence, the number of trainable parameters is approximately three times the other alternatives.

Bhawal et al. (2021) also observed that transformer based approaches consistently performed better on both Tamil and Malayalam text. Various models, including Logistic Regression, Support Vector Machine, etc., were implemented on the Tamil dataset, and the highest F1-score achieved was 0.82. A simple deep neural network was implemented on the same dataset, and it achieved an F1-Score of 0.89 on the Tamil text. The MuRIL model, however, outperformed both of these techniques and achieved an F1-Score of 0.91.

An ensemble approach was adopted by Roy et al. (2022). Initially, many traditional machine learning models and transformer based models were implemented individually. However, it was found that the individual models had a high misclassifictaion rate. Hence, in order to improve the accuracy, a combination of any three of the high scoring models were used for ensembling. Two different approaches were considered to ensemble the models. The first approach involved averaging the outcomes of the models and the second approach involved using custom weights which were determined by grid search method for each member of the ensemble model.

Table 1: Dataset Distribution for Caste and Migration Hate Speech Detection Task

Dataset	**Label**		**Total**
	0	**1**	
Dev	594	351	945
Train	3,303	2,052	5,355

3 Dataset Description

The dataset was provided by the organizers of the competition (Chakravarthi, 2020, 2022; Chakravarthi et al., 2022). The train and dev dataset is comprised of three fields, namely, id, text, and label. The test set comprised of only id and text. The labels for the dataset were 0 or 1, where 0 denoted absence and 1 denoted presence of no caste and migration hate speech, respectively. The distributions of the dev and train datasets have been shown in Table 1.

4 Methodology

Text classification is one of the most prominent tasks in NLP. It can be defined as the segregation

Table 2: Model Performance Comparison

Model	Before Pre-processing		After Pre-processing	
	F1 Score	Accuracy	F1 Score	Accuracy
MuRIL cased	0.60	0.62	0.60	0.61
XLM RoBERTa Large	0.38	0.62	0.61	0.65
Multilingual DistilBERT Base cased	0.28	0.38	0.57	0.65
XLM RoBERTa Base	0.61	0.65	0.61	0.62
Multilingual BERT Base cased	0.59	0.62	0.59	0.60
Indic BERT	0.60	0.60	0.52	0.62

of texts into different classes. Various models using a variety of word representations have been introduced in the past to tackle the text classification problem. Many of these models were based on the transformer architecture and have been pre-trained on large corpora of text and made available for solving problems, including text classification. These models perform tokenization using their own tokenizers and vocabularies. However, the corpora of text these models are trained on are limited to high-resourced languages like English. Hence, this issue was solved using cross-lingual transfer learning. The proposed methodology in this paper uses these models to cater to the needs of the problem presented in the shared tasks.

Many transformer models were trained using the training data and dev data to test the performance, as shown in Table 2. After testing the performance of various transformer models, the top three models with the best performance were selected. The models, XLM RoBERTa base (XLMR) (Conneau et al., 2019), multilingual-cased BERT base (mBERT) (Devlin et al., 2019), MuRIL cased (MuRIL) (Khanuja et al., 2021) were selected. The selected models were trained after concatenating the train and the dev dataset for the final predictions.

XLMR is an unsupervised model which has been trained on 100 different languages. This model was based on Facebook's 2019 RoBERTa (Liu et al., 2019) model. This is a large multi-lingual model which was trained on 2.5TB of filtered data from CommonCrawl.

MuRIL cased temp model is an NLP model that has been trained in the transformers library implemented using Python.

mBERT is a self-supervised transformer model which was pre-trained on a large multilingual corpus. The model was not trained on data labeled by humans instead, it was trained on raw texts. This model was trained on 104 languages with the largest Wikipedia. This model is case sensitive in nature.

It was observed that the performance of the selected models used in the ensemble model suffered after pre-processing the text, where the pre-processing included the removal of numbers, special characters and emojis. Hence, no pre-processing was done before training the models. The performances of the various models that were implemented have been shown in Table 2 both before and after preprocessing the training data and testing its performance on the dev data. The Adam optimizer was used with a learning rate of 1e-5 and cross entropy function was used as the loss function for all the models.

For performing tokenization, different tokenizers were used, which were specific to each model. The XLMRoBERTaTokenizer was used for XLMR, the BertTokenizer was used for mBERT, and the AutoTokenizer was used for MuRIL.

For evaluating the label, as shown in Figure 1, the data was first passed through the three models individually. Then the predictions of these three models were combined by using majority voting. The label with the highest frequency was finally predicted as the output of the ensemble model.

5 Results and Discussion

The ensemble model was designed by selecting the top three models with the best performance on the training data. The performance of all the models that were implemented on the training data has been shown in Table 2.

The base models and transformer models were both trained and tested. The transformer models consistently performed better than the base machine learning models. Each of the transformer models was trained for 5 to 50 epochs each. The highest F1 score and its corresponding accuracy have been mentioned in Table 2 for the transformer models.

The proposed ensembling technique achieved the highest F1 score of 0.82. This also shows that combining the various transformer-based techniques can lead to improved performance.

6 Conclusion and Future Work

In this work, an ensembling technique was proposed to automatically detect whether a given text in Tamil contains caste and migration hate speech for the Caste and Migration Hate Speech Detection in Tamil shared task by the LT-EDI 2024 workshop at EACL 2024. The technique was based on transformer models and utilized transfer learning.

The performance of the ensemble model can be further improved by taking the predictions from more transformer models or other traditional machine learning and deep learning techniques. Also, taking a weighted vote of the models according to their performance on the training data can help give better results than majority voting, where each model is given equal importance irrespective of their performance relative to the other models.

References

Snehaan Bhawal, Pradeep Roy, and Abhinav Kumar. 2021. Hate speech and offensive language identification on multilingual code mixed text using BERT. In *Working Notes of FIRE 2021-Forum for Information Retrieval Evaluation (Online). CEUR.*

Asoka Chakravarthi and Bharathi Raja. 2020. *Leveraging orthographic information to improve machine translation of under-resourced languages*. Ph.D. thesis, NUI Galway.

Bharathi Raja Chakravarthi. 2020. "HopeEDI: A Multilingual Hope Speech Detection Dataset for Equality, Diversity, and Inclusion". In *Proceedings of the Third Workshop on Computational Modeling of People's Opinions, Personality, and Emotion's in Social Media*, pages 41–53, Barcelona, Spain (Online). Association for Computational Linguistics.

Bharathi Raja Chakravarthi. 2022. Hope speech detection in YouTube comments. *Social Network Analysis and Mining*, 12(1):75.

Bharathi Raja Chakravarthi, Vigneshwaran Muralidaran, Ruba Priyadharshini, Subalalitha Cn, John McCrae, Miguel Ángel García, Salud María Jiménez-Zafra, Rafael Valencia-García, Prasanna Kumaresan, Rahul Ponnusamy, Daniel García-Baena, and José García-Díaz. 2022. "Overview of the Shared Task on Hope Speech Detection for Equality, Diversity, and Inclusion". In *Proceedings of the Second Workshop on Language Technology for Equality, Diversity and Inclusion*, pages 378–388, Dublin, Ireland. Association for Computational Linguistics.

Junyoung Chung, Caglar Gulcehre, KyungHyun Cho, and Yoshua Bengio. 2014. Empirical evaluation of gated recurrent neural networks on sequence modeling. *arXiv preprint arXiv:1412.3555*.

Alexis Conneau, Kartikay Khandelwal, Naman Goyal, Vishrav Chaudhary, Guillaume Wenzek, Francisco Guzmán, Edouard Grave, Myle Ott, Luke Zettlemoyer, and Veselin Stoyanov. 2019. Unsupervised cross-lingual representation learning at scale. *arXiv preprint arXiv:1911.02116*.

Jacob Devlin, Ming-Wei Chang, Kenton Lee, and Kristina Toutanova. 2019. "BERT: Pre-training of Deep Bidirectional Transformers for Language Understanding". In *Proceedings of the 2019 Conference of the North American Chapter of the Association for Computational Linguistics: Human Language Technologies, Volume 1 (Long and Short Papers)*, pages 4171–4186, Minneapolis, Minnesota. Association for Computational Linguistics.

Nikhil Ghanghor, Parameswari Krishnamurthy, Sajeetha Thavareesan, Ruba Priyadharshini, and Bharathi Raja Chakravarthi. 2021. "IIITK@DravidianLangTech-EACL2021: Offensive Language Identification and Meme Classification in Tamil, Malayalam and Kannada". In *Proceedings of the First Workshop on Speech and Language Technologies for Dravidian Languages*, pages 222–229, Kyiv. Association for Computational Linguistics.

Sepp Hochreiter and Jürgen Schmidhuber. 1997. Long short-term memory. *Neural computation*, 9(8):1735–1780.

Simran Khanuja, Diksha Bansal, Sarvesh Mehtani, Savya Khosla, Atreyee Dey, Balaji Gopalan, Dilip Kumar Margam, Pooja Aggarwal, Rajiv Teja Nagipogu, Shachi Dave, Shruti Gupta, Subhash Chandra Bose Gali, Vish Subramanian, and Partha Talukdar. 2021. MuRIL: Multilingual Representations for Indian Languages.

Yinhan Liu, Myle Ott, Naman Goyal, Jingfei Du, Mandar Joshi, Danqi Chen, Omer Levy, Mike Lewis, Luke Zettlemoyer, and Veselin Stoyanov. 2019. RoBERTa: A Robustly Optimized BERT Pretraining Approach. *arXiv preprint arXiv:1907.11692*.

Saranya Rajiakodi, Bharathi Raja Chakravarthi, Rahul Ponnusamy, Prasanna Kumar Kumaresan, Sathiyaraj Thangasamy, Bhuvaneswari Sivagnanam, and Charmathi Rajkumar. 2024. Overview of Shared Task on Caste and Migration Hate Speech Detection. In *Proceedings of the Fourth Workshop on Language Technology for Equality, Diversity and Inclusion*, Malta.

European Chapter of the Association for Computational Linguistics.

Pradeep Kumar Roy, Snehaan Bhawal, and Chinnaudayar Navaneethakrishnan Subalalitha. 2022. Hate speech and offensive language detection in Dravidian languages using deep ensemble framework. *Computer Speech Language*, 75:101386.

Kogilavani Shanmugavadivel, Malliga Subramanian, Prasanna Kumar Kumaresan, Bharathi Raja Chakravarthi, B Bharathi, Subalalitha Chinnaudayar Navaneethakrishnan, Lavanya Sambath Kumar, Thomas Mandl, Rahul Ponnusamy, Vasanth Palanikumar, et al. 2022. Overview of the Shared Task on Sentiment Analysis and Homophobia Detection of YouTube Comments in Code-Mixed Dravidian Languages.

Kogilavani Shanmugavadivel, Malliga Subramanian, Shri Durga R, Srigha S, Sree Harene J S, and Yasvanth Bala P. 2023. "KEC_AI_NLP@DravidianLangTech: Abusive Comment Detection in Tamil Language". In *Proceedings of the Third Workshop on Speech and Language Technologies for Dravidian Languages*, pages 293–299, Varna, Bulgaria. INCOMA Ltd., Shoumen, Bulgaria.

Malliga Subramanian, Rahul Ponnusamy, Sean Benhur, Kogilavani Shanmugavadivel, Adhithiya Ganesan, Deepti Ravi, Gowtham Krishnan Shanmugasundaram, Ruba Priyadharshini, and Bharathi Raja Chakravarthi. 2022. Offensive language detection in Tamil YouTube comments by adapters and cross-domain knowledge transfer. *Computer Speech Language*, 76:101404.

Ashish Vaswani, Noam Shazeer, Niki Parmar, Jakob Uszkoreit, Llion Jones, Aidan N Gomez, Łukasz Kaiser, and Illia Polosukhin. 2017. Attention is all you need. *Advances in neural information processing systems*, 30.

Algorithm Alliance@LT-EDI-2024: Caste and Migration Hate Speech Detection

Saisandeep Sangeetham, Shreyamanisha C Vinay, Kavin Rajan G, Abishna A & B Bharathi
Department of Computer Science and Engineering
Sri Sivasubramaniya Nadar College of Engineering
Tamil Nadu, India
saisandeep2210495@ssn.edu.in
shreyamanisha2210857@ssn.edu.in
kavinrajan2210227@ssn.edu.in
abishna2210385@ssn.edu.in
bharathib@ssn.edu.in

Abstract

Caste and Migration speech refers to the use of language that distinguishes the offense, violence, and distress on their social, caste, and migration status. Here, caste hate speech targets the imbalance of an individual's social status and focuses mainly on the degradation of their caste group. While the migration hate speech imposes the differences in nationality, culture, and individual status. These speeches are meant to affront the social status of these people. To detect this hate in the speech, our task on Caste and Migration Hate Speech Detection has been created which classifies human speech into genuine or stimulate categories. For this task, we used multiple classification models such as the train test split model to split the dataset into train and test data, Logistic regression, Support Vector Machine, MLP (Multilayer Perceptron) classifier, Random Forest classifier, KNN classifier, and Decision tree classification. Among these models, The SVM gave the highest macro average F1 score of 0.77 and the average accuracy for these models is around 0.75.

1 Introduction

In the age of rapid globalization and digital interconnectedness, social media platforms have become powerful tools for communication and community engagement. However, this unprecedented accessibility has also given rise to a darker aspect of online discourse – the proliferation of hate speech. Of particular concern is the manifestation of hate speech related to caste and migration issues, which not only perpetuates discrimination but also poses a significant threat to social harmony. As our world embraces the Digital Age, technology plays a pivotal role in connecting people through platforms like Facebook and Twitter (Drus and Khalid, 2019).

Despite its positive aspects, social media harbors drawbacks, with users sometimes engaging in discouragement or targeted hate speech. Detrimental speech on these platforms has a lasting psychological impact on victims (Gongane et al., 2022). This study highlights the surge in hate speech on social media, fuelled by anonymity and the absence of stringent controls, particularly targeting religion, gender, and race. Online communities offer insights into understanding and combating online hate speech, suggesting new dimensions for future research (Nazmine and Khan Tareen, 2021).

Social media platforms struggle to manage the constant flood of comments and posts, making it challenging to effectively monitor and control content due to the sheer volume. Finding a balance between limiting excessive posts and preserving freedom of speech poses a significant predicament. Additionally, the diverse user base, representing various backgrounds, cultures, and beliefs, further complicates the issue, contributing to the widespread problem of hate speech. (Al-Hassan, 2019).

The paper's structure includes a literature review in Section 2, task and data description in Section 3, methodology in Section 4, results and analysis in Section 5, and a conclusion in Section 6.

2 Related Works

Numerous studies have explored hate speech detection, including those focused on caste and migration (Kim et al., 2018). Davidson et al. emphasized the subjective biases in hate speech classification, highlighting the need for objective methodologies. In caste-based hate speech detection, Malmasi and Zampieri addressed challenges using lexical properties like n-grams, character n-grams, word embeddings, and paragraph embeddings (Kim et al., 2018).

Research on migration-related hate speech includes traditional and deep learning-based hate speech classification methods proposed by (Subramanian et al.,

Proceedings of the Fourth Workshop on Language Technology for Equality, Diversity, Inclusion, pages 254–258
March 21, 2024 ©2024 Association for Computational Linguistics

2023). Sanguinetti et al. conducted automatic hate speech detection research, creating datasets annotated with hate labels and related dimensions (Jahan and Oussalah, 2023). The overview of the hope speech detection task is given in (Kumaresan et al., 2023).

In sentiment analysis, (Vijayakumar et al., 2022) used the transformer model ALBERT for hope speech detection in multiple languages like English, Tamil, Kannada, etc. (Chakravarthi et al., 2020) proposed a Convolutional Neural Network (CNN) model outperforming traditional models for hope-speech detection. The authors of(Balouchzahi et al., 2022) performed binary and multi-class hope-speech classification. The binary task involved only two labels whereas the multi-class task involved three labels.

In the paper, (Velankar et al., 2021) used HASOC 2021 Hindi and Marathi hate speech datasets for algorithm comparison. Marathi uses binary labels; Hindi has both binary and detailed labels. Transformer models excelled, and basic models with fastText embeddings showed competitive performance. Intriguingly, after standard hyper-parameter tuning, basic models outperformed BERT-based models, especially on the fine-grained Hindi dataset.

The authors of (Roy et al., 2022) examined code-mixed language use on social media, focusing on Hindi-English, Tamil-English, Malayalam-English, Telugu-English, etc. They proposed a weighted ensemble model combining transformer-based BERT models and a deep neural network for offensive and hate speech detection. Experimental results showed the framework outperformed state-of-the-art models, achieving 0.802 and 0.933 weighted F1 scores for Malayalam and Tamil code-mixed datasets.

The authors of (Saumya and Mishra, 2021) used LSTM, deep learning, and hybrid models on Tamil and Malayalam datasets. In the paper (Ghanghor et al., 2021) applied transformer models like m-BERTcased and XLM-RoBERTa for hope speech detection, with m-BERT-cased achieving the highest F1-score. The top model for the English dataset was the 2-parallel CNN-LSTM using GloVe and Word2Vec embeddings, while the 3-parallel Bi-LSTM excelled on the Malayalam dataset.

In recent years, there's been a rise in studies addressing hate speech targeting specific groups, like caste and migration status. In today's digital age, hate speech based on caste or migration has become a significant concern. These studies showcase versatile models for sentiment analysis on social media comments. To enhance text classification accuracy, we opted for traditional models alongside a basic transformer model based on the literature survey.

3 Task and Data Description

The overview paper for this task is explained in (Rajiakodi et al., 2024). The shared Task on Caste and Migration Hate Speech detection at LT-EDI-EACL 2024 is intended to determine whether the speech text format was legitimate or imposed hate towards Caste and Migration. The dataset consists of two fields namely speech text and a label. Here, the Label indicates the above-mentioned category, and it is represented in hate and non-hate speech. The training dataset consists of around 5,355 text-converted speeches out of which 3,303 instances were labelled as non-hate speech and 2,052 instances were labelled as hate speech. The Development dataset consisted of 945 instances out of which 594 instances were labelled as non-hate speeches and 351 instances were labelled as hate speeches. Here, we used 1576 test data instances for testing the model.

4 Methodology

Several machine learning approaches may be used to achieve this task, but we chose the most effective one for the classification problems, i.e., detection of hate speech related to caste and migration.

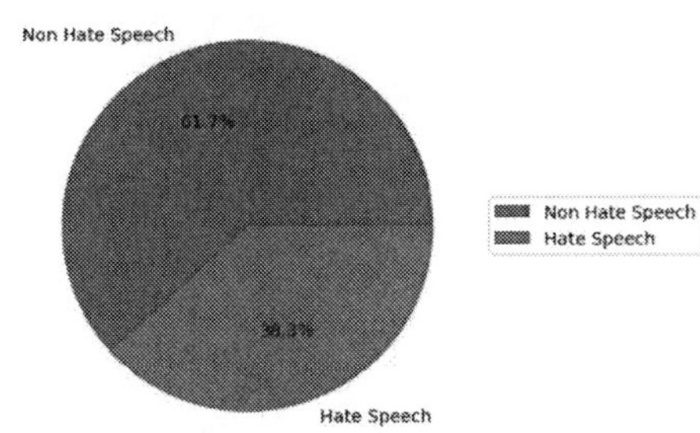

Figure 1: Data distribution in datasets

Label	Train Instances	Dev Instances
Non Hate speech(0)	3303	594
Hate speech(1)	2053	351

Table 1: Description of the Data Distribution

As shown in Figure 1, the distribution of data in the datasets indicates that 38.3% of collected data contains hate speech. Table 1 describes the data distribution of hate speech among the training and development instances.

4.1 Data Preprocessing and Cleaning

Data cleaning procedures were the first step for getting the raw data ready for use in any of the models in machine learning.
The raw data usually consists of many punctuation marks, emojis, and multiple spaces which would affect the performance of the model, hence, to ensure the uniformity of the Data, we are considering the elimination

of these. Using the popular libraries of Python such as the "Demoji" for removing all the emoji's in the dataset, and "re" for removing the special characters, symbols, and multiple spaces in the datasets. This comprehensive pipeline of data preparation and cleaning establishes the foundation that supports subsequent phases of our research, creating a conducive environment for machine learning models to function well.
The uniform and standardized, feature-rich dataset makes the model easier to extract valuable patterns and insights, which improves the model's overall performance.

4.2 Text Tokenization

We addressed the challenge of text vectorization by converting the raw data into a numerical format that could be utilized for a machine-learning model. Initially, we used the popular library "IndicNLP" tokenizer for tokenizing the Tamil language text to clean text. Then we transformed the entire text data into numerical vectors by utilizing the Term Frequency-Inverse Document Frequency (TF-IDF) vectorizer. Therefore TF-IDF vectorization offers an accurate depiction of the text data by encoding the meaning of words in context. Specifically, we limited the feature space for the (TF-IDF) to a maximum of 5000 features. This methodological choice tries to achieve a balance between computational efficiency and the retention of essential information. This forms the foundation for the subsequent application of machine learning models in our research.

4.3 Model Selection

Selecting an appropriate machine learning model is essential, therefore our main goal is to build a model that can deal with various linguistic nuances that are present in hate speech. While still maintaining high accuracy and good classification abilities. So we chose the best suitable algorithm for this task such as by implementing some of the popular classifications such as Logistic Regression, Support Vector Machine(SVM), Multi-Layer Perceptron(MLP), Random Forest Classifier(RFC), Decision Tree, KNN.

5 Results and Analysis

5.1 Performance Metrics

In the field of Machine learning, it is critical to get the predictive model's performance in need to determine its efficiency and suitability for practical uses. Here We determine our model performance by considering metrics such as accuracy, F1-Score, recall, precision, etc. These function as a crucial benchmark for our model.

1) Accuracy is defined as the ratio of the correctly predicted instances to the total number of instances in a dataset. It acts as a straightforward for the model's correctness.

$$\text{Accuracy} = \frac{\text{Number of Correct Predictions}}{\text{Total Number of Predictions}} \tag{1}$$

2) Precision is the ability of a classification model in which it is not to label irrelevant instances as positive in normal terms it is defined as the ratio of true positives to the sum of true and false positives.

$$\text{Precision} = \frac{\text{TP}}{\text{TP} + \text{FP}} \tag{2}$$

3) Recall which is also called sensitivity or true positive rate is defined as the ratio of true positives to the sum of true positives and false negatives.

$$\text{Recall} = \frac{\text{TP}}{\text{TP} + \text{FN}} \tag{3}$$

4) F1-Score is defined as the harmonic mean of the precision and recall. It provides a balanced measure that considers both the false positives and false negatives.

$$\text{F1-Score} = 2 \times \frac{\text{Precision} \times \text{Recall}}{\text{Precision} + \text{Recall}} \tag{4}$$

5.2 Results and Observation

For this task, we investigated the involved application of several machine learning algorithms such as Logistic regression, Support Vector Machines (SVM), Random Forest Classifier, Decision Tree, KNN, and Multi-Layer Perceptron (MLP). Our main aim is to improve the efficiency of the models in automatically classifying the texts that are related to the cast/migration-related hate speech.

5.2.1 Comparative Model Accuracies

By evaluating the performance of various machine learning models on the given datasets. We observed the distinct accuracies across the classifiers. Logistic Regression which we achieved an accuracy of 0.711, surpassing this Support Vector Machines (SVM) outperformed this, exhibiting better discriminate power with an accuracy of 0.797, Random Forest classifier came in close to second by achieving an accuracy of 0.793, The Multi-Layer Perceptron (MLP) exhibited the competitive accuracy at 0.737, suggesting its capacity to capture sophisticated relationships within the textual data. Decision Tree achieved an accuracy of 0.746, showcasing its robustness in discerning hate speech nuances. Unfortunately, given the accuracy of 0.6402, KNN might not be performing at its best.

Tables 2, 3, and 4 show the classification reports for SVM, RFC, and Decision Tree models on the test data, respectively. Figure 2 illustrates the F1-Accuracy scores of different models.

	Precision	Recall	F1 Score	Support
0	0.80	0.91	0.85	594
1	0.80	0.61	0.69	351
Accuracy			0.80	945
Macro Avg	0.80	0.76	0.77	945
Weighted Avg	0.80	0.80	0.79	945

Table 2: Classification Report for SVM on Test Data

	Precision	Recall	F1 Score	Support
0	0.79	0.92	0.85	594
1	0.82	0.57	0.67	351
Accuracy			0.79	945
Macro Avg	0.80	0.75	0.76	945
Weighted Avg	0.80	0.79	0.78	945

Table 3: Classification Report for RFC on Test Data

	Precision	Recall	F1 Score	Support
0	0.79	0.81	0.80	594
1	0.66	0.64	0.65	351
Accuracy			0.77	945
Macro Avg	0.73	0.73	0.73	945
Weighted Avg	0.74	0.75	0.75	945

Table 4: Classification Report for Decision Tree on Test Data

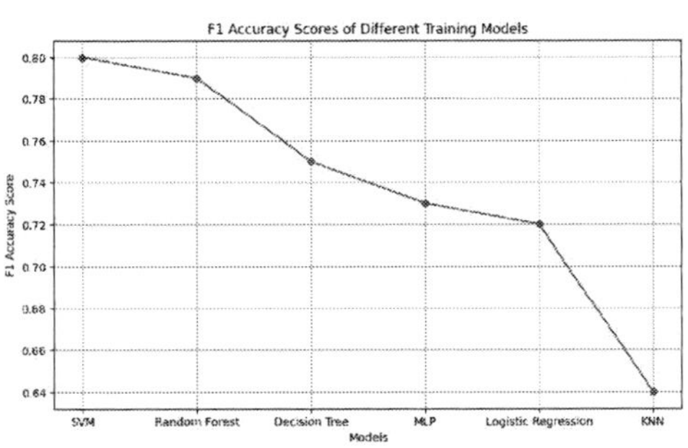

Figure 2: : F1-Accuracy Scores of Different models

6 Limitations

Our research on hate speech detection using SVM and other ML models has shown promise, but it also has notable limitations. The biased training data may not fully represent real-world instances, which challenges the models' ability to generalize. Moreover, subjective hate speech labeling introduces inconsistencies, which affects the reliability of the data.

Another limitation is class imbalance, where hate speech instances are outnumbered by non-hate speech instances, making it difficult to accurately identify and potentially leading to misclassifications. Additionally, linguistic complexity further complicates detection, as SVM and other ML models may struggle with nuances such as sarcasm, irony, and cultural references that are common in hate speech.

Furthermore, SVM models heavily rely on feature engineering, which limits the selection of features that robustly represent diverse hate speech characteristics. The "black box" nature of SVM models also raises concerns about explainability, making it difficult to interpret predictions.

To overcome these limitations, exploring innovative solutions such as improved feature engineering, diverse training datasets, and interpretable ML models is crucial. These steps will enhance the reliability of hate speech detection systems, urging future research to address these challenges.

7 Ethics Statement

"Avoid harm" our model only detects hate speech but doesn't mentally and physically affect anyone. "Be fair and take action not to discriminate". Equality for all and no discrimination on any grounds was done while detecting hate speech. We create opportunities for members of the organization or group to grow as professionals and for team growth.

8 Conclusion

In conclusion, we applied supervised learning models such as Random Forest, SVM, and Logistic regression to investigate hate speech identification and migration speech, with a macro F1 score of 0.77, the SVM model stood out and demonstrated its efficiency by classifying the hate speech in these specific contexts. The following research could investigate the integration of deep learning models to boost accuracy. While emphasizing the ongoing need for adaptive and more flexible classification to deal with the evolving dynamics of these conversations.

References

Hmood Al-Hassan, Areej Al-Dossari. 2019. Detection of hate speech in social networks: A survey on multilingual corpus. pages 83–100.

Fazlourrahman Balouchzahi, Grigori Sidorov, and Alexander Gelbukh. 2022. Polyhope: Two-level hope speech detection from tweets.

Bharathi Chakravarthi, Vigneshwaran Muralidaran, Ruba Asoka Chakravarthi, and John McCrae. 2020. Corpus creation for sentiment analysis in code-mixed tamil-english text.

Zulfadzli Drus and Haliyana Khalid. 2019. Sentiment analysis in social media and its application: Systematic literature review. *Procedia Computer Science*,

161:707–714. The Fifth Information Systems International Conference, 23-24 July 2019, Surabaya, Indonesia.

Nikhil Ghanghor, Rahul Ponnusamy, Prasanna Kumar Kumaresan, Ruba Priyadharshini, Sajeetha Thavareesan, and Bharathi Raja Chakravarthi. 2021. IIITK@LT-EDI-EACL2021: Hope speech detection for equality, diversity, and inclusion in Tamil , Malayalam and English. In *Proceedings of the First Workshop on Language Technology for Equality, Diversity and Inclusion*, pages 197–203, Kyiv. Association for Computational Linguistics.

Vaishali U. Gongane, Mousami V. Munot, and Alwin D. Anuse. 2022. Detection and moderation of detrimental content on social media platforms: current status and future directions. *Social Network Analysis and Mining*, 12(1):129.

Md Saroar Jahan and Mourad Oussalah. 2023. A systematic review of hate speech automatic detection using natural language processing.

Geewook Kim, Kazuki Fukui, and Hidetoshi Shimodaira. 2018. Word-like character n-gram embedding. In *Proceedings of the 2018 EMNLP Workshop W-NUT: The 4th Workshop on Noisy User-generated Text*, pages 148–152, Brussels, Belgium. Association for Computational Linguistics.

Prasanna Kumar Kumaresan, Bharathi Raja Chakravarthi, Subalalitha Cn, Miguel Angel García-Cumbreras, Salud Maria Jimenez Zafra, José Antonio García-Díaz, Rafael Valencia-García, Momchil Hardalov, Ivan Koychev, Preslav Nakov, Daniel García-Baena, and Kishore Kumar Ponnusamy. 2023. Overview of the shared task on hope speech detection for equality, diversity, and inclusion. In *LTEDI*.

Manan Nazmine and Hannan Khan Tareen. 2021. Hate speech and social media: A systematic review. *Turkish Online Journal of Qualitative Inquiry*, 12:5285–5294.

Saranya Rajiakodi, Bharathi Raja Chakravarthi, Rahul Ponnusamy, Prasanna Kumar Kumaresan, Sathiyaraj Thangasamy, Bhuvaneswari Sivagnanam, and Charmathi Rajkumar. 2024. Overview of Shared Task on Caste and Migration Hate Speech Detection. In *Proceedings of the Fourth Workshop on Language Technology for Equality, Diversity and Inclusion*, Malta. European Chapter of the Association for Computational Linguistics.

Pradeep Bhawal Roy, Snehaan Cn, and Subalalitha. 2022. Hate speech and offensive language detection in dravidian languages using deep ensemble framework. *Computer Speech Language*, 75:101386.

Sunil Saumya and Ankit Kumar Mishra. 2021. IIIT_DWD@LT-EDI-EACL2021: Hope speech detection in YouTube multilingual comments. In *Proceedings of the First Workshop on Language Technology for Equality, Diversity and Inclusion*, pages 107–113, Kyiv. Association for Computational Linguistics.

Malliga Subramanian, Veerappampalayam Easwaramoorthy Sathiskumar, G. Deepalakshmi, Jaehyuk Cho, and G. Manikandan. 2023. A survey on hate speech detection and sentiment analysis using machine learning and deep learning models. *Alexandria Engineering Journal*, 80:110–121.

A. Velankar, H. Patil, A. Gore, S. Salunke, and R. Joshi. 2021. Hate and offensive speech detection in hindi and marathi.

Praveenkumar Vijayakumar, S Prathyush, P Aravind, Angel Suseelan, Rajalakshmi Sivanaiah, Sakaya Milton Rajendram, and T. T. Mirnalinee. 2022. Ssn_armm@ lt-edi -acl2022: Hope speech detection for equality, diversity, and inclusion using albert model. In *LTEDI*.

MEnTr@LT-EDI-2024: Multilingual Ensemble of Transformer Models for Homophobia/Transphobia Detection

Adwita Arora[1], **Aaryan Mattoo**[1], **Divya Chaudhary**[2], **Ian Gorton**[2] and **Bijendra Kumar**[1]
[1] Netaji Subhas University of Technology, New Delhi, India
[2] Northeastern University, Boston, MA 02115, United States
{adwita.ug20, aaryan.mattoo.ug20}@nsut.ac.in
{d.chaudhary, i.gorton}@northeastern.edu
bizender@nsut.ac.in

Abstract

Detection of Homophobia and Transphobia in social media comments serves as an important step in the overall development of Equality, Diversity and Inclusion (EDI). In this research, we describe the system we formulated while participating in the shared task of Homophobia/Transphobia detection as a part of the Fourth Workshop On Language Technology For Equality, Diversity, Inclusion (LT-EDI-2024) at EACL 2024[1]. We used an ensemble of three state-of-the-art multilingual transformer models, namely Multilingual BERT (mBERT), Multilingual Representations for Indic Languages (MuRIL) and XLM-RoBERTa to detect the presence of Homophobia or Transphobia in YouTube comments. The task comprised of datasets in ten languages - Hindi, English, Telugu, Tamil, Malayalam, Kannada, Gujarati, Marathi, Spanish and Tulu. Our system achieved rank 1 for the Spanish and Tulu tasks, 2 for Telugu, 3 for Marathi and Gujarati, 4 for Tamil, 5 for Hindi and Kannada, 6 for English and 8 for Malayalam. These results speak for the efficacy of our ensemble model as well as the data augmentation strategy we adopted for the detection of anti-LGBT+ language in social media data.

1 Introduction

Homophobia is defined as intentional discrimination against those who identify as a part of the LGBT+ community. It can be demonstrated in many ways, which can include abuse or social ignorance. Transphobia, on the other hand, refers to the targeted hatred towards transgender individuals whose current gender identity and the one assigned to them during birth differ. Both of these forms of hate speech have negative repercussions on the mental health as well as the overall well-being of people who are a part of the LGBT+ community (Chakravarthi et al., 2022a). This highlights a critical need to build systems that identify this form of prejudice and bigotry.

Pre-trained language models (PLMs) like BERT (Devlin et al., 2018) and GPT (Brown et al., 2020), built on transformer architectures have gained recognition for their ability to interpret languages in a manner similar to humans by displaying state-of-the-art results in many NLP tasks such as document classification and language modelling. PLMs undergo unsupervised training on a large corpus of text data which can then be fine-tuned on domain and task-specific corpora for downstream tasks, such as the shared task on Homophobia and Transphobia detection by LT-EDI@EACL 2024. BERT, specifically, introduced the concept of bidirectional context understanding which considers both the succeeding and preceding word for a particular word to capture a more elaborate and nuanced meaning within the language. For our system, we propose an ensemble consisting of three such popular BERT-based transformer architectures, namely Multilingual BERT (mBERT) (Devlin et al., 2018), Multilingual Representations for Indic Languages (MuRIL) (Khanuja et al., 2021) and XLM-RoBERTa (Conneau et al., 2019).

1.1 Task Description

As specified in (Chakravarthi et al., 2024), participants of this shared task were required to submit systems that classify a given YouTube comment into one of the three categories - Homophobia, Transphobia or None. We were provided with the train and development datasets containing manually annotated posts in English, Hindi, Malayalam, Tamil, Telugu, Kannada, Marathi, Gujarati and Spanish. The dataset described by Kumaresan et al. (2023) forms the seed data for this task. This year, the workshop also introduced a code-mixed dataset on Tulu. Being an under-resourced language, Tulu lacks extensive data and resources

[1]https://sites.google.com/view/lt-edi-2024/

Proceedings of the Fourth Workshop on Language Technology for Equality, Diversity, Inclusion, pages 259–264
March 21, 2024 ©2024 Association for Computational Linguistics

Language		Non anti-LGBT+ content	Homophobia	Transphobia
Tamil	train	2,064	453	145
	dev	507	118	41
	test	634	152	47
Telugu	train	3,496	2,907	2,647
	dev	747	588	605
	test	744	624	571
Kannada	train	4,463	2,765	2,835
	dev	955	585	617
	test	951	599	606
Gujarati	train	3,848	2,267	2,004
	dev	788	498	454
	test	794	510	436
Spanish	train	700	250	250
	dev	200	93	93
	test	300	150	150
Hindi	train	2,423	45	92
	dev	305	2	13
	test	308	3	10
English	train	2,978	179	7
	dev	748	42	2
	test	931	55	4
Malayalam	train	2,468	476	170
	dev	937	197	79
	test	674	140	52
Marathi	train	2,572	551	377
	dev	541	129	80
	test	569	112	69

Table 1: Statistics of the train, dev and train dataset

		Non H/T Content	H/T Content
Tulu	train	542	188
	test	312	67

Table 2: Statistics of the Tulu train and test dataset

for language models. This scarcity leads to a few-shot learning scenario. For the Tulu task, we were required to build a binary classifier that predicts whether a post contains hate-speech relating to homophobia or transphobia. The overall task hence is to develop a multiclass (binary in case of Tulu) classifier that predicts whether a given post contains instances of homophobia or transphobia in 10 different language categories. The systems were weighed using the average macro F1 score for each language across all classes on the test dataset.

2 Related Work

Transformer models have been popular in various classification tasks, including hate speech detection. Roy et al. (2021) experimented with the XLM-RoBERTa model for hate-speech detection in Twitter data in English, German and Hindi. Top submissions to competitions like HASOC (Hate Speech and Offensive Content Identification in Multiple Languages) which provide datasets for hate-speech detection in a multilingual setting also utilised transformer models, such as Farooqi et al. (2021) who used IndicBERT, XLM-RoBERTa and Multilingual BERT with hard voting.

The task presented at this workshop is the third shared task on Homophobia and Transphobia detection in social media comments. In the previous shared tasks, Chakravarthi et al. (2022b) and Chakravarthi et al. (2023), the majority of the submissions received used transformer models, such as Nozza (2022) who used weighted majority voting on the predictions received from BERT, RoBERTa and HateBERT and Maimaitituoheti (2022) who used the pre-trained transformer model RoBERTa for classification. Other submissions also experimented with neural networks and support vector machines such as (García-Díaz et al., 2022) and (Ashraf et al., 2022) respectively. Bhandari and Goyal (2022) experimented with various multilingual BERT models, including mBERT, XLM-RoBERTa, IndicBERT and HateBERT, with a data augmentation strategy of random insertion, deletion or swapping of words in a sentence.

3 Methodology

Language	Homophobia	Transphobia
Tamil	1,146	1,049
Telugu	2,907	2,647
Kannada	2,765	2,835
Gujarati	2,267	2,004
Spanish	316	316
Hindi	837	820
English	1,223	953
Malayalam	1,277	1,189
Marathi	1,209	1,259

Table 3: Train corpora after augmentation

The distribution of labels in the train and dev splits are shown in Table 1 and Table 2. From looking at the balance of classes in the train dataset, it is inferred that the Homophobia and Transphobia classes are highly imbalanced, especially for Hindi, English, Tamil, Malayalam, Marathi and Spanish.

3.1 Handling Class Imbalance

To provide a balance between the classes of the dataset across all languages, we use a translation strategy where we take the positive samples from Kannada, Gujarati and Telugu and translate them into each of our target languages i.e., Hindi, English, Tamil, Malayalam, Marathi and Spanish. This is done for both Homophobia and Transphobia classes. We used the `googletrans`[2] library in Python for the translation process. The distribution of the modified dataset is shown in Table 3.

3.2 Ensemble of Transformer Models

For this classification task, we propose an ensemble of three of the most popular multilingual transformer models built on top of the BERT architecture, as described below:

- **mBERT:** Multilingual BERT (mBERT) (Devlin et al., 2018) is a pre-trained model which is trained using data belonging to 104 languages. We used the `bert-base-multilingual-case`[3] pre-trained model.
- **MuRIL:** Multilingual Representations for Indian Languages (MuRIL) (Khanuja et al., 2021) is a BERT-based model that has been

[2]https://pypi.org/project/googletrans/
[3]https://huggingface.co/bert-base-multilingual-cased

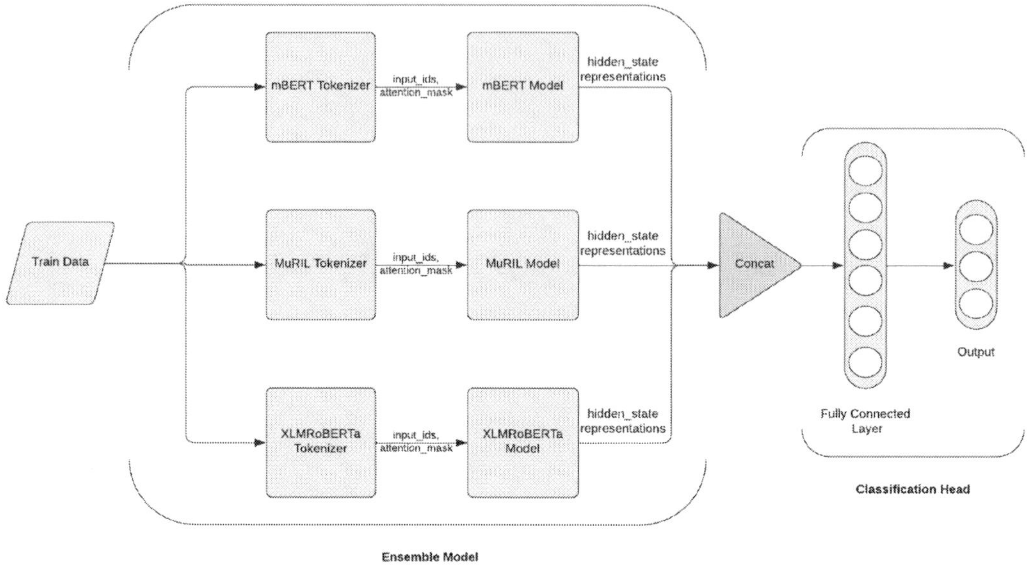

Figure 1: System Architecture

pre-trained on 16 Indian languages. We used the `google/muril-base-cased`[4] model. We removed the MuRIL layer while fine-tuning for the Spanish language condition, given the fact that MuRIL is pre-trained on Indic Languages specifically.

- **XLMRoBERTa:** XLMRoBERTa (Conneau et al., 2019) is a cross-linguistic pre-trained linguistic model built by Meta. We used the `xlm-roberta-base`[5] model.

These models are used with the help of the HuggingFace library [6] for transformer models.

Figure 1 depicts our system, where the train dataset is first tokenized and fed to its corresponding transformer model. The hidden state representation obtained from each of the three models is concatenated and fed as input to a simple classification head consisting of a feed-forward neural network which outputs the predicted class.

We fine-tune the ensemble model on the Google Colab GPU on the train dataset for each language task. We train each language model for 3 epochs using Binary Cross Entropy as the loss function and AdamW (Loshchilov and Hutter, 2017) as the optimizer. We kept the learning rate at 2e-5. The fine-tuned model then generated the predicted classes for test data in each language, which was submitted for evaluation.

4 Results and Discussions

The results obtained for each language task are given in Table 4. This shows the final average macro F1 score obtained for each language on the test dataset as shared by the organizers. The best results were seen in the case of Spanish and Tulu where we achieved a rank of 1. In the Telugu language task, our system ranked second with an average macro F1 score of 0.960 which also was the overall best average macro F1 score across all languages for our system. This can be explained by Telugu having the best class distribution across all languages. Even though we used translation as a data augmentation strategy, it does not ensure that all the linguistic features of the source text are retained in the target text. Our system performs well with Marathi and Gujarati as well, ranking third with average macro F1 scores of 0.488 and 0.960 respectively. For the rest of the languages we see varying performance with Tamil ranking fourth with an average macro F1 score of 0.746

[4]https://huggingface.co/google/muril-base-cased

[5]https://huggingface.co/xlm-roberta-base

[6]https://huggingface.co/

Language	Average Macro F1	Rank
Tulu	0.707	1
Spanish	0.582	1
Telugu	0.960	2
Gujarati	0.960	3
Marathi	0.488	3
Tamil	0.746	4
Hindi	0.325	5
Kannada	0.935	5
English	0.407	6
Malayalam	0.744	8

Table 4: Results showing the average macro F1 score

and Hindi and Kannada ranking fifth with an average macro F1 score of 0.325 and 0.935. For English and Malayalam the performance was not at par with the other languages with ranks 6 and 8 and average macro F1 scores 0.407 and 0.744 respectively. There is a direct link between the average macro F1 score and the distribution of classes in the train dataset, even after data augmentation. The translation schemes, while improving the diversity of the dataset to a certain extent, do not guarantee an improvement in the quality of the dataset. Languages like Hindi and English that had the poorest class balance in the train dataset also resulted in the poorest average macro F1 scores of 0.325 and 0.407 on the test dataset. For the languages having a more diverse distribution like Telugu and Gujarati, we also see a higher average macro F1 score. Results for Tulu are also impressive considering that none of the pre-trained BERT models were trained on corpora containing text data in Tulu. However, given the linguistic and phonetic similarities between Tulu, Kannada and Malayalam, the ensemble model was able to capture the features of this language to a certain extent, resulting in an average macro F1 score of 0.707, ranking first.

5 Conclusions and Future Work

Our submission for the shared task on Homophobia and Transphobia detection in social media comments demonstrates how pre-trained language models (PLMs) specifically those built on a BERT-based architecture can be effectively used in the case of text classification. Our ensemble model consisting of mBERT, MuRIL and XLMRoBERTa, has shown consistent results by achieving the top three ranks for 5 language tasks, ranking first for Spanish and the under-resourced language Tulu. We have been able to achieve average macro F1 scores of 0.707, 0.582, 0.960, 0.960, 0.488, 0.746, 0.325, 0.935, 0.407 and 0.744 for Tulu, Spanish, Telugu, Gujarati, Marathi, Tamil, Hindi, Kannada, English and Malayalam respectively. In the future, we would like to experiment with the following aspects in further detail :

- **Better data augmentation strategies:** Simple translation from one language to another does not consider the linguistic nuances of these languages, which is required to build a diverse and high-quality dataset. We would like to experiment with more sophisticated, language-dependent data augmentation strategies.
- **Attention mechanisms:** Addition of attention modules to the ensemble model to further capture complex positional dependencies in multilingual code-mixed data.

6 Limitations

The data presented in the shared task comprised 10 different languages, each with its own linguistic and cultural nuance, and we recognise that bringing forth a common end-to-end approach for text classification may miss some of these nuances. However, the system we presented stands a baseline which can easily be extended to include language and context specific modules before training.

References

Nsrin Ashraf, Mohamed Taha, Ahmed Abd Elfattah, and Hamada Nayel. 2022. NAYEL @LT-EDI-ACL2022: Homophobia/Transphobia Detection for Equality, Diversity, and Inclusion using SVM. In *Proceedings of the Second Workshop on Language Technology for Equality, Diversity and Inclusion*, pages 287–290, Dublin, Ireland. Association for Computational Linguistics.

Vitthal Bhandari and Poonam Goyal. 2022. bitsa_nlp@LT-EDI-ACL2022: Leveraging Pretrained Language Models for Detecting Homophobia and Transphobia in Social Media Comments. In *Proceedings of the Second Workshop on Language Technology for Equality, Diversity and Inclusion*, pages 149–154, Dublin, Ireland. Association for Computational Linguistics.

Tom B. Brown, Benjamin Mann, Nick Ryder, Melanie Subbiah, Jared Kaplan, Prafulla Dhariwal, Arvind Neelakantan, Pranav Shyam, Girish Sastry, Amanda Askell, Sandhini Agarwal, Ariel Herbert-Voss, Gretchen Krueger, Tom Henighan, Rewon Child,

Aditya Ramesh, Daniel M. Ziegler, Jeffrey Wu, Clemens Winter, Christopher Hesse, Mark Chen, Eric Sigler, Mateusz Litwin, Scott Gray, Benjamin Chess, Jack Clark, Christopher Berner, Sam McCandlish, Alec Radford, Ilya Sutskever, and Dario Amodei. 2020. Language models are few-shot learners.

Bharathi Raja Chakravarthi, Adeep Hande, Rahul Ponnusamy, Prasanna Kumar Kumaresan, and Ruba Priyadharshini. 2022a. How can we detect homophobia and transphobia? experiments in a multilingual code-mixed setting for social media governance. *International Journal of Information Management Data Insights*, 2(2):100119.

Bharathi Raja Chakravarthi, Prasanna Kumar Kumaresan, Ruba Priyadharshini, Paul Buitelaar, Asha Hegde, Hosahalli Lakshmaiah Shashirekha, Saranya Rajiakodi, Miguel Ángel García-Cumbreras, Salud María Jiménez-Zafra, José Antonio García-Díaz, Rafael Valencia-García, Kishore Kumar Ponnusamy, Poorvi Shetty, and Daniel García-Baena. 2024. Overview of third shared task on homophobia and transphobia detection in social media comments. In *Proceedings of the Fourth Workshop on Language Technology for Equality, Diversity and Inclusion*, Malta. European Chapter of the Association for Computational Linguistics.

Bharathi Raja Chakravarthi, Rahul Ponnusamy, S Malliga, Paul Buitelaar, Salud Mar ıa Jimenez-Zafra, José Antonio García-Díaz, Rafael Valencia-García, Nitesh Jindal, et al. 2023. Overview of second shared task on homophobia and transphobia detection in social media comments. In *Proceedings of the Third Workshop on Language Technology for Equality, Diversity and Inclusion*, pages 38–46.

Bharathi Raja Chakravarthi, Ruba Priyadharshini, Thenmozhi Durairaj, John McCrae, Paul Buitelaar, Prasanna Kumaresan, and Rahul Ponnusamy. 2022b. Overview of The Shared Task on Homophobia and Transphobia Detection in Social Media Comments. In *Proceedings of the Second Workshop on Language Technology for Equality, Diversity and Inclusion*, pages 369–377, Dublin, Ireland. Association for Computational Linguistics.

Alexis Conneau, Kartikay Khandelwal, Naman Goyal, Vishrav Chaudhary, Guillaume Wenzek, Francisco Guzmán, Edouard Grave, Myle Ott, Luke Zettlemoyer, and Veselin Stoyanov. 2019. Unsupervised cross-lingual representation learning at scale. *CoRR*, abs/1911.02116.

Jacob Devlin, Ming-Wei Chang, Kenton Lee, and Kristina Toutanova. 2018. BERT: pre-training of deep bidirectional transformers for language understanding. *CoRR*, abs/1810.04805.

Zaki Mustafa Farooqi, Sreyan Ghosh, and Rajiv Ratn Shah. 2021. Leveraging transformers for hate speech detection in conversational code-mixed tweets. *arXiv preprint arXiv:2112.09986*.

José García-Díaz, Camilo Caparros-Laiz, and Rafael Valencia-García. 2022. UMUTeam@LT-EDI-ACL2022: Detecting homophobic and transphobic comments in Tamil. In *Proceedings of the Second Workshop on Language Technology for Equality, Diversity and Inclusion*, pages 140–144, Dublin, Ireland. Association for Computational Linguistics.

Simran Khanuja, Diksha Bansal, Sarvesh Mehtani, Savya Khosla, Atreyee Dey, Balaji Gopalan, Dilip Kumar Margam, Pooja Aggarwal, Rajiv Teja Nagipogu, Shachi Dave, Shruti Gupta, Subhash Chandra Bose Gali, Vish Subramanian, and Partha Talukdar. 2021. MuRIL: Multilingual Representations for Indian Languages.

Prasanna Kumar Kumaresan, Rahul Ponnusamy, Ruba Priyadharshini, Paul Buitelaar, and Bharathi Raja Chakravarthi. 2023. Homophobia and transphobia detection for low-resourced languages in social media comments. *Natural Language Processing Journal*, page 100041.

Ilya Loshchilov and Frank Hutter. 2017. Decoupled weight decay regularization. *arXiv preprint arXiv:1711.05101*.

Abulimiti Maimaitituoheti. 2022. ABLIMET @LT-EDI-ACL2022: A RoBERTa based Approach for Homophobia/Transphobia Detection in Social Media. In *Proceedings of the Second Workshop on Language Technology for Equality, Diversity and Inclusion*, pages 155–160, Dublin, Ireland. Association for Computational Linguistics.

Debora Nozza. 2022. Nozza@LT-EDI-ACL2022: Ensemble Modeling for Homophobia and Transphobia Detection. In *Proceedings of the Second Workshop on Language Technology for Equality, Diversity and Inclusion*, pages 258–264, Dublin, Ireland. Association for Computational Linguistics.

Sayar Ghosh Roy, Ujwal Narayan, Tathagata Raha, Zubair Abid, and Vasudeva Varma. 2021. Leveraging multilingual transformers for hate speech detection. *arXiv preprint arXiv:2101.03207*.

CUET_DUO@StressIdent_LT-EDI@EACL2024: Stress Identification Using Tamil-Telugu BERT

Abu Bakkar Siddique Raihan, Tanzim Rahman, Md. Tanvir Rahman, Jawad Hossain, Shawly Ahsan, Avishek Das and **Mohammed Moshiul Hoque**
Department of Computer Science and Engineering
Chittagong University of Engineering & Technology, Chattogram-4349, Bangladesh
{u1804004, u1804015, u1804002, u1704039, u1704057}@student.cuet.ac.bd
{avishek, moshiul_240}@cuet.ac.bd

Abstract

The pervasive impact of stress on individuals necessitates proactive identification and intervention measures, especially in social media interaction. This research paper addresses the imperative need for proactive identification and intervention concerning the widespread influence of stress on individuals. This study focuses on the shared task, "Stress Identification in Dravidian Languages," specifically emphasizing Tamil and Telugu code-mixed languages. The primary objective of the task is to classify social media messages into two categories: stressed and non stressed. We employed various methodologies, from traditional machine-learning techniques to state-of-the-art transformer-based models. Notably, the Tamil-BERT and Telugu-BERT models exhibited exceptional performance, achieving a noteworthy macro F1-score of **0.71** and **0.72**, respectively, and securing the 15th position in Tamil code-mixed language and the 9th position in the Telugu code-mixed language. These findings underscore the effectiveness of these models in recognizing stress signals within social media content composed in Tamil and Telugu.

1 Introduction

Along with the hectic pace of contemporary life, stress has become an unavoidable force impacting the mental well-being of humans. It is a complicated emotional state produced by multiple events that might inspire displeasure, rage, or worry. Recognizing and resolving stress in its early stages is crucial since persistent stress may lead to devastating diseases, including depression (Masood et al., 2012). Recent surveys indicate that 48% of Gen Z individuals experience depression symptoms, often triggered by the pervasive impact of social media. Issues like the fear of missing out heightened concerns about judgment, and increased insecurity further contribute to stress levels (Milyavskaya et al., 2018). This highlights the need for efficient stress detection and support methods within online platforms. Global stress statistics emphasize the importance of proper stress management, impacting various aspects of people's lives, from businesses and educational institutions to family contexts (Mahmud et al., 2021). Automatic stress detection provides an effective solution to address this global health crisis, offering help and resources to individuals dealing with stress-related challenges.

This research addresses the problem of stress identification in Tamil and Telugu code-mixed languages. This proposed study consists of the following key contributions:

- Investigate various machine learning (ML), deep learning, and transformer-based models for stress identification from code-mixed Tamil and Telugu texts.
- Fine-tuned Tamil-BERT and Telugu-BERT models on respective datasets to enhance stress identification performance from code-mixed data.

2 Related Work

While various studies have studied stress detection in English and other high-resource languages, attention to low-resource languages like Tamil and Telugu has been sparse (Hegde et al., 2022). Chauhan et al. (2017) conducted a study using electrocardiogram data to analyze mental stress. They employed discrete wavelet transform for preprocessing and feature extraction techniques. Nijhawan et al. (2022) used the application of Unsupervised Topic Modeling using Latent Dirichlet Allocation has facilitated the identification of emotions in online user data. This approach has proven effective in analyzing stress or depression, which achieved a high detection rate. Another study (Jadhav et al., 2019) focused on social media stress detection using textual data, highlighting the effectiveness of combining BiLSTM with an attention

Proceedings of the Fourth Workshop on Language Technology for Equality, Diversity, Inclusion, pages 265–270
March 21, 2024 ©2024 Association for Computational Linguistics

mechanism. Dreaddit, a corpus of 190K Reddit posts with 3.5K labeled for stress identification, was introduced by (Elsbeth, 2019). Few studies (Li and Liu (2020), Oryngozha et al. (2023)) demonstrated high accuracy rates in stress identification through the application of conventional and neural supervised learning techniques on the Dreaddit dataset. Ahuja and Banga (2019) focused on exam pressure and recruitment stress frequently ignored factors and aimed to determine the extent of stress experienced by college students. The researchers utilized four classification algorithms (LR, NB, RF, and SVM) with a dataset comprising 206 student records from the Jaypee Institute of Information Technology. Their study yielded the highest accuracy for SVM. In another study conducted by (Lin et al., 2017), the relationship between users' stress states and their friends on social media was investigated using a large-scale real-world social platform dataset.

Researchers enhanced transformer-based models, including BERT and MentalBERT, by incorporating extra-linguistic data for depression and stress detection in social media (Ilias et al., 2023). Their approach involved a multimodal adaptation gate for combined embeddings, inputting data into a BERT (or MentalBERT) model, and model calibration through label smoothing (Aspillaga et al., 2020). The study highlighted the robustness of transformer-based models like RoBERTa, XLNet, and BERT in stress tests but also identified fragility and unexpected behaviors, suggesting potential directions for further advancements in the field.

3 Task & Dataset Descriptions

The task organizers curated a standardized dataset for identifying stress-related statements in Tamil and Telugu code-mixed social media texts. This effort aims to develop a system that proficiently recognizes stress expressions within a given social media text. The dataset is derived from the organizers' corpus (S et al., 2022), categorized into *Stressed (St)* and *Non Stressed (NSt)*. Table 1 displays the dataset distribution summary for Stress Identification Dataset in Tamil, including details on the train, test, and validation datasets, along with the total word count for each class. The same information is presented in Table 2 for Stress Identification Dataset in Telugu.

Class	**Train**	**Validation**	**Test**	W_T
St	1784	439	370	238434
NSt	3720	939	650	30876
Total	**5504**	**1378**	**1020**	269310

Table 1: Summary of SID in Tamil where W_T denotes total words

Class	**Train**	**Validation**	**Test**	W_T
St	1783	440	400	267320
NSt	3314	799	650	26663
Total	**5097**	**1239**	**1050**	293983

Table 2: Summary of SID in Telugu where W_T denotes total words

4 Methodology

The suggested methodology encompasses assessing diverse feature extraction techniques, integrating ML and DNN, and exploring various transformer-based architectures. The comprehensive approach aims to explore the effectiveness of different strategies in addressing the challenge of stress identification in the specified linguistic context. Figure 1 illustrates an overall outline of the stress identification technique in Tamil and Telugu code-mixed texts.

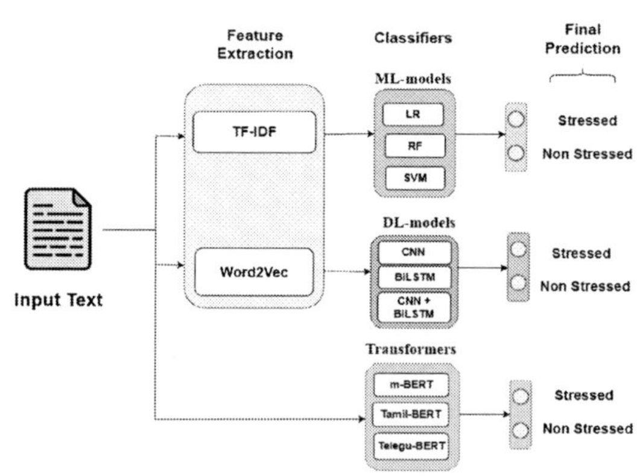

Figure 1: Schematic process of Stress Identification

4.1 Textual Feature Extraction

This study adopted several feature extraction methods to facilitate the training of classifier models for stress identification. We have employed TF-IDF (Sundaram et al., 2021) for ML models and Word2Vec embeddings (Rashid et al., 2020) for

DL models. The Keras embedding layer is vital in generating 100-dimensional embedding vectors, which encode the semantic meaning of words in the document.

4.2 ML Approaches

Various ML-based approaches (including LR, DT, and NB) are explored in developing a robust stress recognition system. Meticulous parameterization was applied to optimize each algorithm's efficiency. For instance, logistic regression underwent fine-tuning with a regularization parameter of 0.01, and the decision tree was configured with a maximum depth of 10. Naive Bayes incorporated an RBF kernel with a gamma value of 0.001, enhancing algorithm effectiveness in stress pattern recognition.

4.3 DL Approaches

A hybrid CNN and LSTM architecture (Wu et al., 2020) is employed, featuring seven layers. The model starts with a 200-length sequence vector input into the embedding layer, followed by two convolution layers with 'relu' activation and downsampling via a max-pooling layer. The Bidirectional LSTM layer, with 128 units, addresses complex patterns, and a dropout rate of 0.5 mitigates overfitting. The final layer uses a sigmoid activation function for binary classification. Pre-trained word vectors are explored, and training spans 20 epochs with a batch size of 64, achieving a balance between performance and computational efficiency in stress identification.

4.4 Transformer-based Approaches

This research exploited three pre-trained transformer models, namely M-BERT (Devlin et al., 2018), Tamil-BERT (Joshi, 2022), and Telugu-BERT (Joshi, 2022). These models, sourced from the Hugging Face[1] transformers library, underwent fine-tuning using the Ktrain (Maiya, 2022) package. Pre-trained versions of the transformer-based models are used with a maximum sequence length of 100 and a batch size of 16. The training spanned three epochs with a learning rate of $1e^{-4}$, enhancing their effectiveness for the specific task of stress identification.

5 Results and Analysis

Table 3 demonstrates the performance of the employed techniques for stress identification on the test set for Tamil code-mixed language and Table 4 for Telugu code-mixed language. The macro F1-score (F) was employed as a significant metric to determine model dominance, while we also evaluated the models on accuracy (A), precision (P), and recall (R) scores.

Method	Classifier	P	R	F	A
ML	LR	0.72	0.57	0.64	0.76
	DT	0.58	0.94	0.71	0.73
	NB	0.52	0.99	0.68	0.67
DL	CNN	0.61	0.82	0.68	0.68
	BiLSTM	0.59	0.88	0.65	0.67
	CNN+BiLSTM	0.54	0.99	0.70	0.72
Transformers	m-BERT	0.77	0.75	0.68	0.68
	Tamil-BERT	0.78	0.77	**0.71**	0.71

Table 3: Performance for stress identification for Tamil code-mixed language

Method	Classifier	P	R	F	A
ML	LR	0.66	0.17	0.27	0.65
	DT	0.58	0.91	0.70	0.72
	NB	0.56	0.97	0.70	0.70
DL	CNN	0.52	0.90	0.69	0.70
	BiLSTM	0.60	0.92	0.71	0.71
	CNN+BiLSTM	0.58	0.96	0.71	0.72
Transformers	m-BERT	0.72	0.73	0.70	0.70
	Telugu-BERT	0.78	0.76	**0.72**	0.72

Table 4: Performance for stress identification in Telugu code-mixed language

The LR displays competitive performance across ML models, reaching an accuracy of 0.72, a balanced recall of 0.57, and a macro F1-score of 0.64 for the Tamil dataset. DT excels in recall (0.94), resulting in a higher macro F1-score (0.71), whereas NB displays high recall (0.99) but poorer accuracy, generating a macro F1-score of 0.68. The DL model gets a competitive macro F1-score of 0.70. Among Transformers, m-BERT and Tamil-BERT demonstrate comparable performance, with macro F1-scores of 0.68 and 0.71, respectively.

For Telugu code-mixed language, LR obtains a moderate accuracy of 0.66, paired with a reduced recall, resulting in a macro F1-score of 0.27. Decision Tree stands out with solid recall (0.91) and a large macro F1-score of 0.70. Naive Bayes displays excellent recall (0.97) but poorer accuracy, pro-

[1] https://huggingface.co/

viding a macro F1-score of 0.70. CNN+BiLSTM delivers balanced accuracy, recall, and the greatest macro F1-score (0.71). Transformer models, m-BERT and Telugu-BERT, demonstrate decent performance, with Telugu-BERT (0.72) marginally beating m-BERT (0.70) in the macro F1-score.

The comparison analysis underlines the different performance of models in stress identification tasks for Tamil and Telugu code-mixed languages. LR and DT demonstrate different strengths in Tamil, whereas in Telugu, DT and CNN+BiLSTM do exceptionally well. The transformer models exhibit competitive performance but with variances in efficacy throughout the two languages.

6 Error Analysis

The stress detection performance of the BERT model in both Tamil and Telugu code-mixed languages demonstrates excellent accuracy in recognizing stressed situations, with a large true positive count in both datasets. However, a substantial difficulty develops in the form of false positives, indicating examples incorrectly categorized as stressed, particularly within an environment of class imbalance when non-stressed instances outweigh stressed ones. Figures 2 and 3 illustrate the performance of Tamil-BERT and Telugu-BERT models concerning the confusion matrix for the stress identification task.

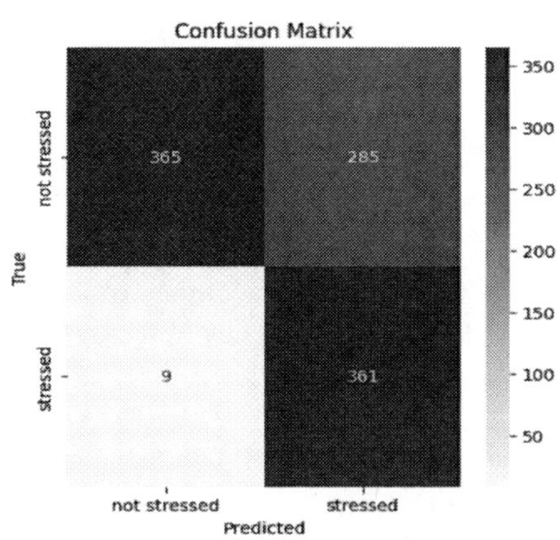

Figure 2: Confusion matrix of stress identification in Tamil using Tamil-BERT

Figure 2 illustrates the Tamil-BERT model's robust performance, accurately classifying 365 not stressed and 361 stressed samples out of 650 and 400, respectively. Despite this, precision is limited, with 285 not stressed samples misclassified as stressed and 9 stressed samples misclassified as not stressed, indicating susceptibility to false positives, particularly in identifying not stressed samples. In Figure 3, the Telugu-BERT model demonstrates strong performance, correctly tagging 371 not stressed and 378 stressed samples out of 650 and 400, respectively. However, precision is limited, with 279 not stressed samples misclassified as stressed and 22 stressed samples misclassified as not stressed. This highlights a vulnerability to false positives, especially in identifying not stressed samples.

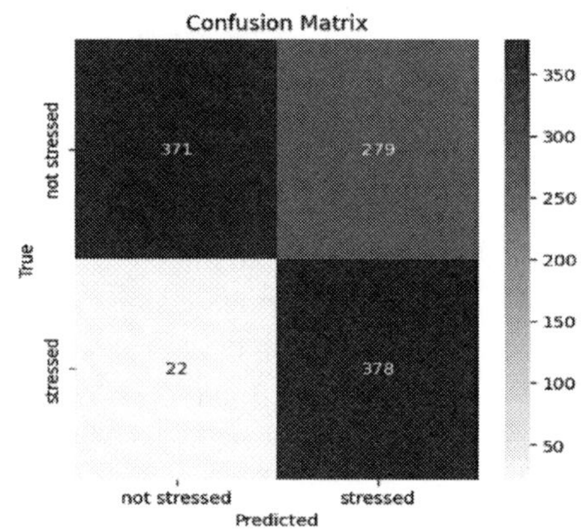

Figure 3: Confusion matrix of stress identification in Telugu using Telugu-BERT

Text Sample	Actual	Predicted
Sample1. நா யார் என்பதற்காக நா நேசிக்கப்பட விரும்புகிறேன், nA ennavAgha இருப்பேன் என்று நா உறுதியளிக்கவில்லை: யென்ன nA adhai ஒருபோதும் கடைப்பிடிக்க மாட்டேன், நீ என்னை vèRughghiRIrghaL.	stressed	Non stressed
Sample2. One of my favourite song ஒரு பெண் தான் கொண்ட காதலை மிகவும் அழகாகவும், அமைதியாகவும் வெளிப்படுத்தும் விதமாகவும் அமைந்துள்ளது.	Non stressed	Non stressed
Sample3. அம்மாவின் அழகு இவர்களிடம்.	Non stressed	Non stressed

Figure 4: Few examples of predicted outputs by the best performing model (Tamil-BERT)

Text Sample	Actual	Predicted
Sample1. మరణం గురించి ఆందోళన : నేను తెల్లవారుజామున 3:30 గంటలకు ఆందోళన చెందడం ఇష్టపడతాను ఎందుకంటే నేను మరణం గురించి ఆలోచిస్తాను మరియు ఏమీ పట్టింపు లేదు మరియు ప్రతిదీ ఒక రోజు నల్లగా మారుతుంది. .	stressed	stressed
Sample2. Kajal enti ni voice agarbathila undiiiiKajal enti ni voice agarbathila undiiii	Non stressed	Non stressed
Sample3. Raktha Sambandam ఎంత కరుణా మూర్తివయ్యా ఎంత చల్లని తండ్రివయ్యా	Non stressed	Non stressed

Figure 5: Few examples of predicted outputs by the best performing model (Telugu-BERT)

Figures 4 and 5 illustrates some correct and incorrect predicted outcomes by the best-performed models (**Tamil-BERT and Telugu-BERT**).

Limitations

Several challenges were encountered in the stress identification task, primarily from using code-mixed language and an imbalanced dataset. The major limitations of the developed models are as follows:

- Incorporating multiple languages in code-mixed text introduces linguistic variations, making it intricate for models to discern stress-related patterns precisely.
- The dataset exhibits an imbalance, with a prevalence of non-stressed instances compared to stressed ones, potentially affecting the model's generalization capabilities. These factors collectively contribute to the task's intricacy, necessitating strategic approaches for enhanced model adaptability and accurate stress identification.

7 Conclusion

This work presented a comprehensive study of stress detection within the code-mixed languages of Tamil and Telugu by exploiting various ML, DL, and transformer-based models. Remarkably, the transformer model Tamil-BERT emerges as a remarkable performer, achieving the most significant macro F1 score of 0.71 in the context of Tamil. Meanwhile, in the domain of Telugu, the leading model is Telugu-BERT, exhibiting a substantial macro F1 score of 0.72. Future endeavors may involve the integration of culturally sensitive features, thereby enhancing the effectiveness of stress detection in social media interactions within specific linguistic contexts.

References

Ravinder Ahuja and Alisha Banga. 2019. Mental stress detection in university students using machine learning algorithms. *Procedia Computer Science*, 152:349–353.

Carlos Aspillaga, Andrés Carvallo, and Vladimir Araujo. 2020. Stress test evaluation of transformer-based models in natural language understanding tasks. *arXiv preprint arXiv:2002.06261*.

Monika Chauhan, Shivani V Vora, and Dipak Dabhi. 2017. Effective stress detection using physiological parameters. In *2017 International Conference on Innovations in Information, Embedded and Communication Systems (ICIIECS)*, pages 1–6. IEEE.

Jacob Devlin, Ming-Wei Chang, Kenton Lee, and Kristina Toutanova. 2018. BERT: pre-training of deep bidirectional transformers for language understanding. *CoRR*, abs/1810.04805.

Turcan Elsbeth. 2019. Dreaddit: A reddit dataset for stress analysis in social media. In *Proceedings of the 10th International Workshop on Health Text Mining and Information Analysis*.

Asha Hegde, Mudoor Devadas Anusha, Sharal Coelho, Hosahalli Lakshmaiah Shashirekha, and Bharathi Raja Chakravarthi. 2022. Corpus creation for sentiment analysis in code-mixed tulu text. In *Proceedings of the 1st Annual Meeting of the ELRA/ISCA Special Interest Group on Under-Resourced Languages*, pages 33–40.

Loukas Ilias, Spiros Mouzakitis, and Dimitris Askounis. 2023. Calibration of transformer-based models for identifying stress and depression in social media. *IEEE Transactions on Computational Social Systems*.

Sachin Jadhav, Apoorva Machale, Pooja Mharnur, Pratik Munot, and Shruti Math. 2019. Text based stress detection techniques analysis using social media. In *2019 5th International Conference On Computing, Communication, Control And Automation (ICCUBEA)*, pages 1–5. IEEE.

Raviraj Joshi. 2022. L3cube-hindbert and devbert: Pre-trained bert transformer models for devanagari based hindi and marathi languages. *arXiv preprint arXiv:2211.11418*.

Russell Li and Zhandong Liu. 2020. Stress detection using deep neural networks. *BMC Medical Informatics and Decision Making*, 20:1–10.

Huijie Lin, Jia Jia, Jiezhong Qiu, Yongfeng Zhang, Guangyao Shen, Lexing Xie, Jie Tang, Ling Feng, and Tat-Seng Chua. 2017. Detecting stress based on social interactions in social networks. *IEEE Transactions on Knowledge and Data Engineering*, 29(9):1820–1833.

Sultan Mahmud, Sorif Hossain, Abdul Muyeed, Md Mynul Islam, and Md Mohsin. 2021. The global prevalence of depression, anxiety, stress, and, insomnia and its changes among health professionals during covid-19 pandemic: A rapid systematic review and meta-analysis. *Heliyon*, 7(7).

Arun S Maiya. 2022. ktrain: A low-code library for augmented machine learning. *The Journal of Machine Learning Research*, 23(1):7070–7075.

Khalid Masood, Beena Ahmed, Jongyong Choi, and Ricardo Gutierrez-Osuna. 2012. Consistency and validity of self-reporting scores in stress measurement surveys. In *2012 Annual International Conference of the IEEE Engineering in Medicine and Biology Society*, pages 4895–4898. IEEE.

Marina Milyavskaya, Mark Saffran, Nora Hope, and Richard Koestner. 2018. Fear of missing out: prevalence, dynamics, and consequences of experiencing fomo. *Motivation and emotion*, 42(5):725–737.

Tanya Nijhawan, Girija Attigeri, and T Ananthakrishna. 2022. Stress detection using natural language processing and machine learning over social interactions. *Journal of Big Data*, 9(1):1–24.

Nazzere Oryngozha, Pakizar Shamoi, and Ayan Igali. 2023. Detection and analysis of stress-related posts in reddit acamedic communities. *arXiv preprint arXiv:2312.01050*.

Umar Rashid, Muhammad Waseem Iqbal, Muhammad Akmal Skiandar, Muhammad Qasim Raiz, Muhammad Raza Naqvi, and Syed Khuram Shahzad. 2020. Emotion detection of contextual text using deep learning. In *2020 4th International symposium on multidisciplinary studies and innovative technologies (ISMSIT)*, pages 1–5. IEEE.

Kayalvizhi S, Thenmozhi Durairaj, Bharathi Raja Chakravarthi, and Jerin Mahibha C. 2022. Findings of the shared task on detecting signs of depression from social media. In *Proceedings of the Second Workshop on Language Technology for Equality, Diversity and Inclusion*, pages 331–338, Dublin, Ireland. Association for Computational Linguistics.

Varun Sundaram, Saad Ahmed, Shaik Abdul Muqtadeer, and R Ravinder Reddy. 2021. Emotion analysis in text using tf-idf. In *2021 11th International Conference on Cloud Computing, Data Science & Engineering (Confluence)*, pages 292–297. IEEE.

Jheng-Long Wu, Yuanye He, Liang-Chih Yu, and K Robert Lai. 2020. Identifying emotion labels from psychiatric social texts using a bi-directional lstm-cnn model. *IEEE Access*, 8:66638–66646.

dkit@LT-EDI-2024: Detecting Homophobia and Transphobia in English Social Media Comments

Sargam Yadav, Abhishek Kaushik and **Kevin McDaid**
d00263026@student.dkit.ie, abhishek.kaushik@dkit.ie and kevin.mcdaid@dkit.ie
Dundalk Institute of Technology,
Dublin Rd, Marshes Upper
Dundalk, Co. Louth, A91 K584

Abstract

Machine learning and deep learning models have shown great potential in detecting hate speech from social media posts. This study focuses on the homophobia and transphobia detection task of LT-EDI-2024 in English. Several machine learning models, a Deep Neural Network (DNN), and the Bidirectional Encoder Representations from Transformers (BERT) model have been trained on the provided dataset using different feature vectorization techniques. We secured top rank with the best macro-F1 score of 0.4963, which was achieved by fine-tuning the BERT model on the English test set.

1 Introduction

The increase in popularity of social media has fostered hate speech in online discourse Paz et al. (2020) Fortuna and Nunes (2018). Social media posts produce a great volume of data which can be hard to moderate manually. Artificial Intelligence tools have proven to be useful in combating trolling Cheng et al. (2017), misinformation, cyberbullying Moreno et al. (2019), etc. Specifically, Large Language Models (LLMs) such as BERT, Cross-Lingual RoBERTa (XLM-RoBERTa) Conneau et al. (2019), and Multilingual Representations for Indian Languages (MuRIL) Khanuja et al. (2021) have been used in recent studies to counter different types of hate speech Mozafari et al. (2020a,b); Kumaresan et al. (2023). The Lesbian, Gay, Bisexual, and Transgender (LGBT+) community has been a prominent target for online hate speech in the past Hinduja and Patchin (2020). Homophobia is the expression of hate and negative attitudes towards people who identify as homosexuals. Transphobia is the expression of negative beliefs towards people who identify as transgenders. It is imperative to filter such toxic and abusive language towards the LGBT+ community, as it can be the cause of severe psychological distress, and can silence their online voices. Very few datasets are available online for homophobia and transphobia detection in code-mixed languages such as Malayalam and Hindi Kumaresan et al. (2023) Chakravarthi et al. (2023). In recent years, shared tasks have been conducted to promote research for different types of hate speech such as misogyny (Automatic Misogyny Identification) Fersini et al. (2020), hate speech in low-resource languages (Hate Speech and Offensive Content Identification in English and Indo-Aryan Languages) Mandl et al. (2021), and code-mixed languages Satapara et al. (2021).

In this study, we focus on our participation in the LT-EDI-2024 shared task, which was was the detection of homophobia and transphobia from social media comments[1]. We have selected English data set for the task Kumaresan et al. (2024). The provided datasets were converted into feature vectors using techniques such as Term Frequency - Inverse Document Frequency (TF-IDF), count vectorizer, Word2Vec. Machine learning and deep learning models were then trained and evaluated on the datasets using empirical metrics such as accuracy, macro-F1 score, etc. The rest of the article is structured as follows: Section 2 discusses the relevant literature in sentiment analysis and hate speech detection. Section 3 provides details of the dataset, and the steps involved in the experiment such as feature vectorization, model training, fine-tuning, and evaluation. Section 4 discusses the results and findings of the study, and Section 5 concludes the study.

2 Related Works

In this section, we will discuss the relevant literature and previous work conducted in sentiment analysis and hate speech detection.

[1] https://codalab.lisn.upsaclay.fr/competitions/16056

Proceedings of the Fourth Workshop on Language Technology for Equality, Diversity, Inclusion, pages 271–276
March 21, 2024 ©2024 Association for Computational Linguistics

2.1 Sentiment Analysis

Natural Language Processing (NLP) tools have been extensively utilised to perform sentiment analysis on datasets in English and other languages Shah and Kaushik (2019); Shah et al. (2020); Kazhuparambil and Kaushik (2020a,b). Code-mixed languages present several challenges due to factors such as inconsistent spelling, lack of grammatical rules, and more Mathur et al. (2018). A novel dataset in code-mixed Hinglish was introduced by Kaur et al. (2019), who performed sentiment analysis on comments about cookery channels using machine learning models. Additionally, deep learning approaches such as multilayer perceptron Donthula and Kaushik (2019) and Transformer-based models were also explored Yadav et al. (2021); Yadav and Kaushik (2022).

2.2 Hate Speech Detection

NLP models have seen significant success in hate speech detection Yadav et al. (2023a); Kumar et al. (2018); Yadav et al. (2023b); Chinnaudayar Navaneethakrishnan et al. (2022). Forum for Information Retrieval Evaluation (FIRE) 2022 organized task A for detecting sentiment analysis and task B for detecting homophobia Chinnaudayar Navaneethakrishnan et al. (2022). The highest accuracy of 93% and 91% was achieved by using XLM-RoBERTa and BERT respectively Manikandan et al. (2022). Authors Kumaresan et al. (2023) presented a novel dataset of YouTube comments for homophobia and transphobia in the following languages: Malayalam, Hindi, Tamil, English, and code-mixed Tamil and English. Chakravarthi (2023) introduce a dataset for homophobia and transphobia detection in English, Tamil and code-mixed Tamil and English. Another study Chakravarthi et al. (2022) expands on the baseline in Chakravarthi (2023) by evaluating the performance of multilingual language models. The second shared task on Homophobia and Transphobia Detection in Social Media Comments (LT-EDI@RANLP-2023) Chakravarthi et al. (2023) was conducted in the following 5 languages: English, Spanish, Tamil, Hindi, and Malayalam. For task A in Malayalam, Spanish, and Tamil, the best weighted F1 score achieved was 0.9976, 0.8883, and 0.9496 respectively, using a weight-space ensembling technique Ninalga (2023). A multilingual model was trained on the complete dataset consisting of all languages, and individual models were fine-tuned for each language. Linear interpolation was then performed between the weights of the fine-tuned and multilingual models. For task B in Malayalam, the best score of 0.8842 was achieved using a custom XLM-RoBERTa model, which was pre-trained with a random sample of 50,000 tweets. For Hindi, Malayalam, and Tamil, one-fourth of the tweets were Romanized to accommodate code-mixing Wong et al. (2023). The literature review suggests that machine learning and deep learning models should be further studied to develop efficient systems for detecting different aspects of hate speech, such as homophobia and transphobia.

Category	Train	Test	Dev
Non-anti-LGBT+	2,978	748	931
Homophobia	179	42	55
Transphobia	7	2	4

Table 1: Class distribution of the English datasets

3 Methodology

In the section, the methodology used in the task is discussed.

3.1 Task and Dataset Description

The Homophobia/Transphobia Detection in social media comments shared task at LT-EDI@EACL-2024 was available in several languages such as Hindi, Tamil, Telugu, Kannada, Gujarathi, Malayalam, Marathi and Tulu. The training dataset for English consisted of a total of 3,164 samples which was divided into the following three classes: 'Non-anti-LGBT+ content', 'Homophobia', and 'Transphobia'. The development set consists of a total of 792 samples, and the test set of 990 samples. Table 1 displays the class distribution of all the sets. Figure 1 displays an example comment from each class in the dataset. In Phase-1 of the study, the training and development sets were released. In Phase-2 of the study, the test comments were released and predictions on these comments were submitted to the shared task organisers for evaluation. Later on, the test set with labels was released so that the performance of all the models could be evaluated.

3.2 Experiment

In this subsection, we will discuss the steps involved in preprocessing the data, feature extraction, and model training. The free version of Google Co-

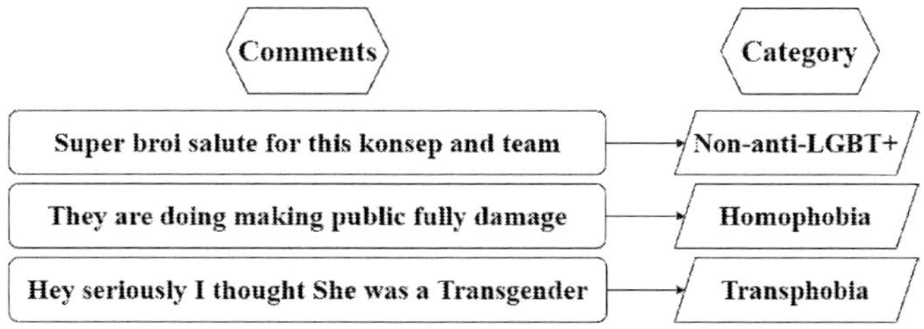

Figure 1: Example comments from each class for English

lab with GPU was used for experimentation. For all models, the training (TS) and development sets (DS) were combined into the merged training set (MTS), and finally split as a stratified sample into training and validation sets consisting of 70% and 30% of the data respectively. Stratified 10-fold cross validation (CV) and parameter tuning was performed using GridSearch CV on the 70% training set for machine learning models to find best parameters. The best models with optimal parameters are selected based on the macro-F1 score obtained by evaluating on the 30% validation set. Finally, the best model with optimal parameters trained on the 70% training set is used to evaluate model performance on the unseen test set (UTS). The results of top two models for each vectorization technique have been recorded. Figure 2 depicts the various steps of the experiment proposed in this study.

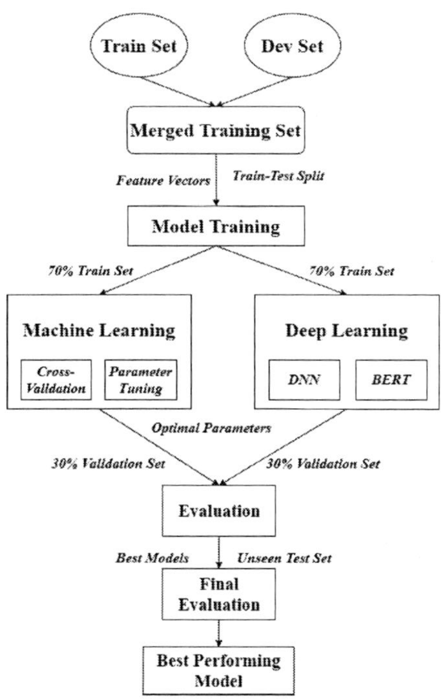

Figure 2: Flowchart of Experimental Methodology

3.2.1 Feature Engineering

For training the machine learning models, data cleaning and pre-processing was performed by removing all non-ASCII characters, user handles, hyperlinks, punctuation, extra whitespaces, stop-words, and newlines. The pre-processing steps were handled by the Natural Language Toolkit (NLTK) library[2]. The 'category' columns for all the sets were converted into numeric labels using Label Encoder. The following feature vectorization techniques were tested for machine learning models: TF-IDF, count vectorizer, and Word2Vec. For TF-IDF and count vectorizer, the maximum number of features has been limited to 2000. A custom Word2Vec model was trained on the merged training set with a vector size of 300, window of 10, and the skip-gram architecture McCormick (2016). The Word2Vec model was trained using the Gensim library[3]. Min-Max scaling to a feature range of 0 to 1 was performed on the Word2Vec embeddings to remove any negative values in the training data.

3.2.2 Machine Learning

The following machine learning models were trained on the resulting vectors: Logistic Regression (LR), Naive Bayes Bernoulli (NB-B), Gaussian (NB-G), and Multinomial (NB-M), Support Vector Machine Linear (SVM-L) and Radial Basis Function (SVM-R), Decision Trees (DT), and Random Forests (RF). For LR, SVM-L, and SVM-R, the value of the parameter C ranges from 10^{-3} to 10^{+3}. For LR, the lbfgs and liblinear solvers are considered. For NB-B and NB-M, the value of α considered is in the range of 10^{-3} to 10^{+3}. For SVM-R, a range of 10^{-3} to 10^{+3} is considered for the value of γ. For DT and RF, gini and entropy are considered as criterion. For DT, the maximum depth of the nodes is considered in the range of 40

[2]https://www.nltk.org/
[3]https://radimrehurek.com/gensim/models/word2vec.html

Model	Acc	Macro-F1	Prec	Rec
BERT	**0.9556**	**0.4963**	**0.5794**	**0.4585**
TF-IDF + DNN	0.9202	0.4295	0.4302	0.4288
TF-IDF + RF	0.9282	0.3482	0.3696	0.3461
TF-IDF + DT	0.8939	0.3551	0.3535	0.3567
Count Vec + DT	0.8797	0.3731	0.3667	0.3859
Count Vec + RF	0.8888	0.3707	0.3661	0.3778
Word2Vec + NB-G	0.6975	0.3428	0.3679	0.4797
Word2Vec + NB-M	0.9418	0.3233	0.3139	0.3333

Table 2: Top Model Results on the Unseen Test Set

to 60. For RF, the no. of estimators are considered in a range of 10 to 100 in steps of 10. For NB-G, var smoothing has been applied.

3.2.3 Deep Neural Network

The DNN model has been trained and evaluated using Tensorflow[4]. TF-IDF vectors have been used to train a DNN consisting of seven layers. The dense input layer has 128 neurons, 'relu' activation, and is followed by a dropout layer (dropout = 0.2). Next is another dense layer with 64 neurons and 'relu' activation, followed by a dropout layer (dropout = 0.2). This is followed by another dense layer with 32 neurons and 'relu' activation, followed by a dropout layer (dropout = 0.2). The final layer is a dense layer with 'softmax' activation to predict the classes. The Adam optimiser with a learning rate of 0.001 is used for optimization. The sparse categorical cross-entropy loss is used while training. The model is then trained for 15 epochs. A class weight dictionary has been calculated and used while training to account for the class imbalance.

3.2.4 Transformer-based models

The BERT (bert-base-uncased)[5] Devlin et al. (2018) English model consists of 12 layers and 110M parameters. It was fine-tuned using HuggingFace[6] and Pytorch[7]. All the comments have been encoded using a BERT tokenizer with the maximum sequence length of 128. The encodings have been converted into TensorDataset and batched using data loader. The hyperparamters used are as followings: number of epochs = 3, learning rate = 3e-5, and training and evaluation batch size = 2. The fine-tuned model was then evaluated on the 30% validation set and finally used to make predictions on the unseen test set.

[4]https://www.tensorflow.org/
[5]https://huggingface.co/bert-base-uncased
[6]https://huggingface.co/
[7]https://pytorch.org/

4 Results and Analysis

In this section, we will discuss the results of the experiment and analyse the findings. Table 2 displays the performance of the best two models for each vectorization technique based on the following evaluation criteria: Accuracy (Acc), Macro-F1, Precision (Prec), and Recall (Rec). The highest macro-F1 score of 0.4963 is achieved by the BERT model, followed by 0.4295 achieved by the DNN + TF-IDF model. Out of the machine learning models, DT performs the best with count vectorizer, achieving a macro-F1 score of 0.3731. Thus, the BERT model can be considered as the best model for homophobia and transphobia detection on this English dataset. The model has been made available[8]

5 Conclusion

In this study, homophobia and transphobia detection in English is conducted using different machine learning models, a DNN, and BERT. The highest macro-F1 score achieved is 0.4963 using the BERT model through simple fine-tuning. Transformer-based models have outperformed traditional machine learning models in this task of homophobia and transphobia detection. Further exploration can be carried out for online inclusivity through experimentation on different datasets and more complex model architectures.

Limitations

The dataset consists of YouTube comments in informal English. Informal English on social media platforms does not follow the linguistic rules of proper English. NLP models and tools have been pre-trained on internet sources written in formal English. Additionally, there is a scarcity of datasets that focus on homophobia and transphobia detection.

[8]https://huggingface.co/sam34738/BERT_homo

Ethics Statement

The annotated dataset used in this study has been taken from the LT-EDI@EACL 2024 shared task. The authors did not re-annotate the data, and only performed feature vectorization and model training. We respect all communities mentioned in the study.

References

Bharathi Raja Chakravarthi. 2023. Detection of homophobia and transphobia in YouTube comments. *International Journal of Data Science and Analytics*, pages 1–20.

Bharathi Raja Chakravarthi, Adeep Hande, Rahul Ponnusamy, Prasanna Kumar Kumaresan, and Ruba Priyadharshini. 2022. How can we detect Homophobia and Transphobia? Experiments in a multilingual code-mixed setting for social media governance. *International Journal of Information Management Data Insights*, 2(2):100119.

Bharathi Raja Chakravarthi, Rahul Ponnusamy, Malliga Subramanian, Paul Buitelaar, Miguel Ángel García-Cumbreras, Salud María Jiménez-Zafra, José Antonio García-Díaz, Rafael Valencia-García, and Nitesh Jindal. 2023. Overview of Second Shared Task on Homophobia and Transphobia Detection in English, Spanish, Hindi, Tamil, and Malayalam. In *Proceedings of the Third Workshop on Language Technology for Equality, Diversity and Inclusion*, Varna, Bulgaria. Recent Advances in Natural Language Processing.

Justin Cheng, Michael Bernstein, Cristian Danescu-Niculescu-Mizil, and Jure Leskovec. 2017. Anyone can become a troll: Causes of trolling behavior in online discussions. In *Proceedings of the 2017 ACM conference on computer supported cooperative work and social computing*, pages 1217–1230.

Subalalitha Chinnaudayar Navaneethakrishnan, Bharathi Raja Chakravarthi, Kogilavani Shanmugavadivel, Malliga Subramanian, Prasanna Kumar Kumaresan, Bharathi, Lavanya Sambath Kumar, and Rahul Ponnusamy. 2022. Findings of shared task on Sentiment Analysis and Homophobia Detection of YouTube Comments in Code-Mixed Dravidian Languages. In *Proceedings of the 14th Annual Meeting of the Forum for Information Retrieval Evaluation*, pages 18–21.

Alexis Conneau, Kartikay Khandelwal, Naman Goyal, Vishrav Chaudhary, Guillaume Wenzek, Francisco Guzmán, Edouard Grave, Myle Ott, Luke Zettlemoyer, and Veselin Stoyanov. 2019. Unsupervised cross-lingual representation learning at scale. *arXiv preprint arXiv:1911.02116*.

Jacob Devlin, Ming-Wei Chang, Kenton Lee, and Kristina Toutanova. 2018. BERT: Pre-training of deep bidirectional transformers for language understanding. *arXiv preprint arXiv:1810.04805*.

Suraj Kumar Donthula and Abhishek Kaushik. 2019. Man is what he eats: A research on Hinglish sentiments of YouTube cookery channels using deep learning. *International Journal of Recent Technology and Engineering (IJRTE)*, 8(2S11):930–937.

Elisabetta Fersini, Debora Nozza, Paolo Rosso, et al. 2020. AMI@ EVALITA2020: Automatic misogyny identification. In *Proceedings of the 7th evaluation campaign of Natural Language Processing and Speech tools for Italian (EVALITA 2020)*. (seleziona...).

Paula Fortuna and Sérgio Nunes. 2018. A survey on automatic detection of hate speech in text. *ACM Computing Surveys (CSUR)*, 51(4):1–30.

Sameer Hinduja and Justin W Patchin. 2020. Bullying, cyberbullying, and LGBTQ students. *Cyberbullying Research Center. http://hdl. handle. net/20.500*, 11990:2073.

Gagandeep Kaur, Abhishek Kaushik, and Shubham Sharma. 2019. Cooking is creating emotion: A study on Hinglish sentiments of YouTube cookery channels using semi-supervised approach. *Big Data and Cognitive Computing*, 3(3):37.

Subramaniam Kazhuparambil and Abhishek Kaushik. 2020a. Classification of Malayalam-English mix-code comments using current state of art. In *2020 IEEE International Conference for Innovation in Technology (INOCON)*, pages 1–6. IEEE.

Subramaniam Kazhuparambil and Abhishek Kaushik. 2020b. Cooking is all about people: Comment classification on cookery channels using BERT and classification models (Malayalam-English mix-code). *arXiv preprint arXiv:2007.04249*.

Simran Khanuja, Diksha Bansal, Sarvesh Mehtani, Savya Khosla, Atreyee Dey, Balaji Gopalan, Dilip Kumar Margam, Pooja Aggarwal, Rajiv Teja Nagipogu, Shachi Dave, et al. 2021. MuRIL: Multilingual representations for Indian languages. *arXiv preprint arXiv:2103.10730*.

Ritesh Kumar, Guggilla Bhanodai, Rajendra Pamula, and Maheshwar Reddy Chennuru. 2018. TRAC-1 shared task on aggression identification: IIT (ISM)@ COLING'18. In *Proceedings of the first workshop on trolling, aggression and cyberbullying (TRAC-2018)*, pages 58–65.

Prasanna Kumar Kumaresan, Rahul Ponnusamy, Ruba Priyadharshini, Paul Buitelaar, and Bharathi Raja Chakravarthi. 2023. Homophobia and transphobia detection for low-resourced languages in social media comments. *Natural Language Processing Journal*, page 100041.

Prasanna Kumar Kumaresan, Ruba Priyadharshini, Bharathi Raja Chakravarthi, Paul Buitelaar, Asha Hegde, Hosahalli Lakshmaiah Shashirekha, Saranya Rajiakodi, Miguel Ángel García-Cumbreras,

Salud María Jiménez-Zafra, José Antonio García-Díaz, Rafael Valencia-García, Kishore Kumar Ponnusamy, Poorvi Shetty, and Daniel García-Baena. 2024. Overview of Third Shared Task on Homophobia and Transphobia Detection in Social Media Comments. In *Proceedings of the Fourth Workshop on Language Technology for Equality, Diversity and Inclusion*, Malta. European Chapter of the Association for Computational Linguistics.

Thomas Mandl, Sandip Modha, Gautam Kishore Shahi, Hiren Madhu, Shrey Satapara, Prasenjit Majumder, Johannes Schäfer, Tharindu Ranasinghe, Marcos Zampieri, Durgesh Nandini, et al. 2021. Overview of the HASOC subtrack at FIRE 2021: Hate speech and offensive content identification in English and Indo-aryan languages. *arXiv preprint arXiv:2112.09301*.

Deepalakshmi Manikandan, Malliga Subramanian, and Kogilavani Shanmugavadivel. 2022. A System For Detecting Abusive Contents Against LGBT Community Using Deep Learning Based Transformer Models. In *Working Notes of FIRE 2022-Forum for Information Retrieval Evaluation (Hybrid). CEUR*.

Puneet Mathur, Ramit Sawhney, Meghna Ayyar, and Rajiv Shah. 2018. Did you offend me? classification of offensive tweets in Hinglish language. In *Proceedings of the 2nd workshop on abusive language online (ALW2)*, pages 138–148.

Chris McCormick. 2016. Word2vec tutorial-the skip-gram model. *Apr-2016.[Online]. Available: http://mccormickml. com/2016/04/19/word2vec-tutorial-the-skip-gram-model*.

Megan A Moreno, Aubrey D Gower, Heather Brittain, and Tracy Vaillancourt. 2019. Applying natural language processing to evaluate news media coverage of bullying and cyberbullying. *Prevention science*, 20(8):1274–1283.

Marzieh Mozafari, Reza Farahbakhsh, and Noel Crespi. 2020a. A BERT-based transfer learning approach for hate speech detection in online social media. In *Complex Networks and Their Applications VIII: Volume 1 Proceedings of the Eighth International Conference on Complex Networks and Their Applications COMPLEX NETWORKS 2019 8*, pages 928–940. Springer.

Marzieh Mozafari, Reza Farahbakhsh, and Noël Crespi. 2020b. Hate speech detection and racial bias mitigation in social media based on BERT model. *PloS one*, 15(8):e0237861.

Dean Ninalga. 2023. Cordyceps@ LT-EDI: Patching Language-Specific Homophobia/Transphobia Classifiers with a Multilingual Understanding. *arXiv preprint arXiv:2309.13561*.

María Antonia Paz, Julio Montero-Díaz, and Alicia Moreno-Delgado. 2020. Hate speech: A systematized review. *Sage Open*, 10(4):2158244020973022.

Shrey Satapara, Sandip Modha, Thomas Mandl, Hiren Madhu, and Prasenjit Majumder. 2021. Overview of the HASOC subtrack at FIRE 2021: Conversational hate speech detection in code-mixed language. *Working Notes of FIRE*, pages 13–17.

Sonali Rajesh Shah and Abhishek Kaushik. 2019. Sentiment analysis on Indian indigenous languages: a review on multilingual opinion mining. *arXiv preprint arXiv:1911.12848*.

Sonali Rajesh Shah, Abhishek Kaushik, Shubham Sharma, and Janice Shah. 2020. Opinion-mining on Marglish and Devanagari comments of YouTube cookery channels using parametric and non-parametric learning models. *Big Data and Cognitive Computing*, 4(1):3.

Sidney Wong, Matthew Durward, Benjamin Adams, and Jonathan Dunn. 2023. cantnlp@ LT-EDI-2023: Homophobia/Transphobia Detection in Social Media Comments using Spatio-Temporally Retrained Language Models. In *Proceedings of the Third Workshop on Language Technology for Equality, Diversity and Inclusion*, pages 103–108.

Sargam Yadav and Abhishek Kaushik. 2022. Contextualized Embeddings from Transformers for Sentiment Analysis on Code-Mixed Hinglish Data: An Expanded Approach with Explainable Artificial Intelligence. In *International Conference on Speech and Language Technologies for Low-resource Languages*, pages 99–119. Springer.

Sargam Yadav, Abhishek Kaushik, and Kevin McDaid. 2023a. Hate Speech is not Free Speech: Explainable Machine Learning for Hate Speech Detection in Code-Mixed Languages. In *2023 IEEE International Symposium on Technology and Society (ISTAS)*, pages 1–8. IEEE.

Sargam Yadav, Abhishek Kaushik, and Shubham Sharma. 2021. Cooking well, with love, is an art: Transformers on YouTube Hinglish data. In *2021 International Conference on Computational Performance Evaluation (ComPE)*, pages 836–841. IEEE.

Sargam Yadav, Abhishek Kaushik, and Surbhi Sharma. 2023b. Comprehensive Analysis of the Artificial Intelligence Approaches for Detecting Misogynistic Mixed-Code Online Content in South Asian Countries: A Review. *Cyberfeminism and Gender Violence in Social Media*, pages 350–368.

KEC_AI_MIRACLE_MAKERS@LT-EDI-2024: Stress Identification in Dravidian Languages using Machine Learning Techniques

Kogilavani Shanmugavadivel[1], Malliga Subramanian[1], Monika R J[1], Monishaa S[1], Rishibalan M B[1]

[1]Department of AI, Kongu Engineering College, Perundurai, Erode.

{kogilavani.sv, mallinishanth72}@gmail.com

{monikarj.22aid, monishaas.22aid}@kongu.edu

rishibalanmb.22aid@kongu.edu

Abstract

Identifying an individual where he/she is stressed or not stressed is our shared task topic. we have used several machine learning models for identifying the stress. This paper presents our system submission for the task 1 and 2 for both Tamil and Telugu dataset, focusing on using supervised approaches. For Tamil dataset, we got highest accuracy for the Support Vector Machine model with macro f1-score of 0.98 and for Telugu dataset, we got highest accuracy for Random Forest algorithm with macro f1-score of 0.99. By using this model, Stress Identification System will be helpful for an individual to improve their mental health in optimistic manner.

1 Introduction

Stress, anxiety, and depression (SAD) are psychological disorders that have a serious negative impact on mental stability. These disorders interfere with an individual's ability to go about their everyday life normally and can sometimes worsen into trauma. The human body releases a variety of chemicals when under stress, despair, or worry, and this results in alterations to nonverbal body language. These psychological diseases can be generically categorised as stress, anxiety, and depression according to the different stages involved in their exploration. Stress is the second stage of mental illness, during which psychological illnesses become more moderate since anxiety is a persistent factor. The third most serious psychological condition that can have a long-term negative impact on a person's physical and mental health is depression.An individual's level of discomfort is a result of stress, and this discomfort manifests as anxiety or depressive episodes. Stress is the culmination of all the things that can make someone feel stressed out. Exercises, additional work, a task overload, shallow breathing, insufficient sleep, questionnaires, etc. are examples of stressors. According to a study, stress can have a beneficial or negative effect depending on the circumstances. The study looked at people's social media posts, where they shared their feelings and emotions, to determine whether or not they were stressed. Social media posts in code-mixed Tamil and Telugu should be classified as either Stressed or Not stressed by the system. Numerous machine learning methods, including the Random Forest, Naive Bayes, and Support Vector Machine (SVC) algorithms, have been employed. This is how the rest of the paper is structured. The literature on work linked to stress identification is briefly discussed in Section 2. Section 3 provides a detailed description of our system, and Section 4 presents the findings and conclusions from the experiments. We wrap off the work by discussing potential implications for further research.

2 Literature Review

In Singh and Kumar (2022), the researchers have used some existing computer vision models for systematic review and used machine learning algorithms to detect SAD, which is more efficient than medical investigations because machine learning is fast and best for computing stress.

The proceedings in Robles et al. (2022),The researchers have used surface electromyography signals (sEMG) for detecting stress with the help of convolutional neural networks, and they got moderate range of the macro f1-score for a bi-class and multi-class classification. But they didn't provide necessary information about the size or diversity of the dataset used for training and testing, and insights into the interpretability of the model.

S and Karthick (2022) have also used the deep learning modal with a convolutional-based network approach and multimodel data with the help of sensors in which the data are collected, such as heartbeat, body temperature, respiration, electromyographic (EMG) data, and additional long and short-term Memory is used. They didn't provide any

Proceedings of the Fourth Workshop on Language Technology for Equality, Diversity, Inclusion, pages 277–281
March 21, 2024 ©2024 Association for Computational Linguistics

limitations or drawbacks.

In Tahira and Vyas (2023) a hybrid deep learning model that combines bidirectional long short-term memory (BLSTM) and convolutional neural networks (CNN) is presented for exploiting EEG signals to determine stress. Even though the modality got higher accuracy, they didn't explore other potential factors that are responsible for the stress.

In Gowtham et al. (2023), the researchers used the BERT model for text-based research and achieved better range of the f1-score, and they combined stacked transformer encoder layers with stacked bi-directional LSTM. But it did not explore other modalities such as signal- or speech-based analysis, and it is not clear how the model's performance compares to other existing state-of-the-art models in stress analysis.

In Suba Raja et al. (2023), they will send the test data through SMS alerts using a GSM module by extracting facial expression and mapped onto the emotion space and the EEG signal value is evaluated. The accuracy and robustness have been limited for the evaluation of this system and have not been discussed the potential limitations.

Saputra and Nafi'Iyah (2022) used feature extraction techniques including mean, standard deviation, and MAV, were applied to the EEG signals to capture relevant information. They have used several machine learning models to features, but the KNN algorithm achieved the highest accuracy in distinguishing between stressed and normal individuals. But they did not provide information about demographic characteristics and also not investigate the impact of external factors.

Garg et al. (2021) aimed to identify the stress among individuals using machine learning and wearable sensors with a random forest model in both binary and three-class classifications, achieving macro f1-scores of 83.34 and 65.73, respectively.But this paper fails to discuss the ethical considerations and privacy concerns related to the use of the wearable sensors.

Sharma et al. (2021) provides a comprehensive review and analysis of supervised learning (SL) and soft computing (SC) techniques used in diagnosis and the potential use of the hybrid technique gives a more accurate stress diagnosis. Their limitations are due to the factors such as real-time data collection, bias, integrity, multi-dimensional data, and data privacy.

Kul (2021) focuses on predicting and detecting stress in individuals by using IoT technology and body sensors, and that uses deep learning algorithms to analyze this data and suggest sending alerts, messages to the individual's relatives for support. But they didn't compare with any other existing methods and didn't provide any real-world validations of the proposed modal in practical scenarios.

3 Problem and system description

From the given dataset, we have to train the model whether the given sentence is stressed or not stressed. This shared task is to detect the individuals whether he/she affected by stress from their social media postings by analysing their shared feelings and emotions. Given dataset of social media postings consists of both Tamil and Telugu languages with this, we have to classify the given test data with 2 labels namely "stressed" or "not stressed".

3.1 Dataset description

The shared dataset consists of 2 languages namely Tamil and Telugu. In Tamil, the training dataset consists of 1,784 Stressed class labels and 3,720 Non-Stressed class labels out of 5,504 labels and the test dataset consists of 1,020 labels. The Telugu training dataset consists of 1,783 Stressed class labels and 3,314 Non-Stressed class labels out of 5,097 labels and the test dataset consists of 1,050 labels. Additionally, they are provided with the development dataset to check the model.

Dataset	No. of Comments
Train	5,504
Test	1,020

Table 1: Tamil Dataset Description

Dataset	No. of Comments
Train	5,097
Test	1,050

Table 2: Telugu Dataset Description

3.2 Work flow of the proposed system

1.Data pre-processing 2.Encoding module 3.Model description

The above mentioned are the major sub categories in the work flow which is explained below with detailed description.

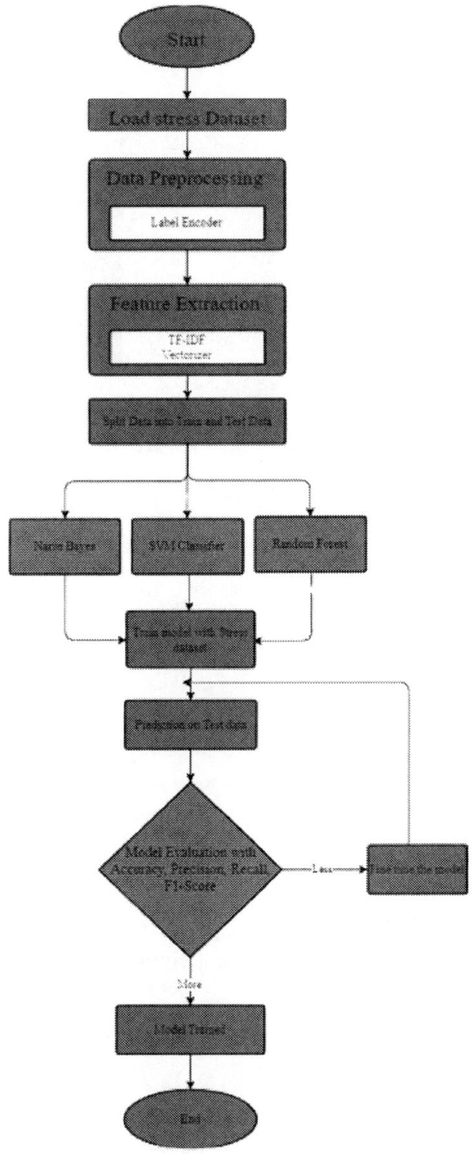

Figure 1: Proposed System Workflow

3.2.1 Data pre-processing

For the given dataset, we have used label encoder which is used to convert the categorical data into the numerical data. It will assign a unique integer to each category which helps the algorithm assume categorical data as numerical data so it makes easier for the models to process the given dataset.

3.2.2 Encoding module

For our dataset, we have used tfidfvectorizer which is imported from sklearn.feature-extraction. The feature extraction is used to makes the dataset in more efficient manner and is very helpful for better predictions by enhancing the model performance and reducing complexity. The TfidfVectorizer accepts the given dataset as input and which transforms the text into matrix where the rows are represented as documents and the columns are represented as unique word and TF-IDF will be calculated to create the matrix. The main use of vectorizer is the conversion of text data into the numerical representations such as matrix to get better model performance.

3.2.3 Model description

To predict where the person is stressed or not stressed by their social media postings, we used three machine learning models for both the dataset i.e., Tamil and Telugu dataset to find the highest accuracy model. The three machine learning models are namely,

Naive Bayes classifier algorithm works based on the Bayes theorem which gives equal importance to all the features to predict the class label. In training dataset, it calculates the class and feature probabilities. During prediction, it computes the likelihood probability of each class given the features, assigning the highest probability class.

Random forest algorithm is a machine learning method that construction of the multiple decision trees by randomly selecting features and samples and handles the high dimensional data. It excels in accuracy for classification, regression and feature selection tasks. It can be used for finding both classification and regression the given dataset.

Support vector machine(SVM) is an algorithm which is also used for both classification and regression. It has diverse domains like text classification and image detection . It identifies the hyperplane that maximizes the margin between classes and can also handle the non-linear classification. It can enable SVM to learn complex decision boundaries.

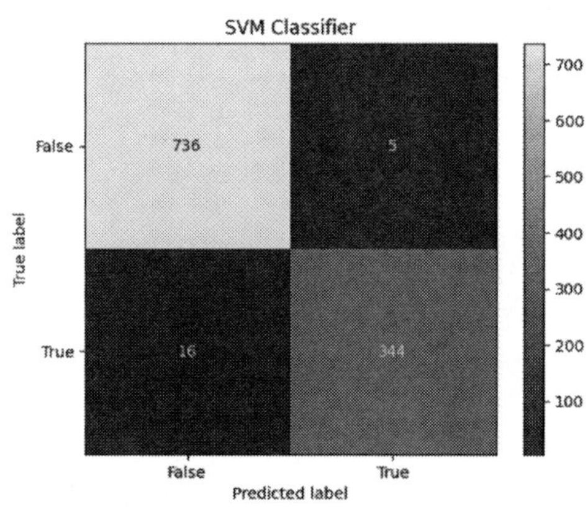

Figure 2: Confusion Matrix Of Support Vector Classifier Model- Tamil Data

4 Experimental Analysis

In this experiment we have used 2 different languages of dataset and 3 machine learning model to predict the class label whether it is "stressed" or "non-stressed". In Tamil dataset, we have gotten accuracy of 98.09% in SVM classifier,97.27% in random forest algorithm and 89.19% in Naïve Bayes algorithm. As of our accuracy result, all the model

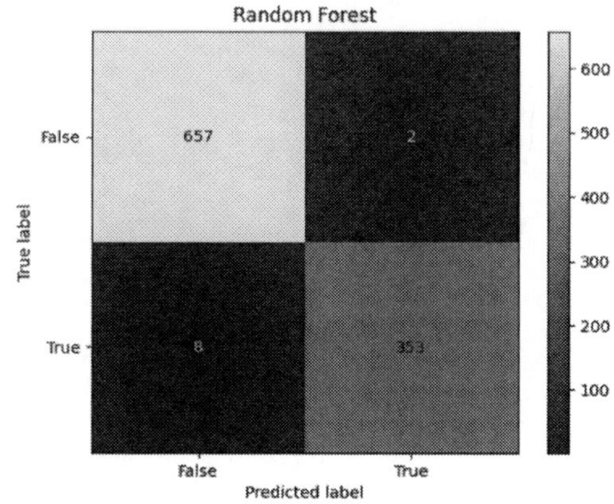

Figure 3: Confusion Matrix Of Random Forest Model- Telugu Data

will have the high accuracy hence we considered the support vector machine algorithm as the best algorithm among the other algorithm and it also have 0.98 macro f1-score. In Telugu dataset, we have got accuracy of 98.9% in SVM classifier,99.01% in random forest algorithm and 92.9% in naïve Bayes algorithm. As of our accuracy result, all the model will have the high accuracy hence we considered the random forest algorithm as the best algorithm among the other algorithm and it have macro 0.99 f1-score.

Model	Macro F1-Score
Support Vector Classifier	0.98
Random Forest	0.97
Naive Bayes	0.89

Table 3: Macro F1-Score Metrics for Tamil Data

Model	Macro F1-Score
Support Vector Classifier	0.98
Random Forest	0.99
Naive Bayes	0.93

Table 4: Macro F1-Score Metrics for Telugu Data

5 Conclusion

Stress Identification is a very sensitive topic where many people around us and we also got stressed now-a-days. Some peoples are handling the things in practical ways but most of 80% of peoples are going to the depression state and they are pushed to take the wrong decision by the surroundings. Hence stress identification system will help an individual to improve their mental health in positive manner. For both the datasets, we got the highest accuracy points and high macro f1-score. So, we got SVM for Tamil dataset with 98% and random forest algorithm for Telugu dataset with accuracy 99% as best predicting models. Therefore,we got more accuracy rate while comparing with any machine learning model and deep learning model,

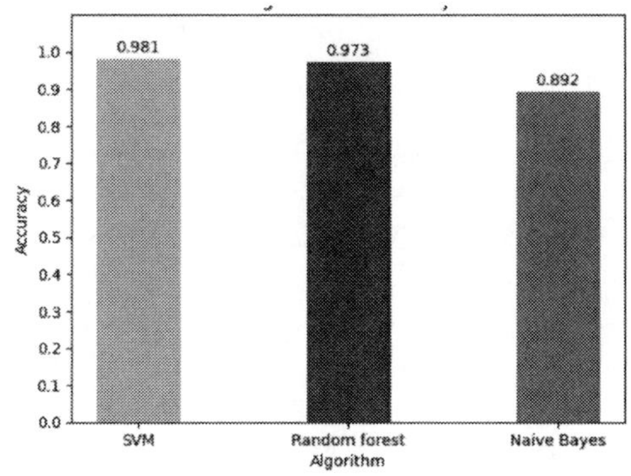

Figure 4: Accuracy - Tamil Data

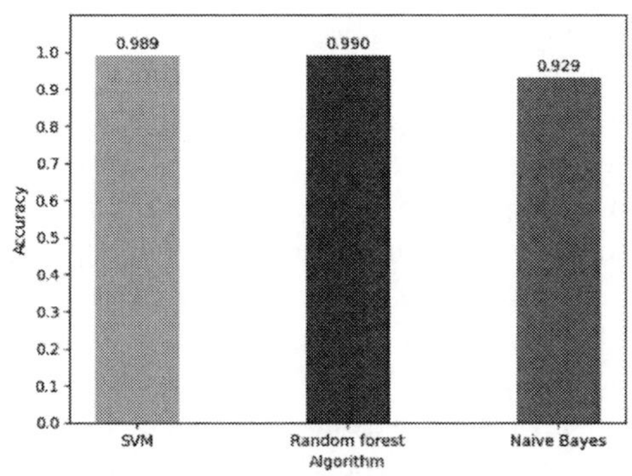

Figure 5: Accuracy - Telugu Data

Model	Accuracy
Support Vector Classifier	0.98
Random Forest	0.97
Naive Bayes	0.89

Table 5: Accuracy for Tamil Dataset

Model	Accuracy
Support Vector Classifier	0.98
Random Forest	0.99
Naive Bayes	0.92

Table 6: Accuracy for Telugu Dataset

References

2021. Stress prediction and detection using iot and deep learning: A comprehensive review. *International Journal for Research in Applied Science and Engineering Technology*, 9(9):1874–1880.

Prerna Garg, Jayasankar Santhosh, Andreas Dengel, and Shoya Ishimaru. 2021. Stress detection by machine learning and wearable sensors. In *26th International Conference on Intelligent User Interfaces - Companion*, IUI '21 Companion, page 43–45, New York, NY, USA. Association for Computing Machinery.

B Gowtham, H Subramani, D Sumathi, and BKSP Kumar Raju Alluri. 2023. Stress analysis using machine learning. In *Applied Computing for Software and Smart Systems: Proceedings of ACSS 2022*, pages 227–234. Springer.

Diego Robles, Mouna Benchekroun, Vincent Zalc, Dan Istrate, and Carla Taramasco. 2022. Stress detection from surface electromyography using convolutional neural networks. In *2022 44th Annual International Conference of the IEEE Engineering in Medicine Biology Society (EMBC)*, pages 3235–3238.

Praveenkumar. S and T. Karthick. 2022. Automatic stress recognition system with deep learning using multimodal psychological data. In *2022 International Conference on Electronic Systems and Intelligent Computing (ICESIC)*, pages 122–127.

Nophaz Hanggara Saputra and Nur Nafi'Iyah. 2022. Identification of human stress based on eeg signals using machine learning. In *2022 1st International Conference on Information System Information Technology (ICISIT)*, pages 176–180.

Samriti Sharma, Gurvinder Singh, and Manik Sharma. 2021. A comprehensive review and analysis of supervised-learning and soft computing techniques for stress diagnosis in humans. *Computers in Biology and Medicine*, 134:104450.

Astha Singh and Divya Kumar. 2022. Computer assisted identification of stress, anxiety, depression (sad) in students: A state-of-the-art review. *Medical Engineering Physics*, 110:103900.

S. Kanaga Suba Raja, Durai Arumugam S S L, R. Praveen Kumar, and J. Selvakumar. 2023. Recognition of facial stress system using machine learning with an intelligent alert system. In *2023 7th International Conference on Computing Methodologies and Communication (ICCMC)*, pages 1–4.

Maryam Tahira and Prerna Vyas. 2023. Eeg based mental stress detection using deep learning techniques. In *2023 International Conference on Distributed Computing and Electrical Circuits and Electronics (ICDCECE)*, pages 1–7.

MUCS@LT-EDI-2024: Exploring Joint Representation for Memes Classification

Sidharth Mahesh[a], Sonith D[b], Gauthamraj[c],
Kavya G[d], Asha Hegde[e], H L Shashirekha[f]
Department of Computer Science, Mangalore University, Mangalore, Karnataka, India
{[a]sidharthmaheshedu, [b]sonithksd, [c]gauthamrajdataspace}@gmail.com,
[d]kavyamujk, [e]hegdekasha}@gmail.com, [f]hlsrekha@mangaloreuniversity.ac.in

Abstract

Misogynistic memes are a category of memes which contain disrespectful language targeting women on social media platforms. Hence, detecting such memes is necessary in order to maintain a healthy social media environment. To address the challenges of detecting misogynistic memes, "Multitask Meme classification - Unraveling Misogynistic and Trolls in Online Memes: LT-EDI@EACL 2024" shared task organized at European Chapter of the Association for Computational Linguistics (EACL) 2024, invites researchers to develop models to detect misogynistic memes in Tamil and Malayalam. The shared task has two subtasks and in this paper, we - team MUCS, describe the learning models submitted to Task 1 - Identification of Misogynistic Memes in Tamil and Malayalam. As memes represent multi-modal data of image and text, three models: i) Bidirectional Encoder Representations from Transformers (BERT)+Residual Network (ResNet)-50, ii) Multilingual Representations for Indian Languages (MuRIL)+ResNet-50, and iii) multilingual BERT (mBERT)+ResNet-50, are proposed based on joint representation of text and image, for detecting misogynistic memes in Tamil and Malayalam. Among the proposed models, mBERT+ResNet-50 and MuRIL+ ResNet-50 models obtained macro F1 scores of 0.73 and 0.87 for Tamil and Malayalam datasets respectively securing 1st rank for both the datasets in the shared task.

1 Introduction

Memes, in the digital age, have become a common form of cultural expression, often shared widely across social media platforms and internet communities. These memes typically comprising of images/videos and text embedded on them, started with the idea of sharing humor (Suryawanshi et al., 2020). But these days, memes are often being misused to spread hateful, troll, and misogynistic content. Misogynistic memes are a category of memes that propagate negative attitude towards women. These memes often promote dangerous or harmful pranks, challenges, or behaviors which leads to physical harm, injury, or legal consequences (Guest et al., 2021; Hegde et al., 2021). Hence, it is necessary to detect such content to protect users from getting harmed and also to maintain a safe and inclusive online environment.

Detecting misogynistic memes on social media is challenging due to the combination of text, image/video, and sometimes audio also, which exhibits a multi-modal nature. This problem becomes more challenging when the embedded text belongs to low-resource languages like Tamil, Malayalam etc., where lack of digital resources and computational tools is the common issue. "Multitask Meme Classification - Unraveling Misogynistic and Trolls in Online Memes: LT-EDI@EACL 2024" (Chakravarthi et al., 2024) shared task encourages the researchers to develop models to detect misogynistic and trolling content in Tamil and Malayalam memes. The shared task has two subtasks and in this paper, we - team MUCS, describe the learning models submitted to Task 1 - Identification of Misogynistic Memes in Tamil and Malayalam. As memes are made up of textual and visual components, they can be represented as multi-modal data of textual and visual features integrated into a single representation known as joint representation. Three models: i) BERT+ResNet-50, ii) MuRIL+ResNet-50, and iii) mBERT+ResNet-50, are proposed based on joint representation, for detecting misogynistic memes in Tamil and Malayalam.

The rest of the paper is arranged as follows: a review of related work is included in Section 2 and the methodology is discussed in Section 3. Experiments and results are described in Section 4 followed by concluding the paper with future work in Section 5.

Proceedings of the Fourth Workshop on Language Technology for Equality, Diversity, Inclusion, pages 282–287
March 21, 2024 ©2024 Association for Computational Linguistics

2 Related work

Researchers have explored several models for detecting memes by representing the visual and textual components of memes as two uni-modal data as well as integrating visual and textual components into a single joint representation. Few of such relevant research works are described below: Raha et al. (2022) have explored uni-modal (Image-Grid, Image-Region, Text BERT, Text Robustly Optimized BERT Pre-training Approach (RoBERTa), Uni-modal fusions (Concat-BERT, Late Fusion), Multi-modal transformers (Multi-Modal BiTransformer (MMBT)-Grid, MMBT-Region, Vision-and-Language BERT (ViLBERT), Visual BERT) and pre-trained models (ViLBERT CC, Visual BERT COCO, ViLBERT HM, Visual BERT HM), for identifying misogynous memes in Conceptual Captions (CC), Common Objects in Context (COCO), Hateful Memes (HM) datasets. Among all the proposed models, the VilBERT HM model outperformed all other models obtaining macro F1 score of 0.712 for HM dataset. Muti et al. (2022) proposed uni-modal and multi-modal approaches for identifying misogynistic memes in English dataset. The multi-modal system is implemented by fusing image and text embeddings through MMBT which is used to jointly fine-tune uni-modal pre-trained text and image encoders by projecting image embeddings to the text token space. Their proposed multi-modal system obtained a macro average F1 score of 0.727.

Maheshwari and Nangi (2022) experimented various Machine Learning (ML), Deep Learning (DL) and Transfer Learning (TL) based models for the identification of misogynous memes in English. Their ML models (Support Vector Machine (SVM), Naive Bayes (NB) and Logistic Regression (LR)) are trained with Term Frequency-Inverse Document Frequency (TF-IDF) of word unigrams (text representation) and pre-trained Visual Geometry Group-16 (VGG-16) (image representation), DL models (LSTM and Convolutional Neural Network (CNN)) are trained with GloVe embeddings (text representation) and VGG-16 (image representation) and TL models are trained with BERT variants (Concat BERT, Average BERT, and Gated BERT) (text representation) and Common World Knowledge (CWK) and Contrastive Language-Image Pre-training (CLIP) (image representation). The authors experimented all the models with uni-modal feature space, i.e, training the classifiers with only text and only image features and also with joint learning i.e., training the classifiers with shared embedding layer for both text and image features. Among all their models, TL model with joint learning using Average BERT + CLIP achieved a macro F1 score of 0.671.

Sean and Kanchana (2022) presented multi-modal models, namely InceptionV3+BERT backbone as Model A, EfficientNetB7+BERT as Model B, CLIP Image+CLIP Text Backbone as Model C, SVM and an Ensemble model (Model A, Model B, SVM), for identifying misogynous memes in English. Among the proposed models, Ensemble model achieved a macro F1 score of 0.718. Rao and Rao (2022) experimented text-based (Bidirectional Long Short Term Memory (BiLSTM)+Glove embeddings, RoBERTa, Ernie-2.0), image-based (VGG-16, ResNet-50, ResNet-152, Vision Transformer), and multi-modal (VGG-16+BiLSTM, MMBT, VisualBERT, MMBT with tRoBERTa, and Average (Avg) Ensemble (RoBERTa and ResNet-152 models with soft voting)) models, for misogynous meme identification in English language. Among their proposed models, the Avg Ensemble model outperformed other models with a macro F1 score of 0.761. Gu et al. (2022) employed an ensemble of ML models (Multinomial NB (MNB) and Gradient Boosting classifiers trained with TF-IDF of word bigrams and unigrams respectively, and Random forest (RF) classifier trained with various image features (Hu moment invariants, Haralick textures, and image histograms), for the identification of misogynous memes. In addition, the ML models of the ensemble are also trained independently with the respective features as mentioned. Among all their models, RF classifier trained with various image features outperformed other models by achieving a macro F1 score of 0.665.

The above literature reveals that the joint representation of image and text exhibits promising performances for meme detection tasks. However, most of the meme detection tasks focus on English language giving less importance for low-resource languages like Tamil and Malayalam.

3 Methodology

The objective of this work is to identify misogynistic memes in the given Tamil and Malayalam datasets. This is achieved by proposing learning models based on the joint representation of image and text components in the given memes. The steps

Language	Image	Text	English Translation	Label
Malayalam	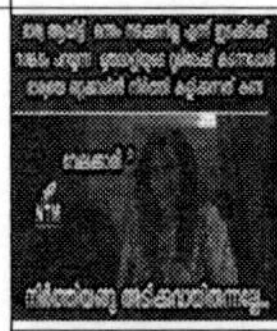	ഭാര്യ ആയിട്ട് ഒന്നും നടക്കുന്നില്ല എന്ന് ഇടക്കിടക്ക് സങ്കടം പറയുന്ന മുതലാളിയുടെ റൂമിലേക്ക് കടന്നപ്പോൾ ഭാര്യയെ ഒറ്റക്കാലിൽ നിർത്തി കളിക്കുന്നത് കണ്ട വേലക്കാരി* നിർത്തിയങ്ങു അടിക്കുവായിരുന്നല്ലേ...	When she entered the boss's room, who often complained that nothing was going on as a wife, the maid stopped and saw her playing on one leg.	Misogyny
		ഐഡിയ 4G ഹമ്പിൽ - മലയാളം വീടിന്റെ മുറ്റത്ത് 2G വിടിന്റെ ഹാളിൽ എന്റെ റൂമിൽ	Idea 4G Humpil - Malayalam In the yard of the house 2G in the hall of the house in my room	Not Misogyny
Tamil		~மாமியார் சமைக்க தெரியுமா? புதுமருமகள் தெரியுமாவா அடுப்ப பத்தவச்சு சுடுதண்ணிய காயவச்சு மேகி பக்கெட்ட கொட்டி அப்டியே கரண்டிய வச்சு அலசுவம்	~ Does mother-in-law know how to cook? Do you know, newlyweds that the stove is heated, the water is heated, the water is dry, the bucket is poured, and the spoon is cleaned?	Misogyny
		ஈட எரிச்சாலும் திரும்ப திரும்ப எழுந்து வர phoenix bird எங்க SILUKKU DOT COM முட்டை போட்டதுக்கே குண்டி வலிக்குதுனுபுலம்புற நீ எங்க	Get up again and again with irritation phoenix bird where sila silukku dot com Where are you after laying the eggs and the pain in the stomach?	Not Misogyny

Table 1: Sample Malayalam and Tamil memes (image and text data) with corresponding labels

Tamil		
Label	**Train set**	**Dev set**
Misogyny	**274**	**76**
Not Misogyny	**863**	**209**
Malayalam		
Misogyny	**256**	**64**
Not Misogyny	**384**	**96**

Table 2: Class-wise distribution of memes in Tamil and Malayalam datasets

involved in the methodology are explained below:

3.1 Pre-processing

Pre-processing is a crucial step that cleans the data and prepares it for further processing. Usually, images will be of varying sizes as they will be collected from different sources and hence they are resized to a standard size. Further, images not in RGB format are converted to RGB format. Punctuation, digits, urls, and hashtags are considered as noise and hence are removed from the textual component. English stopwords (memes may also include English words), available at NLTK[1] library and Tamil stopwords from a GitHub[2] repository are utilized as references for removing English and Tamil stopwords from Tamil dataset respectively and only English stopwords are removed from Malayalam datasets.

3.2 Construction of Learning Models

In DL, feature extraction and classifier construction go hand-in-hand. As memes contain image and embedded text, a joint representation of integrating image and text features is used in this work. The image and text encoders used to represent image and text respectively are described below:

- **Text Representation** - Transformer models have emerged as promising pre-trained models for extracting features from text due to their ability to capture intricate contextual relationships between words in the given input sequence. Their self-attention mechanisms enable a comprehensive understanding of word dependencies, allowing for the creation of context-rich embeddings that enhance the performance of many downstream natural language processing tasks. In this work, BERT[3] (Devlin et al., 2018), MuRIL[4] (Khanuja et al., 2021), and mBERT[5] (Devlin et al., 2018), are used to represent text as three different models. BERT is pre-trained on a large amount of English text in a self-supervised fashion

[1]https://pythonspot.com/nltk-stop-words

[2]https://gist.github.com/arulrajnet/e82a5a331f78a5cc9b6d372df13a919c

[3]https://huggingface.co/bert-base-uncased

[4]https://huggingface.co/google/muril-base-cased

[5]https://huggingface.co/bert-base-multilingual-cased

Language	Tamil					
Model	Dev set			Test set		
	Precision	Recall	F1 score	Precision	Recall	F1 score
BERT+ResNet-50	0.72	0.70	0.71	0.68	0.65	0.66
MuRIL+ResNet-50	0.77	0.72	0.74	0.75	0.64	0.66
mBERT+ResNet-50	0.75	0.72	0.73	0.77	0.72	**0.73**
Language	**Malayalam**					
BERT+ResNet-50	0.82	0.80	0.81	0.82	0.83	0.82
MuRIL+ResNet-50	0.86	0.80	0.81	0.90	0.87	**0.87**
mBERT+ResNet-50	0.77	0.75	0.76	0.85	0.84	0.84

Table 3: Performances of the proposed models for identifying misogynistic memes in Tamil and Malayalam datasets

using a Masked Language Modeling (MLM) objective whereas MuRIL and mBERT are multilingual pre-trained models which support Tamil and Malayalam lamguages. While MuRIL supports 17 Indian languages in their native and transliterated scripts, mBERT supports 104 languages in their native script. BERT is used as the given Tamil and Malayalam datasets contain English texts along with Tamil and Malayalam text in their native script.

- **Image Representation** - ResNet-50[6] (He et al., 2016) - a CNN with 48 Convolution layers along with 1 Max Pool and 1 Average Pool layer and a fully connected layer, is a variant of ResNet which is pre-trained on ImageNet (Deng et al., 2009) dataset at a resolution of 224x224. ReseNet-50 is used as image encoder to obtain the image features.

Dual-encoder architecture which is based on joint representation approach is used to concatenate image and text encoders and the joint encodings are passed through linear layers to build the classifier model for identifying misogynistic memes in Tamil and Malayalam.

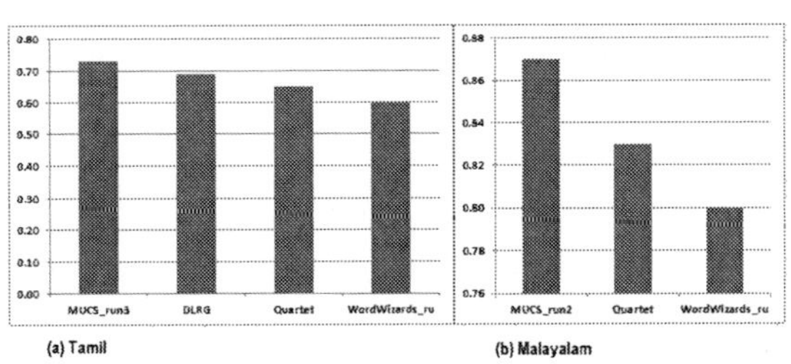

Figure 1: Comparison of macro F1 scores of the participating teams in the shared task

[6] https://iq.opengenus.org/resnet50-architecture/

4 Experiments and Results

Tamil and Malayalam memes datasets provided by the organizers of the shared task are labeled as 'Misogyny' and 'Not Misogyny' memes, for the task of binary classification (Chakravarthi et al., 2024). The sample memes with their corresponding labels and class-wise distribution of Tamil and Malayalam memes datasets are shown in Tables 1 and 2 respectively. Table 3 shows the performances of the proposed models. Among the proposed models, mBERT+ResNet-50 and MuRIL+ResNet-50 models obtained better macro F1 scores of 0.73 and 0.87 for Tamil and Malayalam datasets respectively, securing 1st rank for both the datasets in the shared task. Figure 1 gives a comparison of macro F1 scores of all the participating teams in the shared task.

4.1 Error Analysis

Few misclassified memes along with the actual and predicted labels obtained from mBERT+ResNet-50 and MuRIL+ResNet-50 for Tamil and Malayalam datasets respectively, are shown in Table 4. Misclassifications are due to the limitations of image and text encoders. Text encoders may fail to capture the domain specific meaning of the ambiguous words. Further, there are a few content words or phrases that are often used in the context of one polarity; however, the ground truth of the Test data with same words or phrases has a different polarity. For example, during training, the words or phrases 'quick', 'show', and 'in front of' are often used in the context of 'Misogyny' and the ground truth of this transcription is 'Not Misogyny'. From the image point of view, features that affect the identification of misogynistic memes include noise in the image, image quality, size of the training image dataset, and architecture of the image encoder.

Language	Tamil		Malayalam	
Meme				
Transcription	South Indian Aunties during சண்டை & குழாயடி சண்டை நீஎவன் கூட எல்லாம் தொடர்பு வச்சிருக்கனு எனக்கு தெரியும்டி தெரு	அவ என்னை ஏமாத்துனத கூட மன்னிச்சிடுவேன் டா ஆனா? அவ புள்ளய விட்டு என்னை மாமாயன்னு கூப்பிட வச்சா பாரு ~ மறக்கவே முடியல dude	ബ്ലൗസും പാവാടയുമുടുത്തു ള്ള സിൻ കാണുമ്പോൾ	പെട്ടെന്ന് ദേഷ്യപെടുന്നവർ, എത്ര വലിയ കലിപ്പ് കാണിച്ചാലും ആ കലിപ്പ് അവർ ഇഷ്ടപ്പെടുന്നവരുടെ മുന്നിൽ മാത്രമായിരിക്കും കാണിക്കുള്ളു!
English Translation	South Indian Aunties during fight & Pipe fight I know that even you are connected to the street	Even if she cheated on me, I will forgive her. She left the room and called me Mamayan ~ never forget dude	Seeing Sin in a blouse and skirt	People who are quick to anger, no matter how much anger they show, that anger is only shown in front of those they love!
Actual Label	Misogyny	Not Misogyny	Misogyny	Not Misogyny
Predicted Label	Not Misogyny	Misogyny	Not Misogyny	Misogyny

Table 4: Few misclassified Tamil and Malayalam memes with actual and predicted labels

Added to this is the imbalance nature of the given datasets where both Tamil and Malayalam datasets contain less number of 'Misogyny' memes.

5 Conclusion and Future Work

This paper describes, three models: i) BERT+ResNet-50, ii) MuRIL+ResNet-50, and iii) mBERT+ResNet-50, based on joint representation of text and image features, for detecting misogynistic memes in Tamil and Malayalam datasets, submitted by our team - MUCS to "Multitask Meme classification - Unraveling Misogynistic and Trolls in Online Memes: LT-EDI@EACL 2024" shared task. Among the proposed models, mBERT+ResNet-50 and MuRIL+ResNet-50 models obtained macro F1 scores of 0.73 and 0.87 for Tamil and Malayalam datasets respectively, securing 1st rank for both the datasets in the shared task. More efficient joint representations that improve the performance of the learning models will be explored further.

References

Bharathi Raja Chakravarthi, Saranya Rajiakodi, Rahul Ponnusamy, Kathiravan Pannerselvam, Anand Kumar Madasamy, Ramachandran Rajalakshimi, Hariharan RamakrishnaIyer LekshmiAmmal, Anshid Kizhakkeparambil, Susminu S Kumar, Bhuvaneswari Sivagnanam, and Charmathi Rajkumar. 2024. Overview of Shared Task on Multitask Meme Classification - Unraveling Misogynistic and Trolls in Online Memes. In *Proceedings of the Fourth Workshop on Language Technology for Equality, Diversity and Inclusion*, Malta. European Chapter of the Association for Computational Linguistics.

Jia Deng, Wei Dong, Richard Socher, Li-Jia Li, Kai Li, and Li Fei-Fei. 2009. Imagenet: A large-scale hierarchical image database. In *2009 IEEE Conference on Computer Vision and Pattern Recognition*, pages 248–255.

Jacob Devlin, Ming-Wei Chang, Kenton Lee, and Kristina Toutanova. 2018. BERT: pre-training of deep bidirectional transformers for language understanding. In *CoRR*, volume abs/1810.04805.

Qin Gu, Nino Meisinger, and Anna-Katharina Dick. 2022. QiNiAn at SemEval-2022 Task 5: Multi-Modal Misogyny Detection and Classification. In *Proceedings of the 16th International Workshop on Semantic Evaluation (SemEval-2022)*, pages 736–741.

Ella Guest, Bertie Vidgen, Alexandros Mittos, Nishanth Sastry, Gareth Tyson, and Helen Margetts. 2021. An Expert Annotated Dataset for the Detection of Online Misogyny. In *Proceedings of the 16th Conference of the European Chapter of the Association for Com-*

putational Linguistics: Main Volume, pages 1336–1350.

Kaiming He, Xiangyu Zhang, Shaoqing Ren, and Jian Sun. 2016. Deep Residual Learning for Image Recognition. In *Proceedings of the IEEE conference on computer vision and pattern recognition*, pages 770–778.

Asha Hegde, Mudoor Devadas Anusha, Sharal Coelho, and Hosahalli Lakshmaiah Shashirekha. 2021. Mum at comma@ icon: Multilingual gender biased and communal language identification using supervised learning approaches. In *Proceedings of the 18th International Conference on Natural Language Processing: Shared Task on Multilingual Gender Biased and Communal Language Identification*, pages 64–69.

Simran Khanuja, Diksha Bansal, Sarvesh Mehtani, Savya Khosla, Atreyee Dey, Balaji Gopalan, Dilip Kumar Margam, Pooja Aggarwal, Rajiv Teja Nagipogu, Shachi Dave, Shruti Gupta, Subhash Chandra Bose Gali, Vish Subramanian, and Partha Talukdar. 2021. Muril: Multilingual representations for indian languages.

Paridhi Maheshwari and Sharmila Reddy Nangi. 2022. TeamOtter at SemEval-2022 Task 5: Detecting Misogynistic Content in Multimodal Memes. In *Proceedings of the 16th International Workshop on Semantic Evaluation (SemEval-2022)*, pages 642–647.

Arianna Muti, Katerina Korre, and Alberto Barrón-Cedeño. 2022. UniBO at SemEval-2022 Task 5: A Multimodal bi-Transformer Approach to the Binary and Fine-grained Identification of Misogyny in Memes. In *Proceedings of the 16th International Workshop on Semantic Evaluation (SemEval-2022)*, pages 663–672.

Tathagata Raha, Sagar Joshi, and Vasudeva Varma. 2022. IIITH at SemEval-2022 Task 5: A Comparative Study of Deep Learning Models for Identifying Misogynous Memes. In *Proceedings of the 16th International Workshop on Semantic Evaluation (SemEval-2022)*, pages 673–678.

Ailneni Rakshitha Rao and Arjun Rao. 2022. ASRtrans at SemEval-2022 Task 5: Transformer-based Models for Meme Classification. In *Proceedings of the 16th International Workshop on Semantic Evaluation (SemEval-2022)*, pages 597–604.

Benhur Sean and Sivanraju Kanchana. 2022. Transformers at SemEval-2022 Task 5: A Feature Extraction based Approach for Misogynous Meme Detection. In *Proceedings of the 16th International Workshop on Semantic Evaluation*, pages 550–554.

Shardul Suryawanshi, Bharathi Raja Chakravarthi, Mihael Arcan, and Paul Buitelaar. 2020. Multimodal Meme Dataset (MultiOFF) for Identifying Offensive Content in Image and Text. In *Proceedings of the second workshop on trolling, aggression and cyberbullying*, pages 32–41.

MUCS@LT-EDI-2024: Learning Approaches to Empower Homophobic/Transphobic Comment Identification

Sonali[a], Nethravathi Gidnakanala[b], Raksha G[c], Kavya G[d], Asha Hegde[e], H L Shashirekha[f]
Department of Computer Science, Mangalore University, Mangalore, Karnataka, India
{[a]sonalikulal417, [b]nethravathig749, [c]rakshagmangalore}@gmail.com, {[d]kavyamujk, [e]hegdekasha}@gmail.com, [f]hlsrekha@mangaloreuniversity.ac.in

Abstract

Homophobic/Transphobic (H/T) content includes hatred and discriminatory comments directed at Lesbian, Gay, Bisexual, Transgender, Queer (LGBTQ) individuals on social media platforms. As this unfavourable perception towards LGBTQ individuals may affect them physically and mentally, it is necessary to detect H/T content on social media. This demands automated tools to identify and address H/T content. In view of this, in this paper, we - team MUCS describe the learning models submitted to "Homophobia/Transphobia Detection in social media comments:LT-EDI@EACL 2024" shared task at European Chapter of the Association for Computational Linguistics (EACL) 2024. The learning models: i) Homo_Ensemble - an ensemble of Machine Learning (ML) algorithms trained with Term Frequency-Inverse Document Frequency (TF-IDF) of syllable n-grams in the range (1, 3), ii) Homo_TL - a model based on Transfer Learning (TL) approach with Bidirectional Encoder Representations from Transformers (BERT) models, iii) Homo_probfuse - an ensemble of ML classifiers with soft voting trained using sentence embeddings (except for Hindi), and iv) Homo_FSL - Few-Shot Learning (FSL) models using Sentence Transformer (ST) (only for Tulu), are proposed to detect H/T content in the given languages. Among the models submitted to the shared task, the models that performed better for each language include: i) Homo_Ensemble model obtained macro F1 score of 0.95 securing 4th rank for Telugu language, ii) Homo_TL model obtained macro F1 scores of 0.49, 0.53, 0.45, 0.94, and 0.95 securing 2nd, 2nd, 1st, 1st, and 4th ranks for English, Marathi, Hindi, Kannada, and Gujarathi languages, respectively, iii) Homo_probfuse model obtained macro F1 scores of 0.86, 0.87, and 0.53 securing 2nd, 6th, and 2nd ranks for Tamil, Malayalam, and Spanish languages respectively, and iv) Homo_FSL model obtained a macro F1 score of 0.62 securing 2nd rank for Tulu dataset.

1 Introduction

Homophobia and Transphobia are the two terms that refer to negative attitude towards the homosexual and transsexual people like LGBTQ. These attitudes are expressed in terms of H/T comments, insults, and discriminatory language on social media platforms (Chakravarthi, 2023; Hegde et al., 2023a). This unfavourable perceptions towards homosexual and transsexual people can have a very negative effect which can exacerbate mental health issues and give them a sense of helplessness and fear (Chakravarthi et al., 2022). Hence, there is a need to develop automated tools to detect H/T content to maintain healthy social media platforms.

In a multilingual country like India, people prefer to blend English words or sub-words with their native language creating code-mixed texts (Chakravarthi, 2023). The intricate nature of code-mixed text introduces additional complexities, where words or sub-words from different languages may be combined in different ways lacking grammatical rules, making it challenging to establish consistent patterns for classification. The H/T content available on social media may also be in code-mixed form (Hegde and Shashirekha, 2022b).

To address the challenges of H/T content detection in social media text, in this paper, we - team MUCS, describe the models submitted to "Homophobia/Transphobia Detection in social media comments:LT-EDI@EACL 2024" shared task[1] (Chakravarthi et al., 2024; Kumaresan et al., 2023). While the shared task is modeled as a multi-class text classification problem for H/T content detection in English, Hindi, Tamil, Telugu, Kannada, Gujarathi, Malayalam, Marathi, and Spanish languages, by employing ML and TL approaches, H/T content detection in Tulu is modeled as binary text classification problem using FSL approach.

The rest of the paper is structured as follows:

[1]https://codalab.lisn.upsaclay.fr/competitions/16056

Proceedings of the Fourth Workshop on Language Technology for Equality, Diversity, Inclusion, pages 288–293
March 21, 2024

Section 2 contains related works and Section 3 explains the methodology. Section 4 describes the experiments and results and the paper concludes in Section 5 with future work.

2 Related Work

Researchers have explored different approaches to detect H/T content on social media platforms. Description of few research works that are carried out to perform similar tasks are given below:
Ashraf et al. (2022) presented ML models (Support Vector Machine (SVM), Random Forest (RF), Passive Aggressive Classifier, Gaussian Naïve Bayes (GNB), Multi-Layer Perceptron) trained with TF-IDF of word bigrams, for H/T content detection in English, Tamil and Tamil-English. Out of their proposed models, SVM classifier outperformed the other classifiers with weighted F1 scores of 0.91, 0.92, and 0.88 for English, Tamil, and Tamil-English respectively. Singh and Motlicek (2022) fine-tuned Cross Lingual Language Models Robustly Optimised BERT (XLM-RoBERTa) model in the Zero-Shot learning framework for detecting H/T contents in English, Tamil, and Tamil-English texts. Their proposed methodology obtained weighted F1 scores of 0.92, 0.94, and 0.89 for English, Tamil, and Tamil-English languages respectively.

Pranith et al. (2022) presented TL based approach with two different BERT variants (IndicBERT and LaBSE (Language-Agnostic BERT Sentence Embedding)) for H/T content detection in English, Malayalam, Tamil-English, and Tamil languages. Their proposed LaBSE model obtained weighted F1 score of 0.46 for English language and IndicBERT model obtained weighted F1 scores of 0.54, 0.39, and 0.28 for Malayalam, Tamil-English, and Tamil languages respectively. Chanda et al. (2022) fine-tuned Multilingual BERT (mBERT) model for detecting sentiment and homophobia content in Malayalam and Kannada code-mixed texts and obtained macro F1 scores of 0.72 and 0.66 for Malayalam and Kannada code-mixed texts respectively. Nozza et al. (2022) fine-tuned different Large Language Models (LLMs) (BERT, RoBERTa, HateBERT) and ensemble modeling with majority voting to combine different fine-tuned LLMs. To handle the class imbalance they performed data augmentation by collecting external dataset to include more H/T instances for the detection of H/T content in English dataset. Their proposed ensemble model outperformed other models with a weighted F1 score of 0.94 for English dataset.

Though there are several models to identify H/T content in social media text, there is still scope for developing models for H/T content detection in low-resource languages like Tamil, Malayalam, Telugu, Tulu, etc., as these languages are not much explored in the realm of code-mixed content.

3 Methodology

The proposed methodology includes implementation of a wide range of learning models including ML, TL, and FSL approaches for identifying H/T content in the datasets provided by the organizers of the shared task. Pre-processing techniques are applied commonly to all the datasets. As the datasets are imbalanced, resampling techniques are used to balance the datasets in some of the learning models. Pre-processing and Resampling steps are explained below:

- **Pre-processing** - play an important role in text processing. Emojis are converted to the corresponding English text allowing them to be used as other text data followed by removing URLs, digits, and punctuation, as they do not contribute to text classification. Further, stopwords are removed using the corresponding references (English[2], Hindi[3], Tamil[4], Telugu[5], Kannada[6], Gujarathi[7], Marathi[8], and Spanish[9]).

- **Resampling** - When the number of instances in a labeled dataset for classification varies noticeably, the situation is referred to as data imbalance (Hegde et al., 2023b). This results in learning models becoming biased towards majority class, exhibiting poor performance for minority class. Resampling techniques are capable to resolve this biased training to

[2]https://www.nltk.org/search.html?q=stopwords

[3]https://github.com/stopwords-iso/stopwords-hi

[4]https://gist.github.com/arulrajnet e82a5a331f78a5cc9b6d372df13a919c

[5]https://github.com/Xangis/extra-stopwords/blob/master/telugu

[6]https://gist.github.com/MSDarshan91/ f97c73435a3ab32a6638436231bf5616

[7]https://github.com/stopwords-iso/stopwords-gu/blob/master/stopwords-gu.txt

[8]https://github.com/stopwords-iso/stopwords-mr/blob/master/stopwords-mr.txt

[9]https://github.com/Alir3z4/stop-words/blob/master/spanish.txt

Language	Train set			Development set		
	None	Homophobia	Transphobia	None	Homophobia	Transphobia
English	2,978	179	7	748	42	2
Hindi	2,423	45	92	305	2	13
Tamil	2,064	453	145	507	118	41
Telugu	3,496	2,907	2,647	747	588	605
Kannada	4,463	2,765	2,835	955	585	617
Gujarathi	3,848	2,267	2,004	788	498	454
Malayalam	2,468	476	170	937	197	79
Marathi	2,572	551	377	541	129	80
Spanish	700	250	250	200	93	93
Tulu	542	188	-	-	-	-

Table 1: Statistics of the datasets

Language	Dev set	Test set
English	0.39	0.37
Hindi	0.33	0.33
Tamil	0.90	0.82
Telugu	0.96	**0.95**
Kannada	0.93	0.93
Gujarathi	0.95	0.99
Malayalam	0.93	0.94
Marathi	0.49	0.51
Spanish	0.78	0.51

Table 2: Performances of proposed Homo_Ensemble model in terms of macro F1 score

Language	Dev set	Test set
English	0.41	0.42
Tamil	0.85	**0.86**
Telugu	0.93	0.93
Kannada	0.32	0.54
Gujarathi	0.95	0.95
Malayalam	0.85	**0.87**
Marathi	0.54	0.52
Spanish	0.74	0.53

Table 3: Performances of the proposed Homo_probfuse model based on macro F1 score

some extent. Oversampling is a resampling technique that duplicates the samples belonging to the minority class and adds them to the Train set until it gets balanced. In this study, oversampling technique is used to balance English, Hindi, Tamil, Malayalam, Marathi, and Spanish datasets.

The description of the proposed learning models to identify H/T content in English, Hindi, Tamil, Telugu, Kannada, Gujarathi, Malayalam, Marathi, Spanish, and Tulu languages is given below:

3.1 Homo_Ensemble model

The proposed Homo_Ensemble model comprises of two modules: Feature Extraction and Classifier Construction as explained below:

3.1.1 Feature Extraction

Feature extraction is the process of extracting distinguishable features that can be used to train the learning models. Syllable representation provides meaningful tokens for Indian languages in native scripts. The given datasets (except English dataset) are syllabalized using IndicNLP[10] library. n-grams are a sequence of 'n' consecutive units, where the units can be characters, syllables or words. Syllable sequences in the range (1, 3) obtained from the given text are vectorized using TFIDFVectorizer[11] and the resultant feature vectors are used to train the classifiers.

3.1.2 Classifier Construction

Ensembling classifiers offers a potent method for overcoming individual classifier shortcomings by utilizing the strengths of other classifiers with the aim of improving the performance of a group of classifiers. This work ensembles ML classifiers (DT, SVM, NB, and Linear Support Vector Classifier (LSVC)) with hard voting.

3.2 Learning Models using Transformers

The proposed strategy of using transformers for classification is described below:

[10] https://indicnlp.ai4bharat.org/pages/home/

[11] https://scikit-learn.org/stable/modules/generated/sklearn.feature_extraction.text.TfidfVectorizer.html

3.2.1 Homo_TL model

TL approach involves utilizing knowledge acquired from one task to improve the performance of other but similar task. Instead of training a model from scratch for a new task, TL model leverages the knowledge using pre-trained models (Hegde and Shashirekha, 2022a). In this work, different BERT variants: Multilingual Bidirectional Encoder Representations from Transformers (mBERT)[12] (Devlin et al., 2018) (Hindi, Tamil, Malayalam, Marathi), gujarathi_sbert[13] (Deode et al., 2023; Joshi et al., 2022) (Gujarathi), KannadaSBERT-STS (kannada_sbert)[14] (Deode et al., 2023; Joshi et al., 2022) (Kannada), BERT[15] (Devlin et al., 2018) (English), Spanish BERT[16] (Cañete et al., 2020) (Spanish), and Homophobia_mBERT[17] (Telugu), are fine-tuned on the given Train sets. As the given Train sets are imbalanced, oversampling technique is used to balance the Train sets of English, Hindi, Tamil, Malayalam, Marathi, and Spanish language, before they are used to fine-tune for the intended task.

3.2.2 Homo_probfuse model

Soft voting is a type of ensemble method that involves assigning a probability score to each class for each model during ensembling. The final prediction is then determined by considering the probabilities of all the models. In this work, SVM and RF classifiers are trained using two Sentence Transformers (ST): mXLMR[18] (Reimers and Gurevych, 2019) and IndicSBERT-STS (indic_sbert)[19] (Deode et al., 2023)respectively, for the all datasets except Spanish, Hindi and Tulu languages. For Spanish language, Spanish BERT[20] and mXLMR are used to train SVM and RF classifiers respectively. The predictions of these classifiers are combined based on the maximum probability values. Additionally, the provided Train sets are oversampled before being trained on SVM and RF classifiers.

[12]https://huggingface.co/bert-base-multilingual-cased

[13]l3cube-pune/gujarati-sentence-similarity-sbert

[14]l3cube-pune/kannada-sentence-similarity-sbert

[15]https://huggingface.co/bert-base-uncased

[16]https://huggingface.co/mrm8488/distill-bert-base-spanish-wwm-cased-finetuned-spa-squad2-es

[17]https://huggingface.co/bitsanlp/Homophobia-Transphobia-v2-mBERT-EDA

[18]https://huggingface.co/sentence-transformers/stsb-xlm- r-multilingual

[19]l3cube-pune/indic-sentence-similarity-sbert

[20]https://huggingface.co/mrm8488/distill-bert-base-spanish-wwm-cased-finetuned-spa-squad2-es

Model	Precision	Recall	Macro F1 score
ST_indic	0.61	0.68	0.61
ST_kan	0.62	0.70	**0.62**

Table 4: Performances of the proposed Homo_FSL models for Tulu Language

3.3 Homo_FSL model

ST framework of Python creates contextualised sentence embeddings for the given sentences. Few-shot and zero-shot approaches have received a great deal of interest in the research community due to the availability of ST and their untapped capacity to use them in resource-constrained domains (Girish et al., 2023). In view of this, Homo_FSL models are implemented to detect H/T content in Tulu text using two distinct ST models: indic_sbert and kannada_sbert for extracting sentence embeddings. The sentences in the given text are represented as sentence embeddings using the ST model and the mean embeddings of the sentence embeddings of a given text are obtained to train the ensemble of ML classifiers (LR, BernoulliNB (BNB), SVC, and RF) with hard voting.

4 Experiments and Results

Statistics of the dataset provided by the organizers (Chakravarthi et al., 2022, 2024, 2023) of the shared task for the detection of H/T contents in social media text for English, Hindi, Tamil, Telugu, Kannada, Gujarathi, Malayalam, Marathi, and Spanish are shown in Table 1. From Table 1, it is clear that the datasets provided are highly imbalanced. To overcome this, Homo_TL and Homo_probfuse models are experimented using resampled data by using oversampling method provided by the sklearn library[21]. Performances of the proposed Homo_Ensemble, Homo_probfuse, and Homo_FSL models are shown in the Tables 2, 3, and 4 respectively. Performances of Homo_TL model before and after oversampling are shown in the Table 5.

5 Conclusion and Future Work

This paper describes the models submitted by our team - MUCS, to the shared task "Homophobia/Transphobia Detection in social media comments: LT-EDI@EACL 2024" shared task at EACL 2024. Four distinct models: i) Homo_Ensemble

[21]https://scikit-learn.org/stable/modules/generated/sklearn.utils.resample.html

Language	Development set		Test set	
	Before Oversampling	After Oversampling	Before Oversampling	After Oversampling
English	0.32	0.45	0.32	**0.49**
Hindi	0.33	0.41	0.33	**0.45**
Tamil	0.29	0.79	0.29	0.83
Telugu	0.95	-	0.95	-
Kannada	0.96	-	**0.94**	-
Gujarathi	0.96	-	**0.95**	-
Malayalam	0.49	0.89	0.49	0.91
Marathi	0.20	0.42	0.19	**0.53**
Spanish	0.82	0.43	0.49	0.42

Table 5: Performances of the proposed Homo_TL models before and after Oversampling

ii) Homo_TL and iii) Homo_probfuse are implemented to identify H/T content in all the given languages except Hindi and Tulu, and iv) Homo_FSL model is implemented only for Tulu dataset.

Among the models submitted to the shared task, only the models that performed better for each language are reported. Homo_Ensemble model obtained macro F1 score of 0.95 securing 4th rank for Telugu, Homo_TL model obtained macro F1 scores of 0.49, 0.53, 0.45, 0.94, and 0.95 securing 2nd, 2nd, 1st, 1st, and 4th ranks for English, Marathi, Hindi, Kannada and Gujarathi languages respectively and proposed Homo_probfuse model obtained macro F1 scores of 0.86, 0.87, and 0.53 securing 2nd, 6th, and 2nd ranks for Tamil, Malayalam, and Spanish languages respectively. Homo_FSL model trained using kannada_sbert obtained macro F1 score of 0.62 securing 2nd rank in the shared task for Tulu language. In the future, data augmentation methods for managing unbalanced classes using efficient feature extraction methods will be explored.

References

Nsrin Ashraf, Mohamed Taha, Ahmed Abd Elfattah, and Hamada Nayel. 2022. NAYEL @LT-EDI-ACL2022: Homophobia/Transphobia Detection for Equality, Diversity, and Inclusion using SVM. In *Proceedings of the Second Workshop on Language Technology for Equality, Diversity and Inclusion*, pages 287–290.

José Cañete, Gabriel Chaperon, Rodrigo Fuentes, Jou-Hui Ho, Hojin Kang, and Jorge Pérez. 2020. Spanish Pre-Trained BERT Model and Evaluation Data. In *PML4DC at ICLR 2020*.

Bharathi Raja Chakravarthi. 2023. Detection of Homophobia and Transphobia in YouTube Comments. In *International Journal of Data Science and Analytics*, pages 1–20. Springer.

Bharathi Raja Chakravarthi, Adeep Hande, Rahul Ponnusamy, Prasanna Kumar Kumaresan, and Ruba Priyadharshini. 2022. How can we Detect Homophobia and Transphobia? Experiments in a Multilingual Code-mixed Setting for Social Media Governance. In *International Journal of Information Management Data Insights*, volume 2, page 100119. Elsevier.

Bharathi Raja Chakravarthi, Prasanna Kumar Kumaresan, Ruba Priyadharshini, Paul Buitelaar, Asha Hegde, Hosahalli Lakshmaiah Shashirekha, Saranya Rajiakodi, Miguel Ángel García-Cumbreras, Salud María Jiménez-Zafra, José Antonio García-Díaz, Rafael Valencia-García, Kishore Kumar Ponnusamy, Poorvi Shetty, and Daniel García-Baena. 2024. Overview of Third Shared Task on Homophobia and Transphobia Detection in Social Media Comments. In *Proceedings of the Fourth Workshop on Language Technology for Equality, Diversity and Inclusion*, Malta. European Chapter of the Association for Computational Linguistics.

Bharathi Raja Chakravarthi, Rahul Ponnusamy, Malliga Subramanian, Paul Buitelaar, Miguel Ángel García-Cumbreras, Salud María Jiménez-Zafra, José Antonio García-Díaz, Rafael Valencia-García, and Nitesh Jindal. 2023. Overview of Second Shared Task on Homophobia and Transphobia Detection in English, Spanish, Hindi, Tamil, and Malayalam. In *Proceedings of the Third Workshop on Language Technology for Equality, Diversity and Inclusion*, Varna, Bulgaria. Recent Advances in Natural Language Processing.

Supriya Chanda, Anshika Mishra, and Sukomal Pal. 2022. Sentiment Analysis and Homophobia Detection of Code-Mixed Dravidian Languages Leveraging Pre-trained Model and Word-level Language Tag. In *Working Notes of FIRE 2022-Forum for Information Retrieval Evaluation (Hybrid). CEUR*.

Samruddhi Deode, Janhavi Gadre, Aditi Kajale, Ananya Joshi, and Raviraj Joshi. 2023. L3Cube-IndicSBERT: A Simple Approach for Learning Cross-Lingual Sentence Representations using Multilingual BERT. In *arXiv preprint arXiv:2304.11434*.

Jacob Devlin, Ming-Wei Chang, Kenton Lee, and Kristina Toutanova. 2018. BERT: Pre-training of Deep Bidirectional Transformers for Language Understanding. In *CoRR*, volume abs/1810.04805.

Kavya Girish, A Hegdev, Fazlourrahman Balouchzahi, and SH Lakshmaiah. 2023. Profiling Cryptocurrency Influencers with Sentence Transformers. In *Working Notes of CLEF*.

Asha Hegde, G Kavya, Sharal Coelho, and Hosahalli Lakshmaiah Shashirekha. 2023a. MUCS@ LT-EDI2023: Homophobic/Transphobic Content Detection in Social Media Text using mBERT. In *Proceedings of the Third Workshop on Language Technology for Equality, Diversity and Inclusion*, pages 287–294.

Asha Hegde, G Kavya, Sharal Coelho, and Hosahalli Lakshmaiah Shashirekha. 2023b. MUCS@ LT-EDI2023: Homophobic/Transphobic Content Detection in Social Media Text using mBERT. In *Proceedings of the Third Workshop on Language Technology for Equality, Diversity and Inclusion*, pages 287–294.

Asha Hegde and Hosahalli Lakshmaiah Shashirekha. 2022a. Learning Models for Emotion Analysis and Threatening Language Detection in Urdu Tweets.

Asha Hegde and Hosahalli Lakshmaiah Shashirekha. 2022b. Leveraging Dynamic Meta Embedding for Sentiment Analysis and Detection of Homophobic. In *Transphobic Content in Code-mixed Dravidian Languages*.

Ananya Joshi, Aditi Kajale, Janhavi Gadre, Samruddhi Deode, and Raviraj Joshi. 2022. L3Cube-MahaSBERT and HindSBERT: Sentence BERT Models and Benchmarking BERT Sentence Representations for Hindi and Marathi. In *arXiv preprint arXiv:2211.11187*.

Prasanna Kumar Kumaresan, Rahul Ponnusamy, Ruba Priyadharshini, Paul Buitelaar, and Bharathi Raja Chakravarthi. 2023. Homophobia and Transphobia Detection for Low-resourced Languages in Social Media Comments. In *Natural Language Processing Journal*, page 100041. Elsevier.

Debora Nozza et al. 2022. Nozza@ LT-EDI-ACL2022: Ensemble Modeling for Homophobia and Transphobia Detection. In *Proceedings of the Second Workshop on Language Technology for Equality, Diversity and Inclusion*. Association for Computational Linguistics.

P Pranith, V Samhita, D Sarath, and Durairaj Thenmozhi. 2022. Homophobia and Transphobia Detection of YouTube Comments in Code-Mixed Dravidian Languages using Deep learning.

Nils Reimers and Iryna Gurevych. 2019. Sentence-BERT: Sentence Embeddings using Siamese BERT-Networks. In *Proceedings of the 2019 Conference on Empirical Methods in Natural Language Processing*. Association for Computational Linguistics.

Muskaan Singh and Petr Motlicek. 2022. IDIAP Submission@ LT-EDI-ACL2022: Homophobia/Transphobia Detection in Social Media Comments. In *Proceedings of the Second Workshop on Language Technology for Equality, Diversity and Inclusion*, pages 356–361.

ASR_TAMIL_SSN@ LT-EDI-2024: Automatic Speech Recognition system for Elderly People

S. Suhasini
Department of CSE
R. M. D. Engineering College
ssi.cse@rmd.ac.in

B. Bharathi
Department of CSE
Sri Sivasubramaniya Nadar College of Engineering
bharathib@ssn.edu.in

Abstract

The results of the Shared Task on Speech Recognition for Vulnerable Individuals in Tamil (LT-EDI-2024) are discussed in this paper. The goal is to create an automated system for Tamil voice recognition. The older population that speaks Tamil is the source of the dataset used in this task. The proposed ASR system is designed with pre-trained model akashsivanandan/wav2vec2-large-xls-r-300m-tamil-colab-final. The Tamil common speech dataset is utilized to fine-tune the pre-trained model that powers our system. The suggested system receives the test data that was released from the task; transcriptions are then created for the test samples and delivered to the task. Word Error Rate (WER) is the evaluation statistic used to assess the provided result based on the task. Our Proposed system attained a WER of 29.297%.

1 Introduction

This shared task tackles a difficult area in Tamil automatic speech recognition system for vulnerable elderly and transgender individuals. To take care of their daily necessities, elderly people go to important places including banks, hospitals, and administrative offices. Many elderly folks are not aware of how to use the tools provided to help people. Similar to how transgender persons lack access to basic schooling due to societal discrimination, speech is the only channel that can help them meet their demands. The data on spontaneous speech is collected from elderly and transgender people who are unable to take benefit of these amenities (Fukuda et al., 2019; Hämäläinen et al., 2015). 2 hours of speech data will be made available for testing, while the speech corpus containing 5.5 hours of transcribed speech will be made available for the training set. Recently, the majority of people have begun using various electronic devices to access the internet. In this situation, the elderly people have also started using smart phones to access the internet (Vacher et al., 2015). Some elderly people attempt to acquire information from the internet using their audio message because they are not well-versed in technology. An acoustic model must be created to handle these types of audio messages from elderly individuals; the model will identify their speech and extract the output of the speech data. As a result, a text file will be the output. The speech's output will be used to determine the WER value. The WER number demonstrates how accurately the model predicted the outcome . No other corpus for elderly people is larger than the Japanese Newspaper Article Sentences (JNAS), Japanese Newspaper Article Sentences Read Speech Corpus of the Aged (S-JNAS), and Corpus of Spontaneous Japanese (CSJ) corpora (Fukuda et al., 2020). It has been determined that Automatic Speech Recognition using some standard models has not achieved a good performance (Nakajima and Aono, 2020). It is challenging to identify conversational speech in public settings since each person may have their own accent and pronunciation. Additionally, the methodology for identifying standard speech cannot be applied to the conversational speech corpus because it raises WER. A transformer model technique is utilised to treat this type of older people's conversational speech. The paper is organised as follows: Section 2 discusses the examination of related literature, Section 3 describes the data set, Section 4 discusses the methodology, Section 5 describes the implementation, Section 6 describes the observations, and Section 7 discusses the discussion. Section 8 of the essay concludes with a section on future research.

Proceedings of the Fourth Workshop on Language Technology for Equality, Diversity, Inclusion, pages 294–298
March 21, 2024

2 Related Work

There have been numerous studies on recognising the speech of elderly persons using the adaption acoustic model for CSJ corpus (Fukuda et al., 2020), which yields the lowest WER values. The performance of continuous word identification and phoneme recognition is measured from the two distinct age groups, and the corpus is collected in Bengali (Das et al., 2011). Prosodic and spectral properties are retrieved for senior people speech.The exploration of additional features (Lin and Yu, 2015), such as the speech's volume level, sampling frequency, fundamental frequency, and sentence segmentation, is also possible. Other measurements were locating the pause in the sentence and calculating how long it lasted (Nakajima and Aono, 2020). Low number of utterances is a sign of inadequate performance. If the recorded voice quality is poor (Iribe et al., 2015), the WER value rises. By integrating the transformers for a broad context (Masumura et al., 2021), the E2E ASR transformer can perform encoding and decoding in a hierarchical manner. The WER is decreased by 25.4% via transfer learning when using the hybrid-based LSTM transformer (Zeng et al., 2021). Additionally, the LSTM decoder lowers WER by 13%. Self-attention and a multi-head attention layer (Lee et al., 2021) can be used to carry out the encoding and decoding of transformer models. The transformer model is utilised for CTC/Attention based End-To-End ASR, and it produces a WER of 23.66% (Miao et al., 2020). Transformers for streaming ASR are the foundation of the end-to-end ASR system, where an output must be produced quickly after each spoken word. Time-restricted self-attention is employed for the encoder, and prompted attention is used for the encoder-decoder attention mechanism. The innovative fusion attention technique results in a WER reduction of 16.7% on the Wall Street Journal test compared to the non-fusion standard transformer and 12.1% compared to other authors' transformer-based benchmarks. Findings of the automatic speech recognition for vulnerable individuals are given in (S and B, 2022) (B et al., 2022), have used transformer models used for transformer based ASR for Vulnerable Individuals in Tamil.

3 Dataset Description

Tamil conversational speech data is collected from the elderly people. The speech corpus contains a total of 6 hours and 42 minutes of speech data (Bharathi et al., 2022). The recorded speech of elderly people contains how the elderly people communicate in primary locations like market, bank, shop, public transport and hospitals. It includes both male and female utterances and also this speech data is collected from the transgender people. Table 1. contains the detailed description about the collected data.

Gender	Avg-Age	Duration(mins)
Male	61	93
Female	59	242
Transgender	30	67

Table 1: Dataset Details

The below Figure 1. shows the sample prediction for the given corpus.

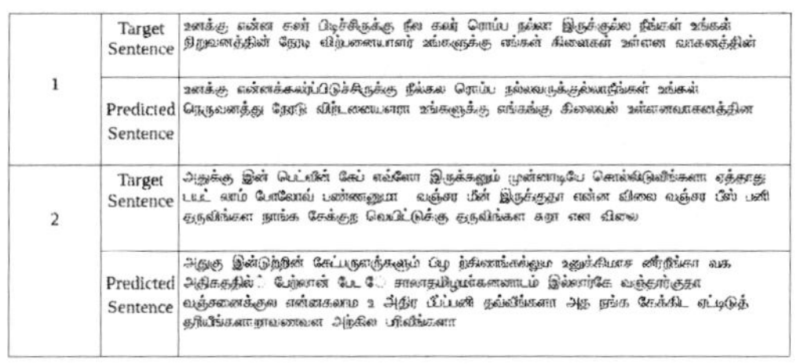

Figure 1: Sample Prediction

4 Proposed Work

In our proposed system, the pretrained transformer model akashsivanandan/wav2vec2-large-xls-r-300m-tamil-colab-final[1] is used. The pretrained model "https://huggingface.co/akashsivanandan/wav2vec2-large-xls-r-300m-tamil-colab-final" is based on the Wav2Vec2 architecture and specifically trained for the Tamil language. Wav2Vec2[2] is a state-of-the-art speech recognition model developed by Facebook AI. It utilizes a self-supervised learning approach, where it learns from large amounts of unlabeled speech data to build representations that capture meaningful information about the audio. The model is based on the transformer architecture, which has proven to be highly effective for various natural language processing tasks. Transformers

[1] https://huggingface.co/akashsivanandan/wav2vec2-large-xls-r-300m-tamil-colab-final

[2] https://huggingface.co/docs/transformers/model_doc/wav2vec2

enable the model to efficiently capture long-range dependencies in the audio input. The model is pretrained on a large corpus of multilingual and monolingual data containing Tamil speech. During pretraining, it learns to predict masked or distorted portions of the input audio, which helps it understand the underlying structure and features of the speech data. After pretraining, the model undergoes fine-tuning using labeled data for specific downstream tasks. Fine-tuning allows the model to adapt to a particular speech recognition task, such as transcription or keyword spotting, in this case, for Tamil language. Although the model is specifically trained for Tamil, it benefits from the multilingual nature of its pretraining data. It can understand and process speech from various languages, making it useful for multilingual applications or tasks involving code-switching. The model has been trained on a vast vocabulary, enabling it to handle a wide range of words and phrases. This makes it suitable for tasks that involve transcribing or recognizing speech with diverse vocabulary. The model's training data and fine-tuning procedure focus on capturing the unique characteristics of the Tamil language, including its phonetics, phonology, and syntax. This enhances its ability to accurately recognize and transcribe Tamil speech.

5 Implementation

Efficient acoustic model can be created based on a pre-trained transformer model as there are many publicly accessible transformer-based pre-trained models. Here, the "https://huggingface.co/akashsivanandan/wav2vec2-large-xls-r-300m-tamil-colab-final" pretrained model for handling Tamil speech corpus is used. This pretrained model is fine-tuned from "facebook/wav2vec2-large-xlsr-53" [3] by common voice dataset in Tamil. The model can be used directly and only accepts input if the voice data is sampled at 16 KHz. It is independent of any language model. The model for creating the wav2vec uses the XSLR (Cross-Lingual Speech Representation), which additionally tests cross-lingual speech data. The quantization of latents, which is common to all languages, can be learned by XLSR. The voice utterance is loaded into the library, saved in a variable, and tokenized using the tokenizer. This process converts the audio to text, and the results are transcripts of the audio file that is loaded into the library. The transcripts are kept in a separate folder after the voice recognition process is complete. Between the transcripts produced by the model and the actual transcripts of the audio written by humans, the WER (Word Error Rate) is determined. The degree of voice recognition can be calculated using the WER value.

[3]https://huggingface.co/facebook/wav2vec2-large-xlsr-53

6 Evaluation of Results

The evaluation metric used by the task to test the results submitted by us is based on the WER computed between the ASR hypotheses submitted by the participants and the ground truth of human speech transcription.

WER (Word Error Rate) = (S + D + I) / N

where,
S = No. of substitutions
D = No. of deletions
I = No. of insertions
N = No. of words in the reference transcription

Word Error Rate (WER) is a commonly used metric in Automatic Speech Recognition (ASR) systems because it provides a straightforward and intuitive measure of the performance of the system. WER is calculated by comparing the recognized words from the ASR system to the reference (ground truth) transcription and counting the number of errors, including substitutions, insertions, and deletions.

7 Observation

The name of the speech data and its WER value are included in the result. Similar to this, the same procedure is used for all audio files. The number of subgroups into which each audio file is divided is also listed in the table. The test set audio files' average WER value, which comprises utterances from men, women, and transgender people, is determined in Table 2.

S.No.	Gender	Count	Avg WER
1	Male	1	33.091
2	Female	2	43.054
3	Transgender	7	40.331

Table 2: Average WER Value for Test Data

S.No.	File Name	Subsets	WER Value
1	Audio-37	15	39.227
2	Audio-38	17	37.872
3	Audio-39	16	46.916
4	Audio-40	17	43.915
5	Audio-41	19	16.792
6	Audio-42	24	17.511
7	Audio-43	30	22.308
8	Audio-44	28	21.545
9	Audio-45	26	31.871
10	Audio-46	47	28.243
11	Audio-47	56	39.192
12	Audio-48	56	22.175

Table 3: WER values for Testing Set

8 Discussion

From the Table 2, the experimental result says that the average WER for the testing dataset. The number of test speech utterances are 351. Similarly, Table 3, says the result of total 351 audio subset files from 12 audio files which is given for testing and the WER measured is 29.297%. We ranked second position in shared task competition.

9 Conclusion

The voice recognition algorithm is able to recognize older people better because to the utilization of conversational speech data. An automatic speech recognition system is developed using a trained model. A dataset pertaining to older folks and transgender individuals who speak Tamil as their mother tongue is being gathered. The utterance in the dataset was recorded in Tamil during a primary site discussion. In the future, the model may be trained using our own dataset and used for testing, which could increase performance, as the pretrained model of the system was refined using a shared speech dataset.

10 Future Work

In Future, instead of using the pretrained model we can fine tune the model with our custom dataset. Fine-tuning an Automatic Speech Recognition (ASR) system with a custom dataset is a promising approach to improve system performance in specific domains or applications, where end-to-end ASR architectures can be used, which directly map input audio to output transcriptions without intermediate steps. This can simplify the training pipeline and potentially improve performance, especially when dealing with limited custom datasets.

References

Bharathi B, Dhanya Srinivasan, Josephine Varsha, Thenmozhi Durairaj, and Senthil Kumar B. 2022. SSNCSE_NLP@LT-EDI-ACL2022:hope speech detection for equality, diversity and inclusion using sentence transformers. In *Proceedings of the Second Workshop on Language Technology for Equality, Diversity and Inclusion*, pages 218–222, Dublin, Ireland. Association for Computational Linguistics.

B Bharathi, Bharathi Raja Chakravarthi, Subalalitha Chinnaudayar Navaneethakrishnan, N Sripriya, Arunaggiri Pandian, and Swetha Valli. 2022. Findings of the shared task on Speech Recognition for Vulnerable Individuals in Tamil. In *Proceedings of the Second Workshop on Language Technology for Equality, Diversity and Inclusion*. Association for Computational Linguistics.

Biswajit Das, Sandipan Mandal, and Pabitra Mitra. 2011. Bengali speech corpus for continuous auutomatic speech recognition system. In *2011 International conference on speech database and assessments (Oriental COCOSDA)*, pages 51–55. IEEE.

Meiko Fukuda, Ryota Nishimura, Hiromitsu Nishizaki, Yurie Iribe, and Norihide Kitaoka. 2019. A new corpus of elderly japanese speech for acoustic modeling, and a preliminary investigation of dialect-dependent speech recognition. In *2019 22nd Conference of the Oriental COCOSDA International Committee for the Co-ordination and Standardisation of Speech Databases and Assessment Techniques (O-COCOSDA)*, pages 1–6. IEEE.

Meiko Fukuda, Hiromitsu Nishizaki, Yurie Iribe, Ryota Nishimura, and Norihide Kitaoka. 2020. Improving speech recognition for the elderly: A new corpus of elderly japanese speech and investigation of acoustic modeling for speech recognition. In *Proceedings of the 12th Language Resources and Evaluation Conference*, pages 6578–6585.

Annika Hämäläinen, António Teixeira, Nuno Almeida, Hugo Meinedo, Tibor Fegyó, and Miguel Sales Dias. 2015. Multilingual speech recognition for the elderly: The aalfred personal life assistant. *Procedia Computer Science*, 67:283–292.

Yurie Iribe, Norihide Kitaoka, and Shuhei Segawa. 2015. Development of new speech corpus for elderly japanese speech recognition. In *2015 International Conference Oriental COCOSDA held jointly with 2015 Conference on Asian Spoken Language Research and Evaluation (O-COCOSDA/CASLRE)*, pages 27–31. IEEE.

Taewoo Lee, Min-Joong Lee, Tae Gyoon Kang, Seokyeoung Jung, Minseok Kwon, Yeona Hong, Jungin Lee, Kyoung-Gu Woo, Ho-Gyeong Kim, Jiseung

Jeong, et al. 2021. Adaptable multi-domain language model for transformer asr. In *ICASSP 2021-2021 IEEE International Conference on Acoustics, Speech and Signal Processing (ICASSP)*, pages 7358–7362. IEEE.

Hui Lin and Yibiao Yu. 2015. Acoustic feature analysis and conversion of age speech. In *IET Conference Proceedings*. The Institution of Engineering & Technology.

Ryo Masumura, Naoki Makishima, Mana Ihori, Akihiko Takashima, Tomohiro Tanaka, and Shota Orihashi. 2021. Hierarchical transformer-based large-context end-to-end asr with large-context knowledge distillation. In *ICASSP 2021-2021 IEEE International Conference on Acoustics, Speech and Signal Processing (ICASSP)*, pages 5879–5883. IEEE.

Haoran Miao, Gaofeng Cheng, Changfeng Gao, Pengyuan Zhang, and Yonghong Yan. 2020. Transformer-based online ctc/attention end-to-end speech recognition architecture. In *ICASSP 2020-2020 IEEE International Conference on Acoustics, Speech and Signal Processing (ICASSP)*, pages 6084–6088. IEEE.

Hideharu Nakajima and Yushi Aono. 2020. Collection and analyses of exemplary speech data to establish easy-to-understand speech synthesis for japanese elderly adults. In *2020 23rd Conference of the Oriental COCOSDA International Committee for the Co-ordination and Standardisation of Speech Databases and Assessment Techniques (O-COCOSDA)*, pages 145–150. IEEE.

Suhasini S and Bharathi B. 2022. SUH_ASR@LT-EDI-ACL2022: Transformer based approach for speech recognition for vulnerable individuals in Tamil. In *Proceedings of the Second Workshop on Language Technology for Equality, Diversity and Inclusion*, pages 177–182, Dublin, Ireland. Association for Computational Linguistics.

Michel Vacher, Frédéric Aman, Solange Rossato, and François Portet. 2015. Development of automatic speech recognition techniques for elderly home support: Applications and challenges. In *International Conference on Human Aspects of IT for the Aged Population*, pages 341–353. Springer.

Zhiping Zeng, Haihua Xu, Yerbolat Khassanov, Eng Siong Chng, Chongjia Ni, Bin Ma, et al. 2021. Leveraging text data using hybrid transformer-lstm based end-to-end asr in transfer learning. In *2021 12th International Symposium on Chinese Spoken Language Processing (ISCSLP)*, pages 1–5. IEEE.

Author Index

Association for Computational Linguistics
209 N. Eighth Street
Stroudsburg, Pennsylvania 18360

ISBN 978-1-7138-9455-1

9 781713 894551

CURRAN ASSOCIATES INC.
proceedings.com